Vital Statistics
on American Politics

Sara Miller McCune founded SAGE Publishing in 1965 to support the dissemination of usable knowledge and educate a global community. SAGE publishes more than 1000 journals and over 800 new books each year, spanning a wide range of subject areas. Our growing selection of library products includes archives, data, case studies and video. SAGE remains majority owned by our founder and after her lifetime will become owned by a charitable trust that secures the company's continued independence.

Los Angeles | London | New Delhi | Singapore | Washington DC | Melbourne

Vital Statistics on American Politics

2017–2020

Jeffrey L. Bernstein
Eastern Michigan University

Amanda C. Shannon
Wright State University

FOR INFORMATION:

SAGE Publications, Inc.
2455 Teller Road
Thousand Oaks, California 91320
E-mail: order@sagepub.com

SAGE Publications Ltd.
1 Oliver's Yard
55 City Road
London, EC1Y 1SP
United Kingdom

SAGE Publications India Pvt. Ltd.
B 1/I 1 Mohan Cooperative Industrial Area
Mathura Road, New Delhi 110 044
India

SAGE Publications Asia-Pacific Pte. Ltd.
18 Cross Street #10-10/11/12
China Square Central
Singapore 048423

Acquisitions Editor: Laura Notton
Production Editor: Megha Negi
Typesetter: Hurix Digital
Proofreader: Eleni-Maria Georgiou
Indexer: Integra
Cover Designer: Candice Harman
Marketing Manager: Gabrielle Perretta

Copyright © 2022 by CQ Press, an Imprint of SAGE Publications, Inc. CQ Press is a registered trademark of Congressional Quarterly Inc.

All rights reserved. Except as permitted by U.S. copyright law, no part of this work may be reproduced or distributed in any form or by any means, or stored in a database or retrieval system, without permission in writing from the publisher.

All third party trademarks referenced or depicted herein are included solely for the purpose of illustration and are the property of their respective owners. Reference to these trademarks in no way indicates any relationship with, or endorsement by, the trademark owner.

Printed in the United States of America

ISBN : 978-1-0718-3686-6

This book is printed on acid-free paper.

22 23 24 25 26 10 9 8 7 6 5 4 3 2 1

Contents

Tables, Figures, and Data Literacy Lessons	vii
Acknowledgments	xix
Introduction	xxi
About the Authors	xxix

1 **Elections and Political Parties**   1
Turnout • Political Parties • Election Results (President, Congress, and State) • Minority Elected Officials • Presidential Nominations • Districting • Voting Rights • Term Limits • Voting Equipment

2 **Campaign Finance and Political Action Committees**   87
Contribution Limits • Presidential Campaign Financing • Party Expenditures • Political Action Committees (PACs)

3 **Public Opinion and Voting**   119
Partisanship • Ideology • Voting by Groups • Presidential and Congressional Approval • Confidence in Government and the Economy • Most Important Problem • Specific Issues

4 **The Media**   181
National Reach • Presence in Washington • Public Use • Coverage and Viewership of Presidential Campaigns, Conventions, and Debates • Newspaper Endorsements

5	**Congress**	219
	Apportionment • Membership Characteristics • Committees • Bills and Laws • Voting Patterns • Current Members	
6	**The Presidency and Executive Branch**	279
	Presidents • Ratings • Backgrounds • Cabinet and Staff • Congressional Relations • Civil Service Employment • Regulations	
7	**The Judiciary**	315
	Federal and State Court Structures • Supreme Court Justices • Ratings • Failed Nominations • Federal Court Judges • Supreme Court Caseloads • Federal Court Caseloads • Laws Overturned	
8	**Federalism**	347
	Historical Data • State Constitutional Provisions • States and the Federal Constitution • State and Local Governments and Employees • Revenues and Spending • Personal Income • Intergovernmental Revenue Flows	
9	**Foreign and Military Policy**	389
	Treaties and Agreements • Military Engagements • Military Personnel • Expenditures • Military Sales and Assistance • Foreign Aid • Investment and Trade	
10	**Social Policy**	419
	Population • Immigration • Medicare and Social Security • Income Levels • Public Aid • Health Insurance • Integration in Schooling • Abortion • Crime and Punishment	
11	**Economic Policy**	461
	Gross Domestic Product (GDP) • Consumer Price Index (CPI) • Federal Budget • National Debt • Tax Rates and Breaks • Income Inequality • Labor Unions • Minimum Wages • Unemployment	

Appendix: Definitions of Regions	497
Index	501

Tables, Figures, and Data Literacy Lessons

Chapter 1	Elections and Political Parties	
T 1-1	Voter Turnout Rates: United States, South, and Non-South, 1789–2020 (percent)	4
F 1-1	Voter Turnout Rates: Presidential and Midterm Elections, 1789–2020	6
F 1-2	Voter Turnout Rates: Presidential Elections, South and Non-South, 1789–2020	7
	Turnout Disparities in the South and Non-South	8
T 1-2	Voting-Age Population Registered and Voting: Cross Sections, 2000–2020 (percent)	10
F 1-3	American Political Parties since 1789	12
T 1-3	Party Competition: Presidency, by State, 1992–2020	13
T 1-4	Party Competition, by Region, 1860–2020 (percent)	14
T 1-5	Party Competition in the States, 1992–2020	15
T 1-6	Partisan Division of Governors and State Legislatures, 2021	16
T 1-7	Popular and Electoral Votes for President, 1789–2020	19
T 1-8	Party Winning Presidential Election, by State, 1789–2020	24
T 1-9	Presidential General Election Returns, by State, 2020	26
F 1-4	Presidential General Election Map, 2020	28
T 1-10	House and Senate Election Results, by Congress, 1788–2020	29
T 1-11	Party Victories in U.S. House Elections, by State, 1860–2020	34
T 1-12	Popular Vote and Seats in House Elections, by Party, 1896–2020	36

vii

	Why Divided Government Matters	38
T 1-13	Divided Government in the United States, by Congress, 1861–2022	40
T 1-14	Split Presidential and House Election Outcomes in Congressional Districts, 1900–2020	42
	The Decline of Split Districts	43
T 1-15	Mean Turnover in the House of Representatives from Various Causes, by Decade and Party System, 1789–2020	45
T 1-16	House and Senate Seats That Changed Party, 1954–2020	46
T 1-17	Losses by President's Party in Midterm Elections, 1862–2018	48
T 1-18	House and Senate Incumbents Retired, Defeated, or Reelected, 1946–2020	49
T 1-19	Incumbent Reelection Rates: Representatives, Senators, and Governors, General Elections, 1960–2020	52
T 1-20	Congressional Districts with a Racial or Ethnic Minority Representative or a "Majority-Minority" Population, 2021	56
T 1-21	Latino Elected Officials in the United States, 1996–2019	61
T 1-22	Blacks, Hispanics, and Women as a Percentage of State Legislators and State Voting-Age Population	62
	Descriptive Representation—What It Is and Why It Matters	64
T 1-23	Presidential Primaries, 1912–2020	66
T 1-24	State Methods for Choosing National Convention Delegates, 1968–2020	67
F 1-5	Democratic and Republican Presidential Nominations, Campaign Lengths, 1968–2020	71
T 1-25	Democratic Presidential Primary Returns, 2020	74
T 1-26	Democratic Presidential Caucus Results, 2020	76
T 1-27	Location and Size of National Party Conventions, 1932–2020	77
T 1-28	Legislative Districting: Deviations from Equality in Congressional and State Legislative Districts (percent)	78
T 1-29	Jurisdictions Subject to Federal Preclearance of Election Law Changes and to Minority Language Provisions of the Voting Rights Act	80
T 1-30	Term Limits on State Legislators	81
T 1-31	Members "Termed Out" of State Legislatures, 2002–2020	83
T 1-32	Types of Voting Equipment Used in U.S. Elections by State, November 2020 (percent)	85

Tables, Figures, and Data Literacy Lessons   ix

Chapter 2	Campaign Finance and Political Action Committees	87
T 2-1	Contribution Limits under the Bipartisan Campaign Reform Act of 2002	90
T 2-2	Contribution Limits on Funding of State Election Campaigns	91
T 2-3	Presidential Campaign Finance, 2020	93
T 2-4	Presidential Campaign Finance, Aggregated Contributions from Individual Donors to Leading Presidential Candidates, 2016 and 2020	95
Making Comparisons over Time		96
T 2-5	Public Funding of Presidential Elections, 1976–2020 (millions)	98
T 2-6	Financial Activity of the National Political Parties, 2001–2020 (millions)	99
T 2-7	Financial Activity of National, State, and Local Party Committees, 2019–2020 (millions)	100
Finding What Isn't There		101
T 2-8	National Party Campaign Finance: "Soft" and "Hard" Money, 2002–2020 (millions)	103
T 2-9	Number of Political Action Committees (PACs), by Type, 1989–2020	104
T 2-10	PACs: Receipts, Expenditures, and Contributions, 1975–2020	105
T 2-11	Spending, by Type of PAC, 1997–2020 (millions)	106
T 2-12	Contributions and Independent Expenditures, by Type of PAC, 2003–2020	107
The Wild Growth of Nonconnected PACs		110
T 2-13	Top Twenty PACs in Overall Spending and in Contributions to Federal Candidates, 2019–2020	112
T 2-14	PAC Congressional Campaign Contributions, by Type of PAC and Incumbency Status of Candidate, 1999–2020 (millions)	114
The Incumbency Advantage and Campaign Finance		117
Chapter 3	Public Opinion and Voting	119
T 3-1	Partisan Identification, American National Election Studies, 1952–2020 (percent)	123
F 3-1	Partisan Identification, American National Election Studies, 1952–2020	124
F 3-2	Partisan Identification, Pew Surveys, 1987–2019	125
T 3-2	Partisan Identification, by Groups, 2012–2020 (percent)	126

T 3-3	Liberal or Conservative Self-Identification, 1973–2018 (percent)	129
F 3-3	Liberal, Moderate, and Conservative Self-Identification, 1973–2018	130
F 3-4	Ideological Self-Identification of College Freshmen, 1970–2019	131
T 3-4	Strength of Party Identification and the Presidential Vote, 1952–2020 (percent)	132
Independent Leaners and the Measure of Partisanship		134
F 3-5	Presidential Preferences during 2020	136
T 3-5	Presidential Vote in General Elections, by Groups, Network Exit Polls, 2004–2020 (percent)	137
T 3-6	Vote in Democratic Presidential Primaries, by Groups, 2000–2020 (percent)	140
T 3-7	Vote in Republican Presidential Primaries, by Groups, 2000–2016 (percent)	142
T 3-8	Congressional Vote in General Elections, by Groups, 2010–2020 (percent)	144
Group Voting in Elections		146
T 3-9	Party-Line Voting in Presidential and Congressional Elections, 1952–2020 (percent)	148
T 3-10	Split-Ticket Voting, 1952–2020 (percent)	149
F 3-6	Presidential Approval, 1993–2021	150
F 3-7	Rating of Congress, 1985–2021	151
F 3-8	Individual Confidence in Government, 1952–2020	152
F 3-9	Satisfaction with "The Way Things Are Going," 1988–2021	153
T 3-11	Importance of Various Political Issues, 2016–2021 (percent)	154
Asking Questions about the (Most) Important Political Issues		155
F 3-10	Favorable Opinions of the Democratic and Republican Parties, 1992–2021	157
F 3-11	Condition of Nation's Economy and Citizens' Personal Financial Situations over the Last Year, 1980–2020 (percent)	158
The Economy and the Vote		159
T 3-12	Public Opinion on Civil Liberties, 1940–2018 (percent)	161
T 3-13	Public Opinion on the Death Penalty, 1972–2018 (percent)	164
F 3-12	Public Opinion on People Living in Integrated Neighborhoods, 1972–2018	165
T 3-14	Public Opinion on Abortion, 1965–2018 (percent)	166

T 3-15	Public Opinion on Gun Control (Requiring Permits to Purchase Guns), 1972–2018 (percent)	167
	Dichotomies and Public Opinion: Abortion and Gun Control	168
F 3-13	Public Opinion on Same-Sex Marriage, 2001–2019	170
F 3-14	Public Opinion on Legalization of Marijuana, 1973–2018	171
F 3-15	Religious Affiliation of the U.S. Population and Political Ideology, by Religious Affiliation, 2014	172
F 3-16	Recent Trends in the Religiously Unaffiliated, by Generation, 2007–2019	173
T 3-16	Public Opinion on the Courts and Criminal Justice, 1972–2018 (percent)	174
T 3-17	Public Opinion on Approval of U.S. Active Involvement in World Affairs, 1987–2019 (percent)	175
T 3-18	Public Opinion on Peace through Military Strength, 1987–2019 (percent)	176
F 3-17	Public Opinion on U.S. Military Involvement in Iraq, 2003–2018	177
T 3-19	Public Opinion on Terrorism, 2001–2016 (percent)	178
Chapter 4	**The Media**	**181**
T 4-1	Reach and Use of Selected Media, 1950–2020	183
T 4-2	Newspaper Circulation, Daily Papers, 1850–2018	184
F 4-1	Growth of Congressional Press Corps, 1864–2020	186
T 4-3	Presidential News Conferences, 1913–2021	187
	Determining What Data to Count	187
T 4-4	Use of Television for News, 1990–2020 (percent)	189
T 4-5	Use of Internet and Newspapers for News, 1990–2020 (percent)	190
T 4-6	Use of Newspaper, Radio, and Television for News, 1993–2020 (percent)	192
T 4-7	Most common platform for political news, Demographics, 2020 (percent)	194
T 4-8	Perceptions of Misinformation in the 2020 Election (percent)	195
T 4-9	Partisan Differences in Media Use and Role Perception, 2020	198
T 4-10	Preference for News with a Point of View, 2004–2020 (percent)	199
T 4-11	Sources of Campaign News, 1992–2020 (percent)	200
	What Are Surveys Asking	201
T 4-12	Use of Digital Platforms by County Political Parties in 2020 (percent)	203

xii   Tables, Figures, and Data Literacy Lessons

T 4-13	Public's Use of Media to Follow Presidential Campaigns, 1960–2012 (percent)	204
T 4-14	Credibility of Television and Print Media, 1998–2019 (percent)	206
T 4-15	National Nominating Conventions: Television Coverage and Viewership, 1952–2020	208
T 4-16	Television Viewership of Presidential and Vice-Presidential Debates, 1960–2020	211
Measuring Trends When Benchmarks Change		212
T 4-17	Newspaper Endorsements of Presidential Candidates, 1948–2020	214
The Relevance of Newspaper Endorsements		216
F 4-2	Newspaper Endorsements of Presidential Candidates: Democratic, Republican, and Uncommitted, 1932–2020	218
Chapter 5	**Congress**	**219**
T 5-1	Apportionment of Membership of the House of Representatives, 1789–2020	221
F 5-1	Apportionment of Membership of the House of Representatives, by Region, 1910 and 2020	226
Reapportionment Data and the State and Regional Level		227
T 5-2	Members of Congress: Female, Black, Hispanic, Marital Status, and Age, 1971–2021	229
T 5-3	Black Members of Congress, 1869–2021	232
T 5-4	Women Nominated, by Party, 1956–2020, and Women Elected to U.S. House of Representatives, by Party, 1916–2020	234
Why Are There So Few Women in Elective Office? And Why Does It Matter?		236
T 5-5	Members of Congress: Seniority and Previous Legislative Service, 2017–2021	238
T 5-6	Congressional Committees and Majority Party Chair Positions, 1983–2023	239
T 5-7	Congressional Measures Introduced and Enacted, 1947–2021	242
F 5-2	Measures Introduced in Congress That Were Passed, 1789–2020 (percent)	243
The Do-Nothing Congress?		244
T 5-8	Record Votes in the House and the Senate, 1947–2020	246
F 5-3	Party Votes in the House, 1878–2020	247
T 5-9	Party Unity and Polarization in Congressional Voting, 1953–2020 (percent)	248

T 5-10	Party Unity in Congressional Voting, 1954–2020 (percent)	249
T 5-11	The 117th Congress: House of Representatives	251
T 5-12	The 117th Congress: Senate	269
	Interest Group Ratings: What They Reveal, What They Obscure	276

Chapter 6 The Presidency and Executive Branch 279

T 6-1	Presidents and Vice Presidents of the United States	282
T 6-2	Ratings of U.S. Presidents	285
	How Do We Rank Presidents? And, Should We Trust These Rankings?	288
T 6-3	Previous Public Positions Held by Presidents, 1788–2021	290
T 6-4	Latest Public Office Held by Candidates for Democratic and Republican Presidential Nominations, 1936–2020	291
T 6-5	The President's Cabinet, 2021	292
T 6-6	White House Staff and Executive Office of the President, 1943–2020	294
T 6-7	Presidential Victories on Votes in Congress, 1953–2020	296
T 6-8	Congressional Voting in Support of the President's Position, 1954–2020 (percent)	299
	What Do Presidential Success in Congress Numbers Really Mean?	301
T 6-9	Presidential Vetoes, 1789–2021, and Signing Statements, 1929–2021	303
T 6-10	Senate Action on Nominations, 1937–2021	305
T 6-11	Senate Rejections of Cabinet Nominations	306
	Interpreting Data on Presidential Nominations, Rejected, and Withdrawn	307
T 6-12	Presidential Executive Orders, 1789–2020	309
	When Counting Executive Orders Isn't Enough	311
T 6-13	Major Regulatory Agencies	313
F 6-1	Number of Pages in *Federal Register*, 1940–2019	314

Chapter 7 The Judiciary 315

F 7-1	The U.S. Court System	317
F 7-2	The Thirteen Federal Judicial Circuits and Ninety-Four District Courts	318
T 7-1	Principal Methods of Judicial Selection for State Courts of Last Resort	319
T 7-2	Supreme Court Justices of the United States	320
T 7-3	Supreme Court Nominations That Failed	327

T 7-4	Characteristics of Federal District and Appellate Court Appointees, Presidents Richard Nixon to Donald Trump (percent)	328
Judicial Characteristics		331
T 7-5	Federal Judicial Appointments of Same Party as President, Presidents Grover Cleveland to Barack Obama	332
T 7-6	Percent of U.S. Circuit and District Court Nominees Confirmed, 1977–2019	333
Political Implications of Confirmations		334
T 7-7	Caseload of the U.S. Supreme Court, 1970–2019 Terms	336
A Case's Path to the Supreme Court		338
F 7-3	Cases Filed in U.S. Supreme Court, 1880–2019 Terms	339
T 7-8	Caseload of U.S. Courts of Appeals, 2000–2020	340
T 7-9	Caseload of U.S. District Courts, 2000–2020	341
T 7-10	Civil and Criminal Cases Filed in U.S. District Courts, 1950–2020	342
T 7-11	Types of Civil and Criminal Cases in U.S. District Courts, 2020	343
T 7-12	Federal, State, and Local Laws Declared Unconstitutional by U.S. Supreme Court, by Decade, 1789–2020	344
F 7-4	Economic and Civil Liberties Laws Overturned by U.S. Supreme Court, by Decade, 1900–2020	345
Chapter 8	**Federalism**	**347**
T 8-1	The States: Historical Data	349
T 8-2	State Constitutions	351
T 8-3	Governors' Terms, Term Limits, and Item Veto	354
T 8-4	State Provisions for Initiative and Referendum	356
T 8-5	Legislative Professionalism in the States	358
Analyzing Legislative Professionalism		361
F 8-1	Initiatives in the States, 1900–2019	363
T 8-6	Incorporation of Bill of Rights to Apply to State Governments	364
T 8-7	Length of Time between Congressional Approval and Actual Ratification of the Twenty-Seven Amendments to the U.S. Constitution	366
F 8-2	Government Employees: Federal, State, and Local, 1929–2019	367
T 8-8	Federal, State, and Local Governments: Number of Units and Employees, 1942–2025	368
What Does "Big Government" Mean, Anyway?		370
T 8-9	State Lottery Revenues (in millions)	372

| T 8-10 | State and Local Government Expenditures, by Function, 1902–2018 (percent) | 374 |
| T 8-11 | Disposable Personal Income per Capita, by State, 1950–2019 | 376 |

Finding Meaning in a Sea of Data ... 378

F 8-3	Surpluses and Deficits in Federal, State, and Local Government Finances, 1948–2019	380
F 8-4	State and Local Government Deficits Compared with Federal Grants-in-Aid, 1948–2019	381
T 8-12	Federal Grants-in-Aid Outlays, 1940–2025	382
T 8-13	Federal Grants-in-Aid to State and Local Governments, by Function, 1950–2025 (percent)	384
T 8-14	Fiscal Dependency of Lower Levels on Higher Levels of Government, 1927–2018	385
T 8-15	Variations in Local Dependency on State Aid, 2018	387

Chapter 9 Foreign and Military Policy 389

T 9-1	Treaties and Executive Agreements Concluded by the United States, 1789–2020	391
T 9-2	Major Arms Control and Disarmament Agreements	392
T 9-3	Use of U.S. Armed Forces Abroad, 1798–2020	394
T 9-4	U.S. Personnel in Major Military Conflicts	395
T 9-5	U.S. Military Forces and Casualties by Conflict 1950–2020	397

Measuring the Cost of War ... 398

| T 9-6 | Sexual Assaults, Amputations, Suicides, and Traumatic Brain Injuries Sustained by U.S. Military Personnel, 2001–2020 | 400 |

Data Collection and Self-Reporting ... 402

T 9-7	U.S. Military Personnel Abroad or Afloat, by Country, 1972–2020 (thousands)	404
T 9-8	U.S. Active Duty Forces, by Sex, Race, and Hispanic Origin, 1965–2019	405
T 9-9	U.S. Defense Spending, 1940–2025	408
F 9-1	U.S. Defense Spending as a Percentage of Federal Outlays and of Gross Domestic Product, 1940–2025	410
T 9-10	Military Expenditures: World, Regional, and Selected National Estimates, 1990–2020	411

Using Data for Comparisons ... 413

| T 9-11 | U.S. Military Sales and Military Assistance to Foreign Governments, Principal Recipients, 1950–2020 (millions) | 414 |

T 9-12	U.S. Foreign Aid, Principal Recipients, 1946-2018 (millions)	415
T 9-13	Foreign Investment in the United States and U.S. Investment Abroad, 1950–2019 (millions)	416
T 9-14	U.S. Balance of Trade, 1946–2020 (in millions)	418
Chapter 10	**Social Policy**	**419**
F 10-1	U.S. Population: Total, Urban, and Rural, 1790–2060	421
T 10-1	U.S. Population, 1790–2010, and State Populations, 2010–2040	422
T 10-2	Foreign-Born and Native-Born U.S. Population, Characteristics, 2017	424
T 10-3	Immigrants to the United States, by Region of Origin, 1820–2019	426
The Importance of Aggregation		427
F 10-2	Immigrants to the United States, by Region of Origin, 1820–2019	428
T 10-4	Legal Status of Immigrants, 2016; Origins of Unauthorized Immigrants, 2016; and State Populations of Unauthorized Immigrants, 1990–2017	429
T 10-5	Hospital Insurance Trust Fund: Income, Expenditures, and Balance, 1970–2029 (billions)	431
T 10-6	Social Security (OASDI)–Covered Workers and Beneficiaries, 1945–2095	432
F 10-3	Social Security Receipts, Spending, and Reserve Estimates, 2020–2030	433
T 10-7	Median Family Income, by Race and Hispanic Origin, 1950–2019	434
Current Dollars and Constant Dollars		436
T 10-8	Persons below the Poverty Line, by Group, 2019	437
T 10-9	Persons below the Poverty Line, by Race and Hispanic Origin, 1959–2019 (percent)	438
F 10-4	Temporary Assistance for Needy Families (TANF) and Food Stamp (SNAP) Benefit Levels as Percentage of Federal Poverty Line, 2020	440
F 10-5	U.S. Population Receiving AFDC/TANF and Food Stamps/SNAP, 1970–2018	441
Identifying Patterns with Data Visualization		442
T 10-10	Health Insurance Coverage U.S. Population, 1987–2019	444
T 10-11	Persons without Health Insurance, by Demographic Characteristics, 2019	446
T 10-12	Persons Who Have Completed High School or College, by Race, Hispanic Origin, and Sex, 1940–2019 (percent)	447

T 10-13	School Desegregation, by Region, 1968–2017		449
T 10-14	Frequency of Legal Abortions, 1972–2017		452
T 10-15	Crime Rates, 1960–2019		453
T 10-16	Death Penalty in the States: Number of Executions, 1930–2020, and Number on Death Row, 2021		454
T 10-17	Number of Executions 1977–2020, by Race of Defendant and Race of Victim(s)		457
T 10-18	Sentenced Federal and State Prisoners, 1925–2019		459
T 10-19	Estimated Number of Persons Supervised by Adult Correctional Systems, by Correctional Status, 2000–2018 (thousands)		460
Chapter 11	**Economic Policy**		**461**
T 11-1	Gross Domestic Product, 1929–2020 (billions)		463
T 11-2	Consumer Price Index, 1950–2020		465
What Is the Consumer Price Index?			468
T 11-3	Federal Budget: Total, Defense, and Nondefense Expenditures, 1940–2025 (billions)		470
T 11-4	Federal Budget Outlays, by Function, 2000–2025 (billions)		472
F 11-1	Federal Outlays as a Percentage of GNP/GDP, 1869–2025		473
T 11-5	Mandatory and Discretionary Federal Budget Outlays, 1975–2025 (billions)		474
T 11-6	The National Debt, 1940–2025		475
F 11-2	National Debt as a Percentage of GDP, 1940–2025		476
T 11-7	Cost of Selected Tax Breaks: Revenue Loss Estimates for Selected Tax Expenditures, 2019–2029 (millions)		477
F 11-3	Mean Income Received by Each Fifth and Top 5 Percent of Families, 1966–2019		479
Analyzing Economic Policy Impacts through Data			480
T 11-8	Membership in Labor Unions, 1900–2020		481
F 11-4	Federal Minimum Wage Rates, 1938–2021		483
Contextualizing Economic Indicators			484
T 11-9	Civilian Labor Force Participation Rate, Overall and by Sex and Race, 1948–2020 (percent)		485
T 11-10	Unemployment Rate Overall, 1929–2019, and by Sex and Race, 1948–2019 (percent)		487
The Importance of Definitions			489
T 11-11	Unemployment, by Race, Sex, and Age, 1955–2020 (percent)		491

T 11-12	Consumer Confidence, Unemployment, and the Stock Market	493
F 11-5	Linking Consumer Confidence to Unemployment and the Stock Market	494
	Thinking about Consumer Confidence	495

Appendix	Definitions of Regions	497
T A-1	Regions as Defined by the U.S. Census Bureau and by Pew Research	497
T A-2	Regions as Defined by Fiscal Note, *New York Times*/CBS News Poll, and Voter Research and Surveys	498
T A-3	Regions for Party Competition Table (Table 1-4) and Apportionment Map (Figure 5-1)	498
T A-4	Regions for School Desegregation Table (Table 10-13)	499

Acknowledgments

Taking on a new edition of a well-known, well-respected volume such as this brings with it challenges. In taking on this challenge, we have benefitted greatly from the support and guidance of many people who have been available to answer questions, talk through ideas, and provide background on why data are collected in a certain way or why collection of certain data changed or stopped. These people, at various times and in myriad ways, pointed us in the right direction, shone lights on what seemed like dead ends, and helped us see when a path really had come to an end.

Help with specific tables or figures was provided by Andrew Adaryukov, Scott Anderson, Lawrence Baum, Chris Bois, Cris De Brey, Peter Conti, Lee Hannah, David Lewis, Chloe Madvig, Suzanne Macartney, Gerhard Peters, Vaughn Shannon, Elliot Slotnick, Tom Tulloch, Paul Villena, Russell Wheeler, John Woolley, and Jennifer Zanoni. Special thanks to Lee Hannah and Vaughn Shannon who provided useful suggestions and shared ideas for chapters 4 and 9. Zachary Bernstein assisted us with updating some tables, and we are grateful for that help.

We are especially grateful to the many, often anonymous, government officials who helped us with this and all previous editions. Say what you will about bureaucracy and government, we have been delighted by the responsiveness, care, and interest those public employees showed us in answering questions we've asked and solving problems we've encountered along the way.

Laura Notton at CQ Press/SAGE Publishing made this process run smoothly and we could not have done this without her. Her careful editing and attention to detail has improved these tables and accompanying essays that comprise the book. We also appreciate her kind and patient approach, even when encountering questions from the authors like "Some of these data are really hard to find! Why isn't there just one place that collects it all?" (We got there eventually and realized that was exactly why we were working on this project, but to her credit Laura didn't even blink an eye when we asked.) Megha Negi was efficient and diligent in handling the production of this book, and we are grateful to her.

Finally, we would like to acknowledge the support and patience of our families: Lisa, Zachary, Solly, Vaughn, Sophia, and Cate have been subjected to more conversations that started with "did you know..." or "fun fact:" and ended in a detailed explanation of a particular data point than they probably ever care to hear again. They have patiently and good-naturedly supported us throughout the process and we are very grateful to them.

Introduction

For more years than we'd care to admit, the two of us have worked, broadly speaking, in the world of information literacy. Mandy has worked as a librarian for much of that time, teaching students how to effectively find appropriate sources to meet different information needs, and to evaluate and contextualize information. Jeff has taught political science classes, including classes on research methods and public opinion, where students spend their time poring over the data and attempting to learn what the data mean, including wrestling with different interpretations of data, and with their implications. The opportunity to edit this book gave us the chance to share our love for data, and our guidance on how it can be used (and misused) with you.

We really do love data. One of the beautiful things about numbers, and data, is that they tell a story. Consider baseball, for example. Imagine we told you that Player A hit forty home runs this year, and Player B stole forty bases. That's a very small bit of information, but based on that information, a baseball fan would be able to form a picture, a story, of each player. Which one is lean and lanky? Which one has thighs the size of tree trunks? Which player is a centerfielder? Which one plays first base, or perhaps is the designated hitter? These simple statistics are interesting to us perhaps because we can look at them and conjure up a story in our head.

In this book, we use numbers to tell the story of American politics in 2021. Our data tell of an electorate in flux, of the cycles in our economy, of how our political institutions function, and of how policies passed in Washington affect the people living in the heartland. Words can convey this picture, and we encourage you to read as much as you can about the narrative others

xxi

have written—and are writing—about politics in contemporary America. But numbers tell this story as well, in a rich and illuminating way.

You will note one thing in this book: we use data in the plural sense (singular: datum). We do this in part because we are, admittedly, somewhat grammatical snobs (not our most endearing quality, but we're also pretty nice people, if that helps). It reminds us that while individual facts matter, it is only when we aggregate these facts and pluralize them (turning datum into data) that a true picture emerges. This was stated quite eloquently over one hundred fifty years ago by William Farr, an early epidemiologist who was investigating the East End cholera outbreak in 1866. Farr wrote that:

> "Facts, however numerous, do not constitute a science. Like innumerable grains of sand on the sea shore, single facts appear isolated, useless, shapeless; it is only when compared, when arranged in their natural relations, when crystallized by the intellect, that they constitute the eternal truths of science."[1]

This book represents one attempt to take the individual facts about American politics (how do Americans feel about same-sex marriage, for example), aggregate the individual facts with others (how we felt about this issue five, or ten years ago) and begin to build theories about public opinion on this issue. When this happens, slowly, we find ourselves using the tools of data analysis to analyze the political world scientifically.

Issues of Data Literacy

Uncovering the "eternal truths of science" that Farr wrote of underpins much of academic exploration. In the political realm, attempts to discover and identify these truths are themselves often politicized. Increasingly, both public debates and political analyses contain points couched in or accompanied by statistics. Democracy turns in part on the ability of an informed public to follow such debates and analyses. Debates in the public forum, whether on social media or broadcast, often hinge on numbers that are treated as definitive answers in and of themselves. Understanding politics requires an ability to comprehend numerical data and the assumptions behind them. It requires that you not merely "buy" the analysis you are being shown, but rather ask tough questions about how much you trust the data, and the way they are presented.[2]

---

[1] Quoted in John Eyler, *Victorian Social Medicine: The Ideas and Methods of William Farr*, Baltimore: Johns Hopkins University Press. This story is shared in Steven Johnson, *Extra Life: A Short History of Living Longer*. New York, Riverhead Books, 2021.

[2] It does not, however, give us license to reject findings merely because we do not like what they say about our favorite politicians, or policies.

Throughout each chapter we have added essays that question and examine some of the assumptions that can be made, and what assumptions we cannot make without additional information. As public discourse has become more polarized, and distrust has grown, statistical data are often hurled about as blunt instruments of "proof." We encourage developing a reflective practice of examining the context of data to focus on understanding rather than proving. We have not provided essays for every table in this volume but, rather, have selected a handful in each chapter that highlight different elements and aspects of these questions useful for developing data literacy.

As we discuss in several essays on aggregation, we rarely encounter data in their original raw form. Considering the way data have been presented to us, and how that shapes our understanding, is useful in developing critical thinking about them. In addition to the presentation of the data themselves, we often encounter them in context far removed from the way the original data were collected. Think of the game of "Telephone" you might have played when you were younger: one person whispers a sentence to the next person in line, who whispers it to the next person, and so on until the last person in line reports what sentence they heard—usually humorously different from the original statement. In the same way, the interpretation of data can change as they're reported: a scholar publishes a study based on an original analysis, which might be shared in a university press release, which is reported on by the local media, which is picked up by another news outlet with claims far removed from the actual statistical analysis.[3]

In a news environment that is increasingly complex, fractured, wide-reaching, and unmediated, we think it's difficult to overstate the importance of careful consideration of data and information that are presented. These essays are intended as guides for developing your skills and practices for reflexive questioning as you encounter new data.

The remainder of this introduction presents four themes to consider. These themes can be summarized as follows:

- Different availability of data over time
- Different ways of reporting results

---

[3] One interesting example of this is presented in the Smithsonian Magazine article "How One Bad Science Headline Can Echo Across the Internet," available at https://www.smithsonianmag.com/science-nature/how-bad-science-headlines-echo-across-internet-180964259. Misrepresentation of a scientific study on the negative effects of synthetic estrogen in water on fish led to reporting claiming that contraceptive pills were causing fish to become transgendered. In addition to misrepresenting the science for political purposes, it also detracted from the actual issues of concern.

- Data collection and reporting as a political process
- Issues of informational/statistical literacy

As authors, we struggled with many of these issues, and believe it is important to convey aspects of how that struggle can be productive to our readers. The themes addressed below in this introduction will all arise frequently in the book, both in the tables and figures we present to you, and in our essays.

Data Availability over Time

Much of the value of a book such as this comes from the trends and patterns over time that become apparent when years (sometimes decades, or even centuries) of data are collected and presented together. However, one of the challenges in developing an understanding of trends and patterns comes when the availability of data used as benchmarks changes.

In some cases, information is simply no longer reported as it once was. For example, Table 8-8 presents data about employment at federal, state, and local government levels. In previous years, the Census reported local government employment data further broken down into two broad categories: general purpose and special purpose; each of those subcategories were further broken down into smaller divisions. Within general purpose designations were county, municipal, and township employee designations, while school district and special district employees were recorded under the special purpose designation. Local employment numbers are no longer reported in that way by the Census Bureau; as a result, we have changed the way we present data in that table. Previous editions of this book included the subdivisions in local government, if you are curious to see an example of what that looked like.

In other cases, the availability of data to share is inexorably intertwined with the reality that collecting data is, itself, an act of scholarship and its availability is dependent on scholars producing it. In Table 7-4, as we explain in much more detail in the accompanying essay, the data were produced by years of effort of a group of dedicated scholars. We are able to present something similar, but not entirely comparable, thanks to the work of a different scholar. These changes in the way data are collected affect what comparisons we're able to make over time. Similarly, we are sometimes able to present new data because new scholars take on new projects and areas of interest. Table 4-12, for example, allows us to explore the ways in which local political parties across the country are using (or not using) various digital platforms because a group of political science scholars spent hours painstakingly checking the digital presence of the Republican and Democratic party of every county in the country (and were kind enough to share those data with us).

Chapter 4, which focuses on the role of the media in American politics, also highlights other challenges inherent in using data to benchmark trends over time: sometimes the very thing you're analyzing itself changes. In a very short period of time the way the world gets news and information has radically changed. There are no comparisons to how voters and politicians used social media in the 1950s or even 1980s because, quite simply, it didn't exist. With the proliferation of digital platforms, social media, and even the fractionalization of television news, the questions that can and should be asked have changed dramatically. As those questions change so, too, do the data that are collected and the way they are presented. In some cases, the very nature of what data are no longer relevant is itself the interesting part of the story.

As we discuss throughout this book, the process of collecting and reporting data is dynamic, plastic, and often political. The careful reader will notice that the reporting periods and years included in the tables and figures vary. This is not a function of careless preparation or editing but, rather, a function of the data that are available at the close date of the book. This is an endeavor that is, by its nature, ongoing; at some point we had to draw the line in the sand and declare this edition complete.

Different Ways of Reporting Data

An additional theme we explore in this book is how different ways of reporting data might yield different interpretations. We note at the beginning that the notion of "the data" speaking clearly in one voice is largely fantasy. Every act we make in collecting, interpreting, and reporting data introduces potential bias into the process; in this section, we focus mostly on how data get reported.

One fascinating historical example of how the ways we report data matters comes from the famous "Connecticut Crackdown on Speeding."[4] In 1955, Connecticut experienced a dramatically higher than normal number of traffic fatalities. Believing that excessive speed was the cause, the state instituted a crackdown on speeding, enforcing existing laws much more stringently. Lo and behold, in 1956, highway fatalities dropped. If you were to look at the comparison between 1955 and 1956, you would see a dramatic decline, and believe that the crackdown on speeding helped. The state of Connecticut did as well. However, if you were to zoom out and look at a larger time series, you would see that the 1956 deaths largely returned to the normal level. The 1955 data were the anomaly, and the crackdown on speeding seems to have

---

[4] See Donald T. Campbell, "Reforms as Experiments." *American Psychologist* 24 (4): 409-429, 1969.

done little more than return to the expected level. Perhaps the crackdown was not all it was cracked up to be.

Questions of how data are reported manifest themselves in other ways. For example, in Chapter 3, one of our data essays talks about the importance voters assign to different political issues. In previous editions of this book, we included figures showing what issue people said was "most important," while in this edition, we show the percentage of people saying an issue was "a very big problem." Both are perfectly valid ways to determine how important an issue is, but the different ways of framing the question can lead to different results. We would imagine, for example, that many people would regard our nation's crumbling infrastructure as a very big problem, but very few would claim it is *the most important* domestic issue facing the nation. Different ways of reporting the results could yield different interpretations, as they do in this case.

In some cases, the way data are presented might have a political edge to it. Democrats might, for example, present graphs that exaggerate the level of decline in unemployment under a Democratic president, and that minimize the level of decline under a Republican president; Republicans likely would do the opposite.[5] This type of partisan manipulation of data is a common trope in politics. Our interest here is less in partisan uses of data and more in the nonpartisan, nonpolitical choices that are made in how data are presented. No single way of reporting data is perfect, and every choice we make gives us certain benefits, but costs us others. We discuss this frequently in the data literacy essays and encourage you to ask these same types of questions as you examine the tables in the book and interpret what they mean.

Data Are Political

One of the challenges data-driven students of political science face is that data, as a general rule, are political. To be sure, some of the data that are reported are straightforward and not at all political—reporting the average age of members of Congress, for example, is a clear measure and one not manipulable by those with a political agenda. But many other data, or presentations of data, or interpretations of data, can be quite political.

We see this in our daily lives. Imagine, for example, that you are trying to convince a friend that climate change is real, or that COVID vaccines are safe

---

[5] This can be done by manipulating the values on the y-axis of the table. Having small gradations (such as by single digits) would exaggerate any year-to-year trends, while larger gradations (such as by five percent increments) would minimize these fluctuations.

and effective. You have data to support your point and are convinced that if your conversation partner would only listen, they would see reason. However, your friend also likely has data to support their argument. They might cite a study or series of studies that "debunk" what you are arguing. You may reject the premise of the study, or the methodology used, or the interpretations of the results. But the critical point to realize is that no matter how correct you think you are, *those on the other side may have data supporting their position*. We are perhaps used to viewing "data" as an unambiguously good thing, which will lead us to truth. A more sophisticated view of data, however, reminds us that while some data are illuminating, others breed confusion and error more than clarity and wisdom. *Caveat emptor* (let the buyer beware) applies to data as well as finance.

Even when we have no reason to believe we are being snookered, different ways of interpreting the same data should give us pause. Consider, for example, Table 3-14, which shows attitudes on abortion. The data have been collected by the highly respected National Opinion Research Center (NORC), as part of the General Social Survey. NORC has no political axe to grind; they simply hope to measure public opinion. One could easily look at the table and see strong support for abortion rights—consider, for example, the large numbers that would allow women to choose an abortion if the health of the mother is at stake, if the pregnancy resulted from rape, or if the baby risked getting a serious birth defect. However, one could easily interpret the table to show support for pro-life policies—majorities, for example, are not willing to allow abortion in some cases, including if the parent was a single-parent or could not afford any more children.

In Table 3-15, the data are the data. The interpretation, however, might be more contested, as might the headlines that various news organizations might run when they report these data. This table reminds us that we need not only worry about the data in terms of how they are collected, but also in how they are presented and interpreted. (Additionally, while harder to assess, we ought to be aware that some data might never see the light of day because they do not say what the person considering sharing them wants them to say.) This not only applies to us as consumers of data, but also as producers of data—it would be good practice, for example, to carefully consider whether our biases affect how we use our data in presenting our arguments. Data, we must repeat, are not always neutral, especially when used in a political context.

Issues of Information Literacy and Statistical Literacy

As we consider the political interpretations of data, we encourage you to consider the broader context in which the data exist. When we talk about data literacy throughout this book, and in our data literacy essays, we are focusing on the critical consumption and assessment of data to be able to use it effectively and ethically.

Data are a type of information and basic ideas of information literacy apply to them. In the same way that you might (and should!) ask questions about information that's presented to you in a narrative form, we encourage you to approach data as they are presented to you with a critical eye. The data literacy essays that we have included throughout the book are based on the same type of questioning practice that we recommend. Some of the questions we explore in these essays, and that we encourage others ask as you encounter data, include:

- From where and when and whom were the data collected?
- What questions were asked that led to the responses or selection of data presented?
- Are the data aggregated in a way that supports conclusions being drawn from them?
- What do we learn about the political system from the presentation of data that we have?
- Moreover, what might we learn from other data that are not presented in the table or figure?

Asking questions such as these does not require sophisticated methodological training or statistical software. Rather, it requires returning to fundamental exploration and inquiry about what the numbers tell us. This isn't to say that statistical knowledge is useless in developing your data literacy skills. Knowing the foundations of quantitative and qualitative methodology will help you ask more sophisticated questions and further understand the data presented to you. Identifying whether an analysis used a one-tailed or two-tailed test, or what the case selection method was for a qualitative case study, are certainly helpful in understanding what conclusions we can draw. But it's not necessary to be a statistician to delve into questions about where data come from and how they're used.

To summarize: There is an important distinction between a critical approach and a cynical one, and we stress that we encourage the former, but not the latter. A critical approach to data means that you approach this new information with curiosity and questions, analyzing information to trust but verify. Developing your own information literacy skills strengthens your ability to learn from political data and information without polarization. In addition to sharing the actual data with you, we hope this book also informs how you approach the data, both in this book and in the larger world.

About the Authors

Jeffrey L. Bernstein is professor of Political Science and director of the Bruce K. Nelson Faculty Development Center at Eastern Michigan University. His main research area is teaching and learning in political science, including citizenship education as well as the teaching of research methods in the political science curriculum.

Amanda C. Shannon is the associate university librarian at Wright State University Libraries. Her primary areas of research interest are the effective integration of information literacy in disciplinary course content, and the implications of data and media literacy for citizenship in the information age.

1
Elections and Political Parties

- Turnout
- Political Parties
- Election Results (President, Congress, and State)
- Minority Elected Officials
- Presidential Nominations
- Districting
- Voting Rights
- Term Limits
- Voting Equipment

In a book about statistics on American politics, elections and campaigns offer us lots and lots of numbers. In fact, if asked for examples of political statistics, most people's minds would go first to election results; many elections are held in any given year, and these elections have extended back to the early years of the country. In this chapter, we share data on voter turnout (Figures 1-1 and 1-2 and Tables 1-1 and 1-2) and on presidential (Table 1-7) and congressional (Table 1-10) election results going back to 1788. This book also provides the most recent results for elections to the governorships and to the state legislatures (Table 1-6), as well as information on presidential primaries and caucuses (Tables 1-23 through 1-26).

As we will discuss in this book, when we have such an abundance of numbers, it behooves us to create some form of summarization. We usually express these summaries in partisan terms, such as comparing a party's share of the vote won and the share of House seats gained (Table 1-12). Wins for the major parties are presented in a variety of ways, but sometimes such results need to be broken down further. In our experience, reporting results by region (Table 1-4 and Figure 1-4) or by state (Tables 1-3, 1-5, and 1-9) is often informative. In addition, historians and political scientists frequently report election results by so-called party systems separated by periods of "realignment"—that is, fundamental shifts in support for parties and the coalitions supporting them. Scholars most often claim that such realignments occurred in the 1850s, 1890s, between 1928 and 1932, and probably in the 1960s.[1] This way of defining party systems is used in the reporting for this analysis (Tables 1-4, 1-8, and 1-11).

We are particularly interested in the current period, as analysis of contemporary election results helps us to understand the world that we see unfolding in front of us. Our data document recent trends in campaigns and elections: the decline in presidential voter turnout between 1960 and 1996 and its recent upsurge (Table 1-1 and Figure 1-1), the electoral advantages of incumbency (Table 1-19), the frequently-lengthened quests for the presidential nominations (Figure 1-5), the greater emphasis on primaries (Tables 1-23 and 1-24), and, in Chapter 2, the growing contributions from political action committees (Table 2-14) and the expense of political campaigns (Tables 2-3 through 2-5).

Besides the arsenal of statistics reporting and summarizing election results by party, other characteristics of the individuals elected to office are of interest. Since we believe it is important to consider the extent to which those who are elected look like those who are voting, we include information on the election of Blacks, Hispanics, and women (Tables 1-21 and 1-22) and on their districts (Table 1-20). Political scientists and others also find it useful to consider the frequency of "divided government" between the presidency and Congress (Table 1-13), to tabulate numbers of House districts in which the votes for president and Congress go to different parties (Table 1-14), to determine individual and partisan turnover rates for members of Congress (Tables 1-15, 1-16, 1-18, and 1-19), and to document the regular pattern of losses by the president's party at midterm elections. The fact that the president's party loses seats in midterm elections is almost taken a given, although this pattern was disrupted in 1998 and 2002 (Table 1-17).

Auxiliary information is often useful in interpreting these election results. One helpful item is a list of political parties that have competed in elections at various times in U.S. history (Figure 1-3). The location and size of presidential nominating conventions (Table 1-27) are also provided, and we also include pertinent information on the election of minorities, as well as on their legislative districts (Table 1-28) and application of the Voting Rights Act (Table 1-29).

While this issue is no longer as hot as it once was, we also consider which states have passed term limits, the length of the limits they have imposed, and the numbers of state representatives who have been "termed out" of office (Tables 1-30 and 1-31). In light of some recent questions about voting equipment, we also present data on the types of voting equipment used throughout the country (Table 1-32). We are quite curious about the issue of voting equipment and procedures, and are interested in how they will evolve in future years.

Despite the large quantity of data in this chapter, there are gaps that reflect the limits on what is known about campaigns, elections, and parties. The lack of survey data on realignments before the 1930s, for example, robs researchers of helpful historical comparisons. Also, not as many sources of data are available on state and local elections as they are on federal elections. Nevertheless, in the area of campaigns and elections, more than anywhere, there is almost an embarrassment of riches.

Note

1. John Aldrich and Richard G. Niemi, "The Sixth American Party System: Electoral Change, 1952–1992," in *Broken Contract? Changing Relationships between Americans and Their Government*, ed. Stephen Craig (Boulder, Colo.: Westview Press, 1996).

Table 1-1 Voter Turnout Rates: United States, South, and Non-South, 1789–2020 (percent)

	Presidential elections[a]				Nonpresidential elections[b]		
Year	United States	Non-South	South[c]	Year	United States	Non-South	South[c]
1789	11.6	11.1	14.3	1790	19.3	18.5	23.5
1792	6.2	6.0	14.4	1794	23.0	22.9	23.5
1796	19.9	19.5	24.9	1798	34.7	33.4	38.0
1800	32.2	40.5	28.7	1802	38.0	36.8	41.0
1804	23.7	27.9	13.1	1806	36.5	35.2	40.2
1808	34.9	42.8	19.1	1810	42.1	40.7	46.8
1812	38.2	43.9	18.9	1814	45.5	45.4	46.0
1816	16.8	20.7	8.1	1818	37.1	33.9	45.8
1820	10.5	12.6	5.2	1822	41.4	38.9	48.0
1824	26.7	26.6	27.2	1826	48.9	46.3	58.9
1828	57.7	62.1	42.5	1830	54.2	55.3	50.6
1832	56.5	64.0	30.1	1834	63.0	63.7	60.7
1836	56.5	58.5	49.2	1838	70.2	72.0	63.7
1840	80.3	81.6	75.4	1842	62.4	63.5	58.3
1844	79.2	80.5	74.2	1846	60.6	62.2	55.2
1848	72.7	74.0	68.0	1850	60.5	61.0	58.5
1852	69.8	72.5	59.3	1854	66.1	65.0	70.0
1856	80.0	81.9	72.2	1858	69.6	71.7	61.5
1860	82.8	84.3	76.7	1862	64.9	64.9	—
1864	77.0	77.0	—	1866	71.2	71.8	51.2[d]
1868	80.9	82.8	71.6	1870	67.0	67.1	66.7
1872	72.5	74.2	67.2	1874	65.0	65.5	63.2
1876	83.4	86.0	75.1	1878	65.1	70.5	48.4
1880	81.2	86.4	65.2	1882	64.2	68.1	58.5
1884	79.1	83.7	64.3	1886	63.9	70.6	42.0
1888	80.9	86.1	64.0	1890	64.6	70.4	44.7
1892	76.2	81.2	59.4	1894	67.5	73.5	47.2
1896	79.9	86.4	57.7	1898	60.1	68.0	33.6
1900	73.9	82.9	43.5	1902	55.7	65.2	23.8
1904	65.8	76.8	29.0	1906	51.4	61.1	18.6
1908	65.9	76.4	30.8	1910	51.8	61.0	20.6
1912	59.0	67.5	27.9	1914	50.1	58.5	18.6
1916	60.7	67.7	31.6	1918	39.9	45.8	14.8
1920	49.3	57.4	21.8	1922	35.8	42.7	11.8
1924	49.0	57.7	19.0	1926	33.0	40.0	8.5
1928	57.1	66.8	23.6	1930	36.9	44.0	12.2
1932	57.3	66.7	24.5	1934	44.8	53.9	13.1
1936	61.4	72.0	25.0	1938	47.0	57.4	11.3
1940	62.9	73.6	26.5	1942	34.1	42.0	7.2
1944	56.2	65.6	24.5	1946	38.8	47.2	10.4
1948	52.2	59.1	23.7	1950	43.6	51.9	13.6
1952	62.3	70.0	38.9	1954	43.5	51.2	17.2
1956	60.2	67.2	37.4	1958	45.0	53.6	16.1
1960	63.8	70.1	40.2	1962	47.7	54.1	24.0
1964	62.8	67.4	45.6	1966	48.7	52.9	33.1
1968	62.5	64.4	51.4	1970	47.3	50.9	34.7
1972	56.2	59.6	44.8	1974	39.1	43.1	26.1
1976	54.8	57.1	47.6	1978[e]	39.0	41.8	30.0
1980	54.2	56.4	47.6	1982[e]	42.1	44.7	31.0
1984	55.2	57.2	49.7	1986	38.1	39.3	34.7
1988	52.8	54.7	47.3	1990	38.4	39.5	35.2

Table 1-1 *(Continued)*

	Presidential elections[a]				*Nonpresidential elections*[b]		
Year	United States	Non-South	South[c]	Year	United States	Non-South	South[c]
1992	58.1	59.9	53.0	1994	41.1	42.8	36.5
1996	51.7	53.1	47.7	1998	38.1	40.1	32.8
2000	54.2	55.5	51.1	2002	39.5	40.2	37.9
2004	60.1	61.1	57.8	2006	40.4	42.4	35.5
2008	61.6	61.8	61.1	2010	41.0	42.1	37.9
2012[f]	58.2	60.0	58.0	2014[f]	35.9	37.2	35.8
2016[f]	60.1	62.3	59.0	2018[f]	50.0	52.0	49.0
2020[f]	66.8	69.1	65.9				

Note: "—" indicates not available. In presidential election years, these turnout figures represent, insofar as possible, the percentage of the eligible electorate that cast votes in presidential elections. In nonpresidential election years through 1946, the figures are the percentage voting in elections for the U.S. House of Representatives. Since 1948, they are the "vote for highest office"—that is, the largest number of votes for a statewide office (U.S. senator or governor) or, if lacking a statewide office, the sum of the votes for the U.S. House of Representatives. In recent years, the problem of estimating turnout for the House has been complicated by the fact that Arkansas, Florida, Louisiana, Oklahoma, and Texas do not tally votes when races are uncontested. The definition of *eligibility* has varied considerably over the years, depending on age, race, gender, felony convictions, and citizenship status. Some states during some periods allowed noncitizens to vote, but this practice has not been permitted nationwide since 1924. Estimating the eligible electorate is especially difficult for the nineteenth century. For details, see Walter Dean Burnham, *Voting in American Elections: The Shaping of the American Political Universe since 1788* (Palo Alto, Calif.: Academia Press, 2010). Also see Curtis Gans, *Vote Turnout in the United States, 1788–2009* (Washington, D.C.: CQ Press, 2011). From 1924 through 1946, the base is what is known as the citizen voting-age population. From 1948 through 2014, the base is the citizen-eligible population, which begins with the voting-age population but removes noncitizens and ineligible felons and adds in overseas eligible voters. Turnout based on the voter-eligible population is higher than that based on the voting-age population. For 2000–2008, the figures for voters living abroad are apportioned between the South and the non-South based on a 2008 estimate, state by state, of the number of citizens living abroad. For the methodology, see George Mason University (*www.electproject.org*), and Michael P. McDonald and Samuel L. Popkin, "The Myth of the Vanishing Voter," *American Political Science Review* 95 (2001): 963–974. Note that the number of people actually going to the polls is slightly higher than these percentages indicate; some voters do not vote for a given office such as president or U.S. representative, and a small number of ballots are spoiled.

[a] Before 1828, only a limited number of states held popular votes for president. Numbers shown reflect turnout in those states.
[b] Before 1880, one or more states held elections for the U.S. House of Representatives in the year following the presidential election year. Before the Civil War, this practice was quite common, especially in the South and New England. Thus, for example, "1840" should be read as "1840/41."
[c] The eleven states of the Confederacy.
[d] Tennessee only.
[e] Because of Louisiana's second ballot system, Louisiana is excluded from the numerator and denominator for 1978 and 1982.
[f] The percentage for the United States includes overseas citizens in the denominator. The percentages for the Non-South and South do not and are therefore slightly inflated.

Sources: 1789–1946: Walter Dean Burnham, *Voting in American Elections: The Shaping of the American Political Universe since 1788* (Palo Alto, Calif.: Academica Press, 2010); 1948–2020: Michael P. McDonald, George Mason University, www.electproject.org; and personal communication.

Figure 1-1 Voter Turnout Rates: Presidential and Midterm Elections, 1789–2020

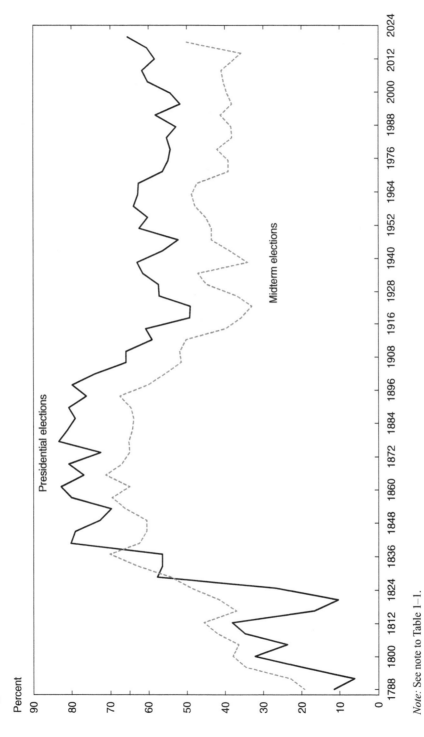

Note: See note to Table 1–1.
Source: Table 1–1, this volume.

Figure 1-2 Voter Turnout Rates: Presidential Elections, South and Non-South, 1789–2020

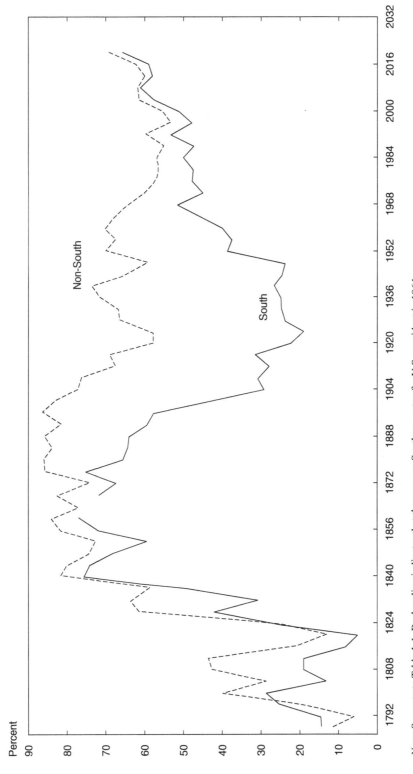

Note: See note to Table 1-1. Broken line indicates that there are no Southern votes for U.S. president in 1864.

Source: Table 1-1, this volume.

A Data Literacy Lesson
Turnout Disparities in the South and Non-South

Take a look at Figure 1-1. It shows voter turnout, differentiated between presidential and off-year elections, which are often called midterm elections since they happen in the middle of the president's term. Not surprisingly, midterm elections have lower turnout, since they lack the excitement and stimulus that presidential elections provide to voters. But, looking at the lines separately, they track a clear trajectory—very low turnout in the early years of the nation, much higher turnout in the second half of the nineteenth century, followed by a decline in the 20th. It may be too early to tell, but we could be seeing a resurgence of turnout in the last few elections.

A figure like this one aggregates the entire nation and shows the results. However, this does not account for sub-groups within the population, and how (or if) their data might differ. If, for example, we found that purchases of hip-hop records increased by 20 percent in the last decade, we would not assume that everyone purchased 20 percent more hip-hop records during that time. For some groups (we imagine younger people), the increase might be even larger, while to balance this off, for others there might be no increase, or perhaps even a decrease.

In presenting longitudinal data (data collected over a long period), a researcher might decide that some separation of the data into its component parts would be valuable. Consider, then, the data reported in Table 1-1, and graphed in Figure 1-2. Following previous editions of this book, we have chosen to break these data out separately by whether a state is in the South (defined as the eleven states of the Confederacy) or not in the South. This was a very important distinction for much of American history. Following the end of Reconstruction in 1877, southern states took drastic steps to limit the political participation of its Black citizens. (Northern states, by the way, were no angels, but the South led the charge in attempting to limit participation.) The Progressive Movement of the late 1800s and early 1900s ushered in some reforms that made it easier to vote, but this movement was concentrated mostly in the North and did not have a significant impact in Southern states.

Table 1-1 and Figure 1-2 both reveal shockingly large gaps in turnout between North and South, in some years exceeding 40 percent. These gaps began to shrink at the beginning of the Civil Rights Movement; while voting rights was not specifically addressed by Congress until the Voting Rights Act of 1965, the growth of the movement and increase in the light that it shed on racial discrimination started to reduce these turnout disparities even before the Voting Rights Act was passed.

Simply put, the Voting Rights Act was successful in reducing turnout gaps between white and Black populations, and between the North and the South. Today, while turnout in the South has not yet matched turnout in the North, the gaps have shrunk considerably, to the point that separating our data down by South and non-South does not explain very much today. The Table and Figure are still quite useful from an historical perspective, so we continue to share it. If we were going to explain deviations in turnout today, however, South versus non-South does not provide us much analytical leverage.

The history lesson that this graph teaches us remains extremely important. The prevalence of racism, an important element in any honest reckoning with American history, reminds us that a common strategy for groups with power is to deny groups that lack power the chance to have their voices heard, and the chance to challenge the status quo. As we write this, even a cursory glance at the news shows us that many states are taking steps to make access to voting harder, done in the name of election security. This movement follows directly from attempts by former president Donald Trump and his supporters to challenge mail-in voting and other aspects of the results of the 2020 election.

We will let you draw your own conclusions about how necessary these laws are. What is beyond dispute is that these laws will make it harder for people (especially those with fewer resources) to vote. Since at least some of the states pursuing these policies are in the South (Georgia and Texas are among the states leading the charge), we may see some of these South versus non-South patterns begin to reemerge. Furthermore, the Supreme Court case of Shelby County v. Holder, which eliminated the Preclearance Provisions from the Voting Rights Act (see the Note to Table 1-30), hearkens back to the older days of North–South distinctions.

We do not know what the future will hold, or what distinctions will be important in separating out key elements of these patterns. The example we show here of how data can be disaggregated into these components provides a useful lesson in how broader national trends do not necessarily affect all subunits equally, and that these differential effects may evolve over time.

Table 1-2 Voting-Age Population Registered and Voting: Cross Sections, 2000–2020 (percent)

	Percentage reporting they registered											Percentage reporting they voted										
	Presidential election years						Congressional election years					Presidential election years						Congressional election years				
	2000	2004	2008	2012	2016	2020	2002	2006	2010	2014	2018	2000	2004	2008	2012	2016	2020	2002	2006	2010	2014	2018
Race/ethnicity																						
White[a]	66	68	67	67	66	74	63	64	62	66	69	56	60	60	58	58	68	44	46	43	44	55
Black[a]	64	64	66	69	65	69	59	57	59	63	64	54	56	61	62	56	63	40	39	41	40	51
Hispanic origin[b]	35	34	38	39	39	44	33	32	34	35	39	28	28	32	32	33	36	19	19	20	18	26
Hispanic citizen[b]	57	58	59	59	57	61	53	54	52	51	54	45	47	50	48	48	54	30	32	31	27	40
Sex																						
Men	62	64	63	63	69	71	59	60	58	63	65	53	56	56	54	59	65	41	42	41	47	55
Women	66	68	67	67	72	74	63	63	61	66	68	56	60	60	59	63	68	43	45	43	51	57
Region[c]																						
Northeast	64	65	64	65	70	74	61	60	60	63	65	55	59	57	57	57	64	41	43	42	45	51
Midwest	70	73	71	71	74	76	66	68	65	66	68	61	65	63	62	64	68	47	51	45	46	50
South	65	65	66	65	70	72	62	62	59	61	64	54	56	58	56	54	60	42	40	39	42	47
West	57	60	59	59	68	71	54	55	55	59	62	50	54	55	52	66	69	39	42	43	45	48
Age																						
18–20 years	41	51	49	44	50	55	33	37	34	34	36	28	41	41	35	39	48	15	17	16	15	23
21–24 years	49	52	56	53	59	63	42	45	47	48	47	35	42	47	40	46	54	19	22	22	19	32
25–34 years	55	56	57	57	65	68	50	50	50	56	52	44	47	48	46	53	60	27	28	27	28	37
35–44 years	64	64	61	62	70	72	60	59	57	65	57	55	57	55	53	60	65	40	40	38	38	44
45–64 years	71	73	70	70	74	75	69	70	66	70	66	64	67	65	63	67	71	53	54	51	49	55
65 years and older	76	77	75	77	78	78	76	75	73	75	73	68	69	68	70	71	74	61	60	59	58	64

Employment																						
Employed	65	67	66	67	72	77	62	63	62	67	68	56	60	60	59	63	70	42	44	43	45	57
Unemployed	46	56	57	57	63	68	48	48	52	56	62	35	46	49	46	50	58	27	28	32	30	44
Not in labor force	64	64	63	63	67	70	61	61	59	63	64	55	56	54	58	58	64	44	44	42	43	52
Education (years)																						
8 or less	36	33	30	29	42	45	32	30	27	44	41	27	24	23	22	32	38	19	17	16	24	25
1–3 of high school	46	45	43	43	47	51	42	38	39	47	44	34	34	32	32	35	42	23	22	21	22	28
4 of high school	60	60	59	59	63	63	57	55	53	58	58	49	50	51	49	52	56	37	36	35	34	42
1–3 of college	70	74	72	71	73	76	67	68	66	67	79	60	66	65	61	63	70	46	47	44	42	55
Total	64	66	65	65	70	73	61	62	60	65	67	55	58	57	61	63	67	42	44	42	42	49

Note: Data for earlier years can be found in previous editions of *Vital Statistics on American Politics.*

[a] In 2002 and after, whites are individuals identifying with that race alone; Blacks are individuals identifying with that race alone.
[b] Persons of Hispanic origin may be of any race.
[c] For composition of regions, see Table A-1, this volume.

Sources: Calculated by the authors from U.S. Census Bureau, "Current Population Reports, Voting and Registration in the Election of November 1994," series P-20, no. PPL-25RV; "November 1996," no. 504; "November 1998," no. 523; "November 2000," no. 542; "November 2002," no. 552; "November 2004," no. 556; "November 2006," no. 557; "November 2008," no. 562; "November 2010"; "November 2012"; "November 2014"; "November 2016"; "November 2018"; "November 2020," www.census.gov.

Figure 1-3 American Political Parties since 1789

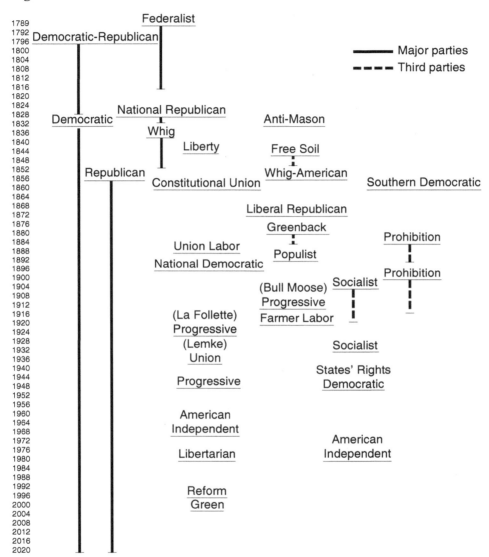

Note: In 1824 and later, the chart indicates the years in which the presidential candidate of a political party received 1.0 percent or more of the popular vote. Minor parties are not included if the minor-party candidate is also the candidate of one of the two major parties (as happened in 1896 when the Populists endorsed William Jennings Bryan, the Democratic candidate). Party candidates sometimes run under different designations in different states (in 1968 George C. Wallace ran for president under at least ten party labels). In such cases, the vote totals for the candidate were aggregated under a single party designation. Sometimes candidates run under no party label as H. Ross Perot did in 1992. (In 1996, Perot ran under the Reform Party label.)

Sources: 1789–1820: U.S. Bureau of the Census, *Historical Statistics of the United States, Colonial Times to 1970* (Washington, D.C.: Government Printing Office, 1975); 1824–2012: *CQ Press Guide to U.S. Elections,* 7th ed. (Washington, D.C.: CQ Press, 2016), 215; 2016–2020: Table 1-9, this volume, and previous editions of *Vital Statistics on American Politics.*

Table 1-3 Party Competition: Presidency, by State, 1992–2020

Number of times Democratic presidential candidate carried the state

0	1	2	3 through 6	7	8
Alabama (9)	Indiana (11)	Arizona (11)	Florida (30) [3 times]	New Hampshire (4)	California (54)
Alaska (3)	Montana (4)	Arkansas (6)		New Mexico (5)	Connecticut (7)
Idaho (4)	North Carolina (16)	Georgia (16)	Ohio (17) [4 times]	Pennsylvania (19)	Delaware (3)
Kansas (6)		Kentucky (8)	Virginia (13) [4 times]	Michigan (15)	District of Columbia (3)
Mississippi (6)		Louisiana (8)		Wisconsin (10)	Hawaii (4)
Nebraska (5)		Missouri (10)	Colorado (10) [5 times]		Illinois (19)
North Dakota (3)		Tennessee (11)	Iowa (6) [5 times]		Maine (4)
Oklahoma (7)		West Virginia (4)			Maryland (10)
South Carolina (9)			Nevada (6) [6 times]		Massachusetts (11)
South Dakota (3)					Minnesota (10)
Texas (40)					New Jersey (14)
Utah (6)					New York (28)
Wyoming (3)					Oregon (8)
					Rhode Island (4)
					Vermont (3)
					Washington (12)
Total electoral votes:					
104	31	74	82	53	194

Note: Numbers of electoral votes for 2024 and subsequent elections are shown in parentheses. For similar data on other periods, see previous editions of *Vital Statistics on American Politics*.

Sources: CQ Press Guide to U.S. Elections, 7th ed. (Washington, D.C.: CQ Press, 2016), 927–932, 1,834; Table 1-9, this volume; and previous editions of *Vital Statistics on American Politics*.

Table 1-4 Party Competition, by Region, 1860–2020 (percent)

Region/office	1860–1895	1896–1931	1932–1965	1966–2020
New England				
President	85.2	85.5	53.7	33.5
Governor	74.3	85.5	63.1	50.2
U.S. representative	86.8	82.8	60.6	24.4
U.S. senator	a	83.3	65.1	37.1
Middle Atlantic				
President	38.9	88.9	47.2	32.9
Governor	34.9	66.7	51.4	51.0
U.S. representative	59.3	68.9	52.9	41.1
U.S. senator	a	76.9	57.7	37.5
Midwest				
President	77.8	84.4	44.4	53.4
Governor	78.8	78.9	46.9	67.1
U.S. representative	61.1	74.5	57.8	52.1
U.S. senator	a	83.3	50.8	37.2
Plains				
President	88.9	77.8	57.4	79.6
Governor	94.4	71.3	70.4	60.1
U.S. representative	88.6	84.2	76.4	60.9
U.S. senator	a	83.9	79.7	54.6
South				
President	18.4	6.1	15.8	77.6
Governor	21.2	4.2	0.0	59.7
U.S. representative	25.0	7.5	7.2	47.5
U.S. senator	a	0.0	1.5	66.3
Border South				
President	8.6	56.8	22.2	60.7
Governor	22.2	38.6	16.7	36.4
U.S. representative	19.4	36.5	18.7	42
U.S. senator	a	42.4	23.4	49.6
Rocky Mountain				
President	73.3	57.8	35.2	80.4
Governor	58.3	51.1	38.5	55.2
U.S. representative	70.0	67.6	30.3	61.2
U.S. senator	a	32.4	20.6	62.1
Pacific Coast				
President	75.0	75.0	37.5	45.3
Governor	47.4	70.8	59.4	35.6
U.S. representative	64.4	85.6	49.0	36.3
U.S. senator	a	73.7	44.4	36.8

Note: Table entries are the percentages of all elections won by Republicans. For composition of regions, see Table A-3, this volume.

[a] Direct election of U.S. senators began after passage of the Seventeenth Amendment in 1913.

Sources: Clerk of the House of Representatives, http://clerk.house.gov; *Congressional Quarterly's Guide to U.S. Elections*, 3rd ed. (Washington, D.C.: Congressional Quarterly, 1994), 1344; *Congressional Quarterly Weekly Report* (*CQ Weekly*) (1996), 3192, 3226, 3238, 3242; (1998), 3002, 3004, 3010–3011; (2000), 2671, 2704–2706; (2002), 3289–3297; (2004), 2653–2660; (2006), 3068–3078, 3132, 3186, 3238, 3381; (2008), 3019, 3043–3052, 3056, 3102, 3153, 3206, 3293, 3374; (2010), 2618–2627, 2716, 2766; (2012), 2284–2293, 2342, 2384, 2430; National Governors Association, www.nga.org; official election results from state websites; Table 1-9, this volume.

Table 1-5 Party Competition in the States, 1992–2020

		Percentage of Democratic wins[a]		
0–20	21–40	41–60	61–80	81–100
Alaska	Georgia	Alabama	Arkansas	California
Arizona	Indiana	Colorado	Delaware	Connecticut
Florida	Iowa	Kentucky	Illinois	Hawaii
Idaho	Michigan	Louisiana	Maine	Maryland
Kansas	Missouri	Mississippi	Minnesota	Massachusetts
Nebraska[b]	Montana	North Carolina	Nevada	New Mexico
North Dakota	New Hampshire	Oklahoma	New Jersey	Rhode Island
Ohio	Wisconsin	Tennessee	New York	Washington
Pennsylvania		Virginia	Oregon	
South Carolina			Vermont	
South Dakota			West Virginia	
Texas				
Utah				
Wyoming				

Note: For similar data on other periods, see previous editions of *Vital Statistics on American Politics*.

[a] The governorship, control of the lower chamber, and control of the upper chamber are figured separately—that is, if in a given state the Democrats won the governorship and control of one chamber, they had 66.7 percent of the wins in that election cycle.

[b] Results are for the governorship only because the legislature is nonpartisan.

Sources: Compiled by the authors. Council of State Governments, *The Book of the States, 1990–91* (Lexington, Ky.: Council of State Governments, 1990), 123; *1992–93* (1992), 141, 269–272; *1996–97* (1996), 68–69, 153–156; *2004* (2004), 269–270; *2006* (2006), 270–271; *2008* (2008), 305–306; *2010* (2010), 332–333; *2012* (2012), 332–333; *2014* (2014), 275–276; *Congressional Quarterly's Politics in America 1994* (Washington, D.C.: CQ Press, 1993); *Congressional Quarterly's Politics in America 1998* (Washington, D.C.: CQ Press, 1997); National Conference of State Legislatures, www.ncsl.org; National Governors Association, www.nga.org; and Richard Scammon and Rhodes Cook, eds., *America Votes 25, 2001–2002: A Handbook of Contemporary American Election Statistics* (Washington, D.C.: CQ Press, 2003).

Table 1-6 Partisan Division of Governors and State Legislatures, 2021

	Governor			Legislature						
				Upper house			Lower house			
State	Name	Party	Next up for election	Democrats	Republicans	Other[a]	Seats up in 2022	Democrats	Republicans	Other[a]	Seats up in 2022
Alabama	Kay Ivey	R	2022	8	26	1v	35	27	76	2v	105
Alaska	Mike Dunleavy	R	2022	7	13		10	15	21	4	40
Arizona	Doug Ducey	R	2022	14	16		30	29	31		60
Arkansas	Asa Hutchinson	R	2022	7	27	1	35	22	78		100
California	Gavin Newsom	D	2022	31	9		20	59	19	1, 1v	80
Colorado	Jared Polis	D	2022	20	15		17	41	24		65
Connecticut	Ned Lamont	D	2022	24	12		36	97	54		151
Delaware	John Carney	D	2024	14	7		10	26	15		41
Florida	Ron DeSantis	R	2022	16	24		20	42	78		120
Georgia	Brian Kemp	R	2022	22	34		56	77	101	2v	180
Hawaii	David Ige	D	2022	23	1	1v	25	47	4		51
Idaho	Brad Little	R	2022	7	28		35	12	58		70
Illinois	JB Pritzker	D[b]	2022	41	18		59	73	45		118
Indiana	Eric Holcomb	R	2024	11	39		25	29	71		100
Iowa	Kim Reynolds	R	2022	18	32		25	41	59		100
Kansas	Laura Kelly	D[b]	2022	11	29		0[c]	39	86		125
Kentucky	Andy Beshear	D	2023	8	30		19	25	75		100
Louisiana	John Bel Edwards	D[b]	2023	12	27		0[d]	35	68	2	0[d]
Maine	Janet Mills	D[b]	2022	22	13		35	80	66	5	151
Maryland	Larry Hogan	R	2022	32	15		47	99	42		141
Massachusetts	Charlie Baker	R	2022	37	3		40	129	30	1	160
Michigan	Gretchen Whitmer	D[b]	2022	16	20	2v	38	52	58		110
Minnesota	Tim Walz	D	2022	31	34	2	67	70	64		134

State	Governor	Party	Year							
Mississippi	Tate Reeves	R	2023	16	36		46	75	1	0[e]
Missouri	Mike Parson	R	2024	10	24	17	49	113	1v	163
Montana	Greg Gianforte	R[b]	2024	19[f]	31[f]	25	33[f]	66[f]	1v	100[f]
Nebraska	Pete Ricketts	R	2022			49				
Nevada	Steve Sisolak	R	2022	12	9	11	26	16		42
New Hampshire	Chris Sununu	R	2022	10	14	24	185	212	3v	400
New Jersey	Phil Murphy	D[b]	2021	25	15	0[g]	52	28		0[g]
New Mexico	Michelle Lujan Grisham	D[b]	2022	27	15	0[h]	44	24	1, 1v	70
New York	Andrew Cuomo	D	2022	43	20	63	106	43	1v	150
North Carolina	Roy Cooper	D[b]	2024	22	28	50	51	69		120
North Dakota	Doug Burgum	R	2024	7	40	24	14	80		48
Ohio	Mike DeWine	R	2022	8	25	17	35	64		99
Oklahoma	Kevin Stitt	R	2022	9	39	24	19	82		101
Oregon	Kate Brown	D	2022	18	11	1	15	37	22	1v	60
Pennsylvania	Tom Wolf	D	2022	21	28	1	25	89	113	1v	203
Rhode Island	Dan McKee	D	2022	33	5	38	65	10		75
South Carolina	Henry McMaster	R	2022	16	30	0[i]	43	81		124
South Dakota	Kristi Noem	R	2022	3	32	35	8	62		70
Tennessee	Bill Lee	R	2022	6	27	17	26	73		99
Texas	Greg Abbott	R	2022	13	18	31	67	83		150
Utah	Spencer Cox	R	2024	6	23	14	17	58		75
Vermont	Phil Scott	R	2022	21	7	2	30	92	46	12	150
Virginia	Ralph Northam	D	2021	21	18	1v	0[j]	55	45		0[j]
Washington	Jay Inslee	D	2024	29	20	24	56	41		98
West Virginia	Jim Justice	R	2024	11	23	17	22	78		100
Wisconsin	Tony Evers	D[b]	2022	12	21	17	38	60	1v	99
Wyoming	Mark Gordon	R	2022	2	28	15	7	51		60
Total	D 23, R 27			848	1,059	1,266	2,448	2,918		4,958

Note: "D" indicates Democratic Party; "R" indicates Republican Party. Governors and legislatures as of June 17, 2021. Data for earlier years can be found in previous editions of *Vital Statistics on American Politics*.

(Table continues)

Table 1-6 *(Continued)*

[a] Indicates number of vacant seats (denoted by a "v" after the number), or number of independents.
[b] Change in party control from previous election.
[c] Forty members of the upper-house are up for election in 2024.
[d] Thirty-nine upper-house seats and 105 lower-house seats are up for election in 2023.
[e] Fifty-two upper-house seats and 122 lower-house seats are up for election in 2023.
[f] Nebraska's forty-nine–member state legislature is nonpartisan and unicameral; twenty-four seats are up for election in 2022.
[g] Forty upper-house seats and eighty lower-house seats are up for election in 2021.
[h] Forty-two seats in the upper house up are for election in 2024.
[i] Forty-six seats in upper house are up for election in 2024.
[j] One hundred lower-house seats are up for election in 2021; forty upper-house seats and 100 lower-house seats are up for election in 2023.

Sources: Governors, name, and party: National Governors Association, www.nga.org; state legislative partisan composition as of 2021: National Conference of State Legislatures, www.ncsl.org, and updated by authors from state government websites; next up for election, governors and state legislatures: calculated by the authors from these sources, previous editions of *Vital Statistics on American Politics*, and state government websites.

Table 1-7 Popular and Electoral Votes for President, 1789–2020

Year	Number of states	Candidates		Electoral vote (number and percent)		Popular vote (number and percent)
1789[a]	10[b]		(Federalist)			
		George Washington		69		
				100%		
1792[a]	15	George Washington		132		
				98%		
1796[a]	16	(Democratic-Republican)	(Federalist)			
		Thomas Jefferson	John Adams	68	71	
				49%	51%	
1800[a]	16	Thomas Jefferson	John Adams	73	65	
				53%	47%	
1804	17	Thomas Jefferson	Charles C. Pinckney	162	14	
		George Clinton	Rufus King	92%	8%	
1808	17	James Madison	Charles C. Pinckney	122	47	
		George Clinton	Rufus King	69%	27%	
1812	18	James Madison	George Clinton	128	89	
		Elbridge Gerry	Jared Ingersoll	59%	41%	
1816	19	James Monroe	Rufus King	183	34	
		Daniel D. Tompkins	John Eager Howard	83%	15%	
		(Democratic-Republican)	(Independent Democratic-Republican)			
1820	24	James Monroe	John Q. Adams	231	1	
		Daniel D. Tompkins	Richard Stockton	98%	0%	
1824[c]	24	Andrew Jackson	John Q. Adams	99	84	
		Nathan Sanford	John C. Calhoun	38%	32%	
		(Democratic-Republican)	(National-Republican)		(National-Republican)	(Democratic-Republican)

(Table continues)

19

Table 1-7 *(Continued)*

Year	Number of states	Candidates		Electoral vote (number and percent)		Popular vote (number and percent)	
1828	24	Andrew Jackson	John Q. Adams	178	83	642,553	500,897
				68%	32%	56.0%	43.6%
1832	24	Andrew Jackson	Henry Clay	219	49	701,780	484,205
		Martin Van Buren	John Sergeant	76%	17%	54.2%	37.4%
		(Democratic)	*(Whig)*	*(Democratic)*	*(Whig)*	*(Democratic)*	*(Whig)*
1836	26	Martin Van Buren	William Henry Harrison	170	73[d]	764,176	550,816
		Richard M. Johnson	Francis Granger	58%	25%	50.8%	36.6%
1840	26	Martin Van Buren	William Henry Harrison	60	234	1,128,854	1,275,390
		Richard M. Johnson	John Tyler	20%	80%	46.8%	52.9%
1844	26	James K. Polk	Henry Clay	170	105	1,339,494	1,300,004
		George M. Dallas	Theodore Frelinghuysen	62%	38%	49.5%	48.1%
1848	30	Lewis Cass	Zachary Taylor	127	163	1,223,460	1,361,393
		William O. Butler	Millard Fillmore	44%	56%	42.5%	47.3%
1852	31	Franklin Pierce	Winfield Scott	254	42	1,607,510	1,386,942
		William R. King	William A. Graham	86%	14%	50.8%	43.9%
		(Democratic)	*(Republican)*	*(Democratic)*	*(Republican)*	*(Democratic)*	*(Republican)*
1856	31	James Buchanan	John C. Fremont	174	114	1,836,072	1,342,345
		John C. Breckinridge	William L. Dayton	59%	39%	45.3%	33.1%
1860	33	Stephen A. Douglas	Abraham Lincoln	12	180	1,380,202	1,865,908
		Herschel V. Johnson	Hannibal Hamlin	4%	59%	29.5%	39.8%
1864	36[e]	George B. McClellan	Abraham Lincoln	21	212	1,809,445	2,220,846
		George H. Pendleton	Andrew Johnson	9%	91%	44.9%	55.1%
1868	37[f]	Horatio Seymour	Ulysses S. Grant	80	214	2,708,744	3,013,650
		Francis P. Blair Jr.	Schuyler Colfax	27%	73%	47.3%	52.7%
1872	37	Horace Greeley	Ulysses S. Grant	g	286	2,835,315	3,598,468
		Benjamin G. Brown	Henry Wilson	g	78%	43.8%	55.6%
1876	38	Samuel J. Tilden	Rutherford B. Hayes	184	185	4,288,191	4,033,497
		Thomas A. Hendricks	William A. Wheeler	50%	50%	51.0%	48.0%

Year	#	Democratic Pres.	Democratic VP	EV	EV%	Popular	Pop%	Republican Pres.	Republican VP	EV	EV%	Popular	Pop%
1880	38	Winfield S. Hancock	William H. English	155	42%	4,445,256	48.2%	James A. Garfield	Chester A. Arthur	214	58%	4,453,611	48.3%
1884	38	Grover Cleveland	Thomas A. Hendricks	219	55%	4,915,586	48.9%	James G. Blaine	John A. Logan	182	45%	4,852,916	48.2%
1888	38	Grover Cleveland	Allen G. Thurman	168	42%	5,539,118	48.6%	Benjamin Harrison	Levi P. Morton	233	58%	5,449,825	47.8%
1892	44	Grover Cleveland	Adlai E. Stevenson	277	62%	5,554,617	46.0%	Benjamin Harrison	Whitelaw Reid	145	33%	5,186,793	43.0%
1896	45	William Jennings Bryan	Arthur Sewall	176	39%	6,370,897	45.8%	William McKinley	Garret A. Hobart	271	61%	7,105,144	51.1%
1900	45	William Jennings Bryan	Adlai E. Stevenson	155	35%	6,357,698	45.5%	William McKinley	Theodore Roosevelt	292	65%	7,219,193	51.7%
1904	45	Alton B. Parker	Henry G. Davis	140	29%	5,083,501	37.6%	Theodore Roosevelt	Charles W. Fairbanks	336	71%	7,625,599	56.4%
1908	46	William Jennings Bryan	John W. Kern	162	34%	6,406,874	43.0%	William Howard Taft	James S. Sherman	321	66%	7,676,598	51.6%
1912	48	Woodrow Wilson	Thomas R. Marshall	435	82%	6,294,326	41.8%	William Howard Taft	James S. Sherman[h]	8	2%	3,486,343	23.2%
1916	48	Woodrow Wilson	Thomas R. Marshall	277	52%	9,126,063	49.2%	Charles E. Hughes	Charles W. Fairbanks	254	48%	8,547,039	46.1%
1920	48	James M. Cox	Franklin D. Roosevelt	127	24%	9,134,074	34.2%	Warren G. Harding	Calvin Coolidge	404	76%	16,151,916	60.3%
1924	48	John W. Davis	Charles W. Bryan	136	26%	8,386,532	28.8%	Calvin Coolidge	Charles G. Dawes	382	72%	15,724,310	54.0%
1928	48	Alfred E. Smith	Joseph T. Robinson	87	16%	15,004,336	40.8%	Herbert C. Hoover	Charles Curtis	444	84%	21,432,823	58.2%
1932	48	Franklin D. Roosevelt	John Nance Garner	472	89%	22,818,740	57.4%	Herbert C. Hoover	Charles Curtis	59	11%	15,760,425	39.6%
1936	48	Franklin D. Roosevelt	John Nance Garner	523	98%	27,750,866	60.8%	Alfred M. Landon	Frank Knox	8	2%	16,679,683	36.5%
1940	48	Franklin D. Roosevelt	Henry A. Wallace	449	85%	27,343,218	54.7%	Wendell L. Willkie	Charles L. McNary	82	15%	22,334,940	44.8%

(Table continues)

21

Table 1-7 *(Continued)*

Year	Number of states	Candidates		Electoral vote (number and percent)		Popular vote (number and percent)	
1944	48	Franklin D. Roosevelt	Thomas E. Dewey	432	99	25,612,610	22,021,053
		Harry S. Truman	John W. Bricker	81%	19%	53.4%	45.9%
1948	48	Harry S. Truman	Thomas E. Dewey	303	189	24,105,810	21,970,064
		Alben W. Barkley	Earl Warren	57%	36%	49.5%	45.1%
1952	48	Adlai E. Stevenson II	Dwight D. Eisenhower	89	442	27,314,992	33,777,945
		John J. Sparkman	Richard Nixon	17%	83%	44.4%	54.9%
1956	48	Adlai E. Stevenson II	Dwight D. Eisenhower	73	457	26,022,752	35,590,472
		Estes Kefauver	Richard Nixon	14%	86%	42.0%	57.4%
1960	50	John F. Kennedy	Richard Nixon	303	219	34,226,731	34,108,157
		Lyndon B. Johnson	Henry Cabot Lodge Jr.	56%	41%	49.7%	49.5%
1964	50	Lyndon B. Johnson	Barry M. Goldwater	486	52	43,129,566	27,178,188
		Hubert H. Humphrey	William E. Miller	90%	10%	61.1%	38.5%
1968	50	Hubert H. Humphrey	Richard Nixon	191	301	31,275,166	31,785,480
		Edmund S. Muskie	Spiro T. Agnew	36%	56%	42.7%	43.4%
1972	50	George S. McGovern	Richard Nixon	17	520	29,170,383	47,169,911
		R. Sargent Shriver Jr.	Spiro T. Agnew	3%	97%	37.5%	60.7%
1976	50	Jimmy Carter	Gerald R. Ford	297	240	40,830,763	39,147,793
		Walter F. Mondale	Robert J. Dole	55%	45%	50.1%	48.0%
1980	50	Jimmy Carter	Ronald Reagan	49	489	35,483,883	43,904,153
		Walter F. Mondale	George H. W. Bush	9%	91%	41.0%	50.7%
1984	50	Walter F. Mondale	Ronald Reagan	13	525	37,577,185	54,455,075
		Geraldine Ferraro	George H. W. Bush	2%	98%	40.6%	58.8%
1988	50	Michael S. Dukakis	George H. W. Bush	111	426	41,809,074	48,886,097
		Lloyd M. Bentsen Jr.	Dan Quayle	21%	79%	45.6%	53.4%
1992	50	Bill Clinton	George H. W. Bush	370	168	44,909,326	39,103,882
		Al Gore	Dan Quayle	69%	31%	43.0%	37.4%
1996	50	Bill Clinton	Robert J. Dole	379	159	47,402,357	39,198,755
		Al Gore	Jack Kemp	70%	30%	49.2%	40.7%

Year		Candidates		Electoral Votes	%	Popular Votes	%
2000	50	Al Gore	George W. Bush	266	49%	50,992,335	48.4%
		Joseph I. Lieberman	Dick Cheney	271	50%	50,455,156	47.9%
2004	50	John Kerry	George W. Bush	251	47%	59,028,439	48.3%
		John Edwards	Dick Cheney	286	53%	62,040,610	50.7%
2008	50	Barack Obama	John McCain	365	68%	69,498,516	52.9%
		Joseph R. Biden Jr.	Sarah Palin	173	32%	59,948,323	45.7%
2012	50	Barack Obama	Mitt Romney	332	62%	65,587,106	51.0%
		Joseph R. Biden Jr.	Paul Ryan	206	38%	60,848,302	47.3%
2016	50	Hillary Clinton	Donald J. Trump	232	43%	65,853,625	48.2%
		Tim Kaine	Mike Pence	306	57%	62,985,106	46.1%
2020	50	Joseph R. Biden Jr.	Donald J. Trump	306	57%	81,282,916	51.3%
		Kamala Harris	Mike Pence	232	43%	74,223,369	46.9%

Note: For details of the electoral system as well as popular and electoral votes polled by minor candidates, see first source. Popular vote returns are shown beginning in 1828 because of availability and because by that time most electors were chosen by popular vote.

[a] The elections of 1789–1800 were held under different rules, which did not include separate voting for president and vice president. Scattered electoral votes are not shown.

[b] Eleven states could have voted, but a dispute between its two chambers prevented the New York state legislature from choosing electors. North Carolina and Rhode Island had not yet ratified the Constitution.

[c] All candidates in 1824 represented factions of the Democratic-Republican Party. Figures are for the two candidates with the highest number of electoral votes. The two other candidates were William H. Crawford and Henry Clay with forty-one and thirty-seven electoral votes, respectively.

[d] Three Whig candidates ran in 1836. Their electoral votes totaled 113.

[e] Eleven southern states had seceded from the Union and did not vote; twenty-five states voted.

[f] Mississippi, Texas, and Virginia were not yet readmitted to the Union and did not vote; thirty-four states voted.

[g] The Democratic presidential nominee, Horace Greeley, died between the popular vote and the meeting of presidential electors. Democratic electors split sixty-three votes among several candidates, Congress refused to count the three Georgians who insisted on casting their votes for Greeley, and an additional fourteen electoral votes were not cast. Congress also did not count the electoral votes from Arkansas and Louisiana because of "disruptive conditions during Reconstruction."

[h] James S. Sherman died on October 12, 1912. Nicholas Murray Butler was nominated as the substitute candidate.

Sources: 1789–2012: *CQ Press Guide to U.S. Elections*, 7th ed. (Washington, D.C.: CQ Press, 2016), 794–840, 876–932; Previous editions of *Vital Statistics in American Politics*; 2016: Federal Election Commission, "Federal Elections 2016: Election Results for the U.S. President, the U.S. Senate and the U.S. House of Representatives (December 2017), https://www.fec.gov/resources/cms-content/documents/federalelections2016.pdf; 2020: Table 1-9, this volume.

Table 1-8 Party Winning Presidential Election, by State, 1789–2020

State	1789–1824 D	F	O	1828–1856 D	R	O	1860–1892 D	R	O	1896–1928 D	R	O	1932–1964 D	R	O	1968–2020 D	R	O
Alabama	2	0	0	8	0	0	6	2	0	9	0	0	7	1	1	1	12	1
Alaska	—	—	—	—	—	—	—	—	—	—	—	—	1	1	0	0	14	0
Arizona	—	—	—	—	—	—	—	—	—	2	3	0	5	4	0	2	12	0
Arkansas	—	—	—	6	0	0	6	1	0	9	0	0	9	0	0	3	10	1
California	—	—	—	2	2	0	2	7	0	1	7	1	6	3	0	8	6	0
Colorado	—	—	—	—	—	—	0	4	1	5	4	0	4	5	0	5	9	0
Connecticut	2	8	0	2	6	0	4	5	0	1	8	0	5	4	0	9	5	0
Delaware	2	8	0	2	6	0	7	1	1	1	8	0	5	4	0	9	5	0
District of Columbia[a]	—	—	—	—	—	—	—	—	—	—	—	—	1	0	0	14	0	0
Florida	—	—	—	2	1	0	4	3	1	8	1	0	6	3	0	4	10	0
Georgia	8	2	0	5	3	0	7	0	1	9	0	0	8	1	0	4	9	1
Hawaii	—	—	—	—	—	—	—	—	—	—	—	—	2	0	0	12	2	0
Idaho	—	—	—	—	—	—	—	—	1	4	5	0	6	3	0	0	14	0
Illinois	2	0	0	8	0	0	1	8	0	1	8	0	7	2	0	8	6	0
Indiana	3	0	0	6	2	0	3	6	0	1	8	0	3	6	0	1	13	0
Iowa	—	—	—	2	1	0	0	9	0	1	8	0	4	5	0	6	8	0
Kansas	—	—	—	—	—	—	0	7	1	3	6	0	3	6	0	0	14	0
Kentucky	8	1	0	2	6	0	8	0	1	6	3	0	7	2	0	3	11	0
Louisiana	4	0	0	6	2	0	5	1	1	9	0	0	6	2	1	3	10	1
Maine	2	0	0	5	3	0	0	9	0	1	8	0	1	8	0	9	5	0
Maryland	4	6	0	1	6	1	7	1	1	4	5	0	6	3	0	11	3	0
Massachusetts	3	7	0	0	8	0	0	9	0	2	7	0	7	2	0	12	2	0
Michigan	—	—	—	4	2	0	0	9	0	0	8	1	5	4	0	11	3	0
Minnesota	—	—	—	—	—	—	0	9	0	0	8	1	7	2	0	13	1	0
Mississippi	2	0	0	7	1	0	5	2	1	9	0	0	6	1	2	1	12	1
Missouri	—	—	—	8	0	0	7	2	0	4	5	0	8	1	0	3	11	0
Montana	—	—	—	—	—	—	0	1	0	4	5	0	6	3	0	1	13	0
Nebraska	—	—	—	—	—	—	0	7	0	4	5	0	3	6	0	0	14	0
Nevada	—	—	—	—	—	—	1	6	1	5	4	0	7	2	0	6	8	0

New Hampshire	4	6	0	6	2	0	0	9	0	2	7	0	4	5	0	7	7	0
New Jersey	5	5	0	3	5	0	7	2	0	1	8	0	6	3	0	8	6	0
New Mexico	—	—	—	—	—	—	—	—	—	2	3	0	7	2	0	7	7	0
New York	6	3	0	5	3	0	4	5	0	1	8	0	6	3	0	11	3	0
North Carolina	8	1	0	5	3	0	5	2	1	8	1	0	9	0	0	2	12	0
North Dakota	—	—	—	—	—	—	—	—	—	—	—	—	3	6	0	0	14	0
Ohio	6	0	0	4	4	0	0	9	0	2	7	0	5	4	0	5	9	0
Oklahoma	—	—	—	—	—	—	—	—	—	—	—	—	6	3	0	0	14	0
Oregon	—	—	—	—	—	—	1	8	0	4	2	0	5	4	0	9	5	0
Pennsylvania	8	2	0	6	2	0	0	9	0	1	8	0	5	4	0	9	5	0
Rhode Island	4	5	0	2	6	0	0	9	0	0	8	1	7	2	0	12	2	0
South Carolina	8	2	0	6	0	2	4	3	1	2	7	0	7	1	1	1	13	0
South Dakota	—	—	—	—	—	—	—	—	—	9	0	0	3	6	0	0	14	0
Tennessee	8	0	0	3	5	0	6	1	0	1	7	0	6	3	0	3	11	0
Texas	—	—	—	3	0	0	7	0	1	7	2	0	7	2	0	2	12	0
Utah	—	—	—	—	—	—	—	—	—	8	1	0	6	3	0	0	14	0
Vermont	6	3	0	7	1	0	0	9	0	2	7	0	1	8	0	8	6	0
Virginia	8	2	0	8	0	0	5	0	1	0	9	0	6	3	0	4	10	0
Washington	—	—	—	—	—	—	—	—	—	8	1	0	6	3	0	10	4	0
West Virginia	—	—	—	—	—	—	5	3	0	2	6	1	8	1	0	6	8	0
Wisconsin	—	—	—	2	1	0	1	8	0	1	7	0	5	4	0	9	5	0
Wyoming	—	—	—	—	—	—	0	1	0	3	6	0	5	4	0	0	14	0
Total[b]	113	61	0	136	79	3	118	189	15	170	244	7	274	158	5	272	437	5

Note: Table entries indicate number of times party indicated won the state. "D" indicates the Democratic-Republican Party from 1796 to 1820 and in 1828, the Jackson faction in 1824, and the Democratic Party in 1832 and later; "F" indicates the Federalists from 1792 to 1816, Independent Democratic-Republicans in 1820, and the Adams faction in 1824; "R" indicates the National Republicans in 1828 and 1832, Whigs from 1836 to 1852, and the Republican Party in 1856 and later. The "O" column refers to other (third) parties. Southern Democrats in 1860 are counted as Democratic. "—" indicates that the state was not yet admitted to the Union.

[a] Residents of the District of Columbia received the presidential vote in 1961.

[b] Fewer total votes for a given state within a party system indicate admission of the state during the party system or nonvoting in certain southern states in 1864, 1868, and 1872.

Sources: Compiled by the authors from *CQ Press Guide to U.S. Elections*, 7th ed. (Washington, D.C.: CQ Press, 2016), 876–932; Table 1-9, this volume; and previous editions of *Vital Statistics on American Politics*.

Table 1-9 Presidential General Election Returns, by State, 2020

	Popular vote										Electoral vote	
	Biden (Democratic)		Trump (Republican)		Other			Plurality[a]				
State	Vote	%	Vote	%	Vote	%	Total vote	Vote	%	Dem.	Rep.
Alabama	849,624	36.6%	1,441,170	62.0%	32,488	1.4%	2,323,282	591,546	25.5%		9
Alaska	153,778	42.8%	189,951	52.8%	15,801	4.4%	359,530	36,173	10.1%		3
Arizona	1,672,143	49.4%	1,661,686	49.1%	53,497	1.6%	3,387,326	10,457	0.3%	11	
Arkansas	423,932	34.8%	760,647	62.4%	34,490	2.8%	1,219,069	336,715	27.6%		6
California	11,110,250	63.5%	6,006,429	34.3%	384,192	2.2%	17,500,871	5,103,821	29.2%	55	
Colorado	1,804,352	55.4%	1,364,607	41.9%	87,993	2.7%	3,256,952	439,745	13.5%	9	
Connecticut	1,080,831	59.3%	714,717	39.2%	28,309	1.6%	1,823,857	366,114	20.1%	7	
Delaware	296,268	58.7%	200,603	39.8%	7,475	1.5%	504,346	95,665	19.0%	3	
District of Columbia	317,323	92.1%	18,586	5.4%	8,447	2.5%	344,356	298,737	86.8%	3	
Florida	5,297,045	47.9%	5,668,731	51.2%	101,680	0.9%	11,067,456	371,686	3.4%		29
Georgia	2,473,633	49.5%	2,461,854	49.3%	62,229	1.2%	4,997,716	11,779	0.2%	16	
Hawaii	366,130	63.7%	196,864	34.3%	11,475	2.0%	574,469	169,266	29.5%	4	
Idaho	287,021	33.1%	554,119	63.9%	26,091	3.0%	867,231	267,098	30.8%		4
Illinois	3,471,915	57.5%	2,446,891	40.6%	114,938	1.9%	6,033,744	1,025,024	17.0%	20	
Indiana	1,242,413	41.0%	1,729,516	57.0%	61,183	2.0%	3,033,112	487,103	16.1%		11
Iowa	759,061	44.9%	897,672	53.1%	34,138	2.0%	1,690,871	138,611	8.2%		6
Kansas	570,323	41.6%	771,406	56.2%	30,574	2.2%	1,372,303	201,083	14.7%		6
Kentucky	772,474	36.2%	1,326,646	62.1%	37,648	1.8%	2,136,768	554,172	25.9%		8
Louisiana	856,034	39.9%	1,255,776	58.5%	36,252	1.7%	2,148,062	399,742	18.6%		8
Maine	435,072	53.1%	360,737	44.0%	23,652	2.9%	819,461	74,335	9.1%	3	1
Maryland	1,985,023	65.4%	976,414	32.2%	75,593	2.5%	3,037,030	1,008,609	33.2%	10	
Massachusetts	2,382,202	65.6%	1,167,202	32.1%	81,998	2.3%	3,631,402	1,215,000	33.5%	11	
Michigan	2,804,040	50.6%	2,649,852	47.8%	85,410	1.5%	5,539,302	154,188	2.8%	16	
Minnesota	1,717,077	52.4%	1,484,065	45.3%	76,029	2.3%	3,277,171	233,012	7.1%	10	
Mississippi	539,508	41.1%	756,789	57.6%	17,597	1.3%	1,313,894	217,281	16.5%		6
Missouri	1,253,014	41.4%	1,718,736	56.8%	54,212	1.8%	3,025,962	465,722	15.4%		10

State	Votes	%	Votes	%	Votes	%	Plurality	Plurality %	EV	EV	EV
Montana	244,786	40.5%	343,602	56.9%	15,286	2.5%	98,816	16.4%			3
Nebraska	374,583	39.4%	556,846	58.5%	20,283	2.1%	182,263	19.2%	1		4
Nevada	703,486	50.1%	669,890	47.7%	32,000	2.3%	33,596	2.4%	6		
New Hampshire	424,921	52.7%	365,654	45.4%	15,607	1.9%	59,267	7.4%	4		
New Jersey	2,608,335	57.3%	1,883,274	41.4%	57,744	1.3%	725,061	15.9%	14		
New Mexico	501,614	54.3%	401,894	43.5%	20,457	2.2%	99,720	10.8%	5		
New York	5,244,886	60.9%	3,251,997	37.7%	119,978	1.4%	1,992,889	23.1%	29		
North Carolina	2,684,292	48.6%	2,758,775	49.9%	81,737	1.5%	74,483	1.3%			15
North Dakota	114,902	31.8%	235,595	65.1%	11,322	3.1%	120,693	33.4%			3
Ohio	2,679,165	45.2%	3,154,834	53.3%	88,203	1.5%	475,669	8.0%			18
Oklahoma	503,890	32.3%	1,020,280	65.4%	36,529	2.3%	516,390	33.1%			7
Oregon	1,340,383	56.5%	958,448	40.4%	75,490	3.2%	381,935	16.1%	7		
Pennsylvania	3,458,229	50.0%	3,377,674	48.8%	79,380	1.1%	80,555	1.2%	20		
Rhode Island	307,486	59.4%	199,922	38.6%	10,349	2.0%	107,564	20.8%	4		
South Carolina	1,091,541	43.4%	1,385,103	55.1%	36,685	1.5%	293,562	11.7%			9
South Dakota	150,471	35.6%	261,043	61.8%	11,095	2.6%	110,572	26.2%			3
Tennessee	1,143,711	37.5%	1,852,475	60.7%	57,665	1.9%	708,764	23.2%			11
Texas	5,259,126	46.5%	5,890,347	52.1%	165,583	1.5%	631,221	5.6%			38
Utah	560,282	37.6%	865,140	58.1%	62,867	4.2%	304,858	20.5%			6
Vermont	242,820	66.1%	112,704	30.7%	11,904	3.2%	130,116	35.4%	3		
Virginia	2,413,568	54.1%	1,962,430	44.0%	84,526	1.9%	451,138	10.1%	13		
Washington	2,369,612	58.0%	1,584,651	38.8%	133,368	3.3%	784,961	19.2%	12		
West Virginia	235,984	29.7%	545,382	68.6%	13,286	1.7%	309,398	38.9%			5
Wisconsin	1,630,866	49.4%	1,610,184	48.8%	56,991	1.7%	20,682	0.6%	10		
Wyoming	73,491	26.6%	193,559	69.9%	9,715	3.5%	120,068	43.4%			3
Total	81,282,916	51.3%	74,223,369	46.9%	2,891,441	1.8%	7,059,547	4.5%	306		232

Note: "—" indicates not available. Based on official returns as of mid-December 2020, subject to amendment. Percentage for "Plurality" calculated by the editors. Data for earlier years can be found in previous editions of *Vital Statistics on American Politics*.

[a] "Plurality" indicates the vote margin between the leader and the second-place finisher.

Source: Federal Election Commission, "Official 2020 Presidential General Election Results," https://www.fec.gov/resources/cms-content/documents/2020presgeresults.pdf.

Figure 1-4 Presidential General Election Map, 2020

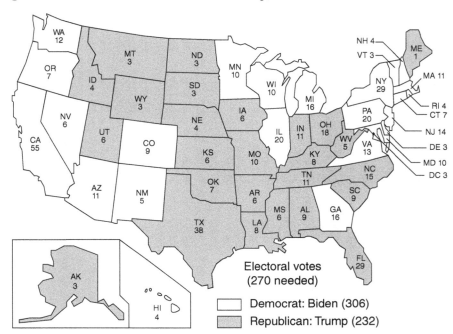

Note: Most states award electoral votes statewide on a winner–take–all basis. Maine and Nebraska award electoral votes by a district system, one for the candidate carrying each congressional district, two for the candidate carrying the state. In 2020, Nebraska awarded four electoral votes to Trump and one to Biden. Maine awarded three electoral votes to Biden and one to Trump.

Source: Table 1-9, this volume.

Table 1-10 House and Senate Election Results, by Congress, 1788–2020

Election year	Congress	House					Senate					President[d]
		Dem.[a]	Rep.[b]	Other	Gains/losses[c]		Dem.[a]	Rep.[b]	Other	Gains/losses[c]		
					Dem.	Rep.				Dem.	Rep.	
1788	1st	26	38		a	b	9	17		a	b	Washington (F)
1790	2nd	33	37		a	b	13	16		a	b	Washington (F)
1792	3rd	57	48		24	11	13	17		0	1	
1794	4th	52	54		−5	6	13	19		0	2	
1796	5th	48	58		−4	4	12	20		−1	1	J. Adams (F)
1798	6th	42	64		−6	6	13	19		1	−1	
1800	7th	69	36		27	−28	18	13		5	−6	Jefferson (DR)
1802	8th	102	39		33	3	25	9		7	−4	
1804	9th	116	25		14	−14	27	7		2	−2	Jefferson (DR)
1806	10th	118	24		2	−1	28	6		1	−1	
1808	11th	94	48		−24	24	28	6		0	0	Madison (DR)
1810	12th	108	36		14	−12	30	6		2	0	
1812	13th	112	68		4	32	27	9		−3	3	Madison (DR)
1814	14th	117	65		5	−3	25	11		−2	2	
1816	15th	141	42		24	−23	34	10		9	−1	Monroe (DR)
1818	16th	156	27		15	−15	35	7		1	−3	
1820	17th	158	25		2	−2	44	4		9	−3	Monroe (DR)
1822	18th	187	26		29	1	44	4		0	0	
1824	19th	105	97		a	b	26	20		a	b	J. Q. Adams (DR)
1826	20th	94	119		−11	22	20	28		−6	8	
1828	21st	139	74		a	b	26	22		a	b	Jackson (D)
1830	22nd	141	58	14	2	−16	25	21	2	−1	−1	
1832	23rd	147	53	60	6	−5	20	20	8	a	b	Jackson (D)
1834	24th	145	98		−2	45	27	25		a	b	
1836	25th	108	107	24	−37	9	30	18	4	3	−7	Van Buren (D)

(Table continues)

29

Table 1-10 *(Continued)*

	House						Senate					
					Gains/losses[c]					Gains/losses[c]		
Election year	Congress	Dem.[a]	Rep.[b]	Other	Dem.	Rep.	Dem.[a]	Rep.[b]	Other	Dem.	Rep.	President[d]
1838	26th	124	118		16	11	28	22		−2	4	
1840	27th	102	133	6	−22	15	28	22	2	0	0	Harrison (W)
1842	28th	142	79	1	40	−54	25	28	1	−3	6	Tyler (W)
1844	29th	143	77	6	1	−2	31	25		6	−3	Polk (D)
1846	30th	108	115	4	−35	38	36	21		5	−4	
1848	31st	112	109	9	4	−6	35	25	2	−1	4	Taylor (W)
1850	32nd	140	88	5	28	−21	35	24	3	0	−1	Fillmore (W)
1852	33rd	159	71	4	19	−17	38	22	2	3	−2	Pierce (D)
1854	34th	83	108	43	−76	37	40	15	5	[a]	[b]	
1856	35th	118	92	26	35	−16	36	20	8	−4	5	Buchanan (D)
1858	36th	92	114	31	−26	22	36	26	4	0	6	
1860	37th	42	106	28	−50	−8	11	31	7	−25	5	Lincoln (R)
1862	38th	80	103		38	−3	12	39		1	8	
1864	39th	46	145		−34	42	10	42		−2	3	Lincoln (R)
1866	40th	49	143		3	−2	11	42		1	0	A. Johnson (R)
1868	41st	73	170		24	27	11	61		0	19	Grant (R)
1870	42nd	104	139		31	−31	17	57		6	−4	
1872	43rd	88	203	3	−16	64	19	54		2	−3	Grant (R)
1874	44th	181	107	3	93	−96	29	46		10	−8	
1876	45th	156	137		−25	30	36	39	1	7	−7	Hayes (R)
1878	46th	150	128	14	−6	−9	43	33		7	−6	
1880	47th	130	152	11	−20	24	37	37	2	−6	4	Garfield (R)
1882	48th	200	119	6	70	−33	36	40		−1	3	Arthur (R)
1884	49th	182	140	2	−18	21	34	41		−2	1	Cleveland (D)

Year	Congress											President
1886	50th	170	151	4	−12	11	37	39		3	−2	Harrison (R)
1888	51st	156	173	1	−14	22	37	47		0	8	
1890	52nd	231	88	14	75	−85	39	47	2	2	0	Cleveland (D)
1892	53rd	220	126	8	−11	38	44	38	3	5	−9	
1894	54th	104	246	7	−116	120	30	44	5	−14	6	McKinley (R)
1896	55th	134	206	16	30	−40	34	46	10	4	2	
1898	56th	163	185	9	29	−21	26	53	11	−8	7	
1900	57th	153	198	5	−10	13	29	56	3	3	3	McKinley (R)
1902	58th	178	207		25	9	32	58		3	2	T. Roosevelt (R)
1904	59th	136	250		−42	43	32	58		0	0	T. Roosevelt (R)
1906	60th	164	222		28	−28	29	61		−3	3	
1908	61st	172	219		8	−3	32	59		3	−2	Taft (R)
1910	62nd	228	162	1	56	−57	42	49		10	−10	
1912	63rd	290	127	18	62	−35	51	44	1	9	−5	Wilson (D)
1914	64th	231	193	8	−59	66	56	39	1	5	−5	
1916	65th	210	216	9	−21	23	53	42	1	−3	3	
1918	66th	191	237	7	−19	21	47	48	1	−6	6	Wilson (D)
1920	67th	132	300	1	−59	63	37	59		−10	11	Harding (R)
1922	68th	207	225	3	75	−75	43	51	2	6	−8	
1924	69th	183	247	5	−24	22	40	54	1	−3	3	Coolidge (R)
1926	70th	195	237	3	12	−10	47	48	1	7	−6	
1928	71st	167	267	1	−28	30	39	56	1	−8	8	Hoover (R)
1930	72nd	220	214	1	53	−53	47	48	1	8	−8	
1932	73rd	313	117	5	93	−97	59	36	1	12	−12	F. Roosevelt (D)
1934	74th	322	103	10	9	−14	69	25	2	10	−11	
1936	75th	333	89	13	11	−14	75	17	4	6	−8	F. Roosevelt (D)
1938	76th	262	169	4	−71	80	69	23	4	−6	6	
1940	77th	267	162	6	5	−7	66	28	2	−3	5	F. Roosevelt (D)
1942	78th	222	209	4	−45	47	57	38	1	−9	10	
1944	79th	243	190	2	21	−19	57	38	1	0	0	F. Roosevelt (D)

(Table continues)

Table 1-10 *(Continued)*

	House				Gains/losses[c]		Senate			Gains/losses[c]		
Election year	Congress	Dem.[a]	Rep.[b]	Other	Dem.	Rep.	Dem.[a]	Rep.[b]	Other	Dem.	Rep.	President[d]
1946	80th	188	246	1	-55	56	45	51		-12	13	Truman (D)
1948	81st	263	171	1	75	-75	54	42		9	-9	Truman (D)
1950	82nd	234	199	2	-29	28	48	47	1	-6	5	
1952	83rd	213	221	1	-21	22	47	48	1	-1	1	Eisenhower (R)
1954	84th	232	203		19	-18	48	47	1	1	-1	
1956	85th	234	201		2	-2	49	47		1	0	Eisenhower (R)
1958	86th	283	154		49	-47	64	34		15	-13	
1960	87th	263	174		-20	20	64	36		0	2	Kennedy (D)
1962	88th	258	176	1	-5	2	67	33		3	-3	
1964	89th	295	140		37	-36	68	32		1	-1	L. Johnson (D)
1966	90th	248	187		-47	47	64	36		-4	4	
1968	91st	243	192		-5	5	58	42		-6	6	Nixon (R)
1970	92nd	255	180		12	-12	55	45		-3	3	
1972	93rd	243	192		-12	12	57	43		2	-2	Nixon (R)
1974	94th	291	144		48	-48	61	38		4	-5	Ford (R)
1976	95th	292	143		1	-1	62	38		1	0	Carter (D)
1978	96th	277	158		-15	15	59	41		-3	3	
1980	97th	243	192		-34	34	47	53		-12	12	Reagan (R)
1982	98th	269	166		26	-26	46	54		-1	1	
1984	99th	253	182		-16	16	47	53		1	-1	Reagan (R)
1986	100th	258	177		5	-5	55	45		8	-8	
1988	101st	259	174	1	1	-3	55	45		0	0	G. H. W. Bush (R)
1990	102nd	267	167	1	8	-7	56	44		1	-1	
1992	103rd	258	176	1	-9	9	57	43		1	-1	Clinton (D)
1994	104th	204	230	1	-54	54	47	53		-10	10	

Year	Congress	House Dem	House Rep		H-Dem gain	H-Rep gain	Senate Dem	Senate Rep	S-Dem gain	S-Rep gain	President
1996	105th	207	227	1	3		45	55	−2	2	Clinton (D)
1998	106th	211	223	1	4		45	55	0	0	
2000	107th	212	221	2	1	−3	50	50	5	−5	G. W. Bush (R)
2002	108th	205	229	1	−7	−4	48	51	−2	1	
2004	109th	201	232	1	−4	3	44	55	−4	4	G. W. Bush (R)
2006	110th	233	202		32	−30	49	49	5	−6	
2008	111th	257	178		24	−24	55	41	5	−8	Obama (D)
2010	112th	193	242		−63	64	51	47	−4	6	
2012	113th	200	233		7	−9	53	45	2	−2	Obama (D)
2014	114th	188	246		−12	13	44	54	−9	9	
2016	115th	194	241		6	−6	46	52	2	−2	Trump (R)
2018	116th[e]	235	199		41	−42	45	53	2	2	
2020	117th	222	213		−13	14	48	50	3	−3	Biden (D)

Note: For parties, see Figure 1-3, this volume.

[a] "Democratic" column indicates Democratic partisans in 1828 and later, "Administration" in 1824 and 1826, "Democratic Republicans" from 1790 to 1822, and "Opposition" in 1788. Consequently, and because of changes within the "Republican" column noted in note b, gains/losses in the "Democratic" column are calculated only for 1792–1822, 1826, 1830, 1836–1852, and 1856 and later.

[b] The "Republican" column indicates Republican partisans in 1854 and later, "Whigs" from 1834 to 1852, "Anti-Masons" in 1832, "National Republicans" in 1828 and 1830, "Jacksonians" in 1824 and 1826, "Federalists" from 1790 to 1822, and "Administration" in 1788. Consequently, gains/losses in the "Republican" column are calculated only for 1792–1822, 1826, 1830, 1836–1852, and 1856 and later.

[c] The seat totals reflect the makeup of the House and Senate at the start of each Congress. Special elections that shifted party ratios between elections are not noted. Because of changes in the overall number of seats in the Senate and House, in the number of seats won by third parties, and in the number of vacancies, a Republican loss is not always matched precisely by a Democratic gain, or vice versa. Partisan seat shares at the start of each Congress need not match postelection seat shares: deaths, resignations, and special elections can cause further changes in party makeup. In the 1930 election, for example, Republicans won majority control, but when Congress organized, special elections held to fill fourteen vacancies resulted in a Democratic majority.

[d] President elected in the year indicated or, if a midterm election year, nonelected president in office at the time of the midterm election.

[e] The results of the election in the 9th congressional district of North Carolina were vacated, leading to a special election called in September of 2019.

Sources: Seat gains and losses calculated by the authors. Other data: 1788–1858: U.S. Bureau of the Census, *Historical Statistics of the United States, Colonial Times to 1970* (Washington, D.C.: Government Printing Office, 1975), 1083–1084; 1860–2008: *CQ Press Guide to U.S. Elections*, 7th ed. (Washington, D.C.: CQ Press, 2016), 1838–1839; 2010–2012: *CQ Weekly* (2011), 119; (2013), 23; 2014: Clerk of the House of Representatives, http://clerk.house.gov; 2016–2020: compiled by authors.

Table 1-11 Party Victories in U.S. House Elections, by State, 1860–2020

State	Total 1860–1895			Total 1896–1931			Total 1932–1965			Total 1966–2020		
	Dem.	Rep.	Other	Dem.	Rep.	Other	Dem.	Rep.	Other	Dem.	Rep.	Other
Alabama	92	19	8	170	0	8	146	5	0	89	110	0
Alaska	—	—	—	—	—	—	4	0	0	2	26	0
Arizona	—	—	—	11	0	0	26	7	0	63	106	0
Arkansas	54	5	6	124	0	0	109	0	0	60	52	0
California[a]	29	46	8	30	133	15	234	212	0	843	501	0
Colorado	1	9	3	21	34	6	43	26	0	80	87	0
Connecticut	33	36	5	11	77	0	58	44	0	109	49	0
Delaware	15	3	2	5	14	0	9	8	0	11	17	0
Florida	18	8	1	57	4	0	111	8	0	273	308	0
Georgia	111	11	12	207	0	1	170	1	0	186	134	0
Hawaii	—	—	—	0	0	1	6	0	0	54	2	0
Idaho	0	4	0	5	42	2	20	14	0	7	49	0
Illinois	118	191	20	136	333	1	220	221	0	319	268	0
Indiana	104	105	17	97	139	0	85	108	0	129	149	0
Iowa	16	131	11	10	193	0	35	105	0	58	93	0
Kansas	0	62	12	30	114	0	16	90	0	28	97	0
Kentucky	133	20	38	151	54	0	122	25	0	78	103	0
Louisiana	69	20	2	136	0	2	139	0	0	107	97	0
Maine	3	76	7	4	71	0	8	41	0	36	20	0
Maryland	74	15	18	63	49	0	87	25	0	157	67	0
Massachusetts	31	165	17	60	211	2	103	136	0	262	34	0
Michigan	33	118	13	12	214	2	112	187	0	241	226	0
Minnesota	11	51	5	8	146	12	44	91	16	132	92	0
Mississippi	70	17	3	142	0	0	110	1	0	81	49	0
Missouri	143	43	38	202	88	0	157	49	0	149	106	0
Montana	1	3	0	13	14	1	23	12	0	17	24	0

Nebraska	3	28	5	36	63	9	21	50	0	6	78	0
Nevada	4	9	4	5	10	4	14	3	0	33	30	0
New Hampshire	11	33	3	3	33	0	3	31	0	20	36	0
New Jersey	53	58	5	66	137	0	84	158	0	225	155	0
New Mexico	—	—	—	7	5	0	29	0	0	36	40	0
New York	236	312	66	328	397	6	387	368	1	598	325	0
North Carolina	78	32	19	157	11	9	189	9	0	181	151	0
North Dakota	0	4	0	0	44	0	2	33	0	16	15	0
Ohio	146	186	39	123	264	0	163	238	0	212	345	0
Oklahoma	—	—	—	70	27	0	112	14	0	72	86	0
Oregon	7	13	2	2	44	0	22	41	0	98	34	0
Pennsylvania	158	300	38	83	522	17	255	291	0	306	305	0
Rhode Island	8	32	2	13	34	0	32	2	0	48	8	0
South Carolina	62	30	6	127	0	0	97	2	0	79	94	0
South Dakota	6	11	0	3	42	2	7	27	0	15	21	0
Tennessee	83	52	13	139	39	4	121	37	1	122	125	0
Texas	110	1	3	295	7	0	365	8	0	470	344	0
Utah	—	—	—	7	23	0	23	11	0	22	59	0
Vermont	0	42	5	0	36	0	1	16	0	8	12	8
Virginia	81	23	23	167	15	0	147	15	0	127	167	1
Washington	0	6	0	8	61	2	54	55	0	155	81	0
West Virginia	37	15	6	23	75	0	84	16	0	76	24	0
Wisconsin	40	94	9	18	176	4	46	105	21	122	123	0
Wyoming	1	2	0	1	17	0	3	14	0	4	24	0
Total	2,283	2,441	494	3,386	4,012	110	4,458	2,960	39	6622	5548	9

Note: Entries indicate the number of U.S. House seats won by the party in the state. "—" indicates that the state was not yet admitted to the Union. The period beginning in 1966 does not include special elections; candidates endorsed by both major and minor parties are counted as major-party candidates.

[a] When it could be determined, candidates who ran as both Republican and Democrat were classified by their usual party affiliation.

Sources: 1860–1964: *Congressional Quarterly's Guide to U.S. Elections*, 2nd ed. (Washington, D.C.: Congressional Quarterly, 1985), 1118–1119; 1966–2008: *CQ Press Guide to U.S. Elections*, 6th ed. (Washington, D.C.: CQ Press, 2010), 1286, 1287, 1306, 1379, 1383, 1750–1755; 2010–2012: Clerk of the House of Representatives, http://clerk.house.gov; *CQ Weekly* (2010), 2618–2627, 2716, 2766; (2012), 2284–2293, 2342, 2384, 2430; 2014–2020: compiled by authors from official election results from state websites.

Table 1-12 Popular Vote and Seats in House Elections, by Party, 1896–2020

	Democratic candidates		Republican candidates		Difference between Democratic percentage of all seats and all votes[a]
Year	Percentage of all votes	Percentage of all seats	Percentage of all votes	Percentage of all seats	
1896	43.3	37.6	46.7	57.9	−5.6
1898	46.7	45.7	45.7	51.8	−1.0
1900	44.7	43.0	51.2	55.6	−1.7
1902	46.7	46.2	49.3	53.8	−0.5
1904	41.7	35.2	53.8	64.8	−6.5
1906	44.2	42.5	50.7	57.5	−1.7
1908	46.1	44.0	49.7	56.0	−2.1
1910	47.4	58.3	46.5	41.4	10.9
1912	45.3	66.7	34.0	29.2	21.3
1914	43.1	53.5	42.6	44.7	10.3
1916	46.3	48.3	48.4	49.7	2.0
1918	43.1	43.9	52.5	54.5	0.8
1920	35.8	30.5	58.6	69.3	−5.4
1922	44.7	47.6	51.7	51.7	2.8
1924	40.4	42.1	55.5	56.8	1.7
1926	40.5	44.8	57.0	54.5	4.3
1928	42.4	37.8	56.5	61.9	−4.5
1930	44.6	49.7	52.6	50.1	5.1
1932	54.5	72.0	41.4	26.9	17.4
1934	53.9	74.0	42.0	23.7	20.1
1936	55.8	76.6	39.6	20.5	20.7
1938	48.6	60.2	47.0	38.9	11.6
1940	51.3	61.4	45.6	37.2	10.1
1942	46.1	51.0	50.6	48.0	5.0
1944	50.6	55.9	47.2	43.7	5.3
1946	44.2	43.2	53.5	56.6	−1.0
1948	51.9	60.5	45.5	39.3	8.6
1950	49.0	53.8	49.0	45.7	4.7
1952	49.7	49.0	49.3	50.8	0.8
1954	52.5	53.3	47.0	46.7	0.8
1956	51.1	53.8	48.7	46.2	2.7
1958	56.3	64.8	43.5	35.2	8.5
1960	54.2	60.2	45.4	39.8	6.0
1962	52.3	59.3	47.4	40.5	7.0
1964	57.4	67.8	42.1	32.2	10.4
1966	50.9	57.0	48.2	43.0	6.1
1968	50.2	55.9	48.5	44.1	5.7
1970	53.4	58.6	45.1	41.4	5.2
1972	51.7	55.9	46.4	44.1	4.2
1974	57.6	66.9	40.6	33.1	9.9
1976	56.2	67.1	42.1	32.9	10.9
1978	53.4	63.7	44.7	36.3	10.3
1980	50.4	55.9	48.0	44.1	5.5
1982	55.6	61.8	42.9	38.2	6.2

Table 1-12 *(Continued)*

Year	Democratic candidates		Republican candidates		Difference between Democratic percentage of all seats and all votes[a]
	Percentage of all votes	Percentage of all seats	Percentage of all votes	Percentage of all seats	
1984	52.1	58.2	47.0	41.8	6.0
1986	54.5	59.3	44.6	40.7	4.8
1988	53.3	59.8	45.5	40.2	6.5
1990	52.9	61.4	45.0	38.4	8.5
1992	50.8	59.3	45.6	40.5	8.5
1994	45.4	46.7	52.4	53.1	1.2
1996	48.5	47.6	48.9	52.2	−1.0
1998	47.8	48.5	48.9	51.3	0.7
2000	47.4	48.7	48.7	50.8	1.3
2002	45.2	47.1	51.6	52.6	1.9
2004	47.4	46.4	50.1	53.3	−1.0
2006	52.8	53.6	44.9	46.4	0.7
2008	53.9	59.1	42.9	40.9	5.2
2010	45.0	44.4	51.8	55.6	−0.7
2012	49.2	46.2	48.0	53.8	−2.9
2014	45.7	43.2	51.4	56.8	−2.5
2016	48.0	44.6	49.1	55.4	−3.6
2018	53.4	54.1	44.8	45.9	0.7
2020	50.8	51.6	47.7	48.4	0.8

Note: In recent years, there has been "built-in" inaccuracy in that some states have chosen not to put uncontested races on the ballot or to require the counting of votes in uncontested races.

[a] Calculated before rounding.

Sources: Votes, 1896–1970: U.S. Bureau of the Census, *Historical Statistics of the United States, Colonial Times to 1970* (Washington, D.C.: Government Printing Office, 1975), part 2, 1084; votes, 1972–1974: U.S. Bureau of the Census, *Statistical Abstract of the United States, 1976* (Washington, D.C.: Government Printing Office, 1976), 460; votes, 1976–1996: *Congressional Quarterly Weekly Report* (1977), 488; (1979), 571; (1981), 713; (1983), 387; (1985), 687; (1987), 484; (1989), 1063; (1991), 487; (1993), 965; (1995), 1079; (1997), 444; votes, 1998 and 2002: "The Rhodes Cook Letter," November 2002, 5; votes, 2000: calculated by the editors using unpublished data provided by Congressional Quarterly; votes, 2004–2010: "The Rhodes Cook Letter," January 2005, 14; December 2006, 16–17; February 2009, 3; December 2010, 5; February 2011, 14, www.rhodescook.com; votes, 2012–2014: David Wasserman, "The Cook Political Report," www.cookpolitical.com; 1896–2014 seats: Clerk of the House of Representatives, http://clerk.house.gov; 2016–2020 votes and seats: Clerk of the House of Representatives, http://history.house.gov; Table 1-10, this volume.

A Data Literacy Lesson
Why Divided Government Matters

This book is full of tables that provide you with information. In some cases, the information in the table speaks for itself, and there is no particular need to push the story further. In most cases, however, the data cry out for more of an investigation. In Table 1-13, we see an example of a table that we think demands more explanation than the mere facts it presents; in this essay, we will highlight two particular questions we think you should always consider when looking at this table in particular, and at much data in general.

On the face of it, Table 1-13 is straightforward. For every two-year period, it lists the president and their party, along with which party controlled the House of Representatives and the Senate. The key column here is the one that lists whether government is unified (the same party controls the White House and both houses of Congress) or whether it is divided. A cursory glance at the table suggests that divided government is becoming more common over time, while the summary at the bottom of the table confirms that this is, in fact, the case. So, divided government is becoming more common.

When we look at data, two of the first questions we think about are basic ones: *Why* and, *so what*? If you ask this question about every table you see in this book, you'll already be a smarter consumer of political data. Of course, the table itself cannot answer the "why" or "so what" questions, but your own knowledge of government, the perspectives of other knowledgeable people and resources that you might consult, and your own independent research may shed some light on these issues.

Let's start with *why*. Why has divided government become so much more common? In the early 1990s, this question spawned a good bit of research—by that point, divided government had moved from unusual to becoming the norm. Perhaps, some scholars suggested, voters intentionally liked to split the control of government, in order to prevent any party from becoming too powerful. Maybe, some argued, voters preferred the Republican Party to handle presidential-level concerns such as foreign policy and international relations, and preferred the Democratic Party to handle issues around policies such as spending and maintaining the social safety net.[1] Perhaps voters liked the thought of giving power to one party in a presidential election, but then reconsidered two years later in the congressional elections (thus creating divided government). This would explain notable recent elections such as 1994, 2010, and 2018.

These potential answers, and many others, are important to contemplate. The prevalence of divided government in our current era would have stunned an observer from a century ago, and it is worth our while to theorize about why this might be the case. When we do, of course, we will learn that some of our theories stand up well against data, while others do not. When we feed additional data back into our theories, over time we end up with better and better explanations for the political phenomena we observe in the world.

Once we have addressed the question of why, a next important question is *so what*. Why does it matter that we are seeing more divided government today than we previously have? A logical answer is that it might affect governmental functioning—is it the case that less gets done when control of government is split between the parties? Logic would suggest this is the case; certainly, recent years have not exactly inspired confidence in our elected officials' ability to cross the partisan divide. And yet, as David Mayhew's influential book from the early 1990s, *Divided We Govern*, shows us, it may not be the case that divided government leads to less getting done. Particularly on less visible and non-wedge issues, bipartisanship does happen in Congress. It may also be the case (at least historically) that divided government forces more compromise and, maybe, better legislation.

We'll leave it to others—perhaps to you—to determine why we have more divided government today, and whether it truly is a bad thing. And we hope you'll internalize these two questions - Why? So what? - as ways to find the larger meaning hiding within the tables and figures in this book.

---

[1] This theory took a hit when it became equally as common to have Democratic presidents facing off against Republican Congresses. Before Bill Clinton, much theorizing about divided government worked from the pattern of Democratic Congresses and Republican White Houses.

Table 1-13 Divided Government in the United States, by Congress, 1861–2022

Years	Congress	Unified/divided	President (party)	Senate majority	House majority
1861–1863	37th	unified	Lincoln (R)	R	R
1863–1865	38th	unified	Lincoln (R)	R	R
1865–1867	39th	unified	Lincoln (R)	R	R
1867–1869	40th	unified	Grant (R)	R	R
1869–1871	41st	unified	Grant (R)	R	R
1871–1873	42nd	divided	Grant (R)	R	D
1873–1875	43rd	unified	Grant (R)	R	R
1875–1877	44th	divided	Grant (R)	R	D
1877–1879	45th	divided	Hayes (R)	R	D
1879–1881	46th	divided	Hayes (R)	D	D
1881–1883	47th	unified	Garfield (R)	even[a]	R
1883–1885	48th	divided	Arthur (R)	R	D
1885–1887	49th	divided	Cleveland (D)	R	D
1887–1889	50th	divided	Cleveland (D)	R	D
1889–1891	51st	unified	Harrison (R)	R	R
1891–1893	52nd	divided	Harrison (R)	R	D
1893–1895	53rd	unified	Cleveland (D)	D	D
1895–1897	54th	divided	Cleveland (D)	R	R
1897–1899	55th	unified	McKinley (R)	R	R
1899–1901	56th	unified	McKinley (R)	R	R
1901–1903	57th	unified	McKinley (R)	R	R
1903–1905	58th	unified	T. Roosevelt (R)	R	R
1905–1907	59th	unified	T. Roosevelt (R)	R	R
1907–1909	60th	unified	T. Roosevelt (R)	R	R
1909–1911	61st	unified	Taft (R)	R	R
1911–1913	62nd	divided	Taft (R)	R	D
1913–1915	63rd	unified	Wilson (D)	D	D
1915–1917	64th	unified	Wilson (D)	D	D
1917–1919	65th	divided	Wilson (D)	D	R
1919–1921	66th	divided	Wilson (D)	R	R
1921–1923	67th	unified	Harding (R)	R	R
1923–1925	68th	unified	Harding (R)	R	R
1925–1927	69th	unified	Coolidge (R)	R	R
1927–1929	70th	unified	Coolidge (R)	R	R
1929–1931	71st	unified	Hoover (R)	R	R
1931–1933	72nd	divided	Hoover (R)	R	D
1933–1935	73rd	unified	F. Roosevelt (D)	D	D
1935–1937	74th	unified	F. Roosevelt (D)	D	D
1937–1939	75th	unified	F. Roosevelt (D)	D	D
1939–1941	76th	unified	F. Roosevelt (D)	D	D
1941–1943	77th	unified	F. Roosevelt (D)	D	D
1943–1945	78th	unified	F. Roosevelt (D)	D	D
1945–1947	79th	unified	F. Roosevelt (D)	D	D
1947–1949	80th	divided	Truman (D)	R	R
1949–1951	81st	unified	Truman (D)	D	D
1951–1953	82nd	unified	Truman (D)	D	D
1953–1955	83rd	unified	Eisenhower (R)	R	R
1955–1957	84th	divided	Eisenhower (R)	D	D
1957–1959	85th	divided	Eisenhower (R)	D	D
1959–1961	86th	divided	Eisenhower (R)	D	D
1961–1963	87th	unified	Kennedy (D)	D	D
1963–1965	88th	unified	Kennedy (D)	D	D
1965–1967	89th	unified	L. Johnson (D)	D	D
1967–1969	90th	unified	L. Johnson (D)	D	D
1969–1971	91st	divided	Nixon (R)	D	D

Table 1-13 *(Continued)*

Years	Congress	Unified/ divided	President (party)	Senate majority	House majority
1971–1973	92nd	divided	Nixon (R)	D	D
1973–1975	93rd	divided	Nixon (R)	D	D
1975–1977	94th	divided	Ford (R)	D	D
1977–1979	95th	unified	Carter (D)	D	D
1979–1981	96th	unified	Carter (D)	D	D
1981–1983	97th	divided	Reagan (R)	R	D
1983–1985	98th	divided	Reagan (R)	R	D
1985–1987	99th	divided	Reagan (R)	R	D
1987–1989	100th	divided	Reagan (R)	D	D
1989–1991	101st	divided	G. H. W. Bush (R)	D	D
1991–1993	102nd	divided	G. H. W. Bush (R)	D	D
1993–1995	103rd	unified	Clinton (D)	D	D
1995–1997	104th	divided	Clinton (D)	R	R
1997–1999	105th	divided	Clinton (D)	R	R
1999–2001	106th	divided	Clinton (D)	R	R
2001–2003	107th	unified	G. W. Bush (R)	even[a]	R
2003–2005	108th	unified	G. W. Bush (R)	R	R
2005–2007	109th	unified	G. W. Bush (R)	R	R
2007–2009	110th	divided	G. W. Bush (R)	D	D
2009–2011	111th	unified	Obama (D)	D	D
2011–2013	112th	divided	Obama (D)	D	R
2013–2015	113th	divided	Obama (D)	D	R
2015–2017	114th	divided	Obama (D)	R	R
2017–2019	115th	unified	Trump (R)	R	R
2019–2021	116th	divided	Trump (R)	R	D
2021–2023	117th	unified	Biden (D)	even[b]	D

	Summary[c]	
	Unified	Divided
1861–1896	9 (50%)	9
1897–1932	14 (78%)	4
1933–1966	13 (76%)	4
1967–2022	10 (36%)	18

Note: "R" indicates Republican; "D" indicates Democrat.

[a] Divided or unified government is as of the start of each Congress. In the 47th Congress (1881), the Senate was initially composed of thirty-seven Republicans and thirty-seven Democrats, one independent (David Davis of Illinois, who voted with the Democrats), and one variously described as an independent or a Readjuster (William Mahone of Virginia, who voted with the Republicans). Vice President Chester A. Arthur's deciding vote resulted in the Republicans organizing the Senate. In the 107th Congress, the Senate was composed of fifty Republicans and fifty Democrats. On January 20, the Republicans organized the Senate. When James M. Jeffords of Vermont switched to independent effective June 6 and caucused with the Democrats, control shifted to the Democrats. This is the only instance for the years indicated in which party control shifted in one chamber after the start of a Congress and led to a change in the organization of that chamber. See the source on party changes in the 83rd Congress.
[b] After the 2020 election, there were fifty Democrats (this includes two independents who caucused with the Democrats) and fifty Republicans. Since the vice president, Kamala Harris, can cast the deciding vote, and she is a Democrat, functionally the Senate was under Democratic control.
[c] 1861–1896 covers the elections of 1860–1894; 1897–1932 covers the elections of 1896–1930; 1933–1966 covers the elections of 1932–1964; 1967–2022 covers the elections of 1966–2020.

Sources: Table 1-10, this volume; information on party switching and party control in evenly divided Congresses: U.S. Senate, "Party Division in the Senate, 1789–Present," www.senate.gov.

Table 1-14 Split Presidential and House Election Outcomes in Congressional Districts, 1900–2020

Year	Total number of districts[a]	Number of districts with split results[b]	Percentage of total
1900	295	10	3.4
1904	310	5	1.6
1908	314	21	6.7
1912	333	84	25.2
1916	333	35	10.5
1920	344	11	3.2
1924	356	42	11.8
1928	359	68	18.9
1932	355	50	14.1
1936	361	51	14.1
1940	362	53	14.6
1944	367	41	11.2
1948	422	90	21.3
1952	435	84	19.3
1956	435	130	29.9
1960	437	114	26.1
1964	435	145	33.3
1968	435	139	32.0
1972	435	192	44.1
1976	435	124	28.5
1980	435	143	32.8
1984	435	196	45.0
1988	435	148	34.0
1992	435	100	23.0
1996	435	111	25.5
2000	435	86	19.8
2004	435	59	13.6
2008	435	83	19.1
2012	435	26	6.0
2016	435	35	8.1
2020	435	16	3.7

[a] For years 1900–1948, data on every congressional district are not available.
[b] Congressional districts carried by a presidential candidate of one party and a House candidate of another party.

Sources: Norman J. Ornstein, Thomas E. Mann, and Michael J. Malbin, eds., *Vital Statistics on Congress, 1993–1994* (Washington, D.C.: Congressional Quarterly, 1994), 64; *Congressional Quarterly Weekly Report (CQ Weekly)* (1997), 862; (2000), 1062; (2005), 879; (2009), 659; David Wasserman, "The Cook Political Report," www.cookpolitical.com; 2016–2020 data compiled by authors.

A Data Literacy Lesson
The Decline of Split Districts

In some of the tables in this book, you've had to look through a lot of numbers to tease out the effect we were hoping you would see. In other tables, the key finding we wanted you to see was really no change at all—stability, sometimes, is the big story. And then there's Table 1-14, in which the effect could not possibly be clearer.

Table 1-14 shows us that in 2020, only sixteen House districts, 3.6 percent of them, supported one party's candidate for president and the other party's candidate for the House. How small a number is that? Consider that in 1984, not all *that* long ago, 196 such districts (45 percent) showed such a split. Something big has happened, and it is worth considering what that might be.

One thing to consider is the nature of our modern political parties. Nowadays, both political parties represent narrow ideological segments of the electorate. A generation ago, it was not at all uncommon for some Democrats to be pro-life and some Republicans to be pro-choice; today, few legislators buck the party orthodoxy on that issue, or many others. Even more structurally, the existence of conservative Democrats (mostly from the South) and liberal Republicans (mostly from the North) meant that each party represented a wider range of beliefs. That range has narrowed considerably over the years. We think of senators such as Joe Manchin (D-W.V.) or Mitt Romney (R-Utah) as being on the fringes of their party, even though they are reliable party votes on most issues. Most senators vote with their parties almost all the time.

It is a question of some dispute within the field of political science whether voters have gotten more polarized (i.e., are Republicans more conservative and Democrats more liberal?). They certainly act that way—we know, for instance, that far fewer voters split their tickets today than was the case in, say, the 1980s. We are less sure that they *think* in a more polarized manner. What we do know is that the choices voters see have become more polarized, as Republican and Democratic officeholders have gotten more conservative and liberal, respectively, even if the voters themselves might be no more partisan. Voters might have had tough choices in the past and might have found candidates from different parties to be preferred for different offices. The rise of negative partisanship, when voters harbor strongly negative attitudes toward the other party, even more than they have positive views toward their own, leads voters to be more likely to cast straight ticket votes, and hence create fewer split districts. This is especially the case when the candidates themselves are so polarizing.

Increased polarization is driven by another factor—partisan gerrymandering. Because more and more congressional districts are drawn to give one party a significant majority, fewer districts are reasonably "in play" from year to year. A district that has a 60–40 Republican split, for example, is unlikely to vote for a Democrat in all but the bleakest years for Republicans. When partisan gerrymandering was less common, more districts could sway back and forth between elections. Today, as Table 1-14 suggests, districts are more likely to be "owned" by one party or the other.

When political parties set out to try to expand their number of House seats, they tend to start with the seats that they carried in the presidential election but lost in the House. These seats are most ripe for the taking; they are, however, harder and harder to find. What is more, these seats are often occupied by the most ideologically diverse members of the party caucus. If we imagine a Democrat who manages to win a House seat in a district carried by Donald Trump, we would assume that the district is fairly conservative, and that the Democrat is a member of the moderate wing of the party. This person is quite vulnerable to defeat in the general election. A strongly progressive Democrat is more likely to represent a very Democratic district and is in less danger in November (although they might be more at risk in the primary). Table 1-14, then, suggests that we should see fewer competitive districts, as well as fewer moderates (and hence more polarization) in Congress.

Trends as dramatic as those we observe in Table 1-14 very rarely happen by chance—as a general rule, when a table shows this big of a change, there are almost always important reasons driving the change, and meaningful impacts of that change. When you encounter data shifts that are this stark, we urge you to explore a little more, and see what's really going on behind the numbers.

Table 1-15 Mean Turnover in the House of Representatives from Various Causes, by Decade and Party System, 1789–2020

Period	Total turnover	Deaths	Retired[a]	Not renominated	General election defeat	Unknown[b]
1790s	0.379	0.017	0.164	0.002	0.027	0.170
1800s	0.361	0.018	0.154	0.001	0.032	0.157
1810s	0.488	0.025	0.181	0.008	0.065	0.209
1820s	0.401	0.018	0.142	0.002	0.079	0.159
1830s	0.483	0.029	0.175	0.006	0.117	0.156
1840s	0.594	0.030	0.253	0.009	0.098	0.205
1850s	0.580	0.018	0.252	0.015	0.140	0.154
1860s	0.492	0.025	0.237	0.026	0.119	0.086
1870s	0.482	0.020	0.220	0.035	0.147	0.060
1880s	0.442	0.023	0.189	0.045	0.130	0.056
1890s	0.394	0.026	0.170	0.043	0.126	0.028
1900s	0.276	0.028	0.114	0.033	0.086	0.015
1910s	0.290	0.029	0.112	0.028	0.114	0.006
1920s	0.223	0.035	0.076	0.026	0.085	0.000
1930s	0.283	0.039	0.084	0.047	0.114	0.000
1940s	0.245	0.025	0.084	0.032	0.104	0.000
1950s	0.168	0.025	0.073	0.014	0.056	0.000
1960s	0.166	0.016	0.073	0.021	0.057	0.000
1970s	0.190	0.010	0.112	0.014	0.053	0.000
1980s	0.120	0.010	0.069	0.007	0.033	0.000
1990s	0.167	0.007	0.106	0.013	0.042	0.000
2000s	0.148	0.006	0.083	0.009	0.051	0.000
2010s	0.164	0.003	0.103	0.016	0.042	0.000
Overall, 1789–2020	0.328	0.021	0.140	0.020	0.083	0.064
Grouped by party system						
First, 1789–1824	0.415	0.020	0.162	0.004	0.048	0.180
Second, 1825–1854	0.524	0.026	0.206	0.007	0.111	0.175
Third, 1855–1896	0.476	0.022	0.215	0.036	0.137	0.067
Fourth, 1897–1932	0.275	0.032	0.103	0.034	0.098	0.008
Fifth, 1933–1964	0.218	0.027	0.080	0.026	0.084	0.000
Sixth, 1965–2020	0.169	0.007	0.100	0.014	0.048	0.000

Note: Figures are proportions of the House membership for each Congress failing to return to the following Congress, averaged across all Congresses within a decade (or a party system). Decades are defined by the first year of a Congress (for example, the 1980s spans 1981–1982 through 1989–1990); each decade mean is based on five Congresses, except for the 1790s (six). Results reflect the final disposition of challenged elections. The overall average represents the average across all congressional elections in the table. Data are current as of June 2021.

[a] Includes retirements from public office, retirements to seek or accept other elective office (including the Senate), retirements to accept federal executive branch appointments, resignations, and expulsions.

[b] "Unknown" are cases in which the member was not a candidate in the next general election, but it could not be determined whether he or she deliberately chose not to seek reelection or was denied renomination.

Sources: Revised from John W. Swain, Stephen A. Borrelli, Brian C. Reed, and Sean F. Evans, "A New Look at Turnover in the U.S. House of Representatives, 1789–1998," *American Politics Quarterly* 28 (2000): 435–457; other data supplied by the authors.

Table 1-16 House and Senate Seats That Changed Party, 1954–2020

		Incumbent defeated		Open seat	
Chamber/ year	Total changes	Democrat to Republican	Republican to Democrat	Democrat to Republican	Republican to Democrat
House					
1954	26	3	18	2	3
1956	20	7	7	2	4
1958	50	1	35	0	14
1960	37	23	2	6	6
1962	19	9	5	2	3
1964	57	5	39	5	8
1966	47	39	1	4	3
1968	11	5	0	2	4
1970	25	2	9	6	8
1972	23	6	3	9	5
1974	55	4	36	2	13
1976	22	7	5	3	7
1978	33	14	5	8	6
1980	41	27	3	10	1
1982	31	1	22	3	5
1984	22	13	3	5	1
1986	21	1	5	7	8
1988	9	2	4	1	2
1990	21	6	9	0	6
1992	43	16	8	11	8
1994	61	35	0	22	4
1996	35	3	18	10	4
1998	17	1	5	5	6
2000	18	2	4	6	6
2002	12	2	2	4	4
2004	10	3	2	2	3
2006	30	0	22	0	8
2008	31	5	14	0	12
2010	69	52	2	14	1
2012	29	6	16	5	2
2014	19	11	2	5	1
2016	12	1	6	2	3
2018	46	0	30	3	13
2020	17	13	0	1	3
Senate					
1954	8	2	4	1	1
1956	8	1	3	3	1
1958	13	0	11	0	2
1960	2	1	0	1	0
1962	8	2	3	0	3
1964	4	1	3	0	0
1966	3	1	0	2	0
1968	9	4	0	3	2

Table 1-16 *(Continued)*

Chamber/ year	Total changes	Incumbent defeated		Open seat	
		Democrat to Republican	Republican to Democrat	Democrat to Republican	Republican to Democrat
1970	6	3	2	1	0
1972	10	1	4	3	2
1974	6	0	2	1	3
1976	14	5	4	2	3
1978	13	5	2	3	3
1980	12	9	0	3	0
1982	4	1	1	1	1
1984	4	1	2	0	1
1986	10	0	7	1	2
1988	7	1	3	2	1
1990	1	0	1	0	0
1992	4	2	2	0	0
1994	8	2	0	6	0
1996	4	0	1	3	0
1998	6	1	2	2	1
2000	8	1	5	1	1
2002	4	2	1	1	0
2004	8	1	0	5	2
2006	6	0	6	0	0
2008	8	0	5	0	3
2010	6	2	0	4	0
2012	3	0	1	1	1
2014	9	5	0	4	0
2016	2	0	2	0	0
2018	6	4	1	0	1
2020	5	1	4	0	0

Note: This table reflects shifts in party control from before to after the November elections. It does not include shifts from the creation of districts or redistricting that result in incumbents from different districts running against each other in the same district.

Sources: 1954–1992: Norman J. Ornstein, Thomas E. Mann, and Michael J. Malbin, eds., *Vital Statistics on Congress, 1993–1994* (Washington, D.C.: Congressional Quarterly, 1994), 54, 56; 1994–2000: *Congressional Quarterly Weekly Report (CQ Weekly)* (1994), 3232–3233, 3240; (1996), 3228, 3238, 3402; (1998), 3004, 3010–3011; (2000), 2646–2647, 2652–2654; 2002: *2003 Congressional Staff Directory* (Washington, D.C.: CQ Press, 2003), 7, 215; 2004: *2005 Congressional Staff Directory* (Washington, D.C.: CQ Press, 2005), 7, 237; 2006: *CQ Weekly* (2006), 3066, 3068–3075, 3132, 3186, 3238, 3381; 2008: *CQ Weekly* (2008), 3043–3052, 3056, 3102, 3153, 3206, 3293, 3374; (2009), 216; 2010: Clerk of the House of Representatives, http://clerk.house.gov; *CQ Weekly* (2010), 2618–2629, 2716, 2717, 2766; 2012: *CQ Weekly* (2012), 2284–2293, 2308–2309, 2342, 2384, 2430; 2014: Clerk of the House of Representatives; *CQ Weekly* (2014), 60–61; 2016–2020: compiled by authors from official election results from state websites.

Table 1-17 Losses by President's Party in Midterm Elections, 1862–2018

Year	Party holding presidency	President's party: gain/loss of seats in House	President's party: gain/loss of seats in Senate
1862	R	−3	8
1866	R	−2	0
1870	R	−31	−4
1874	R	−96	−8
1878	R	−9	−6
1882	R	−33	3
1886	D	−12	3
1890	R	−85	0
1894	D	−116	−14
1898	R	−21	7
1902	R	9[a]	2
1906	R	−28	3
1910	R	−57	−10
1914	D	−59	5
1918	D	−19	−6
1922	R	−75	−8
1926	R	−10	−6
1930	R	−53	−8
1934	D	9	10
1938	D	−71	−6
1942	D	−45	−9
1946	D	−55	−12
1950	D	−29	−6
1954	R	−18	−1
1958	R	−47	−13
1962	D	−5	3
1966	D	−47	−4
1970	R	−12	3
1974	R	−48	−5
1978	D	−15	−3
1982	R	−26	1
1986	R	−5	−8
1990	R	−7	−1
1994	D	−54	−10
1998	D	4	0
2002	R	8	1
2006	R	−30	−6
2010	D	−63	−4
2014	D	−12	−9
2018	R	−42	2

Note: Each entry is the difference between the number of seats held by the president's party at the start of Congress after the midterm election and the number of seats held by that party at the start of Congress after the preceding general election. Special elections that shifted partisan seat totals between elections are not noted. Because of changes in the overall number of seats in the Senate and House, in the number of seats won by third parties, and in the number of vacancies, a Republican loss is not always matched precisely by a Democratic gain, or vice versa.

[a] Although the Republicans gained nine seats in the 1902 elections, they actually lost ground to the Democrats, who gained twenty-five seats after the increase in the overall number of representatives after the 1900 census.

Source: Table 1-10, this volume.

Election Results 49

Table 1-18 House and Senate Incumbents Retired, Defeated, or Reelected, 1946–2020

Chamber/ year	Retired[a]	Number seeking reelection	Defeated Primaries	Defeated General election	Reelected Total	Reelected Percentage of those seeking reelection
House						
1946	32	398	18	52	328	82.4
1948	29	400	15	68	317	79.3
1950	29	400	6	32	362	90.5
1952	42	389	9	26	354	91.0
1954	24	407	6	22	379	93.1
1956	21	411	6	16	389	94.6
1958	33	396	3	37	356	89.9
1960[b, c]	27	405	6	25	375	92.6
1962[d]	24	402	12	22	368	91.5
1964	33	397	8	45	344	86.6
1966	23	411	8	41	362	88.1
1968[e]	24	408	4	9	395	96.8
1970[c]	30	401	10	12	379	94.5
1972[c, f]	40	392	14	13	366	93.4
1974	43	391	8	40	343	87.7
1976	47	384	3	13	368	95.8
1978	49	382	5	19	358	93.7
1980[c]	34	398	6	31	361	90.7
1982	31	387	4	29	354	91.5
1984	22	411	3	16	392	95.4
1986	40	394	3	6	385	97.7
1988	23	409	1	6	402	98.3
1990	27	407	1	15	391	96.1
1992	65	368	19	24	325	88.3
1994[c]	48	387	4	34	349	90.2
1996	49	384	2	21	361	94.0
1998	33	402	1	6	395	98.3
2000	32	403	3	6	394	97.8
2002	35	398	8	8	382	96.0
2004	29	404	2	7	395	97.8
2006[g]	27	404	2	22	380	94.1
2008	32	403	4	19	380	94.3
2010	36	397	4	54	339	85.4
2012	39	391	13	27	351	89.8
2014	41	392	4	14	374	95.4
2016	42	380	6[h]	7	367	96.6
2018	55	376	4	37	337	89.7
2020	36	395	8	13	374	94.7
Senate						
1946	9	30	6	7	17	56.7
1948	8	25	2	8	15	60.0
1950	4	32	5	5	22	68.8
1952	4	31	2	9	20	64.5

(Table continues)

Table 1-18 *(Continued)*

Chamber/year	Retired[a]	Number seeking reelection	Defeated Primaries	Defeated General election	Reelected Total	Reelected Percentage of those seeking reelection
1954	6	32	2	6	24	75.0
1956	6	29	0	4	25	86.2
1958	6	28	0	10	18	64.3
1960	4	29	0	1	28	96.6
1962	4	35	1	5	29	82.9
1964	2	33	1	4	28	84.8
1966	3	32	3	1	28	87.5
1968[c]	6	28	4	4	20	71.4
1970	4	31	1	6	24	77.4
1972	6	27	2	5	20	74.1
1974	7	27	2	2	23	85.2
1976	8	25	0	9	16	64.0
1978	10	25	3	7	15	60.0
1980[c]	5	29	4	9	16	55.2
1982	3	30	0	2	28	93.3
1984	4	29	0	3	26	89.7
1986	6	28	0	7	21	75.0
1988	6	27	0	4	23	85.2
1990	3	32	0	1	31	96.9
1992	7	28	1	4	23	82.1
1994	8	26	0	2	24	92.3
1996	13	21	1	1	19	90.5
1998	5	29	0	3	26	89.7
2000	5	29	0	6	23	79.3
2002	6	28	1	3	24	85.7
2004	8	26	0	1	25	96.2
2006[i]	4	29	1	6	23	79.3
2008	5	30	0	5	25	83.3
2010[j]	12	25	3	2	21	84.0
2012	10	23	1	1	21	91.3
2014	7	28	0	5	23	82.1
2016	5	29	0	2	27	93.1
2018	3	32	0	5	27	84.4
2020	4	31	0	5	26	83.9

[a] Does not include persons who died or resigned from office before the election.
[b] Harold B. McSween, D-La., lost the Democratic primary in 1960 and is counted as an incumbent defeated in the primary. However, his victorious primary opponent, Earl K. Long, died after winning the primary, and McSween was appointed to replace Long in the general election by the Eighth District Democratic Committee. McSween won the general election and is counted as an incumbent winning the general election.
[c] In this year, an incumbent candidate lost the party primary and is counted as an incumbent defeated in the primary. The candidate then ran in the general election on a minor-party label or as a write-in candidate and lost again, but is not also counted (here or in Table 1-19) as an incumbent defeated in the general election. House: 1960, Ludwig Teller, D-N.Y.; 1970, Philip Philbin, D-Mass.; 1972, Emanuel Celler, D-N.Y.; 1980, John Buchanan, R-Ala.; 1994, David A. Levy, R-N.Y. Senate: 1968, Ernest Gruening, D-Alaska; 1980, Jacob K. Javits, R-N.Y.

Table 1-18 *(Continued)*

[d] Clem Miller, D-Calif., was killed in a plane crash on October 7, 1962, but his name remained on the 1962 general election ballot. He won the election posthumously and is counted here as an incumbent winning the general election.

[e] Adam Clayton Powell, D-N.Y., won a special election on April 11, 1967, but he was prevented from taking the oath of office and did not take his seat in Congress. Therefore, he is not counted here (or in Table 1-19) as an incumbent in the 1968 general election.

[f] Bella Abzug, D-N.Y., lost the Democratic primary in 1972 and is counted as an incumbent defeated in the primary. However, her victorious primary opponent, William F. Ryan, died after winning the primary, and Abzug was appointed to replace him in the general election by the local party committee. Abzug won the general election and is counted as an incumbent winning the general election.

[g] In 2006, three representatives withdrew from the general election after winning their primaries: Tom DeLay, R-Texas; Mark Foley, R-Fla.; and Bob Ney, R-Ohio. Because they did not run in the general election, they are not counted as incumbents seeking reelection (here or in Table 1-19).

[h] Mike Honda, D-Calif., lost in the general election to a fellow Democrat, Ro Khanna, D-Calif. We count this as a loss in the primary since the loss was to a member of the same party.

[i] Joseph I. Lieberman, D-Conn., lost the Democratic primary in 2006 and is counted as an incumbent defeated in the primary. He ran as an independent in the general election and won. He is counted as an incumbent winning the general election.

[j] Lisa Murkowski, R-Alaska, lost the Republican primary in 2010 and is counted as an incumbent defeated in the primary. She ran as a write-in candidate in the general election and won. She is counted as an incumbent winning the general election.

Sources: Clerk of the House of Representatives, http://clerk.house.gov; *Congressional Quarterly*; compiled by authors from official election results from state websites.

Table 1-19 Incumbent Reelection Rates: Representatives, Senators, and Governors, General Elections, 1960–2020

Year/office	Number of incumbents			Incumbents winning election (percentage)[a]	Incumbents reelected with 60+ percent of the major-party vote (percentage)[a]
	Ran	Won	Lost		
1960					
House[b, c]	400	375	25	93.5	59.3
Senate	29	28	1	96.6	44.8
Governor	14	8	6	57.1	14.3
1962					
House[d]	390	368	22	96.2	61.0[e]
Senate	34	29	5	85.3	32.4
Governor	26	15	11	57.7	7.7
1964					
House	389	344	45	88.4	58.1
Senate	32	28	4	87.5	46.9
Governor	14	12	2	85.7	50.0
1966					
House	403	362	41	90	67.0
Senate	29	28	1	96.6	44.8
Governor	22	15	7	68.2	22.7
1968					
House[f]	404	395	9	98.8	70.8
Senate[c]	24	20	4	83.3	45.8
Governor	14	10	4	71.4	21.4
1970					
House[c]	391	379	12	96.9	76.7
Senate	30	24	6	79.3	33.3
Governor	22	17	5	77.3	9.1
1972					
House[c, g]	379	366	13	96.6	76.3
Senate	25	20	5	80.0	48.0
Governor	9	7	2	77.8	44.4
1974					
House	383	343	40	89.6	66.6
Senate	25	23	2	92.0	44.0
Governor	21	16	5	76.2	42.9
1976					
House	381	368	13	96.6	72.7
Senate	25	16	9	64.0	44.0
Governor	7	5	2	71.4	28.6
1978					
House	377	358	19	95	75.3
Senate	22	15	7	68.2	31.8
Governor	20	15	5	75.0	30.0
1980					
House[c]	392	361	31	92.1	73.2
Senate[c]	25	16	9	64.0	38.5
Governor	10	7	3	70.0	40.0

Table 1-19 *(Continued)*

Year/office	Number of incumbents			Incumbents winning election (percentage)[a]	Incumbents reelected with 60+ percent of the major-party vote (percentage)[a]
	Ran	Won	Lost		
1982					
House	383	354	29	92.4	69.9
Senate	30	28	2	93.3	46.7
Governor	24	19	5	79.2	45.8
1984					
House	408	392	16	96.1	77.2
Senate	29	26	3	89.7	65.5
Governor	6	4	2	66.7	50.0
1986					
House	391	385	6	98.5	84.4
Senate	28	21	7	75.0	50.0
Governor	17	15	2	88.2	52.9
1988					
House	408	402	6	98.5	87
Senate	27	23	4	85.2	55.6
Governor	9	8	1	88.9	33.3
1990					
House	406	391	15	96.3	74.9
Senate	32	31	1	96.9	62.5
Governor	23	17	6	73.9	47.8
1992					
House	349	325	24	93.1	65.6
Senate	27	23	4	85.2	48.1
Governor	4	4	0	100.0	100.0
1994					
House[c]	383	349	34	91.9	67.2
Senate	26	24	2	92.3	38.5
Governor	21	17	4	81.0	38.1
1996					
House	382	361	21	94.5	67.8
Senate	20	19	1	95.0	30.0
Governor	7	7	0	100.0	71.4
1998					
House	401	395	6	98.5	77.3
Senate	29	26	3	89.6	65.5
Governor	26	24	2	92.3	50.0
2000					
House	400	394	6	98.5	78.0
Senate	29	23	6	79.3	58.6
Governor	6	5	1	83.3	0.0
2002					
House	390	382	8	97.9	86.4
Senate	27	24	3	88.9	65.4
Governor	16	12	4	75.0	25

(Table continues)

Table 1-19 *(Continued)*

Year/office	Number of incumbents			Incumbents winning election (percentage)[a]	Incumbents reelected with 60+ percent of the major-party vote (percentage)[a]
	Ran	Won	Lost		
2004					
House	402	395	7	98.3	85.3
Senate	26	25	1	96.2	69.2
Governor	6	4	2	66.7	33.3
2006					
House[h]	402	380	22	94.5	75.1
Senate[i]	29	23	6	79.3	58.6
Governor	26	25	1	96.1	46.2
2008					
House	399	380	19	95.2	76.4
Senate	30	25	5	83.3	56.7
Governor	8	8	0	100	87.5
2010					
House	393	339	54	86.3	63.9
Senate[j]	23	21	2	91.3	56.5
Governor	13	11	2	84.6	38.5
2012					
House	378	351	27	92.9	66.4
Senate	22	21	1	95.5	54.5
Governor	6	6	0	100	66.7
2014					
House	388	374	14	96.4	77.3
Senate	28	23	5	82.1	46.4
Governor	28	25	3	89.3	28.6
2016					
House	374	367	7	98.1	80.1
Senate	29	27	2	93.1	51.7
Governor	5	4	1	80.0	20.0
2018					
House	372	335	37	90.1	67.2
Senate	32	27	5	84.4	34.4
Governor	18	16	2	88.9	22.2
2020					
House	387	374	13	96.6	67.2
Senate	31	26	5	83.9	32.3
Governor	9	9	0	100	55.6

Note: Percentage gaining more than 60 percent of the vote (among incumbents who ran) is calculated on the basis of the vote for the two major parties. Incumbents running unopposed are considered to have won with over 60 percent of the major-party vote. "Off-off" year gubernatorial elections, held in Kentucky, Louisiana, Mississippi, New Jersey, and Virginia, are not included in the preceding totals. For these gubernatorial election outcomes, see *CQ Press Guide to U.S. Elections*, 7th ed. (Washington, D.C.: CQ Press, 2016).

[a] Percentage is calculated based on all incumbents running in the general election.

[b] Harold B. McSween, D-La., lost the Democratic primary in 1960 and is counted as an incumbent defeated in the primary in Table 1-18. However, his victorious primary opponent, Earl K.

Table 1-19 *(Continued)*

Long, died after winning the primary, and McSween was appointed to replace Long in the general election by the Eighth District Democratic Committee. McSween won the general election and is counted as an incumbent winning the general election.

[c] In this year, an incumbent candidate lost the party primary and is counted as an incumbent defeated in the primary in Table 1-18. The candidate then ran in the general election on a minor-party label or as a write-in candidate and lost again, but is not also counted (here or in Table 1-18) as an incumbent defeated in the general election. House: 1960, Ludwig Teller, D-N.Y.; 1970, Philip Philbin, D-Mass.; 1972, Emanuel Celler, D-N.Y.; 1980, John Buchanan, R-Ala.; 1994, David A. Levy, R-N.Y. Senate: 1968, Ernest Gruening, D-Alaska; 1980, Jacob K. Javits, R-N.Y.

[d] Clem Miller, D-Calif., was killed in a plane crash on October 7, 1962, but his name remained on the 1962 general election ballot. He won the election posthumously and is counted here as an incumbent winning the general election.

[e] Data not available for Alabama. The percentage is calculated excluding the number of incumbents winning House seats in Alabama for this year.

[f] Adam Clayton Powell, D-N.Y., won a special election on April 11, 1967, but he was prevented from taking the oath of office and did not take his seat in Congress. Therefore, he is not counted here (or in Table 1-18) as an incumbent in the 1968 general election.

[g] Bella Abzug, D-N.Y., lost the Democratic primary in 1972 and is counted as an incumbent defeated in the primary in Table 1-18. However, her victorious primary opponent, William F. Ryan, died after winning the primary, and Abzug was appointed to replace him in the general election by the local party committee. Abzug won the general election and is counted as an incumbent winning the general election.

[h] In 2006 three representatives withdrew from the general election after winning their primaries: Tom DeLay, R-Texas; Mark Foley, R-Fla.; and Bob Ney, R-Ohio. Because they did not run in the general election, they are not counted as incumbents seeking reelection (here or in Table 1-18).

[i] Joseph I. Lieberman, D-Conn., lost the Democratic primary in 2006 and is counted as an incumbent defeated in the primary in Table 1-18. He ran as an independent in the general election and won. He is counted as an incumbent winning the general election.

[j] Lisa Murkowski, R-Alaska, lost the Republican primary in 2010 and is counted as an incumbent defeated in the primary in Table 1-18. She ran as a write-in candidate in the general election and won. She is counted as an incumbent winning the general election.

Sources: Clerk of the House of Representatives, http://clerk.house.gov; Congressional Quarterly; National Governors Association, www.nga.gov; compiled by authors from official election results from state websites.

Table 1-20 Congressional Districts with a Racial or Ethnic Minority Representative or a "Majority-Minority" Population, 2021

State	District number	% White	% Black	% Asian	% Other	% Two or more races	% Hispanic	Representative elected in 2020	Party	Representative's race/ethnicity
Racial or ethnic minority representatives in districts with majority-White populations										
California	3	56	7	10	6	5	22	Garamendi	D	Hispanic
California	7	57	8	14	5	5	15	Bera	D	Asian
California	24	66	2	5	4	4	24	Carbajal	D	Hispanic
California	33	68	4	12	3	5	12	Lieu	D	Asian
California	36	51	5	4	20	3	38	Ruiz	D	Hispanic
California	48	60	2	20	7	3	16	Steel	D	Asian
California	49	67	4	7	4	3	19	Levin	D	Hispanic
Colorado	2	87	0	2	1	2	8	Neguse	D	Black
Connecticut	5	74	7	3	4	2	15	Hayes	D	Black
Delaware	At-large	69	22	2	1	3	5	Blunt-Rochester	D	Black
Florida	7	61	11	4	5	2	23	Murphy	D	Asian
Florida	18	73	12	2	2	2	13	Mast	R	Hispanic
Florida	19	78	6	2	2	1	13	Donalds	R	Black
Georgia	6	70	14	9	2	2	6	McBath	D	Black
Illinois	8	62	6	12	8	2	19	Krishnamoorthi	D	Asian
Illinois	14	83	4	3	1	2	9	Underwood	D	Black
Indiana	7	61	30	2	2	3	5	Carson	D	Black
Massachusetts	3	74	4	6	8	2	15	Trahan	D	Hispanic
Massachusetts	7	51	24	9	5	4	16	Pressley	D	Black
Minnesota	5	74	13	4	3	3	4	Omar	D	Black
Missouri	5	70	21	1	2	2	6	Cleaver	D	Black
Nevada	4	53	15	6	9	4	22	Horsford	D	Black
New Jersey	3	78	11	3	1	2	7	Kim	D	Asian
New Jersey	12	56	19	12	3	2	12	Watson Coleman	D	Black
New York	11	64	8	13	4	2	15	Malliotakis	R	Hispanic
New York	17	66	11	6	6	2	16	Jones	D	Black
New York	19	87	5	1	1	2	6	Delgado	D	Black-Hispanic

State	District				Name	Party	Race
Ohio	3	59	31	3	2	3	4	Beatty	D	Black
Ohio	16	92	3	2	0	1	2	Gonzalez	R	Hispanic
Texas	32	61	13	8	4	2	16	Allred	D	Black
Utah	4	82	1	3	6	2	11	Owens	R	Black
Virginia	4	52	41	2	1	2	3	McEachin	D	Black
Washington	3	86	1	3	3	4	5	Herrera-Beutler	R	Hispanic
Washington	7	76	4	10	1	6	5	Jayapal	D	Asian
Washington	10	72	7	7	5	5	8	Strickland	D	Black-Asian
West Virginia	2	92	5	1	0	1	2	Mooney	R	Hispanic
Wisconsin	4	51	32	3	5	3	12	Moore	D	Black

Congressional districts with a majority-minority population

State	District				Name	Party	Race
Alabama	7	35	62	0	0	0	2	Sewell	D	Black
Arizona	3	35	6	2	17	4	53	Grijalva	D	Hispanic
Arizona	7	31	12	2	12	4	51	Gallego	D	Hispanic
California	6	43	14	16	9	6	22	Matsui	D	Asian
California	9	43	10	14	6	8	29	McNerney	D	White
California	12	47	6	31	6	5	12	Pelosi	D	White
California	13	41	18	21	10	6	16	Lee	D	Black
California	14	39	3	35	9	5	18	Speier	D	White
California	15	39	7	31	11	5	19	Swalwell	D	White
California	16	31	7	10	19	3	50	Costa	D	Hispanic
California	17	31	3	48	7	4	16	Khanna	D	Asian
California	19	31	4	30	13	5	32	Lofgren	D	White
California	21	26	6	5	15	4	61	Valadeo	R	Hispanic
California	22	47	3	8	12	4	39	Nunes	R	Hispanic
California	25	49	7	9	11	4	33	Garcia	D	White
California	27	32	5	36	12	3	25	Chu	D	Asian
California	29	28	6	9	23	3	57	Cardenas	D	Hispanic
California	31	33	12	7	12	4	46	Aguilar	D	Hispanic
California	32	19	4	19	16	7	57	Napolitano	D	Hispanic

(Table continues)

57

Table 1-20 *(Continued)*

State	District number	% White	% Black	% Asian	% Other	% Two or more races	% Hispanic	Representative elected in 2020	Party	Representative's race/ethnicity
California	34	18	9	22	27	4	49	Gomez	D	Hispanic
California	35	19	7	8	32	4	65	Torres	D	Hispanic
California	37	31	26	11	11	4	29	Bass	D	Black
California	38	20	4	17	30	3	56	Sanchez	D	Hispanic
California	39	35	3	31	7	3	29	Kim	R	Asian
California	40	8	8	4	33	2	80	Roybal-Allard	D	Hispanic
California	41	27	11	7	24	4	54	Takano	D	Asian
California	42	48	7	9	12	4	33	Calvert	R	White
California	43	19	26	15	15	4	37	Waters	D	Black
California	44	10	22	6	25	3	60	Barragan	D	Hispanic
California	46	27	3	15	20	2	55	Correa	D	Hispanic
California	47	39	9	23	9	4	26	Lowenthal	D	White
California	51	18	9	9	12	4	62	Vargas	D	Hispanic
California	53	46	8	14	5	5	29	Jacobs	D	White
District of Columbia	At-large	42	46	4	2	3	7	Holmes-Norton	D	Black
Florida	5	43	47	2	1	2	6	Lawson	D	Black
Florida	9	46	12	3	6	3	39	Soto	D	Hispanic
Florida	10	42	27	5	5	2	24	Demings	D	Black
Florida	20	21	53	3	3	3	22	Vacant		
Florida	23	45	14	4	5	3	36	Wasserman-Schultz	D	White
Florida	24	12	50	1	6	2	38	Wilson	D	Black
Florida	25	26	6	1	2	1	68	Diaz-Balart	R	Hispanic
Florida	26	19	12	2	5	2	67	Gimenez	R	Hispanic
Florida	27	25	6	2	3	2	68	Salazar	R	Hispanic
Georgia	2	44	51	1	1	2	3	Bishop	D	Black
Georgia	4	28	64	3	1	2	4	Johnson	D	Black

State								Name	Party	Race
Georgia	5	32	59	3	1	2	4	Williams	D	Black
Georgia	13	28	62	2	3	2	6	Scott	D	Black
Hawaii	1	18	3	51	6	20	8	Case	D	White
Hawaii	2	33	2	26	13	22	9	Kahele	D	Asian
Illinois	1	38	52	2	2	1	7	Rush	D	Black
Illinois	2	31	58	1	3	2	10	Kelly	D	Black
Illinois	4	33	5	4	23	3	57	Garcia	D	Hispanic
Illinois	7	32	49	6	4	2	12	Davis	D	Black
Louisiana	2	31	62	2	1	1	4	Carter	D	Black
Maryland	4	29	59	3	5	3	8	Brown	D	Black
Maryland	5	48	40	4	2	3	5	Hoyer	D	White
Maryland	7	36	54	5	1	3	3	Mfume	D	Black
Michigan	13	38	55	1	2	2	4	Tlaib	D	Arab-American
Michigan	14	34	58	3	1	2	3	Lawrence	D	Black
Mississippi	2	33	65	0	0	0	1	Thompson	D	Black
Missouri	1	46	48	2	1	2	2	Bush	D	Black
Nevada	1	43	15	9	15	4	30	Titus	D	White
New Jersey	8	33	12	7	16	4	48	Sires	D	Hispanic
New Jersey	9	46	11	11	11	2	32	Pascrell	D	White
New Jersey	10	23	54	6	7	2	17	Payne	D	Black
New Mexico	1	45	3	2	10	3	44	Vacant		
New Mexico	2	42	3	1	10	2	49	Herrell	R	White
New Mexico	3	42	2	1	27	2	36	Leger-Fernancez	D	Hispanic
New York	5	14	54	13	11	3	15	Meeks	D	Black
New York	6	41	5	33	7	3	19	Meng	D	Asian
New York	7	37	12	14	14	5	36	Velazquez	D	Hispanic
New York	8	28	51	6	6	3	16	Jeffries	D	Black
New York	9	34	48	7	4	3	10	Clarke	D	Black
New York	13	17	33	4	27	6	49	Espaillat	D	Hispanic
New York	14	29	15	15	19	3	41	Ocasio-Cortez	D	Hispanic

(Table continues)

Table 1-20 *(Continued)*

State	District number	% White	% Black	% Asian	% Other	% Two or more races	% Hispanic	Representative elected in 2020	Party	Representative's race/ethnicity
New York	15	4	41	2	34	4	61	Torres	D	Black/Hispanic
New York	16	41	33	5	10	3	22	Bowman	D	Black
North Carolina	1	48	45	1	2	2	3	Butterfield	D	Black
North Carolina	12	48	41	3	3	2	7	Adams	D	Black
Ohio	11	41	51	2	1	3	3	Vacant		
Pennsylvania	2	45	27	6	13	3	22	Boyle	D	White
Pennsylvania	3	35	55	4	1	3	4	Evans	D	White
South Carolina	6	41	55	1	1	2	2	Clyburn	D	Black
Tennessee	9	27	68	1	1	0	2	Cohen	D	White
Texas	9	14	47	11	9	1	27	Green	D	Black
Texas	15	22	3	2	7	1	73	Gonzalez	D	Hispanic
Texas	16	16	4	1	11	3	77	Escobar	D	Hispanic
Texas	18	22	45	4	6	2	28	Jackson Lee	D	Black
Texas	20	25	6	2	6	3	65	Castro	D	Hispanic
Texas	22	44	16	17	2	2	23	Nehls	R	White
Texas	23	29	4	2	7	2	64	Gonzalez	R	Black
Texas	27	45	6	1	4	2	47	Cloud	R	White
Texas	28	22	5	0	4	2	71	Cuellar	D	Hispanic
Texas	29	15	14	2	14	2	69	Garcia	D	Hispanic
Texas	30	22	51	2	3	2	23	Johnson	D	Black
Texas	33	22	24	3	11	2	49	Veasey	D	Black
Texas	34	18	0	0	4	1	79	Velazquez	D	Hispanic
Texas	35	34	10	1	9	3	53	Doggett	D	White
Virginia	3	45	46	2	1	3	4	Scott	D	Black/Asian

Note: "D" indicates Democratic; "R" indicates Republican. Majority-minority districts are those in which the non-Hispanic white population does not constitute a majority of the total population. Population values are based on the 2018 American Community Survey one-year estimates from the U.S. Census Bureau. The six population categories do not sum to 100 percent, due to people being able to count themselves in multiple columns. Data for earlier years can be found in previous editions of *Vital Statistics on American Politics*.

Sources: Derived by the authors from Table 5-11, as well as from U.S. Census Bureau, 2018 American Community Survey 1-Year Estimates, www.census.gov.

Table 1-21 Latino Elected Officials in the United States, 1996–2019

	1996	2000	2005	2007	2010	2012	2014	2019
Members of Congress	17	19	25	26	24	26	31	42
State officials	6	8	9	6	7	8	9	17
State legislators	156	190	232	238	245	258	294	330
County officials	358	398	498	512	563	555	547	517
Municipal officials	1,295	1,469	1,651	1,640	1,707	1,738	1,766	2,258
Judicial and law enforcement	546	465	678	685	874	881	878	882
School board members	1,240	1,392	1,760	1,847	2,071	2,225	2,322	2,535
Special district officials	125	119	188	175	248	237	237	251
Total	3,743	4,060	5,041	5,129	5,739	5,928	6,084	6,832

Sources: 1996–2005: National Association of Latino Elected Officials, "NALEO At-A-Glance" (September 4, 2006), www.naleo.org; 2007: *2007 National Directory of Latino Elected Officials*; 2010: *2010*; 2011: *2011*; 2012: *2012*; 2014: *2014*; 2019: *2019*.

Table 1-22 Blacks, Hispanics, and Women as a Percentage of State Legislators and State Voting-Age Population

State	Total number of legislators	Blacks			Hispanics			Women		
		Legislators	Percentage	Percentage VAP	Ratio[a]	Legislators	Percentage	Percentage VAP	Ratio[a]	Legislators	Percentage	Percentage VAP	Ratio[a]
Alabama	140	32	22.9	26.3	0.871	0	0.0	2.0	0.000	22	15.7	52.5	0.299
Alaska	60	2	3.3	3.1	1.060	1	1.7	5.7	0.292	18	30.0	46.5	0.645
Arizona	90	2	2.2	4.3	0.513	25	27.8	23.2	1.199	40	44.4	50.8	0.875
Arkansas	135	14	10.4	15.1	0.688	1	0.7	3.6	0.208	31	23.0	51.8	0.443
California	120	8	6.7	6.6	1.011	33	27.5	29.8	0.923	38	31.7	51.0	0.621
Colorado	100	8	8.0	3.8	2.092	15	15.0	15.6	0.964	45	45.0	50.3	0.895
Connecticut	187	19	10.2	9.5	1.074	13	7.0	11.9	0.585	64	34.2	52.2	0.656
Delaware	62	12	19.4	21.2	0.912	1	1.6	5.3	0.306	19	30.6	52.6	0.583
Florida	160	27	16.9	14.5	1.166	25	15.6	19.9	0.785	55	34.4	52.0	0.661
Georgia	236	66	28.0	32.1	0.871	3	1.3	4.7	0.272	78	33.1	52.4	0.631
Hawaii	76	2	2.6	2.0	1.334	4	5.3	8.6	0.615	25	32.9	48.6	0.677
Idaho	105	0	0.0	0.5	0.000	1	1.0	8.0	0.119	32	30.5	50.6	0.602
Illinois	177	34	19.2	14.7	1.311	16	9.0	11.2	0.806	71	40.1	51.8	0.774
Indiana	150	14	9.3	8.8	1.057	2	1.3	4.0	0.334	37	24.7	51.6	0.478
Iowa	150	6	4.0	2.9	1.399	1	0.7	3.4	0.198	43	28.7	51.0	0.562
Kansas	165	7	4.2	5.6	0.754	5	3.0	6.9	0.439	49	29.7	50.9	0.583
Kentucky	138	8	5.8	7.7	0.754	1	0.7	1.7	0.418	37	26.8	51.6	0.520
Louisiana	144	36	25.0	31.5	0.793	0	0.0	3.0	0.000	27	18.8	52.0	0.361
Maine	186	3	1.6	0.7	2.254	1	0.5	1.3	0.418	81	43.5	51.6	0.844
Maryland	188	57	30.3	30.1	1.007	6	3.2	5.2	0.614	77	41.0	52.6	0.779
Massachusetts	200	6	3.0	6.1	0.492	9	4.5	8.6	0.525	62	31.0	52.4	0.592
Michigan	148	18	12.2	13.4	0.906	5	3.4	3.3	1.009	53	35.8	51.5	0.695
Minnesota	201	7	3.5	4.7	0.747	5	2.5	2.8	0.880	72	35.8	50.9	0.704
Mississippi	174	54	31.0	36.7	0.845	1	0.6	1.7	0.340	28	16.1	52.5	0.307
Missouri	197	26	13.2	11.0	1.201	0	0.0	2.6	0.000	52	26.4	51.7	0.511
Montana	150	0	0.0	0.4	0.000	1	0.7	2.9	0.229	48	32.0	50.9	0.629
Nebraska	49	2	4.1	4.2	0.972	2	4.1	6.0	0.686	13	26.5	50.9	0.521

Nevada	63	10	15.9	9.3	1.704	8	12.7	19.1	0.665	38	60.3	50.0	1.206
New Hampshire	424	4	0.9	1.1	0.887	7	1.7	2.7	0.616	152	35.8	51.2	0.700
New Jersey	120	19	15.8	13.3	1.194	12	10.0	14.8	0.677	37	30.8	52.3	0.590
New Mexico	112	3	2.7	1.9	1.395	49	43.8	42.7	1.025	49	43.8	51.0	0.858
New York	213	32	15.0	14.4	1.045	21	9.9	14.6	0.677	73	34.3	52.4	0.654
North Carolina	170	37	21.8	21.8	1.000	2	1.2	4.2	0.282	45	26.5	52.3	0.506
North Dakota	141	0	0.0	1.9	0.000	0	0.0	2.8	0.000	32	22.7	48.8	0.465
Ohio	132	18	13.6	11.7	1.169	2	1.5	2.6	0.587	41	31.1	51.8	0.600
Oklahoma	149	8	5.4	7.2	0.744	2	1.3	5.7	0.236	31	20.8	51.3	0.406
Oregon	90	4	4.4	1.7	2.576	4	4.4	7.5	0.591	39	43.3	51.1	0.848
Pennsylvania	253	25	9.9	10.1	0.979	5	2.0	5.2	0.383	73	28.9	51.8	0.557
Rhode Island	113	5	4.4	5.2	0.858	16	14.2	10.6	1.337	51	45.1	52.8	0.855
South Carolina	170	45	26.5	26.6	0.995	0	0.0	2.8	0.000	30	17.6	52.3	0.337
South Dakota	105	1	1.0	1.2	0.828	0	0.0	2.3	0.000	30	28.6	50.3	0.568
Tennessee	132	17	12.9	16.4	0.786	0	0.0	2.3	0.000	22	16.7	52.2	0.319
Texas	181	19	10.5	13.1	0.801	45	24.9	29.9	0.833	48	26.5	51.3	0.517
Utah	104	1	1.0	0.9	1.042	3	2.9	8.7	0.332	25	24.0	50.1	0.480
Vermont	180	2	1.1	0.9	1.227	5	2.8	1.6	1.776	76	42.2	51.2	0.825
Virginia	140	23	16.4	19.4	0.846	1	0.7	5.4	0.132	42	30.0	51.4	0.584
Washington	147	9	6.1	3.5	1.756	6	4.1	7.3	0.557	61	41.5	50.5	0.822
West Virginia	134	3	2.2	3.6	0.626	2	1.5	1.1	1.315	16	11.9	51.1	0.234
Wisconsin	132	10	7.6	5.7	1.328	5	3.8	4.0	0.958	41	31.1	50.9	0.610
Wyoming	90	1	1.1	0.8	1.370	3	3.3	7.1	0.470	16	17.8	49.5	0.359
United States	7,383	766	10.4	12.5	0.830	375	5.1	12.4	0.410	2,285	30.9	51.5	0.601

Note: Hispanics may be of any race. The Black voting-age population (VAP) figures are for the Black-alone racial category. The counts of legislators are as of January 2021.

[a] The ratio between the group's indicated percentage of state legislators and the group's percentage of the state voting-age population. Calculated before rounding.

Sources: Total number of legislators and women legislators: Center for American Women and Politics, "Women in State Legislatures 2021," www.cawp.rutgers.edu; Black legislators: Governing: The Future of States and Localities, "Blacks in State Legislatures: A State-by-State Map," (January 13, 2021), https://www.governing.com; Latino legislators: "Hispanics in State Legislatures: A State-by-State Map," (January 20, 2021); Voting-age population percentages calculated by the authors from U.S. Census Bureau, "Current Population Reports," www.census.gov.

A Data Literacy Lesson
Descriptive Representation—What It Is and Why It Matters

In 1992, one year after the infamous Clarence Thomas and Anita Hill hearings, in which the congressional hearings on the nomination of Clarence Thomas to the Supreme Court featured public allegations of sexual harassment by law professor Anita Hill, American politics experienced the first so-called "Year of the Woman"; subsequently, the year 2018 was referred to in this way as well. Following the 1992 election, the number of women serving in the House of Representatives jumped from thirty to forty-eight, while the number of women serving in the Senate jumped from two to seven.[1] This dramatically increased number of women (although still shockingly low) serving in Congress became the story of that year's contests.

The election of a larger number of women raised the issue of descriptive representation—how important is it that someone be represented by someone who *looks like them*? Before addressing this question, it's worth asking to what extent people actually are represented by people who look like them. Table 1-22 does this at the state level. The Table shows the number (and percentage) of state representatives who are Black, Latino, and women, and compares that to the proportion of the state population that these groups compose. The "ratio" column for each group divides their share of the legislature by their share of the population; a ratio of 1 would indicate that the group is perfectly represented, a ratio below 1 indicates that the group is underrepresented, and a ratio above 1 shows that the group is overrepresented.

As you can see, the larger story of Table 1-22 is one of underrepresentation. Nationwide, Black people are underrepresented by a score of 0.830; while there is substantial variation state-by-state, they are underrepresented in most states. The situation is much worse for Latinos (0.410) and women (0.601), who are underrepresented in far more states than not. Women, in fact, are underrepresented in every state but Nevada!

We can all engage in some speculation about why Black and Latino people, and women, are underrepresented—we engage in some of this speculation in one of these Data Essays in Chapter 5 (focused on women). That these traditionally underrepresented groups may have less access to resources to run a campaign, and/or may face more prejudice from voters, and/or may be less likely to choose to run in the first place, seems important to consider. Table 1-22, however, invites us to speculate at the state level. Why does Nevada overrepresent women? Are they gambling that this would be a good strategy for the state? Why are women so underrepresented in Alabama? (The ratio there is 0.299.) We see similar variance for the other two groups we study here—why would this be the case?

We could speculate on possible reasons—perhaps the political culture of the state (however we might measure it) can explain things? Some states have more progressive traditions than others, which might help to explain these patterns. One additional area in which to look might be legislative professionalism, which we also address in Chapter 8. If a state has a highly professionalized legislature, and pays large salaries, it might attract a wider (and different) pool of candidates than if it were a part-time legislature. This might affect the number of members of traditionally underrepresented groups who are enticed to serve and might also affect their chances of getting elected.

In the end, we are left to ponder why it matters. Can a Black person, for example, be reasonably represented by a white person who shares their convictions on a range of issues? Traditionally, political scientists have argued that, on a simple level, the answer is yes. Every vote counts the same—if a large segment of the Black community wants a "Yes" vote on a particular issue, the race of the person casting the vote doesn't matter, only the way that person votes does. This does not account, however, for the differing levels of intensity people from different groups might bring to the issue, or what other issues they might bring up for vote based on experiences shaped by their demographic characteristics. Legislators are often pulled in multiple directions and cannot prioritize all issues equally. We suspect that descriptive representation explains quite a bit about who participates heavily on some issues versus others, and hence who might be a more effective advocate for the larger group.

Moreover, if it is an ultimate goal to have legislatures look like their populations, one way to get there is by having more diverse political role models for young people who might aspire to office. As a more diverse array of candidates run for office and are elected, future lines of Table 1-22 can be written, and the ratios reported in the table can increase in the years to come.

---

[1] Technically, there were three female Senators at the time of the 1992 election. Two, Nancy Kassenbaum of Kansas and Barbara Mikulski of Maryland, were elected in their own right. The third, Jocelyn Burdick of North Dakota, had been appointed in September of 1992 to fill her late husband's seat until a successor could be elected.

Table 1-23 Presidential Primaries, 1912–2020

	Democratic Party			Republican Party		
Year	Number of primaries	Votes cast	Percentage of delegates selected through primaries	Number of primaries	Votes cast	Percentage of delegates selected through primaries
1912	12	974,775	32.9	13	2,261,240	41.7
1916	20	1,187,691	53.5	20	1,923,374	58.9
1920	16	571,671	44.6	20	3,186,248	57.8
1924	14	763,858	35.5	17	3,525,185	45.3
1928	16	1,264,220	42.2	15	4,110,288	44.9
1932	16	2,952,933	40.0	14	2,346,996	37.7
1936	14	5,181,808	36.5	12	3,319,810	37.5
1940	13	4,468,631	35.8	13	3,227,875	38.8
1944	14	1,867,609	36.7	13	2,271,605	38.7
1948	14	2,151,865	36.3	12	2,653,255	36.0
1952	16	4,928,006	38.7	13	7,801,413	39.0
1956	19	5,832,592	42.7	19	5,828,272	44.8
1960	16	5,687,742	38.3	15	5,537,967	38.6
1964	16	6,247,435	45.7	16	5,935,339	45.6
1968	15	7,535,069	40.2	15	4,473,551	38.1
1972	21	15,993,965	65.3	20	6,188,281	56.8
1976	27	16,052,652	76.0	26	10,374,125	71.0
1980	34	18,747,825	71.8	34	12,690,451	76.0
1984	29	18,009,217	52.4	25	6,575,651	71.0
1988	36	22,961,936	66.6	36	12,165,115	76.9
1992	39	20,239,385	66.9	38	12,696,547	83.9
1996	35	10,996,395	65.3	42	14,233,939	84.6
2000	40	14,045,745	64.6	43	17,156,117	83.8
2004	37	16,182,439	67.5	27	7,940,331	55.5
2008	38	36,995,069[a]	68.9	39	20,840,681	79.8
2012	26	9,187,665	47.2	36	18,767,217	71.3
2016	36	30,642,065	86.4	42	31,183,841	83.0
2020	46	36,917,179	96.7	40	19,321,267	77.6

Note: The number of primaries held include those in which delegates were elected and pledged to specific candidates. A few states also held "beauty contest" primaries that were nonbinding; in those states pledged delegates were selected in caucuses.

[a] Includes 149,181 votes cast in a New Mexico contest in February. That contest was technically a caucus but had many characteristics of a regular primary.

Sources: 1912–2008: *CQ Press Guide to U.S. Elections,* 7th ed. (Washington, D.C.: CQ Press, 2016), 382; 2016 and 2020: updated by authors from news coverage of state contests.

Table 1-24 State Methods for Choosing National Convention Delegates, 1968–2020

State	1968	1972	1976	1980	1984	1988	1992	1996	2000	2004	2008	2012	2016	2020
Alabama	DP	↓	OP	↓	↓	↓	↓	↓	↓	↓	↓	↓	↓	↓
Alaska	CL	↓	↓	↓	↓	↓	↓	↓	↓	↓	↓	↓	CL	(D)P (R)CL
Arizona	(D)CS (R)CL	CL	↓	↓	↓	↓	↓	(D)CL (R)P	P	(D)P (R)CL	P	↓	↓	↓
Arkansas	CS	CL	OP	(D)OP (R)CL	CL	OP	↓	↓	↓	↓	↓	↓	↓	↓
California	P	↓	↓	↓	↓	↓	↓	↓	↓	(D)PI (R)P	↓	P	↓	↓
Colorado	CL	↓	↓	↓	↓	↓	OP	↓	↓	CL	↓	↓	↓	OP
Connecticut	CL	↓	↓	P	(D)P (R)CL	P	↓	↓	↓	↓	↓	↓	↓	↓
Delaware	CL	↓	↓	↓	↓	↓	↓	(D)CL (R)P	(D)X (R)CL	(D)P (R)CL	P	↓	↓	↓
District of Columbia	P	↓	↓	↓	↓	↓	↓	↓	↓	(D)X (R)CL	P	↓	↓	↓
Florida	P	↓	↓	↓	↓	↓	↓	↓	↓	↓	↓	↓	↓	↓
Georgia	(D)CS (R)CL	CL	OP	↓	↓	↓	↓	↓	↓	↓	↓	↓	↓	↓
Hawaii	CL	↓	↓	(D)CL (R)OP	(D)PI (R)OP DP	(D)X (R)OP	↓	↓	(D)X (R)OP, CS	(D)CL (R)OP	↓	↓	↓	P
Idaho	CL	↓	OP	↓	↓	↓	↓	↓	(D)OP	(D)OP	OP	CL	(D)CL R(P)	P
Illinois	DP, CL	P	OP	↓	DP	↓	↓	↓	(R)DP, CS (D)OP	(R)DP	(D)OP (R)DP	↓	OP	↓
Indiana	OP	↓	↓	↓	↓	↓	↓	↓	(R)OP, CS	OP	OP	↓	↓	↓

(Table continues)

Table 1-24 *(Continued)*

State	1968	1972	1976	1980	1984	1988	1992	1996	2000	2004	2008	2012	2016	2020
Iowa	CL	↓	↓	↓	↓	↓	↓	↓	↓	↓	↓	↓	↓	↓
Kansas	CL	↓	↓	PI	CL	↓	PI	↓	↓	CL	↓	↓	↓	P
Kentucky	CL	↓	P	↓	CL	P	↓	↓	↓	↓	↓	↓	↓	↓
Louisiana	CS	CL	↓	P	↓	↓	↓	(D)P (R)CL	P	↓	↓	↓	P	↓
Maine	CL	↓	↓	↓	↓	↓	↓	PI	↓	CL	↓	↓	↓	P
Maryland	(D)CS (R)CL	P	↓	↓	DP	P	↓	↓	(D)P (R)PI	(D)P (R)PI	P	↓	↓	↓
Massachusetts	PI	↓	↓	↓	↓	↓	↓	↓	↓	↓	↓	↓	↓	↓
Michigan	CL	OP	↓	(D)CL (R)OP	CL	(D)CL (R)X	P	(D)CL (R)OP	↓	(D)PI (R)CL	OP	↓	↓	OP
Minnesota	CL	↓	↓	↓	↓	↓	↓	↓	↓	↓	OP	↓	↓	↓
Mississippi	CL	↓	↓	(D)CL (R)DP	CL	OP	↓	↓	↓	↓	↓	↓	↓	↓
Missouri	(D)CL, CS (R)CL	CL	↓	↓	↓	OP	CL	↓	OP	↓	↓	↓	↓	↓
Montana	CL	↓	OP	↓	DP	(D)OP (R)X	↓	↓	↓	↓	↓	CL	OP	↓
Nebraska	OP	↓	↓	↓	P	↓	↓	PI	(D)P (R)DP	(D)P (R)X	(D)CL (R)X	X	(D)CL R(X)	X
Nevada	CL	↓	P	↓	CL	↓	↓	(D)CL (R)P	CL	↓	↓	↓	↓	↓
New Hampshire	PI	↓	↓	↓	↓	↓	↓	↓	↓	↓	↓	↓	↓	↓
New Jersey	PI	↓	↓	↓	DP	↓	↓	(D)PI (R)DP	↓	↓	PI	↓	↓	↓

New Mexico	CL	P	CL	P	↓	↓	↓	↓	(D)CL (R)P	↓	P	↓	↓
New York	DP, CS	↓	DP	(D)P (R)DP, CS	(D)DP (R)DP, CS	↓	↓	↓	P	↓	↓	↓	↓
North Carolina	CL	P	↓	↓	↓	↓	(D)P (R)OP	(D)P (R)PI	PI	PI	↓	↓	↓
North Dakota	CL	↓	↓	↓	DP	(D)X (R)OP	↓	↓	CS	CL	↓	↓	↓
Ohio	OP	↓	↓	↓	PI	↓	↓	↓	OP	↓	PI	(D)PI (R)P	↓
Oklahoma	CL	↓	↓	↓	↓	P	↓	↓	↓	↓	↓	↓	↓
Oregon	P	↓	↓	↓	↓	↓	↓	↓	↓	↓	↓	↓	↓
Pennsylvania	P, CS	P	↓	↓	DP	↓	↓	↓	(D)P (R)DP, CS	↓	P	↓	↓
Rhode Island	(D)CS (R)CL	PI	↓	↓	↓	↓	↓	↓	↓	↓	↓	↓	↓
South Carolina	CL	↓	(D)CL (R)OP	↓	↓	↓	OP	(D)CL (R)OP	OP	OP	↓	↓	↓
South Dakota	P	↓	↓	↓	↓	↓	↓	↓	↓	↓	↓	↓	↓
Tennessee	CL	OP	↓	↓	↓	↓	↓	↓	↓	↓	↓	↓	OP
Texas	CL	↓	OP	P	(D)CL (R)OP	OP	↓	↓	(D)OP, CS (R)OP	OP	↓	OP	OP
Utah	CL	↓	↓	↓	↓	↓	↓	↓	PI	(D)PI (R)CL	OP	CL	OP
Vermont	CL	↓	X	↓	↓	↓	OP	OP	↓	↓	↓	↓	↓
Virginia	CL	↓	↓	↓	↓	(D)OP (R)X	CL	↓	(D)CL (R)OP	(D)OP (R)CL	OP	↓	↓
Washington	(D)CL, CS (R)CL	(D)CL (R)P	↓	↓	CL	↓	P	(D)CL	(D)X	(D)OP (R)CL CL	(D)CL	(D)CL	OP
								(R)OP, CL	(R)P, CL	(R)OP		(D)CL (R)OP	

(Table continues)

Table 1-24 (Continued)

State	1968	1972	1976	1980	1984	1988	1992	1996	2000	2004	2008	2012	2016	2020
West Virginia	P	↓	↓	↓	↓	↓	(D)P (R)PI	↓	(D)P (R)DP	↓	(D)PI (R)PI, CS	PI	↓	↓
Wisconsin	OP	↓	↓	↓	(D)X (R)OP	(D)PI (R)OP	↓	OP	↓	↓	↓	↓	↓	↓
Wyoming	CL	↓	↓	↓	↓		↓	↓	↓	↓	↓	↓	↓	↓
(Puerto Rico)	(D)CL	CL	↓	OP	(D)PI (R)CL	PI	↓	↓	↓	(D)CL (R)OP	↓	OP	OP	OP

Note: "↓" indicates method(s) same as in previous presidential election; "CL" indicates delegates chosen by state party committee; "(D)" indicates Democrats; "DP" indicates delegates chosen directly by voters in primaries with nonbinding presidential preference poll; "OP" indicates delegates chosen or bound by presidential preference primaries open to all registered voters with no regard for party preregistration (or voters can switch party affiliation at the polls on primary day); "P" indicates delegates chosen or bound by presidential preference primaries open only to voters preregistered as members of the particular parties; "PI" indicates delegates chosen or bound by presidential preference primaries open only to voters preregistered as members of the particular parties or as independents; "(R)" indicates Republicans; "X" indicates having nonbinding presidential preference primaries, but delegates are chosen by party caucus and conventions. States with primaries but without voter registration by party are coded "OP."

Sources: 1968–1984: Austin Ranney, ed., *The American Elections of 1984* (Durham, N.C.: Duke University Press, 1985), 330–332; 1988: derived by the authors from Kevin Coleman, "A Summary of National and State Party Rules and State Laws Concerning the Election of Delegates to the 1988 Democratic and Republican National Conventions," Report no. 88-102 GOV, Congressional Research Service, Washington, D.C., 1988; 1992: derived by the authors from Congressional Quarterly, *The First Hurrah: A 1992 Guide to the Nomination of the President* (Washington, D.C.: Congressional Quarterly, 1991); Congressional Quarterly *Weekly Report* (1991); 3478; and Thomas M. Durbin and L. Paige Whitaker, *Nomination and Election of the President and Vice President of the United States, 1992: Including the Manner of Selecting Delegates to National Party Conventions* (Washington, D.C.: Government Printing Office, 1992); 1996: derived by the authors from Congressional Quarterly *Weekly Report* (1995), 2485–2599; 2000–2008: derived by the authors from Rhodes Cook, *Race for the Presidency* (Washington, D.C.: CQ Press, 2000, 2004, and 2008); 2012: derived by the authors from "Presidential Primaries 2012: Democratic Delegate Selection and Voter Eligibility" and "Presidential Primaries 2012: Republican Delegate Selection and Voter Eligibility," www.thegreenpapers.com; 2016 and 2020 updates from websites of state political parties. Because several of the sources of these methods are published prior to the nomination season and because last-minute changes are made in some states' methods, occasionally later publications have led to revisions of a classification for an earlier year.

Presidential Nominations 71

Figure 1-5 Democratic and Republican Presidential Nominations, Campaign Lengths, 1968–2020

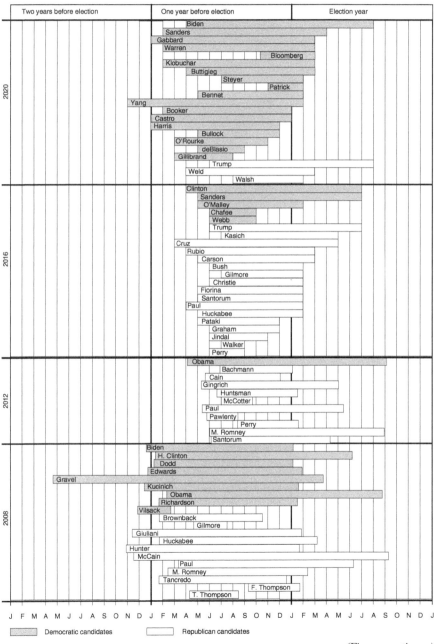

(Figure continues)

72 Elections and Political Parties

Figure 1-5 *(Continued)*

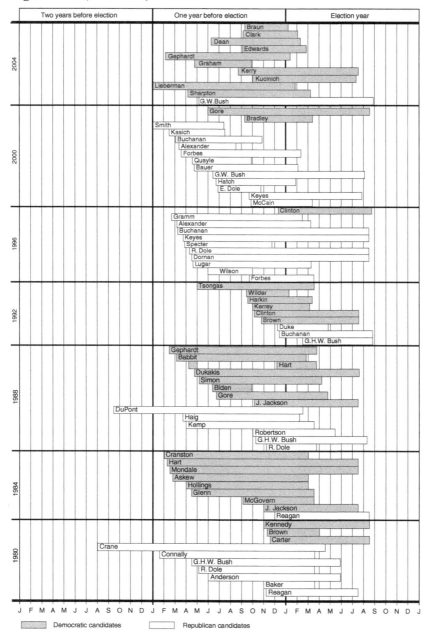

Elections and Political Parties   73

Figure 1-5   *(Continued)*

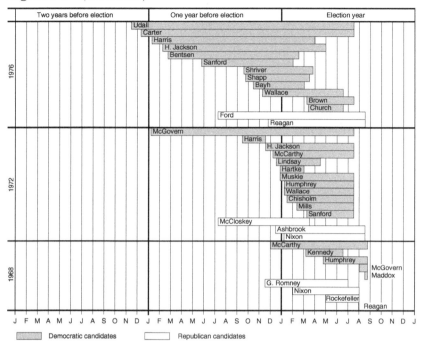

Note: Beginning of campaigns is determined by date of the formal announcement.

Sources: 1968–1984: Congressional Quarterly, *Elections '80* (Washington, D.C.: Congressional Quarterly, 1980), and *Congressional Quarterly's Guide to U.S. Elections,* 2nd ed. (Washington, D.C.: Congressional Quarterly, 1985), 387; 1988–1996: *Congressional Quarterly Weekly Report* (1987), 2732; (1988), 1894, 1896, 1899; (1991), 3735; (1992), 66, 361, 556, 633, 1086; (1995), 2, 13, 15, 3025, 3606; (1996), 641, 716; 2000–2020: compiled by the authors from news reports, various sources.

Table 1-25 Democratic Presidential Primary Returns, 2020

State	Date	Turnout	Biden	Sanders	Warren	Bloomberg	Buttigieg	Klobuchar
New Hampshire	Feb. 11	298,377	8%	26%	9%	2%	24%	20%
South Carolina	Feb. 22	539,263	49	20	7	0	8	3
Alabama	Mar. 3	452,093	63	17	6	12	0	0
Arkansas	Mar. 3	229,122	41	22	10	17	3	3
California	Mar. 3	5,784,364	28	36	13	12	4	2
Colorado	Mar. 3	960,128	25	37	18	19	0	0
Maine	Mar. 3	205,937	33	33	16	12	2	1
Massachusetts	Mar. 3	1,418,180	33	27	21	12	3	1
Minnesota	Mar. 3	744,198	39	30	15	8	1	6
North Carolina	Mar. 3	1,332,382	43	24	11	13	3	2
Oklahoma	Mar. 3	304,281	39	26	13	14	2	2
Tennessee	Mar. 3	516,250	42	25	10	16	3	2
Texas	Mar. 3	2,094,428	35	30	11	14	4	2
Utah	Mar. 3	220,582	18	36	16	15	9	4
Vermont	Mar. 3	158,032	22	51	13	9	2	1
Virginia	Mar. 3	1,323,693	53	23	11	10	1	1
Democrats Abroad	Mar. 3–10	39,984	23	58	14	2	2	1
Idaho	Mar. 10	108,649	49	42	3	2	1	1
Michigan	Mar. 10	1,587,679	53	36	2	5	1	1
Mississippi	Mar. 10	274,391	81	15	1	3	0	0
Missouri	Mar. 10	666,112	60	35	1	2	1	0
Washington	Mar. 10	1,558,776	38	37	9	8	4	2
Arizona	Mar. 17	613,355	44	33	6	—	4	—
Florida	Mar. 17	1,739,214	62	23	2	8	2	1
Illinois	Mar. 17	1,674,133	59	36	2	2	1	—
Wisconsin	Apr. 7	925,065	63	32	1	1	1	1

State	Date	Votes					
Alaska	Apr. 10	19,589	55	45	—	—	—
Ohio	Apr. 28	894,383	72	17	4	3	2	1
Kansas	May 2	143,183	77	23	—	—	—	—
Nebraska	May 12	164,582	77	14	7	—	—	—
Oregon	May 19	618,711	66	21	10	—	—	—
Hawaii	May 22	33,552	63	37	—	—	—	—
District of Columbia	Jun. 2	110,688	76	10	13	—	—	—
Indiana	Jun. 2	497,927	77	14	3	1	4	1
Maryland	Jun. 2	1,050,773	84	8	3	1	1	1
Montana	Jun. 2	149,973	75	15	8	—	—	—
New Mexico	Jun. 2	247,880	73	15	6	—	—	—
Pennsylvania	Jun. 2	1,595,508	79	18	—	—	—	—
Rhode Island	Jun. 2	103,982	77	15	4	—	—	—
South Dakota	Jun. 2	52,661	78	23	—	—	—	—
Georgia	Jun. 9	1,086,729	85	9	2	1	1	0
West Virginia	Jun. 9	187,482	65	12	3	2	2	2
Kentucky	Jun. 23	537,905	68	12	3	—	2	1
New York	Jun. 23	1,759,039	65	16	5	2	1	1
Delaware	Jul. 7	91,682	89	8	3	—	—	—
New Jersey	Jul. 7	958,762	85	15	—	—	—	—
Louisiana	Jul. 11	267,286	80	7	2	2	1	1
Puerto Rico	Jul. 12	7,022	56	13	1	13	2	—
Connecticut	Aug. 11	264,416	85	12	—	—	—	—

Note: "—" indicates that the candidate was not listed on the ballot. Percentages are rounded, and thus do not always sum to 100. Primary results are based on official state returns for all states. Data for earlier years can be found in previous editions of *Vital Statistics on American Politics*.

Source: Compiled by authors from various news reports.

Table 1-26 Democratic Presidential Caucus Results, 2020

State	Date	Turnout	Biden	Sanders	Warren	Bloomberg	Buttigieg	Klobuchar
Iowa	Feb. 3	172,300	14%	26%	20%	0%	25%	12%
Nevada	Feb. 22	101,543	19	40	12	0	17	7
American Samoa	Mar. 3	351	9	11	1	50	0	0
North Dakota	Mar. 10	14,413	39	53	3	1	1	2
Wyoming	Apr. 17	15,118	72	28	0	0	0	0
Guam	Jun. 6	388	70	30	0	0	0	0
U.S. Virgin Islands	Jun. 6	550	91	5	0	0	0	0

Note: Percentages are rounded, and thus do not always sum to 100. Iowa results include only the final alignments, after supporters of nonviable candidates were allowed to caucus with another candidate. Data for earlier years can be found in previous editions of *Vital Statistics on American Politics*.

Source: Compiled by authors from various news reports.

Table 1-27 Location and Size of National Party Conventions, 1932–2020

	Democrats		Republicans	
Year	Location	Delegate votes	Location	Delegate votes
1932	Chicago	1,154	Chicago	1,154
1936	Philadelphia	1,100	Cleveland	1,003
1940	Chicago	1,100	Philadelphia	1,000
1944	Chicago	1,176	Chicago	1,056
1948	Philadelphia	1,234	Philadelphia	1,094
1952	Chicago	1,230	Chicago	1,206
1956	Chicago	1,372	San Francisco	1,323
1960	Los Angeles	1,521	Chicago	1,331
1964	Atlantic City	2,316	San Francisco	1,308
1968	Chicago	2,622	Miami Beach	1,333
1972	Miami Beach	3,016	Miami Beach	1,348
1976	New York	3,008	Kansas City	2,259
1980	New York	3,331	Detroit	1,994
1984	San Francisco	3,933	Dallas	2,235
1988	Atlanta	4,161	New Orleans	2,277
1992	New York	4,288	Houston	2,210
1996	Chicago	4,289	San Diego	1,990
2000	Los Angeles	4,339	Philadelphia	2,066
2004	Boston	4,353	New York	2,509
2008	Denver	4,440	St. Paul	2,380
2012	Charlotte	5,552	Tampa	2,286
2016	Philadelphia	4,763	Cleveland	2,472
2020	Milwaukee[a]	4,749	Charlotte[b]	2,550

Note: The number of delegates (persons attending) may be larger because of fractional votes.

[a] The Democratic National Convention was based at the Milwaukee Center in Milwaukee, Wisconsin, but was largely held remotely. Various other cities "hosted" aspects of the convention.

[b] The first day of the Republican Convention was based in Charlotte, North Carolina, while subsequent days were based in Washington, D.C. Many segments of the convention were held at other remote locations.

Sources: 1932–2008: *CQ Press Guide to U.S. Elections*, 6th ed. (Washington, D.C.: CQ Press, 2010), 489–490, 492; 2012: "The Rhodes Cook Letter," August 2012, 7, 11, www.rhodescook.com; and Rhodes Cook, personal communication; 2016 and 2020: compiled by authors from news reports.

Table 1-28 Legislative Districting: Deviations from Equality in Congressional and State Legislative Districts (percent)

	Congressional districts				State legislative districts							
					Senate				House			
State	1980s	1990s	2000s	2010s	1980s	1990s	2000s	2010s	1980s	1990s	2000s	2010s
Alabama	2.45	[a]	0	0	8.50	9.22	9.73	1.98	9.80	10.20	9.93	1.98
Alaska	AL	AL	AL	AL	9.77	11.70	9.32	2.97	9.99	15.50	9.96	4.25
Arizona	0.08	[a]	0	0	8.40	9.85	3.79	8.78	8.40	9.85	3.79	8.78
Arkansas	0.73	0.73	0.04	0.06	9.15	9.27	9.81	8.20	9.15	9.52	9.87	8.36
California	0.08	0.49	0	[a]	4.60	1.60	0	1.99	3.60	1.80	0	1.98
Colorado	[a]	[a]	0	0	3.98	4.90	4.95	4.99	4.94	4.96	4.88	4.98
Connecticut	0.46	0.05	0	0	3.92	7.98	8.03	9.79	8.35	8.78	9.20	5.99
Delaware	AL	AL	AL	AL	9.78	10.18	9.96	10.73	25.10	9.58	9.98	9.93
Florida	0.13	[a]	0	0	1.05	0.86	0.03	1.92	0.46	4.99	2.79	3.98
Georgia	[a]	0.93	0.01	0	9.99	9.95	1.94	1.84	9.94	9.95	1.96	1.98
Hawaii	[a]	[a]	0.32	0.10	18.60	9.86	38.90	44.23	8.60	9.78	20.10	21.57
Idaho	0.04	[a]	0.60	0.09	5.35	9.88	9.70	9.70	5.35	9.88	9.70	9.70
Illinois	0.03	[a]	0	0	1.75	[a]	0	0	2.80	[a]	0	0
Indiana	2.96	[a]	0.02	0	4.04	2.19	3.80	2.88	4.45	3.36	1.92	1.74
Iowa	0.05	0.05	0.02	0.01	0.71	1.45	1.46	1.65	1.78	1.97	1.89	1.93
Kansas	0.34	0.01	0	0	6.50	6.89	9.27	2.03	9.90	9.72	9.95	2.87
Kentucky	1.39	[a]	0	0	7.52	6.13	9.53	11.02	13.47	9.91	10.00	11.62
Louisiana	0.42	0.04	0.04	0.03	8.40	9.78	9.95	9.86	9.69	9.97	9.88	9.89
Maine	[a]	[a]	0	[a]	10.18	4.16	3.57	9.51	10.94	43.74[b]	9.33	9.90
Maryland	0.35	[a]	0	0	9.80	9.84	9.91	8.87	15.70	10.67	9.89	8.87
Massachusetts	1.09	[a]	0.39	0	—	4.75	9.33	9.77	—	9.92	9.68	9.74
Michigan	[a]	[a]	0	0	16.24	15.83	9.92	9.79	16.34	16.13	9.92	9.96
Minnesota	0.01	[a]	0	0	4.61	3.42	1.35	1.42	3.93	5.90	1.56	1.60
Mississippi	—	0.02	0	0.20	4.61	8.96	9.30	9.77	4.90	9.97	9.98	9.95
Missouri	0.18	0.20	0	0	6.10	8.42	6.81	8.50	9.30	8.96	6.08	7.80
Montana	—	AL	AL	AL	—	9.51	9.82	5.26	—	9.97	9.85	5.44
Nebraska	0.23	0.20	0	0	9.43	3.81	9.21	7.39	[c]	[c]	[c]	[c]
Nevada	0.60	[a]	0	0	8.20	2.28	9.91	0.80	9.70	4.55	1.97	1.33
New Hampshire	0.24	0.07	0.10	[a]	7.60	12.36	9.50	8.83	13.74	14.53	9.26	9.90
New Jersey	0.69	[a]	0	0	7.70	4.60	1.83	5.20	7.70	4.60	1.83	5.20

New Mexico	0.87	0.16	0.03		9.83	9.58	9.60	8.70	9.87	9.89	9.70	6.68
New York	1.64	a	0		5.29	4.29	9.78	8.80	8.17	9.43	9.43	7.94
North Carolina	1.76	a	0		9.46	9.94	9.96	9.49	9.66	9.97	9.98	9.97
North Dakota	AL	AL	AL		9.93	8.71	10.00	8.86	9.93	8.71	10.00	8.86
Ohio	0.68	a	0		8.88	13.60	8.81	9.20	9.67	13.60	12.46	16.44
Oklahoma	0.58		0		5.60	3.93	4.71	2.03	10.98	6.13	2.05	1.81
Oregon	0.15	a	a		3.73	1.69	1.77	2.99	5.34	1.89	1.90	3.10
Pennsylvania	0.24	0.01	0		1.93	1.86	3.98	7.96	2.82	4.94	5.54	7.88
Rhode Island	0.02	0.02	0		—	13.00	9.91	5.01	10.47	14.70	9.88	4.98
South Carolina	0.28	a	0			1.00	9.87	9.55	9.88	5.20	4.99	4.99
South Dakota	AL	AL	AL		12.90	9.47	9.69	9.47	12.40	9.47	9.69	9.64
Tennessee	2.40	a	0		10.22	13.92	9.98	9.17	1.66	9.96	9.99	9.74
Texas	0.28	a	0		1.82	9.98	9.71	8.04	9.95	9.99	9.74	9.85
Utah	0.43	0.02	0		7.80	7.60	7.02	0	5.41	7.94	8.00	0
Vermont	AL	AL	AL		16.18	16.36	14.28	18.01	19.33	17.62	18.99	18.80
Virginia	1.81	a	0		10.65	8.53	4.00	4.00	5.11	9.67	3.90	2.00
Washington	0.06	a	a		5.40	a	0.30	0.07	5.70	a	0.30	0.07
West Virginia	0.50	0.09	0.22		8.96	9.98	10.92	10.00	9.94	9.96	9.98	9.99
Wisconsin	0.14		0		1.23	0.52	0.98	0.62	1.74	0.92	1.60	0.76
Wyoming	AL	AL	AL		63.70	9.60	9.51	9.37	89.40	9.97	9.81	9.84

Note: "AL" indicates at-large district (only one congressional representative); "—" indicates not available. Figures represent the absolute sum of the maximum percentage deviations (positive and negative) from the average district population. 1980s data are as of April 1983; 1990s data are as of August 1994. The 1980 state house plans for Delaware and Rhode Island contained errors that increased total deviation, but had not been corrected. 2000s data are as of March 2005; 2010s data are from February 2019. Data for the 1960s can be found in previous editions of *Vital Statistics on American Politics*.

[a] Less than 0.01 percent.
[b] Apart from two districts, the deviation is 8.15.
[c] Nebraska's state legislature is unicameral.

Sources: 1980s: Election Data Services, Inc.; 1990s: Supreme Judicial Court of Maine, *In re Apportionment of 1993* (Docket #JC–93–229), and unpublished data from the National Conference of State Legislators, Illinois State Board of Elections, Michigan Information Center (Department of Management and Budget), and Tennessee Office of Local Government; 2000s and 2010s: National Conference of State Legislatures, www.ncsl.org.

Table 1-29 Jurisdictions Subject to Federal Preclearance of Election Law Changes and to Minority Language Provisions of the Voting Rights Act

Coverage under preclearance provisions[a]	*Coverage under minority language provisions*[b]	
Alabama	Alaska (15)[c]	Nebraska (3)
Alaska	Arizona (10)	Nevada (1)
Arizona	California	New Jersey (9)
California (4)	Colorado (6)	New Mexico (20)
Florida (5)	Connecticut (10)[c]	New York (7)
Georgia	Florida	Oklahoma (1)
Louisiana	Georgia (1)	Pennsylvania (3)
Michigan (2)[c]	Hawaii (1)	Rhode Island (3)[c]
Mississippi	Illinois (3)	Texas
New York (3)	Iowa (2)	Utah (1)
North Carolina (40)	Kansas (5)	Virginia (1)
South Carolina	Maryland (1)	Washington (4)
South Dakota (2)	Massachusetts (12)[c]	Wisconsin (3)[c]
Texas	Michigan (3)[c]	
Virginia	Mississippi (10)	

Note: "Preclearance" means that changes in election laws must be approved by the U.S. Justice Department. "Language provisions" require covered jurisdictions to provide bilingual voting materials to members of specified minority language groups. Numbers in parentheses indicate the number of counties in the state affected by the provisions. If there are no parentheses, coverage is statewide. The Supreme Court decision in *Shelby County v. Holder,* 133 S. Ct. 2612 (2013) held that Section 4 of the Voting Rights Act, which set out the formula that is used to determine which state and local governments must comply with Section 5's preclearance requirement, is unconstitutional and can no longer be used. Section 5 will have no actual effect unless a jurisdiction is covered by a separate court order entered under Section 3(c) of the VRA or Congress enacts a new statute to determine which jurisdictions should be covered by Section 5. The above table listing jurisdictions subject to federal preclearance indicates the situation immediately before *Shelby County v. Holder.*

[a] Approximately 250 governmental units and jurisdictions once subject to the preclearance provisions of Section 5 were no longer subject to such coverage because they availed themselves of the bailout process set forth in Section 4 of the Voting Rights Act.
[b] Covered jurisdictions under the minority language provisions are determined by the U.S. Census Bureau after each census, based on a formula set out in the Voting Rights Act. The most recent determinations were made on December 5, 2016.
[c] Number of towns, townships, cities, boroughs, or areas.

Sources: U.S. Department of Justice, "Jurisdictions previously covered by Section 5 at the time of the Shelby County decision," Table, https://www.justice.gov/crt/jurisdictions-previously-covered-section-5; U.S. Department of Commerce, Census Bureau, "Voting Rights Act Amendments of 2006, Determinations Under Section 203," *Federal Register,* 81, no. 233 (December 5, 2016), 87532–87538, https://www.govinfo.gov/content/pkg/FR-2016-12-05/pdf/2016-28969.pdf.

Table 1-30 Term Limits on State Legislators

State[a]	Lower house (years)[b]	Upper house (years)[b]	Year adopted	Percent support	Year of first impact Lower house	Year of first impact Upper house	Mechanism[c]	Break in service[d]
Arizona	8	8	1992	74	2000	2000	S	2 years
Arkansas	12	12	1992	60	1998	2000	S	4 years
California	12 years total in legislature		1990	52	1996	1998	S	lifetime
Colorado	8	8	1990	71	1998	1998	S	4 years
Florida	8	8	1992	77	2000	2000	B	2 years
Louisiana	12	12	1995	76	2007	2007	S	4 years[e]
Maine	8	8	1993	68	1996	1996	S	2 years
Michigan	6	8	1992	59	1998	2002	S	lifetime
Missouri[f]	8	8	1992	75	2002	2002	S	lifetime
Montana	8 out of 16	8 out of 16	1992	67	2000	2000	B	contingent
Nebraska	g	8[g]	2000	56	g	2006	S	4 years
Nevada[h]	12	12	1996	70	2010	2010	S	lifetime
Ohio	8	8	1992	68	2000	2000	S	4 years
Oklahoma	12 years total in legislature		1990	67	2004	2004	S	lifetime
South Dakota	8	8	1992	64	2000	2000	S	2 years

Note: States have varying provisions for counting partial terms stemming from appointment or special election. In many states, limits are defined in terms of times elected rather than years served or contain a clause such as "or, but for resignation, would have served."

[a] In addition to the states listed here, Washington, Oregon, and Wyoming passed state legislative term limits in 1992 and Massachusetts, Idaho, and Utah in 1994, but they were overturned by the courts in the first four states (in 1998, 2002, 2004, and 1997, respectively) and by the legislatures in Idaho (in 2002) and Utah (in 2003). In Oregon, some legislators were "termed out" in 1998 and 2000.
[b] Number of years an individual may serve before term limits are applied. In Arkansas and Florida, all senate seats are up for election in the first election of the decade (i.e., after redistricting), so some senators may in fact serve for ten years. In Montana, an individual may not serve more than eight out of sixteen years, whether or not those years are consecutive.
[c] Strict term limits (S) prohibit service in the legislature. Ballot access restrictions (B) prevent a candidate's name from being placed on the ballot, but do not prevent a candidate from being elected on write-in votes.

(Table continues)

Table 1-30 *(Continued)*

[d] Length of time an individual must "sit out" before serving (or having ballot access) again in the same house. The time is "contingent" when the term limit law specifies that an individual may serve no more than a certain number of years over a longer period.
[e] Members may run for the opposite state legislative body without having to sit out any terms.
[f] Because of special elections, term limits were effective in 2000 for eight members of the House and in 1998 for one senator.
[g] Nebraska's legislature is unicameral.
[h] The Nevada Legislative Council and attorney general ruled that Nevada's term limits could not be applied to those legislators elected in the same year term limits were passed (1996). They first applied to persons elected in 1998.

Sources: National Conference of State Legislatures, www.ncsl.org; texts of state measures.

Table 1-31 Members "Termed Out" of State Legislatures, 2002–2020

State	Chamber	Membership	Members termed out in									
			2002	2004	2006	2008	2010	2012	2014	2016	2018	2020
Arizona	House	60	9	5	3	7	13	3	3	5	8	5
	Senate	30	6	2	3	2	10	3	1	1	6	2
Arkansas[a]	House	100	14	36	29	28	34	24	25	0	0	0
	Senate	35	11	0	1	4	13	11	0	0	0	0
California	Assembly	80	20	18	26	24	19	22	16	14	1	0
	Senate	40	7	8	12	10	8	6	6	6	6	6
Colorado	House	65	7	7	11	8	8	8	9	8	5	9
	Senate	35	5	5	4	7	4	9	5	9	7	4
Florida	House	120	14	7	19	28	24	11	15	21	20	18
	Senate	40	12	0	5	5	7	11	0	5	2	7
Louisiana	House	105	—	—	—	[b]	[b]	[b]	[b]	[b]	[b]	[b]
	Senate	39	—	—	—	[b]	[b]	[b]	[b]	[b]	[b]	[b]
Maine	House	151	28	21	19	15	21	26	22	16	21	22
	Senate	35	8	7	1	6	4	9	1	2	8	3
Michigan	House	110	23	37	23	44	34	14	29	38	24	22
	Senate	38	27	[c]	6	[c]	29	[c]	7	[c]	26	[c]
Missouri	House	163	73	15	10	21	52	25	10	22	44	34
	Senate	34	12	10	3	4	10	9	4	3	9	8
Montana	House	100	7	10	16	17	15	17	7	13	14	16
	Senate	50	15	6	5	10	15	8	8	11	6	10
Nebraska	Senate	49	—	—	20	13	1	9	17	11	6	6
Nevada	House	42	—	—	—	—	10	1	2	2	6	1
	Senate	21	—	—	—	—	7	4	1	0	1	2
Ohio	House	99	9	7	14	21	13	7	15	13	20	12
	Senate	33	4	5	7	4	7	2	3	3	10	5

(Table continues)

Table 1-31 *(Continued)*

			Members termed out in								
State	Chamber	Membership	2002	2004	2006	2008	2010	2012	2014	2016	2018	2020
Oklahoma	House	101	—	28	15	7	4	6	7	19	12	4
	Senate	48	—	13	7	5	6	2	4	11	6	1
South Dakota	House	70	7	3	7	13	8	6	6	15	5	8
	Senate	35	4	7	2	6	4	3	2	4	4	6
Total		1,811	322[d]	257[e]	268	309	380	256	225	252	271	211

Note: "—" indicates term limits were not yet applicable.

[a] Arkansas adjusted its term limits in 2014, doubling the amount of time one could serve from six years in the House and eight years in the Senate to twelve years in the House and sixteen years in the Senate. As such, given the extension of time members could serve, none were term-limited in 2016, 2018, or 2020.
[b] Louisiana holds its legislative elections in odd-numbered years. In 2007, forty-four House and sixteen Senate members were termed out; in 2011, the numbers were eleven House members and six Senators, respectively. In 2015, fifteen House and seven Senate members were termed out, while in 2019, thirty-one House and sixteen Senate members were termed out.
[c] No election in this year.
[d] Does not include eight "termed-out" legislators in three states who resigned midterm.
[e] Does not include four "termed-out" legislators in Colorado and Ohio who resigned midterm.

Source: 2002–2014: National Conference of State Legislatures, www.ncsl.org; 2016–2020: updated by authors.

Table 1-32 Types of Voting Equipment Used in U.S. Elections by State, November 2020 (percent)

State	Hand-marked paper ballots, BMDs for Accessibility[a]	Hand-marked paper ballots, DRE systems with VVPAT for accessibility[b, c]	Hand-marked paper ballots with DREs without VVPAT for accessibility	BMDs for all voters	Hybrid BMD/ tabulator	DREs with VVPAT for all voters	DREs without VVPAT for all voters
Alabama	100	0	0	0	0	0	0
Alaska	0	100	0	0	0	0	0
Arizona	100	0	0	0	0	0	0
Arkansas	0	0	0	100	0	0	0
California	68	0	0	32	0	0	0
Colorado	100	0	0	0	0	0	0
Connecticut	100	0	0	0	0	0	0
Delaware	0	0	0	0	100	0	0
District of Columbia	100	0	0	0	0	0	0
Florida	100	0	0	0	0	0	0
Georgia	0	0	0	100	0	0	0
Hawaii	0	5.7	0	0	0	94.3	0
Idaho	81.9	7.2	0	10.9	0	0	0
Illinois	77.1	17.7	0	0	0	5.2	0
Indiana	8.4	0	3.4	34.3	0	14.4	39.6
Iowa	100	0	0	0	0	0	0
Kansas	69.5	0	1.2	25.6	3.6	0.1	0
Kentucky	39.8	0	58	2.2	0	0	0
Louisiana	0	0	0	0	0	0	100
Maine	100	0	0	0	0	0	0
Maryland	100	0	0	0	0	0	0
Massachusetts	100	0	0	0	0	0	0
Michigan	100	0	0	0	0	0	0
Minnesota	100	0	0	0	0	0	0
Mississippi	42.6	0	0	0.3	0	0	57.2
Missouri	94.3	5.7	0	0	0	0	0

Table 1-32 (Continued)

State	Hand-marked paper ballots, BMDs for Accessibility[a]	Hand-marked paper ballots, DRE systems with VVPAT for accessibility[b, c]	Hand-marked paper ballots with DREs without VVPAT for accessibility	BMDs for all voters	Hybrid BMD/tabulator	DREs with VVPAT for all voters	DREs without VVPAT for all voters
Montana	100	0	0	0	0	0	0
Nebraska	100	0	0	0	0	0	0
Nevada	0	0	0	2	0	98	0
New Hampshire	100	0	0	0	0	0	0
New Jersey	0	0	8.8	0	19.4	0.8	71.1
New Mexico	100	0	0	0	0	0	0
New York	100	0	0	13.8	0	0	0
North Carolina	86.2	0	0	0	0	0	0
North Dakota	100	0	0	28.5	0	0	0
Ohio	49.3	0	0	0	5.7	16.5	0
Oklahoma	0	0	100	0	0	0	0
Oregon	100	0	0	0	0	0	0
Pennsylvania	69.1	0	0	12.6	18.3	0	0
Rhode Island	100	0	0	0	0	0	0
South Carolina	0	0	0	100	0	0	0
South Dakota	100	0	0	0	0	0	0
Tennessee	14.1	0	0	26.4	0	0	59.4
Texas	10.4	0	1.7	52.3	0	0	35.6
Utah	64.4	0	0	0	0	35.6	0
Vermont	100	0	0	0	0	0	0
Virginia	100	0	0	0	0	0	0
Washington	97.4	2.6	0	0	0	0	0
West Virginia	0	5.8	0	65.5	0	28.7	0
Wisconsin	88	12	0	0	0	0	0
Wyoming	100	0	0	0	0	0	0

[a] BMD refers to ballot-marking devices.
[b] DREs are direct recording electronic systems.
[c] A VVPAT is a Voter Verified Paper Audit Trail.

Source: Verified Voting, www.verifiedvoting.org. Used with permission.

2
Campaign Finance and Political Action Committees

- **Contribution Limits**
- **Presidential Campaign Financing**
- **Party Expenditures**
- **Political Action Committees (PACs)**

One of the most important aspects of election campaigns, and political activities more generally, is money: who gives it, who spends it, who regulates it, and what effect it has on election results and on policymaking. Surprisingly, a huge quantity of information is available on the subject, and easily accessible through high-quality reporting by the federal agency that regulates it. This abundance stems chiefly from the large number of elections in the United States and the effort over the last four decades to collect data about them and make those data available to the public. This serves the public interest by allowing for more disclosure of who was donating to whose campaign.

Campaign finance law is in flux, as laws that are passed are often challenged in court. One example is the Bipartisan Campaign Reform Act (BCRA) of 2002, a comprehensive attempt to regulate the role of money in campaigns, which enacted new contribution limits (Table 2-1), changed the law on "soft" money (Table 2-8), and otherwise reworked campaign finance law. Likewise, a fairly recent Supreme Court decision, *Citizens United v. Federal Election Commission* in January 2010, allowed the emergence of "super" political action committees. These Super PACs could raise unlimited money from corporations, labor unions, and individuals, and spend that money supporting and opposing presidential or congressional candidates so long as they did not directly coordinate with the campaigns (Table 2-10). In *American Tradition Partnership, Inc. v. Bullock,* a Montana case, the U.S. Supreme Court held that *Citizens United* applied to state elections.[1]

This chapter presents information on the amounts of money collected and spent by individual presidential candidates (Tables 2-3 and 2-4), along with more aggregated information about expenditures by the political parties (Tables 2-6 through 2-8). The most recent campaign expenditures for all 435 representatives and 100 senators can be found in Chapter 5 on Congress (Tables 5-11 and 5-12).

One could easily be intimidated by all of the numbers on campaign finance. The publications of the Federal Election Commission (FEC) alone run to multiple volumes every two years, with detailed accountings of the receipts and expenditures of candidates in federal elections. Additional volumes are produced, though inconsistently and much less systematically, by various state agencies. Because such information is so voluminous, it is often summarized as we do here by how much was spent by various types of political action committees (Table 2-11), which PACs are the biggest contributors (Table 2-13), and so on. We encourage you to explore the FEC site to find more information about any specific campaign (or group of campaigns), or about specific donors.

This wealth of information has been collected since the mid-1970s, when the FEC was established. Although studies of campaign costs were conducted before then, the present time series are often limited to this span of about forty years. Laws regulating campaign contributions, expenditures, and interest group activities change so frequently that longer time series are often unobtainable and would be misleading even if they could be compiled. For example, the growth of PACs dates from 1974 because changes in the laws at that time allowed their establishment (Table 2-9). Similarly, data on public funding of presidential campaigns date from 1976 (Table 2-5). Data from before that would simply not be comparable.

Concern about money is not limited strictly to candidate spending. Indeed, researchers and watchdog groups are probably more concerned about interest group spending and about where candidates' funds come from and what, if anything, that money buys. Fortunately, more and more data are now available on interest group finances and on candidates' fundraising as well as on expenditures. Many of the data are related to PACs, the dominant organizations through which interest groups raise and spend money (Table 2-10). The information presented here is related primarily to the general categories of PACs (Tables 2-9, 2-11, 2-12, and 2-14); the list of the largest PAC contributors illustrates the variety of organizations that fall into these categories (Table 2-13).

Because money is at the heart of interest group activities, matters of campaign finance law are directly relevant to this chapter. At the federal level, these regulations consist mainly of fairly straightforward contribution limits—limits that were recently changed by the BCRA (Table 2-1) and *Citizens*

United (Table 2-10). At the state level, there is a myriad of contribution and expenditure limits (Table 2-2).

Of course, not all questions about efforts to influence the electoral or the political process involve money, at least not in a direct sense. Other aspects of interest group activity that can be quantified are depicted in Chapters 5 and 11, such as the growth and decline of labor unions (Table 11-8) and interest groups' ratings of members of Congress on how favorable their votes were to the groups' interests (Tables 5-11 and 5-12).

For obvious reasons, no one is able to collect systematically what would surely be the most captivating data on organized interests: that on any bribes, threats, and blackmail that may insinuate themselves into campaign finance. Available data provide unprecedented knowledge and research potential about the scope and possible influence of organized interests, and we encourage you to explore them. However, merely saying that a member voted a certain way after receiving money from a particular group is not evidence of bribery or of other untoward influences of money; as one potential explanation, groups often give their financial support to those who have already shown themselves to be supporters. We address these issues in some of the data essays we include in this chapter—linking campaign donations to public policymaking is often far more complicated than most armchair observers believe it to be!

Notes

1. This case is one of the few cases each year decided by per curiam opinion—when the Supreme Court essentially deems the outcome so obvious that there is no need to go through a full process. See Table 7-7 for details on the number of per curiam opinions issued by the Court over time.

Table 2-1 Contribution Limits under the Bipartisan Campaign Reform Act of 2002

	Recipients				
Donors	Candidate committee per election	National party committee per calendar year	State/district/local party committee per calendar year	PAC per calendar year[a]	Additional national party committee accounts per calendar year[b]
Individual	$2,800[c]	$35,500[c]	$10,000 (combined limit)	$5,000	$106,500[c] per account
National party committee	$5,000[d]	Unlimited transfers	Unlimited transfers	$5,000	
State/district/local party committee	$10,000	Unlimited transfers	Unlimited transfers	$5,000 (combined limit)	
PAC multicandidate	$5,000	$15,000	$5,000 (combined limit)	$5,000	$45,000 per account, per year
PAC not multicandidate	$2,800[c]	$35,500[c]	$10,000 (combined limit)	$5,000	$106,500[c] per account
Candidate committee	$2,000	Unlimited transfers	Unlimited transfers	$5,000	

[a] "PAC" here refers to a committee that makes contributions to other federal political committees. Independent expenditure-only political committees (sometimes called "Super PACs") may accept unlimited contributions, including from corporations and labor organizations.

[b] The limits in this column apply to a national party committee's accounts for: (a) the presidential nominating convention; (b) election recounts and contests and other legal proceedings; and (c) national party headquarters buildings. A party's national committee, Senate campaign committee, and House campaign committee are each considered separate party committees with separate limits. Only a national party committee, not the parties' national congressional campaign committees, may have an account for the presidential nominating convention.

[c] These limits will be indexed for inflation. Amounts shown are for the 2019–2020 election cycle.

[d] Additionally, a national party committee and its Senatorial campaign committee may contribute up to $49,600 combined per campaign to each Senate candidate.

Source: Federal Election Commission, "FEC Chart: 2019–2020 Campaign Cycle Contribution Limits," February 7, 2019, www.fec.gov.

Table 2-2 Contribution Limits on Funding of State Election Campaigns

State	Individuals	Corporations	Labor unions	Political action committees	State parties
Alabama	no	no	no	no	no
Alaska	yes	prohibited	prohibited	yes	yes
Arizona	yes	prohibited	prohibited	yes	yes
Arkansas	yes	prohibited	prohibited	yes	yes
California	yes	yes	yes	yes	no
Colorado	yes	prohibited	prohibited	yes	yes
Connecticut	yes	prohibited	prohibited	yes	yes
Delaware	yes	yes	yes	yes	yes
Florida	yes	yes	yes	yes	yes
Georgia	yes	yes	yes	yes	yes
Hawaii	yes	yes	yes	yes	yes
Idaho	yes	yes	yes	yes	yes
Illinois	yes	yes	yes	yes	no[a]
Indiana	no	yes	yes	no[b]	no
Iowa	no	prohibited	no	no	no
Kansas	yes	yes	yes	yes	no[a]
Kentucky	yes	prohibited	prohibited	yes	no
Louisiana	yes	yes	yes	yes	no
Maine	yes	yes	yes	yes	yes
Maryland	yes	yes	yes	yes	yes
Massachusetts	yes	prohibited	prohibited	yes	yes
Michigan	yes	prohibited	prohibited	yes	yes
Minnesota	yes	prohibited	yes	yes	yes
Mississippi	no	yes	no	no	no
Missouri	yes	prohibited	prohibited	yes	yes
Montana	yes	prohibited	prohibited	yes	yes
Nebraska	no	no	no	no	no
Nevada	yes	yes	yes	yes	yes
New Hampshire	yes	yes	prohibited	yes	yes
New Jersey	yes	yes	yes	yes	no
New Mexico	yes	yes	yes	yes	yes
New York	yes	yes	yes	yes	no[a]
North Carolina	yes	prohibited	prohibited	yes	no
North Dakota	no	prohibited	prohibited	no	no
Ohio	yes	prohibited	prohibited	yes	yes
Oklahoma	yes	prohibited	prohibited	yes	yes
Oregon	no	no	no	no	no
Pennsylvania	no	prohibited	prohibited	no	no
Rhode Island	yes	prohibited	prohibited	yes	yes
South Carolina	yes	yes	yes	yes	yes
South Dakota	yes	yes	yes	no	no
Tennessee	yes	yes	yes	yes	yes
Texas	no	prohibited	prohibited	no	no
Utah	no	no	no	no	no

(Table continues)

Table 2-2 *(Continued)*

State	Individuals	Corporations	Labor unions	Political action committees	State parties
Vermont	yes	yes	yes	yes	no
Virginia	no	no	no	no	no
Washington	yes	yes	yes	yes	yes
West Virginia	yes	prohibited	yes	yes	yes
Wisconsin	yes	prohibited	prohibited	yes	no
Wyoming	yes	prohibited	prohibited	yes	no

Note: The definitions of "contributions" and "candidates," as well as the limits on sizes of contributions and other restrictions (for example, from government employees, regulated industries), vary widely across states. For details, see source.

[a] Unlimited, except for primary elections in Illinois (subject to limitations), contested primary elections in Kansas (subject to limitations), and primaries in New York (prohibited).

[b] Unlimited, except for PACs designated for a specific candidate (subject to corporate limitations).

Source: National Conference of State Legislatures, "State Limits on Contributions to Candidates 2019–2020 Cycle," www.ncsl.org.

Table 2-3 Presidential Campaign Finance, 2020

Party/candidate	Federal funds	Contributions from individuals	Contributions from parties	Contributions from other committees	Contributions/loans from the candidate	Other loans	Transfers and offsets[a]	Other receipts	Total
Republicans Trump, Donald J.	$0	$458,351,485	$0	$846,953	$0	$0	$281,551,284	$3,600,506	$744,350,228
Democrats Biden, Joseph R.	0	823,098,083	8,200	563,064	—	—	250,433,267	77,361	1,074,179,975
Others	0	3,900,718	15,499	2,200	12,084	—	10,740	139	3,941,379
Total general election candidates	0	1,285,350,286	23,699	1,412,217	12,084	—	531,995,291	3,678,006	1,811,471,582
Total primary-only candidates	184,988	184,988	670,801,679	16,361	484,339	1,475,658,316	93,595,620	10,660,198	2,251,431,975
Grand total	184,988	1,285,535,274	670,825,378	1,428,578	496,423	1,475,658,316	625,590,911	14,338,204	4,062,903,557

Party/candidate	Operating expenditures	Transfers to other committees	Fundraising disbursements	Total loan repayments	Total contribution refunds	Other disbursements[b]	Total disbursements	Latest cash on hand	Debts owed by campaign[c]
Republicans Trump, Donald J.	$704,895,264	$801	$0	$0	$11,494,581	$36,498,683	$752,889,329	$10,749,402	$2,733,832
Democrats Biden, Joseph R.	1,056,940,034	1192592	0	0	15,783,419	3,456	1,073,919,501	260,475	0

(Table continues)

Table 2-3 *(Continued)*

Party/candidate	Operating expenditures	Transfers to other committees	Fundraising disbursements	Total loan repayments	Total contribution refunds	Other disbursements[b]	Total disbursements	Latest cash on hand	Debts owed by campaign[c]
Others	3,869,601	0	0	10,784	12,045	9,800	3,902,230	39,148	253,840
Total general election candidates	1,765,704,899	1,193,393	0	10,784	27,290,045	36,511,939	1,830,711,060	11,049,026	2,987,672
Total primary-only candidates	2,176,183,477	11,356,081	239,993	16,415,989	16,387,764	20,606,717	2,241,194,549	16,715,639	14,908,162
Grand total	3,941,888,376	12,549,474	239,993	16,426,773	43,677,809	57,118,656	4,071,905,609	27,764,665	17,895,834

Note: General election "Others" category and general election totals include two candidates, Howie Hawkins and Jo Jorgensen, not shown separately. The total for primary-only candidates exclude general election candidates. These data reflect the time period from January 1, 2019 - December 31, 2020. However, the FEC closed its office headquarters in mid-March 2020 due to COVID-19 contingencies, so reports submitted on paper between March 2020 and December 2020 are not included. Approximately 94 percent of reports submitted are done so electronically, and is mandatory for all filers who received contributions or make expenditures exceeding $50,000 in a single year, so most information is included in these estimates.

[a] Although combined here, transfers and offsets are separate totals in the FEC source table.
[b] Includes legal and accounting disbursements, which is presented as a separate category in the FEC source table.
[c] There is also a total of $31,947 in debts owed to campaigns for primary-only candidates (not shown).

Sources: Federal Election Commission, "Table 1: Presidential Campaign Receipts Through December 31, 2020" and "Table 2: Presidential Campaign Disbursements Through December 31, 2020," www.fec.gov.

Table 2-4 Presidential Campaign Finance, Aggregated Contributions from Individual Donors to Leading Presidential Candidates, 2016 and 2020

Candidate	Total number of itemized individual donors	Total net individual contributions (millions)	Percentage of individual contributions from donors aggregating to		
			under $200	$200–999	$1,000 or more[a]
2016					
Clinton	535,305	405.0	3.8	24.1	72.1
Trump	350,273	102.5	10.7	36.4	52.9
Johnson	6,445	3.4	5.3	37.2	57.5
Stein	5,115	2.6	4.0	48.8	47.2
2020					
Biden	4,115,097	886.0	16.5	33.5	50.0
Trump	1,825,158	566.8	13.1	36.6	50.3
Jorgensen	2,389	0.9	9.3	47.0	43.7

Note: Amounts are from FEC data released on November 27, 2017 and March 22, 2021. Similar data for earlier years can be found in previous editions of *Vital Statistics on American Politics*.

[a] The maximum amount an individual donor could give to a candidate was $2,700 in 2016 and $2,800 in 2020. Individuals could contribute up to this amount in the prenomination period and again in the general election period.

Source: OpenSecrets.org, "Donor Demographics," www.opensecrets.org; federal election data from the Federal Election Commission, www.fec.gov.

A Data Literacy Lesson

Making Comparisons over Time

To paraphrase the cinematic philosopher of the 1980s, Ferris Bueller, data comes at you pretty fast. If you don't stop and look around once in a while, you could miss it. We think Table 2-4 provides an interesting example of this: not in the data itself, but in the source and how quickly it can change. If you were trying to find the most recent version of this data, a logical place to start is to look at the source we used. In this case, we found the information from Open Secrets, and (at least as we write this) that's where we'd suggest you start for more details. Depending on when you read this, though, that might not be the case anymore.

If you look at earlier editions of this book, you'll see that the information about individual donors' contributions to presidential campaigns was presented just a little bit differently, and the source was the Campaign Finance Institute (CFI). As of June 2021, the CFI website was still up and running and appeared to have data from as recently as 2019. A little digging though, and you can find that the CFI merged with the National Institute on Money in State Politics in 2018, forming the new National Institute on Money in Politics. In June 2021, the (still relatively new) National Institute on Money in Politics merged with the Center for Responsive Politics, another national nonprofit organization with a focus on tracking the effects of money in politics, to form Open Secrets. That's a lot of organizational change in a short period of time. Each iteration of the organization gathered, aggregated, and presented the data in a slightly different way.

Aside from the scavenger hunt that finding data can become when data-collecting organizations go through institutional mergers and changes, these changes present different options for what data are available. This becomes particularly important when you are working to draw conclusions over long time periods. In Table 2-4, we have presented information about individual donors at the aggregate level for the past two presidential elections. These are both from the same source and present the same information so you can reasonably make comparisons between the 2016 and 2020 election cycles. If this essay were about using data to identify noteworthy changes, we might talk about how changes might be indicators for research questions. (For example, does the increase in the number of individual donors from less than one million combined in 2016 to over six million in 2020 tell us something about political engagement? But we digress because that's not the focus of this essay…)

You can find information about individual donors at the aggregate level in previous editions of this book, but it would be difficult to draw comparisons using the two different volumes because they use two different sources. The Campaign Finance Institute, which is now two-times removed, reported donation levels at $200 or less, while Open Secrets reports a level of $200–$499. (We've collapsed that with the $500–$999 donation levels.) This difference of $1.00 is insignificant in the scope of the thousands of dollars an individual can legally contribute to a candidate. But the difference in reporting is substantial because we no longer have the ability to compare across those elections. We don't know where the split is for those contributions that were $200 exactly and we'd be over-interpreting if we tried. That dollar, as we said, does not make a substantive difference, but it means we cannot make comparisons of today with any election before 2020.

It's possible that by the next edition of this book, we'll be splitting the donation amounts differently again, depending on whether the merged Open Secrets organization reports it differently than it has up to now. And, if it merges with another organization in the meantime, we'll be watching to catch those changes, no matter how fast they occur.

Table 2-5 Public Funding of Presidential Elections, 1976–2020 (millions)

Year	Spending limits Primary[a]	Spending limits Primary plus 20%[a]	Maximum entitlement, primary matching funds[b]	Public funds for each major-party convention[c]	Public funds for each major-party nominee for general election[d]	Coordinated party spending limit[e]
1976	$10.9	$13.1	$5.5	$2.2	$21.8	$3.2
1980	14.7	17.7	7.4	4.4	29.4	4.6
1984	20.2	24.2	10.1	8.1	40.4	6.9
1988	23.1	27.7	11.5	9.2	46.1	8.3
1992	27.6	33.1	13.8	11.0	55.2	10.3
1996	30.9	37.1	15.5	12.4	61.8	12.0
2000	33.8	40.5	16.9	13.5	67.6	13.7
2004	37.3	44.8	18.7	14.9	74.6	16.2
2008	42.1	50.5	21.0	16.8	84.1	19.1
2012	45.6	54.7	22.8	18.2	91.2	21.7
2016	48.1	57.7	24.1	—	96.1	23.8
2020	51.9	62.3	25.6	—	103.7	26.5

Note: Amounts are in current dollars, and reflect what public funding limits are, but are not indicative of whether candidates used the public funding option.

[a] $10 million + COLA. (COLA is the cost-of-living adjustment over the base year of 1974.) Campaigns are also allowed to exempt fundraising costs up to 20 percent of the overall limit, which, in effect, raises their total spending limit by 20 percent. Legal and accounting costs, up to 15 percent of the overall limit, if incurred to comply with the law, are also exempt from the limit.

[b] Eligible candidates in the presidential primaries may receive public funds to match the individual contributions they raise up to half of the national spending limit. Contributions from political action committees (PACs) and party committees are not matchable. Although an individual has been able to give up to $1,000 to a primary candidate (before the Bipartisan Campaign Reform Act of 2002 raised that limit to $2,000), only the first $250 of that contribution is matchable. Presidential candidates become eligible for matching funds by raising more than $5,000 in matchable contributions in each of twenty different states. Candidates must agree to use these public funds only for campaign expenses.

[c] From 1976 to 2012, each major party convention committee was entitled to $4 million plus a cost-of-living adjustment, and minor parties were entitled to partial funding based on their party's share of the vote in the prior presidential election. In 2014, this public funding was eliminated by Section II of Public Law 113–94, the "Gabriella Miller Kids First Research Act."

[d] $20 million + COLA. Legal and accounting costs incurred to comply with the law are exempt from the limit and may be defrayed from private monies raised in separate compliance funds (subject to contribution limitations and prohibitions). The major party candidates who win their party's nominations for president are each eligible to receive a grant to cover all the expenses of their general election campaigns. Nominees who accept the funds must agree not to raise private contributions (from individuals, PACs, or party committees) and to limit their campaign expenditures to the amount of public funds they receive. They may use the funds only for campaign expenses. The last year a major party candidate accepted the general election grant was in 2008. A third-party presidential candidate may qualify for some public funds after the general election if he or she receives at least 5 percent of the popular vote.

[e] The amount the national party may spend on behalf of its nominee is set by a formula: $.02 multiplied by voting-age population of the United States multiplied by the price index and rounded to the nearest $100. The party may work in conjunction with the campaign, but the money is raised, spent, and reported by the national party committee.

Source: Federal Election Commission, www.fec.gov.

Table 2-6 Financial Activity of the National Political Parties, 2001–2020 (millions)

Party	2001–2002	2003–2004	2005–2006	2007–2008	2009–2010	2011–2012	2013–2014	2015–2016	2017–2018	2019–2020
Democratic										
Raised	$217.2	$688.8	$483.1	$763.3	$618.1	$800.1	$657.2	870.1	783.2	1,527.5
Spent	208.7	665.6	472.4	746.5	603.5	784.1	634.6	843.2	750.4	1,424.3
Contributions	2.3	1.8	4.1	2.5	2.0	2.3	1.8	2.3	2.2	2.9
Coordinated expenditures[a]	7.1	33.1	20.7	38.0	24.9	39.5	13.1	37.5	20.1	40.6
Independent expenditures[b]	1.7	176.5	108.1	156.2	107.4	113.8	123.6	141.2	114.5	183.4
Republican										
Raised	424.1	782.4	599.0	792.9	542.1	803.5	565.7	752.4	766.2	1,662.1
Spent	427.0	752.6	608.2	766.1	546.4	786.9	552.9	706.7	745.0	1,579.2
Contributions	4.7	2.6	1.9	8.6	2.4	2.6	2.6	1.9	1.9	4.0
Coordinated expenditures[a]	16.0	29.1	14.2	32.0	27.1	36.3	14.5	39.2	17.8	46.6
Independent expenditures[b]	1.9	88.0	115.6	124.7	76.1	140.3	105.3	113.3	118.2	209.3

Note: Amounts in current dollars. This table includes only federal activity. Total receipts and disbursements do not include monies transferred among committees. Building funds and state and local election spending are not reported to the Federal Election Commission. Data for earlier years can be found in previous editions of *Vital Statistics on American Politics.* Comparisons with earlier years must be made cautiously since subsequent data revisions can differ appreciably from previously published data.

[a] Party committees are also allowed to spend money on behalf of federal candidates, in addition to the money party committees may contribute directly. This spending may be coordinated with a candidate.
[b] The 1996 election cycle was the first in which party committees were permitted to make independent expenditures.

Sources: Federal Election Commission, "Party Table 2a: Democratic Party Committees' Federal Financial Activity through December 31 of the Election Year," "Party Table 3: Republican Party Committees' Federal Financial Activity through December 31 of the Election Year," www.fec.gov.

Table 2-7 Financial Activity of National, State, and Local Party Committees, 2019–2020 (millions)

Committee	Raised			Spent				Cash on hand	Debts owed
	From individuals	From other committees	Total	Contributions made	Coordinated expenditures	Independent expenditures	Total		
Democratic National Committee	$231.7	$1.4	$491.7	$0.00	$17.1	$0.00	$461.5	$38.8	$3.2
Democratic Senatorial Campaign Committee	240.8	12.0	303.9	0.7	15.3	91.2	300.3	9.8	20.0
Democratic Congressional Campaign Committee	211.6	53.2	345.8	0.8	7.3	90.8	330.4	21	14.0
Democratic state and local committees	117.8	63.5	599.5	1.4	0.8	1.3	545.4	37.6	3.1
Total Democratic	802.0	130.0	1,527.5	2.9	40.6	183.4	1,424.3	107.1	40.3
Republican National Committee	469.1	0.7	890.6	0	25.4	7.1	833.5	80.5	0
National Republican Senatorial Committee	225.5	13.3	338.3	1.3	9.8	120.6	331.4	14.4	9.0
National Republican Congressional Committee	159.9	45.5	280.9	0.5	5.6	80.7	284.9	12.6	0
Republican state and local committees	81.1	58.6	478.1	2.2	5.8	0.8	455.2	23.0	1.3
Total Republican	935.6	118.2	1,662.1	4.0	46.6	209.3	1,579.2	130.5	10.3

Note: See notes to Table 2-6, this volume.

Sources: Federal Election Commission, "Party Table 2a: Democratic Party Committees' Federal Financial Activity through December 31 of the Election Year," "Party Table 3a: Republican Party Committees' Federal Financial Activity through December 31 of the Election Year," www.fec.gov.

> ## A Data Literacy Lesson
>
> ### Finding What Isn't There
>
> When we look at things, we're trained to describe and explain and get meaning from what we see. If someone asks you to explain a flower, you might describe the color, the shape, the size, and even the feel. If someone asks you to explain a table of data (let's say one about the financial activity of national, state, and local parties) you might identify descriptive data and attempt to interpret relationships, commonalities, and differences. As you look at Table 2-7 (and also, by the way, at Table 2-8, which presents similar data over a longer time period), you might be inclined to draw some conclusions about the Democratic and Republican parties' spending and fundraising habits. You might note, for example, that the Republican Party both raised and spent more money than the Democratic Party in 2019–2020, but that the amounts for both are in the same ballpark. You might note the differences in how the parties raise money at different levels, with the Republicans raising most from individuals at the National Committee level and progressively raising less down to the state and local levels, while the Democrats collected the most from individual donations to their Senatorial Campaign Committee, followed by the National Committee, then the Congressional Campaign Committee and finally the state and local committees. These all suggest interesting questions that are worth further exploration, but we think there's another interesting thing to consider. It might seem counterintuitive, but we wonder what we'd find if we look for what isn't there.
>
> It's certainly harder to see what isn't included but, as we've said elsewhere throughout this book, data rarely stand alone in a singular table. If you're interested in exploring how major political parties raise and spend money this table is certainly a good place to start. But does this table include all the information you need to continue that exploration? Consider the very first row: as you look at Democratic National Committee money raised, $231.7 million were raised from individuals and $1.4 million were raised from other committees, with a total of $491.7 million raised. Do any questions come to mind as you look at those?
>
> If we were approaching this for the first time, we might question the math: 231.7 +1.4 does *not* equal $491.7. Where did the rest of the money raised by the DNC come from? We also might wonder about the $1.4 million raised from "other committees." What other committees, exactly?
>
> We could start by going to the table the FEC shares. While we get some minor pieces of the puzzle (there are $26.4 million in transfers from "other national" and "state/local" committees that add to the money raised, but still don't come close to the total of $491.7 million), the source for these data might lead to more questions (What are the other national and state/local committees that are sending money to the DNC? What are Levin Funds and what do they have to do with the relationship between different levels of political party organizations?) that lead us, in turn, to other sources, like federal legislation and scholarly articles that provide insight and analysis on these questions.
>
> We've noticed that numbers are often treated as conclusive, as if the final answer to everything will be a number. There would certainly be a satisfying simplicity in that.[1] But we think there's a power in the numerical data that isn't in them
>
> *(Continued)*

(Continued)

providing answers but, rather, suggesting questions. Some of the most interesting questions to explore are found in the space of what isn't reported.

---

[1] Of course, if you're a fan of Douglas Adams' *The Hitchhiker's Guide to the Galaxy*, we will concede that the answer is 42, but we still wonder what the question is for that answer.

Table 2-8 National Party Campaign Finance: "Soft" and "Hard" Money, 2002–2020 (millions)

Committee	2002	2004	2006	2008	2010	2012	2014	2016	2018	2020
Democratic National Committee	$73.3	$399.9	$133.2	$258.3	$223.9	$292.3	$160.7	$347.0	$177.7	$461.5
Democratic Senatorial Campaign Committee	49.8	88.3	121.7	162.6	129.1	144.9	169.2	177.4	145.8	300.3
Democratic Congressional Campaign Committee	47.0	92.4	140.8	176.5	163.6	183.2	206.1	216.4	297.5	330.4
Democratic state and local committees	97.8	153.7	147.6	272.3	161.8	294.8	182.6	366.0	232.8	545.4
Total Democratic	208.7	665.6	472.4	746.5	603.5	784.1	634.6	843.2	750.4	1424.3
Republican National Committee	$186.8	$382.6	$254.6	$415.5	$210.8	$386.2	$194.6	$323.1	$326.7	$833.5
Republican Senatorial Campaign Committee	59.6	78.7	89.7	93.8	112.5	113.8	129.0	133.9	151.2	331.3
Republican Congressional Campaign Committee	130.7	184.8	178.1	118.2	132.1	156.7	153.5	160.6	200.6	284.9
Republican state and local committees	111.1	164.2	152.5	208.3	125.8	241.7	136.0	189.7	148.7	455.2
Total Republican	427.0	752.6	608.2	766.1	546.4	786.9	552.9	706.7	745.0	1579.2

Note: Amounts in current dollars. Totals do not include transfers among national party committees.

Sources: Federal Election Commission, "Party Table 2a: Democratic Party Committees' Federal Financial Activity through December 31 of the Election Year," "Party Table 2b: Republican Party Committees' Federal Financial Activity through December 31 of the Election Year," www.fec.gov.

Table 2-9 Number of Political Action Committees (PACs), by Type, 1989–2020

Year	Corporate	Labor	Trade/ membership/ health[a]	Cooperative	Corporation without stock	Independent expenditure-only committees[b]	Political committees with non-contribution accounts[c]	Leadership PACs	Other nonconnected	Total
1989–1990	1,098	166	590	31	107	—	—	—	877	2,869
1991–1992	1,140	185	603	33	114	—	—	—	992	3,067
1993–1994	1,160	196	616	29	114	—	—	—	984	3,099
1995–1996	1,838	358	1,168	45	134	—	—	—	1,075	4,618
1997–1998	1,824	352	1,083	45	133	—	—	—	1,156	4,593
1999–2000	1,726	350	1,028	41	120	—	—	—	1,231	4,496
2001–2002	1,743	337	1,070	41	117	—	—	—	1,265	4,573
2003–2004	1,757	329	1,068	38	110	—	—	—	1,562	4,864
2005–2006	1,808	312	1,083	37	115	—	—	—	1,657	5,012
2007–2008	1,794	299	1,128	44	114	—	—	—	1,841	5,220
2009–2010	1,816	311	1,102	40	121	—	—	—	2,041	5,431
2011–2012	1,851	300	993	41	118	1,251	65	532	2,160	7,311
2013–2014	1,804	288	967	41	114	1,618	105	558	2,053	7,548
2015–2016	1,803	289	97	42	104	2,722	180	572	1,981	7,790
2017–2018	1,732	279	961	46	103	2,217	343	664	2,318	8,663
2019–2020	1,669	275	951	46	94	2,319	522	727	2,252	8,855

Note: "—" indicates not available. Counts for other years can be found in earlier editions of *Vital Statistics on American Politics*. The counts reflect federally registered PACs. Registration does not necessarily imply financial activity.

[a] As of July 2011, health organizations are no longer an organization type but are included in either the trade or membership category.
[b] Independent expenditure-only committees may receive unlimited contributions from individuals, corporations, and labor unions for the purpose of financing independent expenditures and other independent political activity.
[c] Committees with non-contribution accounts, permitted to make contributions to federal candidates, solicit and accept unlimited contributions from individuals, corporations, labor organizations, and other political committees. These contributions are in a segregated bank account for the purpose of financing independent expenditures, other ads that refer to a federal candidate, and generic voter drives in federal elections, while maintaining a separate bank account, subject to all of the statutory amount limitations and source prohibitions.

Source: Federal Election Commission, "PAC Table 1: Summary of PAC Activity" for each respective year, www.fec.gov.

Table 2-10 PACs: Receipts, Expenditures, and Contributions, 1975–2020

Election cycle[a]	Receipts[b] (millions)	Expenditures[b] (millions)	Contributions to congressional candidates[c] (millions)	Percentage of receipts contributed to congressional candidates
1975–1976	$54.0	$52.9	$22.6	42
1977–1978	80.0	77.4	34.1	43
1979–1980	137.7	131.2	60.2	44
1981–1982	199.5	190.2	87.6	44
1983–1984	288.7	266.8	113.0	39
1985–1986	353.4	340.0	139.8	40
1987–1988	384.6	364.2	159.2	41
1989–1990	372.1	357.6	159.1	43
1991–1992	385.5	394.8	188.9	49
1993–1994	391.8	388.1	189.6	48
1995–1996	437.4	429.9	217.8	50
1997–1998	502.6	470.8	219.9	44
1999–2000	604.9	579.4	259.8	43
2001–2002	685.3	656.5	282.0	41
2003–2004	915.7	842.9	310.5	34
2005–2006	1,085.5	1,055.3	372.1	34
2007–2008	1,212.4	1,180.0	412.8	34
2009–2010	1,197.8	1,174.1	431.5	36
2011–2012	2,259.1	2,198.4	444.5	20
2013–2014	2,368.6	2,304.8	435.9	18
2015–2016	4,046.3	3,973.3	444.0	11
2017–2018	4,674.2	4,554.1	465.6	10
2019–2020	13,227.9	12,947.1	448.8	3

Note: Amounts in current dollars. The 2012 presidential election was the first after a Supreme Court decision, *Citizens United v. Federal Election Commission* in January 2010, allowed the emergence of "super" political action committees (PACs). Super PACs can raise unlimited money from corporations, labor unions, and individuals, spending that money supporting and opposing presidential or congressional candidates, but cannot directly coordinate with the campaigns.

[a] Data cover January 1 of the odd-numbered year to December 31 of the even-numbered year.
[b] Receipts and expenditures for 1975–1984 exclude funds transferred between affiliated committees.
[c] Primarily contributions to candidates for election in the even-numbered year, made during the two-year election cycle. Some contributions went to candidates running for office in future years, or to debt retirement for candidates in past cycles.

Sources: 1975–1976: Joseph E. Cantor, "Political Action Committees: Their Evolution and Growth and Their Implications for the Political System," Report no. 83, Congressional Research Service (Washington, D.C., 1982), 87–88; 1977–1978: Federal Election Commission, "FEC Releases First PAC Figures for 1985–86," press release, May 21, 1987, 1; 1979–1988: "PAC Activity Falls in 1990 Elections," press release, March 31, 1991, 10; 1989–2010: "Table 4: Summary of PAC Activity, 1990–2010"; 2011–2020: "PAC Table 1: Summary of PAC Activity," "PAC Table 2: PAC Contributions to Candidates," www.fec.gov.

Table 2-11 Spending, by Type of PAC, 1997–2020 (millions)

Election cycle[a]	Separate Segregated Funds (SSFs)					Nonconnected committees			Total
	Corporate	Labor	Trade/ membership[b]	Cooperative	Corporations without stock	Independent expenditure-only committees[c]	Committees with non-contribution accounts[c]	Other PACs[d]	
1997–1998	$141.4	$103.0	$141.5	$4.3	$8.6	—	—	$94.8	$493.7
1999–2000	162.8	129.4	178.6	3.3	12.2	—	—	125.2	$611.5
2001–2002	184.3	159.3	175.9	3.7	9.6	—	—	153.8	$686.5
2003–2004	225.3	184.4	219.8	3.9	9.3	—	—	495.9	$1,138.5
2005–2006	272.9	198.5	251.9	4.6	11.1	—	—	328.7	$1,067.7
2007–2008	299.7	252.3	294.9	9.9	12.7	—	—	310.7	$1,180.3
2009–2010	302.8	256.9	268.8	6.3	15.9	90.9	—	333.1	$1,274.6
2011–2012	343.0	279.4	264.5	6.7	16.2	796.9	175.3	316.3	$2,198.4
2013–2014	370.7	289.2	290.5	7.0	19.4	687.2	312.6	328.0	$2,304.8
2015–2016	385.7	331.5	300.2	7.0	15.7	1805.9	769.0	358.2	$3,973.3
2017–2018	404.8	342.2	261.7	8.4	14.4	1540.7	1458.2	523.6	$4,554.1
2019–2020	408.5	385.6	280.7	7.3	13.2	3385.9	7656.5	809.2	$12,947.1

Note: "—" indicates not available. Amounts in current dollars. Detail may not add to totals because of rounding. Data for earlier years may be found in previous editions of *Vital Statistics on American Politics*.

[a] Data cover January 1 of the odd-numbered year to December 31 of the even-numbered year.
[b] This category combines the Federal Election Commission categories of trade and membership.
[c] For details, see notes for Table 2-9, this volume.
[d] This category includes the Federal Election Commission category of leadership PACs (initiated in 2011–2012).

Sources: 1997–2012: Federal Election Commission, "PAC Table 1: Summary of PAC Activity through December 31 of the Election Year"; 2013–2014: "PAC Table 1: Summary of PAC Activity, January 1, 2013 through December 31, 2014"; 2015–2016: "PAC Table 1: Summary of PAC Activity, January 1, 2015 through December 31, 2016"; 2017–2018: "PAC Table 1: Summary of PAC Activity, January 1, 2017 through December 31, 2018"; 2019–2020: "PAC Table 1: Summary of PAC Activity, January 1, 2019 through December 31, 2020." 2013–2020 sources available at www.fec.gov.

Table 2-12 Contributions and Independent Expenditures, by Type of PAC, 2003–2020

			Contributions to federal candidates[c]		Independent expenditures[d]	
Election cycle/PAC type	Number[a]	Receipts[b]	Amount	Percentage of receipts	Amount	Percentage of receipts
2003–2004						
Corporate	1,402	$238,984,115	$115,641,547	48%	$223,729	0.1%
Labor	206	191,651,043	52,103,572	27	20,737,373	10.8
Trade/membership/health	722	181,837,429	83,221,870	46	18,138,069	10.0
Cooperative	34	4,187,378	2,872,363	69	4,993	0.1
Corporations without stock	75	9,639,838	4,182,321	43	111,095	1.2
Nonconnected	819	289,423,580	52,467,328	18	18,159,133	6.3
Total	3,258	915,723,383	310,489,001	34	57,374,392	6.3
2005–2006						
Corporate	1,464	278,345,927	135,925,970	49	250,345	0.1
Labor	204	218,185,504	55,815,069	26	10,056,447	4.6
Trade/membership/health	745	218,448,147	101,803,507	47	19,050,740	8.7
Cooperative	35	6,166,566	3,454,915	56	3,865	0.1
Corporations without stock	89	11,441,713	4,885,718	43	377,849	3.3
Nonconnected	887	352,947,674	70,217,568	20	8,083,013	2.3
Total	3,424	1,085,535,531	372,102,747	34	37,822,259	3.5
2007–2008						
Corporate	1,470	313,350,975	158,323,496	51	221,207	0.1
Labor	203	262,055,837	62,675,294	24	58,630,780	22.4
Trade/membership/health	794	240,983,640	112,897,919	47	44,911,854	18.6
Cooperative	39	10,283,949	6,861,823	67	0	0.0
Corporations without stock	84	13,025,360	5,461,525	42	582,735	4.5
Nonconnected	1,023	372,720,837	66,627,495	18	30,834,925	8.3
Total	3,613	1,212,420,598	412,847,552	34	135,181,501	11.1

(Table continues)

Table 2-12 (Continued)

Election cycle/PAC type	Number[a]	Receipts[b]	Contributions to federal candidates[c]		Independent expenditures[d]	
			Amount	Percentage of receipts	Amount	Percentage of receipts
2009–2010						
Corporate	1,470	316,954,250	165,455,021	52	360,039	0.1
Labor	203	259,066,268	64,162,708	25	25,881,237	10.0
Trade/membership/health	794	227,397,841	115,335,850	51	31,734,037	14.0
Cooperative	39	10,060,381	4,959,203	49	0	0.0
Corporations without stock	84	14,253,911	7,488,570	53	712,598	5.0
Nonconnected	1,023	451,730,393	74,089,193	16	10,308,213	2.3
Total	3,613	1,279,469,044	431,490,545	34	68,996,124	5.4
2011–2012						
Corporate	1,851	361,088,386	181,141,433	50	—	—
Labor	300	282,589,623	57,476,379	20	—	—
Trade/membership[e]	993	270,443,042	121,324,660	45	—	—
Cooperative	41	7,318,621	5,345,052	73	—	—
Corporations without stock	118	17,343,198	7,529,555	43	—	—
Nonconnected[f]	4,008	1,320,350,343	73,532,041	6	—	—
Total	7,311	2,259,133,213	446,349,121	20	78,044,150	3.5
2013–2014						
Corporate	1,804	384,831,590	178,086,417	46	—	—
Labor	288	305,740,812	50,647,727	17	—	—
Trade/membership[e]	967	302,705,703	119,232,896	39	—	—
Cooperative	41	7,699,678	4,928,775	64	—	—
Corporations without stock	114	19,705,058	7,025,307	36	—	—
Nonconnected[f]	4,334	1,347,934,933	76,025,813	6	—	—
Total	7,548	2,368,617,774	435,946,935	18	47,449,852	2.0
2015–2016						
Corporate	1,803	$405,476,939	$182,762,062	45	—	—
Labor	389	342,382,387	46,728,402	14	—	—
Trade/membership[e]	973	319,722,996	123,074,945	38	—	—
Cooperative	42	8,021,080	4,726,798	59	—	—
Corporations without stock	104	15,707,065	7,527,678	48	—	—
Nonconnected[f]	5,455	2,954,949,795	79,192,956	3	—	—
Total	8,766	3,726,537,266	444,012,840	12	52,125,823	1.4

2017–2018					
Corporate	1,732	$417,247,320	$178,089,875	43	—
Labor	279	365,802,911	53,817,857	15	—
Trade/membership[e]	961	274,735,696	120,321,020	44	—
Cooperative	46	9,069,475	5,096,426	56	—
Corporations without stock	103	14,326,066	7,444,232	52	—
Nonconnected[f]	5,542	3,593,033,432	100,808,176	3	—
Total	8,663	4,674,214,900	464,577,585	10	57,854,221 1.2
2019–2020					
Corporate	1,669	$429,563,082	$165,747,241	39	—
Labor	275	384,279,535	51,824,216	13	—
Trade/membership[e]	951	303,134,221	117,317,488	39	—
Cooperative	46	7,775,702	5,133,600	66	—
Corporations without stock	94	14,258,153	6,650,350	47	—
Nonconnected[f]	5,820	12,088,845,195	102,086,283	1	—
Total	8,855	13,257,855,888	448,759,178	3	65,040,522 0.5

Note: "—" indicates not available. Amounts in current dollars. Data for earlier years can be found in previous editions of *Vital Statistics on American Politics*.

[a] For 2003–2010, the numbers shown are those PACs that actually made contributions.

[b] Not adjusted for money transferred between affiliated committees. Receipts are for all PACs whether or not they made contributions to candidates in the election cycle.

[c] Figures include contributions to all federal candidates, including those who did not run for office during the years indicated.

[d] Independent expenditures include money spent for candidates and against candidates.

[e] As of July 2011, health organizations are no longer an organization type but are included in either the trade or the membership category.

[f] This category includes independent expenditure-only committees which are prohibited from making contributions to candidates.

Sources: Federal Election Commission, "PAC Activity Increases for 2004 Elections," press release, April 13, 2005; "PAC Activity Continues Climb in 2006," press release, October 5, 2007; "Growth in PAC Financial Activity Slows," press release, April 24, 2009; "PAC Financial Activity, 2009–2010," "Table 3: 2009–2010 Summary of Independent Expenditures," "Independent Expenditure Table 1: Independent Expenditures Made for or against Candidates through December 31 of the Election Year (2012 and 2010)," "PAC Table 1: Summary of PAC Activity through December 1 of the Election Year," "PAC Table 2: PAC Contributions to Candidates, January 1, 2011–December 31, 2012," "PAC Table 1: Summary of PAC Activity, January 1, 2013 through December 31, 2014," "PAC Table 2: PAC Contributions to Candidates, January 1, 2013–December 31, 2014," "Independent Expenditure Table 2: Independent Expenditures Made For or Against Congressional Candidates, January 1, 2013 through December 31, 2014," www.fec.gov.

A Data Literacy Lesson

The Wild Growth of Nonconnected PACs

It is not a typo—we checked it multiple times. The bottom of Table 2-12 shows that so-called "Nonconnected" Political Action Committees (PACs) gave about $1.3 million to candidates in 2013–2014, a shade under $3 million in 2015–2016, about $3.5 million from 2017–2018, and then an astonishing $12 million from 2019–2020. Sometimes, when we look at a table, we have to work hard to find the key numbers hidden within the rows and columns. This number, a more than three-fold increase in a two-year period, jumps right out at us, and begs for explanation.

Let's start with a definition. There are two kinds of political action committees (organizations that pool funds from their members and donate them to candidates or campaigns). So-called connected PACs are affiliated with a political party, a candidate, or exist as a separate segregated fund that is established by a labor union or corporation.[1] A nonconnected PAC is a political committee that is not a party committee, an authorized committee of a candidate, or a separate segregated fund established by a corporation or labor organization. When the idea of a political action committee was first introduced into the lexicon in the 1970s, most of these PACs were associated with parties, candidates, unions, or corporations. As recently as 2003–2004, only about one-quarter of PACs were nonconnected. If we look at Table 2-12, that number is now close to two-thirds. (Out of 8,855 PACs donating to candidates in 2019–2020, 5,820 were classified as nonconnected.)

There are two significant consequences to this trend. First, the barriers to entry for those who wish to raise money for or against candidates have been lowered. If you wish to use your money to affect the results of elections, you no longer need to be associated with a campaign, a corporation, or a union to start a political action committee. Anyone who wishes to start an unconnected PAC can do so, relatively easily. (We do recommend consulting a good lawyer before doing so, as campaign finance laws are rather complex, and we don't want you to end up in prison.)

Voters, of course, are far more likely to give money to PACs rather than starting their own, and here we see another critical difference between nonconnected and connected PACs. PACs connected to labor unions and corporations are permitted to seek their contributions from a "restricted class" of donors, which generally consists of managers and shareholders of the corporation or members of the labor union. Nonconnected PACs are free to seek money from anyone, giving them a significant leg up in the drive to raise money and, in so doing, gain influence.

A second consequence of the growth of nonconnected PACs concerns political polarization. Nonconnected PACs are more likely to represent ideological and/or single-issue constituencies. This can have the effect of pulling political activity away from the center and toward the ideological poles. If we consider an issue such as abortion, an increasing number of single-issue pro-life or pro-choice groups means more money being raised on the issue, and increased ability to use this money to enforce ideological rigidity. Candidates know that if they depart even a little bit from the orthodoxy of these single-issue nonconnected PACs, large amounts of money can be raised to support their opponents, or (more likely) to fund a primary challenger who will toe the group's line on this issue. Abortion, of course, is just one such issue on which nonconnected PACs make moving to the center to find common ground an electorally dangerous act.

In our experience, numbers tell us something real. When a type of political action committee goes from representing about one-quarter of the PACs to representing two-thirds of them in a short period of time, and when their contributions increase by almost a factor of ten in a six-year period, that should tip us off that something big is changing. A few minutes spent visiting the FEC site to see what these different categories mean, followed by a few minutes reading about this concept of a nonconnected PAC and the challenges associated with them, have now led us to more evidence of the potential causes of polarization and the collapse of the center in American politics.

All of this from just noticing one very large, and anomalous, number.

---

[1] The Federal Election Commission (FEC) has helpful resources explaining the different types of political action committees, particularly at https://www.fec.gov/help-candidates-and-committees/registering-pac/understanding-nonconnected-pacs.

Table 2-13 Top Twenty PACs in Overall Spending and in Contributions to Federal Candidates, 2019–2020

Rank	PAC	Overall spending
1	Win The Era PAC	$104,963,611
2	Emily's List	$79,603,956
3	SEIU COPE (Service Employees International Union Committee on Political Education)	$75,441,290
4	The Good Land Committee, Inc.	$45,341,044
5	End Citizens United	$42,245,587
6	Democracy Engine, Inc., PAC	$29,393,358
7	National Rifle Association of America Political Victory Fund	$22,739,549
8	UAW - V - CAP (UAW Voluntary Community Action Program)	$22,639,912
9	American Federation Of State County & Municipal Employees PEOPLE	$21,421,473
10	People Powered Action	$18,568,037
11	Democratic Action	$16,769,222
12	D.R.I.V.E.—Democrat, Republican, Independent Voter Education (The PAC of The International Brotherhood of Teamsters)	$16,326,214
13	CHC Bold PAC	$15,024,503
14	UA Union Plumbers & Pipefitters Vote! PAC (United Association of Journeymen and Apprentices of the Plumbing & Pipefitting Industry of the United States and Canada)	$13,217,494
15	1199 Service Employees Int'l Union Federal Political Action Fund	$13,110,706
16	National Association of Realtors Political Action Committee	$12,607,348
17	United Food and Commercial Workers International Union Active Ballot Club	$12,312,480
18	Engineers Political Education Committee (EPEC)/ International Union of Operating Engineers	$12,077,559
19	Let America Vote PAC	$12,031,578
20	Laborers' International Union of North America (LIUNA) PAC	$11,603,313

Rank	PAC	Contributions to federal candidates and other committees[a]
1	Democracy Engine, Inc., PAC	$28,250,918
2	SEIU COPE (Service Employees International Union Committee on Political Education)	$26,026,821
3	National Rifle Association of America Political Victory Fund	$11,036,600

Table 2-13 *(Continued)*

Rank	PAC	Contributions to federal candidates and other committees[a]
4	Laborers' International Union of North America (LIUNA) PAC	$10,871,200
5	Engineers Political Education Committee (EPEC)/ International Union of Operating Engineers	$10,635,142
6	Jstreet PAC	$9,770,821
7	UAW - V - CAP (UAW Voluntary Community Action Program)	$8,672,852
8	National Association of Realtors Political Action Committee	$7,076,213
9	National Association of Letter Carriers of U.S.A. Political Fund (Letter Carrier Political Fund)	$7,043,750
10	National Air Traffic Controllers Association PAC	$5,938,600
11	Votesane PAC	$5,852,282
12	United Food and Commercial Workers International Union Active Ballot Club	$5,629,708
13	D.R.I.V.E.—Democrat, Republican, Independent Voter Education (The PAC of the International Brotherhood of Teamsters)	$5,539,563
14	Communications Workers of America-COPE Political Contributions Committee	$5,222,523
15	Comcast Corporation & NBC Universal Political Action Committee—Federal	$5,109,000
16	CHC BOLD PAC	$5,079,425
17	International Brotherhood of Electrical Workers Political Action Committee	$4,585,900
18	AT&T Inc./Warnermedia LLC Federal Political Action Committee (AT&T/Warnermedia Federal PAC)	$4,521,000
19	Air Line Pilots Association PAC	$4,504,000
20	Club for Growth PAC	$4,454,519

Note: Amounts in current dollars. Information for earlier years can be found in previous editions of *Vital Statistics on American Politics*.

[a] Includes contributions to candidate committees, other PACs, and party committees.

Source: Federal Election Commission, "PAC Table 4b: Top 50 PACs by Disbursements, January 1, 2019–December 31, 2020" and "PAC Table 4c: Top 50 PACs by Contributions to Candidates and Other Committees, January 1, 2019–December 31, 2020," www.fec.gov.

Table 2-14 PAC Congressional Campaign Contributions, by Type of PAC and Incumbency Status of Candidate, 1999–2020 (millions)

	House							Senate						
	Candidate party		Type of contest					Candidate party		Type of contest				
Election cycle/PAC type	Dem.	Rep.	Incum-bent	Chal-lenger	Open seat[a]	Total		Dem.	Rep.	Incum-bent	Chal-lenger	Open seat[a]	Total
1999–2000													
Corporate	$22.0	$40.0	$54.50	$2.30	$5.30	$62.10		$5.10	$16.90	$16.00	$1.50	$4.60	$22.10
Trade/membership/health	22.3	32.6	45.7	3.4	5.7	55		3.8	9.4	9.3	1.2	2.8	13.3
Labor	39.9	3.5	30.1	8	5.3	43.5		6.2	0.4	2.3	2.8	1.5	6.6
Nonconnected	11.4	15.6	15.0	5.7	6.2	27.1		3	5.5	4.9	1.5	2.2	8.6
Total[b]	98.2	94.7	150.1	19.8	23	193.4		18.7	33.2	33.5	7.1	11.3	51.9
2001–2002													
Corporate	23.6	44.6	59.7	1.6	6.9	68.2		7.0	16.4	15.8	4.3	3.4	23.4
Trade/membership/health	23.0	34.2	47.1	2.1	8	57.2		4.9	9.3	9.5	3.1	1.7	14.3
Labor	39.9	4.3	31.4	5.2	7.7	44.4		7.0	0.5	4.1	2.4	1.1	7.5
Nonconnected	14.0	18.1	18.5	4.8	8.9	32.2		5.8	6.6	6.6	4.1	1.8	12.5
Total[b]	102.6	104.2	160.9	13.8	32	206.9		25.4	33.8	37	14.2	8.1	59.2
2003–2004													
Corporate	24.8	54.3	72.6	1.9	4.6	79.1		8.9	16.3	17.2	1.2	6.7	25.2
Trade/membership/health	23.0	40.1	55.4	2.3	5.4	63.2		5.7	9.3	9.9	1.1	4	15
Labor	37.3	5.4	32.9	5.2	4.6	42.8		6.8	0.8	4.3	0.9	2.3	7.6
Nonconnected	11.4	23.8	21.6	6	7.6	35.2		6.3	8.3	6.9	2.2	5.4	14.6
Total[b]	98.6	126.6	187.1	15.6	22.5	225.4		28.4	35.3	39.3	5.6	18.8	63.7
2005–2006													
Corporate	31.7	64.2	90.0	1.7	4.2	95.9		9.1	17.1	21.9	1.7	2.6	26.2
Trade/membership/health	30.3	49.0	70.2	3.4	5.7	79.3		6.0	9.8	12.1	1.8	2.0	15.8
Labor	42.1	5.5	32.2	10.3	5.1	47.6		5.8	0.5	3.3	2.1	0.9	6.3
Nonconnected	18.2	32.0	31.5	10.5	8.2	50.2		7.1	9.4	9.5	4.3	2.7	16.5
Total[b]	124.9	154.2	229.3	26.2	23.5	279.2		28.6	37.5	47.7	10	8.3	66.1

2007–2008												
Corporate	57.3	54.4	103.2	5.0	3.6	111.7	11.4	21.8	27.4	2.7	3.1	33.3
Trade/membership/health	48.0	40.0	76.0	7.2	4.8	88.0	7.3	12.5	15.2	2.6	2.0	19.8
Labor	49.9	3.9	37.9	11.3	4.6	53.8	6.6	0.5	2.8	3.0	1.2	7.1
Nonconnected	25.3	19.6	27.9	11.6	5.4	44.9	7.8	10	10.9	4.4	2.5	17.8
Total[b]	185.6	122.4	253.5	35.7	18.8	308.1	33.9	45.9	57.7	13.0	9.1	79.8
2009–2010												
Corporate	58.0	55.7	102.1	6.4	5.3	113.7	13.6	23.2	22.6	3.2	11	36.8
Trade/membership/health	45.6	40.8	74.2	6.7	5.5	86.4	8.3	13.1	12.6	2.2	6.6	21.4
Labor	50.8	3.5	46.6	3.7	3.9	54.2	7.1	0.6	2.9	1.4	3.4	7.7
Nonconnected	25.1	24.7	31.8	12.4	5.6	49.8	9.9	10.9	9.6	3.4	7.8	20.8
Total[b]	184.4	129.2	262.8	30	20.7	313.6	39.9	49	48.9	10.4	29.5	88.8
2011–2012												
Corporate	45.1	88.9	125.4	5.0	4.1	134.5	20.9	24.7	34.9	4.4	6.5	45.8
Trade/membership[c]	34.2	62.4	84.8	7.2	4.9	96.9	11.5	12.5	16.8	2.7	4.6	24.2
Labor	44.1	5.2	32.2	11.8	5.4	49.4	7.3	0.5	4.8	1.2	2.1	8.1
Nonconnected	21	29.4	34.1	11.5	4.9	50.6	12.4	9.8	12.3	4.2	5.8	22.3
Total[b]	148.1	192.1	285.4	36.1	19.8	341.3	53.5	48.9	70.7	12.8	19.7	103.2
2013–2014												
Corporate	49.2	89.7	130.7	2.2	6.0	138.9	14.9	24.3	28.5	5.3	5.4	39.1
Trade/membership[c]	36.8	60.7	88.1	2.9	6.5	97.6	8.2	13.5	14.8	3.3	3.6	21.7
Labor	39.3	5.2	35.3	4.3	4.8	44.5	5.8	0.3	4.3	0.5	1.3	6.2
Nonconnected	19.6	30.8	35.3	7.9	7.3	50.4	12.1	13.5	14.9	5.5	5.3	25.6
Total[b]	149.3	192.3	298.9	17.6	25.1	341.6	41.8	52.5	63.6	14.8	15.9	94.3
2015–2016												
Corporate	49.3	94.0	138.0	1.3	4.0	143.3	8.9	28.4	32.3	1.0	4.0	37.3
Trade/membership[c]	35.6	64.0	92.1	2.6	4.9	99.6	5.9	16.2	18.0	1.4	2.7	22.1
Labor	34.8	6.0	30.5	6.3	3.9	40.8	4.9	0.6	1.7	2.6	1.3	5.5
Nonconnected	21.2	33.4	40.6	7.2	6.8	54.5	9.2	13.9	15.0	4.3	3.8	23.1
Total[b]	140.8	197.4	301.2	17.5	19.6	338.2	28.9	59.2	67.1	9.3	11.8	88.1

(Table continues)

Table 2-14 (Continued)

	House							Senate						
	Candidate party		Type of contest					Candidate party		Type of contest				
Election cycle/PAC type	Dem.	Rep.	Incumbent	Challenger	Open seat[a]	Total		Dem.	Rep.	Incumbent	Challenger	Open seat[a]	Total
2017–2018													
Corporate	52.3	95.6	142.3	0.8	4.9	147.9		16.6	12.7	23.4	3.2	2.8	29.4
Trade/membership[c]	37.5	63.7	92.5	2.4	6.2	101.2		10.1	8.4	13.6	2.9	2.0	18.5
Labor	39.8	7.3	33.3	7.5	6.4	47.1		5.9	0.4	5.0	0.6	0.7	6.4
Nonconnected	33.6	41.9	50.1	13.5	12.0	75.6		14.2	10.2	16.0	5.2	3.3	24.5
Total[b]	163.3	208.5	318.2	24.1	29.5	371.8		46.8	31.8	57.9	11.9	8.8	78.7
2019–2020													
Corporate	63.5	69.3	128.6	1.7	2.5	132.8		7.3	25.5	30.3	0.8	1.7	32.8
Trade/membership[c]	48.0	49.4	89.2	4.0	4.2	97.4		5.0	14.6	16.7	1.2	1.6	19.5
Labor	40.9	5.6	39.7	4.4	2.4	46.5		4.4	0.6	2.6	2.0	0.4	5.0
Nonconnected	38.2	35.9	51.4	15.3	7.4	74.0		11.6	15.0	18.1	6.4	2.2	26.6
Total[b]	190.6	160.1	308.9	25.3	16.5	350.7		28.3	55.6	67.6	10.4	5.9	84.0

Note: Amounts are current dollar amounts contributed during the two-year election cycle indicated to all candidates in primary, general, runoff, and special elections. Figures are for all House and Senate candidates, not just those up for election in the two-year cycle. Data for earlier years can be found in previous editions of *Vital Statistics on American Politics*.

[a] "Open seat" refers to candidates in elections in which an incumbent did not seek reelection.
[b] Includes PACs classified by the Federal Election Commission as cooperatives and corporations without stock.
[c] As of July 2011, health organizations are no longer an organization type but are included in either the trade or membership category.

Sources: Federal Election Commission, "PAC Contributions to Candidates 1996 through 2010 Election Cycles," "PAC Table 2: PAC Contributions to Candidates, January 1, 2011–December 31, 2012," "PAC Table 2: PAC Contributions to Candidates, January 1, 2013 through December 31, 2014," "PAC Table 2: PAC Contributions to Candidates, January 1, 2015 through December 31, 2016," "PAC Table 2: PAC Contributions to Candidates, January 1, 2017 through December 31, 2018," "PAC Table 2: PAC Contributions to Candidates, January 1, 2019 through December 31, 2020." 2013–2020 sources available at www.fec.gov.

A Data Literacy Lesson

The Incumbency Advantage and Campaign Finance

As an institution, the U.S. Congress is wildly unpopular.[1] And yet, as Tables 1-18 and 1-19 show, members of Congress manage to get reelected at shockingly high rates. There are many familiar explanations for this "incumbency advantage." For example, gerrymandering sometimes is done in a way that protects incumbent members of Congress. Additionally, members of Congress have many resources at their disposal to advertise their name or perform constituent services for their voters that help them buck the institutional unpopularity. In the end, as political scientist Richard Fenno argued long ago, it may well be that people hate Congress, but actually like their own individual member.

One other source of the incumbency advantage is campaign finance. Take a look at Table 2-14, particularly the columns labeled "Type of Contest." Here, we see the distribution of money based upon whether the candidate is an incumbent, a challenger seeking to defeat the incumbent, or a candidate for an open seat (i.e., where there is no incumbent). From 2019–2020, for example, $308.9 million of the $350.7 million spent by political action committees on House elections went to incumbents. (For the Senate, it was $67.6 million out of $84 million.) If Congress is so unpopular, why do so many political action committees give so much money to return incumbents to office?

Understanding this might require us to reorient ourselves around this topic. It is a common belief—perhaps a misconception—that members of Congress "follow the money"; that is, they vote whichever way their donors want them to vote. This belief does not come from nowhere; we can all point to examples of this unsavory behavior occurring. And yet, we should be a little bit skeptical about this supposition. While quantitative data are hard to come by on this question, it seems fair to posit that the vast majority of people running for office would not be willing to abandon long-held positions for the possibility of gaining a little bit of extra campaign money (especially when the identity of donors is publicly available on the Federal Election Commission website at www.fec.gov). While some mercenaries may exist in Congress, we believe the vast majority of members are devoted to advocating for their deepest beliefs, not selling them out for a campaign donation. (We hope we're right.)

Instead of believing that votes follow money, it might be useful to reverse the causal arrow—money might follow votes. Imagine a political action committee is drawing up their list of who to support. They can use multiple strategies. On the one hand, they can donate to members of Congress who have opposed them, in an attempt to change their mind. On the other hand, they could restrict their giving to those who have supported them, hoping to keep them in office. The latter strategy strikes us as far more sensible, in light of what we argue above.

There is, however, a second level to the decision, one that more directly connects to Table 2-14. PACs could choose to support members who are already in office (incumbents) and have been supportive of them, or they could choose to support candidates who are challenging members who have opposed their PAC. While the latter is more satisfying (how cool would it be to orchestrate the defeat of a political opponent?!), such a strategy is not as cost-effective. For the reasons noted above, it is hard to defeat an incumbent member of Congress. Most political action committees, then, tend to concentrate their donations on reelecting their supporters, rather than defeating or converting their opponents.[2]

When looking at data, we often like to see relationships where the direction is clear. In this case, such clarity eludes us. Incumbents get more money because they are more likely to win their elections; moreover, incumbents are more likely to win because they get more money. Table 2-14 tells us that PACs prefer to give to incumbents; in doing so, the PACs are both responding to the fact that incumbents are more likely to win, and creating that fact. More sophisticated data analysis could help unpack this relationship somewhat, but it cannot obscure the fact that these complexities exist, and have real-world implications.

---

[1] For a fun story about some unpleasant things that get even higher polling numbers than Congress, see https://www.washingtonpost.com/news/wonk/wp/2013/01/10/graph-of-the-day-congress-is-less-popular-than-lice-colonoscopies-and-nickelback.

[2] Open-seat elections provide opportunities to elect new friends without dealing with the incumbency advantage, and hence tend to attract large amounts of donations. Because there are so few of these elections, the amount of money spent on open-seat elections appears relatively small in the table.

3
Public Opinion and Voting

- **Partisanship**
- **Ideology**
- **Voting by Groups**
- **Presidential and Congressional Approval**
- **Confidence in Government and the Economy**
- **Most Important Problem**
- **Specific Issues**

Public opinion is one of the most studied areas within political science; everywhere you look, it seems you can find a public opinion poll on one issue or another. Polling may be done to give us a sense of who is winning and who is losing in an election; websites like realclearpolitics.com or fivethirtyeight.com not only present these polls, but also aggregate survey results to provide a meta-analysis of the data. Polling can also be done around specific issues, to help us understand how the public feels about policy matters and about potential changes in public policy. Surveys may also be used by political actors in an attempt to "educate" the public and bring the electorate around to their views on policies. This chapter explores the world of public opinion surveys to represent public opinion on issues that are broad, such as the government and the economy, and on those that are more specific, such as gun control and the death penalty.

This chapter also includes tables and figures that reveal how specific groups of voters cast their ballots in elections, both presidential and congressional. Chapter 1 presented overall election results, indicating which party or individual won an election, whereas this chapter shows votes by region, gender, race, religion, and so on, as well as for groups of ideologues, such as liberals and conservatives, partisan groups, and sometimes special groups such as first-time voters. The dividing line we use is that Chapter 1 focused on actual election outcomes, while this chapter focuses on data that come from sample surveys and indicate group opinions rather than overall election outcomes.

Figures 3-1 through 3-4 and Tables 3-1 through 3-3 cover two of the most frequently cited components of public opinion—partisanship and political ideology. These characteristics merit emphasis because of their practical political significance—knowing whether someone is a Democrat or Republican, or a liberal or conservative, provides a great deal of information. These data are of interest not only to analysts who wish to understand scientifically why people behave as they do, but also to those who assess long-term political and social trends, as well as those who track day-to-day politics.

From another perspective, these results are important because they illustrate the reliability and validity of public opinion polling, as well as the hazards of gauging personal opinion. Figures 3-1 and 3-2, showing self-proclaimed party identification, are reasonably similar for the period they jointly cover; each, however, is derived from different surveys done by separate polling organizations. The similarity of the results should boost our confidence in the whole enterprise of public opinion polling, for two reasons. First, these data are based on polling as few as fifteen hundred people and using them as a window to the opinion of the entire population. Since both organizations, as well as many others, take great care in how they use scientific survey procedures, we should not be surprised (but should be pleased!) that they end up with similar results. Moreover, this example shows that poll results are not completely dependent on exact question wording. The Pew question (Figure 3-2) focuses on the immediate situation ("In politics today . . . "), while the American National Election Studies question (Table 3-1) is broader ("Generally speaking . . . "), suggesting that the Pew question might pick up more short-term fluctuations in partisanship. Yet the results are quite similar.

Both the American National Election Studies and Pew surveys probe those who claim to be independents to determine whether they lean toward one party or the other. The responses to this question, as well as other evidence (see Table 3-4) raise the question of whether independents are really closet partisans (we include an essay here that addresses this point). How that question is answered, as the contrast between the two plots in Figures 3-1 and 3-2 shows, has major implications for conclusions about the relative strengths of the parties. As emphasized in earlier introductions, even simple data descriptions involve interpretation.

One challenge with doing surveys is "sampling error," which arises because surveys are not exact counts of the whole population. The potential for sampling error suggests that any polling result we get will likely be accurate, plus or minus a certain percentage. That percentage is based on sample size and, in high quality surveys, is usually around plus or minus 3 percent. If we could increase the size of the sample, even to the point of surveying every American adult simultaneously to ask whether they are a Democrat, an independent, or a Republican, we would eliminate sampling error. We would, however, still end up having to ask what the results mean—for instance, as noted above, what does it mean to be an independent? (And, needless to say, surveys with such large pools of respondents are prohibitively expensive.)

We can illustrate a similar point when we examine the "don't know" responses to the ideology question about liberal or conservative self-identification in Table 3-3. Results in this, and other, public opinion tables illustrate a similar point. Whether pollsters ask about a general position or a specific issue, some proportion of the sample—often as much as 15 percent and sometimes even more—responds "I don't know." It is not immediately apparent how to interpret such responses. Some people have information about the subject matter but no opinion; some have no information and no opinion; and a few have no information but have an opinion anyway. The pollster's decision about how to treat such responses can make a large difference. For example, in a preelection poll, we might assume that respondents who have not yet chosen candidates to support will eventually act in one of four ways. They may split votes between candidates in similar proportions as those who have already decided, stay home and not vote, divide themselves evenly between the candidates, or overwhelmingly support another candidate. Assessing the likelihood of each of these options is important if we hope to understand the public's sentiments.

Public officials who seek guidance on public sentiment have another challenge—understanding intensity. Consider, for example, gun control. Majorities of Americans—at times approaching two-thirds—thought it was more important to "control gun ownership" than to "protect the right to own guns," according to polls between 1993 and 2008 (Table 3-15). If that is true, why were more stringent gun control laws not enacted? The answer has to do, in part, with intensity of those who oppose-gun control, and with how well-organized and well-funded they were. Those supporting Second Amendment rights have historically been much better organized and have outspent those who would restrict gun ownership, presumably because gun advocates have traditionally felt more strongly about the issue. Understanding the importance of public opinion in politics requires more than a simple nose count. The salience of an opinion to the person holding it also counts. This may account for why much of the work of the gun control lobby concerns trying to increase the intensity of feeling on the part of supporters, and getting them to make this one of the issues on which they vote, and donate money.

Another factor in polling is that a particular survey result usually says little in isolation. Our most solid interpretations depend on several surveys stretching over time, often over a period of years. When patterns recur across different years, this lets us speak with confidence about a public mood rather than a potential blip in the long-term trend. Consider the decline and partial recovery in public confidence in government (Figure 3-8). The confidence level at a particular time is one data point, often difficult to interpret. Yet when that point is viewed with comparable points from similar surveys over the years, now we may be able to identify a trend, be it a decline, upsurge, or consistency. Reports of public opinion increasingly emphasize extended time series, as is done here (Figures 3-15, 3-16, and 3-17, and Tables 3-11 through 3-18). Such time series data can be usefully supplemented by cross sections (Table 3-2). Such within-survey contrasts convey whether and how groups differ in attitudes. Where long time series are impossible because of the nature of the event—such as the U.S. military actions in Iraq (Figure 3-17) and the war on terrorism (Table 3-19)—comparison of multiple time series can aid interpretation.

The issues most salient in the public's mind vary across time. This fact itself has been measured by asking people what they regard as the nation's most important problem, as is done in Table 3-11. Yet many issues are of perennial interest, and over-time assessments (which sometimes require the use of earlier editions of this volume) often date back to the 1940s (Tables 3-12 and 3-17). From the point of view of elections, the significance of public opinion lies chiefly in how the public translates its feelings into summary judgments of the president (Figure 3-6), Congress (Figure 3-7), and government and society as a whole (Figures 3-8 and 3-9). Yet another set of data consists of favorable versus unfavorable opinions of the two parties (Figure 3-10). Finally, public satisfaction with the status quo and evaluations of the economy, both personal and national, and present and future, are perennial concerns in politics (Figure 3-9).

The most direct and important judgments about political leaders, candidates, and parties occur in elections, but election results tell us only the overall results (and outcomes in different geographical areas). Surveys are the prime means of looking into the behavior of individuals and groups. This chapter reveals how various kinds of individuals voted for president, both in the general election (Table 3-5) in presidential primaries (Tables 3-6 and 3-7), and for Congress (Table 3-8). These data also answer questions of great theoretical and practical interest, such as the extent to which individuals vote in accordance with their general party preference and in straight or split tickets (Tables 3-4, 3-9, and 3-10).

Table 3-1 Partisan Identification, American National Election Studies, 1952–2020 (percent)

	Democrat				Republican				
Year	Strong	Weak	Independent	Independent	Independent	Weak	Strong	Total[a]	Number of interviews
1952	23	26	10	5	8	14	14	100	1,689
1954	23	26	9	8	6	15	13	100	1,088
1956	22	24	7	9	9	15	16	102	1,690
1958	28	23	7	8	5	17	12	100	1,737
1960	21	26	6	10	7	14	16	100	1,864
1962	24	24	8	8	6	17	13	100	1,237
1964	27	25	9	8	6	14	11	100	1,536
1966	18	28	9	12	7	15	10	99	1,263
1968	20	26	10	11	9	15	10	101	1,531
1970	20	24	10	13	8	15	9	99	1,490
1972	15	25	11	15	10	13	10	99	2,695
1974	18	21	13	18	9	14	8	101	2,492
1976	15	25	12	16	10	14	9	101	2,833
1978	15	24	14	16	10	13	8	100	2,269
1980	18	23	11	15	10	14	9	100	1,612
1982	20	24	11	13	8	14	10	100	1,403
1984	17	20	11	13	12	15	12	100	2,228
1986	18	22	10	14	11	15	11	101	2,157
1988	18	18	12	12	13	14	14	101	2,026
1990	20	19	12	12	12	15	10	100	1,965
1992	18	17	14	13	12	14	11	99	2,473
1994	15	18	13	11	12	15	15	99	1,780
1996	18	19	14	10	12	15	12	100	1,706
1998	19	18	14	12	11	16	10	100	1,267
2000	19	15	15	13	13	12	12	99	1,790
2002	17	17	16	7	13	16	15	101	1,466
2004	17	16	17	10	12	12	16	100	1,194
2008	19	15	17	11	12	13	13	100	2,293
2012	20	15	12	14	12	12	15	100	5,892
2016	21	13	12	14	12	12	17	101	4,270
2020	24	11	12	12	11	10	21	101	8,280

Note: Question: "Generally speaking, do you consider yourself a Republican, a Democrat, an Independent, or what?" If Republican or Democrat: "Would you call yourself a strong (R/D) or a not very strong (R/D)?" If Independent or other: "Do you think of yourself as closer to the Republican or Democratic party?" Regarding the data: "The percentages above for the 7-category party identification variable reflect the following: 1) the apolitical category is eliminated, 2) respondents who fail or refuse to say whether they are a 'strong' partisan are not imputed to be a 'weak' partisan, ... 3) respondents who identify as members of other parties are coded as missing from the Democrat-Independent-Republican scale." For further consideration, see "Clarification of 'apolitical' codes in the party identification summary variable on ANES datasets," December 8, 2009, www.electionstudies.org. There was no update of the American National Election Studies series in 2006, 2010, 2014, and 2018. Data from 2016 and 2020 are from the preelection wave of the survey.

[a] Totals may not add to 100 due to rounding.

Source: American National Election Studies data, University of Michigan, Ann Arbor, Mich., and Stanford University, Palo Alto, Calif., www.electionstudies.org.

Figure 3-1 Partisan Identification, American National Election Studies, 1952–2020

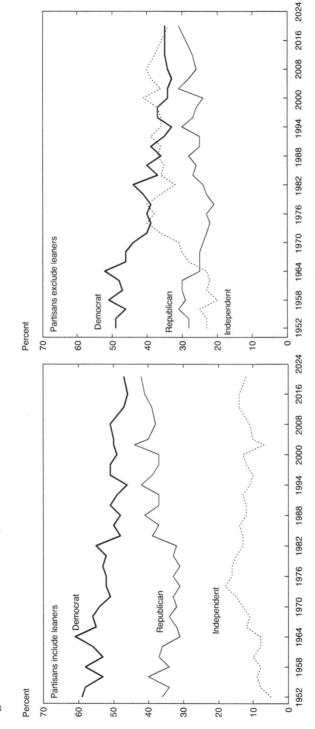

Note: See Table 3-1, this volume, for question. "Leaners" are independents who consider themselves closer to one party. There was no update of the American National Election Studies series in 2006, 2010, and 2014.

Source: American National Election Studies data, University of Michigan, Ann Arbor, Mich., and Stanford University, Palo Alto, Calif., www.electionstudies.org.

Figure 3-2 Partisan Identification, Pew Surveys, 1987–2019

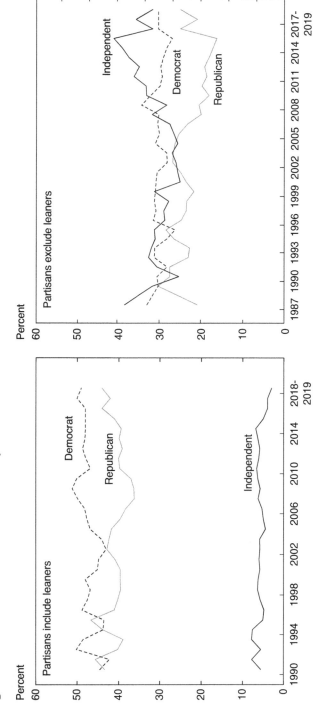

Note: Question: "In politics today, do you consider yourself a Republican, Democrat, or Independent?" If answered other than Republican or Democrat: "As of today do you lean more to the Republican Party or more to the Democratic Party?" Related data for additional years can be found in previous editions of *Vital Statistics on American Politics*.

Source: Pew Research Center, "In Changing U.S. Electorate, Race and Education Remain Stark Dividing Lines," June 2, 2020; "Wide Gender Gap, Growing Educational Divide in Voters' Party Identification," March 20, 2018; "2016 Party Identification Detailed Tables," September 13, 2016, https://www.pewresearch.org.

Table 3-2 Partisan Identification, by Groups, 2012–2020 (percent)

	2012				2016				2020			
	Dem.	Ind.	Rep.	Democratic advantage	Dem.	Ind.	Rep.	Democratic advantage	Dem.	Ind.	Rep.	Democratic advantage
Sex												
Men	43	9	48	−5	41	8	51	−10	42	8	50	−8
Women	52	8	39	13	54	8	38	16	56	6	38	18
Age												
18–29 years	55	9	36	19	—	—	—	—	—	—	—	—
30–49 years	47	8	45	2	—	—	—	—	—	—	—	—
50–64 years	48	8	43	5	—	—	—	—	—	—	—	—
65 years and over	45	7	48	−3	—	—	—	—	—	—	—	—
Generation[a]												
Millennial	—	—	—	—	57	7	36	21	54	8	38	26
Generation X	—	—	—	—	48	9	42	6	48	7	45	3
Baby Boomer	—	—	—	—	45	6	49	−4	46	7	47	−1
Silent Generation	—	—	—	—	40	7	53	−13	48	5	49	−1
Race and ethnicity												
White	40	8	52	−12	39	7	54	−15	42	5	53	−11
All others	73	8	20	53	70	8	22	48	69	7	24	45
Black	87	5	8	79	87	6	7	80	83	7	10	73
Hispanic	61	10	29	32	63	10	27	36	63	8	29	34
Region[b]												
Northeast	54	9	37	17	54	7	39	15	—	—	—	—
Midwest	47	9	43	4	45	8	47	−2	—	—	—	—
South	45	8	47	−2	45	8	48	−3	—	—	—	—
West	49	9	43	6	52	8	40	12	—	—	—	—
Education												

High school graduate[c]	—	—	—	—	46[c]	8[c]	45[c]	1	44[c]	8[c]	48[c]	-4
Some college	46	8	46	0	45	9	46	-1	46	8	46	0
College graduate	48	7	45	3	50	6	44	6	53	7	40	13
Postgraduate	54	7	39	15	55	6	39	15	61	6	33	28
Income												
<$20,000[d]	57	11	32	25	60[d]	8[d]	32[d]	28	—	—	—	—
$20,000–29,999	54	9	37	17	—	—	47	-1	—	—	—	—
$30,000–49,999	49	7	44	5	46	7	49	-5	—	—	—	—
$50,000–74,999	46	7	46	0	44	6	48	-4	—	—	—	—
$75,000–99,999	46	7	46	0	44	8	48	-4	—	—	—	—
$100,000+	45	5	49	-4	46	5	49	-3	—	—	—	—
Community type												
Urban	57	8	35	22	60	7	33	27	62	7	31	31
Suburban	46	8	46	0	44	7	48	-4	46	7	47	-1
Rural	40	9	51	-11	37	8	55	-18	35	7	58	-23
Religious preference												
White, evangelical Protestant	22	7	71	-49	20	4	76	-56	17	5	78	-61
White, mainline Protestant	40	8	52	-12	37	8	55	18	39	7	54	-15
White, non-Hispanic Catholic	41	8	50	-9	37	6	58	21	38	5	57	-19
Marital status												
Married	42	8	50	-8	44	6	51	7	—	—	—	—
Unmarried	—	—	—	—	56	8	36	20	—	—	—	—
Divorced/separated	54	11	35	19	—	—	—	—	—	—	—	—
Widowed	48	9	44	4	—	—	—	—	—	—	—	—
Never married	58	9	33	25	—	—	—	—	—	—	—	—
Living with partner	62	9	29	33	—	—	—	—	—	—	—	—

Note: "—" indicates not available. For 2012, the percentages are from 13,429 registered voters interviewed from January through July of 2012. Not all characteristics were available in each of the pooled surveys, making sample sizes vary. A Democratic gain is not always matched precisely by a Republican loss, or vice versa. Related data for additional years can be found in previous editions of *Vital Statistics on American Politics*. For partisan identification question, see Figure 3-2, this volume. Percentages in the table count leaners as partisans.

[a] These data are reported by generation for 2016 and 2020. The top line is Millennials (ages 18–35 in 2016), the second line is Generation X (ages 36–51), the third line are Baby Boomers (ages 52–70), and the bottom line is the Silent Generation (ages 71–88).
[b] For composition of regions, see Table A-1, this volume.
[c] For 2016 and 2020, refers to high school graduate or less.
[d] For 2016, refers to incomes below $30,000

Sources: 2012: Pew Research Center"A Closer Look at the Parties in 2012," August 23, 2012, 6–7; "The Parties on the Eve of the 2016 Election: Two Coalitions, Moving Further Apart," September 13, 2016; "In Changing U.S. Electorate, Race and Education Remain Stark Dividing Lines," June 2, 2020, https://www.pewresearch.org.

Table 3-3 Liberal or Conservative Self-Identification, 1973–2018 (percent)

Year	Extremely liberal	Liberal	Slightly liberal	Moderate	Slightly conservative	Conservative	Extremely conservative	Don't know	Number of interviews
1973	4	14	13	36	13	13	3	6	1,484
1975	3	12	13	38	16	11	2	5	1,478
1978	2	9	16	37	18	13	2	4	1,509
1980	3	8	14	40	19	12	3	1	1,451
1983	2	8	12	40	18	13	2	3	802
1985	2	11	11	37	18	14	3	4	1,526
1986	2	9	11	39	17	15	3	4	1,468
1987	2	12	13	37	16	12	2	4	1,436
1988	2	12	12	35	17	16	2	4	1,472
1989	3	12	12	37	16	13	2	5	1,532
1990	3	10	13	34	18	14	4	4	1,369
1991	2	10	14	39	14	14	3	3	1,512
1993	2	12	13	35	17	16	3	3	1,598
1994	2	11	13	35	16	16	3	3	2,981
1996	2	10	12	36	16	16	3	5	2,898
1998	2	12	12	36	15	15	3	5	2,824
2000	4	11	10	38	14	15	3	5	2,797
2002	3	11	12	38	15	16	3	3	1,362
2004	3	9	12	37	16	17	4	2	1,325
2006	3	11	11	37	14	15	4	3	1,323
2008	3	12	11	37	14	16	4	4	2,010
2010	4	13	12	37	13	16	4	3	3,752
2012	4	12	11	36	14	15	3	4	1,961
2014	4	12	10	39	13	14	4	3	2,514
2016	5	12	11	36	13	15	4	3	2,867
2018	5	12	11	36	12	15	4	3	2,348

Note: General Social Survey interviews are conducted in the spring of the year indicated, usually March–June. Question: "We hear a lot of talk these days about liberals and conservatives. I'm going to show you a seven-point scale on which the political views that people might hold are arranged from extremely liberal—point 1—to extremely conservative—point 7. Where would you place yourself on this scale?" Data for additional years can be found in previous editions of *Vital Statistics on American Politics*.

Source: General Social Survey, National Opinion Research Center, University of Chicago.

Figure 3-3 Liberal, Moderate, and Conservative Self-Identification, 1973–2018

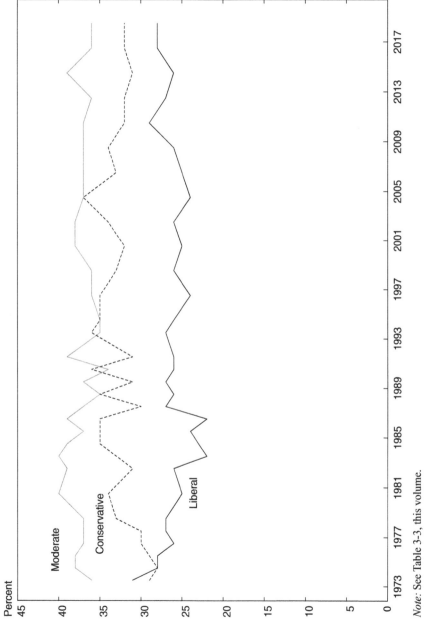

Note: See Table 3-3, this volume.

Source: Table 3-3, this volume.

Figure 3-4 Ideological Self-Identification of College Freshmen, 1970–2019

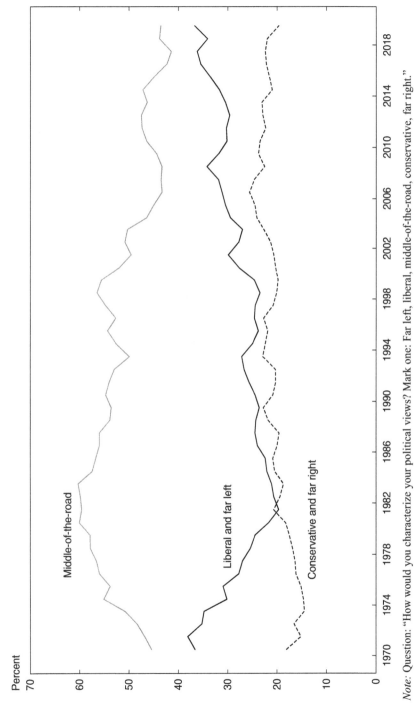

Note: Question: "How would you characterize your political views? Mark one: Far left, liberal, middle-of-the-road, conservative, far right."

Sources: Alexander Astin et al., *The American Freshman: Thirty Year Trends* (Los Angeles: Higher Education Research Institute, University of California, Los Angeles, 1997); *The American Freshman: National Norms for Fall 1997–* (Los Angeles: Higher Education Research Institute, University of California, Los Angeles, annual).

Table 3-4 Strength of Party Identification and the Presidential Vote, 1952–2020 (percent)

Year/candidate	Strong Democrat	Weak Democrat	Independent Democrat	Independent	Independent Republican	Weak Republican	Strong Republican	Total
1952								
Stevenson (D)	84	62	61	20	7	6	2	42
Eisenhower (R)	16	38	39	80	93	94	98	58
1956								
Stevenson (D)	85	63	67	17	6	7	0	40
Eisenhower (R)	15	37	33	83	94	93	100	60
1960								
Kennedy (D)	91	72	90	46	12	13	2	49
Nixon (R)	9	28	10	54	88	87	98	51
1964								
L. Johnson (D)	95	82	90	77	25	43	10	68
Goldwater (R)	5	18	10	23	75	57	90	32
1968								
Humphrey (D)	92	68	64	30	5	11	3	46
Nixon (R)	8	32	36	70	95	89	97	54
1972								
McGovern (D)	73	48	61	30	13	9	3	36
Nixon (R)	27	52	39	70	87	91	97	64
1976								
Carter (D)	92	75	76	44	14	22	3	51
Ford (R)	8	25	24	56	86	78	97	49
1980								
Carter (D)	89	65	60	26	13	5	5	44
Reagan (R)	11	35	40	74	87	95	95	56
1984								
Mondale (D)	89	68	79	28	7	6	3	42
Reagan (R)	11	32	21	72	93	94	97	58
1988								
Dukakis (D)	94	72	88	35	15	17	2	47
G. H. W. Bush (R)	6	28	12	65	85	83	98	53

1992								
Clinton (D)	97	84	92	65	15	20	2	58
G. H. W. Bush (R)	3	16	8	35	85	80	98	42
1996								
Clinton (D)	98	91	93	49	23	23	5	58
Dole (R)	2	9	7	51	77	77	95	42
2000								
Gore (D)	97	85	78	45	14	16	2	52
G. W. Bush (R)	3	15	22	55	86	84	98	48
2004								
Kerry (D)	98	85	88	58	15	11	3	50
G. W. Bush (R)	2	15	12	42	85	89	97	50
2008								
Obama (D)	95	86	91	57	18	12	4	55
McCain (R)	5	14	9	43	82	88	96	45
2012								
Obama (D)	99	85	91	54	9	12	3	54
Romney (R)	1	15	9	46	91	88	97	46
2016								
Clinton (D)	98	83	91	42	9	18	2	52
Trump (R)	2	17	9	58	91	82	98	48
2020								
Biden (D)	98	92	98	63	17	23	3	57
Trump (R)	2	8	2	37	83	77	97	43

Note: "D" indicates Democrat; "R" indicates Republican. Results are from surveys in which voters are asked with which party they identify and for whom they voted. For the party identification questions, see Table 3-1, this volume. Votes for candidates other than Democratic or Republican were excluded.

Source: American National Election Studies data, University of Michigan, Ann Arbor, Mich., and Stanford University, Palo Alto, Calif., www.electionstudies.org.

A Data Literacy Lesson

Independent Leaners and the Measure of Partisanship

Political party identification has long been a topic of interest to political scientists. In a complex world, in which multiple issues and candidates compete for our attention, political party labels provide a useful organizing framework for summarizing lots of information. As just one example, if I told you that Mary was a Republican and Barbara was a Democrat, you would be able to form highly educated guesses about where they stood on the issues. Who is pro-choice? Who is on good terms with the National Rifle Association? Party identification would be enough to answer these questions, with a high degree of certainty. Armed with nothing more than their party identification, most of us would know exactly who they were voting for.

The traditional way we measure party identification is with a seven-point scale, as reflected in Table 3-1. (See the note about the questions used in operationalizing this concept.) After asking someone if they are a Democrat, Republican, or Independent, we ask the partisans if they are strong or weak Democrats (or Republicans) and ask the independents if they are closer to the Republicans (or Democrats), or neither. Those who are closer to one party are said to lean that way (and hence are often called "independent leaners") while those who are closer to neither party are often called "pure Independents."

We might anticipate the steps in the seven-point scale are on what is called an "interval" scale—the steps between each increment on the scale are equidistant from one another. If you believe this to be the case, you're incorrect on this particular measurement. If we look at the last four elections reported on in Table 3-4, we see an interesting pattern. Strong partisans are most likely to vote for their own party, although not unanimously. (We've not met any of the 3 percent of strong Republicans who voted for Joe Biden or Barack Obama, but the table tells us they're out there.) Weak partisans are actually slightly *more* likely to defect than are the independent leaners, although this pattern is not terribly strong. But what becomes clear from this table is that, in recent years, those who identify as independent leaners are, simply speaking, partisans.

This has significant implications for understanding the concept of partisanship. We imagine that many of you have encountered voters who claim to be independent ("I don't vote for any party. I look at each election and choose the best candidate, regardless of party!") and yet *always* vote for the same party. Some societal value, it seems, is attached to claiming to be independent, unencumbered by a tie to a particular party, even if their behavior is overwhelmingly partisan. This is a reminder that while firmly identifying with a political party is a point of pride and identity to some highly engaged political people, *not doing so* is equally important to others.

This finding is also important for thinking about electoral strategy. Table 3-1, and Figures 3-1 and 3-2, might suggest to the uninitiated that there are very large numbers of independent voters out there, not tied to any political party. These voters, the strategist might conclude, are up for grabs in the campaign. Table 3-4, however, reminds us that most of these voters are not really up for grabs. If approximately one-third of the Independents lean Democratic, one-third of them lean Republican, and one-third are pure independents, the number of Independents who are in play is much less than we might think. If elections are being fought over the undecideds, it seems there are fewer than we might have expected.

A scale like the seven-point scale for party identification might imply to use that it is an interval scale, and that the independent leaners might be expected to behave "halfway between" weak partisans and pure independents. That they clearly do not has implications for how we think about this measurement technique, and how we think about campaign strategies.

Figure 3-5 Presidential Preferences during 2020

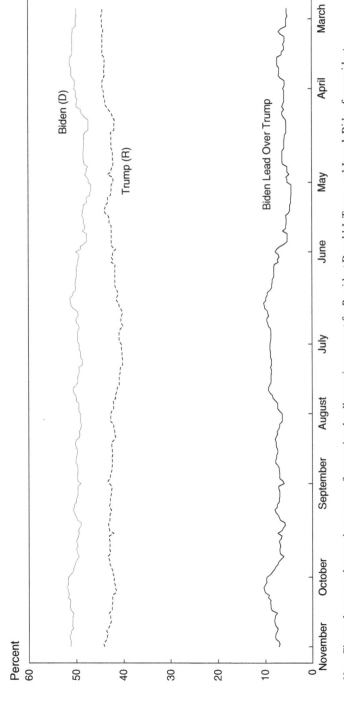

Note: Figure shows ten-day moving average from national polls gauging support for President Donald J. Trump and Joseph Biden for president.

Source: Real Clear Politics, www.realclearpolitics.com.

Table 3-5 Presidential Vote in General Elections, by Groups, Network Exit Polls, 2004–2020 (percent)

	Percentage of voters					2004		2008		2012		2016		2020	
	2004	2008	2012	2016	2020	D	R	D	R	D	R	D	R	D	R
Sex															
Men	46	47	47	47	48	44	55	49	48	45	52	41	52	45	53
Women	54	53	53	53	52	51	48	56	43	55	44	54	41	57	42
Race/ethnicity															
White	77	74	72	71	67	41	58	43	55	39	59	37	57	41	58
Black	11	13	13	12	13	88	11	95	4	93	6	89	8	87	12
Hispanic/Latino	8	9	10	11	13	53	44	67	31	71	27	66	28	65	32
Age															
Younger than 30 years	17	18	19	19	17	54	45	66	32	60	37	55	36	60	36
30–44 years	29	29	27	25	23	46	53	52	46	52	45	51	41	52	46
45–64 years	30[a]	37	38	40	38	48[a]	51[a]	50	49	47	51	44	52	49	50
65 years and older	24[b]	16	16	16	22	46[b]	54[b]	45	53	44	56	45	52	47	52
Education															
Not high school graduate	4	4	3	—	—	50	49	63	35	64	35	—	—	—	—
High school graduate	22	20	21	18[c]	19[d]	47	52	52	46	51	48	46[c]	51[c]	46[d]	54[d]
College incomplete	32	31	29	32	39[e]	46	54	51	47	49	48	43	51	49[e]	48[e]
College graduate	42	45	47	32	27	49	49	53	45	50	48	49	44	51	47
Postgraduate	—	—	—	18	15	—	—	—	—	—	—	58	37	62	37
Religion															
White Protestant	41	42	39	—	—	32	67	34	65	30	69	—	—	—	—
White fundamentalist	23	26	26	—	—	21	78	24	74	21	78	—	—	—	—
Catholic	27	27	25	23	25	47	52	54	45	50	48	46	50	52	47
Jewish	3	2	2	3	2	74	25	78	21	69	30	71	23	—	—
Region															
East	22	21[f]	—	—	20	56	43	59[f]	40[f]	—	—	—	—	58	41
Midwest	26	24	—	—	23	48	51	54	44	—	—	—	—	47	51
South	32	32	—	—	35	42	58	45	54	—	—	—	—	46	53
West	20	23	—	—	22	50	49	57	40	—	—	—	—	57	41

(Table continues)

137

Table 3-5 *(Continued)*

	Percentage of voters					2004		2008		2012		2016		2020	
	2004	2008	2012	2016	2020	D	R	D	R	D	R	D	R	D	R
Union household	24	21	18	18	20	59	40	59	39	58	40	51	42	56	40
Family income															
Under $15,000	8	6	—	—	—	63	36	73	25	—	—	—	—	—	—
$15,000–29,999	15	12	20[g]	17[g]	15[g]	57	42	60	37	63[g]	35[g]	53[g]	40[g]	54[g]	46[g]
$30,000–49,999	22	19	21	19	20	50	49	55	43	57	42	52	41	56	43
$50,000–74,999	23	21	31[h]	30[h]	39[h]	43	56	48	49	46[h]	52[h]	46[h]	49[h]	57[h]	42[h]
Over $75,000	32	41	28[i]	34[i]	26[i]	43	57	50	49	44[i]	54[i]	47[i]	47[i]	42[i]	54[i]
Party															
Democratic	37	39	38	36	37	89	11	89	10	92	7	89	8	94	6
Independent	26	29	29	31	26	49	48	52	44	45	50	42	46	54	41
Republican	37	32	32	33	36	6	93	9	90	6	93	8	88	6	94
Ideology															
Liberal	21	22	25	26	24	85	13	89	10	86	11	84	10	89	64
Moderate	45	44	41	39	38	54	45	60	39	56	41	52	40	64	34
Conservative	34	34	35	35	38	15	84	20	78	17	82	16	81	14	85
Previous presidential vote															
Democratic	37	37	—	—	40	90	10	89	9	—	—	—	—	95	4
Independent/third party	3	4	—	—	5	71	21	66	24	—	—	—	—	60	25
Republican	43	46	—	—	43	9	91	17	82	—	—	—	—	7	92
Congressional vote															
Democratic	49	54	50	49	51	88	11	88	10	93	6	90	5	95	4
Republican	50	44	48	50	48	9	91	9	89	7	92	8	87	4	95
First-time voter	11	11	—	10	14	53	46	69	30	—	—	57	38	64	32
Total	100	100	100	100	100	48	51	53	45	50	48	48	46	51	47

Note: "D" indicates Democrat; "R" indicates Republican. "—" indicates not available. Data based on questionnaires completed by voters leaving polling places around the nation on election day. Differing questions and question formats make comparability across elections of some of these groups problematic. For example, in some years the "white fundamentalist" category is "evangelicals," "born-again Christians," or members of the "religious right." See sources for details. The number of respondents in 2004 was 13,660; in 2008, 17,836; in 2012, 26,565; in 2016, 24,558; and in 2020, 15,590. Data for earlier years can be found in previous editions of *Vital Statistics on American Politics*.

[a] Age category is 45–59 years for 2004.
[b] Age category is 60 years and older for 2004.
[c] Education category is "high school or less" for 2016.
[d] Education category is "never attended college" for 2020.
[e] Education category is a weighted combination of "some college" and "associate's degree" for 2020.
[f] Region is "Northeast" for 2008.
[g] Income category is under $30,000 for 2012 through 2020.
[h] Income category is $50,000–$99,999 for 2012 through 2020.
[i] Income category is over $100,000 for 2012 through 2020.

Sources: Percentages calculated by the authors from National Election Pool General Election Exit Polls, 2004, National Data; CNN Presidential Election National Exit Poll, 2008, www.cnn.com; National Election Pool, National Exit Poll, 2012, as reported by Fox News, www.foxnews.com; 2016 and 2020 CNN Presidential Election National Exit Polls; some data obtained through the Inter-university Consortium for Political and Social Research, www.icpsr.umich.edu. Neither the collectors of the original data nor the consortium bear any responsibility for the results presented here.

Table 3-6 Vote in Democratic Presidential Primaries, by Groups, 2000–2020 (percent)

Group	Percentage of voters					2000		2004				2008		2016		2020			
	2000	2004	2008	2016	2020	Bradley	Gore	Edwards	Kerry	Others		Clinton	Obama	Clinton	Sanders	Biden	Sanders	Warren	Bloomberg
Sex																			
Men	43	46	43	42	41	27	71	25	54	21		43	50	50	49	39	32	6	5
Women	57	54	57	58	59	22	76	26	55	20		52	43	62	37	44	26	8	6
Race/ethnicity																			
White	69	73	65	62	62	29	69	28	53	19		55	39	48	50	41	27	8	5
Black	17	16	19	27	22	12	86	19	56	25		15	82	78	21	63	18	4	8
Hispanic	10	8	12	7	12	11	89	13	70	17		61	35	62	38	35	47	3	5
Age																			
Younger than 30 years	9	10	14	17	14	26	72	25	48	27		38	58	28	71	13	54	12	4
30–44 years	26	23	—	23	21	24	74	25	52	23		—	—	50	49	27	43	11	4
45–59 years	31	34	—	40	33	27	71	27	56	18		—	—	65	33	48	21	7	6
60 years and older	33	33	18[a]	21	32	21	77	25	63	12		59[a]	34[a]	72	26	57	11	5	7
Religion																			
Catholic	29	29	—	—	—	26	72	23	61	16		—	—	—	—	—	—	—	—
White Protestant	49	—	—	—	—	26	71	—	—	—		—	—	—	—	—	—	—	—
Jewish	8	5	—	—	—	31	68	17	70	13		—	—	—	—	—	—	—	—
Party																			
Democratic	84	73	76	74	73	21	77	23	60	17		51	45	66	33	46	25	8	5
Independent	14	22	19	24	25	42	55	31	42	28		40	52	36	62	18	40	17	6
Ideology																			
Liberal	47	46	47	61	62	21	72	22	58	20		47	48	55	44	35	37	9	5
Moderate	41	39	40	32	32	22	77	28	54	18		50	45	65	34	54	16	3	7
Conservative	12	15	13	9	6	27	68	30	43	26		47	44	73	26	44	19	4	17

| Union household | 28 | 32 | — | — | — | 22 | 75 | 23 | 58 | 19 | — | — | — | — |
| Total | 100 | 100 | 100 | 100 | 100 | 24 | 74 | 25 | 54 | 21 | | | | |

Note: "—" indicates data not available. Entries are derived from exit poll data in twenty contested delegate selection primaries in 2000, eighteen in 2004; thirty-nine in 2008, twenty-eight in 2016, and twenty-three in 2020. In 2012, President Obama was uncontested for renomination.

[a] Age 65 years and older for 2008.

Sources: Percentages calculated by the authors from Voter News Service, Presidential Primary Exit Polls, 2000; Edison Media Research, Mitofsky International, National Election Pool Democratic Presidential Preference Primary Exit Polls, 2004; ABC News Presidential Primary Exit Polls, http://abcnews.go.com; 2008: obtained through the Inter-university Consortium for Political and Social Research, www.icpsr.org, and calculated by the authors from CNN Exit Polls in 2016 and 2020, www.cnn.com. Neither the collectors of the original data nor the consortium bear any responsibility for the results presented here.

Table 3-7 Vote in Republican Presidential Primaries, by Groups, 2000–2016 (percent)

	Percentage of voters				2000		2008			2012					2016			
Group	2000	2008	2012	2016	G. W. Bush	McCain	Huckabee	McCain	Romney	Gingrich	Paul	Romney	Santorum	Trump	Cruz	Rubio	Kasich
Sex																		
Men	51	54	52	51	55	38	21	43	25	22	12	38	26	47	24	11	12
Women	49	46	48	49	60	35	24	41	25	20	8	41	29	39	25	15	14
Race/ethnicity																		
White	—	89	93	90	—	—	22	42	25	21	10	40	28	44	25	12	13
Black	—	2	1	2	—	—	27	42	17	—	—	—	—	—	—	—	—
Hispanic	—	6	—	4	—	—	19	46	19	25	5	46	10	24	26	41	2
Age																		
Younger than 30 years	10	11	9	12	56	34	29	34	21	13	27	30	28	32	26	19	12
30–44 years	26	—	18	19	59	33	—	—	—	18	15	34	31	40	25	15	13
45–64 years	31[a]	—	46	44	55[a]	39[a]	—	—	—	21	8	40	29	47	24	11	12
65 years and older	34[a]	23	27	25	60[a]	37[a]	16	48	26	25	5	46	22	44	23	12	15
Party																		
Democrat	6	3	5	4	18	77	22	48	16	6	17	22	46	—	—	—	—
Independent	25	21	26	30	38	55	19	42	20	16	20	36	25	40	22	13	15
Republican	70	76	70	66	67	27	23	42	26	23	6	42	28	44	26	13	12
Ideology																		
Liberal	11	9	3	3	40	54	15	55	16	6	17	22	46	—	—	—	—
Moderate	33	27	33[b]	22	46	50	14	55	18	15[b]	16[b]	44[b]	21[b]	43	12	15	21
Conservative	55	63	67	75	68	25	27	35	29	23	7	38	30	43	27	13	10
Evangelical or member of religious right																		
No	72	56	48	46	52	43	10	49	28	15	13	49	20	45	17	15	16
Yes	23	44	52	54	74	17	39	33	20	26	8	31	34	40	29	12	11

Military veteran										
Yes	—	22	—	19	—	19	47	25	—	—	49	19	16	7
No	—	78	—	81	—	23	41	25	—	—	40	22	20	9
Total vote	100	100	100	100	36	58	22	42	25	21	10	40	27	43	24	13	13

Notes: "—" indicates not available. The small percentage of votes going to other candidates is not shown. For 2000, based on combined vote totals and results from exit polls conducted by Voter News Service in twenty-five primary states between February 1 and March 14. Some questions were not asked in each state. There was no exit poll in Washington State. There were no exit polls for the 2004 primaries when President Bush was uncontested for renomination. For 2008, based on combined vote totals and results from exit polls conducted by Edison Media Research/Mitofsky International in twenty-seven primaries and two caucuses (Iowa and Nevada) between January 8 and March 11. There were no exit polls for primaries held in Rhode Island, the District of Columbia, and Washington State. For 2012, based on combined vote totals and results from exit polls conducted by Edison Research for the National Election Pool in eighteen primaries and two caucuses (Iowa and Nevada) held between January 3 and April 3. There were no exit polls for primaries held in Missouri and the District of Columbia. For 2016, results are based on exit polling conducted in twenty-seven states. There were no exit polls for the 2020 primaries when President Trump was uncontested for renomination.

[a] The two oldest age categories in 2000 are 45 to 59 and 60 years and older.
[b] In 2012, moderate and liberal responses are combined.

Sources: Calculated by the authors from data in previous editions of *Vital Statistics on American Politics* and exit poll data as reported by CNN, www.cnn.com, ABC News, http://abcnews.go.com, and MSNBC, www.nbcnews.com.

Table 3-8 Congressional Vote in General Elections, by Groups, 2010–2020 (percent)

	Percentage of voters						2010		2012		2014		2016		2018		2020	
Group	2010	2012	2014	2016	2018	2020	D	R	D	R	D	R	D	R	D	R	D	R
Sex																		
Men	48	47	49	48	48	48	41	55	45	53	42	56	43	55	47	51	45	54
Women	52	53	51	52	52	52	48	49	55	44	52	47	54	44	59	40	57	43
Race/ethnicity																		
White	77	72	75	71	72	66	37	60	39	59	38	60	38	60	44	54	41	59
Black	11	13	12	12	11	13	89	9	91	8	89	10	88	10	90	9	87	12
Hispanic/Latino	8	10	8	11	11	14	60	38	68	30	63	35	67	32	69	29	63	36
Asian	2	3	3	4	3	4	58	40	73	25	50	49	65	34	77	23	68	32
Age																		
18–29 years	12	19	13	19	13	17	55	42	60	38	54	43	56	42	67	32	62	36
30–44 years	24	26	22	25	22	23	46	50	51	46	50	48	52	46	58	39	53	46
45–64 years	43	38	43	40	39	38	45	53	47	51	45	53	44	54	49	50	48	51
65 years and older	21	17	22	16	26	22	38	59	44	55	42	57	45	53	48	50	46	54
Education																		
Not a high school graduate	3	3	2	—	—	—	57	36	62	35	54	44	—	—	—	—	—	—
High school graduate	17	21	18	18[a]	23[a]	20[a]	46	52	52	46	46	53	46[a]	52[a]	48[a]	51[a]	46[a]	52[a]
College incomplete	28	29	29	31	36	38[b]	43	53	48	50	45	53	46	52	51	48	51[b]	48[b]
College graduate	51	47	50	50	41	42	45	53	49	49	48	50	51	47	50	39	53	46
Region																		
East	21[c]	—	21	—	—	21	54[c]	44[c]	—	—	55	43	—	—	—	—	56	44
Midwest	25	—	24	—	—	22	44	53	—	—	45	53	—	—	—	—	47	52
South	31	—	33	—	—	34	37	61	—	—	39	58	—	—	—	—	47	52
West	23	—	22	—	—	22	49	48	—	—	51	47	—	—	—	—	57	41
Religion																		
White Protestant	44	39	39	—	—	—	28	69	29	70	27	71	—	—	—	—	—	—
White fundamentalist	25	26	26	—	—	—	19	77	20	78	21	78	—	—	—	—	—	—
Catholic	23	25	24	23	26	25	44	54	50	49	45	53	46	53	50	49	52	48
Jewish	2	2	3	3	2	2	—	—	69	29	65	33	72	26	79	17	—	—
Union household	17	18	17	18	—	19	49	48	—	—	51	47	—	—	—	—	60	40

Family income												
Less than $30,000	17	16	17	17	16	57	40	63	35	59	39[g]	56	41	63	34	54	46
$30,000–49,999	20	20	19	21	20	51	46	56	42	51	47	55	44	57	41	56	44
$50,000–99,999	21[d]	34	30	29	39	45[d]	51[d]	46	52	44	54	47	51	52	47	57	42
More than $100,000	42[e]	30	34	33	26	41[e]	58[e]	42	56	42	57	45	52	47	52	44	56
Party																	
Democratic	35	39	36	37	37	91	7	94	6	92	7	92	7	95	4	95	5
Independent	29	28	30	30	27	37	56	44	51	42	54	45	51	54	42	53	44
Republican	35	33	33	33	36	5	94	5	94	5	94	4	94	6	94	5	94
Ideology																	
Liberal	20	25	26	27	24	90	8	86	12	87	11	87	11	91	8	89	11
Moderate	38	40	38	37	38	55	42	57	41	53	44	52	46	62	36	64	35
Conservative	42	35	35	36	39	13	84	16	82	13	85	15	83	16	83	14	85
Previous presidential vote																	
Democratic	45	—	—	43	—	84	14	—	—	—	—	—	—	94	5	—	—
Independent/third party	4	—	—	8	—	33	58	—	—	—	—	—	—	54	41	—	—
Republican	45	—	—	40	—	7	91	—	—	—	—	—	—	8	91	—	—
First-time voter	3	—	—	10	16[f]	45	43	—	—	—	—	59	40	62[f]	36[f]	66	34
Total	100	100	100	100	100	45	52	50	48	47	51	48	49	53	45	51	48

Note: "D" indicates Democrat; "R" indicates Republican; "—" indicates not available. Percentages based on Democratic, Republican, and other (not shown) votes. Data based on questionnaires completed by voters leaving polling places around the nation on Election Day. Differing questions and question formats make comparability across elections of some of these groups problematic. For example, in some years the "white fundamentalist" category is "evangelicals," "born-again Christians," or members of the "religious right." See sources for details. The number of respondents in 2010 was 17,504; in 2012, 25,058; in 2014, 19,436; in 2016, 23,447; in 2018, 18,778; in 2020, 15,087. Data for earlier years can be found in previous editions of *Vital Statistics on American Politics*.

[a] Education level is "high school or less" for 2016 and 2018, and "never attended college" for 2020.
[b] Combines "some college" and "Associate's degree" in 2020.
[c] Region is "Northeast" for 2010.
[d] Income category is $50,000–74,999 for 2010.
[e] Income category is more than $75,000 for 2010.
[f] Specifies first-time midterm election voter for 2018.

Sources: Percentages calculated by the authors from CNN U.S. House National Exit Poll, 2010, www.cnn.com; National Election Pool, House National Exit Poll, 2012 and 2014, as reported by Fox News, www.foxnews.com; CNN U.S. House National Exit Poll, 2016, 2018, and 2020. Neither the collectors of the original data nor the consortium bears any responsibility for the results presented here.

A Data Literacy Lesson
Group Voting in Elections

For someone who finds politics fascinating, tables such as 3-5, 3-6, 3-7, and 3-8 can be sources of endless fun. Throw a table like these onto the screen in front of a group of political science students (as one of us frequently does in campaigns and election classes), and you can provoke fabulous discussion.[1] "Wow, look how strongly political parties predict votes!" some students might say, or "I wonder what explains the increasing age gap in voting behavior?" or "How come Jewish people are so strongly Democratic in their voting?" The tables provide no shortage of opportunities to use data to note interesting trends, or to raise questions about results that might, at first glance, not make complete sense.

While it might be most fascinating to concentrate our attention on the voting patterns shown on the right-hand side of the table, we would like to point out two other aspects of data in these tables, one of which can easily be seen in the table, and one of which cannot. Understanding these two aspects of the tables will enable you to have even more fun looking at the results, and to be a wiser consumer of all things political.

First, look to the left side of the table, to the section labeled "percentage of voters." This information is frequently presented in tables such as these, but often attracts little notice. These data tell us that it is important not just to know how people in different groups vote, but also to know how large these groups are (and how large they once were). As one example, consider race/ethnicity and voting behavior. Table 3-4 tells us that Black voters are overwhelmingly supportive of the Democratic Party, Latino voters are also strong Democrats, and white voters tilt Republican. These numbers fluctuate somewhat from election to election, but the overall behavior of these groups seems clear (and not surprising to people who study this). When we look at who the voters are in American elections, however, we see that white voters make up a much smaller percentage of the electorate than they used to. In 2004, white voters were 77 percent of the presidential electorate; in 2020, they were just 67 percent of the electorate.[2] Demographers are doing interesting research to explain these patterns, and predict what the future might be, but for political folks, the implication is clear. If the bulk of Republican support is coming from a steadily shrinking share of the electorate, the current Republican coalition (or turnout levels) will need to change if Republicans hope to be competitive in future elections.

We note as well that these distinctions become even more important when we consider voting in presidential primaries (see Tables 3-5 and 3-6). Looking at the percentage of primary voters in different demographic categories is instructive—we see, for example, how Republican primary voters are more likely to be older, white, and male than Democratic primary voters. Calling the Republicans the party of the "old white men" is frequently used as a pejorative; the table indicates, however, that there is more than a shred of truth to this statement. This demographic difference has profound implications for who the Republican Party nominates, and who their core constituency is.

A second factor to consider when looking at one of these tables is the notion of intersectionality. Each section of this table considers one aspect of an individual's identity—their sex, race, age, etc. But we are, as the idea of intersectionality teaches us, a product of all pieces of our identity, and how they intersect with one another. The lived experience of being a woman in America, for example, is different if you are white or Black; hence, feminism in white America looks different from feminism in Black America. We might, therefore, expect to see somewhat different voting patterns for white women and for Black women.

Similarly, an interesting finding from the 2008 and 2016 Democratic primaries was that while older women gravitated toward Hillary Clinton (perhaps seeing her as an opportunity to shatter the glass ceiling keeping women from the presidency), younger women were more attracted to Barack Obama and Bernie Sanders. Gender certainly matters in explaining political behavior, but a full understanding of its impact needs to consider intersectional aspects of identity, in this case age and political generation.

The polling data we present here do a good job addressing each group's share of the electorate, but do less to show intersections among the groups. CNN does provide some of these results in its reporting on exit polls; other results can be calculated by the enterprising reader if they gather the raw data and do these analyses. Increasingly, polling organizations make these data available. While there is a learning curve one must climb in figuring out how to download data and run analyses, the payoff can be well worth it in the end. Perhaps your results could one day be featured on placemats at the finest political eateries in the land!

---

[1] While we are aware of no restaurants or bars that provide data such as these on their placemats, we see a great deal of potential in this idea.
[2] In 1996, (before the time period in the table), white voters represented 83 percent of the electorate. A sixteen-point reduction in a 24-year period is a big deal.

Table 3-9 Party-Line Voting in Presidential and Congressional Elections, 1952–2020 (percent)

Year	Presidential elections			U.S. Senate elections			U.S. House elections		
	Party-line voters[a]	Defectors[b]	Independents	Party-line voters[a]	Defectors[b]	Independents	Party-line voters[a]	Defectors[b]	Independents
1952	77	18	5	79	16	5	80	15	5
1956	76	15	9	80	12	8	82	9	9
1960	79	13	8	79	12	9	80	11	8
1964	79	15	5	78	16	6	79	15	5
1968	69	24	7	73	20	7	74	19	7
1972	67	25	8	69	22	9	74	17	8
1976	73	16	11	69	19	12	72	19	9
1980	68	24	8	71	21	8	69	23	8
1984	79	13	8	72	20	9	70	23	7
1988	81	12	7	72	20	7	74	19	7
1992	68	24	9	74	20	7	71	21	7
1996	78	16	5	77	16	7	77	17	5
2000	79	12	8	79	13	7	76	17	7
2004	85	10	5	81	14	5	79	15	6
2008	84	9	7	81	12	7	80	13	6
2012	83	8	9	82	9	9	82	9	8
2016	85	7	7	79	14	7	78	14	8
2020	86	6	8	85	8	7	82	11	7

Note: "—" indicates not available. In presidential elections, the base for percentages is all voters. In Senate and House elections, the base for percentages is all voters supporting Democratic or Republican candidates. Data for additional years may be found in previous editions of *Vital Statistics on American Politics*.

[a] Democratic or Republican identifiers who vote for the candidate of their party. Party identification is based on surveys in which voters are asked with which party they identify. See Table 3-1, this volume, for question. "Independent partisans," or "leaners," are included here as party-line voters or defectors.
[b] Democratic or Republican identifiers who do not vote for the candidate of their party.

Source: American National Election Studies data, University of Michigan, Ann Arbor, Mich., and Stanford University, Palo Alto, Calif., www.electionstudies.org.

Table 3-10 Split-Ticket Voting, 1952–2020 (percent)

Year	President–House	Senate–House	State–local
1952	13	9	26
1956	16	10	29
1958		10	31
1960	14	9	27
1962		—	42
1964	14	18	41
1966		21	50
1968	17	21	47
1970		20	51
1972	30	22	58
1974		24	61
1976	25	23	—
1978		35	—
1980	28	31	59
1982		24	55
1984	25	20	52
1986		28	—
1988	25	27	—
1990		25	—
1992	22	25	—
1994		24	—
1996	18	19	—
1998		23	—
2000	19	18	—
2002		21	—
2004	17	16	—
2008	17	16	—
2012	14	14	—
2016	16	17	—
2020	11	13	—

Note: "—" indicates not available. Entries are the percentages of voters who "split" their ticket by supporting candidates of different parties for the offices indicated. Those who cast ballots for other than Democratic and Republican candidates are excluded in presidential and congressional calculations. The state–local figure is based on a general question: "Did you vote for other state and local offices? Did you vote a straight ticket or did you vote for candidates from different parties?" There was no update of the American National Election Studies series in 2006, 2010, 2014, and 2018.

Source: American National Election Studies data, University of Michigan, Ann Arbor, Mich., and Stanford University, Palo Alto, Calif., www.electionstudies.org.

Figure 3-6 Presidential Approval, 1993–2021

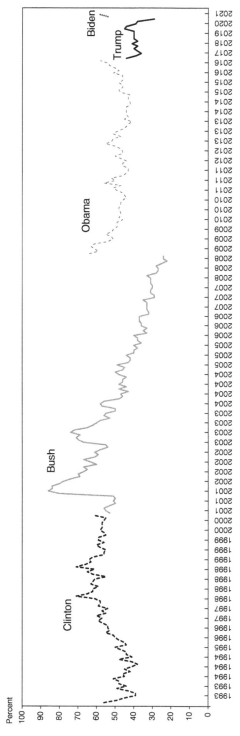

Note: Data for 2021 are through April. Question: "Do you approve or disapprove of the way _____ (Bill Clinton/George W. Bush/Barack Obama/Donald J. Trump/Joseph Biden) is handling his job as president? Related data for additional years can be found in previous editions of *Vital Statistics on American Politics*.

Sources: Clinton: Pew Research Center, "It's the Economy Again!: Clinton Nostalgia Sets in, Bush Reaction Mixed," January 11, 2001, 27–28; Bush: "Reviewing the Bush Years and the Public's Final Verdict: Bush and Public Opinion," December 18, 2008, 24–25; Obama: "Obama Leaves Office on High Note, but Public Has Mixed Views of his Accomplishments," December 14, 2016, 25; Trump: "Biden Begins Presidency with Positive Ratings; Trump Departs with Lowest Ever Job Mark," January 15, 2021, 44; Biden: "Biden Nears 100-Day Mark with Strong Approval, Positive Rating for Vaccine Rollout," April 15, 2021, 38, https://www.pewresearch.org.

Figure 3-7 Rating of Congress, 1985–2021

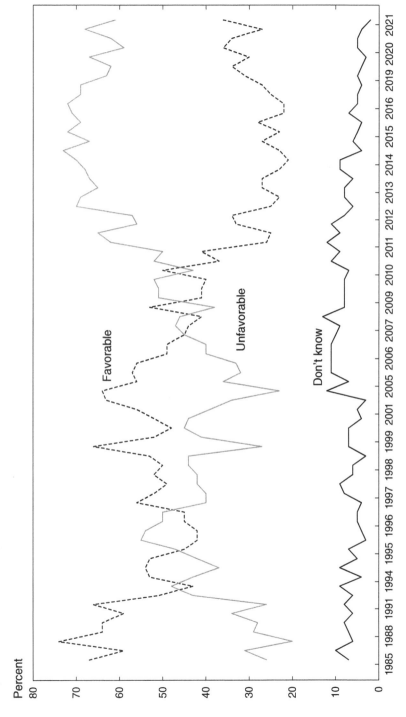

Note: Data for 2021 are through April. Question: "Is your overall opinion of Congress very favorable, mostly favorable, mostly unfavorable, or very unfavorable?" Related data for additional years can be found in previous editions of *Vital Statistics on American Politics*.

Source: Pew Research Center, "Biden Nears 100-Day Mark with Strong Approval, Positive Rating for Vaccine Rollout," 46–47, https://www.pewresearch.org.

Figure 3-8 Individual Confidence in Government, 1952–2020

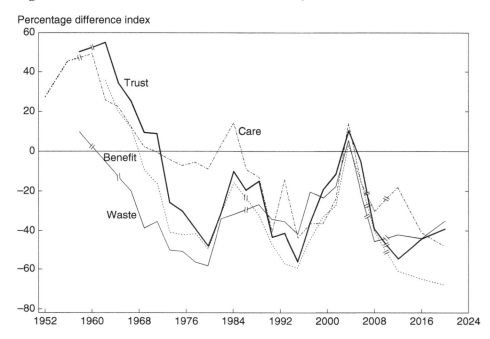

Note: Broken line indicates question not asked that year in the biennial American National Election Studies. Questions: (Care) "I don't think public officials care much about what people like me think." (Trust) "How much of the time do you think you can trust the government in Washington to do what is right—just about always, most of the time, or only some of the time?" (Benefit) "Would you say the government is pretty much run by a few big interests looking out for themselves or that it is run for the benefit of all people?" (Waste) "Do you think that people in the government waste a lot of money we pay in taxes, waste some of it, or don't waste very much of it?" The percentage difference index is calculated by subtracting the percentage giving a nontrusting response from the percentage giving a trusting response. There was no update of the American National Election Studies series in 2006, 2010, 2014, and 2018.

Source: American National Election Studies, University of Michigan, Ann Arbor, Mich., and Stanford University, Palo Alto, Calif., www.electionstudies.org.

Figure 3-9 Satisfaction with "The Way Things Are Going," 1988–2021

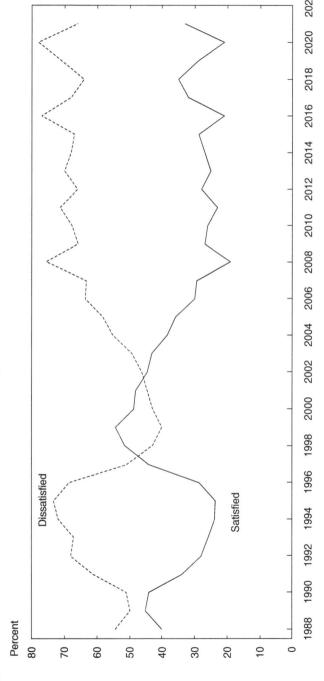

Note: Data for 2021 are through March. Question: "All in all, are you satisfied or dissatisfied with the way things are going in this country today?" Related data for additional years can be found in previous editions of *Vital Statistics on American Politics*.

Sources: Pew Research Center, "Biden Viewed Positively on Many Issues, but Public Is Less Confident He Can Unify Country." March 11, 2021, 29, https://www.pewresearch.org.

Table 3-11 Importance of Various Political Issues, 2016–2021 (percent)

Issue	November 2016	October 2018	December 2018	March 2019	September 2019	June 2020	April 2021
Budget Deficit		55			53	47	49
Climate Change	40	43		46	48	40	40
Coronavirus						58	47
Economic Inequality[a]	57	54		51	44		43
Gun Violence	48	53					48
Health Care (affordability)		70		67	66	57	56
Illegal Immigration	44	42		38	43	28	48
Public Schools			36				39
Racism	39	46		40	43		45
Roads, Bridges, Infrastructure	37		33				34
Sexism	23	34		26	26		23
Terrorism[b]	53	35		34	39	25	35
Unemployment						50	41
Violent Crime			52	49		41	48

Note: The number in each cell indicates percentage of respondents indicating the issue is "A very big problem." Other answer choices were "A moderately big problem," "A Small Problem," or "Not a Problem at All."

[a] In February 2019 and earlier, this question asked about "The gap between the rich and the poor."
[b] In April 2021, this question was changed to read "International Terrorism."

Source: Pew Research Center, "Biden Nears 100 Day Mark with Strong Approval, Positive Ratings for Vaccine Rollout," April 15, 2021, 44–45, https://www.pewresearch.org.

A Data Literacy Lesson

Asking Questions about the (Most) Important Political Issues

Table 3-11 takes a variety of political issues, ranging from old standbys (the affordability of health care or the size of the budget deficit) to new issues (no pollster was asking about the importance of the coronavirus before 2020). The table arrays these issues over time and shows how important respondents felt these issues were, on a scale that included options ranging from "a very big problem" to "not a problem at all." The table reports the percentage of respondents indicating the issue was a very big problem.

This table is a new one for this book, replacing two previous figures in which respondents were asked to note the "Most Important Problem" facing the nation, with separate figures for international and domestic problems. Our reasons for making this shift are twofold. First, as is a common theme in essays here, the availability of data changed. The "Most Important Problem" question is reported less by the Pew Research Center (our source for these data); instead, Pew is now using surveys where they give respondents a set of issues and ask them to rate their importance. We cannot keep reporting data if those data are not being collected regularly; as such, we need to adapt to the data that are readily available for us to use.

However, it is not just the availability of data that led us to make this change—if we did not like the way the new data addressed the underlying issue, they would not be in the book. The new way of reporting the data gives us far more information. Imagine, for example, that you were asked what the most important issue facing the nation is. You might say climate change, or the budget deficit, or gun violence. In so doing, you would give us a tremendous amount of data on one issue—you believe, for example, that climate change is THE TOP issue. But your answer would not tell us anything about how important you felt the budget deficit, or gun violence, is. The only thing we would know is that you believed the deficit, or gun violence, was less important than climate change. That's just not a lot of information.

The newer version of the question provides a good bit more information. For each topic, we can now determine how important the respondent believes that issue to be. So, if the respondent believes that

(Continued)

(Continued)

the budget deficit is "a small problem" but gun violence is a "moderately big problem," we now have the basis for rating which one is more important than the other. We can compare across issues to see how many rated a particular issue "a big problem" versus how many said it was "not a problem at all." And, as we also do in the table, we can look over time to see when issues become more important, and when they become less important. The table tells us, for example, that the relative importance respondents place on terrorism as an issue has fluctuated quite a bit, while the percent believing racism in a big problem has remained fairly steady. Findings such as these can be grist for the research mill.

We do lose something with this new format of the question, however. A respondent could, in theory, indicate that six different issues are big problems. Frankly, we understand that—as we scan the list of problems in the table, we each think many of them are really big problems. The table, as constructed here, allows respondents to indicate that many things are big problems, but does not force them to prioritize among these big problems. This is certainly a drawback. Voters often choose to vote based upon the one issue that matters most to them—the table does not allow us to identify who might be single issue voters on climate, or on racism, for example. In a world where presidents typically have very little political capital to spend, the table does not tell us enough about where voters might want the president to spend their limited capital—if, for example, President Trump or President Biden were only able to address one issue, which would you want it to be? The older language speaks to this point in a way that the newer language does not.

No survey question is perfect; the way we frame each question gives us various bits of information, but also denies us other useful information. On balance, we prefer the formatting of the newer question, and believe it contains many useful insights. This is a fortunate development, since as of now, this is the format in which we see the most useful data!

Figure 3-10 Favorable Opinions of the Democratic and Republican Parties, 1992–2021

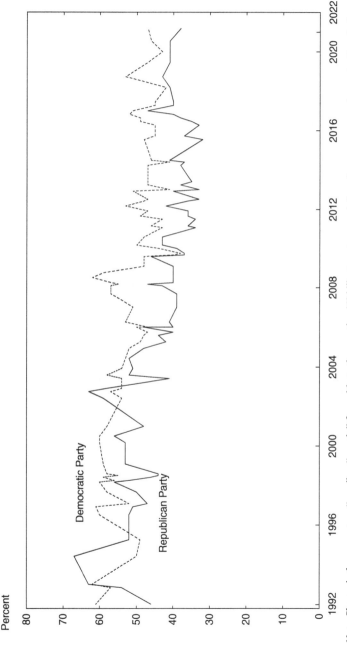

Note: Shown is the percentage "very" or "mostly" favorable to the question "I'd like to get your opinion of some groups and organizations in the news. Is your overall opinion of the [Democratic] [Republican] Party very favorable, mostly favorable, mostly unfavorable, or very unfavorable?" Typically, 5 to 10 percent of the respondents volunteer that they cannot rate the parties.

Source: Pew Research Center, "Voter Enthusiasm at Record High in Nationalized Midterm Environment," September 26, 2018, 43–44; "Biden Viewed Positively on Many Issues, but Public Is Less Confident He Can Unify Country," March 11, 2021, 31, http://people-press.org.

158 Public Opinion and Voting

Figure 3-11 Condition of Nation's Economy and Citizens' Personal Financial Situations over the Last Year, 1980–2020 (percent)

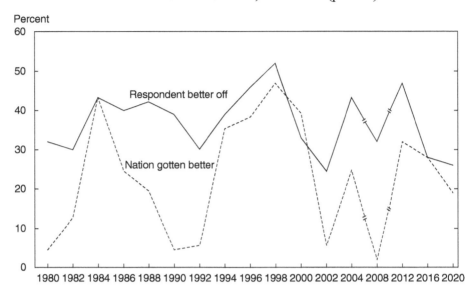

Note: Broken line indicates question not asked that year in the biennial American National Election Studies. Questions: Nation's economy: "How about (1996–later: Now thinking about) the economy (1990, 1994–later: in the country as a whole)?" All years except 2000: "Would you say that over the past year the nation's economy has gotten better, stayed (all years except 1984: about) the same, or gotten worse?" (2000:) "Would you say that over the past year the nation's economy has gotten worse, stayed about the same, or gotten better?"; personal financial situation: 1962–1998, 2004–2008: "We are interested in how people are getting along financially these days. Would you say that (1962, 1966–1974: you [and your family]; 1976 and later: you [and your family living here]) are better off or worse off financially than you were a year ago?"; 2000–2002: "We are interested in how people are getting along financially these days. Would you say that you (and your family [2000 face-to-face only: living here]) are better off, worse off, or just about the same financially as you were a year ago?" There was no update of the American National Election Studies series in 2006, 2010, 2014, and 2018.

Source: American National Election Studies data, University of Michigan, Ann Arbor, Mich., and Stanford University, Palo Alto, Calif., www.electionstudies.org.

A Data Literacy Lesson

The Economy and the Vote

One of us is old enough to remember the line, delivered with the timing and skill of a Hollywood actor, that Ronald Reagan used to thoroughly disarm Jimmy Carter's reelection bid in 1980: "Are you better off now than you were four years ago?" Reagan asked during a presidential debate. In the context of a debate taking place within a campaign in which the voters were trying to determine whether to keep the incumbent or fire him, asking voters this simple question was illuminative and predictive. If you're not happy with the last four years, fire the guy who's been in charge and replace him with someone else. If you're happy, stay the course. Reagan was smart enough to realize that given the national situation at the time, more voters than not would reply, "No, I am not better off than I was four years ago. I want to throw Carter out and try Reagan."

Do voters actually behave in this way? As we do throughout this book, we can bring in some data to address this question. In Figure 3-11, we see some interesting evidence for this point. Consider first the presidential elections in which voters chose to change the party that controlled the White House. In those years, we see the following percentages of people who said the nation's economy had gotten better in the last four years:[1]

1980 (4); 1992 (5); 2000 (39); 2008 (2); 2016 (28); 2020 (19)

Compare this to the percentages in the years in which the nation chose to keep the same party in charge:

1984 (43); 1988 (19); 1996 (38); 2004 (24); 2012 (32)

The pattern is not perfect, but it strongly suggests that people's perceptions of how the national economy is doing very much colors how they will respond to the incumbent party in a presidential election. When people perceive the national economy is doing poorly, they choose to change the leadership in the White House.[2] When things are perceived to be going better, the voters choose a different party for the White House.

Interestingly, the relationship between vote choice and the perception of national economic conditions is stronger than between the respondent's personal economic situation and their vote choice. Even in the worst of economic situations, at least a quarter of people believe their economic situation has gotten better. This is not surprising—economic downturns rarely hit all segments of the economy, and some people have the ability to thrive even as the national economic situation changes for the worse. There is a lot more variance in public perceptions of the economy, which enables it to have more explanatory power.

While the link between economic perceptions and the vote seems clear, it is worth noting one additional pattern—increasingly, people's perceptions of how the economy is doing are conditioned by their partisan identification. When a Democrat

(Continued)

(Continued)

controls the White House, Democrats are more likely to believe the national economy is doing well than they would be if a Republican was in charge, *even if the underlying economic conditions were exactly the same.* We see a similar pattern for Republicans. The same Republicans who thought the economy was booming in early January 2021 (while Donald Trump was president) are likely to believe it was lagging by late January 2021 (when Joe Biden had taken over). Democrats, not surprisingly, showed the opposite pattern.

Of course, we are all sophisticated enough to understand that presidents do not have total control over how the economy is doing, that people have imperfect ways of judging how well the economy actually is doing, and that other things matter in judging presidential performance rather than the economy. Still, looking at figures like Figure 3-11 can show us these kinds of patterns, and can help us narrow down our understanding of the mechanism by which the economy drives vote choice.

---

[1] These numbers are from the raw data used to populate the table.

[2] Interestingly, the 2000 and 2016 elections, both of which led to a different party occupying the White House, showed relatively high scores for how well people thought the economy was doing. In each case, the Democrats (the incumbent party) actually did win the popular vote, even though they lost the electoral vote.

Table 3-12 Public Opinion on Civil Liberties, 1940–2018 (percent)

Issue/year	Allow[a]	Don't forbid[b]
Public speeches against democracy		
1940	25	46
1974	56	72
1976	55	80
1976	52	79

Issue/year	Allow to speak	Allow to teach college	Keep book in library
Atheist[c]			
1954	37	12	35
1964[d]	—	—	61
1972	66	41	61
1973[a]	66	42	62
1973[b]	62	39	57
1974	62	42	60
1976	65	42	60
1977	63	40	59
1978	63	—	60
1980	66	46	62
1982	65	46	61
1985	65	46	61
1987	70	47	67
1988	70	46	64
1989	72	52	68
1990	73	51	67
1991	73	51	68
1993	71	53	68
1994	73	53	70
1996	74	56	68
1998	75	58	70
2000	75	57	68
2002	77	60	72
2004	76	64	72
2006	77	60	71
2008	76	61	71
2010	76	60	73
2012	77	63	75
2014	79	66	77
2016	79	65	76
2018	80	65	77
Admitted communist[c]			
1954	27	6	27
1972	53	33	53
1973[a]	61	40	59
1973[b]	53	30	54
1974	58	42	59
1976	55	42	57
1977	56	39	56
1978	60	—	61
1982	56	43	57
1985	58	46	58
1987	60	46	62

(Table continues)

Table 3-12 (Continued)

Year			
1988	61	48	60
1989	65	51	63
1990	65	53	64
1991	68	54	67
1993	70	57	68
1994	67	55	67
1996	64	58	65
1998	67	57	67
2000	66	57	66
2002	69	59	69
2004	69	63	70
2006	67	60	68
2008	65	58	67
2010	64	61	69
2012	66	62	73
2014	68	63	71
2016	69	64	72
2018	67	61	71
Racist[c]			
1943[e]	17	—	—
1976	61	41	60
1977	59	41	62
1978	62	—	64
1980	62	42	64
1982	59	43	60
1985	56	42	60
1987	60	43	64
1988	61	41	61
1989	62	46	65
1990	64	45	65
1991	62	41	65
1993	61	45	65
1994	62	43	66
1996	61	46	64
1998	62	47	63
2000	60	46	63
2002	62	52	65
2004	62	46	65
2006	61	46	64
2008	59	45	63
2010	56	47	65
2012	59	47	64
2014	60	47	63
2016	60	45	64
2018	57	42	61
Admitted homosexual[c]			
1973	61	48	54
1974	63	51	56
1976	63	53	56
1977	62	50	55
1980	66	55	58
1982	65	55	56
1985	67	58	56
1987	68	57	58

1988	70	57	61
1989	77	64	66
1990	75	65	65
1991	77	63	69
1993	79	69	67
1994	80	71	69
1996	81	75	69
1998	81	75	70
2000	81	76	71
2002	83	78	75
2004	83	79	73
2006	82	78	74
2008	82	79	76
2010	86	84	78
2012	86	83	77
2014	89	87	80
2016	89	87	82
2018	88	86	83

Note: "—" indicates not available.

[a] Question: "Do you think the United States should allow public speeches against democracy?"
[b] Question: "Do you think the United States should forbid public speeches against democracy?"
[c] Question: "There are always some people whose ideas are considered bad or dangerous by other people. For instance, somebody who (is against all churches and religion/admits he is a communist/believes that Blacks are genetically inferior/admits that he is a homosexual). If such a person wanted to make a speech in your (city/town/community), should he be allowed to speak or not? Should such a person be allowed to teach in a college or university or not? If some people in your community suggested that a book he wrote (against churches and religion/promoting communism/which said Blacks are inferior/in favor of homosexuality) should be taken out of your public library, would you favor removing this book or not?" (Slight variations in wording across groups.) A "don't know" response is considered a "no."
[d] In 1964 the question was as follows: "Suppose a man admitted in public that he did not believe in God. Do you think a book he wrote should be removed from a public library?"
[e] In 1943 the question was as follows: "In peacetime, do you think anyone in the United States should be allowed to make speeches against certain races in this country?"

Sources: Public speeches against democracy: Howard Schuman and Stanley Presser, *Questions and Answers in Attitude Surveys* (New York: Academic Press, 1981), 277; Atheist: 1943, 1964, and 1973a: National Opinion Research Center surveys; 1954: Samuel A. Stouffer, *Communism, Conformity, and Civil Liberties* (Garden City, N.Y.: Doubleday, 1955), 32–34, 40–43; 1973b: Clyde Z. Nunn et al., *Tolerance for Nonconformity* (San Francisco: Jossey-Bass, 1978), 40–43; data for all other years from General Social Survey, National Opinion Research Center, University of Chicago.

Table 3-13 Public Opinion on the Death Penalty, 1972–2018 (percent)

Year	Favor	Oppose	Don't know
1972	53	39	8
1973	60	35	5
1974	63	32	5
1975	60	33	7
1976	66	29	5
1977	68	26	6
1978	67	28	5
1980	68	27	5
1982	74	21	5
1983	74	21	5
1984	72	23	5
1985	75	20	5
1986	72	23	5
1987	69	25	6
1988	71	22	7
1989	74	21	5
1990	75	20	6
1991	72	22	6
1993	72	21	7
1994	75	19	6
1996	72	21	7
1998	68	25	7
2000	64	28	8
2002	67	29	4
2004	65	30	5
2006	64	30	5
2008	64	31	5
2010	65	30	5
2012	61	33	7
2014	61	34	6
2016	57	38	5
2018	60	35	5

Note: General Social Survey interviews are conducted in the spring of the year indicated, usually March–June. Question: "Do you favor or oppose the death penalty for persons [or: "people"] convicted of murder?" Data for additional years can be found in previous editions of *Vital Statistics on American Politics*.

Source: General Social Survey, National Opinion Research Center, University of Chicago.

Figure 3-12 Public Opinion on People Living in Integrated Neighborhoods, 1972–2018

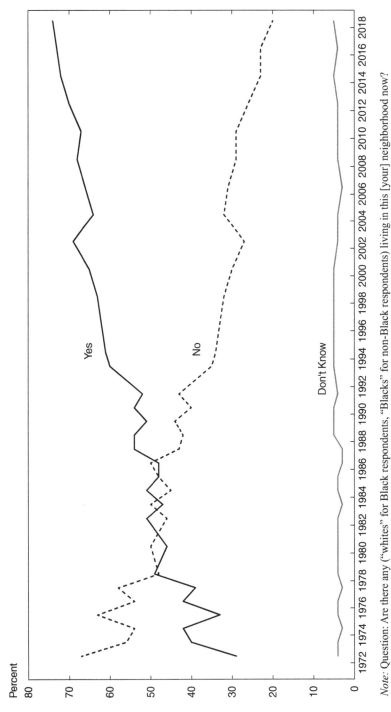

Note: Question: Are there any ("whites" for Black respondents, "Blacks" for non-Black respondents) living in this [your] neighborhood now?

Source: General Social Survey, National Opinion Research Center, University of Chicago.

Table 3-14 Public Opinion on Abortion, 1965–2018 (percent)

	Abortion should be legal under these circumstances						
Year	Mother's health	Rape	Birth defect	Low income	Single mother	As form of birth control	Any reason
1965	70	56	55	21	17	15	—
1972	84	75	75	46	41	38	—
1973	90	81	82	52	47	47	—
1974	91	83	82	52	48	45	—
1975	88	80	80	50	46	43	—
1976	89	81	82	51	48	45	—
1977	89	81	83	51	47	44	36
1978	88	80	80	45	39	38	32
1980	88	80	81	50	46	45	39
1982	90	84	82	49	45	46	38
1983	87	78	76	41	36	37	32
1984	88	76	78	45	42	41	37
1985	88	78	77	42	40	39	36
1987	86	77	76	43	40	40	37
1988	86	77	76	40	38	39	35
1989	88	80	79	46	43	43	39
1990	90	81	78	45	43	43	42
1991	88	83	80	46	43	42	41
1993	86	79	77	47	45	44	42
1994	88	81	79	48	46	46	45
1996	88	80	78	44	43	44	42
1998	84	76	74	41	39	39	38
2000	85	76	75	39	36	38	37
2002	89	76	75	42	39	41	40
2004	83	73	69	39	40	39	38
2006	84	73	70	40	37	40	38
2008	85	72	70	41	40	43	40
2010	84	77	72	44	41	47	41
2012	84	73	72	43	41	45	43
2014	86	75	73	44	42	46	44
2016	86	76	73	44	42	46	45
2018	88	77	75	48	45	50	49

Note: "—" indicates not available. Question: "Please tell me whether or not you think it should be possible for a pregnant woman to obtain a legal abortion [in the order asked in the survey] if there is a strong chance of serious defect in the baby? If she is married and does not want any more children? If the woman's own health is seriously endangered by the pregnancy? If the family has a very low income and cannot afford any more children? If she became pregnant as a result of rape? If she is not married and does not want to marry the man? The woman wants it for any reason?" A "don't know" response is considered a "no." Data for additional years can be found in previous editions of *Vital Statistics on American Politics*.

Sources: 1965: National Opinion Research Center surveys; 1972–2018: General Social Survey, National Opinion Research Center, University of Chicago.

Table 3-15 Public Opinion on Gun Control (Requiring Permits to Purchase Guns), 1972–2018 (percent)

Date	Favor requiring police permit before gun purchase	Oppose requiring police permit before gun purchase	Don't know
1972	70	27	3
1973	74	25	2
1974	75	23	1
1975	74	24	3
1976	72	27	1
1977	72	27	2
1980	69	29	2
1982	73	25	2
1984	70	27	3
1985	72	27	1
1987	72	26	2
1988	74	24	3
1989	78	21	2
1990	79	20	2
1991	81	18	1
1993	81	17	2
1994	78	20	2
1996	80	18	2
1998	82	16	2
2000	80	18	2
2002	80	19	1
2004	79	20	1
2006	78	20	2
2008	78	21	1
2010	74	25	1
2012	72	26	2
2014	72	27	1
2016	71	28	1
2018	70	28	2

Note: Question: "Would you favor or oppose a law which would require a person to obtain a police permit before he or she could buy a gun?

Source: General Social Survey, National Opinion Research Center, University of Chicago.

A Data Literacy Lesson
Dichotomies and Public Opinion: Abortion and Gun Control

When we discuss public opinion on a variety of political issues, we are used to noting that for many issues, political views are not a simple dichotomy (a division into two mutually exclusive groups). We understand that we do not easily divide into groups that favor or oppose national health insurance, for example, or that favor or oppose gun control. Within each of these issues, there are gradations of political support. Some people might favor some limited forms of national health insurance (like the Affordable Care Act), others might want to the see the United States develop a single-payer national model, while others might favor absolutely no government intervention at all. On gun control, issues regarding waiting periods for gun-purchases, or limitations on the number of guns one may own, or closing the so-called gun-show loopholes, or on outright bans of certain types of weapons, all divide us. Many people might favor some of these restrictions while opposing others.

Table 3-15 offers a good approach, in which we examine public opinion on the issue of gun control as a dichotomy. The people writing this question are forcing the issue, asking people which they thought was more important—to protect the right of Americans to own guns, or to control gun ownership. There is clearly a good bit of room for a respondent to say "both" to this question—one could easily imagine a staunch advocate of gun rights who also believes, for example, that ex-felons should not be allowed to own machine guns, or that second graders should not be allowed to purchase a handgun.[1] But on this particular question, the reader is forced into a choice. We have two competing goals—do we prioritize protecting gun rights, or controlling gun ownership? While Pew can (and does) ask other questions on more specific areas of gun control, this one serves its own unique purpose, and is interesting enough that we chose to include these data.

Finally, consider Table 3-14. Here, we include information on a wide range of questions concerning public opinion on abortion. Instead of asking simply, "Are you pro-life or pro-choice," this table reproduces results from the General Social Survey, in which people are asked about whether abortion should be legal in a variety of cases, including if the health of the mother was endangered, if there was a strong chance of a serious birth defect, or if the woman is married and does not want any more children. The responses for each question are shown in Table 3-14, revealing that three basic categories emerge. Public opinion is most pro-choice when the health of the mother is at stake, followed closely by a second category of cases where the woman has been raped, or where there is a serious risk of birth defects in the baby. While public opinion is not as pro-choice in these two areas as it is for the health of the mother, it is still strongly pro-choice. Public opinion turns more toward pro-life when other considerations are raised, including if the mother is low-income, a single mother, or just simply does not want more children.

Digging a little deeper into the numbers, if in 2018, 12 percent of the people were unwilling to allow abortion if the mother's health was at risk (historically the case where pro-choice attitudes were highest) and 49 percent were willing to allow abortion for any reason, it stands to reason that around

39 percent (or even slightly higher) were willing to allow abortion for some reasons but not for others.[2] These results suggest that treating abortion as a dichotomous, yes-no issue is probably not accurate. While abortion does clearly polarize much of the country, a large part of the nation looks at an issue like this and responds, "It depends."

It is wise to assume that even on our most contentious, two-sided issues, a large chunk of the country is not prepared to take a firm stance on one side or the other, preferring to seek a middle ground. The figure and tables referenced here offer a variety of ways that this middle ground might (or might not) be reflected in how we ask survey questions, and how we present the results.

---

[1] For the record, arming second graders is a very bad idea. Very bad.
[2] We calculate this by taking 100 percent of the population and subtracting both the 49 percent who favored abortion in all circumstances and the 12 percent who opposed it in the most stringent case (and by extension most likely opposed it in all cases).

Figure 3-13 Public Opinion on Same-Sex Marriage, 2001–2019

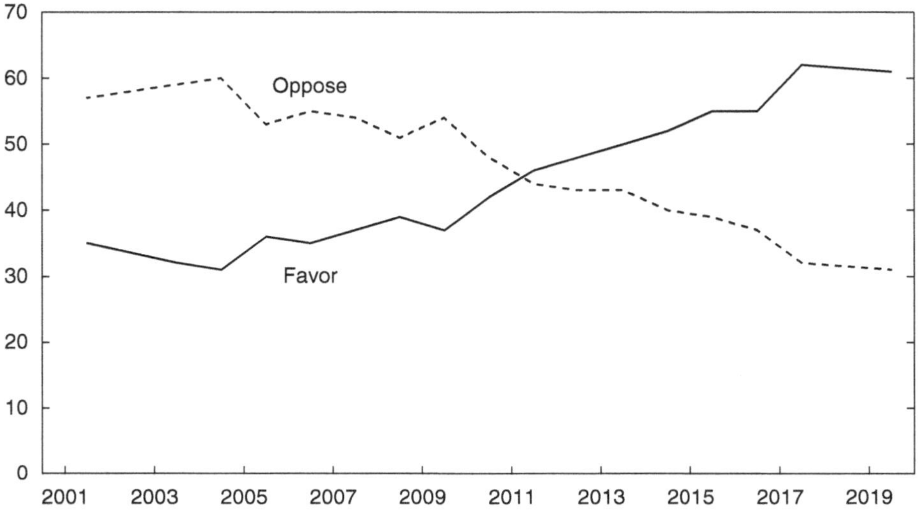

Note: Question: 1996–2013: "Do you strongly favor, favor, oppose, or strongly oppose allowing gay and lesbian couples to marry legally?" In some surveys, the question asked about "allowing gays and lesbians to marry legally." 2014: "Do you agree or disagree with the following statement: Homosexuals should have the right to marry one another." 2015: "Do you favor or oppose allowing gay and lesbian couples to enter into same-sex marriages?" Typically, 8 to 12 percent of the respondents volunteer that they don't know.

Source: Pew Research Center, "Fact Sheet: Attitudes on Same-Sex Marriage," May 14, 2019, https://www.pewresearch.org.

Figure 3-14 Public Opinion on Legalization of Marijuana, 1973–2018

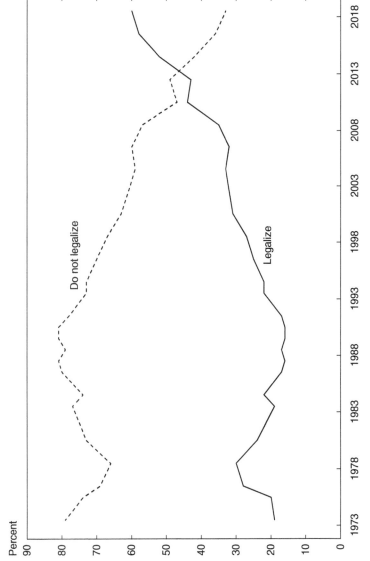

Note: Question: "Do you think the use of marijuana should be made legal, or not?" Typically, 3 to 8 percent of the respondents volunteer that they don't know.

Source: General Social Survey, National Opinion Research Center, University of Chicago.

Figure 3-15 Religious Affiliation of the U.S. Population and Political Ideology, by Religious Affiliation, 2014

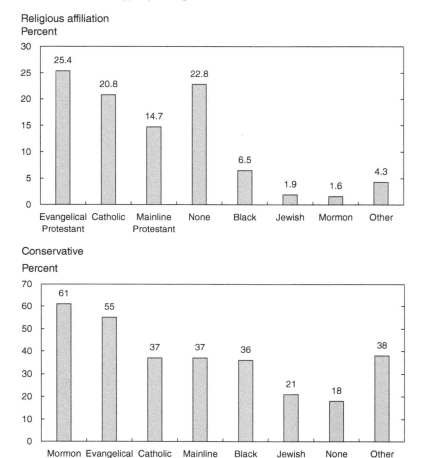

Note: Other affiliations (each less than 1 percent of the population) are Buddhist, Jehovah's Witness, Hindu, Orthodox, Muslim, and "others." The bottom figure shows the percentages responding "very conservative" or "conservative" in response to the question "In general, would you describe your political views as very conservative, conservative, moderate, liberal, or very liberal?"

Source: Pew Research Center, "U.S. Religious Landscape Survey," https://www.pewresearch.org.

Figure 3-16 Recent Trends in the Religiously Unaffiliated, by Generation, 2007–2019

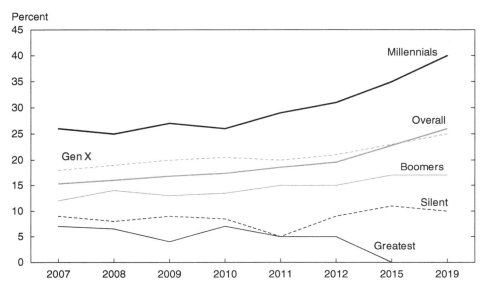

Sources: 2007–2012: Pew Research Center's Forum on Religion and Public Life, "'Nones' on the Rise: One-in-Five Adults Have No Religious Affiliation," October 9, 2012, 13, 16; 2015: "American's Changing Religious Landscape," May 12, 2015, 70; 2019: "In U.S., Decline of Christianity Continues at a Rapid Pace," October 17, 2019, 8, https://www.pewresearch.org.

Table 3-16 Public Opinion on the Courts and Criminal Justice, 1972–2018 (percent)

Year	Too harsh	About right	Not harsh enough	Don't know
1972	8	16	66	11
1973	5	13	73	9
1974[a]	5	6	60	29
1974	6	10	78	6
1975	4	10	79	7
1976	3	10	82	6
1977	3	8	83	5
1978	3	7	85	5
1980	3	7	84	5
1981 (Jan.)	3	13	77	7
1982[a]	4	5	76	14
1982	3	6	86	4
1983	4	6	85	4
1984	3	11	82	4
1985	3	10	84	3
1986	3	8	85	4
1987	3	12	80	5
1988	4	10	82	4
1989	3	9	84	5
1990	4	10	82	4
1991	4	11	80	5
1993	4	9	82	5
1994	3	8	85	4
1996	5	10	78	7
1998	6	13	75	6
2000	7	15	69	8
2002	9	17	67	6
2004	9	20	65	6
2006	9	21	64	5
2008	12	19	63	6
2010	14	18	61	8
2012	14	19	58	9
2014	15	19	57	8
2016	18	16	55	10
2018	19	15	54	12

Note: General Social Survey interviews are conducted in the spring of the year indicated, usually March–June. Question: "In general, do you think the courts in this area deal too harshly or not harshly enough with criminals?" Data for additional years can be found in previous editions of *Vital Statistics on American Politics*.

[a] In 1974 and 1982, half of the General Social Survey sample was asked the question as noted above and half the sample was asked the same question but with the phrase "or don't you have enough information about the courts to say" added at the end. The "don't know" column for these rows includes those saying "not enough information."

Sources: 1981: *Los Angeles Times* survey; others years: General Social Survey, National Opinion Research Center, University of Chicago.

Table 3-17 Public Opinion on Approval of U.S. Active Involvement in World Affairs, 1987–2019 (percent)

	Agree		Disagree		
Date	Completely	Mostly	Mostly	Completely	Don't know
May 1987	32	55	7	1	5
May 1988	47	43	6	1	3
February 1989	51	42	3	1	3
May 1990	39	50	6	1	4
November 1991	54	38	4	2	2
June 1992	47	44	5	2	2
May 1993	33	54	9	1	3
July 1994	51	39	7	2	1
November 1997	48	43	6	2	1
September 1999	45	43	8	2	2
August 2002	49	41	5	3	2
August 2003	50	40	6	2	2
January 2007	42	44	7	3	4
April 2009	51	39	5	2	3
April 2012	42	41	9	4	3

	Best to be active in word affairs	Should pay less attention to problems overseas	No answer
December 2004	44	49	7
March 2011	33	58	8
March 2014	35	60	5
July 2017	47	47	6
March 2019	44	49	6
September 2019	48	47	5

Note: Question: One version of this question has read: "Now I am going to read you another series of statements on some different topics. For each statement, please tell me if you completely agree with it, mostly agree with it, mostly disagree with it, or completely disagree with it. It's best for the future of our country to be active in world affairs." At other times a slightly different question has been used: "Which statement comes closer to your own views, 'It's best for the future of our country to be active in world affairs,' versus 'We should pay less attention to problems overseas and concentrate on problems here at home.'" Related data for additional years can be found in previous editions of *Vital Statistics on American Politics*.

Sources: Pew Research Center, "Partisan Polarization Surges in Bush, Obama Years: Trends in American Values: 1987–2012," June 4, 2012, 152–153; "Beyond Red vs. Blue: The Political Typology," June 26, 2014, 152, 155; "In a Politically Polarized Era, Sharp Divides in Both Partisan Coalitions," December 17, 2019, 122, https://www.pewresearch.org.

Table 3-18 Public Opinion on Peace through Military Strength, 1987–2019 (percent)

	Best Way to Assure Peace		
Date	Military Strength	Diplomacy	Other[a]
July 1994	36	58	6
October 1994	40	52	8
April 1995	35	58	7
October 1995	36	59	5
October 1996	36	53	11
August 1999	33	55	12
December 2004	30	55	15
October 2006	28	57	15
March 2011	31	58	11
December 2013	31	57	12
March 2014	30	62	8
July 2015	30	58	12
October 2015	36	56	9
September 2016	36	57	7
June 2017	30	61	9
September 2019	28	62	10

Note: Question: "Now I am going to read you another series of statements on some different topics. For each statement, please tell me if you completely agree with it, mostly agree with it, mostly disagree with it, or completely disagree with it. The best way to ensure peace is through military strength." Related data for additional years can be found in previous editions of *Vital Statistics on American Politics*.

[a] Other includes respondents who volunteered "Both" or "Neither," as well as Don't Know or No Answer.

Sources: Pew Research Center, "In a Politically Polarized Era, Sharp Divides in Both Partisan Coalitions," December 17, 2019, 123, https://www.pewresearch.org.

Figure 3-17 Public Opinion on U.S. Military Involvement in Iraq, 2003–2018

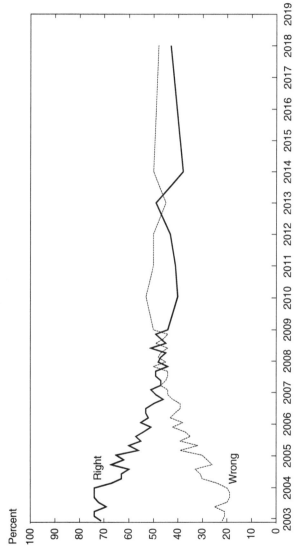

Note: Questions: "Do you think the U.S. made the right decision or the wrong decision in using military force in Iraq?" (In earlier years, the question wording was, ". . . in using military force against Iraq?") "How well is the U.S. military effort in Iraq going—very well, fairly well, not too well, or not at all well?" Related data for additional years can be found in previous editions of Vital Statistics on American Politics.

Sources: Pew Research Center, "Obama's Ratings Little Affected by Recent Turmoil," June 24, 2010, 35–36; "More Now See Failure than Success in Iraq, Afghanistan," January 30, 2014, 9–10; "In a Politically Polarized Era, Sharp Divides in Both Partisan Coalitions," December 17, 2019, https://www.pewresearch.org.

Table 3-19 Public Opinion on Terrorism, 2001–2016 (percent)

Terrorists' Ability to launch another major attack on the United States

Date	Greater	The same	Less	Don't know, refused
August 2002	22	39	34	5
July 2004	24	39	34	3
July 2005	28	40	29	3
January 2006	17	39	39	5
August 2006	25	37	33	5
December 2006	23	41	31	5
February 2008	16	41	39	4
February 2009	17	44	35	4
October–November 2009	29	38	29	4
January 2010	33	35	29	3
August 2011	23	39	35	3
October–November 2013	34	36	29	2
July 2014	34	34	30	2
August–September 2016	40	31	25	5

Concerns about Government's Anti-Terrorism Policies

Date	Gone too far in restricting civil liberties	Not done enough to protect the country	Both / neither approve of policies (volunteered)	Don't know, refused (volunteered)
July 2004	29	49	11	11
July 2005	31	52	10	7
Late October 2005	34	48	10	8
January 2006	33	46	12	9
February 2006	33	50	10	7
August 2006	26	55	11	8
Late February 2008	36	47	9	8
February 4–8, 2008	36	42	9	13
October 28–November 8, 2009	36	40	13	11
January 6–10, 2010	27	58	8	8
October 13–18, 2010	32	47	11	10
July 17–21, 2013	47	35	11	7
October 30–November 6, 2013	44	39	9	7
September 2–9, 2014	35	50	9	6
January 7–11, 2015	37	49	8	6
December 8–13, 2015	28	56	11	5
April 12–19, 2016	35	50	11	4
August 23–September 2, 2016	33	49	13	5

Note: Questions: "Overall, do you think the ability of terrorists to launch another major attack on the U.S. is greater, the same, or less than it was at the time of the September 11th terrorist attacks?" and "What concerns you more about the government's anti-terrorism policies: that they have gone too far in restricting the average person's civil liberties, or that they have not gone far enough to adequately protect the country?" Related data for additional years can be found in previous editions of *Vital Statistics on American Politics*.

Sources: Pew Research Center, "Most Think the U.S. Has No Responsibility to Act in Iraq," July 18, 2014, 9–10; "Terrorism Worries Little Changed; Most Give Government Good Marks for Reducing Threat," January 12, 2015, 14–15, http://people-press.org, "15 Years After 9/11, a Sharp Partisan Divide on Ability of Terrorists to Strike U.S.," September 7, 2016.

4
The Media

- **National Reach**
- **Presence in Washington**
- **Public Use**
- **Coverage and Viewership of Presidential Campaigns, Conventions, and Debates**
- **Newspaper Endorsements**

Acknowledging that the media have a tremendous role and influence on the American political system is certainly not a groundbreaking statement. Aside from the First Amendment recognition that a free press is essential to a functioning democracy, its role is perceived as so important and influential that it's not unusual to see the media referred to as the "fourth branch" of government. Perhaps more than any other aspect of the American political system, the role of the media has changed dramatically in the past ten to fifteen years. Just *how* it has changed and continues to evolve is something that we can begin to explore through the vast amount of data collected on mass media.

The role of the media can be viewed from different perspectives. First, where are Americans getting information? The reach and use of television and Internet (Table 4-1) introduces a shift that can be seen throughout this chapter and in all questions about the relationship between media and politics in the modern context: the growth of Internet use over the past thirty years is obvious. We see this not just in broad use of different media, but in where people get their news generally (Tables 4-5 and 4-6) and where they get their political (Table 4-7) and campaign (Table 4-11) news, specifically. Coinciding with the rise in new types of media, we also see changes in the number and reach of traditional media outlets, such as newspapers (Table 4-2). Television has played a prominent role in politics since the mid-20th century, but even there we see changes in how people use that medium as a source of news (Table 4-4), from the advent of cable news channels, to recent declines in TV use as other media have garnered more focus.

The question of where the public gets information is, of course, related to what is made available to them through various platforms. The political public has many more options than in previous decades, which were limited to nightly network news programs, newspapers, and radio broadcasts. With the rise of social media, the number of potential media outlets is unlimited. As media experienced tremendous diffusion, we see the effects on individual platforms not only in how much attention audiences give to them, but also in how much attention each platform devotes to specific political coverage. We note that network television devotes less coverage to elements of the political system, such as the hours of nominating conventions that are aired on network television (Table 4-15). Do fewer hours of convention coverage mean that the public are no longer interested in watching the conventions? Does it maybe mean that they continue to be interested but prefer watching on cable news channels with more of a point of view in their coverage, or catching up on the hot issues of the convention on social media channels?

Another question that's become relevant for many media and politics scholars is the perception the public has of media and whether it contributes to, or is affected by, increased polarization. We note that there are more similarities than differences in what platforms different demographic groups turn to for political news (Table 4-7) but more variation in specific news sources based on partisan affiliation (Table 4-8). In the past few years, with the rise of social media and websites, there is a great deal of area for study in the spread and velocity of misinformation, disinformation, and malinformation in shaping political outcomes. A relatively new topic, there is a lot of room for confusion and questions about its role, including how the public perceives its role and intent (Table 4-8).

The rise of social media and the Internet as an influential part of American politics is undeniable, but, as it has shifted relatively quickly, comparisons over time are difficult to make. This adds complication to questions of interpretation. As the landscape of political media shifts, researchers continue to update and shift their focus to ask new questions, collect different data, and adjust methods used to update their understanding of the topic. The Pew Research Foundation, from which much of the data in this chapter comes, offered an in-depth view of this in their December 2020 report, "Measuring News Consumption in a Digital Era," which we recommend reading as a companion to this chapter. As the number and types of data available change, and researchers update data collection practices, the types of questions we'll be able to explore using data will also change.

Table 4-1 Reach and Use of Selected Media, 1950–2020

Year	Percentage of households with Telephone service[a]	Percentage of households with Television sets	Percentage of adults who use Internet[b]	Percentage of TV households with Cable television	Percentage of TV households with Satellite television[c]	Average hours viewing per TV home per day
1950	62.0	9.0	—	—	—	4.6
1960	78.5	87.1	—	—	—	5.1
1970	87.0	95.3	—	6.7	—	5.9
1975	—	97.1	—	12.6	—	6.1
1980	93.0	97.9	—	19.9	—	6.6
1985	91.8	98.1	—	42.8	—	7.2
1990	93.3	98.2	—	56.4	—	6.9
1995	93.9	98.3	14.0	63.4	—	7.3
2000	94.1	98.2	52.0	70.2	11.4	7.6
2001	94.9	98.2	55.0	70.5	13.9	7.7
2002	95.3	98.2	59.0	69.1	16.5	7.7
2003	94.7	98.2	61.0	67.4	18.2	8.0
2004	93.5	98.2	63.0	66.4	19.2	8.0
2005	92.9	98.2	68.0	64.8	20.8	8.2
2006	93.4	98.2	71.0	62.1	24.5	8.2
2007	94.9	98.2	74.0	61.3	28.0	8.2
2008	95.0	98.2	74.0	61.3	28.7	8.3
2009	95.7	98.9	76.0	61.7	29.3	8.3
2010	95.9	98.9	76.0	60.7	30.5	—
2011	95.6	98.9	79.0	60.4	31.1	—
2012	95.8	96.7	83.0	59.6	31.5	—
2013	95.7	95.8	84.0	58.5	31.8	—
2014	96.1	96.4	84.0	56.9	32.9	4.2
2015	96.3	96.1	86.0	55.9	30.1	4.1
2016	96.3	95.2	88.0	53.3	30.3	4.1
2017	95.8	96.0	—	48.7	29.8	3.6
2018	96.0	96.5	89.0	48.7	28.0	3.4
2019	—	95.9	90.0	47.3	24.2	2.3
2020	—	96.1	93.0	46.1	22.9	2.5

Note: "—" indicates not available. Data for additional years can be found in previous editions of *Vital Statistics on American Politics*.

[a] Includes cell phone service. It is estimated that 85 percent of U.S. adults had a cell phone in 2010. As early as 2003, less than 2 percent were estimated to have no phone service at all.
[b] Questions have varied over the years. The data reflected here are based on a pooled analysis of all surveys conducted in that year. In previous editions of this book, in years with multiple surveys, the highest value was shown, which accounts for slight variations between this edition and prior years.
[c] Includes a small number of other delivery systems.

Sources: Telephone service: ProQuest Statistical Abstract of the United States, 2021 (Rowman and Littlefield, 2021), Table "Utilization and Number of Selected Media," and earlier editions of *Statistical Abstract*; television sets, cable and satellite television, 1950–2020, viewing 1950–2011: Television Bureau of Advertising, https://www.tvb.org, various years; Internet: Pew Research Center, "Core Trends Survey," January 2021, https://www.pewresearch.org; viewing 2014–2020: https://www.emarketer.com via *Statista*.

Table 4-2 Newspaper Circulation, Daily Papers, 1850–2018

Year	Number	Circulation (thousands)	Circulation as a percentage of population
1850	254	758	3.3
1860	387	1,478	4.7
1870	574	2,602	6.5
1880	971	3,566	7.1
1890	1,610	8,387	13.3
1900	2,226	15,102	19.8
1904	2,452	19,633	23.4
1909	2,600	24,212	26.2
1914	2,580	28,777	28.6
1919	2,441	33,029	31.0
1921	2,334	33,742	31.7
1923	2,271	35,471	30.6
1925	2,116	37,407	32.3
1927	2,091	41,368	35.7
1929	2,086	42,015	34.1
1931	2,044	41,294	33.6
1933	1,903	37,630	29.6
1935	2,037	40,871	32.1
1937	2,065	43,345	34.1
1939	2,040	42,966	32.4
1947	1,854	53,287	37.0
1950	1,772	53,800	35.3
1954	1,820	56,410	34.6
1958	1,778	58,713	33.6
1960	1,763	58,900	32.6
1963	1,766	63,831	33.7
1965	1,751	60,400	31.1
1967	—	66,527	33.5
1970	1,748	62,100	30.3
1975	1,756	60,700	28.1
1978	1,756	62,000	27.9
1979	1,763	62,200	27.6
1980	1,745	62,200	27.3
1981	1,730	61,400	26.7
1982	1,711	62,500	26.9
1983	1,701	62,600	26.7
1984	1,688	63,300	26.8
1985	1,676	62,800	26.3
1986	1,657	62,500	26.0
1987	1,645	62,826	25.9
1988	1,642	62,695	25.6
1989	1,626	62,649	25.3
1990	1,611	62,328	24.9
1991	1,586	60,687	24.4
1992	1,570	60,164	23.1

Table 4-2 *(Continued)*

Year	Number	Circulation (thousands)	Circulation as a percentage of population
1993	1,556	59,812	22.6
1994	1,548	59,305	22.2
1995	1,533	58,193	21.9
1996	1,520	56,983	21.1
1997	1,509	56,728	20.7
1998	1,489	56,182	20.3
1999	1,483	55,979	20.2
2000	1,480	55,773	19.8
2001	1,468	55,578	19.2
2002	1,457	55,186	18.9
2003	1,456	55,185	18.6
2004	1,457	54,626	18.6
2005	1,452	53,345	18.0
2006	1,437	52,329	17.5
2007	1,422	50,742	16.8
2008	1,408	48,598	15.9
2009	1,397	46,278	15.1
2010	—	—	—
2011	1,381	44,243	14.0
2012	1,425	43,154	13.8
2013	1,395	40,712	12.9
2014	1,331	40,420	13.0
2015	1,338	34,901	11.0
2016	1,286	33,419	10.0
2017	1,277	29,185	9.0
2018	1,279	25,705	8.0

Note: "—" indicates not available. Data are for English language newspapers only. In 1900 and earlier, figures include a small number of periodicals. From 1970–2012, the number of newspapers is for February of the following year; in 2013 and later, the number of newspapers is as of January the following year. Circulation figures are as of September 30 of the year indicated.

Sources: Daily papers, 1850–1967: U.S. Bureau of the Census (Washington, D.C.: Government Printing Office, 1975), 810; 1970–2009: *Editor & Publisher International Yearbook* (New York: Editor & Publisher, annual); 2012–2013: *Editor & Publisher Newspaper Data Book*; population, 1850–1990, 1998–1999, 2004–2009: U.S. Bureau of the Census, *Statistical Abstract of the United States* (Washington, D.C.: Government Printing Office, annual); 1991–1997, 2000–2003: estimated by *Editor & Publisher*; population, 2012–2017: Proquest LLC, *Proquest Statistical Abstract of the United States, 2021* (Bethesda, MD: Bernan, 2021).

186 The Media

Figure 4-1 Growth of Congressional Press Corps, 1864–2020

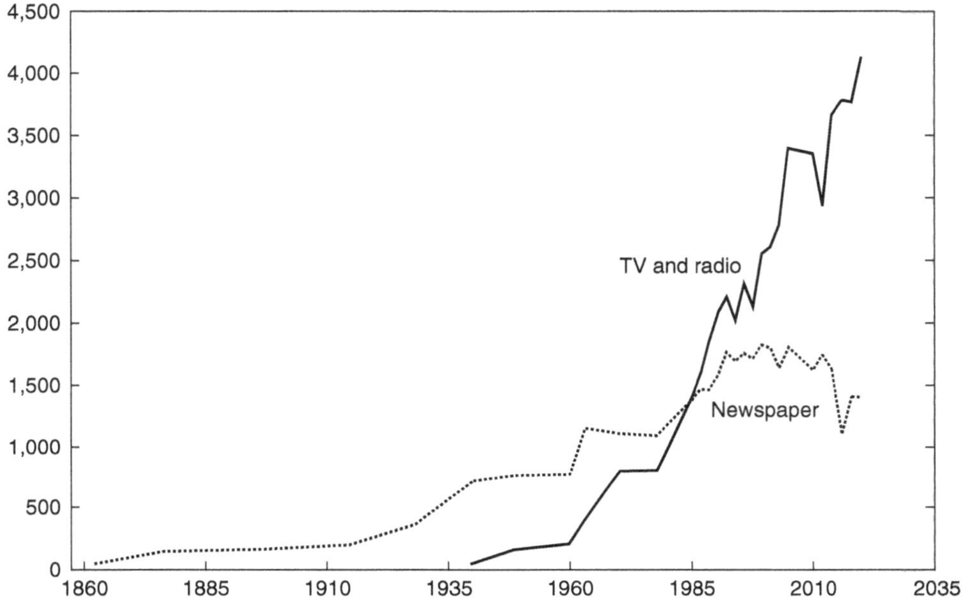

Note: Press corps members are those correspondents entitled to admission to the Senate and House press galleries and radio and television galleries. Before 1986, the number of press corps members was recorded about every ten years. Since 2000, the numbers are from the revised, online edition of the *Official Congressional Directory* (see source) for the year indicated.

Sources: Samuel Kernell, *Going Public: New Strategies of Presidential Leadership* (Washington, D.C.: CQ Press, 1986), 57; updated by the editors from successive volumes of U.S. Congress Joint Committee on Printing, *Official Congressional Directory* (Washington, D.C.: Government Printing Office); as of 2000 from the online version, www.gpo.gov.

Table 4-3 Presidential News Conferences, 1923–2021

President	Total number of solo press conferences	Total number of press conferences	Average number of press conferences per month
Coolidge (1923–1929)	407	407	6.1
Hoover (1929–1933)	267	268	5.6
F. Roosevelt (1933–1945)	881	881	6.1
Truman (1945–1953)	324	324	3.5
Eisenhower (1953–1961)	193	193	2.0
Kennedy (1961–1963)	65	65	1.9
L. Johnson (1963–1969)	135	135	2.2
Nixon (1969–1974)	29	39	0.6
Ford (1974–1977)	36	40	1.4
Carter (1977–1981)	52	59	1.2
Reagan (1981–1989)	15	46	0.5
G. H. W. Bush (1989–1993)	89	137	3.0
Clinton (1993–2001)	59	193	2.0
G. W. Bush (2001–2009)	49	210	2.2
Obama (2009–2017)	64	163	1.7
Trump (2017–2021)	44	88	1.8

Sources: Gerhard Peters, "Presidential News Conferences," *The American Presidency Project,* ed. John T. Woolley and Gerhard Peters (Santa Barbara, CA: University of California), https://www.presidency.ucsb.edu/node/323900.

A Data Literacy Lesson

Determining What Data to Count

Tallying the number of times a president holds a press conference, as we've done in Table 4-3, seems on the surface like it should be a clear-cut task. Certainly, there are instances when it is apparent that an interaction between a president and the press is clearly a press conference. On June 16, 2021, for example, President Joe Biden's official public schedule included an entry at 1:20 p.m. that read, "The President holds a Press Conference." Add one tally to the "press conferences" column.

But, if we continue on the president's schedule a bit, we notice a different entry for a week later. On June 24, 2021, at 1:05 p.m., the schedule read, "The President and a bipartisan group of Senators gaggle with the press." A gaggle, generally, is a less formal, off-camera (but usually on-record) conversation between an official and a group of pool reporters. It's the White House Press Secretary who holds press gaggles but occasionally, as on June 24, 2021, even the president will gaggle. Should that count as a press conference?

Access to the public has changed tremendously since Dwight Eisenhower held the first televised press conference in 1955 and, of course, even more dramatically since Woodrow Wilson held the first press conference in 1913. Should the data that represent the number of press conferences be updated as well? In this case (and, we'd argue, any time you're trying to draw substantive conclusions from raw data), consider what it is that you're attempting to measure. Are the data that you're using the best way to measure what you're investigating? (Or, as you might have learned in an introductory research methods class—how are you operationalizing the variable and is it appropriate for testing your hypothesis?) We think that press conferences are one of the valuable aspects of considering how the president attempts to interact with the public through the media. They have historically been a valuable means to the "bully pulpit" that allows presidents to share information and policies, and to persuade the public. As we consider that relationship, though, we also need to consider how complete the interactions we count are and how they help us understand the questions we're trying to answer.[1]

What about the casual, unscheduled (if not entirely spontaneous) interactions between the president and the press on the walk between the Oval Office and the Marine One helicopter? When a president gives a long-form interview to one reporter, where does that fit in? And, in the modern era, how do we account for social media as politicians and elected officials increasingly rely on direct communication with the public through their social media channels?

As you use data to understand political relationships, take a moment before you dive into the data to ask yourself what, exactly, you're trying to understand. To better understand whether the data provide enough information to explore that relationship, explore what goes into the tally marks you're counting. Different ways of measuring the same phenomena may cause you to reach different conclusions, even if they represent the same underlying behaviors.

---

[1] Martha Joynt Kumar, an expert on presidential press conferences, explicitly examines different types of interactions between presidents and the press and the importance of those differences in understanding different presidencies in a 2020 article, "Contemporary Presidency: Presidents Meet Reporters: Is Donald Trump an Outlier among Recent Presidents?" *Presidential Studies Quarterly,* 50 (1), 193–215.

Table 4-4 Use of Television for News, 1990–2020 (percent)

Date	TV	Local TV news[a]	Network TV news[b]	Cable news channels[c]	Cable News Network (CNN)[d]	Fox News Cable Channel[e]	MSNBC[f]	CNBC[g]
January 1990	—	—	—	—	51	—	—	—
June 1990	—	—	—	—	57	—	—	—
February 1993	—	92	81	—	—	—	—	—
May 1993	—	93	88	—	69	—	—	—
March 1995	—	90	76	—	58	—	—	—
April 1996	—	88	71	—	59	—	—	—
February 1997	—	88	72	—	58	—	—	—
April 1998	—	86	67	—	57	47	31	39
August 1999	—	—	73	—	—	—	—	—
April 2000	—	80	58	—	55	45	38	42
April 2002	—	81	61	68	56	48	45	43
April 2004	—	82	62	71	55	54	42	41
April 2006	—	77	54	65	54	51	40	37
May 2008	—	77	54	67	57	50	46	38
June 2010	—	76	55	70	50	49	39	35
May–June 2012	—	73	53	64	50	48	39	—
August–September 2013[h]	—	72	59	52	—	—	—	—
January–February 2016[h]	—	73	57	58	—	—	—	—
August 2017[h]	—	64	51	55	—	—	—	—
July–August 2018[h]	—	64	50	53	—	—	—	—
August–September 2020[h]	68	—	—	—	—	—	—	—

Note: "—" indicates not available. Data for other months can be found in previous editions of *Vital Statistics on American Politics.*

[a] Question: "How often do you watch the local news about your viewing area which usually comes on before or after the national news in the evening and again later at night—regularly, sometimes, hardly ever, or never?" (Prior to 2002, the question was, "How often do you watch the local news about your viewing area? This usually comes on before the national news and then later at night at 10 or 11.") In 2013–2018, the question was, "How often do you watch local television news—often, sometimes, hardly ever, or never?"
[b] Question: "How often do you watch the national nightly network news on CBS, ABC, or NBC? This is different from local news shows about the area where you live—regularly, sometimes, hardly ever, or never?" In 2013–2018, the question was, "How often do you watch national evening network television news (such as ABC World News, CBS Evening News, or NBC Nightly News)—often, sometimes, hardly ever, or never?"
[c] Question: "How often do you watch cable news channels such as CNN, MSNBC, or the Fox News Cable Channel—regularly, sometimes, hardly ever, or never?" In 2013–2018, the question was, "How often do you watch cable television news (such as CNN, The Fox News Cable channel, or MSNBC)—often, sometimes, hardly ever, or never?"
[d] Question: "How often do you watch CNN—regularly, sometimes, hardly ever, or never?" (Prior to 2008, the question was, "How often do you watch Cable News Network (CNN)—regularly, sometimes, hardly ever, or never?")
[e] Question: "How often do you watch the Fox News Cable Channel—regularly, sometimes, hardly ever, or never?"
[f] Question: "How often do you watch MSNBC—regularly, sometimes, hardly ever, or never?"
[g] Question: "How often do you watch CNBC—regularly, sometimes, hardly ever, or never?"
[h] Responses are for "often or sometimes watch."

Sources: Pew Research Center, "Americans Spending More Time Following the News," September 12, 2010, 107–109; "In Changing News Landscape, Even Television Is Vulnerable," September 27, 2012, 59–61; "The Role of News on Facebook," October 24, 2013, 2; 2016–2018: *American Trends Panel,* Wave 37; 2020: *American Trends Panel,* Wave 73, https://www.pewresearch.org.

Table 4-5 Use of Internet and Newspapers for News, 1990–2020 (percent)

Date	Ever go online?[a]		Frequency of going online to get news[b]					Read newspaper regularly?[c]	
	Yes	No	Every day	3–5 days/week	1–2 days/week	Every few weeks	Less often	No/never (volunteered)	Yes	No
November 1990	—	—	—	—	—	—	—	—	74	26
July 1991	—	—	—	—	—	—	—	—	73	27
June 1992	—	—	—	—	—	—	—	—	75	25
October 1994	—	—	—	—	—	—	—	—	73	27
March 1995	—	—	—	—	—	—	—	—	71	29
June 1995	14	86	6	9	15	13	28	29	69	34
April 1996	21	79	—	—	—	—	—	71	28	—
April 1998	36	64	18	17	20	15	21	9	68	32
September 1998	42	58	23	16	21	14	19	7	—	—
November 1998	—	—	—	—	—	—	—	—	70	30
August 1999	52	48	22	15	19	15	20	9	—	—
May 2000	52	48	27	15	19	12	18	9	63	37
July 2002	59	41	25	16	16	13	21	9	63	37
March 2004	69	31	27	18	15	12	17	11	60	40
April 2006	73	27	27	20	17	12	16	8	59	41
May 2008	73	27	37	18	16	8	13	8	54	46
May 2010	79	21	39	17	13	8	15	7	49	51
April 2012	82	18	37	16	13	7	19	7	49	50

Table 4-5 *(Continued)*

	Frequency of getting news on computer[d]				Frequency of getting news on a mobile device[e]			
	Often	Sometimes	Hardly ever	Never	Often	Sometimes	Hardly ever	Never
May 2013	35	30	17	18	21	19	13	46
July 2015	—	—	—	—	—	—	—	—
May 2016	33	30	16	21	36	24	12	28
March 2017	31	34	20	15	45	29	10	15
January 2018	—	—	—	—	—	—	—	—
February 2019	30	31	22	18	5	23	9	11
September 2020	60	26	7	7	—	—	—	—

Prior values (first column of numbers before Often): May 2013: 85, 15; July 2015: 87, 13; May 2016: 87, 13; March 2017: —, —; January 2018: 89, 11; February 2019: 90, 10; September 2020: 93, 7.

Additional columns (before mobile): May 2013: 54, 46; July 2015: —, 52; May 2016: 48, —; March 2017: —, —; January 2018: 43, 57; February 2019: 41, 59; September 2020: 32, 68.

Note: "—" indicates not available. Data for other months can be found in previous editions of *Vital Statistics on American Politics*.

[a] Questions: Prior to 2005, the question was, "Do you ever go online to access the Internet or World Wide Web or to send and receive email?"; 2005–2012, a "yes" was recorded for anyone who answered "yes" to either "Do you use the Internet, at least occasionally?" or "Do you send or receive email, at least occasionally?"; 2012: "Do you use the Internet, at least occasionally?"; —; "Do you send or receive email, at least occasionally?"; "Do you access the Internet on a cell phone, tablet, or other mobile handheld device, at least occasionally?" A "yes" response to any question is considered a "yes" to "Ever go online?"; 2013–2020: "Do you use the Internet or email, at least occasionally?" and "Do you access the Internet on a cellphone, tablet or other mobile handheld device, at least occasionally?"

[b] Question: Asked only of those who "ever" go online, "How frequently do you get news online or on a mobile device.... Would you say every day, 3 to 5 days per week, 1 or 2 days per week, once every few weeks, or less often?" (For June 2010 and earlier, the question did not include the phrase, "or on a mobile device." For May 2008 and earlier, the question wording was, "How frequently do you go online to get news...?")

[c] Questions: 1990–2012: "Do you happen to read any daily newspaper or newspapers regularly, or not?"; 2013–2020: "How often do you read any newspapers in print—often, sometimes, hardly ever, or never?" (responses shown for often and sometimes). (Dates Aug - Sept 2013, Jan - Feb 2016, Aug 2017, Jul - Aug 2018, Aug-Sept 2020.)

[d] Question: 2013–2019: "How often do you get news on a desktop or laptop computer?"; 2020: "How often do you get news from a smartphone, computer, or tablet?" (Note that previous categories have been combined.) (Dates Aug - Sept 2013, Jan - Feb 2016, March 2017, July 2019.)

[e] Question: 2013–2019: "How often do you get news on a mobile device (such as a smartphone or tablet)?" (Dates Aug - Sept 2013, Jan - Feb 2016, March 2017, July 2019.)

Source: 1990–2012: Pew Research Center; Frequency of getting news on computer and mobile device 2013–2019: *American Trends Panel*, Wave 51; Internet use 2000–2021: "January 2021 Core Trends Survey"; newspaper use 2013–2020: *American Trends Panel*, Wave 37; newspaper use 2020: *American Trends Panel*, Wave 73, https://www.pewresearch.org.

Table 4-6 Use of Newspaper, Radio, and Television for News, 1993–2020 (percent)

	Read/listened often			Often watch				Often use	
Year	Newspaper[a]	Radio news[b]	TV[c]	Cable TV news[d]	Local TV news[e]	Nightly network news[f]	Morning network news[g]	News websites or apps[h]	Social media[i]
1993	58[j]	47[j]	—	—	77	60	—	—	—
1996	50	44	—	—	65	42	—	—	—
1998	48	49	—	—	64	38	23	—	—
2000	47	43	—	—	56	30	20	—	—
2002	41	41	—	33	57	32	22	—	—
2004	42	40	—	38	59	34	22	—	—
2006	40	36	—	34	54	28	23	—	—
2008	34	35	—	39	52	29	22	—	—
2010	31	34	—	39	50	28	20	—	—
2012	29	33	—	34	48	27	19	—	—
2013	27	26	—	24	46	31	—	—	—
2016	20	25	—	31	46	30	—	28	18
2017	18	25	—	28	37	26	—	33	20
2018	16	26	—	30	37	25	—	33	20
2020	10	16	40	—	—	—	—	34	23

Note: "—" indicates not available.

[a] Questions: 1993–2012: "Did you get a chance to read a daily newspaper yesterday, or not?"; 2013–2018: "How often do you read any newspapers in print—often, sometimes, hardly ever, or never?"; 2020: "How often do you get news from print publications—often, sometimes, rarely, or never?" Responses are for "often."

[b] Questions: 2008 and earlier: "About how much time, if any, did you spend listening to any news on the radio yesterday or didn't you happen to listen to the news on the radio yesterday?"; 2009–2010: "About how much time, if any, did you spend listening to a radio news program or any news on the radio yesterday, or didn't you happen to listen to any news on the radio yesterday?"; 2011–2012: "About how much time, if any, did you spend listening to a radio news program or any news on the radio yesterday, or didn't you happen to listen to any radio news yesterday?"

Table 4-6 (*Continued*)

c Question: "How often do you get news from television—often, sometimes, rarely, or never?"
d Questions: 1993–2012: "Tell me if you watch cable news channels such as CNN, MSNBC, or the Fox News Cable Channel—regularly, sometimes, hardly ever, or never."; 2013–2018: "How often do you watch cable television news (such as CNN, The Fox News Cable channel, or MSNBC)—often, sometimes, hardly ever, or never?"
e Questions: 1993–2012: "Tell me if you watch the local news about your viewing area which usually comes on before or after the national news in the evening and again later at night—regularly, sometimes, hardly ever, or never."; 2013–2018: "How often do you watch local television news—often, sometimes, hardly ever, or never?"
f Questions: 1993–2012: "Tell me if you watch the national nightly network news on CBS, ABC, or NBC—regularly, sometimes, hardly ever, or never."; 2013–2018: "How often do you watch national evening network television news (such as ABC World News, CBS Evening News, or NBC Nightly News)—often, sometimes, hardly ever, or never?"
g Question: "Now I'd like to know how often you watch or listen to certain TV and radio programs. For each that I read, tell me if you watch or listen to it regularly, sometimes, hardly ever or never….The Today Show, Good Morning America, or CBS This Morning." From 2000 through 2010, this item referred to "The Today Show, Good Morning America, or The Early Show."
h Question: 2016–2018: "How often do you get news from a social media site (such as Facebook, Twitter, or Snapchat)—often, sometimes, hardly ever, or never?"; 2020: "Now thinking about the news you get on a smartphone, computer, or tablet, how often do you get news from social media such as Facebook, Twitter, or Instagram—often, sometimes, rarely, or never?"
i Question: 2016–2018: "How often do you get news from a news website or app—often, sometimes, hardly ever, or never?"; 2020: "Now thinking about the news you get on a smartphone, computer, or tablet, how often do you get news from news websites or apps—often, sometimes, rarely, or never?"
j Data from 1994.

Sources: Pew Research Center, "In Changing News Landscape, Even Television Is Vulnerable," September 27, 2012, 50, 52, 59, 61–62; "The Role of News on Facebook," October 24, 2013, 2; 2016–2018: *American Trends Panel*, Wave 37; 2020: *American Trends Panel*, Wave 73, https://www.pewresearch.org.

Table 4-7 Most common platform for political news, Demographics, 2020 (percent)

	Print	Radio	Network TV	Local TV	Cable TV	News website or app	Social Media
Gender[a]							
Men	3	7	13	12	15	33	16
Women	3	6	16	17	16	23	18
Age							
18–29 years	2	4	6	9	7	30	41
30–49 years	2	9	9	11	9	37	22
50–64 years	3	6	18	23	18	23	6
65 years and older	6	6	24	16	30	16	3
Race							
White non-Hispanic	3	8	14	13	17	29	15
Black non-Hispanic	2	2	16	29	16	18	15
Hispanic	3	3	16	15	12	24	24
Asian non-Hispanic	3	7	8	12	8	38	26
Education							
High school graduate or less	3	5	15	22	18	19	16
Some college	3	7	14	14	15	26	21
College graduate	3	7	12	10	13	37	17
Postgraduate	5	9	13	6	13	41	13
Family income							
Lower income	3	5	14	20	13	19	24
Middle income	2	7	14	14	16	29	16
Higher income	5	7	13	8	17	38	11
Party identification							
Democrat/Lean Democrat	4	6	15	14	13	29	13
Republican/Lean Republican	2	8	13	16	18	26	15
Political Knowledge							
High political knowledge	41	42	29	10	35	45	17
Middle political knowledge	29	34	35	21	29	31	27
Low political knowledge	31	24	36	69	35	23	57
Total	3	6	14	15	15	28	17

Note: Percentages are those responding to the question "What is the most common way you get political and election news?" Categories may not total 100 percent due to respondent refusal to answer some questions. Survey was conducted August 21–September 7, 2020.

[a] The group of respondents who answered "other" was too small to analyze.

Source: Pew Research Center, *American News Pathways* data tool, https://www.pewresearch.org/pathways-2020/NEWS_MOST.

Table 4-8 Perceptions of Misinformation in the 2020 Election (percent)

	Believe they encountered made-up news[a]				Believe misinformation played a role in which candidate people voted for[b]			Believe made-up news was mostly intended to hurt a particular party[c]			
	A lot	Some	Not much	None	Major impact	Minor impact	Not much	Republican Party	Democratic Party	Both parties equally	Neither party in particular
All adults	28	45	20	6	53	31	15	34	35	21	8
Primary news platform											
Print	26	48	16	10	50	29	20	35	43	19	3
Radio	27	49	20	3	51	35	13	41	35	18	6
Local TV	24	39	24	11	51	28	28	38	25	23	12
Network TV	25	48	21	6	53	32	16	35	38	18	9
Cable TV	31	43	18	7	57	29	13	41	37	15	6
Social media	25	44	22	8	52	32	16	28	34	30	8
Website or app	30	48	18	3	55	32	12	32	43	19	6
Party											
Democrat/Lean Democrat	23	46	23	8	47	35	17	5	63	22	9
Republican/Lean Republican	34	44	17	4	61	27	11	69	6	19	5
News Diet Republican/Lean Republican											
Only Fox or talk radio	47	41	10	2	71	23	5	94	1	4	1
Fox/talk radio and other sources	32	41	18	8	61	24	14	65	6	18	10
No Fox/talk radio; only other sources	19	48	27	5	48	35	16	44	15	33	7

(Table continues)

Table 4-8 (Continued)

	Believe they encountered made-up news[a]				Believe misinformation played a role in which candidate people voted for[b]			Believe made-up news was mostly intended to hurt a particular party[c]			
	A lot	Some	Not much	None	Major impact	Minor impact	Not much	Republican Party	Democratic Party	Both parties equally	Neither party in particular
None of the sources asked about	31	47	17	3	60	28	11	68	4	21	6
Democrat/Lean Democrat Only MSNBC, CNN, NPR, *The New York Times*, or *The Washington Post*	27	50	19	4	54	33	13	1	83	12	4
MSNBC/CNN/NPR, *The New York Times/The Washington Post*, and other sources	24	45	22	9	49	33	16	8	66	18	8
No MSNBC/CNN/ NPR/*NYT*/*The Washington Post*; only other sources	15	46	27	11	38	41	21	4	58	28	10
None of the sources asked about	19	45	26	9	41	36	23	7	52	29	12
Gender											
Men	31	44	19	5	53	33	14	38	36	20	6
Women	25	45	21	7	54	29	16	31	35	23	10

Table 4-8 (Continued)

Age									
18–29 years	23	45	26	6	53	31	15	26	37	28	9
30–49 years	24	46	21	7	51	33	15	28	35	27	9
50–64 years	33	43	17	7	54	29	16	40	34	17	7
65 years and older	33	44	17	6	60	26	14	45	36	12	6
Education											
High school graduate or less	28	40	21	10	50	29	20	38	26	23	11
Some college	29	45	20	5	56	30	13	36	34	23	7
College graduate	27	48	19	4	55	33	12	31	44	20	5
Postgraduate	25	51	19	4	55	34	11	25	53	16	6

[a] Question: "How much, if any, news and information have you seen or heard about the 2020 presidential election that seemed completely made up—a lot, some, not much, or none at all?"

[b] Question: "Thinking about the presidential election, how much of an impact, if any, do you think made-up news and information had on which candidate people decided to vote for—a major impact, a minor impact, or not much of an impact at all?"

[c] Question: "Do you think made-up news and information related to the presidential election was mostly intended to hurt the Republican Party, the Democratic Party, both parties about equally, or neither party in particular?"

Source: Calculated by the authors from Pew Research Center, *American News Pathways* Data Tool, November 18–20, 2020, https://www.pewresearch.org/pathways-2020.

Table 4-9 Partisan Differences in Media Use and Role Perception, 2020

	All U.S. Adults	Republican/ Lean Republican	Democrat/ Lean Democrat
News Fatigue[a]			
Like the amount of news	32	24	40
Worn out by the amount of news	66	75	59
Media role in fact checking candidates[b]			
A major responsibility	67	54	79
A minor responsibility	21	28	14
Not a responsibility	12	17	7
Amount of election news[c]			
Too much attention	25	28	21
Too little attention	17	19	15
Right amount of attention	58	52	64
Most common way to get news[d]			
Print	3	2	4
Radio	6	8	6
Local television	15	16	14
Network television	14	13	15
Cable television	15	18	13
News website or app	28	26	29
Social media	17	15	19
Main source of news[e]			
ABC	4	4	4
CBS	3	2	3
CNN	12	5	18
Fox News	16	34	2
MSNBC	4	0	7
NBC	4	4	5
NPR	5	1	8
Social media sites	4	3	4
The New York Times	2	0	4
Other Sources	33	34	33
Refused/don't know	13	12	12

[a] Questions: "Which of the following statements come closer to your view? 'I like seeing a lot of coverage of the campaign and candidates.' Or 'I am worn out by so much coverage of the campaign and candidates.'"
[b] Question: "More broadly, in covering political campaigns and candidates, how much of a responsibility is it of the news media to correct statements that a candidate makes that are inaccurate?"
[c] Question: "Thinking about some major events in the news, how much attention do you think news organizations are giving each of the following? The 2020 presidential election—too much attention, too little attention, or right amount of attention?"
[d] Question: "What is the most common way you get political and election news?"
[e] Question: "What news sources do you turn to most often for political and election news? Please list the name of the specific news organization or source."

Source: Compiled by the authors from Pew Research Center, *American News Pathways* Data Tool, 2020, https://pewresearch.org/pathways-2020.

Table 4-10 Preference for News with a Point of View, 2004–2020 (percent)

	Prefer news from		
	My point of view	No point of view	Don't know
2004	25	67	8
2006	23	68	9
2008	23	66	11
2010	25	62	13
2012	26	64	10
2013	27	71	—
2020	30	60	—[a]

Note: "—" indicates not available. Question: 2004–2013: "Thinking about the different kinds of political news available to you, what do you prefer… getting news from sources that share your political point of view or getting news from sources that don't have a particular political point of view?"; 2013: "Thinking about the different kinds of news you get, do you mostly… get news from sources that share [your] point of view or get news from sources that don't have a particular point of view?"; 2020: "Thinking about the different kinds of news available to you, do you prefer getting news from sources that share, challenge, or have no point of view?"

[a] The remaining 10 percent of respondents indicated that they prefer news that challenges their point of view.

Sources: Pew Research Center, "Americans Spending More Time Following the News," September 12, 2010, 47; "In Changing News Landscape, Even Television Is Vulnerable," September 27, 2012, 32; "The Role of News on Facebook," October 24, 2013, 20; "Topline," 3, https://www.pewresearch.org; 2020: Reuters Institute, *Digital News Report 2020,* 15, https://reutersinstitute.politics.ox.ac.uk/sites/default/files/2020-06/DNR_2020_FINAL.pdf.

Table 4-11 Sources of Campaign News, 1992–2020 (percent)

	1992	1996	2000	2004	2008	2012	2016	2020
Main source of campaign news[a]								
Television	82	72	70	76	68	67	78	44
Newspapers	57	60	39	46	33	27	36	3
Radio	12	19	15	22	16	20	44	6
Magazines	9	11	4	6	3	3	—	—
Campaign news from the Internet[b]								
Yes	—	10	30	41	56	67	65	45
No	—	90	70	59	44	33	35	55

Note: "—" indicates not available. Results are based on adults who voted. For purposes of comparison, note the change in question format in 2020, shifting from using a source and having an option to indicate multiple selections, to indicating only one primary type of source. Data for additional years can be found in earlier editions of *Vital Statistics on American Politics*.

[a] Question: 1992–2012: "How did you get most of your news about the presidential election campaign?" Sum may exceed 100 percent due to multiple responses. Respondents were allowed to give two responses 1992–2012, and were able to give multiple responses in 2016.

[b] Questions: 2008 and earlier: "Did you happen to get any news or information about the [year] elections from the Internet, or not?"; 2012: "Did you happen to get any news or information about the 2012 elections online on a computer, tablet, cell phone, or other device, or not?"; 2016: "In the past week did you learn something about the presidential campaign or candidates from each of the following sources?"; 2020: "What is the most common way you get political and election news?"

Source: Pew Research Center, "Low Marks for the 2012 Election: Voters Pessimistic about Partisan Cooperation," November 15, 2012, 38–39; "The 2016 Presidential Campaign—A News Event That's Hard to Miss," February 5, 2016, 7; 2020 data: *American News Pathways* data tool, https://www.pewresearch.org.

A Data Literacy Lesson

What Are Surveys Asking?

It's not a particularly bold statement to say that the relationship between media and the political system has changed dramatically, and quickly, in recent years. Consider that the Internet has only been widely available for the past twenty-five years and smart phones, which have brought the Internet to a much more prominent place in our lives, have only been available for the past four presidential elections.

As the world changes, scholars and experts have to update their approaches to studying and understanding it accordingly. The Internet was not widely used enough to include questions about its use for keeping up with campaign news in 1992. Less than thirty years later, the idea of not including a multitude of questions about how campaigns and the American public use websites, social media, and news apps for campaign news is inconceivable. While these updates are essential and useful for understanding how the world works as it is, they also provide other challenges.

Table 4-11 provides an interesting example of this. We've provided an overview of how Americans get their campaign news in each presidential election since 1992. There are a lot of useful ways that these data could be used. But, as we make comparisons over time, it's important to pay close attention to whether we're comparing the same question or different questions over time.

We've noted elsewhere throughout this book the importance of checking how data were collected. In cases where results are from surveys (as in many of the tables throughout this chapter), it's important to know the question wording that was used, so you know what respondents were answering. If you look only at the numbers in Table 4-11 without examining the question wording in the survey questions that were used to collect the data, you might come to a set of conclusions that isn't accurate. For the first example of this, look at the use of newspapers and radio across time: it looks like they were a fairly steady source of campaign news until there was a sudden and precipitous drop in their use between 2016 and 2020. The second place where, without context, we might draw some erroneous conclusions, is in Internet use. Moving along the timeline, it looks as though people were using it as a source of campaign news at a steadily increasing pace between 1996 and 2012, when it plateaued and then dropped between 2016 and 2020. The growth in its use seems reasonable and intuitive, but the plateau and subsequent decrease in use would be surprising and might lead to some unfounded conclusions.

The reality is that these patterns are a function of the question wording. Look at the footnotes, which include the questions that were used in surveys over the years. You can see that the question wording for the survey was the same from 1992–2012 for television, newspapers, radio, and magazines. Specifically, the question asked how respondents got most of their news about the election—and let them provide up to two answers. Internet use for campaign news was asked separately and from 1996–2012 simply asked if respondents got any news from the Internet.

In 2016, the question changed: here, Internet was combined with television, radio, and newspapers (magazines were no longer offered as a separate category), and respondents were asked if they'd learned anything about the election in the past

(Continued)

(Continued)

week from any of the sources. Respondents could provide as many answers as they had used.

Finally, the question changed again in 2020. As in 2020, the source types were all considered together, but respondents were asked to identify the most common way they got political and election news. This was closer to the question wording in 1992–2012, but forced respondents to pick only one, rather than allowing two or more responses.

Going back to the patterns we observed, without considering the context of question wording, would you feel comfortable saying there was a sudden and precipitous decline in newspaper use between 2012 and 2016? We wouldn't. The more accurate (if less succinct) statement would be, "Between 1992–2012, there was a steady decrease in the number of respondents who identified newspapers as one of their two primary news sources. In 2016, slightly more than a third had gotten at least some information from a newspaper at some point in the past week, and by 2020, only 3 percent of respondents identified newspapers as their most common source of political or campaign news." Similarly, for the pattern in Internet use, we could more accurately say, "Between 1996 and 2012, the percentage of Americans that ever used the Internet for news steadily grew. By 2016, 65 percent had gotten some political news online in the past week, and by 2020, 45 percent had identified the Internet as their primary source of news." Such headlines, of course, do not fit nicely onto websites, or as teasers on the network news.

It's nice when the same question can be asked in the same way of the same group of people each year over time—it provides a much simpler comparison over time. But, the reality is that as the world changes, the questions we ask to understand the world need to change to keep up. To make sure our understanding is accurate, we need to make sure we know what questions are being answered.

Table 4-12 Use of Digital Platforms by County Political Parties in 2020 (percent)

Region	Email	Website	Facebook	Twitter	Instagram
New England					
Democratic Party	76.9	55.9	77.8	34.0	7.0
Republican Party	68.9	42.7	69.7	27.5	0.0
Middle Atlantic					
Democratic Party	98.0	92.0	94.7	53.2	27.1
Republican Party	84.9	74.5	90.6	43.3	9.9
East North Central					
Democratic Party	87.2	59.3	87.9	38.8	13.2
Republican Party	69.9	51.2	86.4	32.2	6.9
West North Central					
Democratic Party	80.4	46.3	64.7	17.2	5.1
Republican Party	49.2	18.4	56.5	9.5	0.7
South Atlantic					
Democratic Party	88.9	56.1	82.3	44.6	23.5
Republican Party	75.8	65.7	82.4	39	16.3
East South Central					
Democratic Party	83.2	60.4	62.3	20.6	6.3
Republican Party	69.6	40.5	68.3	16.6	1.6
West South Central					
Democratic Party	47.7	20.5	58.2	13.0	4.7
Republican Party	73.1	23.7	55.6	9.2	2.4
Mountain					
Democratic Party	77.3	59.7	77.6	28.9	11.4
Republican Party	76.9	45.0	69.0	21.1	4.5
Pacific					
Democratic Party	72.4	69.6	67.9	32.9	8.4
Republican Party	75.0	55.9	79.1	24.5	5.9
Total					
Democratic Party	79.1	57.8	74.8	31.5	11.9
Republican Party	71.5	46.4	73.1	24.8	5.4

Note: Local parties in each start are organized by county lines with the exception of Alaska, Connecticut, Massachusetts, Minnesota, North Dakota, and Virginia. Local parties in those states are organized along different divisions such as township lines or state house districts. For states included in each region, see Appendix A.

Source: Whitesell, Anne M., Kevin Reuning, and A. Lee Hannah, "Local Political Party Presence Online." Forthcoming at *Party Politics*. A. Lee Hannah, Department of Political Science, Wright State University, personal communication.

Table 4-13 Public's Use of Media to Follow Presidential Campaigns, 1960–2012 (percent)

Media	1960	1964	1968	1972	1976	1980	1984	1988	1992	1996	2000	2004	2008	2012	2016[a]	2020[b]
Read newspaper articles about the election																
Yes															50	41
Regularly	44	40	37	26	28	—	—	—	—	—	—	—	—	14	—	—
Often[c]	12	14	12	14	17	27	24	—	—	—	—	—	—	20	—	—
From time to time[d]	16	18	19	16	24	29	34	—	—	—	—	—	—	—	—	—
Once in a great while[e]	7	6	7	4	10	17	19	—	—	—	—	—	—	15	—	—
None	21	22	25	40	22	27	23	—	—	—	—	—	—	51	—	—
Paid attention to newspaper articles about the presidential campaign																
Great deal	—	—	—	—	—	—	8	6	9	5	6	8	9	—	—	—
Quite a bit	—	—	—	—	—	—	14	12	15	11	10	14	18	—	—	—
Some	—	—	—	—	—	—	28	22	20	19	19	21	31	—	—	—
Very little	—	—	—	—	—	—	20	9	6	7	6	6	9	—	—	—
None	—	—	—	—	—	—	31	52	50	58	60	51	33	—	—	—
Listened to speeches or discussions on radio																
Yes															45	52
Good many[f]	15	12	12	8	12	14	10	5	7	7	8	15	13	10	—	—
Several[g]	17	23	16	21	20	22	20	10	11	14	14	18	19	14	—	—
One or two[h]	10	12	12	13	16	15	16	17	18	18	15	18	15	13	—	—
None	58	52	59	59	52	50	55	69	64	61	62	49	53	64	—	—
Watched programs about the campaign on television																
Yes															84	85
Good many[f]	47	41	42	33	37	28	25	—	31	15	24	27	29	20	—	—
Several[g]	29	34	34	41	38	37	37	—	39	32	35	37	37	28	—	—
One or two[h]	11	13	13	16	15	22	24	—	19	28	23	22	20	28	—	—
None	13	11	11	9	10	13	14	—	11	25	18	14	14	24	—	—

Table 4-13 (Continued)

Paid attention to television news about the presidential campaign																
Great deal	—	—	—	—	12	9	7	—	17	15	20	—	27	—	—	—
Quite a bit	—	—	—	—	15	12	15	—	24	26	29	—	31	—	—	—
Some	—	—	—	—	13	15	14	—	28	29	28	—	23	—	—	—
Very little	—	—	—	—	13	15	12	—	11	13	11	—	8	—	—	—
None	—	—	—	—	59	61	64	—	20	17	13	—	11	—	—	—
Read about the campaign in magazines																
Good many[f]	12	10	9	7	12	7	7	—	—	—	—	—	—	—	—	—
Several[g]	15	16	12	15	24	19	16	—	—	—	—	—	—	—	—	—
One or two[h]	13	13	15	14	15	12	11	—	—	—	—	—	—	—	—	—
None	59	61	64	64	49	62	66	—	—	—	—	—	—	—	—	—
Paid attention to magazine articles about the presidential campaign																
Great deal	—	—	—	—	—	—	3	3	4	3	—	—	4	3	—	—
Quite a bit	—	—	—	—	—	—	4	6	7	7	—	—	7	8	—	—
Some	—	—	—	—	—	—	7	11	10	15	—	—	12	17	—	—
Very little	—	—	—	—	—	—	2	3	3	7	—	—	6	7	—	—
None	—	—	—	—	—	—	84	76	77	68	—	—	72	65	—	—
Used Internet to follow presidential campaign																
Yes	—	—	—	—	—	—	—	—	—	—	—	—	—	—	61	70

Note: "—" indicates question not asked or response category not offered. Data for earlier years can be found in previous editions of *Vital Statistics on American Politics*.

[a] Question: "From which of the following sources have you heard anything about the presidential campaign—Television news programs; newspapers; Internet sites, chat rooms, or blogs; or radio news or talk shows?"
[b] Question: "From which of the following sources have you heard anything about the presidential campaign—TV Programs, Newspapers, Internet Sites, Radio News, or None?"
[c] "Quite a lot, pretty much" in 1952; "yes" in 1956; "good many" in 1980–1984 and 2012.
[d] "Not very much" in 1952; "several" in 1980–1984 and 2012.
[e] "One or two" in 1980–1984 and 2012.
[f] "Quite a lot, pretty much" in 1952; "yes" in 1956; "good many" in 1980–1984.
[g] "Yes" in 1956.
[h] "Not very much" in 1952.

Source: American National Election Studies data, University of Michigan, Ann Arbor, Mich., and Stanford University, Palo Alto, Calif., https://www.electionstudies.org.

Table 4-14 Credibility of Television and Print Media, 1998–2019 (percent)

	1998	2000	2002	2004	2006	2008	2010	2012	Not rated, 2012[a]	2014	2019
TV news outlets											
60 Minutes (CBS)	34	34	34	32	27	30	33	30	10	50	48
ABC News	30	30	24	24	22	24	21	22	7	46	45
CBS News	28	29	26	24	22	22	21	20	6	54	47
CNN	43	39	37	32	28	31	29	25	6	—	—
C-SPAN	32	34	30	27	25	25	22	—	—	44	43
Fox News	—	25	24	24	25	24	27	22	8	—	—
Local TV news	34	32	28	24	23	28	29	28	5	38	34
MSNBC	—	28	27	21	20	24	22	19	10	50	47
NBC News	30	29	25	23	23	24	19	20	5	38	42
NewsHour/PBS	29	24	26	23	23	23	—	—	—	29	31
National Public Radio	18	25	23	22	22	27	28	24	21	—	—
Print news outlets											
Associated Press	18	21	17	18	17	16	—	—	—	—	—
The National Enquirer	3	4	3	5	6	5	—	—	—	—	35
The New York Times	—	—	—	21	20	18	21	17	19	34	—
Newsweek	24	24	20	19	18	16	—	—	—	—	—
People	10	10	9	7	8	8	—	—	—	—	—
Time	27	29	23	22	21	21	—	—	—	—	—
U.S. News	—	—	26	24	21	20	17	14	17	33	28
USA Today	23	23	20	19	19	16	25	21	19	31	31
The Wall Street Journal	41	41	33	24	26	25	21	20	8	—	—
Your daily newspaper	29	25	22	18	19	23	—	—	—	—	—

Table 4-14 *(Continued)*

Note: "—" indicates not available. The 1998–2012 percentages are, of respondents who could rate each organization, those who believe all or most of what the organization says. Question: "As I name some organizations, please rate how much you think you can believe each that I name on a scale of 4 to 1. On this four-point scale, '4' means you can believe all or most of what the organization says, and '1' means you believe almost nothing of what they say. First, how would you rate the believability of _____ on this scale of 4 to 1?" 2014-2019 percentages are, of respondents who have heard of each organization, those who indicate they trusted them. Question, "Of the sources you have heard of, click on all that you generally TRUST for political and election news."

a "Not rated" combines "never heard of" and "can't rate" responses.

Sources: Pew Research Center, "Audience Segments in a Changing News Environment," August 17, 2008, 122–126; "Americans Spending More Time Following the News," September 12, 2010, 138–141; "Further Decline in Credibility Ratings for Most News Organizations," August 16, 2012, 11–14; *American Trends Panel*, Wave 1, 45, https://www.pewresearch.org.

Table 4-15 National Nominating Conventions: Television Coverage and Viewership, 1952–2020

Year/party	Audience rating[a] (percent)	Average hours viewed by household	Network hours telecast[b]
1952			
Republican	—	10.5	57.5
Democratic	—	13.1	61.1
1956			
Republican	—	6.4	22.8
Democratic	—	8.4	37.6
1960			
Republican	28.0	6.2	25.5
Democratic	29.2	8.3	29.3
1964			
Republican	21.8	7.0	36.5
Democratic	28.8	6.4	23.5
1968			
Republican	26.4	6.5	34.0
Democratic	28.5	8.5	39.1
1972			
Republican	23.4	3.5	19.8
Democratic	18.3	5.8	36.7
1976			
Republican	31.5	6.3	29.5
Democratic	25.2	5.2	30.4
1980			
Republican	21.6	3.8	22.7
Democratic	27.0	4.4	24.1
1984			
Republican	19.2	1.9	11.9
Democratic	23.4	2.5	12.9
1988			
Republican	18.3	—	—
Democratic	19.8	—	—
1992			
Republican	20.5	—	7.3
Democratic	22.0	—	8.0
1996			
Republican	16.5	—	5.0
Democratic	17.2	—	5.0
2000			
Republican	13.9	—	5.2
Democratic	15.3	—	5.3
2004			
Republican	15.3	—	3.0
Democratic	14.3	—	3.0
2008			
Republican	21.9	1.4	3.0[c]
Democratic	19.9	1.4	4.0
2012			
Republican	19.3[d]	—	3.0
Democratic	22.7[e]	—	3.0

Table 4-15   *(Continued)*

Year/party	Audience rating[a] (percent)	Average hours viewed by household	Network hours telecast[b]
2016			
Republican	20.2[f]	—	3.0
Democratic	18.7[g]	—	3.0
2020			
Republican	14.7[h]	—	3.0
Democratic	15.6[i]	—	3.0

Note: "—" indicates not available.

[a] Sum of the percentage of television households viewing the convention during an average minute of common coverage periods. Through 1988, based on viewing of ABC, CBS, and NBC; for 1992 and 1996, based on viewing the three networks plus PBS and CNN (the 1996 Republican convention was also televised on the Family Channel, but that is not included in the rating); for 2000, includes the three networks, CNN, Fox News Channel, and MSNBC; for 2004, includes the three networks, CNN, Fox News Channel, and MSNBC; for 2008, includes the three networks, CNN, Fox News Channel, MSNBC, BET (Democratic convention only), TV One (Democratic convention only), Univision (day four only), and Telemundo (day four only). C-SPAN viewing not included.

[b] Number of hours during which one or more of ABC, CBS, or NBC was broadcasting the convention. PBS has provided three hours each night of the convention. CNN, Fox News Channel, and MSNBC provided extensive coverage, often entailing regular news programming anchored from the convention site. Extensive streaming coverage has also been available in recent elections.

[c] Four hours of network coverage of the Republican convention was originally planned. However, because of Hurricane Gustav the convention's first night was scaled back and networks aired storm coverage instead.

[d] Day four ratings. There was no common coverage, and thus no rating calculated, for the first day of the convention due to Hurricane Isaac. For day two of the convention, the audience rating for all households was 14.7; and for day three, 14.7.

[e] Day three ratings. For day one of the convention, the audience rating for all households was 17.3; for day two, 16.7.

[f] Day four ratings. For day one of the convention, the average rating for all households was 14.8; for day two, 12.7; and for day three, 15.0.

[g] Day four ratings. For day one of the convention, the average rating for all households was 16.6; for day two, 16.2; and for day three, 15.8.

[h] Day four ratings. For day one of the convention, the average rating for all households was 10.7; for day two, 12.2; and for day three, 11.0.

[i] Day four ratings. For day one of the convention, the average rating for all households was 12.7; for day two, 12.6; and for day three, 14.6.

Sources: Audience rating, 1960–2004: The Nielsen Company, "Historical TV Ratings: Democratic Conventions" and "Historical TV Ratings: Republican Conventions," August 27, 2008; audience rating, 2008: The Nielsen Company, "Audience Estimates for the 2008 Republican Convention," September 5, 2008, https://www.nielsen.com/us/en/insights; audience rating, 2012: The Nielsen Company, "Final Night of Republican National Convention Draws 30.3 Million Viewers," August 31, 2012, https://www.nielsen.com/us/en/insights, The Nielsen Company, "Closing Night of Democratic National Convention Draws 35.7 Million Viewers," September 7, 2012, https://www.nielsen.com/us/en/insights; audience rating 2016–2020: The Nielsen Company, "Media Advisory: Television Audience Estimates," nielsen.com/us/en/press-releases/2020; Hours viewed, hours telecast, 1952–1980: Christopher Sterling, *Electronic Media: A Guide to Trends in Broadcasting and Newer Technologies, 1920–1983* (Praeger,

(Table continues)

Table 4-15 *(Continued)*

1984), 169; hours viewed, hours telecast, 1984: *Network Television Audiences to Primaries, Conventions, and Elections: 1987 Update Edition* (Northbrook, Ill.: A. C. Nielsen, 1987), 13, 17; hours telecast, 1992: A. C. Nielsen Co., *Nielsen Tunes in to Politics: Tracking the Presidential Election Years (1960–1992)* (New York: Nielsen Media Research, 1993), 2–3; hours telecast, 1996: John Carmody, "Convention Low-Show," *The Washington Post*, August 19, 1996, B1; hours telecast, 2000: Robin Toner, "The Conventions Are Over, the Party's Just Starting," *The New York Times,* August 20, 2000, iv; hours telecast, 2004: Michael Janofsky, "Each Convention to Get 3 Hours of Prime Time on TV Networks," *The New York Times,* July 13, 2004, A16; hours telecast, 2008: "Networks Rethink Conventions," *The Baltimore Sun,* August 25, 2008, 11A, and "TV Cameras Turn from G.O.P. to Storm," *The New York Times,* September 1, 2008; hours viewed, 2008: The Nielsen Company, "Nielsen Examines TV Viewers to the Political Convention," September 2008, 3; hours telecast, 2012: "CBS, NBC and ABC Announce Just Three Hours of Primetime Coverage," *The Tampa Bay Times,* August 20, 2012, www.tampabay.com; Copyrighted information of The Nielsen Company, licensed for use herein

Table 4-16 Television Viewership of Presidential and Vice-Presidential Debates, 1960–2020

Year	Candidates	Date	Audience rating[a] (percentage)	Viewers (millions)
1960	Kennedy–Nixon	Sept. 26	59.5	—
		Oct. 7	59.1	—
		Oct. 13	61.0	—
		Oct. 21	57.8	—
1976	Carter–Ford	Sept. 23	53.5	69.7
		Oct. 6	52.4	63.9
		Oct. 22	47.8	62.7
	Mondale–Dole	Oct. 15	35.5	43.2
1980	Carter–Reagan	Oct. 28	58.9	80.6
1984	Mondale–Reagan	Oct. 7	45.3	65.1
		Oct. 21	46.0	67.3
	Ferraro–G. H. W. Bush	Oct. 11	43.6	56.7
1988	Dukakis–G. H. W. Bush	Sept. 25	36.8	65.1
		Oct. 13	35.9	67.3
	Bentsen–Quayle	Oct. 5	33.6	46.9
1992	Clinton–G. H. W. Bush–Perot	Oct. 11	38.3	62.4
		Oct. 15	46.3	69.9
		Oct. 19	45.2	66.9
	Gore–Quayle–Stockdale	Oct. 13	35.9	51.2
1996	Clinton–Dole	Oct. 6	31.6	36.1
		Oct. 16	26.1	36.3
	Gore–Kemp	Oct. 9	19.7	26.6
2000	Gore–G. W. Bush	Oct. 3	31.7	46.6
		Oct. 11	26.8	37.6
		Oct. 17	25.9	37.7
	Lieberman–Cheney	Oct. 5	21.0	29.0
2004	Kerry–G. W. Bush	Sept. 30	39.4	62.5
		Oct. 8	29.6	46.7
		Oct. 13	32.6	51.2
	Edwards–Cheney	Oct. 5	28.1	43.6
2008	Obama–McCain	Sept. 26	31.6	52.4
		Oct. 7	38.8	63.2
		Oct. 15	35	56.5
	Biden–Palin	Oct. 2	41.7	70.0
2012	Obama–Romney	Oct. 3	40.4	67.2
		Oct. 16	40.0	65.6
		Oct. 22	35.9	59.2

Table 4-16 *(Continued)*

Year	Candidates	Date	Audience rating[a] (percentage)	Viewers (millions)
	Biden–Ryan	Oct. 11	31.9	51.4
2016	Clinton–Trump	Sept. 26	47.6	84.0
		Oct. 9	37.1	66.6
		Oct. 19	41.7	71.6
	Kaine–Pence	Oct. 4	23.5	37.1
2020	Biden–Trump	Sept. 29	40.2	73.1
		Oct. 22	35.3	63.0
	Harris–Pence	Oct. 7	33.7	57.9

Note: "—" indicates not available. Vice presidential candidates are in italics. 1976–1988 debates include ABC, CBS, and NBC only; 1992 includes ABC, CBS (not Oct. 11), NBC, and CNN; 1996 includes ABC, CBS, NBC, CNN, and Fox (only Oct. 6); 2000 includes ABC, CBS, NBC (some affiliates on tape delay Oct. 3), CNN, Fox (some affiliates on tape delay Oct. 3, not included Oct. 5 or Oct. 11), Fox News Channel, and MSNBC; 2004 includes ABC, CBS, NBC, CNN, Fox (not Oct. 5 or Oct. 13), Fox News Channel, and MSNBC; 2008 includes ABC, CBS, Fox (not Oct. 15), NBC, Telefutura (not Oct. 7 or Oct. 15), Telemundo, Univision (not Sept. 26 or Oct. 2), BBC-America, CNBC, CNN, Fox News Channel, MSNBC, and MUN2 (only Oct. 15); 2012 includes ABC, CBS, Fox (not Oct. 22), NBC, Telemundo, Univision, PBS, CNN, Fox News Channel, MSNBC, CurrentTV, and CNBC; 2016 includes ABC, CBS, FOX, Univision (not Oct. 4), NBC (not Oct. 9), Telemundo (not Oct. 4 or Oct. 9), Azteca America (not Oct. 4; on tape delay Oct. 19), PBS, CNBC (not Oct. 4), CNN, Fox Business Network, Fox News Channel, and MSNBC; 2020 includes ABC, CBS, NBC, FOX (not Oct. 22), Telemundo, Univision, PBS, CNN, CNNe, Fox Business Network, Fox News Channel, MSNBC, Newsmax, Newsy, Vice, and WGNA. Vice Presidential Debate in 2020 also included BET and BET HER. PBS (before 2012) and C-SPAN data not included. Combined audience estimates are based on comparable durations.

[a] Percentage of television households viewing the debates during an average minute.

Sources: Presidential debates, 1960–2004: Nielsen Media Research, "Political Debates: Presidential Debates;" 2008: "Media Advisory: 56.5 Million Watch the Final 2008 Presidential Debate;" 2012: "Final Presidential Debate Draws 59.2 Million Viewers"; 2016 and 2020: "Media Advisory: Final Presidential Debate of 2020 Draws 63 Million Viewers"; vice presidential debates, 1976–2004: "Political Debates: Vice Presidential Debates"; 2008: "Media Advisory: 69.6 Million Watch the 2008 Vice Presidential Debate"; 2012: "51.4 Million Viewers Tune into Biden and Ryan's VP Debate"; 2016–2020: "Media Advisory: 2020 Vice Presidential Debate Draws 57.9M Viewers," nielsen.com. Copyrighted information of The Nielsen Company, licensed for use herein.

A Data Literacy Lesson

Measuring Trends When Benchmarks Change

We've talked about it throughout this chapter—the influence of the Internet generally, and social media specifically, on the modern political system is hard to overstate. Barack Obama was the first presidential candidate to use social media as a central strategy of his 2008 campaign. His popular Facebook, YouTube, MySpace, and Twitter accounts dwarfed both the number of followers and success with the medium his competitor John McCain experienced.[1] Since that election, social media has been an essential part of any campaign, providing candidates a means to connect directly with voters through paid advertisements but also through less formal, more personal connections.

Determining what to measure and its effect on campaign success is difficult. Some social media sites rise and fall quickly—MySpace, which had more unique users in the United States than Facebook during the 2008 campaign, is now relegated to relative obscurity. Other sites such as Facebook and Twitter have maintained a steady presence but have had dramatic changes in their use and audience—Facebook was predominantly a platform for young people in 2008. As we noted in the essay accompanying Table 4-11, this poses challenges for following changes in media use over time.

As we consider the direct effect of social media and ways to measure its influence, we also want to consider the effect it has on consumption of political information from other media. Consider tables 4-15 and 4-16. In table 4-15, we can clearly see a dramatic decrease in the number of hours of nominating conventions that network television aired from the 1950s to modern elections. Does that mean, though, that American voters have less access to watching the conventions? Aside from cable news coverage, what about clips from the convention on YouTube or direct messages from and about the conventions on social media? And, where should the line be drawn on what constitutes campaign coverage—is it convention content only if it's coming from a mainstream news channel social media account, or should that include the national party accounts? Do behind-the-scenes pictures and videos from delegates or candidates' family members count?

Similarly, when looking at table 4-16, we see that the television viewership numbers for debates are expansive in including a variety of network and cable news channels with a variety of targeted audiences. What we can't answer from this table, though, is whether and how this was the primary way for voters to watch the debates. We know from Table 4-11 that the Internet is increasingly an access point for political information, but whether that is comparable to sitting down to watch a full debate on television or is through sound bites and memes isn't something we can clearly delineate in a table at this point.

Social media is a means of political communication that is both direct and diffuse. There are a variety of considerations to consider both in how to measure its direct effect as well as its effect on measures of traditional methods of media consumption. Data on what news sources people use, and on how they use these sources, are rarely as straightforward as they seem at first glance.

---

[1] We'd be remiss if we didn't note that 2008 was also the first year in which an official campaign videogame was launched. While Howard Dean's Iowa-focused game was the first, John McCain took it to the general election with the game Pork Invaders, in which a McCain icon used vetoes to shoot pork, while the score reflected millions of tax dollars saved.

Table 4-17 Newspaper Endorsements of Presidential Candidates, 1948–2020

	Papers		Circulation	
Year/candidate endorsed	Number	Percentage	Number	Percentage
1948				
Dewey (R)	771	65	35,152,807	79
Truman (D)	182	15	4,489,851	10
Thurmond	45	4	537,730	1
Wallace	3	0	60,233	0
Uncommitted	182	15	4,454,557	10
1952				
Eisenhower (R)	933	67	40,129,237	80
Stevenson (D)	202	15	5,466,781	11
Uncommitted	250	18	4,417,102	9
1956				
Eisenhower (R)	740	62	34,538,755	72
Stevenson (D)	189	15	6,122,491	13
Uncommitted	270	23	7,079,846	15
1960				
Nixon (R)	731	58	38,006,203	71
Kennedy (D)	208	16	8,448,677	16
Uncommitted	328	26	7,135,954	13
1964				
Goldwater (R)	359	35	8,977,214	21
L. Johnson (D)	440	42	26,997,400	62
Uncommitted	237	23	7,638,727	18
1968				
Nixon (R)	634	61	34,559,385	70
Humphrey (D)	146	14	9,572,948	19
1972				
Nixon (R)	753	71	30,560,535	77
McGovern (D)	56	5	3,044,534	8
Uncommitted	245	23	5,864,548	15
1976				
Ford (R)	411	62	20,951,798	62
Carter (D)	80	12	7,607,739	23
Uncommitted	168	26	5,074,069	15
1980				
Reagan (R)	443	42	17,561,333	49
Carter (D)	126	12	7,782,078	22
Anderson	40	4	1,614,740	4
Uncommitted	439	42	9,131,940	25
1984				
Reagan (R)	381	58	18,357,512	52
Mondale (D)	62	9	7,568,639	21
Uncommitted	216	33	9,611,058	27
1988				
G. H. W. Bush (R)	241	31	18,186,225	40

Table 4-17 *(Continued)*

	Papers		Circulation	
Year/candidate endorsed	Number	Percentage	Number	Percentage
Dukakis (D)	103	13	11,644,600	25
Uncommitted	428	55	16,224,807	35
1992[a]				
G. H. W. Bush (R)	121	15	7,134,599	18
Clinton (D)	149	18	10,961,415	27
Uncommitted	542	67	22,225,342	55
1996[b]				
Dole (R)	111	19	4,741,645	13
Clinton (D)	65	11	4,581,337	13
Uncommitted	415	70	26,173,692	74
2000				
G. W. Bush (R)	93	48	—	—
Gore (D)	44	23	—	—
Uncommitted	56	29	—	—
2004				
G. W. Bush (R)	205	48	15,743,799	41
Kerry (D)	213	50	20,882,889	55
Uncommitted	12[c]	3	1,650,819[c]	4
2008				
McCain (R)	159	34	9,301,511	29
Obama (D)	287	61	23,086,607	71
Uncommitted	26	6	—	—
2012[d]				
Romney (R)	212	45	17,660,553[e]	46
Obama (D)	191	41	12,897,157[e]	34
Uncommitted	66	14	7,718,757[e]	20
2016[f]				
Trump (R)	2	2	315,666	2
Clinton (D)	57	67	13,095,067	67
Uncommitted	26	31	6,102,180	31
2020				
Trump (R)	7	7	862,860	6
Biden (D)	47	47	9,580,450	61
Uncommitted	44	44	5,241,419	33

Note: "D" indicates Democrat; "R" indicates Republican; "—" indicates not available. In 2000, Editor & Publisher changed the method used to conduct its poll of newspaper endorsements, which resulted in a much smaller number of responses, with an unknown but probably larger bias; also, circulation numbers were not indicated. Circulation numbers were not provided for all papers in 2012. 2012 was the last presidential election year for which Editor and Publisher compiled endorsement data. Data for 2016 and 2020 are from the American Presidency Project and represent only the 100 newspapers with the highest circulation in the United States, resulting in smaller number of responses. Data for additional years can be found in previous editions of *Vital Statistics on American Politics*.

[a] One newspaper—circulation 9,075—endorsed H. Ross Perot, independent.
[b] One newspaper—circulation 3,300—endorsed Harry Browne, Libertarian.

(Table continues)

Table 4-17 *(Continued)*

---

c Based on the 2008 listing, which indicated those uncommitted in 2004.
d Two newspapers endorsed Gary Johnson, Libertarian (combined circulation 103,186).
e Usually Sunday circulation (except for weekly paper).
f Four newspapers endorsed Gary Johnson, Libertarian (combined circulation 738,750); three newspapers explicitly endorsed "Not Trump" (combined circulation 3,243,140); five newspapers endorsed "None of the above" (combined circulation 440,796).

Sources: 1948–2012: Editor & Publisher, October 30, 1948, 11; November 1, 1952, 9; November 3, 1956, 11; November 5, 1960, 10; October 31, 1964, 10; November 2, 1968, 9; November 7, 1972, 9; October 30, 1976, 5; November 1, 1980, 10; November 3, 1984, 9; November 5, 1988, 9; October 24, 1992, 9; October 26, 1996, 8; November 6, 2000, 9; November 5, 2004; November 7, 2008; November 2012, www.editorandpublisher.com; 2016–2020: The American Presidency Project, "Newspaper Editorial Endorsements," https://www.presidency.ucsb.edu/statistics/data.

A Data Literacy Lesson

The Relevance of Newspaper Endorsements

Political scientists focus a great deal of attention, energy, and pages of scholarly journals trying to understand, explain, and predict what sways the minds of American voters. Relatedly, many actors in American political discourse try to be influential in being the swaying factor. Whether they're trying to influence voters or simply state their opinions for the public record, each election season many newspaper editorial boards publish their endorsement of one candidate over the others.

Some large newspapers, such as *The Wall Street Journal* and *USA Today,* have a longstanding practice of not endorsing candidates.[1] *The Wall Street Journal* has not offered an endorsement since 1928. Other publications, including *The New York Times* and *The Washington Post* and many local newspapers, regularly offer their editorial opinion on the best candidate for the job.

When we look at the data in Table 4-18, there are two trends that we notice and think are worth exploring. First, and perhaps most starkly, is the dwindling number of newspapers to compare. Through the mid-1960s, we have data from over 1,000 different newspapers; by the last two elections we are able to consider a set of 100 newspapers. As we identify in the note at the bottom of this table, part of this is a function of the way data are collected and reported, as in a shift in 2000. Part of this is a function of changing standards of what information is collected. After the 2012 presidential election, *Editor & Publisher,* the long-standing trade publication about newspapers, no longer collected or published information about newspaper endorsements. We have shifted the focus of our reporting to the 100-top circulating newspapers in the country, based on data from the American Presidency Project. And, as exploring the editorial policies of those newspapers reveals, more newspapers are opting out of offering endorsements over time.

There are several questions that we can ask that might be relevant to understanding the diminishing number of newspapers offering endorsements. Often shifting standards of data availability and reporting are themselves a function of bigger substantive issues. For example, while we don't know why *Editor & Publisher*, which called itself "the bible of the newspaper industry," stopped printing information about newspaper endorsements, we might reasonably ask if they view it as a less important role for newspapers than in the past. Perhaps the number of editorial boards ending the practice of endorsing candidates is in response to concerns about trust in mainstream media and potential bias. More simply, as we see in Table 4-2, the number of newspapers has decreased to a number of newspapers not seen since the late 19th century, indicating that there are fewer newspapers to have the option of offering editorials.

If it were only the raw number of newspapers offering endorsements that were declining, that would tell us one story. But, when we look at the percentage of newspapers offering endorsements, there are different questions we can explore: are newspapers more likely to offer an endorsement in tightly contested races or when there's a clear front runner? Do endorsements consistently favor one party over another? And, the second trend we think is important to spend some time on: How often do newspaper endorsements align with vote outcome? That is, are there indications that newspaper endorsements might be influential in swaying voters' minds and influencing the election? Or, perhaps, might newspapers follow (rather than lead) public opinion in order to remain popular and relevant within their communities?

We note that in 2016, only 2 percent of the 100 top-circulating newspapers in the country endorsed Donald Trump. Notably, more newspapers explicitly endorsed "none of the above" and "Not Trump" than endorsed his candidacy. Whether the endorsements were intended for the effect of swaying votes, it's safe to say that the endorsements in 2016 didn't translate into similar voting outcomes.

As Americans have access to a multitude of media outlets, and the number of newspapers opting out of endorsing candidates grows, there are many avenues to explore the fluctuating influence of editorial endorsements over time. Ultimately, while the number and percentage of endorsements has decreased, it's easy to overlook that a majority of the top-circulating newspapers do still offer endorsements, suggesting they still see value in publishing them. What that value might be can't be answered by this table alone, but we think it's an interesting question for further exploration.

---

[1] *USA Today* notably broke with their practice in 2016 when they endorsed "Not Trump" and in 2020 when they endorsed Joe Biden.

Figure 4-2 Newspaper Endorsements of Presidential Candidates: Democratic, Republican, and Uncommitted, 1932–2020

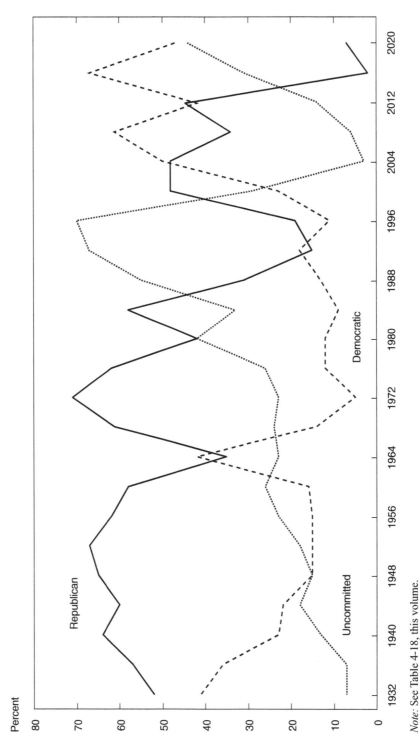

Note: See Table 4-18, this volume.

Source: Table 4-18, this volume.

5
Congress

- **Apportionment**
- **Membership Characteristics**
- **Committees**
- **Bills and Laws**
- **Voting Patterns**
- **Current Members**

While the U.S. Congress is fundamentally an "N" of 1, it offers far more data for all of us to examine than the small N would suggest. Any given Congress has 535 members, for whom we can find biographical information, as well as background on their districts, in lengthy treatments (see, for example, the *Almanac of American Politics*, published by the National Journal Group, which comes out every two years). Washington insiders often have these books on their shelves, and thumb through these biographies frequently. Among political science geeks, being able to know off the top of one's head who represents the second congressional district of Nebraska provides immediate street cred.

Moreover, congressional elections are held every two years, providing us with copious amounts of data on vote totals, shifts in partisan control of the institutions, and data on campaign contributions and spending. A political junkie could get lost for hours in data from the Federal Elections Commission (www.fec.gov) on who raises and spends campaign money. And, once we shift our focus from the electoral realm to the legislative realm, the hundreds of annual votes taken in the House and Senate provide further data for examination; roll-call voting in Congress is one of the most-studied aspects of American politics.

Congressional elections, not surprisingly, provide one of the largest collections of data on Congress. Generally, these data are found elsewhere in this book—election results, including material associated specifically with congressional elections such as losses by the president's party at midterm, are provided in Chapter 1, while information on the funding of congressional campaigns is provided in Chapter 2. Some of the tables and figures in Chapter 3 focus on individual-level voting behavior in congressional elections, as well as on how the public views the job performance of Congress.

This chapter begins with a focus on the apportionment of seats among the states within the House of Representatives (Table 5-1 and Figure 5-1). While this may not seem, at first glance, like the most riveting topic, it has significant real-world implications, as we note in one of our data literacy essays. We also include material here on the increasing diversity among members of Congress, focusing specifically on increasing numbers of women and racial and ethnic minorities serving in Congress (Tables 5-2 through 5-5).

We then move on to discuss how Congress does its work, in the way we might assess the operations of any large organization. We consider information about the numbers of committees and their leadership (Table 5-6), the numbers of measures considered and passed (Figure 5-2 and Table 5-7), and numbers of recorded votes Congress takes (Table 5-8). Organization matters in legislative politics—the way committee systems are structured, and power dispersed or concentrated, can affect the results of legislative battles. Legislative output is important to consider as well, given concerns about how well (or poorly) Congress does its job, and about potential executive overreach, such as through executive orders.

Voting by the members of Congress on pending legislation is of obvious interest. Indeed, cohesion within and contrasts between the political parties were the topics of some of the first statistical treatments of political subjects.[1] The following section of the chapter considers the numbers of roll calls and other record votes (Table 5-8), as well as determinants of that voting, such as party unity and presidential support by individual representatives and senators (Tables 5-11 and 5-12) and for parties in the aggregate. Understanding this kind of voting is a standard part of congressional analyses, as we note in a data essay.

Congress remains a fascinating area of study for those who like getting their hands on data. Old theories and topics provide continued grist for analysis, since the turnover in personnel, the ongoing change in congressional leadership and of the president, the changes in regional strength, and so on make Congress anything but static. In addition, the ongoing reforms of congressional procedures and of campaign finance, begun during and after the Watergate scandal in the 1970s and continuing today, the technological changes that have resulted in electronic voting and the televising of proceedings in both chambers, and the changes in the size and scope of the government bureaucracy that Congress must deal with are reason enough to scrutinize anew the data underlying one's understanding of Congress.

Notes

1. Stuart Rice, *Quantitative Methods in Political Science* (New York: Knopf, 1928).

Table 5-1 Apportionment of Membership of the House of Representatives, 1789–2020

1789–1890

State	1789[a]	1790	1800	1810	1820	1830	1840	1850	1860	1870	1880	1890
Alabama	—	—	—	—	3	5	7	7	6	8	8	9
Alaska	—	—	—	—	—	—	—	—	—	—	—	—
Arizona	—	—	—	—	—	—	—	—	—	—	—	—
Arkansas	—	—	—	—	—	—	1	2	3	4	5	6
California	—	—	—	—	—	—	—	2	3	4	6	7
Colorado	—	—	—	—	—	—	—	—	—	—	1	2
Connecticut	5	7	7	7	6	6	4	4	4	4	4	4
Delaware	1	1	1	2	1	1	1	1	1	1	1	1
Florida	—	—	—	—	—	—	—	1	1	2	2	2
Georgia	3	2	4	6	7	9	8	8	7	9	10	11
Hawaii	—	—	—	—	—	—	—	—	—	—	—	—
Idaho	—	—	—	—	—	—	—	—	—	—	—	1
Illinois	—	—	—	—	1	3	7	9	14	19	20	22
Indiana	—	—	—	—	3	7	10	11	11	13	13	13
Iowa	—	—	—	—	—	—	—	2	6	9	11	11
Kansas	—	—	—	—	—	—	—	—	1	3	7	8
Kentucky	—	2	6	10	12	13	10	10	9	10	11	11
Louisiana	—	—	—	—	3	3	4	4	5	6	6	6
Maine	—	—	—	—	7	8	7	6	5	5	4	4
Maryland	6	8	9	9	9	8	6	6	5	6	6	6
Massachusetts	8	14	17	20	13	12	10	11	10	11	12	13
Michigan	—	—	—	—	—	—	3	4	6	9	11	12
Minnesota	—	—	—	—	—	—	—	—	2	3	5	7
Mississippi	—	—	—	—	1	2	4	5	5	6	7	7
Missouri	—	—	—	—	1	2	5	7	9	13	14	15
Montana	—	—	—	—	—	—	—	—	—	—	—	1
Nebraska	—	—	—	—	—	—	—	—	—	1	3	6
Nevada	—	—	—	—	—	—	—	—	—	1	1	1
New Hampshire	3	4	5	6	6	5	4	3	3	3	2	2

(Table continues)

Table 5-1 (Continued)

1789–1890

State	1789[a]	1790	1800	1810	1820	1830	1840	1850	1860	1870	1880	1890
New Jersey	4	5	6	6	6	6	5	5	5	7	7	8
New Mexico	—	—	—	—	—	—	—	—	—	—	—	—
New York	6	10	17	27	34	40	34	33	31	33	34	34
North Carolina	5	10	12	13	13	13	9	8	7	8	9	9
North Dakota	—	—	—	—	—	—	—	—	—	—	—	1
Ohio	—	—	—	6	14	19	21	21	19	20	21	21
Oklahoma	—	—	—	—	—	—	—	—	—	—	—	—
Oregon	—	—	—	—	—	—	—	—	1	1	1	2
Pennsylvania	8	13	18	23	26	28	24	25	24	27	28	30
Rhode Island	1	2	2	2	2	2	2	2	2	2	2	2
South Carolina	5	6	8	9	9	9	7	6	4	5	7	7
South Dakota	—	—	—	—	—	—	—	—	—	—	—	2
Tennessee	—	—	—	6	9	13	11	10	8	10	10	10
Texas	—	—	3	—	—	—	—	2	4	6	11	13
Utah	—	—	—	—	—	—	—	—	—	—	—	—
Vermont	—	2	4	6	5	5	4	3	3	3	2	2
Virginia	10	19	22	23	22	21	15	13	11	9	10	10
Washington	—	—	—	—	—	—	—	—	—	—	—	2
West Virginia	—	—	—	—	—	—	—	—	—	3	4	4
Wisconsin	—	—	—	—	—	—	—	3	6	8	9	10
Wyoming	—	—	—	—	—	—	—	—	—	—	—	1
Representatives apportioned by census count	65	105	141	181	213	240	223	234	241	292	325	356
Apportionment population[c]	[d]	3,615,823	4,879,820	6,584,231	8,972,396	11,930,987	15,908,376	21,766,691	29,550,038	38,115,641	49,371,340	61,908,906
Apportionment ratio[e]	30,000[f]	34,436	34,609	36,377	42,124	49,712	71,338	93,020	122,614	130,533	151,912	173,901

1900–2020

State	1900	1910	1930[b]	1940	1950	1960	1970	1980	1990	2000	2010	2020
Alabama	9	10	9	9	9	8	7	7	7	7	7	7
Alaska	—	—	—	—	—	1	1	1	1	1	1	1
Arizona	—	1	1	2	2	3	4	5	6	8	9	9
Arkansas	7	7	7	7	6	4	4	4	4	4	4	4
California	8	11	20	23	30	38	43	45	52	53	53	52
Colorado	3	4	4	4	4	4	5	6	6	7	7	8
Connecticut	5	5	6	6	6	6	6	6	6	5	5	5
Delaware	1	1	1	1	1	1	1	1	1	1	1	1
Florida	3	4	5	6	8	12	15	19	23	25	27	28
Georgia	11	12	10	10	10	10	10	10	11	13	14	14
Hawaii	—	—	—	—	—	2	2	2	2	2	2	2
Idaho	1	2	2	2	2	2	2	2	2	2	2	2
Illinois	25	27	27	26	25	24	24	22	20	19	18	17
Indiana	13	13	12	11	11	11	11	10	10	9	9	9
Iowa	11	11	9	8	8	7	6	6	5	5	4	4
Kansas	8	8	7	6	6	5	5	5	4	4	4	4
Kentucky	11	11	9	9	8	7	7	7	6	6	6	6
Louisiana	7	8	8	8	8	8	8	8	7	7	6	6
Maine	4	4	3	3	3	2	2	2	2	2	2	2
Maryland	6	6	6	6	7	8	8	8	8	8	8	8
Massachusetts	14	16	15	14	14	12	12	11	10	10	9	9
Michigan	12	13	17	17	18	19	19	18	16	15	14	13
Minnesota	9	10	9	9	9	8	8	8	8	8	8	8
Mississippi	8	8	7	7	6	5	5	5	5	4	4	4
Missouri	16	16	13	13	11	10	10	9	9	9	8	8
Montana	1	2	2	2	2	2	2	2	1	1	1	2
Nebraska	6	6	5	4	4	3	3	3	3	3	3	3
Nevada	1	1	1	1	1	1	1	2	2	3	4	4
New Hampshire	2	2	2	2	2	2	2	2	2	2	2	2
New Jersey	10	12	14	14	14	15	15	14	13	13	12	12
New Mexico	—	1	1	2	2	2	2	3	3	3	3	3
New York	37	43	45	45	43	41	39	34	31	29	27	26

(Table continues)

223

Table 5-1 *(Continued)*

1900–2020

State	1900	1910	1930[b]	1940	1950	1960	1970	1980	1990	2000	2010	2020
North Carolina	10	10	11	12	12	11	11	11	12	13	13	14
North Dakota	2	3	2	2	2	2	1	1	1	1	1	1
Ohio	21	22	24	23	23	24	23	21	19	18	16	15
Oklahoma	—	8	9	8	6	6	6	6	6	5	5	5
Oregon	2	3	3	4	4	4	4	5	5	5	5	6
Pennsylvania	32	36	34	33	30	27	25	23	21	19	18	17
Rhode Island	2	3	2	2	2	2	2	2	2	2	2	2
South Carolina	7	7	6	6	6	6	6	6	6	6	7	7
South Dakota	2	3	2	2	2	2	2	1	1	1	1	1
Tennessee	10	10	9	10	9	9	8	9	9	9	9	9
Texas	16	18	21	21	22	23	24	27	30	32	36	38
Utah	1	2	2	2	2	2	2	3	3	3	4	4
Vermont	2	2	1	1	1	1	1	1	1	1	1	1
Virginia	10	10	9	9	10	10	10	10	11	11	11	11
Washington	3	5	6	6	7	7	7	8	9	9	10	10
West Virginia	5	6	6	6	6	5	4	4	3	3	3	2
Wisconsin	11	11	10	10	10	10	9	9	9	8	8	8
Wyoming	1	1	1	1	1	1	1	1	1	1	1	1
Representatives apportioned by census count	386	435	435	435	435	435	435	435	435	435	435	435
Apportionment population[c]	74,562,608	91,603,772	122,093,455	131,006,184	149,895,183	178,559,217	204,053,025	225,867,174	249,022,783	281,424,177	309,183,463	331,449,281
Apportionment ratio[e]	193,167	210,583	280,675	301,164	344,587	410,481	469,088	519,235	572,466	646,952	710,767	761,952

Note: "—" indicates state not yet admitted to Union. States mentioned in the decennial apportionment law or report are listed for that year. Several territories were counted in the census and admitted after the census year, but before the apportionment law. These states are included in that apportionment decade. The remaining states were admitted during the decade after an apportionment law or report. All new states were admitted with one seat unless noted. These states were, after the 1790 apportionment, Tennessee; after 1800, Ohio; after 1810, Alabama, Illinois, Indiana, Louisiana, and Mississippi; after 1830, Arkansas and Michigan; after 1840,

224

California, Florida, Iowa, and Wisconsin; after 1870, Colorado; after 1880, Idaho, Montana, North Dakota, South Dakota, Washington, and Wyoming; after 1890, Utah; after 1900, Oklahoma; after 1950, Alaska and Hawaii. Twenty members were assigned to Massachusetts in the 1810 apportionment; seven of these were credited to Maine when that area became a state. Virginia had eleven representatives in 1860; three of these were credited to West Virginia when that area became a state. The only exception to the census apportionment or new state admittance manner of securing a representative was when California was given one additional representative for the Thirty-seventh Congress (1861–1863).

[a] Original apportionment made in Constitution, pending first census.
[b] No apportionment was made in 1920.
[c] Excludes the population of District of Columbia; the population of the territories; prior to 1940, the number of American Indians not taxed; and, prior to 1870, two-fifths of the slave population. In 1970 and 1990 includes selected segments of Americans abroad.
[d] No census prior to 1790.
[e] The ratio of apportionment population to the number of representatives apportioned by census.
[f] The minimum ratio of population to representative, as stated in Article I, section 2, of the U.S. Constitution.

Sources: Apportionment of membership, 1788–1990: Kenneth C. Martis and Greg A. Elmes, *The Historical Atlas of State Power in Congress, 1790–1990* (Washington, D.C.: Congressional Quarterly, 1993); apportionment population, 1790–1990: U.S. Census Bureau, "Population Base for Apportionment and the Number of Representatives Apportioned: 1790 to 1990"; 2000: "Apportionment Population and Number of Representatives, by State: Census 2000"; 2010: "Apportionment Population and Number of Representatives, by State: 2010 Census"; 2020: "2020 Census: Apportionment of the U.S. House of Representatives," www.census.gov. Apportionment ratios calculated by the authors.

Figure 5-1 Apportionment of Membership of the House of Representatives, by Region, 1910 and 2020

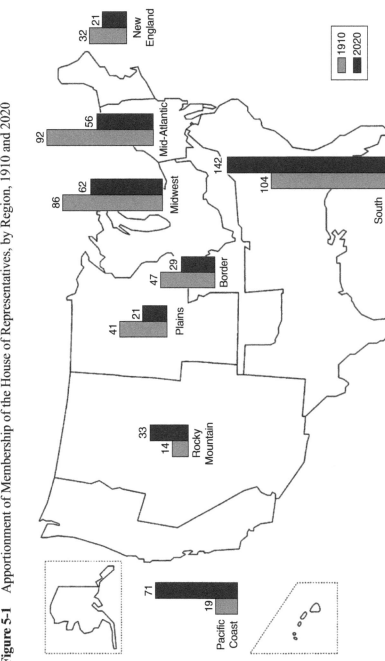

Note: For composition of regions, see Table A-3, this volume.

Source: Table 5-1, this volume.

A Data Literacy Lesson

Reapportionment Data and the State and Regional Level

When we present data to illustrate a point, one technique we might use would be to present all the data, put them in a table, and have the reader make sense of it all. This is what we do in Table 5-1, where we show the apportionment of seats in the House of Representatives since the beginning of the nation. If one steps back from the table to take a long view, patterns emerge quite clearly. California, for example, has dramatically increased its electoral votes—in fact, 2010 was the first year in which it did not gain House seats, and 2020 was the first year in which it lost a seat. New York, which peaked at 45 House seats in the 1930s and 1940s, is now down to 26, having lost at least one House seat in every census since 1950. A broad shift of electoral power away from the North and Midwest and toward the South and the West is apparent, if one takes the time to look closely at the data.

Figure 5-1 presents another approach to these data, this time breaking the data up into categories. In this comparison, we can see evidence in support of the final sentence in the last paragraph, this time much more quickly and graphically. New England has lost one-third of its congressional representation over that time, while the Mid-Atlantic states have lost about 40 percent of their seats. The power has shifted most to the South (moving from 104 to 142 seats) and the Pacific Coast (from 19 to 71, more than tripling their power). Categorization is a useful tool for making sense of data—rather than forcing the reader to go through an entire table and mentally tally these calculations, Figure 5-1 does that for you. You're welcome; glad to help!

And yet, the process of categorization adds its own challenges—what fits into which category? Fortunately, we have engaged in the business of categorizing states for long enough that these categories do have some inherent meaning. (The categories we use for this table can be seen on the map—states in each region are also listed in Appendix A-3, in case you do not have the map of the United States memorized.) We know what the New England states are, for example. Most of us have a concept in our head of the Midwest, or of the South. In all of cases, these descriptions not only connote a list of states, but also a certain regional culture and vibe, for want of a better word. We recognize that states can be somewhat blunt levels for categorization. For example, Pittsburgh might be more similar to Cleveland—in another state and another region—than it is to Philadelphia, but apportionment is done at the state level. We think these divisions are useful and capture general regional similarities that are useful for understanding how individual, state-level changes can lead to bigger cultural shifts in Congress.

The reapportionment of congressional seats (and, by extension, electoral votes) is important, and well worth the attention it receives when results are announced every ten years. Apportionment tells us where political power goes. To take just two examples, if all the states were to vote the same way in 2024 as they did in 2020, the Republicans would gain three electoral votes (based on shifts in electoral vote totals among the states) based on the most recent reapportionment. This could certainly matter in a very close election. The House of Representatives is very tightly divided between Democrats and Republicans in 2021; shifting seats out of Democratic states into Republican states could change the 2022 congressional electoral results at the margins, which might be enough to shift partisan control of the House.

Apportionment matters; the two ways in which we document the over-time shift in political power offer different perspectives on how to view these shifts, each of them with their own value, and their own limitations.

Table 5-2 Members of Congress: Female, Black, Hispanic, Marital Status, and Age, 1971–2021

Congress		Female	Black	Hispanic	Not married[a]	Age[b]					
						Under 40	40–49	50–59	60–69	70–79	80 and older
Representatives											
92nd	(1971)	12	12	5	26	40	133	152	86	19	3
93rd	(1973)	14	15	5	34	45	132	154	80	20	2
94th	(1975)	18	16	5	54	69	138	137	75	14	2
95th	(1977)	18	16	5	56	81	121	147	71	15	0
96th	(1979)	16	16	6	69	86	125	145	63	14	0
97th	(1981)	19	16	6	86	94	142	132	54	12	1
98th	(1983)	21	20	10	86	86	145	132	57	13	1
99th	(1985)	22	19	11	68	71	154	131	59	17	2
100th	(1987)	23	22	11	69	63	153	137	56	24	2
101st	(1989)	25	23	11	64	41	163	133	74	20	2
102nd	(1991)	28	25	10	—	39	153	133	86	20	4
103rd	(1993)	47	38	17	—	47	152	129	91	13	3
104th	(1995)	47	39	18	—	53	153	136	80	12	1
105th	(1997)	51	37	18	—	47	145	147	82	10	2
106th	(1999)	56	39	19	—	32	131	171	80	20	0
107th	(2001)	59	36	19	—	36	118	175	78	26	0
108th	(2003)	59	37	23	—	26	111	175	102	21	0
109th	(2005)	65	40	23	—	25	97	176	111	23	3
110th	(2007)	71	40	23	—	20	93	171	117	30	4
111th	(2009)	78	41	25	—	23	84	156	128	40	3
112th	(2011)	72	42	24	—	22	89	138	132	42	12
113th	(2013)	78	40	28	—	26	74	138	143	42	10
114th	(2015)	84	44	29	—	26	69	141	147	44	7
115th	(2017)	84	47	37	—	24	64	141	136	60	10
116th	(2019)	101	53	43	—	33	72	120	123	68	9
117th	(2021)	118	57	44	—	30	77	117	122	70	14

(Table continues)

Table 5-2 *(Continued)*

					Not		Age[b]				
Congress		Female	Black	Hispanic	married[a]	Under 40	40–49	50–59	60–69	70–79	80 and older
Senators											
92nd	(1971)	1	1	1	3	4	24	32	23	16	1
93rd	(1973)	0	1	1	4	3	25	37	23	11	1
94th	(1975)[c]	0	1	1	6	5	21	35	24	15	0
95th	(1977)	0	1	0	9	6	26	35	21	10	2
96th	(1979)	1	0	0	5	10	31	33	17	8	1
97th	(1981)	2	0	0	7	9	35	36	14	6	0
98th	(1983)	2	0	0	10	7	28	39	20	3	3
99th	(1985)	2	0	0	8	4	27	38	25	4	2
100th	(1987)	2	0	0	11	5	30	36	22	5	2
101st	(1989)	2	0	0	—	0	30	40	22	6	2
102nd	(1991)	2	0	0	—	0	22	47	24	5	2
103rd	(1993)	6	1	0	—	1	16	49	22	11	1
104th	(1995)	8	1	0	—	1	14	41	27	16	1
105th	(1997)	9	1	0	—	1	21	39	26	12	1
106th	(1999)	9	0	0	—	2	16	42	27	11	2
107th	(2001)	13	0	0	—	0	17	43	31	7	2
108th	(2003)	14	0	0	—	2	16	33	36	11	2
109th	(2005)	14	1	2	—	0	17	29	33	16	5
110th	(2007)	16	0	3	—	0	11	26	36	21	6
111th	(2009)	17	0	3	—	0	7	32	37	18	4
112th	(2011)	17	0	2	—	0	9	29	38	21	3
113th	(2013)	20	1	3	—	1	9	30	35	23	3
114th	(2015)	20	2	3	—	0	13	24	39	18	5
115th	(2017)	21	3	4	—	0	14	22	39	17	8
116th	(2019)	25	3	4	—	0	13	19	40	22	6
117th	(2021)[d]	24	4	6	—	1	9	19	42	24	6

Note: "—" indicates not available. As of beginning of first session of each Congress. Figures for representatives exclude vacancies. The counts exclude nonvoting delegates and commissioners from American Samoa, Guam, Puerto Rico, the Virgin Islands, and Washington, D.C.

a Single, widowed, or divorced.
b Age is calculated as of January 1 of the year the first session of a particular Congress begins.
c Includes Senator John Durkin, D-N.H., seated September 1975.
d Includes Senator Alex Padilla, D-Calif., who was appointed to the Senate on December 22, 2020, to replace Kamala Harris, who was slated to become vice president of the United States.

Sources: Hispanic (1971–1985): Congressional Quarterly, *American Leaders, 1789–1987* (Washington, D.C.: Congressional Quarterly, 1987), 55; female and Black (1971–2009) and Hispanic (1987–2009), *Congressional Quarterly Weekly Report* (CQ Weekly) (1970), 2756; (1972), 2991; (1974), 3104; (1976), 3155; (1978), 3252; (1980), 3318; (1982), 2805; (1984), 2921; (1986), 2863; (1988), 3294; (1990), 3835–3836; (January 16, 1993, Supplement), 12; (November 12, 1994, Supplement), 10; (1997), 28; (1999), 62; (2001), 178; (2003), 192; (2005), 243; (2006), 3008, 3064; (2008), 2998, 3374; female, Black, and Hispanic (2011–2015): CQ Roll Call, "Guide to the New Congress," November 4, 2010, 15; November 12, 2012, 17; November 6, 2014, 59, updated by the editors; not married and age (1971–1989): U.S. Bureau of the Census, *Statistical Abstract of the United States, 1988* (Washington, D.C.: Government Printing Office, 1987), 244; 1990, 257; age (1991–2015): calculated by the editors from *Congressional Quarterly Weekly Report* (CQ Weekly) (1991) 118–127; (January 16, 1993, Supplement), 12, 160–168; (1995), 541–549; (1997), 497–505; *Congressional Biographical Directory*, http://bioguide.congress.gov; Congressional Quarterly, unpublished data; women (2017, 2019, and 2021): Center for American Women and Politics, https://cawp.rutgers.edu; Black (2017, 2019, and 2021): Pew Research Center, "Black Americans have made gains in U.S. political leadership, but gaps remain," https://www.pewresearch.org/fact-tank/2021/01/22/black-americans-have-made-gains-in-u-s-political-leadership-but-gaps-remain; Hispanic (2017, 2019, and 2021): U.S. House of Representatives, Office of the Clerk, "Hispanic-American Representatives, Senators, Delegates, and Resident Commissioners by Congress, 1822–Present," https://history.house.gov/Exhibitions-and-Publications/HAIC/Historical-Data/Hispanic-American-Representatives,-Senators,-Delegates,-and-Resident-Commissioners-by-Congress.

Table 5-3 Black Members of Congress, 1869–2021

Congress		Black members of U.S. House of Representatives	Black members of U.S. Senate	Total Black members
41st	(1869–1871)	2	1	3
42nd	(1871–1873)	5	0	5
43rd	(1873–1875)	7	0	7
44th	(1875–1877)	7	1	8
45th	(1877–1879)	3	1	4
46th	(1879–1881)	0	1	1
47th	(1881–1883)	2	0	2
48th	(1883–1885)	2	0	2
49th	(1885–1887)	2	0	2
50th	(1887–1889)	0	0	0
51st	(1889–1891)	3	0	3
52nd	(1891–1893)	1	0	1
53rd	(1893–1895)	1	0	1
54th	(1895–1897)	1	0	1
55th	(1897–1899)	1	0	1
56th	(1899–1901)	1	0	1
57th	(1901–1903)	0	0	0
58th	(1903–1905)	0	0	0
59th	(1905–1907)	0	0	0
60th	(1907–1909)	0	0	0
61st	(1909–1911)	0	0	0
62nd	(1911–1913)	0	0	0
63rd	(1913–1915)	0	0	0
64th	(1915–1917)	0	0	0
65th	(1917–1919)	0	0	0
66th	(1919–1921)	0	0	0
67th	(1921–1923)	0	0	0
68th	(1923–1925)	0	0	0
69th	(1925–1927)	0	0	0
70th	(1927–1929)	0	0	0
71st	(1929–1931)	1	0	1
72nd	(1931–1933)	1	0	1
73rd	(1933–1935)	1	0	1
74th	(1935–1937)	1	0	1
75th	(1937–1939)	1	0	1
76th	(1939–1941)	1	0	1
77th	(1941–1943)	1	0	1
78th	(1943–1945)	1	0	1
79th	(1945–1947)	2	0	2
80th	(1947–1949)	2	0	2
81st	(1949–1951)	2	0	2
82nd	(1951–1953)	2	0	2
83rd	(1953–1955)	2	0	2
84th	(1955–1957)	3	0	3
85th	(1957–1959)	4	0	4
86th	(1959–1961)	4	0	4
87th	(1961–1963)	4	0	4
88th	(1963–1965)	5	0	5
89th	(1965–1967)	6	0	6
90th	(1967–1969)	5	1	6

Congress		Black members of U.S. House of Representatives	Black members of U.S. Senate	Total Black members
91st	(1969–1971)	10	1	11
92nd	(1971–1973)	13	1	14
93rd	(1973–1975)	16	1	17
94th	(1975–1977)	17	1	18
95th	(1977–1979)	17	1	18
96th	(1979–1981)	17	0	17
97th	(1981–1983)	19	0	19
98th	(1983–1985)	21	0	21
99th	(1985–1987)	21	0	21
100th	(1987–1989)	23	0	23
101st	(1989–1991)	24	0	24
102nd	(1991–1993)	27	0	27
103rd	(1993–1995)	39	1	40
104th	(1995–1997)	40	1	41
105th	(1997–1999)	39	1	40
106th	(1999–2001)	39	0	39
107th	(2001–2003)	39	0	39
108th	(2003–2005)	39	0	39
109th	(2005–2007)	42	1	43
110th	(2007–2009)	42	1	43
111th	(2009–2011)	41	1	42
112th	(2011–2013)	42	0	42
113th	(2013–2015)	41	2	43
114th	(2015–2017)	44	2	46
115th	(2017–2019)	49	3	52
116th	(2019–2021)	56	3	59
117th	(2021–2023)	59	3	62

Note: The numbers reflect the highest number of Black members to serve in the House of Representatives or Senate at any one time during a Congress. For example, a record forty-six Black members were elected to the 110th Congress, but only forty-three served at any one time during the Congress.

Sources: 41st–110th Congresses: Mildred L. Amer, "African American Members of the United States Congress: 1870–2008," RL30378, Congressional Research Service, Washington, D.C., July 23, 2008; 111th Congress: CQ Weekly (2008), 2998; (2009), 132; 112th Congress: CQ Roll Call, "Guide to the New Congress," November 4, 2010, 15; 113th Congress: CQ Roll Call, "Guide to the New Congress," November 8, 2012, 17; 114th Congress: *CQ Weekly* (2014), 59, updated by the authors; 115th–117th Congresses: U.S. House of Representatives, Office of the Clerk, "Black-American Members by Congress, 1870–Present," https://history.house.gov/Exhibitions-and-Publications/BAIC/Historical-Data/Black-American-Representatives-and-Senators-by-Congress.

Table 5-4 Women Nominated, by Party, 1956–2020, and Women Elected to U.S. House of Representatives, by Party, 1916–2020

Election year	Congress	Major-party nominees			Elected			Success rate (percent)			Serving		
		Democratic	Republican	Total	Democratic	Republican	Total	Democratic	Republican	Total	Democratic	Republican	Total
1916	65th	—	—	—	0	1	1	—	—	—	0	1	1
1918	66th	—	—	—	0	0	0	—	—	—	0	0	0
1920	67th	—	—	—	0	1	1	—	—	—	0	3	3
1922	68th	—	—	—	0	1	1	—	—	—	0	1	1
1924	69th	—	—	—	1	0	1	—	—	—	1	2	3
1926	70th	—	—	—	1	3	4	—	—	—	2	3	5
1928	71st	—	—	—	4	4	8	—	—	—	5	4	9
1930	72nd	—	—	—	3	3	6	—	—	—	4	3	7
1932	73rd	—	—	—	3	2	5	—	—	—	4	3	7
1934	74th	—	—	—	4	2	6	—	—	—	4	2	6
1936	75th	—	—	—	4	1	5	—	—	—	5	1	6
1938	76th	—	—	—	2	2	4	—	—	—	4	4	8
1940	77th	—	—	—	3	4	7	—	—	—	5	4	9
1942	78th	—	—	—	1	6	7	—	—	—	2	6	8
1944	79th	—	—	—	4	5	9	—	—	—	6	5	11
1946	80th	—	—	—	3	4	7	—	—	—	3	4	7
1948	81st	—	—	—	4	4	8	—	—	—	5	4	9
1950	82nd	—	—	—	2	6	8	—	—	—	4	6	10
1952	83rd	—	—	—	5	6	11	—	—	—	5	6	11
1954	84th	—	—	—	9	6	15	—	—	—	10	6	16
1956	85th	15	14	29	9	6	15	60.0	43.0	51.7	9	6	15
1958	86th	13	14	27	8	8	16	61.5	57.1	59.3	9	8	17
1960	87th	15	8	23	9	6	15	60.0	75.0	65.2	11	7	18
1962	88th	12	11	23	6	5	11	50.0	45.5	47.8	6	6	12
1964	89th	11	7	18	6	4	10	54.5	57.1	55.6	7	4	11
1966	90th	10	13	23	6	5	11	60.0	38.5	47.8	6	5	11
1968	91st	13	6	19	6	4	10	46.2	66.7	52.6	6	4	10
1970	92nd	14	10	24	9	3	12	64.3	30.0	50.0	10	3	13
1972	93rd	23	10	33	12	2	14	52.2	20.0	42.4	14	2	16
1974	94th	27	16	43	14	4	18	51.9	25.0	41.9	14	5	19

Year	Congress										
1976	95th	34	20	54	13	18	38.2	25.0	33.3	13	5	18
1978	96th	26	18	44	10	15	38.5	27.8	34.1	11	5	16
1980	97th	27	26	53	10	19	37.0	34.6	35.8	11	10	21
1982	98th	27	27	54	12	21	44.4	33.3	38.9	13	9	22
1984	99th	28	36	64	11	22	39.3	30.6	34.4	12	11	23
1986	100th	30	34	64	12	23	40.0	32.4	35.9	13	11	24
1988	101st	33	25	58	14	25	42.4	44.0	43.1	16	13	29
1990	102nd	38	29	67	19	28	50.0	31.0	41.8	20	9	29
1992	103rd	69	35	104	35	47	50.7	34.3	45.2	35	12	47
1994	104th	72	42	114	31	51	43.1	38.1	41.2	32	17	49
1996	105th	78	42	120	35	56	44.9	38.1	42.5	37	18	55
1998	106th	73	45	118	39	59	53.4	37.8	47.5	39	17	56
2000	107th	81	43	124	41	59	50.6	41.9	47.6	42	18	60
2002	108th	77	44	121	38	59	49.4	47.7	48.8	39	21	60
2004	109th	85	52	137	42	65	49.4	44.2	47.4	43	25	68
2006	110th	94	42	136	50	71	53.2	50.0	52.2	55	21	76
2008	111th	95	38	133	58	75	61.1	44.7	56.4	58	17	75
2010	112th	91	47	138	48	72	52.7	51.1	52.2	51	24	75
2012	113th	118	48	166	58	78	49.1	41.7	47.0	61	20	81
2014	114th	109	50	159	62	84	56.9	44.0	52.8	63	22	84
2016	115th	120	47	167	62	83	51.7	44.7	49.7	64	21	85
2018	116th	182	52	234	88	101	48.4	25.0	43.1	89	13	102
2020	117th	204	94	298	89	119	43.6	32.0	39.9	87	31	118

Notes: "___" indicates not available. "Major-party nominees," "elected," and "success rate" refer to women candidates in regularly scheduled elections for the election year indicated. "Serving" includes women elected in regularly scheduled elections in the election year indicated as well as those elected in special elections over the course of the congressional session. One woman was elected as an independent: Jo Ann Emerson was elected simultaneously as a Republican to the 104th Congress and as an independent to the 105th Congress by special election to fill the vacancy caused by the death of her husband, U.S. Representative Bill Emerson. She changed from an independent to a Republican on January 8, 1997, and was elected as a Republican to the 106th and subsequent Congresses. In the counts, Emerson is considered a Republican.

Data for the 2020 election cycle are current as of May 14, 2021. One woman, Republican Julia Letlow (La.-5), was elected to Congress in a special election on March 20, 2021. Other special elections are pending. Democratic representatives Marcia Fudge and Debra Haaland left to serve in Joseph Biden's administration after the 117th Congress was sworn in.

Source: Unpublished data, Barbara Palmer, Baldwin Wallace University, and Dennis Simon, Southern Methodist University, published with permission. Data for 2016, 2018, and 2020 found in reports from the Center for American Women and Politics, https://cawp.rutgers.edu.

A Data Literacy Lesson

Why Are There So Few Women in Elective Office? And Why Does It Matter?

Why are there so few women holding elective office? This question never fails to elicit interesting discussion in the classroom. Politics, it may be said, is a "man's game," and women are at a disadvantage when they run for office. Perhaps women lack the levels of formal education and advanced degrees that men have, or lack the money that men have (or can access) to fund their campaigns. Women might be perceived by some as weaker than men, which could cost them support; they might also suffer at the polls from sexist male (or even female) voters. Women may be more likely to face criticism for their appearance, or for aspects of their persona unrelated to governing ability; they simply may not "look" or "seem" the way some believe a senator or president should look or seem. Regardless of the merit of these beliefs, all of these are reasonable hypotheses for what might drive voters' behavior, which we could test against data if we wished to do so.

Table 5-4 tells us a potentially different story. Look first at the first set of columns, representing the number of women running as a major party nominee for Congress. Over the years represented in the table, more women have always run for Congress as Democrats rather than as Republicans, no doubt reflecting higher levels of identification as Democrats among women. The numbers in the table have gone up over time, from an almost incomprehensible twenty-nine back in 1956 to 204 in 2020. The second set of columns, not surprisingly, show that the number of women representatives has also risen dramatically during this time. Only one woman was elected to the House in 1916[1], and the number of women serving did not hit double figures until 1952. Today, 119 women serve in the House of Representatives; while we are not yet at (or even close to) parity, this is undeniably a dramatic increase, particularly in recent years. Thirty years ago, women made up less than 5 percent of the House; today, that number is above 25 percent. Slow progress is still progress.

When we combine these numbers, in the third set of columns, we see some interesting results. While the table does reveal year-to-year variation, sometimes quite significant, we can see that the overall trend is fairly steady over time, and that it hovers close to (and sometimes edges above) 50 percent. When women get nominations for congressional seats, they consistently have almost as good a chance of winning as men. To go back to our first question, voters refusing to support women candidates seems a less compelling answer given these data. An important area of investigation, then, echoing work by Jennifer Lawless and Richard Fox, realizes that a key reason for the underrepresentation of women is that women just don't run for office as much as men do. Their book seeks to explore why this is the case.[2] Among the key insights from this area of scholarship is that women need to be asked to run more than men do. An average male candidate sees an opportunity, looks in the mirror, sees an ideal candidate, and throws his hat in the ring. An average female candidate needs more convincing to believe that she is a viable candidate; the table indicates, however, that once she decides to run, she has a virtually equal chance of success compared to her male colleague.

What this table does not tell us, of course, is why it matters. If Steve can do an equivalent job as Sarah in representing "the interests of women" (however we define them), does it matter that Steve is not a woman? Most observers would say that it does—the lived experiences of women give them an important perspective that even the most sympathetic and supportive man has not experienced. Men may vote the same as women, but they may not necessarily approach some issues with the same intensity that women might. Some even argue that women legislate in a different style than men do, and that a legislature composed of more women would operate in a more consensual, less conflictual style than one dominated by men.

In a world where the notion of gender as a nonbinary construct is increasingly being understood and accepted, it is worth noting that this table (and essay) present gender as binary, male or female. This is because, to this point (and to our knowledge), there are no members of Congress who are transgender, or whose gender identity is nonbinary. This will change over time, as our societal conception of gender, and of different ways of gender expression, evolves. One day, a table such as Table 5-4 will incorporate nonbinary perspectives on gender, offering up more questions and explanations for who gets elected to Congress, and who does not.

---

[1]This was Jeannette Rankin of Montana, who served two nonconsecutive terms in Congress (1917–1918 and 1941–1942), and voted against United States entry into both World War I and World War II.
[2]Jennifer L. Lawless and Richard L. Fox. *It Takes a Candidate: Why Women Don't Run for Office.* New York: Cambridge University Press, 2005.

Table 5-5 Members of Congress: Seniority and Previous Legislative Service, 2017–2021

	Representatives									Senators								
	115th (2017)			116th (2019)			117th (2021)			115th (2017)			116th (2019)			117th (2021)		
	Dem.	Rep.	Total	Dem.	Rep.	Total	Dem.	Rep.	Total	Dem.	Rep.	Total	Dem.	Rep.	Total	Dem.	Rep.	Total
Seniority																		
Under 2 years	30	38	68	60	41	101	16	50	66	5	3	8	3	8	11	6	4	10
2–9 years	79	135	214	81	112	193	114	96	210	24	27	51	20	26	46	18	22	40
10–19 years	45	39	84	47	36	83	44	54	98	14	11	25	17	10	27	16	18	34
20–29 years	35	19	54	34	9	43	36	8	44	5	4	9	6	5	11	9	3	12
30 years or more	8	7	15	10	5	15	8	4	12	1	6	7	1	4	5	1	3	4
Total	197	238	435	232	203	435	218	212	430	49	51	100	47	53	100	50	50	100
Previous Service in U.S. House																		
Yes							Not Applicable			28	28	56	25	27	52	24	22	46
No										21	23	44	22	26	48	26	28	54

Note: Seniority represents consecutive years of service. Senators Bernie Sanders (I-Vt.) and Angus King (I-Maine) are listed as Democrat. Representative Justin Amash (I-Mich.) is listed as a Republican. House totals for the current session include five vacancies, two due to deaths (Ron Wright, R-Texas, and Alcee Hastings, D-Fla.), and three due to members of the House accepting positions in the Biden Administration (Deb Haaland, D-N.M, Marcia Fudge, D-Ohio, and Cedric Richmond, D-La.). For previous Congresses, if the seat holder changed during the term, the table reflects the person who held the seat for the largest part of the term.

Sources: Compiled by authors.

Table 5-6 Congressional Committees and Majority Party Chair Positions, 1983–2023

Congress		Number of committees[a]	Party in majority	Number of majority party members	Number of majority party members chairing standing committees and subcommittees	Percentage of majority party members chairing standing committees and subcommittees	Number of majority party members chairing all committees and subcommittees	Percentage of majority party members chairing all committees and subcommittees
House								
98th	(1983–1985)	172	D	267	124	46.4	127	47.6
99th	(1985–1987)	191	D	253	129	51.0	131	51.8
100th	(1987–1989)	192	D	258	128	49.6	132	51.2
101st	(1989–1991)	189	D	260	134	51.5	137	52.7
102nd	(1991–1993)	185	D	267	130	48.7	135	50.6
103rd	(1993–1995)	146	D	258	113	43.8	116	45.0
104th	(1995–1997)	110	R	230	86	37.4	86	37.4
105th	(1997–1999)	112	R	225	100	44.4	100	44.4
106th	(1999–2001)	108	R	222	100	45.0	100	45.0
107th	(2001–2003)	116	R	221	109	49.3	109	49.3
108th	(2003–2005)	122	R	228	89	39.0	97	42.5
109th	(2005–2007)	121	R	230	107	46.5	112	48.7
110th	(2007–2009)	131	D	232	114	49.1	119	51.3
111th	(2009–2011)	131	D	254	109	42.9	117	46.1
112th	(2011–2013)	130	R	241	121	50.2	122	50.6
113th	(2013–2015)	123	R	232	106	45.7	107[b]	46.1
114th	(2015–2017)	124	R	245	112	45.7	115[b]	46.9
115th	(2017–2019)	129	R	241	113	46.9	116	48.1
116th	(2019–2021)	130	D	235	115	49.0	119	50.6
117th	(2021–2023)	132	D	222	114	51.3	120	54.1

(Table continues)

Table 5-6 (Continued)

Congress		Number of committees[a]	Party in majority	Number of majority party members	Number of majority party members chairing standing committees and subcommittees	Percentage of majority party members chairing standing committees and subcommittees	Number of majority party members chairing all committees and subcommittees	Percentage of majority party members chairing all committees and subcommittees
Senate								
98th	(1983–1985)	137	R	54	52	96.3	52	96.3
99th	(1985–1987)	120	R	53	49	92.5	49	92.5
100th	(1987–1989)	118	D	54	47	87.0	47	87.0
101st	(1989–1991)	118	D	55	46	83.6	46	83.6
102nd	(1991–1993)	119	D	56	50	89.3	50	89.3
103rd	(1993–1995)	111	D	57	46	80.7	46	80.7
104th	(1995–1997)	92	R	54	44	81.5	44	81.5
105th	(1997–1999)	92	R	54	49	90.7	49	90.7
106th	(1999–2001)	94	R	55	52	94.5	52	94.5
107th	(2001–2003)	92	R[c]	50	49	98.0	49	98.0
108th	(2003–2005)	92	R	51	50	98.0	50	98.0
109th	(2005–2007)	96	R	55	52	94.5	53	96.4
110th	(2007–2009)	96	D	50[d]	40	80.0	40	80.0
111th	(2009–2011)	89	D	58[d]	46	79.3	46	79.3
112th	(2011–2013)	98	D	53[d]	49	92.5	49	92.5
113th	(2013–2015)	96	D	55[e]	49	89.1	49[b]	89.1
114th	(2015–2017)	97	R	54[e]	50	92.6	51[b]	94.4
115th	(2017–2019)	94	R	52[e]	48	92.3	49	94.2
116th	(2019–2021)	92	R	53[e]	49	92.5	50	94.3
117th	(2021–2023)	92	D	50[e]	45	90.0	45	90.0

Note: "D" indicates Democratic; "R" indicates Republican. Data for additional years can be found in previous editions of *Vital Statistics on American Politics*. Information for the 117th Congress is current as of May 13, 2021.

[a] Includes standing committees, subcommittees of standing committees, select and special committees, subcommittees of select and special committees, joint committees, and subcommittees of joint committees. The counts may exclude a few late-forming committees or subcommittees.

[c] Split 50–50 at the start of the session, the Senate was controlled by Republicans by virtue of Vice President Dick Cheney's vote. On May 24, 2001, Senator James M. Jeffords, Vt., announced that he would switch from Republican to independent and that he would caucus with the Democrats. This change shifted control of the Senate to the Democratic Party.

[d] Includes Joseph I. Lieberman, Conn., elected in 2006 under the label "Connecticut for Lieberman," and Bernard Sanders, Vt., elected as an independent, both of whom caucused with the Democrats.

[e] Includes Angus S. King Jr, Md., and Bernard Sanders, Vt., elected as independents, both of whom caucus with the Democrats.

Sources: 98th–103rd: Norman J. Ornstein, Thomas E. Mann, and Michael J. Malbin, eds., *Vital Statistics on Congress, 1993–1994* (Washington, D.C.: Congressional Quarterly, 1994), 113, 117–118; 104th–111th: calculated by the editors from *Congressional Quarterly Weekly Report* (CQ Weekly), supplement to volumes 53 (March 25, 1995); (March 22, 1997); 57 (March 13, 1999); 59 (April 28, 2001); 61 (April 12, 2003); 63 (April 11, 2005); 65 (April 16, 2007); 67 (April 13, 2009); 1 (March 25, 2013); 112th–114th: calculated by www.contactingthecongress.org, supplemented by House committee list (www.house.gov) and Senate committee list (www.senate.gov); 115th–117th Congress compiled by authors from House committee list and Senate committee list.

Table 5-7 Congressional Measures Introduced and Enacted, 1947–2021

Congress			Measures introduced			Measures enacted	
		Bills	Joint resolutions	Total	Public	Private	Total
80th	(1947–1949)	10,108	689	10,797	906	457	1,363
81st	(1949–1951)	14,219	769	14,988	921	1,103	2,024
82nd	(1951–1953)	12,062	668	12,730	594	1,023	1,617
83rd	(1953–1955)	14,181	771	14,952	781	1,002	1,783
84th	(1955–1957)	16,782	905	17,687	1,028	893	1,921
85th	(1957–1959)	18,205	907	19,112	936	784	1,720
86th	(1959–1961)	17,230	1,031	18,261	800	492	1,292
87th	(1961–1963)	17,230	1,146	18,376	885	684	1,569
88th	(1963–1965)	16,079	1,401	17,480	666	360	1,026
89th	(1965–1967)	22,483	1,520	24,003	810	473	1,283
90th	(1967–1969)	24,786	1,674	26,460	640	362	1,002
91st	(1969–1971)	24,631	1,672	26,303	695	246	941
92nd	(1971–1973)	21,363	1,606	22,969	607	161	768
93rd	(1973–1975)	21,950	1,446	23,396	651	123	774
94th	(1975–1977)	19,762	1,334	21,096	588	141	729
95th	(1977–1979)	18,045	1,342	19,387	633	170	803
96th	(1979–1981)	11,722	861	12,583	613	123	736
97th	(1981–1983)	10,582	908	11,490	473	56	529
98th	(1983–1985)	10,134	1,022	11,156	623	54	677
99th	(1985–1987)	8,697	1,188	9,885	664	24	688
100th	(1987–1989)	8,515	1,073	9,588	713	48	761
101st	(1989–1991)	9,257	1,095	10,352	404	7	411
102nd	(1991–1993)	9,601	909	10,510	589	14	603
103rd	(1993–1995)	7,883	661	8,544	465	8	473
104th	(1995–1997)	6,545	263	6,808	234	2	236
105th	(1997–1999)	7,532	200	7,732	394	10	404
106th	(1999–2001)	8,968	190	9,158	580	24	604
107th	(2001–2003)	8,956	178	9,134	377	6	383
108th	(2003–2005)	8,468	157	8,625	498	6	504
109th	(2005–2007)	10,560	143	10,703	395	1	396
110th	(2007–2009)	11,081	147	11,228	416	0	416
111th	(2009–2011)	10,621	149	10,770	336	2	338
112th	(2011–2013)	10,439	173	10,612	238	1	239
113th	(2013–2015)	8,915	178	9,093	296	0	296
114th	(2015–2017)	10,074	149	10,222	329	0	329
115th	(2017–2019)	14,281	205	14,486	442	1	443
116th	(2019–2021)	14,150	192	14,342	283	0	283

Note: Measures exclude simple and concurrent resolutions.

Sources: 80th–99th: U.S. Congress, Calendars of the U.S. House of Representatives and History of Legislation, 99th Cong., final ed., 19–57 through 19–68; 100th–106th: successive issues of *Congressional Quarterly Almanac* (Washington, D.C.: CQ Press); 107th–113th: "Résumé of Congressional Activity," *Congressional Record—Daily Digest*, various issues, 2005–2020.

Turnout 243

Figure 5-2 Measures Introduced in Congress That Were Passed, 1789–2020 (percent)

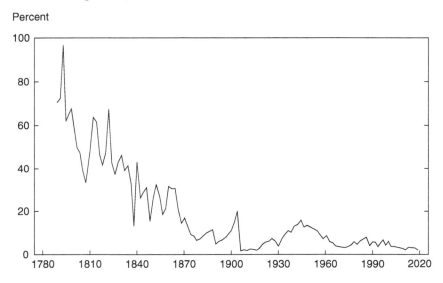

Note: Measures include bills and joint resolutions. Before 1824, only bills are included. Figures are for each Congress.

Sources: 1789–1968: U.S. Bureau of the Census, *Historical Statistics of the United States,* Series Y189-198 (Washington, D.C.: Government Printing Office, 1975), 1081–1082; 1969–2020: Table 5-7, this volume.

> ### A Data Literacy Lesson
>
> #### The Do-Nothing Congress?
>
> Even just a quick glance at Table 5-7 (or especially Figure 5-2) will reveal a stark pattern—fewer and fewer bills are getting through Congress and being enacted as laws. Whereas sixty years ago Congress was enacting over 1,000 bills per session, that number is closer to 300 nowadays. This begs the question of why this is happening.
>
> One reason that becomes immediately clear from the table is that Congress is passing fewer private bills these days (only one since 2013). Unlike public bills, which are intended to apply to the general public or to groups of citizens, private bills affect only specific individuals, or organizations. These were commonly passed to make exceptions to immigration laws (such as to change an individual's immigration status, as a way to stave off deportation proceedings against an individual). Private bills are used much less in recent years, which accounts for much of the total reduction in measures enacted.
>
> If we limit our focus to just public bills, however, we still see a significant reduction in the number of bills that were passed—on average, this number is now around half of what we might have seen in the 1960s and 1970s. "That darned do-nothing Congress!" we might exclaim. Looking a little closer, however, we see that the percentage of bills passed back then is, roughly speaking, pretty close to what it is now. If we turn our attention away from Table 5-7 and toward Figure 5-2, we can see that starting about 1960, the percentage of measures introduced in Congress that were passed seems to be about equivalent to what it is today. The stark decline displayed in Figure 5-2 reflects the fact that before 1840, it was typical to have more than 40 percent of bills passed; today, that figure is below 5 percent. The length of the time series displayed in Figure 5-2, and the decline it shows, obscures the fact that the graph for the last sixty years is pretty level. (Although, to be clear, the last two Congresses have hit lower levels than was previously the case.)
>
> One could easily imagine political pundits looking at Figure 5-2 and complaining about how inefficient Congress has become. They might decry the excessive partisanship within Congress, the increased tendency toward divided government, the inability and unwillingness of members of Congress to cross the aisle and put country above party, and the increased time and attention members of Congress give to reelection concerns at the expense of legislating. Such complaints, however, might be misguided; Congress is doing as well now on this measure as it was in the 1960s, when partisan differences were less prevalent in Congress. Why members of Congress are proposing fewer bills, of course, begs asking. That question, and not the legislative "batting average" of Congress, seems to warrant the lion's share of the attention, based on these data.
>
> And yet, as we have said often in this book, what you see in a table tells only part of the story. What is the nature of the bills that Congress is passing? A Pew Foundation report asks about whether the bills Congress passes are substantive (such as overhauling the immigration system), or ceremonial (such as naming a post office). Close to one-third of the bills Congress passes, the report tells us, are ceremonial bills, a proportion that has been roughly the same over the last thirty years. While this report does not say that congressional productivity has changed in recent years, it does remind us that not all bills are created equal, and that any

analysis based solely on a raw count of the number of bills passed risks missing something.

The trends and patterns we see in Table 5-7 and Figure 5-2 tell us something, as this essay has noted. However, we sometimes need to dig a little deeper to define our historical frame of reference (do we want to compare the modern Congress to those of two hundred years ago or fifty years ago?) and to define the terms we are using (public versus private bills, or substantive versus ceremonial bills?). Asking a few key questions about any table or figure we see can help us to refine the questions we are asking, and to determine what further data we need to address them.

Table 5-8 Record Votes in the House and the Senate, 1947–2020

Year	House	Senate	Year	House	Senate
1947	84	138	1984	408	292
1948	79	110	1985	439	381
1949	121	226	1986	451	359
1950	154	229	1987	488	420
1951	109	202	1988	451	379
1952	72	129	1989	368	312
1953	71	89	1990	510	326
1954	76	181	1991	428	280
1955	73	88	1992	473	270
1956	74	136	1993	597	395
1957	100	111	1994	497	329
1958	93	202	1995	867	613
1959	87	215	1996	454	306
1960	93	207	1997	633	298
1961	116	207	1998	533	314
1962	124	227	1999	609	374
1963	119	229	2000	600	298
1964	113	312	2001	507	380
1965	201	259	2002	483	253
1966	193	238	2003	675	459
1967	245	315	2004	543	216
1968	233	280[a]	2005	669	366
1969	177	245	2006	539	279
1970	266	422	2007	1177	442
1971	320	423	2008	688	215
1972	329	532	2009	987	397
1973	541	594	2010	660	299
1974	537	544	2011	946[b]	235
1975	612	611	2012	657	251
1976	661	700	2013	640	291
1977	706	636	2014	563	366
1978	834	520	2015	705	339
1979	672	509	2016	622	163
1980	604	546	2017	710	325
1981	353	497	2018	497	274
1982	459	469	2019	701	428
1983	498	381	2020	253	292

[a] The Senate record vote total does not include one yea-and-nay vote that was ruled invalid for lack of a quorum.
[b] The House record vote total includes one roll call vote that was vacated by unanimous consent.

Note: In the House, record votes are defined as yea-and-nay (roll call) votes plus so-called recorded votes, which refers to votes cast electronically using the system introduced in the House after the Legislative Reorganization Act of 1970. In the Senate, there is no electronic system, so record votes are simply yea-and-nay (roll call) votes. Quorum votes are excluded for both the House and the Senate.

Source: U.S. Congress, "Résumé of Congressional Activity," *Congressional Record—Daily Digest*, various issues, Eightieth Congress (1947) through 116th Congress (2020).

Figure 5-3 Party Votes in the House, 1878–2020

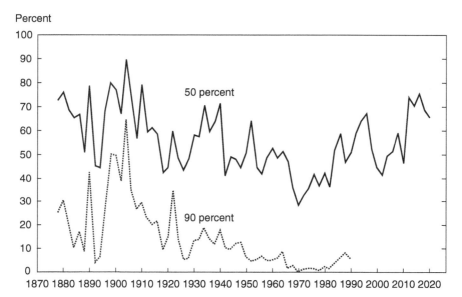

Note: Figures shown by Congress. A party vote occurs when the specified percentage (or more) of one party votes against the specified percentage (or more) of the other party.

Sources: 1878–1886 and 90 percent vote for 1972–1990: Brinck Kerr, "Structural Determinants of Party Voting in the U.S. Congress, 1877–1990," PhD diss., Texas A&M University, 1993; 1887–1969: Joseph Cooper, David William Brady, and Patricia A. Hurley, "The Electoral Basis of Party Voting: Patterns and Trends in the U.S. House of Representatives, 1887–1969," in *The Impact of the Electoral Process,* Louis Maisel and Joseph Cooper (Beverly Hills, Calif.: Sage Publications, 1977), 139; 1970–1990: *Congressional Quarterly Almanac* (Washington, D.C.: Congressional Quarterly, annual); 1991–2010: *Congressional Quarterly Weekly Report (CQ Weekly)* (1992), 3906; (1993), 3480; (1994), 3658; (1996), 199, 3432; (1998), 18; (1999), 79; (2000), 2975; (2001), 56; (2002), 114, 3240; (2004), 11, 2907; (2006), 93; (2007), 33; (2008), 144, 3333; (2010), 123; (2011), 30 (2012), 111; (2013), 132–136; (2014), 183; (2015), 37; 2016–2020: *CQ Weekly* (February 8, 2016); (October 17, 2016); (February 12, 2018); (February 25, 2019); (February 24, 2020); (March 1, 2021).

Table 5-9 Party Unity and Polarization in Congressional Voting, 1953–2020 (percent)

Year	House	Senate	Year	House	Senate
1953	52	52	1987	64	41
1954	38	48	1988	47	43
1955	41	30	1989	56	35
1956	44	53	1990	49	54
1957	59	36	1991	55	49
1958	40	44	1992	65	53
1959	55	48	1993	66	67
1960	53	37	1994	62	52
1961	50	62	1995	73	69
1962	46	41	1996	56	62
1963	49	47	1997	50	50
1964	55	36	1998	56	56
1965	52	42	1999	47	63
1966	42	50	2000	43	49
1967	36	35	2001	40	55
1968	35	32	2002	43	46
1969	31	36	2003	52	67
1970	27	35	2004	47	52
1971	38	42	2005	49	63
1972	27	37	2006	55	57
1973	42	40	2007	62	60
1974	29	44	2008	53	52
1975	48	48	2009	51	72
1976	36	37	2010	40	79
1977	42	42	2011	76	51
1978	33	45	2012	73	60
1979	47	47	2013	69	70
1980	38	46	2014	73	67
1981	37	48	2015	75	73
1982	36	43	2016	76	48
1983	56	44	2017	76	69
1984	47	40	2018	59	50
1985	61	50	2019	68	54
1986	57	52	2020	70	64

Note: Data indicate the percentage of all record votes on which a majority of voting Democrats opposed a majority of voting Republicans.

Source: 1953: *CQ Weekly* (2011), 37; 1954–1955: (2013), 138; 1956–2014: (2015), 42; 2015–2020: *CQ Magazine,* (February 8, 2016); (October 17, 2016); (February 2, 2018); (February 25, 2019); (February 24, 2020); (March 1, 2021).

Table 5-10 Party Unity in Congressional Voting, 1954–2020 (percent)

	House			Senate		
Year	All Democrats	Southern Democrats	Republicans	All Democrats	Southern Democrats	Republicans
1954	80	—	84	77	—	89
1955	84	68	78	82	78	82
1956	80	79	78	80	75	80
1957	79	71	75	79	81	81
1958	77	67	73	82	76	74
1959	85	77	85	76	63	80
1960	75	62	77	73	60	74
1961	—	—	—	—	—	—
1962	81	—	80	80	—	81
1963	85	—	84	79	—	79
1964	82	—	81	73	—	75
1965	80	55	81	75	55	78
1966	78	55	82	73	52	78
1967	77	53	82	75	59	73
1968	73	48	76	71	57	74
1969	71	47	71	74	53	72
1970	71	52	72	71	49	71
1971	72	48	76	74	56	75
1972	70	44	76	72	43	73
1973	75	55	74	79	52	74
1974	72	51	71	72	41	68
1975	75	53	78	76	48	71
1976	75	52	75	74	46	72
1977	74	55	77	72	48	75
1978	71	53	77	75	54	66
1979	75	60	79	76	62	73
1980	78	64	79	76	64	74
1981	75	57	80	77	64	85
1982	77	62	76	76	62	80
1983	82	67	80	76	70	79
1984	81	68	77	75	61	83
1985	86	76	80	79	68	81
1986	86	76	76	74	59	80
1987	88	78	79	85	80	78
1988	88	81	80	85	78	74
1989	86	77	76	79	69	79
1990	86	78	78	82	75	77
1991	86	78	81	83	73	83
1992	86	79	84	82	70	83
1993	89	83	87	87	78	86
1994	88	83	87	86	77	81
1995	84	75	93	84	76	91
1996	84	76	90	86	75	91
1997	85	78	91	86	75	88
1998	86	79	89	90	85	88
1999	86	77	88	91	86	90
2000	86	80	90	90	80	91
2001	86	77	94	90	79	90

(Table continues)

Table 5-10 *(Continued)*

	House			Senate		
Year	All Democrats	Southern Democrats	Republicans	All Democrats	Southern Democrats	Republicans
2002	90	82	93	85	69	88
2003	91	85	95	90	76	95
2004	91	83	93	88	76	93
2005	91	84	93	90	81	90
2006	90	82	92	89	77	87
2007	95	85	90	92	93	84
2008	97	—	92	92	—	87
2009	94	—	90	94	—	87
2010	93	—	94	94	—	93
2011	91	—	94	94	—	89
2012	92	—	93	93	—	83
2013	92	—	95	96	—	89
2014	95	—	95	99	—	89
2015	95	—	87	88	—	93
2016	95	—	89	84	—	94
2017	89	—	91	87	—	92
2018	93	—	92	92	—	97
2019	93	—	91	83	—	91
2020	92	—	93	89	—	91

Note: "—" indicates not available. Data show percentage of members voting with a majority of their party on party unity votes. Party unity votes are those roll calls on which a majority of Democrats vote against a majority of Republicans. Percentages are calculated to eliminate the impact of absences as follows: unity = (unity)/(unity + opposition).

Sources: 1954–1992: Norman J. Ornstein, Thomas E. Mann, and Michael J. Malbin, eds., V*ital Statistics on Congress, 1993–1994* (Washington, D.C.: Congressional Quarterly, 1994), 201–202; 1993–2016: *Congressional Quarterly Weekly Report (CQ Weekly)* (1993), 3479; (1994), 3659; (1996), 245, 3461; (1998), 33; (1999), 92, 2993; (2001), 67; (2002), 142, 3281; (2004), 48, 2952; (2006), 97; (2007), 38; (2008), 147, 3337; (2011), 36; (2013), 137; (2015), February 8, 2016; (2016), February 14, 2017; 2017–2020: *CQ Magazine,* (February 12, 2018); (February 25, 2019); (February 24, 2020); (March 1, 2021).

Table 5-11 The 117th Congress: House of Representatives

State/district/ representative	Party	Year born	Year entered the House	Percentage vote in 2020 Primary	Percentage vote in 2020 General	Campaign expenditures (2019–2020)	Voting ratings[a] VP	PS	PU	ADA	ACU	CCUS	LCV
Alabama													
1 Carl	R	1958	2021	52	65	2,232,544	—	—	—	—	—	—	—
2 Moore	R	1966	2021	60	65	856,277	—	—	—	—	—	—	—
3 Rogers	R	1958	2003	U	67	1,228,340	93	94	97	10	83	77	4
4 Aderholt	R	1965	1997	U	82	1,352,138	89	91	96	5	81	77	4
5 Brooks	R	1954	2011	75	96	223,707	99	96	99	0	97	68	2
6 Palmer	R	1954	2015	U	97	921,542	95	92	100	0	96	65	0
7 Sewell	D	1965	2011	U	97	1,498,832	89	11	98	85	6	69	94
Alaska													
AL Young	R	1933	1973	76	54	1,817,837	92	94	85	10	61	91	22
Arizona													
1 O'Halleran	D	1946	2017	59	51	3,359,687	98	10	97	80	7	67	99
2 Kirkpatrick	D	1950	2019	76	55	1,433,662	54	12	98	85	2	70	94
3 Grijalva	D	1948	2003	U	65	691,288	74	6	100	95	0	39	99
4 Gosar	R	1958	2011	63	70	759,239	90	83	99	0	94	51	4
5 Biggs	R	1958	2017	99	59	1,338,432	98	94	98	0	100	59	0
6 Schweikert	R	1962	2011	U	52	2,283,321	99	88	92	0	88	82	14
7 Gallego	D	1979	2015	U	77	1,668,669	97	10	99	90	4	60	99
8 Lesko	R	1958	2018	U	60	996,782	95	93	98	0	90	80	2
9 Stanton	D	1970	2019	U	62	1,019,971	99	11	99	90	4	75	99
Arkansas													
1 Crawford	R	1966	2011	U	100	1,095,518	91	92	98	0	88	70	9
2 Hill	R	1956	2015	U	55	3,059,236	99	94	95	5	74	94	15
3 Womack	R	1957	2011	U	64	924,121	100	93	95	5	74	86	9
4 Westerman	R	1967	2015	U	79	1,123,312	98	95	99	5	89	79	7

(Table continues)

Table 5-11 *(Continued)*

State/district/representative	Party	Year born	Year entered the House	Percentage vote in 2020 Primary	Percentage vote in 2020 General	Campaign expenditures (2019–2020)	Voting ratings[a] VP	PS	PU	ADA	ACU	CCUS	LCV
California													
1 LaMalfa	R	1960	2013	55	57	1,179,454	96	91	97	0	82	86	6
2 Huffman	D	1964	2013	68	76	821,813	91	11	100	100	2	46	100
3 Garamendi	D	1945	2009	59	55	717,060	78	10	99	90	2	63	99
4 McClintock	R	1956	2009	51	56	2,130,296	96	92	95	0	98	58	2
5 Thompson	D	1951	1999	68	76	2,044,727	94	10	98	95	0	64	95
6 Matsui	D	1944	2005	70	73	1,077,825	100	10	99	95	0	56	99
7 Bera	D	1965	2013	50	57	1,126,436	93	10	98	90	4	70	99
8 Obernolte	R	1970	2021	35	56	1,958,786	—	—	—	—	—	—	—
9 McNerney	D	1951	2007	57	58	1,128,096	93	10	100	95	0	62	99
10 Harder	D	1986	2019	44	55	4,091,139	98	9	95	80	9	77	99
11 DeSaulnier	D	1952	2015	71	73	442,547	69	9	100	100	0	44	98
12 Pelosi	D	1940	1987	74	78	22,681,810	11	17	100	—	—	45	—
13 Lee	D	1946	1998	93	90	1,810,132	95	12	99	100	2	44	100
14 Speier	D	1950	2008	77	79	920,752	83	10	99	95	2	55	97
15 Swalwell	D	1980	2013	59	71	4,113,001	85	11	99	95	0	68	81
16 Costa	D	1952	2005	38	59	1,846,494	90	11	95	80	4	69	90
17 Khanna	D	1976	2017	69	71	2,535,202	81	14	99	95	2	46	99
18 Eshoo	D	1942	1993	62	63	2,078,652	96	10	100	95	0	55	97
19 Lofgren	D	1947	1995	63	72	1,771,846	68	10	99	95	0	53	92
20 Panetta	D	1969	2017	66	77	1,596,716	99	10	98	90	4	60	99
21 Valadao	R	1977	2021	50	51	4,018,146	—	—	—	—	—	—	—
22 Nunes	R	1973	2003	56	54	20,201,845	99	94	97	0	79	83	5
23 McCarthy	R	1965	2007	67	62	25,148,570	96	96	95	5	78	90	9
24 Carbajal	D	1964	2017	58	59	1,490,231	99	10	99	90	2	63	99
25 Garcia	R	1976	2020	24	50	9,762,756	—	—	—	—	—	—	—
26 Brownley	D	1952	2013	56	61	1,351,679	88	9	99	90	2	67	99
27 Chu	D	1953	2009	71	70	963,130	91	11	99	95	2	48	99

28 Schiff	D	1960	2001	60	73	10,404,171	100	10	99	95	0	56	99
29 Cardenas	D	1963	2013	59	57	1,219,561	82	8	99	100	2	53	100
30 Sherman	D	1954	1997	58	70	1,112,586	98	10	98	90	0	62	97
31 Aguilar	D	1979	2015	62	61	1,915,174	99	10	98	95	6	58	97
32 Napolitano	D	1936	1999	52	67	256,047	70	8	100	95	0	50	96
33 Lieu	D	1969	2015	61	68	1,601,806	68	9	99	90	0	51	94
34 Gomez	D	1974	2017	52	53	1,273,472	92	13	99	95	2	47	99
35 Torres	D	1965	2015	71	69	667,057	98	10	99	95	7	54	96
36 Ruiz	D	1972	2013	61	60	1,796,927	91	10	99	90	0	65	99
37 Bass	D	1953	2011	88	86	1,220,423	94	9	100	90	0	49	97
38 Sanchez	D	1969	2003	78	74	1,157,773	92	10	100	95	0	56	96
39 Kim	R	1962	2021	48	51	6,070,017	—	—	—	—	—	—	—
40 Roybal-Allard	D	1941	1993	51	73	750,770	81	10	100	95	2	49	96
41 Takano	D	1960	2013	51	64	962,989	98	9	99	95	2	50	99
42 Calvert	R	1953	1993	58	57	1,552,252	95	96	92	5	70	93	14
43 Waters	D	1938	1991	78	72	1,947,129	97	12	99	95	0	53	99
44 Barragan	D	1976	2017	64	68	727,579	86	10	100	100	2	45	100
45 Porter	D	1974	2019	51	54	6,717,188	76	10	95	85	2	63	95
46 Correa	D	1958	2017	58	69	666,547	99	9	98	85	2	67	97
47 Lowenthal	D	1941	2013	45	62	859,602	71	9	99	100	2	40	100
48 Steel	R	1955	2021	35	51	6,271,739	—	—	—	—	—	—	—
49 Levin	D	1978	2019	57	53	2,959,856	99	10	99	85	4	62	99
50 Issa	R	1953	2021	23	54	16,521,430	—	—	—	—	—	—	—
51 Vargas	D	1961	2013	71	68	801,671	88	10	100	95	0	51	98
52 Peters	D	1958	2013	49	62	2,160,222	89	9	96	85	7	63	99
53 Jacobs	D	1989	2021	29	60	7,608,203	—	—	—	—	—	—	—
Colorado													
1 DeGette	D	1957	1997	U	74	1,080,589	92	11	100	95	0	49	99
2 Neguse	D	1984	2019	U	61	690,025	97	11	100	95	0	56	99
3 Boebert	R	1986	2021	55	51	2,632,716	—	—	—	—	—	—	—
4 Buck	R	1959	2015	U	60	540,092	90	86	97	0	98	53	0
5 Lamborn	R	1954	2007	U	58	390,061	95	91	100	0	96	75	6

(Table continues)

253

Table 5-11 (Continued)

State/district/representative	Party	Year born	Year entered the House	Percentage vote in 2020 Primary	Percentage vote in 2020 General	Campaign expenditures (2019–2020)	Voting ratings[a] VP	PS	PU	ADA	ACU	CCUS	LCV
6 Crow	D	1979	2019	U	57	2,973,215	99	10	95	85	6	69	99
7 Perlmutter	D	1953	2007	U	59	1,345,447	95	10	99	80	2	65	99
Connecticut													
1 Larson	D	1948	1999	U	64	1,336,604	97	10	99	90	0	61	98
2 Courtney	D	1953	2007	U	59	1,002,505	99	10	99	90	0	62	97
3 DeLauro	D	1943	1991	U	59	1,813,322	98	10	99	90	0	53	99
4 Himes	D	1966	2009	U	62	2,199,740	98	10	98	90	0	66	99
5 Hayes	D	1973	2019	U	55	1,605,008	92	10	99	90	0	60	99
Delaware													
AL Blunt Rochester	D	1962	2010	U	58	1,327,604	99	10	100	95	0	65	96
Florida													
1 Gaetz	R	1982	2017	81	65	4,602,509	84	86	91	5	93	59	17
2 Dunn	R	1953	2017	U	98	656,913	87	96	97	5	81	85	8
3 Cammack	R	1988	2021	25	57	1,104,894	—	—	—	—	—	—	—
4 Rutherford	R	1952	2017	80	61	1,284,766	96	95	91	10	71	94	16
5 Lawson	D	1948	2017	56	65	731,878	69	10	98	80	6	68	99
6 Waltz	R	1974	2019	U	61	2,036,834	93	87	90	20	72	89	24
7 Murphy	D	1978	2017	U	55	1,828,522	99	14	93	80	7	73	96
8 Posey	R	1947	2009	63	61	1,127,339	98	88	93	0	77	78	17
9 Soto	D	1978	2017	U	56	949,960	98	10	99	90	4	65	99
10 Demings	D	1957	2011	U	64	1,198,213	99	10	99	90	4	68	99
11 Webster	R	1949	2011	U	67	588,604	90	89	95	0	79	75	12
12 Bilirakis	R	1963	2007	U	63	1,553,942	97	93	91	5	77	95	20
13 Crist	D	1956	2017	U	53	4,059,148	98	10	97	80	6	70	99
14 Castor	D	1966	2007	U	60	1,209,194	96	10	99	95	0	60	99

15 Franklin	R	1964	2021	51	55	1,639,817	—	—	—	—	—	—	—
16 Buchanan	R	1951	2007	U	56	3,649,491	92	86	87	15	65	95	32
17 Steube	R	1978	2019	U	65	629,763	95	92	98	0	99	70	4
18 Mast	R	1980	2017	86	56	5,369,800	96	89	88	15	68	86	34
19 Donalds	R	1978	2021	23	61	2,738,685	—	—	—	—	—	—	—
20 Vacant[b]													
21 Frankel	D	1948	2013	86	59	1,330,993	68	10	99	90	2	61	98
22 Deutsch	D	1966	2010	U	59	1,283,607	84	10	99	95	0	67	99
23 Wasserman Schultz	D	1966	2005	72	58	1,992,619	98	10	99	85	4	58	97
24 Wilson	D	1942	2011	85	76	321,019	61	10	99	95	0	52	94
25 Diaz-Balart	R	1961	2003	U	U	811,379	97	88	86	25	58	93	29
26 Gimenez	R	1954	2021	60	52	2,206,564	—	—	—	—	—	—	—
27 Salazar	R	1961	2021	79	51	3,682,371	—	—	—	—	—	—	—
Georgia													
1 Carter	R	1963	2015	82	58	1,766,880	98	94	98	0	86	77	16
2 Bishop	D	1947	1993	U	59	1,456,259	95	10	98	90	4	68	97
3 Ferguson	R	1966	2017	U	65	2,166,683	97	93	98	0	84	84	9
4 Johnson	D	1954	2007	68	80	498,219	99	13	99	95	2	64	99
5 Williams	D	1978	2021	U	85	367,104	—	—	—	—	—	—	—
6 McBath	D	1960	2019	U	55	8,757,259	100	12	98	80	6	71	96
7 Bourdeaux	D	1970	2021	53	51	5,331,900	—	—	—	—	—	—	—
8 Scott	R	1969	2011	90	65	730,669	94	93	98	10	84	76	9
9 Clyde	R	1963	2021	56	79	1,925,863	—	—	—	—	—	—	—
10 Hice	R	1960	2015	U	62	462,698	94	92	99	0	99	68	0
11 Loudermilk	R	1963	2015	U	60	723,066	78	92	100	5	95	77	4
12 Allen	R	1951	2015	U	58	666,048	97	95	100	5	90	74	4
13 Scott	D	1945	2003	53	77	1,147,252	97	10	99	85	6	67	99
14 Greene	R	1974	2021	57	75	2,709,893	—	—	—	—	—	—	—
Hawaii													
1 Case	D	1952	2019	U	72	570,675	95	12	96	85	4	66	99
2 Kahele	D	1974	2021	77	63	1,059,753	—	—	—	—	—	—	—

(Table continues)

255

Table 5-11 *(Continued)*

State/district/representative	Party	Year born	Year entered the House	Percentage vote in 2020 Primary	Percentage vote in 2020 General	Campaign expenditures (2019–2020)	Voting ratings[a] VP	PS	PU	ADA	ACU	CCUS	LCV
Idaho													
1 Fulcher	R	1962	2019	80	68	515,965	99	95	100	0	97	67	4
2 Simpson	R	1950	1999	72	64	1,101,104	90	92	89	15	68	87	20
Illinois													
1 Rush	D	1946	1993	72	74	500,779	68	10	100	95	0	65	99
2 Kelly	D	1956	2013	85	79	1,112,900	98	10	100	90	0	66	99
3 Newman	D	1964	2021	47	56	2,732,742	—	—	—	—	—	—	—
4 Garcia	D	1956	2019	U	84	726,422	98	14	99	100	2	44	100
5 Quigley	D	1958	2009	75	71	927,705	97	10	100	95	0	55	99
6 Casten	D	1971	2019	U	53	5,437,739	100	10	99	90	4	58	99
7 Davis	D	1941	1997	60	80	510,806	94	11	100	95	0	55	99
8 Krishnamoorthi	D	1973	2017	80	73	2,259,903	99	10	99	90	0	68	99
9 Schakowsky	D	1944	1999	U	71	1,538,439	96	9	100	95	0	44	96
10 Schneider	D	1961	2017	U	64	3,024,002	92	10	99	90	4	67	99
11 Foster	D	1955	2013	59	63	1,861,113	96	10	99	90	4	68	99
12 Bost	R	1960	2015	U	60	1,540,312	93	87	89	10	64	94	17
13 Davis	R	1970	2013	U	54	4,891,001	98	83	81	15	51	97	28
14 Underwood	D	1986	2019	U	51	7,360,377	100	10	98	80	6	64	99
15 Miller	R	1959	2021	57	73	581,556	—	—	—	—	—	—	—
16 Kinzinger	R	1978	2011	U	65	1,598,081	91	86	85	10	58	91	22
17 Bustos	D	1961	2013	U	52	6,479,373	97	10	98	80	6	69	99
18 LaHood	R	1968	2015	U	70	1,761,973	94	91	97	0	84	85	11
Indiana													
1 Mrvan	D	1969	2021	33	57	476,407	—	—	—	—	—	—	—
2 Walorski	R	1963	2013	79	62	1,696,493	96	94	94	5	73	98	12
3 Banks	R	1979	2017	85	68	791,041	99	88	98	0	99	79	4

4 Baird	R	1945	2019	U	67	233,208	99	94	97	0	81	86	4
5 Spartz	R	1978	2021	40	50	3,161,482	—	—	—	—	—	—	—
6 Pence	R	1956	2019	87	69	2,849,708	97	100	96	5	76	85	10
7 Carson	D	1974	2008	92	62	882,862	95	11	99	85	2	58	97
8 Bucshon	R	1962	2011	U	67	1,084,251	96	91	95	5	75	86	12
9 Hollingsworth	R	1983	2017	U	62	515,280	96	86	86	10	84	84	22
Iowa													
1 Hinson	R	1983	2021	78	51	5,062,131	—	—	—	—	—	—	—
2 Miller-Meeks	R	1955	2021	48	50	1,735,403	—	—	—	—	—	—	—
3 Axne	D	1965	2019	U	49	6,294,921	95	12	92	80	9	72	94
4 Feenstra	R	1969	2021	46	62	1,895,390	—	—	—	—	—	—	—
Kansas													
1 Mann	R	1976	2021	54	71	1,282,296	—	—	—	—	—	—	—
2 LaTurner	R	1988	2021	49	55	1,591,626	—	—	—	—	—	—	—
3 Davids	D	1980	2019	U	54	5,320,319	99	12	97	85	4	72	94
4 Estes	R	1956	2017	U	64	1,429,529	99	96	99	0	93	81	7
Kentucky													
1 Comer	R	1972	2016	U	75	507,694	99	97	98	5	83	81	9
2 Guthrie	R	1964	2009	89	71	1,579,045	98	93	97	5	75	93	12
3 Yarmuth	D	1947	2007	U	63	695,281	98	10	100	95	0	60	97
4 Massie	R	1971	2012	81	67	1,570,704	96	79	91	15	91	42	2
5 Rogers	R	1937	1981	91	84	842,843	97	95	93	5	67	92	9
6 Barr	R	1973	2013	91	57	4,391,220	97	95	97	5	74	93	10
Louisiana													
1 Scalise	R	1965	2008	72	d	33,728,421	98	96	99	5	88	79	7
2 Vacant[c]													
3 Higgins	R	1961	2017	68	d	736,219	90	95	97	0	91	67	7
4 Johnson	R	1972	2017	60	d	1,063,517	90	93	98	5	95	71	2
5 Letlow	R	1981	2021	33	62	1,305,957	—	—	—	—	—	—	—
6 Graves	R	1972	2015	71	d	1,240,249	95	93	94	10	81	84	11

(Table continues)

257

Table 5-11 (Continued)

State/district/representative	Party	Year born	Year entered the House	Percentage vote in 2020 Primary	Percentage vote in 2020 General	Campaign expenditures (2019–2020)	Voting ratings[a] VP	PS	PU	ADA	ACU	CCUS	LCV
Maine													
1 Pingree	D	1955	2009	U	62	276,671	70	8	100	100	0	62	99
2 Golden	D	1982	2019	U	53	5,344,641	100	16	84	75	16	63	96
Maryland													
1 Harris	R	1957	2011	82	63	983,300	98	97	99	0	97	67	0
2 Ruppersberger	D	1946	2003	73	68	938,294	98	10	99	90	4	65	99
3 Sarbanes	D	1962	2007	83	70	692,303	100	10	100	95	0	56	99
4 Brown	D	1961	2017	78	80	855,968	98	9	99	95	4	58	96
5 Hoyer	D	1939	1981	64	69	4,363,891	99	10	99	90	4	63	99
6 Trone	D	1955	2019	72	59	2,980,058	94	10	99	90	4	71	99
7 Mfume	D	1948	2020	74	72	715,394	—	—	—	—	—	—	—
8 Raskin	D	1962	2017	87	68	1,438,142	100	11	99	100	0	43	100
Massachusetts													
1 Neal	D	1949	1989	59	97	5,957,631	98	10	100	95	0	63	99
2 McGovern	D	1959	1997	U	65	1,093,205	100	13	99	100	0	41	100
3 Trahan	D	1973	2019	U	U	1,499,562	95	10	100	95	0	54	96
4 Auchincloss	D	1988	2021	22	61	2,415,437	—	—	—	—	—	—	—
5 Clark	D	1963	2013	U	74	1,542,099	99	12	100	90	0	53	99
6 Moulton	D	1978	2015	78	65	1,830,883	91	10	96	75	4	68	97
7 Pressley	D	1974	2019	U	87	1,775,676	93	16	98	95	6	42	99
8 Lynch	D	1955	2001	66	81	1,140,250	99	10	99	85	2	60	99
9 Keating	D	1952	2011	U	61	652,598	96	10	99	90	2	63	96
Michigan													
1 Bergman	R	1947	2017	U	62	1,850,481	98	95	92	5	76	93	16
2 Huizenga	R	1969	2011	U	59	1,920,126	95	92	94	10	85	81	15
3 Meijer	R	1988	2021	50	53	3,412,998	—	—	—	—	—	—	—

4 Moolenaar	R	1961	2015	U	65	1,042,444	100	92	94	5	77	92	17
5 Kildee	D	1958	2013	U	54	1,511,290	100	12	100	95	0	60	99
6 Upton	R	1953	1987	63	56	3,494,801	99	68	73	20	48	98	54
7 Walberg	R	1951	2011	U	59	1,601,506	97	92	97	5	83	86	8
8 Slotkin	D	1976	2019	U	51	7,587,944	99	10	92	85	6	69	96
9 Levin	D	1960	2019	U	58	919,437	97	11	99	100	0	43	100
10 McClain	R	1966	2021	42	66	2,362,181	—	—	—	—	—	—	—
11 Stevens	D	1983	2019	U	50	5,815,453	100	10	97	85	6	72	97
12 Dingell	D	1953	2015	81	66	1,692,360	97	11	100	85	0	53	99
13 Tlaib	D	1976	2019	66	78	3,769,569	95	17	97	95	5	40	96
14 Lawrence	D	1954	2015	93	79	792,122	87	10	99	75	0	58	95
Minnesota													
1 Hagedorn	R	1962	2019	U	49	2,342,968	98	95	97	0	80	83	6
2 Craig	D	1972	2019	U	48	4,731,914	99	10	93	80	6	70	99
3 Phillips	R	1969	2019	91	56	2,215,322	100	10	97	85	6	72	99
4 McCollum	D	1952	2001	84	63	1,001,041	100	10	100	90	2	55	99
5 Omar	D	1982	2019	58	64	5,697,934	96	17	97	95	6	40	96
6 Emmer	R	1951	2015	87	66	2,579,117	90	90	95	0	83	77	9
7 Fischbach	R	1965	2021	59	53	2,608,186	—	—	—	—	—	—	—
8 Stauber	R	1966	2019	94	57	2,618,059	97	90	83	10	67	95	18
Mississippi													
1 Kelly	R	1966	2015	U	69	837,436	97	91	100	5	93	74	6
2 Thompson	D	1948	1993	94	66	1,099,404	91	12	99	90	2	62	93
3 Guest	R	1970	2019	90	65	554,150	97	94	97	5	86	79	10
4 Palazzo	R	1970	2011	67	U	758,749	90	93	98	0	85	82	9
Missouri													
1 Bush	D	1976	2021	49	79	1,345,334	—	—	—	—	—	—	—
2 Wagner	R	1962	2013	U	52	6,568,320	96	91	90	15	71	98	16
3 Luetkemeyer	R	1952	2009	75	69	2,085,423	97	92	95	10	74	84	6
4 Hartzler	R	1960	2011	77	68	1,343,060	98	92	94	5	78	84	9
5 Cleaver	D	1944	2005	85	59	950,094	86	11	99	90	4	64	92

(Table continues)

259

Table 5-11 (Continued)

State/district/representative	Party	Year born	Year entered the House	Percentage vote in 2020 Primary	Percentage vote in 2020 General	Campaign expenditures (2019–2020)	Voting ratings[a] VP	PS	PU	ADA	ACU	CCUS	LCV
6 Graves	R	1963	2001	80	67	1,655,930	98	89	98	15	82	87	9
7 Long	R	1955	2011	66	69	1,534,977	98	94	97	0	86	80	9
8 Smith	R	1980	2013	U	77	1,516,930	99	96	99	0	93	78	3
Montana													
AL Rosendale	R	1960	2021	48	56	3,848,140	—	—	—	—	—	—	—
Nebraska													
1 Fortenberry	R	1960	2005	U	60	2,465,446	96	87	81	5	63	93	39
2 Bacon	R	1963	2017	91	51	3,755,144	99	84	86	0	68	99	29
3 Smith	R	1970	2007	83	79	1,153,644	99	93	98	0	84	88	4
Nevada													
1 Titus	D	1950	2013	83	62	589,979	88	10	99	95	0	53	98
2 Amodei	R	1958	2011	81	57	1,048,739	96	93	92	5	72	93	17
3 Lee	D	1966	2019	83	49	4,781,543	98	11	96	80	6	77	96
4 Horsford	D	1973	2019	75	51	3,048,785	89	10	98	85	4	58	99
New Hampshire													
1 Pappas	D	1980	2019	U	51	3,122,214	100	11	96	95	2	68	99
2 Kuster	D	1956	2013	93	54	3,055,351	84	11	99	95	2	70	99
New Jersey													
1 Norcross	D	1958	2014	U	63	1,102,257	98	9	99	95	2	56	99
2 Van Drew	R	1953	2019	82	52	4,138,861	97	38	75	75	35	76	80
3 Kim	D	1982	2019	U	53	6,869,994	93	10	95	80	7	71	99
4 Smith	R	1953	1981	95	60	1,288,378	97	56	64	40	46	87	77
5 Gottheimer	D	1975	2017	67	53	3,593,230	98	12	90	80	7	73	99
6 Pallone	D	1951	1988	79	61	2,030,033	100	9	100	100	2	44	100
7 Malinowski	D	1965	2019	U	51	7,503,597	99	10	98	90	4	69	99

8 Sires	D	1951	2006	70	74	551,325	89	11	100	90	2	65	97
9 Pascrell	D	1937	1997	81	66	1,842,259	85	9	100	95	0	52	100
10 Payne	D	1958	2012	89	83	457,252	63	11	99	95	0	62	88
11 Sherrill	D	1972	2019	U	53	3,807,868	98	10	94	85	6	69	97
12 Watson Coleman	D	1945	2015	89	66	848,942	71	10	99	100	0	49	100
New Mexico													
1 Vacant[e]													
2 Herrell	R	1964	2021	45	54	2,984,196	—	—	—	—	—	—	—
3 Leger Fernandez	D	1959	2021	43	59	2,143,697	—	—	—	—	—	—	—
New York													
1 Zeldin	R	1980	2015	U	55	8,282,563	99	92	90	15	68	83	26
2 Garbarino	R	1984	2021	64	53	1,664,776	—	—	—	—	—	—	—
3 Suozzi	D	1962	2017	67	56	2,350,872	97	10	97	90	4	68	99
4 Rice	D	1965	2015	U	56	1,228,432	97	9	97	80	8	75	92
5 Meeks	D	1953	1998	76	U	1,495,900	96	10	100	95	0	59	97
6 Meng	D	1975	2013	66	68	1,876,468	80	13	98	100	2	43	100
7 Velazquez	D	1953	1993	80	85	694,477	95	10	99	100	0	46	100
8 Jeffries	D	1970	2013	U	85	3,325,841	99	9	100	95	4	56	99
9 Clarke	D	1964	2007	54	83	1,205,205	99	13	99	100	0	43	100
10 Nadler	D	1947	1992	68	75	1,960,860	79	13	99	95	4	47	100
11 Malliotakis	R	1980	2021	69	53	3,483,560	—	—	—	—	—	—	—
12 Maloney	D	1946	1993	4	82	3,061,752	98	12	99	100	0	46	100
13 Espaillat	D	1964	2017	59	91	1,256,042	100	13	99	100	0	43	100
14 Ocasio-Cortez	D	1989	2019	75	72	17,310,936	98	20	96	95	6	38	96
15 Torres	D	1988	2021	32	89	1,831,234	—	—	—	—	—	—	—
16 Bowman	D	1976	2021	55	84	2,837,899	—	—	—	—	—	—	—
17 Jones	D	1987	2021	42	59	2,207,871	—	—	—	—	—	—	—
18 Maloney	D	1966	2013	U	56	1,769,856	99	10	97	85	4	65	99
19 Delgado	D	1977	2019	U	55	3,034,333	100	10	96	80	4	71	99
20 Tonko	D	1949	2009	U	61	1,424,285	96	10	99	95	0	46	100

(Table continues)

261

Table 5-11 *(Continued)*

State/district/representative	Party	Year born	Year entered the House	Percentage vote in 2020 Primary	Percentage vote in 2020 General	Campaign expenditures (2019–2020)	Voting ratings[a] VP	PS	PU	ADA	ACU	CCUS	LCV
21 Stefanik	R	1984	2015	U	59	11,718,617	99	72	75	20	58	98	52
22 Tenney	R	1961	2021	60	48	2,800,346	—	—	—	—	—	—	—
23 Reed	R	1971	2010	U	58	3,202,933	97	83	79	20	53	99	40
24 Katko	R	1962	2015	U	53	3,615,241	96	62	67	20	49	95	55
25 Morelle	D	1957	2018	68	59	1,317,025	96	11	99	85	6	62	94
26 Higgins	D	1959	2005	U	70	988,667	96	10	100	90	2	59	99
27 Jacobs	R	1966	2020	60	60	2,089,855	—	—	—	—	—	—	—
North Carolina													
1 Butterfield	D	1947	2004	U	54	887,752	92	12	99	95	5	58	97
2 Ross	D	1963	2021	70	63	1,840,264	—	—	—	—	—	—	—
3 Murphy	R	1963	2019	U	63	1,612,718	45	44	49	—	44	33	5
4 Price	D	1940	1997	87	67	1,030,191	82	10	99	95	2	57	99
5 Foxx	R	1943	2005	U	67	1,963,676	96	92	97	5	88	74	10
6 Manning	D	1956	2021	48	62	1,769,590	—	—	—	—	—	—	—
7 Rouzer	R	1972	2015	U	60	1,052,925	98	92	97	0	84	70	11
8 Hudson	R	1971	2013	U	53	4,404,938	91	91	96	0	85	88	8
9 Bishop	R	1964	2019	U	56	4,350,727	48	44	50	—	50	27	0
10 McHenry	R	1975	2005	71	69	2,351,361	86	92	94	5	77	92	19
11 Cawthorn	R	1995	2021	66	54	4,577,527	—	—	—	—	—	—	—
12 Adams	D	1946	2014	88	U	669,627	96	10	100	95	2	55	98
13 Budd	R	1971	2017	U	68	1,324,659	97	94	98	0	95	77	9
North Dakota													
AL Armstrong	R	1976	2019	U	69	1,083,764	96	95	91	15	5	79	83
Ohio													
1 Chabot	R	1953	2011	U	52	2,888,369	1	100	92	98	5	84	85
2 Wenstrup	R	1958	2013	94	61	1,764,298	2	98	92	98	0	90	86

3 Beatty	D	1950	2013	68	71	2,551,302	3	93	10	100	95	0	68
4 Jordan	R	1964	2007	U	68	13,268,968	4	98	91	100	0	100	62
5 Latta	R	1956	2007	U	78	1,490,979	5	99	92	99	5	88	79
6 Johnson	R	1954	2011	87	74	1,852,525	6	98	94	96	0	75	88
7 Gibbs	R	1954	2011	U	68	453,928	7	94	93	97	0	84	82
8 Davidson	R	1970	2016	91	69	854,735	8	98	89	95	0	97	64
9 Kaptur	D	1946	1983	91	63	987,298	9	91	9	99	85	4	61
10 Turner	R	1960	2003	86	58	1,748,901	10	99	90	88	10	62	97
11 Vacant[f]													
12 Balderson	R	1962	2018	84	55	1,999,773	12	99	90	95	10	70	85
13 Ryan	D	1973	2003	U	53	2,089,545	13	82	11	99	85	0	65
14 Joyce	R	1957	2013	83	60	2,526,145	14	98	88	84	10	57	97
15 Stivers	R	1965	2011	88	63	2,305,320	15	94	88	88	10	68	95
16 Gonzalez	R	1984	2019	U	63	1,895,208	16	98	90	86	10	65	92
Oklahoma													
1 Hern	R	1961	2018	U	64	1,160,066	99	94	99	0	97	77	2
2 Mullin	R	1977	2013	80	75	1,088,384	72	92	98	0	45	76	3
3 Lucas	R	1960	1994	U	79	1,045,126	95	95	94	5	67	91	9
4 Cole	R	1949	2003	76	68	1,757,230	99	94	90	10	62	99	14
5 Bice	R	1973	2021	53	52	3,567,879	—	—	—	—	—	—	—
Oregon													
1 Bonamici	D	1954	2012	84	63	867,301	90	14	100	95	0	48	99
2 Bentz	R	1952	2021	31	60	1,363,581	—	—	—	—	—	—	—
3 Blumenauer	D	1948	1996	81	73	1,963,949	91	12	99	95	4	47	97
4 DeFazio	D	1947	1987	84	52	5,884,593	90	8	99	100	0	46	99
5 Schrader	D	1951	2009	69	52	1,937,977	97	16	90	85	11	73	90
Pennsylvania													
1 Fitzpatrick	R	1973	2017	63	57	4,309,028	98	45	56	60	32	90	85
2 Boyle	D	1977	2015	U	73	760,250	94	12	99	90	0	58	99
3 Evans	D	1954	2016	U	91	786,063	98	10	100	95	0	60	99
4 Dean	D	1959	2019	U	60	1,147,079	96	10	100	95	0	67	99

(Table continues)

263

Table 5-11 (Continued)

State/district/representative	Party	Year born	Year entered the House	Percentage vote in 2020 Primary	Percentage vote in 2020 General	Campaign expenditures (2019–2020)	Voting ratings[a] VP	PS	PU	ADA	ACU	CCUS	LCV
5 Scanlon	D	1959	2018	U	65	1,374,969	99	10	100	90	2	58	99
6 Houlahan	D	1967	2019	U	56	1,419,800	99	10	96	80	6	70	99
7 Wild	D	1957	2018	U	52	4,591,501	99	12	95	80	7	64	96
8 Cartwright	D	1961	2013	U	52	4,214,643	97	10	99	90	2	63	98
9 Meuser	R	1964	2019	U	66	945,604	95	94	98	0	81	82	9
10 Perry	R	1962	2013	U	53	3,905,340	97	93	96	5	97	68	4
11 Smucker	R	1964	2017	U	63	671,774	95	94	95	5	80	79	11
12 Keller	R	1965	2019	U	71	1,087,701	50	42	50		47	34	3
13 Joyce	R	1957	2019	U	74	477,893	97	94	99	0	92	76	7
14 Reschenthaler	R	1983	2019	U	65	1,594,661	93	93	92	5	73	89	11
15 Thompson	R	1959	2009	U	74	1,866,009	97	94	92	5	77	90	9
16 Kelly	R	1948	2011	U	59	1,380,453	97	94	95	5	84	79	13
17 Lamb	D	1984	2018	U	51	3,486,882	94	16	88	80	9	67	93
18 Doyle	D	1953	1995	67	69	1,003,463	93	12	100	95	0	52	96
Rhode Island													
1 Cicilline	D	1961	2011	U	71	1,755,649	99	10	100	95	0	58	99
2 Langevin	D	1964	2001	70	58	1,428,508	81	10	99	90	4	62	99
South Carolina													
1 Mace	R	1977	2021	58	51	5,813,666	—	—	—	—	—	—	—
2 Wilson	R	1947	2001	74	56	1,762,180	95	92	96	5	80	87	9
3 Duncan	R	1966	2011	U	71	1,289,578	94	96	99	0	95	70	6
4 Timmons	R	1984	2019	U	62	1,368,033	81	88	99	0	94	75	9
5 Norman	R	1953	2017	U	60	910,151	96	93	100	0	100	66	4
6 Clyburn	D	1940	1993	U	68	2,372,934	92	11	99	90	2	66	96
7 Rice	R	1957	2013	U	62	1,252,458	98	92	97	0	87	67	8
South Dakota													
AL Johnson	R	1976	2019	77	81	700,356	99	89	97	5	81	81	9

Tennessee											
1 Harshbarger	R	1960	2021	19	75	1,870,826.67	—	—	—	—	—
2 Burchett	R	1964	2019	U	68	889,218.07	99	94	97	5	86	75	10
3 Fleischmann	R	1962	2011	U	67	387,211.20	100	95	94	0	76	89	9
4 DesJarlais	R	1964	2011	71	67	393,314.56	94	92	99	0	93	78	7
5 Cooper	D	1954	2003	57	U	1,335,309.99	98	11	97	90	6	66	97
6 Rose	R	1965	2019	U	74	1,158,244.67	97	93	99	0	91	75	7
7 Green	R	1964	2019	U	70	1,025,487.64	87	89	99	0	91	77	3
8 Kustoff	R	1966	2017	U	69	1,076,430.14	98	94	98	10	79	85	10
9 Cohen	D	1949	2007	84	77	458,671	85	9	100	95	0	56	98
Texas												
1 Gohmert	R	1953	2005	90	73	592,388	90	89	99	0	97	63	4
2 Crenshaw	R	1984	2019	U	56	17,654,095	99	92	95	0	79	94	15
3 Taylor	R	1972	2019	U	55	3,277,899	99	90	96	0	91	82	11
4 Fallon	R	1967	2021	None	75	95,068	—	—	—	—	—	—	—
5 Gooden	R	1982	2019	83	62	1,311,983	98	93	99	0	98	79	4
6 Vacant[g]												
7 Fletcher	D	1975	2019	U	51	6,386,610	97	14	96	75	5	79	90
8 Brady	R	1955	1997	81	73	3,200,482	93	93	97	0	85	74	6
9 Green	D	1947	2005	83	76	502,386	99	10	99	95	0	57	99
10 McCaul	R	1962	2005	U	53	3,927,931	98	90	88	15	60	95	27
11 Pfluger	R	1978	2021	52	80	2,004,400	—	—	—	—	—	—	—
12 Granger	R	1943	1997	58	64	3,358,466	85	93	93	15	36	88	12
13 Jackson	R	1967	2021	56	79	1,764,055	—	—	—	—	—	—	—
14 Weber	R	1953	2013	U	62	929,317	94	92	100	0	97	70	2
15 Gonzalez	D	1967	2017	U	51	908,000	90	11	97	75	6	69	91
16 Escobar	D	1969	2019	U	65	1,089,250	92	9	99	95	2	56	96
17 Sessions	R	1955	2021	54	56	1,696,588	—	—	—	—	—	—	—
18 Jackson Lee	D	1950	1995	77	73	838,414	97	10	100	95	0	55	97
19 Arrington	R	1972	2017	89	75	1,970,964	97	95	98	0	93	75	4
20 Castro	D	1974	2013	92	65	718,442	94	11	100	85	0	58	97
21 Roy	R	1972	2019	U	52	4,771,750	97	88	95	0	95	45	0
22 Nehls	R	1968	2021	70	52	1,798,160	—	—	—	—	—	—	—

(Table continues)

265

Table 5-11 (Continued)

State/district/representative	Party	Year born	Year entered the House	Percentage vote in 2020 Primary	Percentage vote in 2020 General	Campaign expenditures (2019–2020)	VP	PS	PU	ADA	ACU	CCUS	LCV
23 Gonzalez	R	1980	2021	50	51	2,851,613	—	—	—	—	—	—	—
24 Van Duyne	R	1970	2021	64	49	3,361,913	—	—	—	—	—	—	—
25 Williams	R	1949	2013	88	56	3,358,151	98	93	99	10	88	85	5
26 Burgess	R	1950	2003	74	61	2,102,030	97	93	98	0	86	77	10
27 Cloud	R	1975	2018	U	63	834,592	98	89	98	0	100	70	0
28 Cuellar	D	1955	2005	52	58	3,747,550	99	13	92	70	11	75	85
29 Garcia	D	1950	2019	U	71	795,553	100	12	99	90	0	54	95
30 Johnson	D	1935	1993	71	78	496,547	72	10	100	90	2	62	96
31 Carter	R	1941	2003	82	53	2,223,167	84	95	96	10	40	80	7
32 Allred	D	1983	2019	U	52	5,721,623	95	11	98	85	4	77	97
33 Veasey	D	1971	2013	64	67	1,631,328	94	9	99	85	2	64	99
34 Vela	D	1963	2013	75	55	1,034,382	97	12	98	85	4	64	93
35 Doggett	D	1946	1995	73	65	425,737	88	11	99	95	2	46	99
36 Babin	R	1948	2015	90	74	1,310,866	95	93	99	0	95	71	4
Utah													
1 Moore	R	1980	2021	31	70	835,315	—	—	—	—	—	—	—
2 Stewart	R	1960	2013	U	59	929,210	95	91	97	0	84	82	9
3 Curtis	R	1960	2017	U	69	718,455	93	88	97	0	80	82	4
4 Owens	R	1951	2021	44	48	5,068,996	—	—	—	—	—	—	—
Vermont													
AL Welch	D	1947	2007	95	67	869,591	71	11	100	95	0	49	99
Virginia													
1 Wittman	R	1959	2007	U	58	2,190,582	99	93	98	5	86	88	11
2 Luria	D	1975	2019	U	52	6,556,704	98	16	90	80	11	72	96
3 Scott	D	1947	1993	U	68	835,219	99	10	99	90	2	59	99
4 McEachin	D	1961	2017	80	62	988,771	70	12	98	95	6	54	100

5 Good	R	1965	2021	58	52	1,328,693	—	—	—	—	—	—
6 Cline	R	1972	2019	U	65	680,286	99	94	99	5	93	77	0
7 Spanberger	D	1979	2019	U	51	7,959,481	99	13	88	80	11	72	96
8 Beyer	D	1950	2015	U	76	2,077,823	97	9	99	95	2	58	99
9 Griffith	R	1958	2011	U	94	467,455	94	91	95	5	87	71	11
10 Wexton	D	1968	2019	U	57	1,901,912	99	10	98	85	6	65	99
11 Connolly	D	1950	2009	78	71	1,832,941	99	10	98	90	2	59	99
Washington													
1 DelBene	D	1962	2012	55	59	1,903,677	96	10	100	90	0	67	99
2 Larsen	D	1965	2001	49	63	1,227,914	98	10	99	95	4	64	97
3 Herrera Beutler	R	1978	2011	56	56	4,586,794	86	74	83	20	10	93	29
4 Newhouse	R	1955	2015	57	66	1,002,461	95	88	90	0	73	88	14
5 McMorris Rodgers	R	1969	2005	53	61	3,503,094	96	90	92	5	77	86	12
6 Kilmer	D	1974	2013	47	59	2,564,803	97	10	98	90	2	71	99
7 Jaypal	D	1965	2017	80	83	1,555,769	84	15	98	100	4	42	98
8 Schrier	D	1968	2019	43	52	3,804,549	91	10	98	85	2	68	99
9 Smith	D	1965	1997	74	74	933,145	96	10	100	85	0	51	99
10 Strickland	D	1962	2021	20	49	1,802,662	—	—	—	—	—	—	—
West Virginia													
1 McKinley	R	1947	2011	U	69	1,088,039	100	88	89	5	69	90	18
2 Mooney	R	1971	2015	72	63	859,927	99	88	96	0	91	75	10
3 Miller	R	1950	2019	70	71	763,796	98	98	97	0	79	89	13
Wisconsin													
1 Steil	R	1981	2019	U	59	3,172,845	99	89	91	10	80	86	20
2 Pocan	D	1964	2013	U	70	1,017,815	81	13	99	100	2	44	100
3 Kind	D	1963	1997	81	51	4,450,117	89	11	96	90	8	65	94
4 Moore	D	1951	2005	U	75	1,181,901	70	10	99	95	0	50	99
5 Fitzgerald	R	1963	2021	77	60	969,890	—	—	—	—	—	—	—
6 Grothman	R	1955	2015	U	59	1,750,819	97	91	96	0	91	72	8
7 Tiffany	R	1957	2020	U	61	2,529,735	—	—	—	—	—	—	—
8 Gallagher	R	1984	2017	U	64	2,935,204	94	79	89	10	74	83	17

(Table continues)

267

Table 5-11 *(Continued)*

Wyoming								
AL Cheney	R	1966	2017	73	69	3,066,535	94	92	97	5	77	78	4

Note: "—" indicates a newly elected representative (no basis for voting ratings) or data unavailable; "AL" indicates "at large"; "D" indicates Democrat; "R" indicates Republican; "U" indicates the candidate received more than 99 percent of the vote or was unopposed and did not appear on the ballot. Information as of May 11, 2021. Table entries reflect those initially elected to serve in the 117th Congress.

[a] Two types of voting ratings are provided: CQ Roll Call's vote studies and interest group ratings. CQ Roll Call calculates "VP," "PS," and "PU" scores for 2020 for members of the 116th Congress. "VP" indicates voting participation score (percentage of recorded votes on which a representative voted "yea" or "nay"). "PS" indicates presidential support score (percentage of votes on which the president took a position that the representative supported). "PU" indicates party unity score (percentage of votes on which a representative supported his or her party when a majority of voting Democrats opposed a majority of voting Republicans). Interest group ratings indicate the percentage of time a representative supported the group-preferred position on votes the group selects. The ratings are the average of the 2019 and 2020 scores provided by each group for anyone who qualified under each group's own rules. "ADA" (Americans for Democratic Action) is a liberal group, and their scores are only provided for 2019; "ACU" (American Conservative Union) is a conservative group; "CCUS" (Chamber of Commerce of the United States) is a business group; and "LCV" (League of Conservation Voters) is an environmental group. Voting participation and "ADA" scores are lowered by a member's failure to vote. Failure to vote does not lower the other scores.

[b] Alcee Hastings (D-Fla.) was reelected in 2020 but passed away on April 6, 2021.

[c] Cedric Richmond (D-La.) was reelected in 2020 but resigned his seat in January 2021 to become senior advisor to President Biden and director of the White House Office of Public Engagement.

[d] In Louisiana, all candidates appear on the initial ballot (a blanket primary). If one candidate gets more than 50 percent, there is no general election for that seat.

[e] Deb Haaland (D-N.M.) was reelected in 2020 but resigned on March 16, 2021, after her confirmation as secretary of the Interior.

[f] Marcia Fudge (D-Ohio) was reelected in 2020 but resigned on March 10, 2021, following her confirmation as secretary of Housing and Urban Development.

[g] Ron Wright (R-Texas) was reelected in 2020 but passed away on February 7, 2021. His wife, Susan, placed first in a special election to fill his seat but lost to Jake Ellzey in a runoff election held on July 27, 2021.

Sources: "Biographical Directory of the United States Congress," http://bioguide.congress.gov; CQ Press, Congress Collection database, interest group ratings data compiled by J. Michael Sharp; CQ Roll Call, 2019 Vote Studies; campaign finance data: Federal Election Commission, www.fec.gov.

Table 5-12 The 117th Congress: Senate

					% vote in last election			Voting ratings[b]						
State/senator	Party	Year born	Assumed Office	Next Election	Primary	General	Last campaign expenditures[a]	VP	PS	PU	ADA	ACU	CCUS	LCV
Alabama														
Shelby	R	1934	1987	2022	65	64	$12,083,489	99	97	98	0	73	75	15
Tuberville	R	1954	2021	2026	61	60	9,432,335	—	—	—	—	—	—	—
Alaska														
Murkowski	R	1957	2002	2022	72	44	7,167,503	94	94	90	10	49	92	26
Sullivan	R	1964	2015	2026	U	54	10,145,559	97	96	98	0	74	95	11
Arizona														
Sinema	D	1976	2019	2024	79	50	24,735,382	91	66	60	65	17	82	67
Kelly	D	1964	2020	2022	U	51	99,704,060	—	—	—	—	—	—	—
Arkansas														
Boozman	R	1950	2011	2022	76	60	496,399	100	96	98	5	69	93	18
Cotton	R	1977	2015	2026	U	67	6,846,753	99	95	98	5	74	77	15
California														
Feinstein	D	1933	1992	2024	44	54	24,497,309	98	45	92	100	2	67	96
Padilla	D	1973	2021	2022	None	None	Not applicable	—	—	—	—	—	—	—
Colorado														
Bennet	D	1964	2009	2022	U	50	16,480,485	84	39	96	75	8	70	82
Hickenlooper	D	1952	2021	2026	59	54	42,604,035	—	—	—	—	—	—	—
Connecticut														
Blumenthal	D	1946	2011	2022	U	63	6,607,689	99	24	99	95	2	60	96
Murphy	D	1973	2013	2024	U	60	104,976,473	99	51	82	100	3	63	93
Delaware														
Carper	D	1947	2001	2024	65	60	4,887,154	100	49	84	100	7	52	96
Coons	D	1963	2010	2026	73	59	6,095,494	97	45	89	90	5	62	96

(Table continues)

269

Table 5-12 *(Continued)*

					% vote in last election		Last campaign	Voting ratings[b]						
State/senator	Party	Year born	Assumed Office	Next Election	Primary	General	expenditures[a]	VP	PS	PU	ADA	ACU	CCUS	LCV
Florida														
Rubio	R	1971	2011	2022	72	52	21,289,500	95	94	99	10	74	85	11
Scott	R	1952	2019	2024	89	50	83,771,112	96	94	99	0	91	78	4
Georgia														
Ossoff	D	1987	2021	2026	48	51	151,813,794	—	—	—	—	—	—	—
Warnoock	D	1969	2021	2022	33	51	103,595,578	—	—	—	—	—	—	—
Hawaii														
Schatz	D	1972	2012	2022	86	74	2,549,166	94	28	99	100	2	53	100
Hirono	D	1947	2013	2024	U	71	4,024,270	98	27	100	100	2	50	96
Idaho														
Crapo	R	1951	1999	2022	U	66	5,851,739	100	97	99	0	82	88	4
Risch	R	1943	2009	2026	U	63	2,284,606	97	96	100	0	87	78	4
Illinois														
Durbin	D	1944	1997	2026	U	55	10,204,830	98	42	94	100	2	65	96
Duckworth	D	1968	2017	2022	64	55	16,761,919	97	37	96	95	5	60	96
Indiana														
Young	R	1972	2017	2022	67	52	11,394,679	98	94	95	5	69	92	22
Braun	R	1954	2019	2024	41	51	25,878,621	99	94	99	0	93	67	4
Iowa														
Grassley	R	1933	1981	2022	U	60	10,804,669	99	96	99	0	77	89	8
Ernst	R	1970	2015	2026	U	52	30,265,789	99	96	98	0	74	93	11
Kansas														
Moran	R	1954	2011	2022	79	62	5,715,751	90	94	94	15	79	89	15
Marshall[c]	R	1960	2021	2026	40	53	7,171,199	—	—	—	—	—	—	—

Kentucky														
McConnell	R	1942	1985	2026	83	58	67,388,725	100	97	96	0	69	91	19
Paul	R	1963	2011	2022	85	57	11,142,100	91	86	89	30	98	70	4
Louisiana														
Cassidy	R	1957	2015	2026	59	U	10,727,747	95	96	98	0	83	83	4
Kennedy	R	1951	2017	2022	25	61	5,050,026	98	97	98	5	89	71	4
Maine														
Collins	R	1952	1997	2026	U	51	30,417,005	100	87	81	50	29	90	55
King	I	1944	2013	2024	U	54	5,150,506	100	51	83	85	11	76	85
Maryland														
Cardin	D	1943	2007	2024	79	65	4,386,408	98	41	94	90	2	57	96
Van Hollen	D	1959	2017	2022	53	61	11,481,663	100	32	99	100	2	49	96
Massachusetts														
Warren	D	1949	2013	2024	U	60	24,406,936	64	13	100	75	3	53	71
Markey	D	1946	2013	2026	55	66	15,051,879	88	15	100	100	3	32	89
Michigan														
Stabenow	D	1950	2001	2024	U	52	17,225,717	95	30	99	95	5	54	96
Peters	D	1958	2015	2026	U	50	50,890,960	100	41	94	95	5	56	96
Minnesota														
Klobuchar	D	1960	2007	2024	96	60	9,571,860	74	16	100	80	6	44	71
Smith	D	1958	2018	2026	87	49	16,100,432	99	33	99.5	95	2	57	96
Mississippi														
Wicker	R	1951	2007	2024	83	59	7,069,901	100	97	98	5	74	95	11
Hyde-Smith	R	1959	2018	2026	U	54	3,292,471	99	98	98	0	73	91	19
Missouri														
Blunt	R	1050	2011	2022	73	49	16,182,432	98	97	98	5	71	96	18
Hawley	R	1979	2019	2024	83	51	11,470,517	100	94	98	5	78	60	4

(Table continues)

271

Table 5-12 (Continued)

State/senator	Party	Year born	Assumed Office	Next Election	% vote in last election		Last campaign expenditures[a]	Voting ratings[b]						
					Primary	General		VP	PS	PU	ADA	ACU	CCUS	LCV
Montana														
Tester	D	1956	2007	2024	U	50	20,822,247	96	49	87	95	7	62	96
Daines	R	1962	2015	2026	88	55	34,075,789	99	95	97	5	82	80	22
Nebraska														
Fischer	R	1951	2013	2024	76	58	6,048,167	96	96	100	0	78	89	4
Sasse	R	1972	2015	2026	75	63	5,168,783	97	94	99	5	91	66	0
Nevada														
Cortez Masto	D	1964	2017	2022	81	47	19,005,870	100	40	94	95	5	66	96
Rosen	D	1957	2019	2024	77	50	26,079,221	100	43	92	95	5	69	96
New Hampshire														
Shaheen	D	1947	2009	2026	94	57	18,861,334	99	47	86	100	2	69	96
Hassan	D	1958	2017	2022	U	48	18,564,772	100	49	84	95	2	71	96
New Jersey														
Menendez	D	1954	2006	2024	62	54	13,664,479	99	32	97	95	5	59	96
Booker	D	1969	2013	2026	88	57	11,579,012	65	17	100	60	2	40	75
New Mexico														
Heinrich	D	1971	2013	2024	U	54	8,030,924	96	33	99	95	7	65	89
Luján[c]	D	1972	2021	2026	U	52	9,596,963	—	—	—	—	—	—	—
New York														
Schumer	D	1950	1999	2022	U	70	24,771,506	100	24	100	95	2	41	100
Gillibrand	D	1966	2009	2024	U	67	12,540,956	87	15	100	95	5	23	97
North Carolina														
Burr	R	1955	2005	2022	61	51	10,212,664	88	98	98	0	68	92	22
Tillis	R	1960	2015	2026	78	49	26,370,206	95	97	98	0	78	96	18

Senator	Party	Born	Elected	Term ends		%	Population							
North Dakota														
Hoeven	R	1957	2011	2022	U	78	2,628,140	98	96	99	0	71	94	15
Cramer	R	1961	2019	2024	88	55	6,231,101	97	96	99	0	71	96	15
Ohio														
Brown	D	1952	2007	2024	U	53	27,997,834	98	37	96	100	5	61	96
Portman	R	1955	2011	2022	82	58	26,987,259	99	96	97	10	65	99	22
Oklahoma														
Inhofe	R	1934	1994	2026	74	63	5,761,858	97	95	100	0	83	68	0
Lankford	R	1968	2015	2022	U	68	2,800,373	100	94	100	0	91	68	0
Oregon														
Wyden	D	1949	1996	2022	83	56	9,782,114	99	26	99	95	2	51	96
Merkley	D	1956	2009	2026	U	57	8,277,385	99	25	99	100	2	37	96
Pennsylvania														
Casey	D	1960	2007	2024	U	56	21,412,915	100	41	95	90	9	67	96
Toomey	R	1961	2011	2022	U	49	31,622,034	96	94	99	5	92	68	4
Rhode Island														
Reed	D	1949	1997	2026	U	67	3,984,162	100	41	94	100	5	40	100
Whitehouse	D	1955	2007	2024	77	62	6,783,166	91	43	91	95	2	44	93
South Carolina														
Graham	R	1955	2003	2026	68	55	102,199,337	95	98	96	5	68	91	22
Scott	R	1965	2013	2022	U	61	4,795,257	100	95	99	0	83	81	11
South Dakota														
Thune	R	1961	2005	2022	U	72	7,109,178	100	96	100	0	71	93	11
Rounds	R	1954	2015	2026	75	66	3,246,188	87	96	99	0	83	90	11
Tennessee														
Blackburn	R	1952	2019	2024	84	55	16,572,478	98	93	99	0	94	68	11
Hagerty	R	1959	2021	2026	51	62	15,717,519	—	—	—	—	—	—	—

(Table continues)

Table 5-12 (Continued)

State/senator	Party	Year born	Assumed Office	Next Election	% vote in last election		Last campaign expenditures[a]	Voting ratings[b]							
					Primary	General		VP	PS	PU	ADA	ACU	CCUS	LCV
Texas														
Cornyn	R	1952	2002	2026	76	54	36,654,082	99	98	98	0	76	83	8
Cruz	R	1970	2013	2024	85	51	45,990,176	95	94	99	0	95	60.5	0
Utah														
Lee	R	1971	2011	2022	U	68	5,822,361	99	89	93	15	98	61	0
Romney	R	1947	2019	2024	71	63	5,294,219	99	94	97	5	68	87	7
Vermont														
Leahy	D	1940	1975	2022	89	61	4,946,359	96	44	91	100	2	48	96
Sanders	I	1941	2007	2024	94	67	8,200,325	44	15	100	60	0	18	66
Virginia														
Warner	D	1954	2009	2026	U	56	17,150,515	97	47	87	95	2	67	96
Kaine	D	1958	2013	2024	U	57	19,571,406	98	45	91	100	3	56	96
Washington														
Murray	D	1950	1993	2022	54	59	10,869,560	94	29	100	90	0	52	93
Cantwell	D	1958	2001	2024	55	58	11,964,267	99	29	98	95	2	67	96
West Virginia														
Manchin	D	1947	2010	2024	70	50	8,998,899	98	69	56	65	29	84	70
Capito	R	1953	2015	2026	83	70	3,967,986	94	97	98	5	66	98	22
Wisconsin														
Johnson	R	1955	2011	2022	U	50	21,228,172	96	95	99	0	89	72	0
Baldwin	D	1962	2013	2024	U	55	31,549,383	100	36	98	100	2	56	96
Wyoming														
Barrasso	R	1952	2007	2024	65	67	6,048,766	98	69	55.5	65	29	84	70
Lummis	R	1954	2021	2026	60	73	3,037,813	100	95	100	0	80	74	4

Note: "—" indicates a newly elected representative (no basis for voting ratings) or data unavailable; "AL" indicates "at large"; "D" indicates Democrat; "R" indicates Republican; "U" indicates the candidate received more than 99 percent of the vote or was unopposed and did not appear on the ballot. Information as of May 11, 2021. Table entries reflect those initially elected to serve in the 117th Congress. Kamala Harris (D-Calif.) is not included in the table because she resigned her seat at the very beginning of the Congress to become vice president of the United States. Her appointed successor, Alex Padilla, is included in the table.

[a] Figures for campaign expenditures can cover as many as six years, from January 1 of the year following the preceding election (or whenever the campaign registered with the Federal Election Commission during the six-year election cycle) through December 31 of the election year.

[b] Two types of voting ratings are provided: CQ Roll Call's vote studies and interest group ratings. CQ Roll Call calculates "VP," "PS," and "PU" scores for 2020 for members of the 116th Congress. "VP" indicates voting participation score (percentage of recorded votes on which a representative voted "yea" or "nay"). "PS" indicates presidential support score (percentage of votes on which the president took a position that the representative supported). "PU" indicates party unity score (percentage of votes on which a representative supported his or her party when a majority of voting Democrats opposed a majority of voting Republicans). Interest group ratings indicate the percentage of time a representative supported the group-preferred position on votes the group selects. The ratings are the average of the 2019 and 2020 scores provided by each group for anyone who qualified under each group's own rules. "ADA" (Americans for Democratic Action) is a liberal group, and their scores are only provided for 2019; "ACU" (American Conservative Union) is a conservative group; "CCUS" (Chamber of Commerce of the United States) is a business group; and "LCV" (League of Conservation Voters) is an environmental group. Voting participation and "ADA" scores are lowered by a member's failure to vote. Failure to vote does not lower the other scores.

[c] The voting ratings for Roger Marshall (R-Kans.) and Ben Ray Luján (D-N.M.) pertain to their prior House service.

Sources: "Biographical Directory of the United States Congress," http://bioguide.congress.gov; CQ Press, Congress Collection database, interest group ratings data compiled by J. Michael Sharp; CQ Roll Call, 2019 Vote Studies; campaign finance data: Federal Election Commission, www.fec.gov.

275

A Data Literacy Lesson

Interest Group Ratings: What They Reveal, What They Obscure

The interest group ratings in Tables 5-11 and 5-12 serve three different functions. For scholars doing research, they serve as a tool we can use to determine the ideology of members. Researchers interested in testing hypotheses against data—as one example, are women more liberal than men?—could use these scores to test these hypotheses. One might also hope to gain some leverage on longitudinal questions, such as by comparing a representative's scores over time to see if one becomes more liberal or more conservative as they age and gain in seniority.

Voters can use them to help make voting decisions—liberals could choose to vote for the candidate with the highest score from the ADA (Americans for Democratic Action) while conservatives might follow the ACU (American Conservative Union). More specifically, voters who wish to support labor unions might be guided by the ratings from the AFL-CIO, while those inclined to support the interests of the business community might be guided by ratings from the Chamber of Commerce. Campaigns use this information for their purposes, as might be expected: candidates put out press releases, for example, claiming to have received a perfect score from the NRA, or boasting of how their score from an environmental group is higher than their opponent's.

Interest groups, however, have their own purposes in using these scores. As shocking as it is that they do not always use them to help scholars do their work (shocking!), they also do not always use them to help voters make better decisions. Instead, interest group ratings serve as a tool by which interest groups can influence the behavior of members of Congress and get them to vote in accord with the group's preferences.

It is common knowledge, for example, that when interest groups perceive a particular vote as important, they will make it known that they are "scoring" the vote. This puts members of Congress on notice that this vote will be counted in the ratings that these groups assign to them. Members who were unsure how to vote might be swayed by this realization. A member who seeks to advertise that they are a supporter of gun rights might zealously guard their NRA rating, and tread carefully in any vote where support for gun rights is being assessed. Interest group scores are also a signal to potential donors; as Emily Charlock notes, the ADA and ACU have historically used their scores to help steer campaign resources (including campaign donations) to those they rated highly. This creates a political version of the Hawthorne Effect, wherein members of Congress might change their behavior simply as a result of their being observed.

Do interest groups scores measure something useful? Absolutely! A member who gets a high score from the NRA is almost certainly more in favor of gun rights than one who gets a low score. Someone who gets an 80 from the League of Conservation Voters is likely more of an environmentalist than one who gets a 20. As we look at these scores, though, it is worth remembering that they are created with a purpose in mind. Such a purpose is likely to maximize small differences in voting, and to highlight areas of difference rather than similarity. As you consider using them, remember their purpose. They are used to create more uniformity and unanimity among the supporters of these interest groups, not necessarily to help you with your research!

6
The Presidency and Executive Branch

- **Presidents**
- **Ratings**
- **Backgrounds**
- **Cabinet and Staff**
- **Congressional Relations**
- **Civil Service Employment**
- **Regulations**

On the one hand, studying the presidency poses a special problem for those interested in collecting statistical data. The scope and variety of data available on the presidency are limited by the singularity of the office and how individual presidents change the office's organization and operation. The modern presidency has evolved since Franklin D. Roosevelt took office in the 1930s. Since FDR, the end of the Cold War and the rise of terrorism, the rapid developments in modes of communication, the growth of government power, and the shift in emphasis from conventions to primaries as a way of nominating presidential candidates have further changed the nature of the presidency and the characteristics of incumbent presidents. Analysts wishing to collect data on the presidency have often found that there have been too few modern-day occupants of the Oval Office to sustain statistical analysis when we use the individual president as the unit of analysis.

In spite of this seemingly insurmountable problem, the visibility of the president provides a considerable amount of relevant data. Of all elected officials, for example, only for presidents are public judgments about how well they are doing displayed prominently and repeatedly: the twists and turns in the public approval ratings of a president's job performance are themselves news items. Consequently, elsewhere in this book a graph is devoted to this subject alone—Figure 3-6 shows the overall presidential approval scores for our most recent presidents. But presidents are not judged only by the public or only while they are in office. At various times and in various ways, historians and political scientists have rated all the U.S. presidents (Table 6-2), an exercise that is both fascinating and problematic.

Apart from approval ratings (and, of course, presidential elections), the presidency has not been subjected to extensive statistical scrutiny. However, perhaps because the number of presidents has now reached forty-six (Table 6-1), some additional areas are beginning to receive systematic study.[1] The president's relationship with Congress is one such area. Information about presidential "victories" on votes in Congress (Table 6-7), the extent to which the president is supported by his own party and by the other party (Table 6-8), the number of vetoes presidents from Washington to Trump have exercised (Table 6-9), and presidents' success in securing approval of their nominations (Tables 6-10 and 6-11) are all regularly tabulated and increasingly analyzed.

As discussed in Chapter 4, analysts are beginning to study media coverage of the president more systematically. In part, this study results from the extreme visibility of the president and of the federal government in general (Figure 4-1 and Table 4-17); it also stems from the changing relationships between the president and the press, as indicated, for example, by the considerable decline in press conferences since the 1930s (Table 4-3).

Compilations of various presidential characteristics and activities also have become more numerous or more meaningful as the number of presidents has grown. How individuals get to be president, for example, has been a subject of considerable interest (Tables 6-3 and 6-4). As shown in Chapter 7, presidential appointments have been assessed for their partisan characteristics (Table 7-6) and increasingly for their racial and sex distributions (Table 7-5).

The executive branch, apart from the president, has received little statistical analysis. Yet here too there is ample opportunity for meaningful tabulations, if not for t-tests and correlations. The tremendous size of the federal government (Tables 6-5 and 6-12) necessitates such an interest. The expanded involvement of the government in regulation (Table 6-13 and Figure 6-1) also compels attention. But these data also contain other more subtle and more significant messages. For example, the changing priorities of the nation and of particular presidents are reflected in such mundane listings as the size of the White House staff over time (Table 6-6).

Thus, although the presidency is a source of data for conventional statistical analyses in only a few areas, the increasing numerical data available provide considerable insight into what traditionally has been viewed as an office of impressive singularity.

Note

1. Only forty-five persons have served as president, but President Joseph Biden is known as the forty-sixth president because President Grover Cleveland is counted twice—his nonconsecutive terms make him the twenty-second and twenty-fourth president (www.whitehouse.gov/about/presidents).

Table 6-1 Presidents and Vice Presidents of the United States

President (political party)	Born	Died	Age at inauguration	Native of...	Elected from...	Term of service	Vice president
George Washington (F)	1732	1799	57	Va.	Va.	April 30, 1789–March 4, 1793	John Adams
George Washington (F)			61			March 4, 1793–March 4, 1797	John Adams
John Adams (F)	1735	1826	61	Mass.	Mass.	March 4, 1797–March 4, 1801	Thomas Jefferson
Thomas Jefferson (D-R)	1743	1826	57	Va.	Va.	March 4, 1801–March 4, 1805	Aaron Burr
Thomas Jefferson (D-R)			61			March 4, 1805–March 4, 1809	George Clinton
James Madison (D-R)	1751	1836	57	Va.	Va.	March 4, 1809–March 4, 1813	George Clinton
James Madison (D-R)			61			March 4, 1813–March 4, 1817	Elbridge Gerry
James Monroe (D-R)	1758	1831	58	Va.	Va.	March 4, 1817–March 4, 1821	Daniel D. Tompkins
James Monroe (D-R)			62			March 4, 1821–March 4, 1825	Daniel D. Tompkins
John Q. Adams (NR)	1767	1848	57	Mass.	Mass.	March 4, 1825–March 4, 1829	John C. Calhoun
Andrew Jackson (D)	1767	1845	61	S.C.	Tenn.	March 4, 1829–March 4, 1833	John C. Calhoun
Andrew Jackson (D)			65			March 4, 1833–March 4, 1837	Martin Van Buren
Martin Van Buren (D)	1782	1862	54	N.Y.	N.Y.	March 4, 1837–March 4, 1841	Richard M. Johnson
W. H. Harrison (W)	1773	1841	68	Va.	Ohio	March 4, 1841–April 4, 1841	John Tyler
John Tyler (W)	1790	1862	51	Va.	Va.	April 6, 1841–March 4, 1845	
James K. Polk (D)	1795	1849	49	N.C.	Tenn.	March 4, 1845–March 4, 1849	George M. Dallas
Zachary Taylor (W)	1784	1850	64	Va.	La.	March 4, 1849–July 9, 1850	Millard Fillmore
Millard Fillmore (W)	1800	1874	50	N.Y.	N.Y.	July 10, 1850–March 4, 1853	
Franklin Pierce (D)	1804	1869	48	N.H.	N.H.	March 4, 1853–March 4, 1857	William R. King
James Buchanan (D)	1791	1868	65	Pa.	Pa.	March 4, 1857–March 4, 1861	John C. Breckinridge
Abraham Lincoln (R)	1809	1865	52	Ky.	Ill.	March 4, 1861–March 4, 1865	Hannibal Hamlin
Abraham Lincoln (R)			56			March 4, 1865–April 15, 1865	Andrew Johnson
Andrew Johnson (R)	1808	1875	56	N.C.	Tenn.	April 15, 1865–March 4, 1869	
Ulysses S. Grant (R)	1822	1885	46	Ohio	Ill.	March 4, 1869–March 4, 1873	Schuyler Colfax
Ulysses S. Grant (R)			50			March 4, 1873–March 4, 1877	Henry Wilson

President	Born	Died	Age	State	Term	Vice President
Rutherford B. Hayes (R)	1822	1893	54	Ohio	March 4, 1877–March 4, 1881	William A. Wheeler
James A. Garfield (R)	1831	1881	49	Ohio	March 4, 1881–Sept. 19, 1881	Chester A. Arthur
Chester A. Arthur (R)	1830	1886	50	Vt.	Sept. 20, 1881–March 4, 1885	
Grover Cleveland (D)	1837	1908	47	N.J.	March 4, 1885–March 4, 1889	Thomas A. Hendricks
Benjamin Harrison (R)	1833	1901	55	Ohio	March 4, 1889–March 4, 1893	Levi P. Morton
Grover Cleveland (D)	1837	1908	55		March 4, 1893–March 4, 1897	Adlai E. Stevenson
William McKinley (R)	1843	1901	54	Ohio	March 4, 1897–March 4, 1901	Garret A. Hobart
William McKinley (R)			58		March 4, 1901–Sept. 14, 1901	Theodore Roosevelt
Theodore Roosevelt (R)	1858	1919	42	N.Y.	Sept. 14, 1901–March 4, 1905	
Theodore Roosevelt (R)			46		March 4, 1905–March 4, 1909	Charles W. Fairbanks
William H. Taft (R)	1857	1930	51	Ohio	March 4, 1909–March 4, 1913	James S. Sherman
Woodrow Wilson (D)	1856	1924	56	Va.	March 4, 1913–March 4, 1917	Thomas R. Marshall
Woodrow Wilson (D)			60		March 4, 1917–March 4, 1921	Thomas R. Marshall
Warren G. Harding (R)	1865	1923	55	Ohio	March 4, 1921–Aug. 2, 1923	Calvin Coolidge
Calvin Coolidge (R)	1872	1933	51	Vt.	Aug. 3, 1923–March 4, 1925	
Calvin Coolidge (R)			52		March 4, 1925–March 4, 1929	Charles G. Dawes
Herbert C. Hoover (R)	1874	1964	54	Iowa	March 4, 1929–March 4, 1933	Charles Curtis
Franklin D. Roosevelt (D)	1882	1945	51	N.Y.	March 4, 1933–Jan. 20, 1937	John N. Garner
Franklin D. Roosevelt (D)			55		Jan. 20, 1937–Jan. 20, 1941	John N. Garner
Franklin D. Roosevelt (D)			59		Jan. 20, 1941–Jan. 20, 1945	Henry A. Wallace
Franklin D. Roosevelt (D)			63		Jan. 20, 1945–April 12, 1945	Harry S. Truman
Harry S. Truman (D)	1884	1972	60	Mo.	April 12, 1945–Jan. 20, 1949	
Harry S. Truman (D)			64		Jan. 20, 1949–Jan. 20, 1953	Alben W. Barkley
Dwight D. Eisenhower (R)	1890	1969	62	Texas	Jan. 20, 1953–Jan. 20, 1957	Richard Nixon
Dwight D. Eisenhower (R)			66	Pa.	Jan. 20, 1957–Jan. 20, 1961	Richard Nixon
John F. Kennedy (D)	1917	1963	43	Mass.	Jan. 20, 1961–Nov. 22, 1963	Lyndon B. Johnson
Lyndon B. Johnson (D)	1908	1973	55	Texas	Nov. 22, 1963–Jan. 20, 1965	
Lyndon B. Johnson (D)			56		Jan. 20, 1965–Jan. 20, 1969	Hubert H. Humphrey
Richard Nixon (R)	1913	1994	56	Calif.	Jan. 20, 1969–Jan. 20, 1973	Spiro T. Agnew

(Table continues)

Table 6-1 *(Continued)*

President (political party)	Born	Died	Age at inauguration	Native of . . .	Elected from . . .	Term of service	Vice president
Richard Nixon (R)			60			Jan. 20, 1973–Aug. 9, 1974	Spiro T. Agnew Gerald R. Ford
Gerald R. Ford (R)	1913	2006	61	Neb.	Mich.	Aug. 9, 1974–Jan. 20, 1977	Nelson A. Rockefeller
Jimmy Carter (D)	1924		52	Ga.	Ga.	Jan. 20, 1977–Jan. 20, 1981	Walter F. Mondale
Ronald Reagan (R)	1911	2004	69	Ill.	Calif.	Jan. 20, 1981–Jan. 20, 1985	George H. W. Bush
Ronald Reagan (R)			73			Jan. 20, 1985–Jan. 20, 1989	George H. W. Bush
George H. W. Bush (R)	1924	2018	64	Mass.	Texas	Jan. 20, 1989–Jan. 20, 1993	Dan Quayle
Bill Clinton (D)	1946		46	Ark.	Ark.	Jan. 20, 1993–Jan. 20, 1997	Al Gore
Bill Clinton (D)			50			Jan. 20, 1997–Jan. 20, 2001	Al Gore
George W. Bush (R)	1946		54	Conn.	Texas	Jan. 20, 2001–Jan. 20, 2005	Dick Cheney
George W. Bush (R)			58			Jan. 20, 2005–Jan. 20, 2009	Dick Cheney
Barack Obama (D)	1961		47	Hawaii	Ill.	Jan. 20, 2009–Jan. 20, 2013	Joseph R. Biden Jr.
Barack Obama (D)			51			Jan. 20, 2013–Jan. 20, 2017	Joseph R. Biden Jr.
Donald J. Trump (R)	1946		70	New York	New York	Jan. 20, 2017–Jan. 20, 2021	Michael R. Pence
Joseph R. Biden Jr. (D)	1942		78	Pennsylvania	Delaware	Jan. 20, 2021–	Kamala D. Harris

Note: "D" indicates Democrat; "D-R" indicates Democratic-Republican; "F" indicates Federalist; "NR" indicates National Republican; "R" indicates Republican; "W" indicates Whig.

Source: Congressional Quarterly, *Presidential Elections, 1789–2004* (Washington, D.C.: CQ Press, 2005), 3; updated by the authors.

Table 6-2 Ratings of U.S. Presidents

Schlesinger (1948)	Schlesinger (1962)	Maranell-Dodder (1970)	Murray-Blessing (1982)[a]	Ridings-McIver (1989, 1996)	Schlesinger (1997)	Federalist Society/Wall Street Journal (2005)[b]	C-SPAN (2009)[b]	Rottinghaus-Vaughn (2015)	C-SPAN (2017)	Siena College Research Institute (2018)
Great	Great	Accomplishments of administration	Great	Overall ranking	Great	Great	Overall ranking	Overall ranking	Overall ranking	Overall ranking
1. Lincoln	1. Lincoln	1. Lincoln	1. Lincoln	1. Lincoln	1. Lincoln	1. Washington	1. Lincoln	1. Lincoln	1. Lincoln	1. Washington
2. Washington	2. Washington	2. F. Roosevelt	2. F. Roosevelt	2. F. Roosevelt	2. Washington	2. Lincoln	2. Washington	2. Washington	2. Washington	2. F. Roosevelt
3. F. Roosevelt	3. F. Roosevelt	3. Washington	3. Washington	3. Washington	3. F. Roosevelt	3. F. Roosevelt	3. F. Roosevelt	3. F. Roosevelt	3. F. Roosevelt	3. Lincoln
4. Wilson	4. Wilson	4. Jefferson	4. Jefferson	4. Jefferson			4. T. Roosevelt	4. T. Roosevelt	4. T. Roosevelt	4. T. Roosevelt
5. Jefferson	5. Jefferson	5. T. Roosevelt		5. T. Roosevelt	Near great	Near great	5. Truman	5. Jefferson	5. Eisenhower	5. Jefferson
6. Jackson		6. Truman	Near great	6. Wilson	4. Jefferson	4. Jefferson	6. Kennedy	6. Truman	6. Truman	6. Eisenhower
	Near great	7. Wilson	5. T. Roosevelt	7. Truman	5. Jackson	5. T. Roosevelt	7. Jefferson	7. Eisenhower	7. Jefferson	7. Madison
Near great	6. Jackson	8. Jackson	6. Wilson	8. Jackson	6. T. Roosevelt	6. Reagan	8. Eisenhower	8. Clinton	8. Kennedy	8. Monroe
7. T. Roosevelt	7. T. Roosevelt	9. L. Johnson	7. Jackson	9. Eisenhower	7. Wilson	7. Truman	9. Wilson	9. Jackson	9. Reagan	9. Truman
8. Cleveland	8. Polk/Truman (tie)	10. Polk	8. Truman	10. Madison	8. Truman	8. Eisenhower	10. Reagan	10. Wilson	10. L. Johnson	10. Kennedy
9. J. Adams	9. J. Adams	11. J. Adams		11. J. Adams	9. Polk	9. Polk	11. Polk	11. L. Johnson	11. Reagan	11. Wilson
10. Polk	10. Cleveland	12. Kennedy	Above average	12. L. Johnson		10. Jackson	12. Polk	12. L. Johnson	12. Obama	12. Polk
		13. Monroe	9. J. Adams	13. Monroe	High average		13. Jackson	13. Madison	13. Monroe	13. Reagan
Average	Average	14. Cleveland	10. L. Johnson	14. J. Adams	10. Eisenhower	Above average	14. Monroe	14. Kennedy	14. Polk	14. J. Adams
11. J. Q. Adams	11. Madison	15. Madison	11. Eisenhower	15. Kennedy	11. J. Adams	11. Wilson	15. Clinton	15. J. Adams	15. Clinton	15. Clinton
12. Monroe	12. J. Q. Adams	16. Taft	12. Polk	16. Cleveland	12. Kennedy	12. Cleveland	16. McKinley	16. Monroe	16. McKinley	16. L. Johnson
13. Hayes	13. Hayes	17. McKinley	13. Kennedy	17. McKinley	13. Cleveland	13. J. Adams	17. J. Adams	17. G. H. W. Bush	17. Madison	17. Obama
14. Madison	14. McKinley	18. J. Q. Adams	14. Madison	18. J. Q. Adams	14. L. Johnson	14. McKinley	18. G. H. W. Bush	18. Obama	18. Jackson	18. J. Q. Adams
15. Van Buren	15. Taft	19. Hoover	15. Monroe	19. Carter	15. Monroe	15. Kennedy	19. J. Q. Adams	19. Polk	19. J. Adams	19. Jackson
16. Taft	16. Van Buren	20. Eisenhower	16. J. Q. Adams	20. Taft	16. McKinley	16. Monroe	20. Madison	20. Taft	20. G. H. W. Bush	20. McKinley
17. Arthur	17. Monroe	21. A. Johnson	17. Cleveland	21. Van Buren			21. Cleveland	21. McKinley	21. J. Q. Adams	21. G. H. W. Bush
18. McKinley	18. Hoover	22. Van Buren	Average	22. G. H. W. Bush	Average	Average	22. Ford	22. J. Q. Adams	22. Grant	22. Taft
19. A. Johnson	19. B. Harrison	23. Arthur	18. McKinley	23. Clinton	17. Madison	17. Madison	23. Grant	23. Cleveland	23. Cleveland	23. Cleveland
20. Hoover	20. Eisenhower/Arthur (tie)	24. Hayes		24. Hoover	18. J. Q. Adams	18. L. Johnson	24. Taft	24. Ford	24. Taft	24. Grant

(Table continues)

285

Table 6-2 *(Continued)*

Schlesinger (1948)	Schlesinger (1962)	Maranell-Dodder (1970)	Murray-Blessing (1982)[a]	Ridings-McIver (1989, 1996)	Schlesinger (1997)	Federalist Society–Wall Street Journal (2005)[b]	C-SPAN (2009)[b]	Rottinghaus-Vaughn (2015)	C-SPAN (2017)	Siena College Research Institute (2018)
21. B. Harrison	21. A. Johnson	25. Tyler	19. Taft	25. Hayes	19. B. Harrison	19. G. W. Bush	25. Carter	25. Van Buren	25. Ford	25. Van Buren
Below average	Below average	26. B. Harrison	20. Van Buren	26. Reagan	20. Clinton	20. Taft	26. Coolidge	26. Carter	26. Carter	26. Carter
		27. Taylor	21. Taylor	27. Hoover	21. Ford	21. Taft	27. G. H. W. Bush	27. Nixon	27. Coolidge	27. Ford
22. Tyler	22. Taylor	28. Buchanan	22. Hayes	28. Arthur	22. Van Buren	22. Clinton	28. Garfield	28. Grant	28. Nixon	28. Garfield
23. Coolidge	23. Tyler	29. Fillmore	23. Arthur	29. Taylor	23. Hayes	23. Coolidge	29. Taylor	29. B. Harrison	29. Garfield	29. Nixon
24. Fillmore	24. Fillmore	30. Coolidge	24. Ford	30. Garfield	24. G. H. W. Bush	24. Hayes	30. B. Harrison	30. Hayes	30. B. Harrison	30. Taylor
25. Taylor	25. Coolidge	31. Pierce	25. Carter	31. B. Harrison	25. Reagan	Below average	31. Van Buren	31. Garfield	31. Taylor	31. Coolidge
26. Buchanan	26. Pierce	32. Grant	26. B. Harrison	32. Nixon	26. Arthur	25. J. Q. Adams	32. Arthur	32. Arthur	32. Hayes	32. Hayes
27. Pierce	27. Buchanan	33. Harding		33. Coolidge	27. Carter	26. Arthur	33. Hayes	33. Taylor	33. G. W. Bush	33. G. W. Bush
			Below average	34. Tyler	28. Ford	27. Van Buren	34. Hoover	34. Nixon	34. Van Buren	34. Arthur
Failure	Failure		27. Taylor	35. W. H. Harrison		28. Ford	35. Tyler	35. G. W. Bush	35. Arthur	35. B. Harrison
28. Grant	28. Grant		28. Reagan	36. Fillmore	Below average	29. Grant	36. G. W. Bush	36. Tyler	36. Hoover	36. Hoover
29. Harding	29. Harding		29. Tyler	37. Pierce	29. Taylor	30. B. Harrison	37. Fillmore	37. Fillmore	37. Fillmore	37. Tyler
			30. Fillmore	38. Grant	30. Coolidge		38. Harding	38. Hoover	38. W. H. Harrison	38. Fillmore
			31. Coolidge	39. A. Johnson	31. Fillmore	31. Hoover	39. W. H. Harrison	39. W. H. Harrison	39. Tyler	39. W. H. Harrison
			32. Pierce	40. Buchanan	32. Tyler	32. Nixon	40. Pierce	40. Pierce	40. Harding	40. Pierce
				41. Harding		33. Taylor	41. A. Johnson	41. A. Johnson	41. Pierce	41. Harding
			Failure		Failure	34. Carter	42. Buchanan	42. Harding	42. A. Johnson	42. Trump

286

33. A. Johnson	33. Pierce	35. Tyler	43. Buchanan	43. Buchanan
34. Buchanan	34. Grant			44. A. Johnson
35. Nixon	35. Hoover	Failure		
36. Grant	36. Nixon	36. Fillmore		
37. Harding	37. A. Johnson	37. A. Johnson		
	38. Buchanan	38. Pierce		
	39. Harding	39. Harding		
		40. Buchanan		

Note: These ratings are derived from surveys of scholars. The sample sizes range from 49 to 846. In addition to these ratings, the Siena College Research Institute developed an alternative rating system based on scores given across twenty different categories. Using this method, it rated presidents in 1982, 1990, 1994, 2002, 2010, and 2017. See Siena's 6th Presidential Expert Poll, 1982–2018, https://scri.siena.edu/2019/02/13/sienas-6th-presidential-expert-poll-1982-2018. Additional ratings of the greatest and worst presidents can be found in previous editions of *Vital Statistics on American Politics*.

[a] The rating of President Ronald Reagan was obtained in a separate poll conducted in 1989.
[b] An earlier rating by the same organization, with slightly different results, was conducted in 1999 (C-SPAN) or 2000 (Federalist Society). See previous editions of *Vital Statistics on American Politics*.

Sources: : Henry J. Abraham, *Justices and Presidents: Appointments to the Supreme Court*, 2nd ed. (New York: Oxford University Press, 1985), 380–383; Robert K. Murray and Tim H. Blessing, *Greatness in the White House*, 2nd updated ed. (University Park: Pennsylvania State University Press, 1994), 16–17, 81; Arthur M. Schlesinger Jr., "Rating the Presidents: Washington to Clinton," *Political Science Quarterly* (Summer 1997); "C-SPAN 2009 Historians Presidential Leadership Survey," https://static.c-span.org/assets/documents/presidentSurvey/2009%20C-SPAN%20Presidential%20Survey%20Scores%20and%20Ranks%20FINAL.PDF; "Presidential Leadership: The Rankings," *Federalist Society—The Wall Street Journal*, September 12, 2005, https://www.wsj.com/news/opinion; William J. Ridings Jr. and Stuart B. McIver, *Rating the Presidents* (Secaucus, N.J.: Carol Publishing, 1997), xi; Brandon Rottinghaus and Justin Vaughn, "Expert Survey of Presidential Greatness," (2015); "C-SPAN Presidential Historians Survey, 2017," https://www.c-span.org/presidentsurvey2017; "Siena College 6th Presidential Expert Poll, 1982–2018," https://scri.siena.edu/2019/02/13/sienas-6th-presidential-expert-poll-1982-2018.

> **A Data Literacy Lesson**
>
> How Do We Rank Presidents? And, Should We Trust These Rankings?
>
> It's a favorite parlor game (perhaps for the nerdiest among us): sitting around and debating who the best and worst presidents have been. It can even go beyond that to more specific questions. Of the presidents we have known, who was the best speaker? Who was best at getting their way with Congress? Who would you most like to sit next to at a baseball game? People seem to like ranking things—witness all the "Top Ten XXX of the Year" lists that seem to proliferate in December—and presidents are no different. The labels we give to presidents often provide a useful shorthand for interpreting what we are seeing in real time.
>
> Starting from the work of Arthur Schlesinger in 1948 and continuing to the present day, ranking the president is a common pastime among historians and political scientists. Table 6-2 shows a collection of rankings unfolding over seventy years. The list is notable both for its uniformity (Lincoln, Washington, and Franklin Roosevelt always seem to end up at the top, while Harding, Buchanan, and Andrew Johnson continually occupy the bottom rungs of the ladder) and for its fluctuation. To take just one example, Ulysses S. Grant was one of the two lowest-scoring presidents in every survey we have included through 1982 but has now moved up and established himself in the middle of the pack. Andrew Jackson, however, was #6 (a near great) in earlier rankings but has now moved down into the middle of the pack.
>
> Why do some president's rankings move around so much? One reason might be seeing the long-term effects of the policies they pursued. It is a common adage in the presidential ratings game that we need to wait a while before doing serious ratings; sometimes, a policy that looks like a failure at one point might look better with the passage of time, or vice versa. To cite just one example, the Affordable Care Act, occasionally referred to as Obamacare, might one day be hailed as a highly successful, transformative policy, or as a dismal failure. Only time will tell how the policy is ultimately viewed (we would argue the jury is still out), which makes attempts to rate Barack Obama's presidency arguably premature at this point.
>
> A second reason rankings may change could be due to changing scholarship on the presidents. Dwight Eisenhower had an image as being somewhat of a low-energy bumbler as president, but his reputation was enhanced by revisionist scholarship, starting with Fred Greenstein's 1982 book, *The Hidden-Hand Presidency: Eisenhower as Leader*. While Ulysses S. Grant's reputation was already rising due to recent scholarship, we imagine that the publication of Ron Chernow's largely positive biography, *Grant*, in 2017 will only help his further rise on the list.
>
> Finally, we might see presidential ratings change as our standards for evaluating presidents changes, reflecting a shifting moral consensus in the country. Andrew Jackson is a prime example. To put it mildly, Jackson's reputation on matters concerning Native Americans is not stellar. That deeply troubling fact aside, Jackson's presidency also had many notable successes, especially in comparison with the weak presidents who served in the twenty-four years between Jackson and Lincoln. Earlier historians might have been more willing to forgive Jackson his trespasses;

later historians, acting in a more politically enlightened manner, are punishing him more in the rankings for this aspect of his record.

Presidential rankings are a fun and fascinating way to look at presidents; considering how presidents stack up against their predecessors is an engaging part of armchair study of the presidency. We warn practitioners of this art, and observers of this table, to be aware of the limitations of such examinations, and to be aware of the extent to which presidential ratings represent a snapshot in time rather than a firm, unyielding, historical judgment.

Table 6-3 Previous Public Positions Held by Presidents, 1788–2021

	Number of presidents holding position prior to presidency	
Position	Pre-1900 (24)	Post-1900 (21)
Vice president	7	8
Cabinet member	7	3
U.S. representative	13	5
U.S. senator	9	7
U.S. Supreme Court justice	0	0
Federal judge	0	1
Governor	11	8
State legislator	16	5
State judge	1	2
Mayor	2	1
Diplomat, ambassador	7	2
Military general	11	1

	Last public position held prior to presidency	
Position	Pre-1900 (24)	Post-1900 (21)
Vice president		
Succeeded to presidency	4	5
Won presidency in own right	3	3
Congress		
House	1	0
Senate	3	3
Appointive federal office		
Military general	3	1
Cabinet secretary	3	2
Ambassador	2	0
Other civilian	1	0
Governor	4	6
No public position	0	1

Note: Included in the list of generals are Andrew Johnson, who held the rank of general when serving as military governor of Tennessee, and Chester A. Arthur, who held the rank of general when serving as quartermaster general. President Cleveland is counted only at his first term.

Source: Compiled by the authors from Robert G. Ferris, *The Presidents, rev. ed.* (Washington, D.C.: National Park Service, 1977); updated by the authors through Joseph Biden.

Table 6-4 Latest Public Office Held by Candidates for Democratic and Republican Presidential Nominations, 1936–2020

Public office[a]	Percentage of all persons polling at least 1 percent in Gallup Poll	Percentage of all Democratic and Republican nominees
President[b]	1	32
Vice president	1	16
U.S. senator	38	16
Governor	23	25
Cabinet officer	11	2
U.S. representative	10	0
Mayor	3	0
U.S. Supreme Court justice	1	0
All others	2	0
No public office	11	9
Total	101	100
	(N = 215)	(N = 44)

[a] Last or current office at time person first polled at least 1 percent support for presidential nomination among fellow partisans or was first nominated.

[b] Presidents Harry S. Truman and Gerald R. Ford received poll support for the presidential nomination only after they actually served in the office.

Source: William R. Keech and Donald R. Matthews, *The Party's Choice: With an Epilogue on the 1976 Nominations* (Washington, D.C.: Brookings Institution, 1976), 18; updated by the authors.

Table 6-5 The President's Cabinet, 2021

Cabinet office	Year established[a]	Current secretary[b]	Date confirmed	Number of paid civilian employees			Percentage Change (2020 versus 2014)	Percentage Change (2020 versus 1980)
				1980[c]	2014[c]	2020[c]		
State	1789	Antony Blinken	01/26/2021	23,644	41,768	11,968	−71.3	−49.4
Treasury	1789	Janet Yellen	01/25/2021	123,754	112,461	94,366	−16.1	−23.7
War	1789[c]							
Navy	1798[c]							
Interior	1849	Deb Haaland	03/15/2021	79,505	69,807	66,113	−5.3	−16.8
Agriculture	1862	Tom Vilsack	02/23/2021	122,839	94,083	91,774	−2.5	−25.3
Justice	1870	Merrick Garland	03/10/2021	56,426	114,055	115,882	1.6	105.4
Post Office	1872[d]							
Commerce and Labor	1903[e]							
Commerce	1913	Gina Raimondo	03/02/2021	46,189	43,182	53,939	24.9	16.8
Labor	1913	Marty Walsh	03/22/2021	23,717	16,796	13,976	−16.8	−41.1
Defense	1947	Lloyd Austin	01/22/2021	972,999	723,175	768,307	6.2	−21.0
Health, Education and Welfare	1953[f]							
Health and Human Services	1979	Xavier Becerra	03/18/2021	158,644	71,862	83,514	16.2	−47.4
Housing and Urban Development	1965	Marcia Fudge	03/10/2021	16,890	7,795	7,845	0.6	−53.6
Transportation	1966	Peter Buttigieg	02/02/2021	72,066	54,790	54,343	−0.8	−24.6

Energy	1977	Jennifer Granholm	02/25/2021	21,729	14,802	14,573	−32.9
Education	1979	Miguel Cardona	03/01/2021	7,370	4,123	4,031	−45.3
Veterans Affairs	1989	Denis McDonough	02/08/2021	235,501[g]	339,903	420,048	78.4
Homeland Security	2003[h]	Alejandro Mayorkas	02/02/2021		185,870	210,860	13.4

Note: "—" indicates data unavailable. The Cabinet also includes the vice president. In addition, the following positions have the status of Cabinet-rank: White House chief of staff, Environmental Protection Agency, Office of Management and Budget, U.S. trade representative, U.S. ambassador to the United Nations, National Intelligence, Council of Economic Advisers, and Small Business Administration and Office of Science and Technology Policy Science Advisor to the President.

[a] The year is that in which a department achieved cabinet status. The Offices of Attorney General and Postmaster General were created in 1789, but the executive departments were not created until later. A Department of Agriculture was established in 1862, but the commissioner did not achieve cabinet status until 1889.
[b] As of August 2, 2021.
[c] Incorporated into Defense Department in 1947.
[d] Independent agency as of 1971.
[e] Split into separate departments in 1913.
[f] Split into Health and Human Services and Education in 1979.
[g] Figures are for the Veterans Administration, the agency that was upgraded on March 15, 1989, to the Department of Veterans Affairs.
[h] In January 2003, the Department of Homeland Security was organized with more than 180,000 employees drawn from other agencies.

Sources: "President Obama's Cabinet," www.whitehouse.gov; year established: Ronald C. Moe, "The Federal Executive Establishment: Evolution and Trends," prepared for the U.S. Senate Committee on Governmental Affairs by the Congressional Research Service (Washington, D.C.: Government Printing Office, 1980), 26–27; *Congressional Quarterly Weekly Report* (1988), 3059; U.S. Office of Personnel Management, *Federal Civilian Workforce Statistics, Employment and Trends*, January 1981, 8–9, 11; September 2014, Table 11, www.opm.gov; 2020: Office of Personnel Management, *Federal Workforce Data*, fedscope.opm.gov; Current Cabinet names and confirmation dates from www.senate.gov.

Table 6-6 White House Staff and Executive Office of the President, 1943–2020

Year	White House	Bureau of Budget/OMB[a]	Council of Economic Advisers	National Security Council	Office of Economic Opportunity	Office of Science and Technology Policy	Office of Administration	Office of the U.S. Trade Representative	Domestic Policy Staff/Office of Policy Development[b]	Total, executive office[c]
1943[d]	51	543								703
1944[c]	58	542								683
1945[c]	64	705								820
1946[c]	216	692	26							1,034
1947[c]	228	549	26							1,077
1948[c]	209	521	38	20						1,205
1949	243	517	36	17						1,240
1950	313	509	38	17						1,408
1955	366	422	33	27						1,221
1960	423	441	31	64						2,779
1965	292	506	45	39	1,768					3,307
1970	491	636	57	82	2,633	75		24	26	4,808
1975	525	664	48	85		77		26	55	1,801
1976	534	694	39	79		19		56	43	1,796
1977	387	721	36	68		44		55	41	1,637
1978	381	617	35	76		46	197	52	55	1,679
1979	418	638	36	73		44	180	58	60	1,918
1980	426	631	38	74		50	182	70	68	2,013
1981	378	679	38	65		13	190	131	48	1,674
1982	374	617	35	59		20	196	139	46	1,608
1983	376	619	34	61		23	213	138	39	1,622
1984	371	605	28	63		21	196	139	40	1,593
1985	362	569	32	61		17	193	147	38	1,549
1986	365	537	36	69		11	200	152	40	1,526
1987	375	573	31	56		11	199	144	37	1,604
1988	357	573	35	63		10	232	155	32	1,594
1989	370	536	32	62		20	213	162	37	1,640
1990	391	568	35	60		22	215	164	37	1,729
1991	358	608	36	61		39	241	172	33	1,797
1992	392	553	34	62		47	247	181	42	1,869

Year							
1993	392	522	31	52	35	185	177	42	1,570
1994	381	544	29	49	36	182	166	38	1,577
1995	387	522	28	44	34	182	165	30	1,555
1996	387	527	30	43	33	185	161	28	1,582
1997	389	507	28	43	34	178	154	29	1,591
1998	391	509	27	42	34	170	169	30	1,604
1999	393	525	28	40	33	180	180	28	1,651
2000	398	510	29	45	30	194	174	31	1,665
2001	382	509	32	49	19	198	201	33	1,652
2002	408	506	30	64	28	205	193	30	1,712
2003	401	502	29	57	31	216	198	31	1,717
2004	409	509	29	61	31	216	217	30	1,784
2005	411	473	24	61	30	221	210	27	1,697
2006	414	472	24	64	30	225	233	25	1,739
2007	419	476	23	59	32	224	226	22	1,707
2008	399	487	23	57	31	238	229	22	1,707
2009	423	517	24	63	27	226	234	24	1,769
2010	457	547	28	77	34	224	235	23	1,866
2011	464	545	26	74	35	226	236	23	1,875
2012	451	527	32	72	27	233	248	23	1,852
2013	454	456	27	69	34	236	235	23	1,761
2014	475	480	37	69	38	244	229	23	1,823
2015	474	—	—	—	—	—	—	—	—
2016	472	630	29	58	31	245	235	—	—
2017	359	581	22	51	17	240	229	—	—
2018	354	606	22	60	20	243	254	—	—
2019	382	579	24	51	24	244	275	—	—
2020	376	589	23	54	23	232	269	—	—

Note: "—" indicates data unavailable or calculation cannot be made. In almost all instances, when no figures are shown the office did not exist as a separate entity. Data as of December of the year indicated, except 1947 (January), 1960 (October), 2009 (September), and 2014. White House staff data for 2015–2020 is as of June that year. Data for additional years can be found in previous editions of *Vital Statistics on American Politics*.

[a] The Bureau of the Budget became the Office of Management and Budget (OMB) in 1970.
[b] The Domestic Policy Staff became the Office of Policy Development in 1981.
[c] Includes offices not shown separately.
[d] Total, executive office, excludes personnel in war establishments or emergency war agencies.

Source: U.S. Office of Personnel Management, *Federal Manpower Statistics, Federal Civilian Workforce Statistics, Employment and Trends*, quarterly release, www.opm.gov.

Table 6-7 Presidential Victories on Votes in Congress, 1953–2020

President (political party)/ year	House and Senate victories (percent)	House Victories (percent)	House Number of votes	Senate Victories (percent)	Senate Number of votes
Eisenhower (R)					
1953	89.2	91.2	34	87.8	49
1954	82.8	78.9	38	77.9	77
1955	75.3	63.4	41	84.6	52
1956	69.2	73.5	34	67.7	65
1957	68.4	58.3	60	78.9	57
1958	75.7	74.0	50	76.5	98
1959	52.9	55.6	54	50.4	121
1960	65.1	65.1	43	65.1	86
Average	69.9	68.4		70.7	
Total			354		605
Kennedy (D)					
1961	81.5	83.1	65	80.6	124
1962	85.4	85.0	60	85.6	125
1963	87.1	83.1	71	89.6	115
Average	84.6	83.7		85.2	
Total			196		364
L. Johnson (D)					
1964	87.9	88.5	52	87.6	97
1965	93.1	93.8	112	92.6	162
1966	78.9	91.3	103	68.8	125
1967	78.8	75.6	127	81.2	165
1968	74.5	83.5	103	68.9	164
Average	82.2	85.9		79.7	
Total			497		713
Nixon (R)					
1969	74.8	72.3	47	76.4	72
1970	76.9	84.6	65	71.4	91
1971	74.8	82.5	57	69.5	82
1972	66.3	81.1	37	54.3	46
1973	50.6	48.0	125	52.4	185
1974	59.6	67.9	53	54.2	83
Average	64.3	68.2		61.5	
Total			384		559
Ford (R)					
1974	58.2	59.3	54	57.4	68
1975	61.0	50.6	89	71.0	93
1976	53.8	43.1	51	64.2	53
Average	58.3	51.0		65.0	
Total			194		214

Table 6-7 *(Continued)*

President (political party)/ year	House and Senate victories (percent)	House		Senate	
		Victories (percent)	Number of votes	Victories (percent)	Number of votes
Carter (D)					
1977	75.4	74.7	79	76.1	88
1978	78.3	69.6	112	84.8	151
1979	76.8	71.7	145	81.4	161
1980	75.1	76.9	117	73.3	116
Average	76.6	73.1		79.7	
Total			453		516
Reagan (R)					
1981	82.4	72.4	76	88.3	128
1982	72.4	55.8	77	83.2	119
1983	67.1	47.6	82	85.9	85
1984	65.8	52.2	113	85.7	77
1985	59.9	45.0	80	71.6	102
1986	56.5	33.3	90	80.7	83
1987	43.5	33.3	99	56.4	78
1988	47.4	32.7	104	64.8	88
Average	62.2	45.6		77.9	
Total			721		760
G. H. W. Bush (R)					
1989	62.6	50.0	86	73.3	101
1990	46.8	32.4	108	63.4	93
1991	54.2	43.2	111	67.5	83
1992	43.0	37.1	105	53.3	60
Average	51.8	40.2		65.6	
Total			410		337
Clinton (D)					
1993	86.4	87.3	102	85.4	89
1994	86.4	87.2	78	85.5	62
1995	36.2	26.3	133	49.0	102
1996	55.1	53.2	79	57.6	59
1997	53.6	38.7	75	71.4	63
1998	50.6	36.6	82	66.7	72
1999	37.8	35.4	82	42.2	45
2000	55.0	49.3	69	65.0	40
Average	57.4	50.9		66.0	
Total			700		532
G. W. Bush (R)					
2001	87.0	83.7	43	88.3	77
2002	88.0	82.5	40	91.4	58
2003	78.7	87.3	55	74.8	119
2004	72.6	70.6	34	74.0	50

(Table continues)

Table 6-7 *(Continued)*

President (political party)/ year	House and Senate victories (percent)	House		Senate	
		Victories (percent)	Number of votes	Victories (percent)	Number of votes
2005	78.0	78.3	46	77.8	45
2006	80.9	85.0	40	78.6	70
2007	38.3	15.4	117	66.0	97
2008	47.8	33.8	80	68.5	54
Average	64.1	56.3		76.9	
Total			455		570
Obama (D)					
2009	96.6	94.4	72	98.7	79
2010	85.9	88.1	42	84.4	64
2011	57.1	31.6	95	84.3	89
2012	53.6	19.7	61	79.7	79
2013	56.7	20.9	86	85.2	108
2014	68.7	15.2	66	93.1	145
2015	45.7	14.6	89	82.3	75
2016	39.0	12.2	49	85.7	28
Average	62.5	34.6		85.6	
Total			560		667
Trump (R)					
2017	98.7	100.0	36	98.3	117
2018	93.4	93.3	30	93.5	107
2019	73.0	8.1	62	94.2	190
2020	73.4	17.5	40	93.0	114
Average	82.8	45.2		94.7	
Total			168		528

Note: "R" indicates Republican; "D" indicates Democrat. Percentages based on the number of congressional votes supporting the president divided by the total number of votes on which the president had taken a position. The percentages differ slightly from those found in *Congressional Quarterly Almanac, Congressional Quarterly Weekly Report (CQ Weekly)*, and Norman J. Ornstein et al.'s *Vital Statistics on Congress* because of corrections and consistent rounding of percentages to one decimal place. Averages are weighted by number of roll calls in each year.

Sources: Congressional Quarterly Almanac (Washington, D.C.: Congressional Quarterly, various years); *Congressional Quarterly Weekly Report* (CQ Weekly) (1992), 3894; (1993), 3473; (1994), 3620; (1996), 3428; (1998), 14; (1999), 76, 2972; (2001), 54; (2002), 142, 3237; (2004), 54–55, 2947–2948; (2006), 87; (2007), 50; (2008), 138–139, 3328; (2010), 118; (2011), 26; (2012), 106–107; (2013), 128; (2014), 178–179; 2015–2020, *CQ Magazine,* (February 8, 2016); (October 17, 2016); (February 12, 2018); (February 25, 2019); (Febuary 24, 2020); (March 1, 2021).

Table 6-8 Congressional Voting in Support of the President's Position, 1954–2020 (percent)

	House		Senate	
President (political party)/year	Democrats	Republicans	Democrats	Republicans
Eisenhower (R)				
1954	44	71	38	73
1955	53	60	56	72
1956	52	72	39	72
1957	49	54	51	69
1958	44	67	44	67
1959	40	68	38	72
1960	44	59	43	66
Average	46.3	63.8	43.0	70.0
Kennedy (D)				
1961	73	37	65	36
1962	72	42	63	39
1963	72	32	63	44
Average	72.3	36.7	63.7	39.6
L. Johnson (D)				
1964	74	38	61	45
1965	74	41	64	48
1966	63	37	57	43
1967	69	46	61	53
1968	64	51	48	47
Average	68.4	43.2	58.0	47.6
Nixon (R)				
1969	48	57	47	66
1970	53	66	45	60
1971	47	72	40	64
1972	47	64	44	66
1973	35	62	37	61
1974	46	65	39	57
Average	44.1	64.2	40.9	61.7
Ford (R)				
1974	41	51	39	55
1975	38	63	47	68
1976	32	63	39	62
Average	37.3	59.7	42.5	62.4
Carter (D)				
1977	63	42	70	52
1978	60	36	66	41
1979	64	34	68	47
1980	63	40	62	45
Average	62.6	37.4	66.4	45.6
Reagan (R)				
1981	42	68	49	80
1982	39	64	43	74
1983	28	70	42	73
1984	34	60	41	76
1985	30	67	35	75
1986	25	65	37	78
1987	24	62	36	64

(Table continues)

Table 6-8 *(Continued)*

	House		Senate	
President (political party)/year	Democrats	Republicans	Democrats	Republicans
1988	25	57	47	68
Average	30.5	63.7	41.7	74.0
G. H. W. Bush (R)				
1989	36	69	55	82
1990	25	63	38	70
1991	34	72	41	83
1992	25	71	32	73
Average	29.7	68.7	42.8	77.3
Clinton (D)				
1993	77	39	87	29
1994	75	47	86	42
1995	75	22	81	29
1996	74	38	83	37
1997	71	30	85	60
1998	74	26	82	41
1999	73	23	84	34
2000	73	27	89	46
Average	74.2	31.0	84.3	38.4
G. W. Bush (R)				
2001	31	86	66	94
2002	32	82	71	89
2003	26	89	48	94
2004	30	80	60	91
2005	24	81	38	86
2006	31	85	51	85
2007	7	72	37	78
2008	16	64	34	70
Average	20.9	77.5	50.2	86.5
Obama (D)				
2009	90	26	92	50
2010	84	29	94	41
2011	80	22	92	53
2012	77	17	93	47
2013	83	12	96	40
2014	81	12	95	55
2015	86	11	87	53
2016	88	8	86	49
Average	83.6	17.1	91.9	48.5
Trump (R)				
2017	16	93	37	96
2018	31	89	37	93
2019	5	91	35	93
2020	16	90	34	90
Average	17.0	90.8	35.3	93.0

Note: "R" indicates Republican; "D" indicates Democrat. Entries indicate the percentage of roll calls on which members voted in agreement with the president's position (based on a set of roll calls on which the president took a clear position). Averages are weighted by the number of such roll calls in each year, as shown in Table 6-7, this volume. *Congressional Quarterly* no longer provides information on absences, so "nonsupport" may include not voting on the roll call.

Source: CQ Weekly (May 7, 2015), 31; *CQ Magazine* (February 8, 2016); (February 6, 2017); (February 25, 2019); (February 24, 2020); (March 1, 2021).

A Data Literacy Lesson
What Do Presidential Success in Congress Numbers Really Mean?

"The power of the presidency," wrote political scientist Richard Neustadt over sixty years ago, "is the power to persuade." More recently, in the 1995 movie "The American President," President Andrew Shepherd (played by Michael Douglas) opined, "The White House is the single greatest home court advantage in the modern world."[1] The ability of the president to get his way, particularly when it comes to legislative matters, is well-engrained in the American psyche.

Perhaps the epitome of political power in modern times would be Lyndon Johnson.[2] Not surprisingly, Johnson scores second highest among presidents (since Eisenhower) in the percentage of victories his positions enjoyed in Congress: 82 percent. The only president to outscore Johnson was John F. Kennedy, a strong political figure, to be sure, but one who also did not serve long enough to experience the decline in support that presidents typically face as their tenure in office winds down. The only other presidents to score about 70 percent were Jimmy Carter and Donald Trump.

What lessons can we learn about each one of these presidents? While some scholarship is attempting to rehabilitate the Carter presidency, nobody would consider him to be one of our nation's most powerful presidents. Carter is, however, the last president to serve an entire term under unified government—his party controlled both the House and the Senate during all years of his term. Thus, even though Carter was not especially well-regarded as a persuasive legislative animal, the shared issue positions he had with his co-partisans led to him having a strong record of victories in Congress.

Trump, like Barack Obama, enjoyed the first two years of his term under unified government, and posted record successes during those years—his first-year success figure of 98.7 percent victories in Congress wrested the record from Barack Obama, who had 96.6 percent victories in his first year. Trump's totals declined quite a bit in his third and fourth years when he, like Obama, lost control of the House of Representatives. In Trump's case, he was able to win enough to keep his average above 70 percent. Interestingly, Obama was also above 70 percent after his first term, but fell below that as his tenure continued, and he lost the Senate in 2014. Trump did not serve a second term and was thus immune from the seemingly inevitable second-term slump.

Table 6-8 reaffirms our belief that partisan control of the legislative chambers matters a great deal, particularly recently. Whereas Eisenhower experienced a gap of around 25 points between support from his party and the opposition party, that gap had grown to around 33 points under Reagan, and around 55 points under Obama (the figures we report are an average of House and Senate differences). Persuasion may matter at the margins, but it helps to be tasked with persuading members of the president's party! Furthermore, as noted above, the magical powers of the president to get congressional support fades over time, as the president may wear out his welcome, decline in public approval, and approach lame duck status.

One final note—as we do often, it is worth briefly highlighting not only what the table shows, but what it does not. Strategic presidents may realize that their approval ratings, and influence, decline when they suffer legislative defeats. As such, we wonder about the extent to which the dynamics of presidential support in Congress may be reversed. It might not be the case that presidents announcing their position moves Congress to support them; it might instead be that presidents choose what legislative battles to fight based upon whether or not they have the votes behind them. Tables 6-7 and 6-8 tell us about the legislative wins and losses—they do not tell us about the decision whether to enter the fray in the first place.

---

[1] If you have not seen this movie, put down this essay and go watch it. The essay will still be here for you when you return.

[2] For a visual demonstration of Lyndon Johnson's power to "persuade" others, Google "Lyndon Johnson and Theodore Green" and see how Johnson used his considerable size and willingness to invade one's personal space to his advantage.

Table 6-9 Presidential Vetoes, 1789–2021, and Signing Statements, 1929–2021

						Signing statements[a]	
Years	President	Regular vetoes	Vetoes overridden	Pocket vetoes	Total vetoes	Those raising constitutional concerns	Total
1789–1797	Washington	2	0	0	2	—	—
1797–1801	J. Adams	0	0	0	0	—	—
1801–1809	Jefferson	0	0	0	0	—	—
1809–1817	Madison	5	0	2	7	—	—
1817–1825	Monroe	1	0	0	1	—	—
1825–1829	J. Q. Adams	0	0	0	0	—	—
1829–1837	Jackson	5	0	7	12	—	—
1837–1841	Van Buren	0	0	1	1	—	—
1841–1841	W. H. Harrison	0	0	0	0	—	—
1841–1845	Tyler	6	1	4	10	—	—
1845–1849	Polk	2	0	1	3	—	—
1849–1850	Taylor	0	0	0	0	—	—
1850–1853	Fillmore	0	0	0	0	—	—
1853–1857	Pierce	9	5	0	9	—	—
1857–1861	Buchanan	4	0	3	7	—	—
1861–1865	Lincoln	2	0	5	7	—	—
1865–1869	A. Johnson	21	15	8	29	—	—
1869–1877	Grant	45	4	48	93	—	—
1877–1881	Hayes	12	1	1	13	—	—
1881–1881	Garfield	0	0	0	0	—	—
1881–1885	Arthur	4	1	8	12	—	—
1885–1889	Cleveland	304	2	110	414	—	—
1889–1893	B. Harrison	19	1	25	44	—	—
1893–1897	Cleveland	42	5	128	170	—	—
1897–1901	McKinley	6	0	36	42	—	—
1901–1909	T. Roosevelt	42	1	40	82	—	—
1909–1913	Taft	30	1	9	39	—	—
1913–1921	Wilson	33	6	11	44	—	—
1921–1923	Harding	5	0	1	6	—	—
1923–1929	Coolidge	20	4	30	50	—	—
1929–1933	Hoover	21	3	16	37	—	16
1933–1945	F. Roosevelt	372	9	263	635	—	44
1945–1953	Truman	180	12	70	250	—	107
1953–1961	Eisenhower	73	2	108	181	—	145
1961–1963	Kennedy	12	0	9	21	—	36
1963–1969	L. Johnson	16	0	14	30	—	177
1969–1974	Nixon	26[b]	7	17	43	—	117
1974–1977	Ford	48	12	18	66	—	137
1977–1981	Carter	13	2	18	31	—	228

(Table continues)

Table 6-9 *(Continued)*

						Signing statements[a]	
Years	President	Regular vetoes	Vetoes overridden	Pocket vetoes	Total vetoes	Those raising constitutional concerns	Total
1981–1989	Reagan	39	9	39	78	86	250[c]
1989–1993	G. H. W. Bush	29	1	15[d]	44	107	228
1993–2001	Clinton	36	2	1	37	70	381[e]
2001–2009	G. W. Bush	12	4	0[f]	12	127	161[g]
2009–2017	Obama	12	1	0	12	23	37
2017–2021	Trump	10	1	0	10	63	70
	Total	1,518	112	1,066	2,584	476	1,342

Note: "—" indicates not available.

[a] Presidents issue "signing statements" in writing when signing legislation. Often these statements merely comment on the bill signed. Some statements involve more controversial claims by the president that some part of the legislation is unconstitutional and that he intends to disregard it or to implement it in ways he thinks is constitutional.
[b] Two pocket vetoes, overruled in the courts, are counted here as regular vetoes.
[c] The American Presidency Project lists 249 signing statements for Reagan.
[d] President George H. W. Bush attempted to pocket veto two bills during intrasession recesses. These two disputed vetoes are not included here.
[e] The American Presidency Project lists 383 signing statements for Clinton.
[f] President George W. Bush characterized his veto of H.R. 1585 as a pocket veto; however, the 110th Congress treated it as a normal veto. It is counted as a normal veto here.
[g] The American Presidency Project lists 162 signing statements for George W. Bush.

Sources: Vetoes: Maeve P. Carey, "Regular Vetoes and Pocket Vetoes: An Overview," RS22188, Congressional Research Service, Washington, D.C., June 18, 2014, updated by the authors; signing statements (total), Hoover to Carter, Obama, and Obama: John Woolley and Gerhard Peters, "Presidential Signing Statements," The American Presidency Project, www.presidency.ucsb.edu; signing statements (those raising constitutional concerns and total), Reagan to G. W. Bush: Todd Garvey, "Presidential Signing Statements: Constitutional and Institutional Implications," RL33667, Congressional Research Service, Washington, D.C., January 4, 2012; signing statements (those raising constitutional concerns), Obama and Trump: Garvey, "Presidential Signing Statements."

Table 6-10 Senate Action on Nominations, 1937–2021

Congress		Received[a]	Confirmed	Withdrawn	Rejected[b]	Unconfirmed[c]
75th	(1937–1939)	15,330	15,193	20	27	90
80th	(1947–1949)	66,641	54,796	153	0	11,692
85th	(1957–1959)	104,193	103,311	54	0	828
86th	(1959–1961)	91,476	89,900	30	1	1,545
87th	(1961–1963)	102,849	100,741	1,279	0	829
88th	(1963–1965)	122,190	120,201	36	0	1,953
89th	(1965–1967)	123,019	120,865	173	0	1,981
90th	(1967–1969)	120,231	118,231	34	0	1,966
91st	(1969–1971)	134,464	133,797	487	2	178
92nd	(1971–1973)	117,053	114,909	11	0	2,133
93rd	(1973–1975)	134,384	131,254	15	0	3,115
94th	(1975–1977)	135,302	131,378	21	0	3,903
95th	(1977–1979)	137,509	124,730	66	0	12,713
96th	(1979–1981)	156,141	154,665	18	0	1,458
97th	(1981–1983)	186,264	184,856	55	0	1,353
98th	(1983–1985)	97,893	97,262	4	0	627
99th	(1985–1987)	99,614	95,811	16	0	3,787
100th	(1987–1989)	94,687	88,721	23	1	5,942
101st	(1989–1991)	96,130	88,078	48	1	8,003
102nd	(1991–1993)	76,628	75,802	24	0	802
103rd	(1993–1995)	79,956	76,122	1,080	0	2,754
104th	(1995–1997)	82,214	73,711	22	0	8,481
105th	(1997–1999)	46,290	45,878	40	0	372
106th	(1999–2001)	46,952	44,980	25	0	1,947
107th	(2001–2003)	50,406	48,724	79	0	1,603
108th	(2003–2005)	59,655	48,627	39	0	10,989
109th	(2005–2007)	57,514	55,545	40	0	1,929
110th	(2007–2009)	45,453	44,677	74	0	702
111th	(2009–2011)	48,665	46,377	36	0	2,252
112th	(2011–2013)	44,987	44,111	44	0	832
113th	(2013–2015)	38,872	35,682	27	0	3,163
114th	(2015–2017)	42,009	39,053	350	0	2,604
115th	(2017–2019)	42,101	41,363	62	0	574
116th	(2019–2021)	42,619	41,859	43	0	807

Note: Data for additional years can be found in previous editions of *Vital Statistics on American Politics*.

[a] Count includes those in the second session carried over from the first session.

[b] Category includes only those nominations rejected outright by a vote of the Senate. Most nominations that fail to win approval of the Senate are unfavorably reported by committees and never reach the Senate floor, having been withdrawn. In some cases, the full Senate may vote to recommit a nomination to committee, in effect killing it.

[c] Includes "returned" nominations. Nominations must be returned to the president unless confirmed or rejected during the session in which they are made. If the Senate adjourns or recesses for more than thirty days within a session, all pending nominations must be returned (Senate Rule XXI).

Sources: 1937–1999: *Congressional Quarterly's Guide to Congress, 5th ed.* (Washington, D.C.: CQ Press, 2000), 1: 295; 1999–2001: Congressional Record—Daily Digest, D45; 2001–2003: D456–D457; 2003–2005: D96–D97; 2005–2007: D158, D1173; 2007–2009: D80, D1336–D1337; 2009–2011: D1249; 2011–2013: D11, D210; 2013–2015: D195, D1161; 2016–2021: U.S. Congress, *Congressional Record—Daily Digest, Résumé of Congressional Activity*.

Table 6-11 Senate Rejections of Cabinet Nominations

Presidential Nominees Rejected by Senate				
Nominee	Position	President	Date Rejected	Vote
Roger B. Taney	secretary of treasury	Jackson	6/23/1834	18–28
Caleb Cushing	secretary of treasury	Tyler	3/3/1843	19–27
Caleb Cushing	secretary of treasury	Tyler	3/3/1843	10–27
Caleb Cushing	secretary of treasury	Tyler	3/3/1843	2–29
David Henshaw	secretary of navy	Tyler	1/15/1844	6–34
James M. Porter	secretary of war	Tyler	1/30/1844	3–38
James S. Green	secretary of treasury	Tyler	6/15/1844	a
Henry Stanbery	attorney general	A. Johnson	6/2/1868	11–29
Charles B. Warren	attorney general	Coolidge	10/3/1925	39–41
Charles B. Warren	attorney general	Coolidge	3/16/1925	39–46
Lewis L. Strauss	secretary of commerce	Eisenhower	6/19/1959	46–49
John Tower	secretary of defense	G. H. W. Bush	9/3/1989	47–53

Presidential Nominees Withdrawn before Senate Vote			
Nominee	Position	President	Date Withdrawn
Lucius Stockton	secretary of war	J. Adams	1/29/1801
Henry Dearborn	secretary of war	Madison	3/2/1815
David Tod	secretary of treasury	Lincoln	7/1/1864
Edwin D. Morgan	secretary of treasury	Lincoln	2/13/1865
Benjamin Bristow	attorney general	Grant	1/8/1874
Zoe E. Baird	attorney general	Clinton	1/26/1993
Anthony Lake	director of central intelligence agency	Clinton	4/18/1997
Hershel W. Gober	secretary of veterans affairs	Clinton	10/27/1997
Linda Chavez	secretary of labor	G. W. Bush	1/9/2001
Bernard Kerik	secretary of homeland security	G. W. Bush	12/10/2004
Bill Richardson	secretary of commerce	Obama	1/4/2009
Tom Daschle	secretary of health and human services	Obama	2/9/2009
Judd Gregg	secretary of commerce	Obama	2/12/2009
Andrew Puzder	secretary of labor	Trump	2/28/2017
Ronny Jackson	secretary of veterans affairs	Trump	6/20/2018
Chad Wolf	secretary of homeland security	Trump	1/6/2021
Neera Tanden	director of office of management and budget	Biden	3/2/2021

Source: U.S. Senate, "Cabinet Nominations Rejected, Withdrawn, or No Action Taken," https://www.senate.gov/legislative/NominationsRejectedorWithdrawn.htm.

A Data Literacy Lesson
Interpreting Data on Presidential Nominations, Rejected, and Withdrawn

In previous editions of this book, only the top panel of Table 6-11 was included. A glance at this largely static table would reveal that very few presidential nominations were rejected by the Senate; of the nine unique nominees who have been rejected, Caleb Cushing was rejected three times (all in the same day!), while Charles B. Warren was rejected twice. Most of these took place a long time ago; only three different nominees were rejected after Reconstruction, and only one has been rejected since 1959. While the Constitution gives the presidency the power to nominate the heads of the executive departments and gives the Senate the right to advise and consent to those nominations, the top panel of Table 6-11 suggests that this power is rarely used.

And yet, it seems as if there should be more to the story. For this edition of this book, we added the bottom panel to Table 6-11, which shows those nominees who were put forward by a president and then withdrawn. Now things get more interesting, and more contemporary! Since the Senate rejected George H. W. Bush's nomination of John Tower to be Secretary of Defense in 1989, one dozen nominees have been withdrawn, with all the presidents beginning with Bill Clinton having suffered that fate. The causes have ranked from not paying taxes on household employees (the so-called "nanny tax") to having sent a series of incendiary tweets about key senators, to simply not being judged as qualified for the position in question. In each case, the president and/or the nominees perceived that the votes simply were not there to attain Senate confirmation and pulled the plug on the nomination.

Losing a confirmation vote is damaging to a president. When President Bush lost on the Tower nomination, it painted a picture of an administration stumbling out of the gate, and of a president who did not have the strength or influence to get a nominee through the process. (That Tower was a former senator who presumably still had friends in the chamber made this defeat even more noteworthy.) Learning from this lesson, presidents know how important the decision is to go all-in behind a nominee, or to fold their hand and try their luck with the next one. In the case of President Joseph Biden and his director of the Office of Management and Budget nominee, Neera Tanden, Biden did not have the votes to get Tanden through. His desire to push the limits on this nomination were no doubt constrained by his need to put all of his political capital behind the COVID stimulus bill; Biden could not afford a highly visible loss while trying to get this signature piece of legislation through, and while trying to preserve political capital for future battles.

We can conclude, at one level, that merely considering nominees who get rejected paints an incomplete picture—presidents are inclined nowadays not to push a nomination all the way to defeat, but rather to step back and withdraw when the votes are not there. But even this would not be a full rendering of the picture, since presidents may be constrained in who they nominate. A president facing opposing party control in the Senate might choose to nominate someone who has a better chance of getting some votes from across the aisle than someone who has little chance of doing so. As an example, when President Obama sought to replace Justice

Antonin Scalia on the Supreme Court while Republicans controlled the Senate, he chose a nominee, Merrick Garland, who was not an extreme liberal but rather was moderate enough to potentially get the Republican votes he needed to be confirmed. (Garland was not even given a hearing by the Senate, and his nomination ultimately was never acted upon.)[1] President Trump, armed with a Republican majority, faced no such constraints.

Looking at direct actions as in Table 6-11 (such as Cabinet nominees rejected, or even those withdrawn for lack of support) tells us something, but it misses the consideration of actions that were not attempted. In many ways, the greatest advice and consent power the Senate may exercise comes not from who they reject, but rather from whose nominations they prevent in the first place. And, unfortunately, there is no table we could produce that shows those data!

---

[1] If judicial confirmations and rejections are interesting to you, you might want to explore Table 7-3, which focuses on unsuccessful Supreme Court nominations, and Table 7-6, which focuses on the percent of Circuit and District Court Nominees confirmed.

Civil Service Employment

Table 6-12 Presidential Executive Orders, 1789-2020

President (Party)	Presidential terms	Executive orders	Years served	Executive orders per year	Executive orders by number
George Washington (F)	Total	8	7.85	1	unnumbered
John Adams (F)	Total	1	4	0.25	unnumbered
Thomas Jefferson (D-R)	Total	4	8	0.5	unnumbered
James Madison (D-R)	Total	1	8	0.13	unnumbered
James Monroe (D-R)	Total	1	8	0.13	unnumbered
John Quincy Adams (D-R)	Total	3	4	0.75	unnumbered
Andrew Jackson (D)	Total	12	8	1.5	unnumbered
Martin van Buren (D)	Total	10	4	2.5	unnumbered
William Henry Harrison (W)	Total	0	0.08	0	unnumbered
John Tyler (W)	Total	17	3.92	4.3	unnumbered
James K. Polk (D)	Total	18	4	4.5	unnumbered
Zachary Taylor (W)	Total	5	1.35	3.7	unnumbered
Millard Fillmore (W)	Total	12	2.65	4.5	unnumbered
Franklin Pierce (D)	Total	35	4	9	unnumbered
James Buchanan (D)	Total	16	4	4	unnumbered
Abraham Lincoln (R)	Total	48	4.12	12	unnumbered
Andrew Johnson (D)	Total	79	3.89	20	unnumbered
Ulysses S. Grant (R)	Total	217	8	27	unnumbered
Rutherford B. Hayes (R)	Total	92	4	23	unnumbered
James Garfield (R)	Total	6	0.55	11	unnumbered
Chester Arthur (R)	Total	96	3.46	28	unnumbered
Grover Cleveland (D, First Term)	Total	113	4	28	unnumbered
Benjamin Harrison (R)	Total	143	4	36	unnumbered
Grover Cleveland (D, Second Term)	Total	140	4	35	unnumbered
William McKinley (R)	Total	185	4.53	41	unnumbered
Theodore Roosevelt (R)	Total	1,081	7.47	145	unnumbered
William Howard Taft (R)	Total	724	4	181	823–1546
Woodrow Wilson (D)	Total	1,803	8	225	1547–3350
Warren G. Harding (R)	Total	522	2.41	217	335–3872
Calvin Coolidge (R)	Total	1,203	5.59	215	3873–5074
Herbert Hoover (R)	Total	968	4	242	5075–6070
Franklin D. Roosevelt (D)	Total	3,721	12.12	307	6071–9537
Harry S. Truman (D)	Total	907	7.78	117	9538–10431
	I	504	3.78	133	9538–10029
	II	403	4	101	10030–10431
Dwight D. Eisenhower (R)	Total	484	8	61	10432–10913
	I	266	4	67	10432–10695A
	II	218	4	55	10696–10913
John F. Kennedy (D)	Total	214	2.84	75	10914–11127
Lyndon B. Johnson (D)	Total	325	5.17	63	11128–11451
Richard Nixon (R)	Total	346	5.55	62	11452–11797
	I	247	4	62	11452–11698
	II	99	1.55	64	11699–11797
Gerald R. Ford (R)	Total	169	2.45	69	11798–11966
Jimmy Carter (D)	Total	320	4	80	11967–12286

(Table continues)

Table 6-12 *(Continued)*

President (Party)	Presidential terms	Executive orders	Years served	Executive orders per year	Executive orders by number
Ronald Reagan (R)	Total	381	8	48	12287–12667
	I	213	4	53	12287–12499
	II	168	4	42	12500–12667
George Bush (R)	Total	166	4	42	12668–12833
William J. Clinton (D)	Total	364	8	46	12834–13197
	I	200	4	50	12834–13033
	II	164	4	41	13034–13197
George W. Bush (R)	Total	291	8	36	13198–13488
	I	173	4	43	13198–13370
	II	118	4	30	13371–13488
Barack Obama (D)	Total	276	8	35	13489–13764
	I	147	4	37	13489–13635
	II	129	4	32	13636–13764
Donald J. Trump (R)	Total	220	4	55	13765–13984

Note: "D" indicates Democrat, "R" indicates Republican, "D-R" indicates Democratic Republican, "W" indicates Whig, and "F" indicates Federalist. Numbering of Executive Orders begins in 1907.

Source: Gerhard Peters and John T. Woolley, "Executive Orders," The American Presidency Project, ed. John T. Woolley and Gerhard Peters (Santa Barbara, CA: University of California), https://www.presidency.ucsb.edu/statistics/data/executive-orders.

A Data Literacy Lesson
When Counting Executive Orders Isn't Enough

We remember learning it in school—or even from Schoolhouse Rock—that the government has three branches: a legislative branch, which makes the laws; an executive branch, which enforces the laws; and a judicial branch, which interprets them. Policy is made by Congress, which negotiates the details and passes legislation, and by the president, who signs the law (or perhaps the law might take effect if a presidential veto is overridden). The courts, if asked, rule on constitutionality.

The more we study American government, however, the more we learn that this basic understanding misses some realities. One of the most common examples of this is the executive order. While the United States Constitution does not directly say the president may issue executive orders, Article II vests the executive power in the president, and in describing the powers of the office gives the president the power to "take Care that the Laws be faithfully executed." An executive order, which is basically the issuance of a federal directive, must be based in a presidential power, whether from a specific power given to the president in the Constitution or delegated to the president by a statute. Executive orders are subject to judicial review.

In recent years, we have seen more and more arguments that presidents are using executive orders to get around Congress, and complaints (from both parties) about legislating by executive order. President Obama, for example, established DACA (Deferred Action for Childhood Arrivals), a means of protecting those who were brought to the country illegally as children, through an executive order. President Trump established the so-called Muslim ban by executive order (in fact, it took three versions of this order to pass muster before the courts). And President Biden signed ten executive orders on his first day in office!

But is it really the case that presidents are making greater use of executive orders? You may not remember from your history classes that two important examples of presidential leadership (Lincoln's Emancipation Proclamation and Truman's desegregation of the armed forces) came not via law, but via executive order. Less nobly, President Roosevelt's policy of moving Japanese Americans on the west coast to internment camps during World War II also came by executive order. It simply is not the case, then, that the use of executive orders to unilaterally make important policy is a modern-day invention.

If you look to Table 6-12, you will see that there is some truth to the idea that presidents are issuing more executive orders than in the past. Early presidents hardly made use of this power; none of our first fourteen presidents issued more than twenty executive orders during their time in office. Andrew Johnson was the first president to average more than twenty per year, but it took until Benjamin Harrison for the average to reach forty. Theodore Roosevelt was the first president to cross one hundred executive orders per year, a figure attained by all presidents between him and Harry Truman. The high, 307 per year, was achieved by FDR. Since then, no president has averaged more than eighty per year; Barack Obama averaged thirty-two per year, while Donald Trump averaged fifty-five.

A simple glance would tell us that presidents are not using *more* executive orders than their predecessors, at least those who served since the dawn of the last century. What is left unsaid by Table 6-12, of course, is the extent to which these executive orders may be "larger" than past years. Are presidents routinely using executive orders to bypass Congress and enact major policy changes? There is certainly some evidence (from above) that presidents are using executive orders in the present day to make big policy steps, but there is also ample evidence that their predecessors did as well. Given partisan gridlock, it may also just be the case that all executive orders feel, at some level, like presidents are legislating by means other than the traditional legislative process.

Table 6-12 tells us a lot. It is important, however, to separate in our minds the questions that it answers, and the questions that it cannot address. And, when the table fails to answer questions about which we care deeply, remember we can use data we collect or find elsewhere to dig further into our questions.

Table 6-13 Major Regulatory Agencies

Agency	Year established	Agency head Number	Agency head Title	Number of employees[a]
Consumer Financial Protection Bureau	2011	1	director	1,540
Consumer Product Safety Commission	1972	3	commissioner	522
Environmental Protection Agency	1970	1	administrator	14,915
Equal Employment Opportunity Commission	1965	5	commissioner	2,045
Federal Communications Commission	1934	5	commissioner	1,486
Federal Deposit Insurance Corporation	1933	5	board of directors	5,860
Federal Election Commission	1975	6	commissioner	310
Federal Energy Regulatory Commission	1977	5	commissioner	1,461
Federal Reserve System	1913	7	governor	1,492
Federal Trade Commission	1914	5	commissioner	1,164
Food and Drug Administration	1906	1	commissioner	16,646
National Labor Relations Board	1935	5	board of directors	1,572
Occupational Safety and Health Administration	1970	1	assistant secretary	2,170
Securities and Exchange Commission	1934	5	commissioner	4,479

Note: The Interstate Commerce Commission, established in 1887, was terminated on December 30, 1995. It was succeeded by the Surface Transportation Board.

[a] All data for FY 2020.

Sources: Year established, agency head: *Federal Regulatory Directory, 16th ed.* (Washington, D.C.: CQ Press, 2014); updated by authors; Number of employees: Office of Personnel Management Federal Workforce Data, www.fedscope.opm.gov; OSHA FY 2020: U.S. Department of Labor, Budget in Brief, https://www.dol.gov/sites/dolgov/files/ETA/budget/pdfs/FY2020BIB.pdf; CFPB FY 2020: U.S. Consumer Financial Protection Bureau, Fiscal Year 2020: *Annual Performance Plan and Report, and Budget Overview,* https://files.consumerfinance.gov/f/documents/cfpb_performance-plan-and-report_fy20.pdf; FDA: Food and Drug Administration, *Supplementary Tables,* "DETAIL OF FULL-TIME EQUIVALENTS," https://www.fda.gov/media/132813/download.

Figure 6-1 Number of Pages in *Federal Register*, 1940–2019

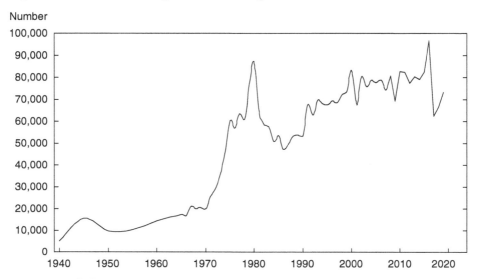

Source: Compiled from successive volumes of the *Federal Register* (Washington, D.C.: Government Printing Office).

7
The Judiciary

- **Federal and State Court Structures**
- **Supreme Court Justices**
- **Ratings**
- **Failed Nominations**
- **Federal Court Judges**
- **Supreme Court Caseloads**
- **Federal Court Caseloads**
- **Laws Overturned**

The judiciary is a co-equal branch to the legislature and executive branches, but occupies a unique space within the American political system. Established by Article III of the Constitution to interpret law by deciding cases of dispute, the federal judiciary includes the Supreme Court and other "inferior" courts established by Congress. As Figure 7-1 and 7-2 illustrate, the system that has developed over the years is organized both hierarchically and geographically, with a variety of rules and interpretations governing the jurisdiction of the different courts. This is to say nothing of the separate judicial systems operating within each state, which we do not address in this chapter.

As arbiters of disputes between other actors in the political systems the judiciary, and the judges and justices who sit on its benches, are expected to be independent from political influence or pressures. However, Article III judges (Supreme Court justices, and federal circuit and district court judges) are inherently part of the political system beginning with their access to the bench, which requires being nominated by the president and confirmed by the U.S. Senate to be seated. Nomination by the president does not guarantee confirmation by the Senate, as illustrated by Tables 7-3 and 7-7. Beyond the political process that governs their appointment to the bench, the rulings made in the judiciary have broad reaching political implications. Whether ruling on the constitutionality of laws passed by legislatures, interpreting executive actions, or changing the boundaries of established civil rights and liberties, the judiciary is certainly political in effect, if not label. The judiciary has had an effect on nearly every aspect of American political life, from campaign finance and PACs (*Citizens United v. FEC, see Table 2-10*) and presidential election outcomes (*Bush v. Gore*) to immigration policy (*Padilla v. Kentucky, Nielsen v. Preap, Niz-Chavez v. Barr, etc.*) and abortion (e.g., *Roe v. Wade, Webster v. Reproductive Health Services, Gonzales v. Planned Parenthood Federation of America, Inc., etc.*).

Beyond statistics about who is nominated to the judiciary (as in Tables 7-4 and 7-5), there are things to be learned and interpreted from statistical data about the judiciary's role in American politics. While most broad media attention focuses on the Supreme Court and its rulings, the cases that are heard and decided at that level represent a very small fraction of the cases heard in the United States each year. This means that for most actors in the judicial system, the district or circuit courts will be the final arbiter. However, even as their caseloads have risen dramatically (Tables 7-7 through 7-9 and Figure 7-3), the number of judges available to hear the cases has not similarly risen, leading to relatively fewer cases being heard by the Supreme Court, and much heavier workloads for lower court judges. Looking at data, we can see that much of this increased workload (and the relatively smaller proportion of cases terminated) each year has been driven largely by a growth in civil cases brought to the district courts (Table 7-10). From 2019 to 2020 alone there was 58 percent increase in civil cases brought to district courts.

We can also use statistics to understand the nature of the disputes being brought to the courts. In 2020, just over half of all cases were tort actions, the bulk of which were personal injury product liability cases. These numbers also inform our understanding of how political issues and social policies have an impact on the courts. In 2020, over a quarter of all criminal cases were drug offenses, while more than a third were related to immigration violations. The policies that are established and implemented by the legislative and executive branches have consequences for the work of the judicial branch.

Collecting statistical data for the judiciary is an interesting endeavor on its own merits. Some information, such as the number and types of cases heard and decided each year, is readily available in a variety of formats from government agencies and the courts themselves. The Federal Judicial Center is the research and education arm of the federal judiciary, and offers a great deal of data about various aspects of the judiciary. Scholars of the judiciary find that some statistics are not readily available, though. Collecting detailed information on the characteristics of federal judges is itself an act of scholarship (as we explore in the essay accompanying Table 7-4) and relies on the work of academics and advocacy organizations. In an effort to maintain an image of judges as apolitical, collecting statistical data about their background poses a challenge.

Figure 7-1 The U.S. Court System

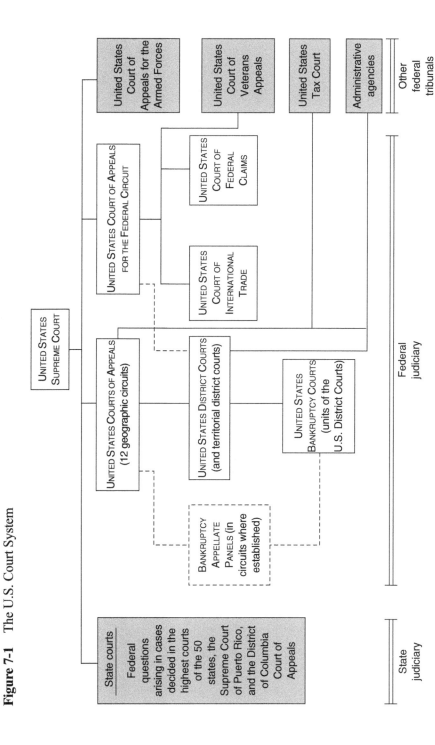

Source: U.S. Courts. *Court Role and Structure*, https://www.uscourts.gov/about-federal-courts/court-role-and-structure.

Figure 7-2 The Thirteen Federal Judicial Circuits and Ninety-Four District Courts

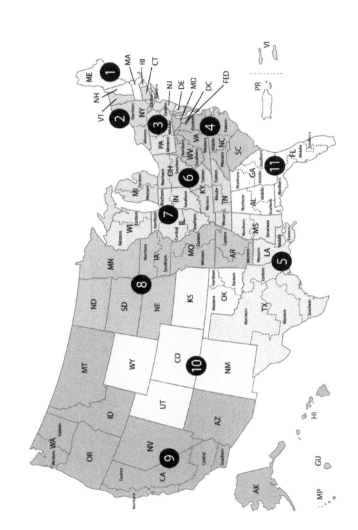

Note: Puerto Rico is part of the 1st Circuit; the Virgin Islands, the 3rd Circuit. The D.C. Circuit, not shown here, is also a geographic circuit. In addition, there is a Federal Circuit (see Figure 7-1, this volume).

Source: Administrative Office of the United States Courts, www.uscourts.gov.

Table 7-1 Principal Methods of Judicial Selection for State Courts of Last Resort

Partisan election	Nonpartisan election	Legislative appointment	Gubernatorial appointment	Merit plan
Alabama	Arkansas	South Carolina	California	Alaska
Illinois	Georgia	Virginia	Maine	Arizona
Louisiana	Idaho		New Hampshire	Colorado
Michigan	Kentucky		New Jersey	Connecticut
New Mexico	Minnesota		Tennessee	Delaware
North Carolina	Mississippi		Puerto Rico	Florida
Ohio	Montana			Hawaii
Pennsylvania	Nevada			Indiana
Texas	North Dakota			Iowa
	Oregon			Kansas
	Washington			Maryland
	West Virginia			Massachusetts
	Wisconsin			Missouri
				Nebraska
				New York
				Oklahoma
				Rhode Island
				South Dakota
				Utah
				Vermont
				Wyoming

Note: "Merit plan" typically involves appointment by the governor from a list of candidates submitted by an independent or quasi-independent judiciary council or commission. For details on all selection methods, see notes in source.

We present the method of selection for a full term. For details on different methods of selection for retention and unexpired terms, which can vary from the full-term method, see original source.

Source: Council of State Governments, *The Book of the States, 2019* (Lexington, Ky.: Council of State Governments, 2019), Table 5-6.

Table 7-2 Supreme Court Justices of the United States

Seat number and justice	Party	Home state	Years on Court	Age at nomination	Years of previous judicial experience
Washington appointees					
1 John Jay	Federalist	New York	1789–1795	44	2
2 John Rutledge	Federalist	South Carolina	1789–1791	50	6
3 William Cushing	Federalist	Massachusetts	1789–1810[a]	57	29
4 James Wilson	Federalist	Pennsylvania	1789–1798[a]	47	0
5 John Blair Jr.	Federalist	Virginia	1789–1795	57	11
6 James Iredell	Federalist	North Carolina	1790–1799[a]	38	0.5
2 Thomas Johnson	Federalist	Maryland	1791–1793	59	1.5
2 William Paterson	Federalist	New Jersey	1793–1806[a]	47	0
1 John Rutledge	Federalist	South Carolina	1795	55	6[b]
5 Samuel Chase	Federalist	Maryland	1796–1811[a]	55	8
1 Oliver Ellsworth	Federalist	Connecticut	1796–1800	51	5
J. Adams appointees					
4 Bushrod Washington	Federalist	Virginia	1798–1829[a]	36	0
6 Alfred Moore	Federalist	North Carolina	1799–1804	44	1
1 John Marshall	Federalist	Virginia	1801–1835[a]	45	3
Jefferson appointees					
6 William Johnson	Jeffersonian	South Carolina	1804–1834[a]	32	6
2 H. Brockholst Livingston	Jeffersonian	New York	1806–1823[a]	49	0
7 Thomas Todd	Jeffersonian	Kentucky	1807–1826[a]	42	6
Madison appointees					
5 Gabriel Duvall	Jeffersonian	Maryland	1811–1835	58	6
3 Joseph Story	Jeffersonian	Massachusetts	1811–1845[a]	32	0
Monroe appointee					
2 Smith Thompson	Jeffersonian	New York	1823–1843[a]	55	16

J. Q. Adams appointee				
7 Robert Trimble	Jeffersonian	Kentucky	1826–1828[a]	49	11
Jackson appointees				
7 John McLean	Democrat	Ohio	1829–1861[a]	44	6
4 Henry Baldwin	Democrat	Pennsylvania	1830–1844[a]	50	0
6 James Wayne	Democrat	Georgia	1835–1867[a]	45	5
1 Roger B. Taney	Democrat	Maryland	1836–1864[a]	59	0
5 Philip P. Barbour	Democrat	Virginia	1836–1841[a]	52	8
Van Buren appointees				
8 John Catron	Democrat	Tennessee	1837–1865[a]	51	10
9 John McKinley	Democrat	Alabama	1837–1852[a]	57	0
5 Peter V. Daniel	Democrat	Virginia	1841–1860[a]	57	0
Tyler appointee				
2 Samuel Nelson	Democrat	New York	1845–1872	52	22
Polk appointees				
3 Levi Woodbury	Democrat	New Hampshire	1845–1851[a]	55	6
4 Robert C. Grier	Democrat	Pennsylvania	1846–1870	52	13
Fillmore appointee				
3 Benjamin R. Curtis	Whig	Massachusetts	1851–1857	41	0
Pierce appointee				
9 John A. Campbell	Democrat	Alabama	1853–1861	41	0
Buchanan appointee				
3 Nathan Clifford	Democrat	Maine	1858–1881[a]	54	0
Lincoln appointees				
7 Noah H. Swayne	Republican	Ohio	1862–1881	57	0
5 Samuel F. Miller	Republican	Iowa	1862–1890[a]	46	0

(Table continues)

321

Table 7-2 *(Continued)*

Seat number and justice	Party	Home state	Years on Court	Age at nomination	Years of previous judicial experience
9 David Davis	Republican	Illinois	1862–1877	47	14
10 Stephen J. Field	Democrat	California	1863–1897	46	6
1 Salmon P. Chase	Republican	Ohio	1864–1873[a]	56	0
Grant appointees					
4 William Strong	Republican	Pennsylvania	1870–1880	61	11
6 Joseph P. Bradley	Republican	New Jersey	1870–1892[a]	56	0
2 Ward Hunt	Republican	New York	1873–1882	62	8
1 Morrison R. Waite	Republican	Ohio	1874–1888[a]	57	0
Hayes appointees					
9 John M. Harlan	Republican	Kentucky	1877–1911[a]	44	1
4 William B. Woods	Republican	Georgia	1880–1887[a]	56	12
Garfield appointee					
7 Stanley Matthews	Republican	Ohio	1881–1889[a]	56	4
Arthur appointees					
3 Horace Gray	Republican	Massachusetts	1881–1902	53	18
2 Samuel Blatchford	Republican	New York	1882–1893[a]	62	15
Cleveland appointees (first term)					
4 Lucius Q. C. Lamar	Democrat	Mississippi	1888–1893[a]	62	0
1 Melville W. Fuller	Democrat	Illinois	1888–1910[a]	55	0
Harrison appointees					
7 David J. Brewer	Republican	Kansas	1889–1910[a]	52	19
5 Henry B. Brown	Republican	Michigan	1891–1906	54	16
6 George Shiras Jr.	Republican	Pennsylvania	1892–1903	60	0
4 Howell E. Jackson	Democrat	Tennessee	1893–1895[a]	60	7

Cleveland appointees (second term)				
2 Edward D. White	Democrat	Louisiana	1894–1910[a]	1.5
4 Rufus W. Peckham	Democrat	New York	1895–1909[a]	9
McKinley appointee				
8 Joseph McKenna	Republican	California	1898–1925	5
T. Roosevelt appointees				
3 Oliver W. Holmes	Republican	Massachusetts	1902–1932	20
6 William R. Day	Republican	Ohio	1903–1922	7
5 William H. Moody	Republican	Massachusetts	1906–1910	0
Taft appointees				
4 Horace H. Lurton	Democrat	Tennessee	1909–1914[a]	26
7 Charles E. Hughes	Republican	New York	1910–1916	0
1 Edward D. White	Democrat	Louisiana	1910–1921[a]	1.5[b]
2 Willis Van Devanter	Republican	Wyoming	1910–1937	8
5 Joseph R. Lamar	Democrat	Georgia	1910–1916[a]	2
9 Mahlon Pitney	Republican	New Jersey	1912–1922	11
Wilson appointees				
4 James C. McReynolds	Democrat	Tennessee	1914–1941	0
5 Louis D. Brandeis	Republican	Massachusetts	1916–1939	0
7 John H. Clarke	Democrat	Ohio	1916–1922	2
Harding appointees				
1 William H. Taft	Republican	Ohio	1921–1930	13
7 George Sutherland	Republican	Utah	1922–1938	0
6 Pierce Butler	Democrat	Minnesota	1923–1939[a]	0
9 Edward T. Sanford	Republican	Tennessee	1923–1930[a]	14
Coolidge appointee				
8 Harlan Fiske Stone	Republican	New York	1925–1941	0

(Table continues)

323

Table 7-2 (*Continued*)

Seat number and justice	Party	Home state	Years on Court	Age at nomination	Years of previous judicial experience
Hoover appointees					
1 Charles E. Hughes	Republican	New York	1930–1941	67	0
9 Owens J. Roberts	Republican	Pennsylvania	1930–1945	55	0
3 Benjamin N. Cardozo	Democrat	New York	1932–1938[a]	61	18
F. Roosevelt appointees					
2 Hugo L. Black	Democrat	Alabama	1937–1971[a]	51	1.5
7 Stanley F. Reed	Democrat	Kentucky	1938–1957	53	0
3 Felix Frankfurter	Independent	Massachusetts	1939–1962	56	0
5 William O. Douglas	Democrat	Connecticut	1939–1975	40	0
6 Frank Murphy	Democrat	Michigan	1940–1949[a]	49	7
4 James F. Byrnes	Democrat	South Carolina	1941–1942	62	0
1 Harlan Fiske Stone	Republican	New York	1941–1946[a]	68	0[b]
8 Robert H. Jackson	Democrat	New York	1941–1954[a]	49	0
4 Wiley B. Rutledge	Democrat	Iowa	1943–1949[a]	48	4
Truman appointees					
9 Harold H. Burton	Republican	Ohio	1945–1958	57	0
1 Fred M. Vinson	Democrat	Kentucky	1946–1953[a]	56	5
6 Tom C. Clark	Democrat	Texas	1949–1967	49	0
4 Sherman Minton	Democrat	Indiana	1949–1956	58	8
Eisenhower appointees					
1 Earl Warren	Republican	California	1953–1969	62	0
8 John M. Harlan	Republican	New York	1955–1971	55	1
4 William J. Brennan	Democrat	New Jersey	1956–1990	50	7
7 Charles E. Whittaker	Republican	Missouri	1957–1962	56	3
9 Potter Stewart	Republican	Ohio	1958–1981	43	4

Kennedy appointees				
7 Byron R. White	Democrat	Colorado	1962–1993	44	0
3 Arthur J. Goldberg	Democrat	Illinois	1962–1965	54	0
L. Johnson appointees				
3 Abe Fortas	Democrat	Tennessee	1965–1969	55	0
6 Thurgood Marshall	Democrat	New York	1967–1991	59	4
Nixon appointees				
1 Warren E. Burger	Republican	Minnesota	1969–1986	61	13
3 Harry A. Blackmun	Republican	Minnesota	1970–1994	61	11
2 Lewis F. Powell Jr.	Democrat	Virginia	1971–1987	64	0
8 William H. Rehnquist	Republican	Arizona	1971–1986	47	0
Ford appointee				
5 John Paul Stevens	Republican	Illinois	1976–2010	55	5
Reagan appointees				
9 Sandra Day O'Connor	Republican	Arizona	1981–2006	51	6.5
1 William H. Rehnquist	Republican	Arizona	1986–2005[a]	61	0[b]
8 Antonin Scalia	Republican	Illinois	1986–2016[a]	50	4
2 Anthony M. Kennedy	Republican	California	1988–2018	51	12
G. H. W. Bush appointees				
4 David H. Souter	Republican	New Hampshire	1990–2009	50	13
6 Clarence Thomas	Republican	Georgia	1991–	43	1
Clinton appointees				
7 Ruth Bader Ginsburg	Democrat	New York	1993–2020[a]	60	13
3 Stephen G. Breyer	Democrat	Massachusetts	1994–	55	15

(Table continues)

325

Table 7-2 (Continued)

Seat number and justice	Party	Home state	Years on Court	Age at nomination	Years of previous judicial experience
G. W. Bush appointees					
1 John G. Roberts Jr.	Republican	Maryland	2005–	50	2
9 Samuel A. Alito Jr.	Republican	New Jersey	2006–	55	15
Obama appointees					
4 Sonia Sotomayor	Democrat	New York	2009–	54	18
5 Elena Kagan	Democrat	New York	2010–	50	0
Trump appointees					
8 Neil M. Gorsuch	Republican	Colorado	2017–	49	11
2 Brett M. Kavanaugh	Republican	Maryland	2018–	53	12
7 Amy Coney Barrett	Republican	Indiana	2020–	48	3

Note: Seat number 1 is always held by the chief justice of the United States.

[a] Died in office.
[b] Prior to appointment to associate justice.

Sources: U.S. Supreme Court, "Justices 1789 to Present" and "Current Members," www.supremecourt.gov.

Table 7-3 Supreme Court Nominations That Failed

Nominee	Date nomination received in Senate[a]	President	Action
William Paterson[b]	1793	Washington	withdrawn
John Rutledge[c]	1795	Washington	rejected, 10–14
Alexander Wolcott	1811	Madison	rejected, 9–24
John J. Crittenden	1828	J. Q. Adams	postponed
Roger B. Taney[b]	1835	Jackson	postponed
John C. Spencer	1844	Tyler	rejected, 21–26
Reuben H. Walworth	1844	Tyler	withdrawn
Edward King	1844	Tyler	tabled, 29–18
John C. Spencer	1844	Tyler	withdrawn
Reuben H. Walworth	1844	Tyler	motion to consider objected to
Reuben H. Walworth	1844	Tyler	withdrawn
Edward King	1844	Tyler	withdrawn
John M. Read	1845	Tyler	motion to consider unsuccessful
George W. Woodward	1845	Polk	rejected, 20–29
Edward A. Bradford	1852	Fillmore	tabled
George E. Badger	1853	Fillmore	postponed, 26–25
William C. Micou	1853	Fillmore	discharged
Jeremiah S. Black	1861	Buchanan	motions to consider unsuccessful
Henry Stanbery	1866	A. Johnson	no record of action
Ebenezer R. Hoar	1869	Grant	rejected, 24–33
George H. Williams[c]	1873	Grant	withdrawn
Caleb Cushing[c]	1874	Grant	withdrawn
Stanley Matthews[b]	1881	Hayes	postponed
William B. Hornblower	1893	Cleveland	no record of action
William B. Hornblower	1893	Cleveland	rejected, 24–30
Wheeler H. Peckham	1894	Cleveland	rejected, 32–41
Pierce Butler[b]	1922	Harding	no record of action
John J. Parker	1930	Hoover	rejected, 39–41
John Marshall Harlan II[b]	1954	Eisenhower	no record of action
Abe Fortas[c]	1968	L. Johnson	withdrawn
Homer Thornberry	1968	L. Johnson	not acted on
Clement F. Haynsworth Jr.	1969	Nixon	rejected, 45–55
G. Harrold Carswell	1970	Nixon	rejected, 45–51
Robert H. Bork	1987	Reagan	rejected, 42–58
Harriet Miers	2005	G. W. Bush	withdrawn
Merrick Garland	2016	Obama	not acted on

Note: Seven individuals were confirmed but declined to serve: Robert H. Harrison, 1789; William Cushing, 1796; John Jay, 1800; Levi Lincoln, 1811; John Quincy Adams, 1811; William Smith, 1837; Roscoe Conkling, 1882. One person, Edwin Stanton (1869), was confirmed but died before he could take his seat. In 1987, the nomination of Douglas Ginsburg was publicly announced by President Ronald Reagan but was withdrawn before the president formally submitted his nomination to the Senate.

[a] The date of the president's nomination and the date the nomination is received in the Senate are often, but not always, the same.
[b] Later nominated and confirmed (Taney as chief justice). See Table 7-2, this volume.
[c] For chief justice.

Sources: U.S. Senate, *Supreme Court Nominations (1789–present)*, https://www.senate.gov/legislative/nominations/SupremeCourtNominations1789present.htm.

Table 7-4 Characteristics of Federal District and Appellate Court Appointees, Presidents Richard Nixon to Donald Trump (percent)

	Nixon appointees	Ford appointees	Carter appointees	Reagan appointees	G. H. W. Bush appointees	Clinton appointees	G. W. Bush appointees	Obama appointees	Trump appointees
District courts									
Occupation									
Politics/government	10.6	21.2	5.0	13.4	10.8	11.5	13.4	18.7	—
Judiciary	28.5	34.6	44.6	36.9	41.9	48.2	48.3	43.7	—
Large law firm[a]	11.2	9.6	13.9	17.9	25.7	16.1	18.8	16.1	—
Moderate law firm[a]	27.9	25.0	19.3	19.0	14.9	13.4	10.0	12.3	—
Small/solo law firm[a]	19.0	9.6	13.9	10.0	4.7	8.2	6.1	6.8	—
Other	2.8	0.0	3.5	2.8	2.0	2.6	3.4	2.6	—
Experience									
Judicial	35.2	42.3	54.0	46.2	46.6	52.1	52.1	47.0	—
Prosecutorial	41.9	50.0	38.1	44.1	39.2	41.3	47.1	42.9	—
Neither	36.3	30.8	31.2	28.6	31.8	28.9	24.9	30.6	—
Immediate prior position									
Judge	—	—	—	—	—	—	—	—	37.3
Federal or state government	—	—	—	—	—	—	—	—	19.7
Private practice	—	—	—	—	—	—	—	—	39.5
Other (usually academic)	—	—	—	—	—	—	—	—	3.4
Political affiliation									
Democrat	7.3	21.2	91.1	4.8	6.1	87.5	8	79.5	—
Republican	92.7	78.8	4.5	91.7	88.5	6.2	83.1	7.5	—
Independent or other	0.0	0.0	4.5	3.4	5.4	6.2	8.8	13.1	—
Past party activism	48.6	50.0	61.4	60.3	64.2	50.2	52.5	50.0	—
Religion									
Protestant	73.2	73.1	60.4	60.3	64.2	—	—	—	—
Catholic	18.4	17.3	27.7	30.0	28.4	—	—	—	—
Jewish	8.4	9.6	11.9	9.3	7.4	—	—	—	—

Race/ethnicity									
White	95.5	88.5	78.2	92.4	89.2	75.1	81.2	63.4	88.1
Black	3.4	5.8	13.9	2.1	6.8	17.4	6.9	19.0	5.7
Asian American	0.0	3.9	0.5	0.7	0.0	1.3	1.5	6.0	2.3
Hispanic	1.1	1.9	6.9	4.8	4.0	5.9	10.3	11.2	4.0
Native American	—	—	0.5	0.0	0.0	0.3	0.0	0.4	0.0
Sex									
Women	0.6	1.9	14.4	8.3	19.6	28.5	20.7	41.0	23.2
Number of appointees	179	52	202	290	148	305	261	268	177
Courts of appeals[b]									
Occupation									
Politics/government	4.4	8.3	5.4	6.4	10.8	6.6	18.6	8.3	—
Judiciary	53.3	75.0	46.4	55.1	59.5	52.5	49.1	60.4	—
Large law firm[a]	4.4	8.3	10.7	14.1	16.2	18.0	11.9	14.6	—
Moderate law firm[a]	22.2	8.3	16.1	9.0	10.8	13.1	6.8	4.2	—
Small/solo law firm[a]	6.7	0.0	5.4	1.3	0.0	1.6	3.4	0.0	—
Other	8.9	0.0	16.1	14.1	2.7	8.2	10.2	12.5	—
Experience									
Judicial	57.8	75.0	53.6	60.3	62.2	59.0	61.0	60.4	—
Prosecutorial	46.7	25.0	30.4	28.2	29.7	37.7	33.9	52.1	—
Neither	17.8	25.0	39.3	34.6	32.4	29.5	25.4	22.9	—
Immediate prior position									
Judge	—	—	—	—	—	—	—	—	42.6
Federal or state government	—	—	—	—	—	—	—	—	24.1
Private practice	—	—	—	—	—	—	—	—	29.6
Other (usually academic)	—	—	—	—	—	—	—	—	3.7

(Table continues)

329

Table 7-4 *(Continued)*

	Nixon appointees	Ford appointees	Carter appointees	Reagan appointees	G. H. W. Bush appointees	Clinton appointees	G. W. Bush appointees	Obama appointees	Trump appointees
Political affiliation									
Democrat	6.7	8.3	82.1	0.0	2.7	85.2	6.8	87.5	—
Republican	93.3	91.7	7.1	96.2	89.2	6.6	91.5	0.0	—
Independent or other	0.0	0.0	10.7	3.8	8.1	8.2	1.7	12.5	—
Past party activism	60.0	58.3	73.2	66.7	70.3	54.1	67.8	45.8	—
Religion									
Protestant	75.6	58.3	60.7	55.1	59.4	—	84.7	—	87.0
Catholic	15.6	33.3	23.2	30.8	24.3	—	10.2	—	0.0
Jewish	8.9	8.3	16.1	14.1	16.3	—	5.1	—	11.0
Race/ethnicity									
White	97.8	100.0	78.6	97.4	89.2	73.8	84.7	66.7	87.0
Black	0.0	0.0	16.1	1.3	5.4	13.1	10.2	18.8	0.0
Asian American	2.2	0.0	1.8	0.0	0.0	1.6	0.0	6.3	11.0
Hispanic	0.0	0.0	3.6	1.3	5.4	11.5	5.1	8.3	2.0
Sex									
Women	0.0	0.0	19.6	5.1	18.9	32.8	25.4	45.8	19.0
Number of appointees	45	12	56	78	37	61	59	48	54

Note: "—" indicates not available. Statistics are for lifetime appointments to courts of general jurisdiction. Data for earlier years can be found in previous editions of *Vital Statistics on American Politics*.

[a] Large law firm: twenty-five or more partners and associates; moderate: five to twenty-four; small: two to four.
[b] Two recess appointments by Presidents G. W. Bush and Clinton are not included in these statistics.

Sources: Sheldon Goldman, "Bush's Judicial Legacy: The Final Imprint," *Judicature* 76 (April–May 1993): 287, 293; Elliot Slotnick, Sara Schiavoni, and Sheldon Goldman, "Obama's Judicial Legacy: The Final Chapter," *Journal of Law and Courts* 5, no. 2 (Fall 2017): 363–422; Russell Wheeler, Visiting Fellow, Government Studies, Brookings Institute, personal correspondence.

> ## A Data Literacy Lesson
>
> ### Judicial Characteristics
>
> If you were to track down the data sources throughout this book, in some instances you would find nearly identical information from the original source. In those cases, the data already exist compiled in the way we have presented it. In other instances, you would find that we've combined information from more than one source, or done calculations from existing data, or both. In some cases, such as in Table 7-4, we have relied on data tables that exist because they have been compiled from many sources by scholars.
>
> Experts provide commentary, analysis, and interpretation in articles and books, which is widely recognized as a scholarly contribution. But, the act of collecting data and putting it into the public realm is an act of scholarship in and of itself. The data that scholars collect and make available are valuable contributions for other scholars to analyze, interpret, and continue to add to our collective understanding of a field.
>
> The information presented in Table 7-4 provides an extensive overview of the characteristics of federal court appointees and is based on a decades-long project from judicial scholars. As you look at the source information, you can see that the information from presidents Nixon through Obama is from articles by Sheldon Goldman, Elliot Slotnick, and Sara Schiavoni. This table of numbers represents hours and years of investigation, including, among other techniques: personal interviews with staffers at the White House, Senate, and Department of Justice; reviewing questionnaires completed by nominees for the Senate Judiciary Committee; and reviewing media reports and Board of Elections data.
>
> From that investigation, we have a great deal of information about characteristics such as the prior political affiliation and experiences of judges, which is not often publicly shared as judges strive to maintain an air of being "apolitical." We also have information about judges' experience not just in the judiciary but as prosecutors and in politics. All of this can be used by other scholars to investigate their own questions about whether and how the characteristics of federal judges have changed over time, and how they affect judicial outcomes. However, after the Obama administration much of the information is simply not available because that project has ended.
>
> We have provided some information on the judicial appointees of the Trump administration by turning to Russell Wheeler, another judicial expert who compiles related (but not identical) information. His techniques are different, and so the categories of information available to us do not align exactly with the data that were available for previous administrations.
>
> Some of the "missing" information can be tracked down by turning to a variety of different agencies and organizations. But, some of the information is simply not available without a scholar, or group of scholars, who turn their attention to asking similar questions in similar ways, and dedicating their efforts to making that information widely available.
>
> We have less information about judicial characteristics about the Trump administration's appointees than for previous administrations because it's simply

no longer available. Over time, as scholars' interests in judicial characteristics change and grow, the information that we present in data tables will reflect those changes.

Table 7-5 Federal Judicial Appointments of Same Party as President, Presidents Grover Cleveland to Barack Obama

President	Party	Percentage
Cleveland	Democratic	97.3
Harrison	Republican	87.9
McKinley	Republican	95.7
T. Roosevelt	Republican	95.8
Taft	Republican	82.2
Wilson	Democratic	98.6
Harding	Republican	97.7
Coolidge	Republican	94.1
Hoover	Republican	85.7
F. Roosevelt	Democratic	96.4
Truman	Democratic	93.1
Eisenhower	Republican	95.1
Kennedy	Democratic	90.9
L. Johnson	Democratic	94.5
Nixon	Republican	92.8
Ford	Republican	81.2
Carter	Democratic	89.1
Reagan	Republican	92.7
G. H. W. Bush	Republican	88.6
Clinton	Democratic	87.2
G. W. Bush	Republican	84.7
Obama	Democratic	80.7

Sources: Cleveland–Kennedy: Henry J. Abraham, *Justices, Presidents, and Senators: A History of U.S. Supreme Court Appointments from Washington to Bush II*, 5th ed. (Lanham, MD: Rowman and Littlefield, 2008), 54; L. Johnson–Obama: calculated from Table 7-4, this volume, and previous editions of *Vital Statistics on American Politics*.

Table 7-6 Percent of U.S. Circuit and District Court Nominees Confirmed, 1977–2019

President	Congress	Senate controlled by same party	Number of Circuit Court nominations	Percentage Circuit Court confirmed	Number of District Court nominations	Percentage District Court appointed	Number of Supreme Court nominations	Percentage Supreme Court appointed
Carter	95th	Yes	12	100.0	50	96.0	—	—
Carter	96th	Yes	48	91.7	216	91.7	—	—
Reagan	97th	Yes	20	95.0	69	98.6	1	100.0
Reagan	98th	Yes	19	73.7	75	81.3	2	100.0
Reagan	99th	Yes	33	100.0	100	95.0	2	50.0
Reagan	100th	No	26	65.4	78	84.6	—	—
G. H. W. Bush	101st	No	23	95.7	50	96.0	1	100.0
G. H. W. Bush	102nd	No	31	64.5	144	69.4	1	100.0
Clinton	103rd	Yes	22	86.4	118	90.7	2	100.0
Clinton	104th	No	20	55.0	85	72.9	—	—
Clinton	105th	No	30	66.7	94	84.0	—	—
Clinton	106th	No	34	44.1	83	68.7	—	—
G. W. Bush	107th	[a]	32	53.1	98	84.7	—	—
G. W. Bush	108th	Yes	34	52.9	94	90.4	—	—
G. W. Bush	109th	Yes	28	57.1	65	53.8	4[c]	50.0
G. W. Bush	110th	No[b]	23	43.5	79	73.4	—	—
Obama	111th	Yes	25	64.0	78	56.4	2	100.0
Obama	112th	Yes	25	56.0	127	76.4	—	—
Obama	113th	Yes	26	88.5	123	88.6	—	—
Obama	114th	No	9	22.2	61	29.5	1	0.0
Trump	115th	Yes	43	69.8	112	47.3	2	100.0
Trump	116th	Yes	—	—	—	—	1	100.0

[a] Control of the Senate was primarily with the Democratic Party with the exception of January 21, 2001, when Vice President Al Gore left office, through May 23, 2001. On May 24, 2001, Senator Jim Jeffords left the Republican Party and began caucusing with the Democratic Party, giving that party control of the Senate.

[b] While there were 49 Democrats and 49 Republicans, two Independent senators caucused with the Democratic Party.

[c] John Roberts, Jr. was originally nominated to fill Sandra Day O'Connor's seat but his nomination was withdrawn and resubmitted to fill the Chief Justice position after William Rehnquist's death. Harriet Miers was subsequently nominated for Justice O'Connor's seat but her nomination was withdrawn. The seat was eventually filled by Justice Samuel Alito.

Sources: Congressional Research Service (2019) *Judicial Nomination Statistics and Analysis: U.S. District and Circuit Courts 1977–2018*, (2019), Table 3, https://crsreports.congress.gov/product/pdf/R/R45622; U.S. Senate, *Supreme Court Nominations (1789–Present)*, https://www.senate.gov/legislative/nominations/SupremeCourtNominations1789present.htm.

> ## A Data Literacy Lesson
>
> ### Political Implications of Confirmations
>
> Historically, the judiciary was presented as the apolitical branch of the federal government. Judges and justices were portrayed as above the fray of political battles, a neutral arbiter. Chief Justice John Roberts famously compared the judiciary's role to that of umpires, who are there to "call balls and strikes" rather than play in the game of politics. The Court's expressed desire not to intrude upon the "political thicket," as expressed in the reapportionment case of *Baker v. Carr* (1962), also speaks to this point.
>
> The role of the judiciary in the political system is, of course, more complex than the neutral umpire analogy would suggest. There are many studies in the field of judicial politics that examine the political effects of the courts on shaping policy and public opinion. We also note from the data in Table 7-6 that the influences of the political climate can shape the judiciary itself.
>
> Article III of the U.S. Constitution gives the Senate the power to vote on presidents' nominees to the judicial branch. The fate of the "apolitical" federal judiciary, then, rests in the hands of the political legislative branch. There are two questions we think are interesting to explore in this table.
>
> First, we wonder if there is a difference in presidents' success in having their nominations approved when the Senate is controlled by the same party. More sophisticated analyses exist to gauge this relationship, such as Sheldon Goldman's Index of Obstruction and Delay, but we think even a simple comparison offers some preliminary insights. For example, if we explore what percentage of Circuit Court nominees were confirmed, we note that the mean confirmation rate was more than 20 points greater in unified Congresses than in divided. The discrepancy is smaller for District Court nomination, but the mean confirmation rate is still nearly seven points higher when the Senate was controlled by the same party as the president. This suggests that there is an observable effect of divided government on judicial nominees' relative success. (Incidentally, this also highlights how preliminary observations in data can lead to further questions for research, such as why the effect is so much greater for Circuit Court nominations than for District Court nominations.)
>
> | | Circuit Court | District Court |
> | --- | --- | --- |
> | Same Party Control | mean 77.93% confirmed | mean 80.52% confirmed |
> | Different Party Control | mean 56.69% confirmed | mean 73.69% confirmed |
>
> The second question that comes to mind as we look at this table is whether there are trends over time that mirror political trends. There has been a great deal of discussion, including in the essays in this book, about growing polarization in our political system. Do the data in this table support the idea that polarization has affected judicial nominees' success? We think this is a worthwhile question, but one

that can't be answered fully by this table. It's important to remember that sometimes questions (and answers) are more complex than can be resolved with one data source. Too often we've seen politicians, pundits, and the public try to shoehorn data to make a claim without adequate support.

Here, for example, as we look over time we could make the case that, on average, the last five sessions of Congress for which we have data had lower success rates for Circuit Court nominees (60 percent) than the first five sessions in this table (92 percent). But, we then note that the first five sessions all were of the same party as the president, while the last five sessions included one where the Senate was controlled by the opposition party. We also note that the 114th was an outlier in the striking lack of success, and the reasons for that cannot be answered by these data. We don't know from this table how many of those nominations were never brought to a vote, and whether these lower percentages mirror an overall decrease in Senate actions over time. Depending on your interest, these are all questions that can be explored elsewhere.

While the picture of the judiciary as an apolitical branch is an appealing one, the reality is that there are myriad ways in which the courts shape the political system and the political system shapes the courts. Tables such as 7-6 can help us begin to understand some, but certainly not all, of the implications of that.

Table 7-7 Caseload of the U.S. Supreme Court, 1970–2019 Terms

Action	1970	1975	1980	1985	1990	1995	2000	2005	2010	2015	2016	2017	2018	2019
Paid cases on docket	1,903	2,352	2,749	2,571	2,351	2,456	2,305	2,025	1,895	1,839	1,850	2,062	1,910	1,818
From prior term	325	431	527	400	365	361	351	354	337	293	300	345	322	327
Docketed during present term	1,578	1,921	2,222	2,171	1,986	2,095	1,954	1,671	1,558	1,546	1,550	1,718	1,593	1,478
Cases acted upon[a]	1,613	1,900	2,324	2,185	2,042	2,130	2,024	1,703	—	—	—	—	—	—
Granted review	214	244	167	166	114	92	85	63	76	66	69	69	74	56
Denied, dismissed, or withdrawn	1,285	1,538	1,999	1,863	1,802	1,945	1,842	1,554	—	—	—	—	—	—
Summarily decided	114	118	90	78	81	62	63	46	—	—	—	—	—	—
Cases not acted upon	290	452	425	386	309	326	281	322	—	—	—	—	—	—
In forma pauperis cases on docket	2,289	2,395	2,371	2,577	3,951	5,098	6,651	7,575	7,167	5,688	5,477	5,320	5,703	4,703
Cases acted upon[a]	1,802	1,997	2,027	2,189	3,436	4,514	5,736	6,533	—	—	—	—	—	—
Granted review	41	28	17	20	27	13	14	15	14	12	5	8	9	4
Denied, dismissed, or withdrawn	1,683	1,903	1,968	2,136	3,369	4,439	5,658	6,459	—	—	—	—	—	—
Summarily decided	78	66	32	24	28	55	61	58	—	—	—	—	—	—
Cases not acted upon	487	398	344	388	515	584	915	1,042	—	—	—	—	—	—
Original cases on docket	20	14	24	10	14	11	9	8	4	8	7	8	9	10
Cases disposed of during term	7	7	7	2	3	5	1	4	2	1	1	1	2	2
Total cases available for argument	267	280	264	276	201	145	138	122	—	—	—	—	—	—
Cases disposed of	160	181	162	175	131	93	89	88	—	—	—	—	—	—
Cases argued	151	179	154	171	125	90	86	90	86	82	71	69	73	73
Cases dismissed or remanded without argument	9	2	8	4	6	3	3	1	2	1	5	5	2	1
Cases remaining	107	99	102	101	70	52	49	31	43	31	32	38	38	51

Cases decided by signed opinion	126	160	144	161	121	87	83	82	83	70	68	63	69
Cases decided per curiam opinion	22	16	8	10	4	3	4	5	3	12	1	6	2	4
Number of signed opinions	109	138	123	146	112	75	77	69	75	62	61	59	66	53
Total cases on docket	4,212	4,761	5,144	5,158	6,316	7,565	8,965	9,608	9,066	7,535	7,334	7,390	7,622	6,534

Note: "—" indicates not available. The Supreme Court begins its regular annual session on the first Monday in October. This session, known as the October term, lasts about nine months. The year shown indicates when the term began. These data were previously provided by the Supreme Court in its unpublished statistical sheets. Beginning with the 2007 term, the Court no longer provides these statistical sheets to the public. Data for additional years can be found in previous editions of *Vital Statistics on American Politics*.

[a] For 1980–2005, includes cases granted review and carried over to next term, not shown separately.

Sources: 1970–1980: U.S. Bureau of the Census, *Statistical Abstract of the United States, 1977* (Washington, D.C.: Government Printing Office, 1976), 184; 1987: 168; 1985–2005: *The United States Law Week* (Washington, D.C.: Bureau of National Affairs), vol. 56, 3102; vol. 61, 3098; vol. 65, 3100; vol. 71, 3080; vol. 76, 3016; 2010–2019: *Journal of the Supreme Court of the United States*, October Term 2010, ii; June 29, 2011, October Term 2015, ii, June 28, 2016; October Term 2016, ii, June 28, 2017; October Term 2017, ii, June 29, 2018, October Term 2018, ii, June 28, 2019; October Term 2019, ii, July 9, 2020, https://www.supremecourt.gov/orders/journal.aspx.

> ## A Data Literacy Lesson
>
> ### A Case's Path to the Supreme Court
>
> "I'll take this all the way to the Supreme Court!" We've heard countless instances of characters in popular culture indicating their commitment to fight something to the bitter end with some version of this statement, with an end goal of having a dispute decided by the Supreme Court. In reality, the path to having a case heard by the highest court in the land is far more complicated than simply having a commitment to the cause and the willingness to fight for it.
>
> As you likely learned in an American Politics course, there are rules about what types of cases the Supreme Court can and cannot hear—that is, where they have jurisdiction. Even within those cases where the Court does have jurisdiction, it is still up to the determination of the justices whether they will grant *certiorari*, or decide to hear it.
>
> A closer look at the data in Table 7-7 shows the odds of a case making it "all the way to the Supreme Court." While the number of petitions has changed over the years, over the past five years an average of over 7,000 cases are placed on the docket each year. Of those, a majority are filed in *forma pauperis*, or in the form of a pauper, which allows petitioners without financial means to pay for legal fees and Court filings to file a petition at no cost. Nearly all of those cases are not granted review. In 2019, for example, we note that 4,703 in *forma pauperis* cases were on the docket, only four of which (or less than 1/10th of one percent) were granted review. While a higher percentage of paid cases were granted review, still less than 4 percent of the paid cases docketed during the 2019 term were granted review.
>
> Being granted *certiorari* for a case to be heard is clearly not common, regardless of the circumstances that led to the case being filed. And, even once that hurdle has been cleared, and *certiorari* is granted, there is no guarantee that a case will move through the Court quickly. We note that each year hundreds of cases remain on the docket from the prior year. At the same time, the number of cases argued has decreased fairly steadily over the past fifty years. Prior to 1995, the Court heard oral arguments in between 125 and 179 cases each term. In 1995, that dipped below 100 cases for the first time and is now regularly below 75 cases per term.
>
> A table of data like this cannot answer the complex questions about why the number of cases argued has gone down, even as the number of cases on the docket has remained steady or even increased, nor can it tell us anything about the kinds of cases the Court does hear. However, a table like this can be useful as part of a larger exploration of what changes have occurred over time, and for understanding the likelihood of a case being heard by the Court in a given year.
>
> As we can clearly see in this table, having a case heard by the Supreme Court is increasingly rare, and often slow. The promise to "take this all the way to the Supreme Court" may be sincerely uttered, but these words are generally an unrealistic threat.

Figure 7-3 Cases Filed in U.S. Supreme Court, 1880–2019 Terms

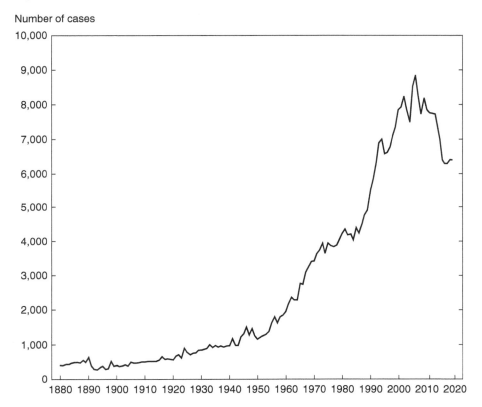

Note: Number of cases filed in term starting in year indicated.

Sources: 1880–2004: Lee Epstein, Jeffrey A. Segal, Harold J. Spaeth, and Thomas G. Walker, *The Supreme Court Compendium: Data, Decisions, and Developments*, 4th ed. (Washington, D.C.: CQ Press, 2007), 62–67; 2005–2013: U.S. Supreme Court, "2006 Year-End Report on the Federal Judiciary," January 1, 2007; "2008," December 31, 2008; "2010," December 31, 2010; "2012," December 31, 2012; "2014," December 31, 2014; "2016," December 31, 2016; "2018," December 31, 2018; "2020," December 31, 2020, www.supremecourtus.gov.

Table 7-8 Caseload of U.S. Courts of Appeals, 2000–2020

	2000	2005	2010	2015	2016	2017	2018	2019	2020
Number of judgeships	167	167	167	167	167	167	167	167	167
Number of sitting senior judges	81	90	88	90	85	92	98	99	100
Number of vacant judgeship months	278.9	165.6	212.3	87.6	114.2	222.4	210.2	142.1	18.7
Appeals filed									
Prisoner	17,252	17,034	15,789	13,900	13,551	14,317	13,475	12,365	11,738
All other civil	23,501	21,666	19,593	20,277	28,801	20,119	19,920	20,191	19,679
Criminal	10,707	16,060	12,797	11,380	11,536	9,917	9,792	10,001	9,668
Administrative	3,237	13,713	7,813	7,141	6,469	6,153	6,089	5,929	7,105
Total	54,697	68,473	55,992	52,698	60,357	50,506	49,276	48,486	48,190
Appeals terminated									
Consolidations and cross appeals	2,740	2,317	2,379	2,788	2,836	2,556	2,381	2,458	2,818
Procedural	26,256	29,745	26,233	18,803	18,361	17,230	16,639	15,693	15,411
On the merits									
Prisoner	5,328	4,435	4,669	8,870	8,010	9,056	8,747	7,777	7,265
All other civil	13,497	12,443	11,025	12,132	17,707	15,192	12,549	12,209	12,311
Criminal	7,236	8,614	9,842	7,770	7,598	7,652	7,000	6,733	7,208
Administrative	1,455	4,421	5,378	2,850	3,232	2,661	3,112	3,019	3,287
Total on the merits	27,516	29,913	30,914	31,622	36,547	34,561	31,408	29,738	30,071
Total	56,512	61,975	59,526	53,213	57,744	54,347	50,428	47,889	48,300
Pending appeals	40,410	57,724	46,351	40,806	43,275	39,400	38,232	38,837	38,731
Per active judge[a]									
Termination on the merits	458	457	463	463	565	502	453	433	427
Procedural terminations	168	170	161	71	78	68	61	57	61

Note: "—" indicates not available. Data are for the twelve-month period ending on September 30. Data for additional years can be found in previous editions of *Vital Statistics on American Politics*.

[a] Includes only judges active during the entire twelve-month period.

Sources: 2000: 2001, 31; 2005–2020: Administrative Office of the United States Courts, www.uscourts.gov.

Table 7-9 Caseload of U.S. District Courts, 2000–2020

	2000	2005	2010	2015	2016	2017	2018	2019	2020
Overall									
Filings	310,346	330,721	394,345	347,822	387,687	365,084	391,345	412,337	562,342
Terminations	306,211	347,196	419,178	369,720	365,842	384,840	375,480	418,643	360,273
Pending	290,167	323,914	377,952	426,042	446,051	425,162	465,787	456,827	656,897
Number (and percentage) of civil cases over three years old	30,434 (12.2)	39,600 (14.9)	45,010 (15.8)	34,377 (10.1)	53,162 (14.7)	57,155 (16.9)	73,938 (19.8)	56,356 (15.8)	53,600 (9.6)
Number of judgeships	655	678	678	677	677	677	677	677	677
Vacant judgeship months	597.5	309.2	964.1	550.6	762.1	1266.8	1541.3	1493.4	928.8
Per judgeship									
Civil filings	396	374	417	412	431	396	418	440	695
Criminal felony filings	78	87	130	105	104	104	119	128	103
Total filings	474	488	582	554	573	539	578	609	831
Pending cases	443	478	557	629	659	628	688	675	970
Terminations	467	512	618	546	540	568	555	618	532
Trials completed	22	19	20	17	17	16	16	17	12
Median time from filing to disposition (months)									
Criminal felony	6.5	7.3	6.9	7.6	7.5	7.6	7.0	7.0	7.2
Civil	8.2	9.5	7.6	8.8	9.2	9.9	9.2	10.8	8.9
Median time from filing to trial (months)									
Civil only[a]	20	23	24	26.8	27	26.3	27.3	27.8	27.1

Note: Data are for the twelve-month period ending on September 30. Data for additional years can be found in previous editions of *Vital Statistics on American Politics*.

[a] Time is computed from the date that the answer or response is filed to the date trial begins.

Sources: Administrative Office of the United States Courts, www.uscourts.gov.

Table 7-10 Civil and Criminal Cases Filed in U.S. District Courts, 1950–2020

Year	Civil cases Commenced	Civil cases Terminated	Criminal cases Commenced	Criminal cases Terminated
1950	44,454	42,482	36,383	37,675
1955	48,308	47,959	35,310	38,990
1960	49,852	48,847	28,137	30,512
1965	67,678	63,137	31,569	33,718
1970	87,321	79,466	38,102	36,356
1975	117,320	103,787	41,108	49,212
1980	168,789	160,481	28,932	29,297
1985	273,670	269,848	39,500	37,139
1990	217,879	213,922	48,904	44,295
1991	207,742	211,713	47,035	41,569
1992	230,509	231,304	48,356	44,147
1993	230,597	227,316	46,098	45,280
1994	238,590	227,015	45,269	44,924
1995	248,335	229,820	45,788	41,527
1996	269,132	250,387	47,889	45,499
1997	272,027	249,641	50,363	46,887
1998	256,787	262,301	57,691	51,428
1999	260,271	272,526	59,923	56,511
2000	259,517	259,637	62,745	58,102
2001	250,907	248,174	62,708	58,718
2002	274,841	259,537	67,000	60,991
2003	252,962	253,015	70,642	65,628
2004	281,338	252,761	71,022	64,621
2005	253,273	271,753	69,575	66,561
2006	259,541	273,193	66,860	67,499
2007	257,507	239,678	68,413	67,851
2008	267,257	234,571	70,896	70,629
2009	276,397	263,703	76,655	75,077
2010	282,895	309,759	78,428	78,069
2011	289,252	303,158	78,440	79,839
2012	278,442	271,572	71,303	74,308
2013	284,604	255,260	68,918	69,279
2014	295,310	258,477	62,722	64,985
2015	279,036	274,627	61,202	61,555
2016	291,851	271,649	59,064	59,365
2017	267,769	289,901	59,788	57,812
2018	282,936	276,311	69,644	63,475
2019	297,877	311,900	75,029	69,122
2020	470,581	271,256	59,884	58,589

Note: Reports vary in the month used. Most are from the period ending on June 30 or September 30 of the year indicated.

Sources: 1950–1975: U.S. Bureau of the Census, *Statistical Abstract of the United States, 1971* (Washington, D.C.: Government Printing Office, 1971), 152; 1976, 168; 1980–1999: Director of the Administrative Office of the United States Courts, *Annual Report of the Director of the Administrative Office of the United States Courts, Judicial Business of the United States Courts 1987* (Washington, D.C.: Government Printing Office, 1987), 7, 13; 1989, 7, 12; 1991, 7, 10; 1992, 4, 6; 1994; 1996; 1998, 16; 1999, 16; 2000–2020, Tables C, D, www.uscourts.gov.

Table 7-11 Types of Civil and Criminal Cases in U.S. District Courts, 2020

Civil cases	Percentage[a]	Criminal cases	Percentage
Contract actions	6.2	Drug offenses	27.5
Recovery of overpayments and enforcements of judgments	0.2	Immigration	36.4
		Fraud	7.4
Insurance	2.6	Traffic offenses	2.0
Other contract actions	3.5	Firearms and explosives	13.3
Tort actions	51.0	Larceny and theft	1.5
Personal injury, not product liability	4.9	Violent Offenses	3.1
		Embezzlement	0.3
Product liability, personal injury	44.9	Forgery and counterfeiting	0.2
Personal property damage	1.0	Justice system offenses (e.g., escape, aiding and abetting, and failure to appear)	0.9
Statutory actions	41.8	Sex offenses	3.6
Prisoner petitions	13.5	Other	3.8
Civil rights	10.0		
Labor laws	3.7		
Social Security	4.3		
Intellectual property rights	2.4		
Bankruptcy	0.5		
Tax suits	0.1		
Other statutory	7.3		
Real property actions	1.4		
Total number of civil cases	421,082	Total number of criminal cases	78,970

Note: Data are for the twelve-month period ending on June 30, 2020. Data for earlier years can be found in previous editions of *Vital Statistics on American Politics*. Categories have changed slightly over the years.

[a] Percentages for subcategories may not sum to the category total due to rounding.

Source: Director of the Administrative Office of the United States Courts, *Annual Report of the Director of the Administrative Office of the United States Courts, Judicial Business of the United States Courts 2020* (Washington, D.C.: Government Printing Office, 2020), Tables C-2, D-2, www.uscourts.gov.

Table 7-12 Federal, State, and Local Laws Declared Unconstitutional by U.S. Supreme Court, by Decade, 1789–2020

Years	Federal	State and local
1789–1799	0	0
1800–1809	1	1
1810–1819	0	7
1820–1829	0	6
1830–1839	0	2
1840–1849	0	7
1850–1859	1	7
1860–1869	4	15
1870–1879	7	36
1880–1889	4	43
1890–1899	5	33
1900–1909	9	39
1910–1919	6	93
1920–1929	15	119
1930–1939	13	77
1940–1949	2	48
1950–1959	4	47
1960–1969	18	125
1970–1979	19	174
1980–1989	16	116
1990–1999	24	49
2000–2009	16	27
2010–2020	24	39
Total	188	1,110

Sources: Lawrence Baum, *The Supreme Court, 14th ed.* (Washington, D.C.: CQ Press, 2022); Lawrence Baum, Department of Political Science, The Ohio State University, personal communication.

Figure 7-4 Economic and Civil Liberties Laws Overturned by U.S. Supreme Court, by Decade, 1900–2020

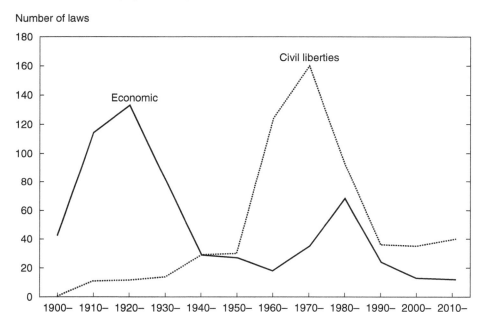

Note: Civil liberties category does not include laws supportive of civil liberties. Laws include federal, state, and local. State and local cases include those in which the Court held that a state law was preempted by federal law.

Source: Lawrence Baum, Department of Political Science, The Ohio State University, personal communication.

8
Federalism

- **Historical Data**
- **State Constitutional Provisions**
- **States and the Federal Constitution**
- **State and Local Governments and Employees**
- **Revenues and Spending**
- **Personal Income**
- **Intergovernmental Revenue Flows**

One salient feature about American government is the federalist system, in which power is shared between the national, state, and local governments. This presents its share of challenges—consider, for example, how many different layers of government have their hands in policies on education, including the local government (through elected school boards), the state government (which sets the curriculum, and provides much of the funding), and the national government, whose laws such as Title IX (of the Education Amendments of 1972) and No Child Left Behind (2001) affect the daily functioning of public schools. It also, however, provides opportunities for policy experimentation; states (or local governments), in essence, can be policy laboratories, trying out policy at a smaller level to evaluate its potential effectiveness on a larger scale.

For scholars wishing to compare salient features across different states, one could look at the different term lengths, term limits, and powers (such as the line-item veto) of the governors of each state. One could also compare aspects of the state legislatures, including their salaries and length of sessions, to determine how "professional" each one of them is. We could also compare the states based upon the extent to which they have adopted progressive-era reforms, including the ability for citizens to legislate through initiatives and referenda.

Another important aspect of federalism concerns fiscal issues, including the relative sizes of federal, state, and local governments, and issues of where each of these governments spend money. We might compare surpluses and deficits across the different states, or also compare sources of revenue (such as lottery revenue), or economic issues in the states, such as through disposal of personal income. As much of federalism is fiscal, a researcher might be interested in studying the historical patterns of federal aid to states and local governments, and the variations in how dependent states are on federal money, and local governments are on state money.

Data to address each of these questions are included in this chapter as a starting point for readers interested in exploring further these aspects of federalism. Studying American government below the federal level is challenging, as the large number of governments often makes it difficult for researchers to procure accurate, up-to-date information about all the relevant jurisdictions. If the researcher were satisfied with state-level data, they could turn to each of the fifty state capitals (fifty-one units if data about the District of Columbia are needed, or even more if Puerto Rico and territories such as the Northern Mariana Islands are included). However, if the researcher wants to study counties, or cities, or school districts, or other such entities, the data collection challenges escalate quickly, far beyond the capacity of any one person.

Fortunately, organizations and publications devoted to data collection have stepped up to the challenge. Some organizations, such as the Council of State Governments and the International City Management Association, are well established. The Council of State Governments has published *The Book of the States* since 1935, and the International City Management Association has issued *The Municipal Year Book* since 1934. Other sources are newer, such as the magazine *GOVERNING*, which began publication in 1987. Such groups and publications make data collection far easier and more systematic, and they ensure higher quality than in the past. The researcher can thus take what we offer here as a starting point, and fairly expeditiously move on and learn more.

Even when data are available, a researcher can still be frustrated (as we have been!) by the inevitable variety that occurs across units. Simple tables or one-sentence summaries are often inadequate. In studying state and local governments, their interrelationships, and their relations with the federal government, a scholar must pay attention to details. Even more than usual, it is essential to read notes and check several sources. Differences in data collection procedures, the timing of data collection, and variations in the detail of reports all become important. The user must also keep in mind the purpose of examining the data. It takes a careful researcher to know when variations can be ignored and when they become so frequent or so large that they must be an explicit part of the analysis.

Despite improvements in data collection, states and localities must be approached directly for some information. Fortunately, this approach, too, has become easier because the many searchable website directories now available provide the names of specific individuals and offices, typically with addresses, phone numbers, and email addresses. Although the availability of such sources will still not make a project involving twenty-five or fifty states easy, at least one can gather missing information or exact details about specific states and localities. We personally have benefitted from the generosity of experts in the field, who offered us their guidance.

As the tables in this chapter demonstrate, students as well as professionals now have access to systematic information about all fifty states and increasingly about localities. Although users may have to make an extra effort to absorb all the details provided by these tables, the rewards for doing so are well worth the challenges inherent in the task.

Table 8-1 The States: Historical Data

State	Date organized as territory	Date admitted to Union	Chronological order of admissions to Union
Alabama	March 3, 1817	December 14, 1819	22
Alaska	August 24, 1912	January 3, 1959	49
Arizona	February 24, 1863	February 14, 1912	48
Arkansas	March 2, 1819	June 15, 1836	25
California	a	September 9, 1850	31
Colorado	February 28, 1861	August 1, 1876	38
Connecticut	—	January 9, 1788[b]	5
Delaware	—	December 7, 1787[b]	1
Florida	March 30, 1822	March 3, 1845	27
Georgia	—	January 2, 1788[b]	4
Hawaii	June 14, 1900	August 21, 1959	50
Idaho	March 4, 1863	July 3, 1890	43
Illinois	February 3, 1809	December 3, 1818	21
Indiana	May 7, 1800	December 11, 1816	19
Iowa	June 12, 1838	December 28, 1846	29
Kansas	May 30, 1854	January 29, 1861	34
Kentucky	a	June 1, 1792	15
Louisiana	March 26, 1804	April 30, 1812	18
Maine	a	March 15, 1820	23
Maryland	—	April 28, 1788[b]	7
Massachusetts	—	February 6, 1788[b]	6
Michigan	January 11, 1805	January 26, 1837	26
Minnesota	March 3, 1849	May 11, 1858	32
Mississippi	April 7, 1798	December 10, 1817	20
Missouri	June 4, 1812	August 10, 1821	24
Montana	May 26, 1864	November 8, 1889	41

(Table continues)

Table 8-1 *(Continued)*

State	Date organized as territory	Date admitted to Union	Chronological order of admissions to Union
Nebraska	May 30, 1854	March 1, 1867	37
Nevada	March 2, 1861	October 31, 1864	36
New Hampshire	—	June 21, 1788[b]	9
New Jersey	—	December 18, 1787[b]	3
New Mexico	September 9, 1850	January 6, 1912	47
New York	—	July 26, 1788[b]	11
North Carolina	—	November 21, 1789[b]	12
North Dakota	March 2, 1861	November 2, 1889	39
Ohio	May 7, 1800	March 1, 1803	17
Oklahoma	May 2, 1890	November 17, 1907	46
Oregon	August 14, 1848	February 14, 1859	33
Pennsylvania	—	December 12, 1787[b]	2
Rhode Island	—	May 29, 1790[b]	13
South Carolina	—	May 23, 1788[b]	8
South Dakota	March 2, 1861	November 2, 1889	40
Tennessee	June 8, 1790[c]	June 1, 1796	16
Texas	[a]	December 29, 1845	28
Utah	September 9, 1850	January 4, 1896	45
Vermont	[a]	March 4, 1791	14
Virginia	—	June 25, 1788[b]	10
Washington	March 2, 1853	November 11, 1889	42
West Virginia	[a]	June 20, 1863	35
Wisconsin	April 20, 1836	May 29, 1848	30
Wyoming	July 25, 1868	July 10, 1890	44

Note: "—" indicates one of the original thirteen states.

[a] No territorial status before admission to Union.
[b] Date of ratification of U.S. Constitution.
[c] Date Southwest Territory (boundaries identical to Tennessee's) was created.

Source: Council of State Governments, *The Book of the States, 2014* (Lexington, Ky.: Council of State Governments, 2014), 505–506.

Table 8-2 State Constitutions

State	Number of constitutions[a]	Dates of adoption	Present constitution Effective date	Estimated length (number of words)	Number of amendments Submitted to voters	Adopted
Alabama	6	1819, 1861, 1865, 1868, 1875, 1901	November 28, 1901	402,852	1,280	946
Alaska	1	1956	January 3, 1959	13,479	43	29
Arizona	1	1911	February 14, 1912	47,306	280	156
Arkansas	5	1836, 1861, 1864, 1868, 1874	October 30, 1874	59,120	208	108[b]
California	2	1849, 1879	July 4, 1879	76,930	909	538
Colorado	1	1876	August 1, 1876	84,239	355	164
Connecticut	2	1818, 1965	December 30, 1965	16,401	35	33
Delaware	4	1776, 1792, 1831, 1897	June 10, 1897	25,445	[c]	150
Florida	6	1839, 1861, 1865, 1868, 1886, 1968	January 7, 1969	49,230	185	137
Georgia	10	1777, 1789, 1798, 1861, 1865, 1868, 1877, 1945, 1976, 1982	July 1, 1983	41,684	107	83
Hawaii	1	1950	August 21, 1959	21,498	140	114
Idaho	1	1889	July 3, 1890	24,626	214	126
Illinois	4	1818, 1848, 1870, 1970	July 1, 1971	16,401	22	15
Indiana	2	1816, 1851	November 1, 1851	11,610	81	49
Iowa	2	1846, 1857	September 3, 1857	11,089	59	54[d]
Kansas	1	1859	January 29, 1861	14,097	128	98
Kentucky	4	1792, 1799, 1850, 1891	September 28, 1891	27,234	76	42
Louisiana	11	1812, 1845, 1852, 1861, 1864, 1868, 1879, 1898, 1913, 1921, 1974	January 1, 1975	76,730	281	196

(Table continues)

351

Table 8-2 (Continued)

State	Number of constitutions[a]	Dates of adoption	Present constitution		Number of amendments	
			Effective date	Estimated length (number of words)	Submitted to voters	Adopted
Maine	1	1819	March 15, 1820	16,313	206	173[e]
Maryland	4	1776, 1851, 1864, 1867	October 5, 1867	43,198	269	233
Massachusetts	1	1780	October 25, 1780	45,283	148	120
Michigan	4	1835, 1850, 1908, 1963	January 1, 1964	31,164	76	32
Minnesota	1	1857	May 11, 1858	12,016	218	121
Mississippi	4	1817, 1832, 1869, 1890	November 1, 1890	26,229	164	126
Missouri	4	1820, 1865, 1875, 1945	March 30, 1945	84,924	193	126
Montana	2	1889, 1972	July 1, 1973	12,790	58	32
Nebraska	2	1866, 1875	October 12, 1875	34,934	354	230
Nevada	1	1864	October 31, 1864	37,418	238	140
New Hampshire	2	1776, 1784	June 2, 1784	13,238	291	147
New Jersey	3	1776, 1844, 1947	January 1, 1948	26,360	88	72
New Mexico	1	1911	January 6, 1912	33,198	306	172[f]
New York	4	1777, 1822, 1846, 1894	January 1, 1895	49,360	305	229
North Carolina	3	1776, 1868, 1970	July 1, 1971	17,177	51	41
North Dakota	1	1889	November 2, 1889	18,746	282	161
Ohio	2	1802, 1851	September 1, 1851	63,140	294	177
Oklahoma	1	1907	November 16, 1907	84,956	373	199[g]
Oregon	1	1857	February 14, 1859	49,430	505	258
Pennsylvania	5	1776, 1790, 1838, 1873, 1968	1968[h]	26,078	39	33
Rhode Island	2	1842, 1986	December 4, 1986	11,407	14	12
South Carolina	7	1776, 1778, 1790, 1861, 1865, 1868, 1895	January 1, 1896	27,421	690	500
South Dakota	1	1889	November 2, 1889	28,840	243	122

State	#	Years	Effective date of present constitution	Estimated length (words)	Submitted	Adopted
Tennessee	3	1796, 1835, 1870	February 23, 1870	13,960	66	43
Texas	5	1845, 1861, 1866, 1869, 1876	February 15, 1876	92,025	676	498
Utah	1	1895	January 4, 1896	20,700	178	122
Vermont	3	1777, 1786, 1793	July 9, 1793	8,565	212	54
Virginia	6	1776, 1830, 1851, 1869, 1902, 1970	July 1, 1971	22,570	60	52
Washington	1	1889	November 11, 1889	32,578	181	107
West Virginia	2	1863, 1872	April 9, 1872	33,324	126	75
Wisconsin	1	1848	May 29, 1848	15,102	197	147
Wyoming	1	1889	July 10, 1890	26,349	130	101

Note: Constitutions as of January 1, 2019. For more details on the constitutions, see source.

a The constitutions include those Civil War documents customarily listed by the individual states. In Connecticut and Rhode Island, colonial charters served as the first constitutions.
b Eight of the approved amendments have been superseded and are not printed in the current edition of the constitution. The total adopted does not include five amendments proposed and adopted since statehood.
c Proposed amendments are not submitted to the voters in Delaware.
d The figure includes three amendments approved by the voters and later nullified by the state Supreme Court.
e This figure does not include one amendment approved by the voters in 1967 that is inoperative until implemented by legislation.
f The total excludes one amendment approved by voters in November 2008 but later declared invalid on single subject grounds by the state Supreme Court.
g The figures include six amendments submitted to and approved by the voters which were, by decisions of the Oklahoma or federal courts, rendered inoperative or ruled invalid, unconstitutional, or illegally submitted.
h Certain sections of the constitution were revised in 1967–1968. Amendments proposed and adopted are since 1968.

Source: Council of State Governments, *The Book of the States, 2019* (Lexington, Ky.: Council of State Governments, 2019), http://knowledgecenter.csg.org/kc/content/book-states-2019-chapter-1-state-constitutions.

Table 8-3 Governors' Terms, Term Limits, and Item Veto

State	Length of term in 1900 (years)	Length of term in 2019 (years)	Year of change	Term limits	Item veto[a]
Alabama	2	4	1902	2–4	yes
Alaska	b	4		2–4	yes[c]
Arizona	b	4	1970	2–4	yes[c]
Arkansas	2	4	1986	2A	yes[c]
California	4	4		2A	yes[c]
Colorado	2	4	1958	2–4	yes[c]
Connecticut	2	4	1950	no limit	yes
Delaware	4	4		2A	yes
Florida	4	4		2–4	yes[c]
Georgia	2	4	1942	2–4	yes[c]
Hawaii	b	4		2–4	yes
Idaho	2	4	1946	no limit	yes[c]
Illinois	4	4		no limit	yes
Indiana	4	4		2–12	no
Iowa	2	4	1974	no limit	yes[c]
Kansas	2	4	1974	2–4	yes[c]
Kentucky	4	4		2–4	yes[c]
Louisiana	4	4		2–4	yes[c]
Maine	2	4	1958	2–4	yes[c]
Maryland	4	4		2–4	yes
Massachusetts	1	4	1920, 1966[d]	no limit	yes
Michigan	2	4	1966	2A	yes[c]
Minnesota	2	4	1962	no limit	yes[c]
Mississippi	4	4		2A	yes[c]
Missouri	4	4		2A	yes[c]
Montana	4	4		2–16	yes[c]
Nebraska	2	4	1966	2–4	yes[c]
Nevada	4	4		2A	no
New Hampshire	2	2		no limit	yes
New Jersey	3	4	1949	2–4	yes[c]
New Mexico	b	4	1916, 1970	2–4	yes[c]
New York	2	4	1938	no limit	yes
North Carolina	4	4		2–4	no
North Dakota	2	4	1964	no limit	yes[c]
Ohio	2	4	1958	2–4	yes[c]
Oklahoma	b	4		2A	yes[c]
Oregon	4	4		2–12	yes[c]
Pennsylvania	4	4		2–4	yes[c]
Rhode Island	1	4	1912, 1994[d]	2–4	no
South Carolina	2	4	1926	2–4	yes[c]
South Dakota	2	4	1974	2–4	yes[c]
Tennessee	1	4	1954	2–4	yes[c]
Texas	2	4	1974	no limit	yes[c]
Utah	4	4		no limit	yes[c]

Table 8-3 *(Continued)*

State	Length of term in 1900 (years)	Length of term in 2019 (years)	Year of change	Term limits	Item veto[a]
Vermont	2	2		no limit	no
Virginia	4	4		1–4	yes[c]
Washington	4	4		no limit	yes
West Virginia	4	4		2–4	yes[c]
Wisconsin	2	4	1970	no limit	yes[c]
Wyoming	4	4		2–16	yes

Note: 2A: Two terms, absolute; 2–4: Two terms, re-eligible after four years; 2–12: Two terms, eligible for eight out of 12 years; 2–16: Two terms, eligible for eight out of 16 years; 1–4: One term, re-eligible after four years.

[a] In all states the governor has the power to veto bills passed by the state legislature. Item veto refers to the power to veto items within a bill. Provisions to override vary, requiring as many as two-thirds of the legislators elected. For details, see *The Book of the States* in source.

[b] Oklahoma was admitted to the Union in 1907, Arizona and New Mexico in 1912, and Alaska and Hawaii in 1959. Oklahoma, Alaska, and Hawaii have always had four-year gubernatorial terms. Arizona started with two years. New Mexico started with four years, went to two years in 1916 and back to four years in 1970.

[c] Over appropriations only. In Wisconsin, the governor has a broader veto on appropriations bills.

[d] Massachusetts went from one year to two years in 1920 and from two years to four years in 1966. Rhode Island went from one year to two years in 1912 and from two years to four years in 1994.

Sources: Length of term in 1900 and year of change: Congressional Quarterly, *Gubernatorial Elections, 1787–1997* (Washington, D.C.: Congressional Quarterly, 1998), 2–3; All others: Council of State Governments, *The Book of the States, 2019* (Lexington, Ky.: Council of State Governments, 2019), http://knowledgecenter.csg.org/kc/content/book-states-2019-chapter-4-state-executive-branch.

Table 8-4 State Provisions for Initiative and Referendum

State	Changes to constitution			Changes to statutes			
	Initiative		Referendum	Initiative		Referendum	
	Direct	Indirect	Legislative	Direct	Indirect	Legislative	Citizen petition
Alabama	no	no	yes	no	no	no	no
Alaska	no	no	yes	no[c]	yes	no	yes
Arizona	yes	no	yes	yes	no	yes	yes
Arkansas	yes	no	yes	yes	no	yes	yes
California	yes	no	yes	yes	no	yes	yes
Colorado	yes	no	yes	yes	no	yes	yes
Connecticut	no	no	yes	no	no	no	no
Delaware	no	no	no	no	no	yes	no
Florida	yes	no	yes	no	no	no	no
Georgia	no	no	yes	no	no	no	no
Hawaii	no	no	yes	no	no	no	no
Idaho	no	no	yes	yes	no	yes	yes
Illinois	yes	no	yes	no	no	yes	no
Indiana	no	no	yes	no	no	no	no
Iowa	no	no	yes	no	no	no	no
Kansas	no	no	yes	no	no	no	no
Kentucky	no	no	yes	no	no	yes	no
Louisiana	no	no	yes	no	no	no	no
Maine	no	no	yes	no	yes	yes	yes
Maryland	no	no	yes	no	no	yes	yes
Massachusetts	no	yes	yes	no	yes	yes	yes
Michigan	yes	no	yes	no	yes	yes	yes
Minnesota	no	no	yes	no	no	no	no
Mississippi	no	yes	yes	no	no	no	no
Missouri	yes	no	yes	yes	no	yes	yes
Montana	yes	no	yes	yes	no	yes	yes
Nebraska	yes	no	yes	yes	no	yes	yes
Nevada	yes	no	yes	no	yes	yes	yes
New Hampshire	no	no	yes	no	no	no	no
New Jersey	no	no	yes	no	no	no	no
New Mexico	no	no	yes	no	no	yes	no
New York	no	no	yes	no	no	no	no
North Carolina	no	no	yes[a]	no	no	no	no
North Dakota	yes	no	yes	yes	no	yes	yes
Ohio	yes	no	yes	no	yes	yes	yes
Oklahoma	yes	no	yes	yes	no	yes	yes
Oregon	yes	no	yes	yes	no	yes	yes
Pennsylvania	no	no	yes	no	no	no	no[b]
Rhode Island	no	no	yes	no	no	no	no
South Carolina	no	no	yes	no	no	no	no
South Dakota	yes	no	yes	yes	no	yes	yes
Tennessee	no	no	yes	no	no	no	no
Texas	no	no	yes	no	no	no	no
Utah	no	no	yes	yes	yes	yes	yes

Table 8-4 (Continued)

	Changes to constitution			Changes to statutes			
	Initiative		Referendum	Initiative		Referendum	
State	Direct	Indirect	Legislative	Direct	Indirect	Legislative	Citizen petition
Vermont	no	no	yes	no	no	no	no
Virginia	no	no	yes	no	no	no	no
Washington	no	no	yes	yes	yes	yes	yes
West Virginia	no	no	yes	no	no	no	no
Wisconsin	no	no	yes	no	no	no	no
Wyoming	no	no	yes	yes[c]	no	no	yes

Note: An *initiative* may propose a constitutional amendment or develop state legislation and may be formed either directly or indirectly. The *direct initiative* allows a proposed measure to be placed on the ballot after a specific number of signatures has been secured on a citizen petition. The *indirect initiative* must be submitted to the legislature for a decision after the required number of signatures has been secured on a petition and prior to placing the proposed measure on the ballot. *Referendum* refers to the process whereby a state law or constitutional amendment passed by the legislature may be referred to the voters before it goes into effect. Three forms of referenda exist: (1) *citizen petition*, whereby the people may petition for a referendum on legislation that has been considered by the legislature; (2) *submission by the legislature* (designated in table as "Legislative"), whereby the legislature may voluntarily submit laws to the voters for their approval; and (3) *constitutional requirement*, whereby the state constitution may require that certain questions be submitted to the voters. For details, see source.

[a] Only the legislature can make statutory changes while in session. Proposed constitutional changes must be passed by the legislature and then are submitted to the citizens to be voted on.
[b] No provision for statewide referenda initiated by citizen petition. There are several county/local referenda that can be initiated by citizen petition.
[c] Alaska and Wyoming's initiative process could be considered either direct or indirect. They require that an initiative cannot be submitted until after a legislative session has convened and adjourned, with the intent to give the legislature the opportunity to address the proposed initiative.

Source: National Counsel of Conference Legislatures, "Initiative and Referendum States," https://www.ncsl.org/research/elections-and-campaigns/chart-of-the-initiative-states.aspx; Legislative referenda from the Initiative and Referendum Institute, http://www.iandrinstitute.org/docs/Legislative-Referendum-States.pdf.

Table 8-5 Legislative Professionalism in the States

Legislative professionalization rank	State	Legislative professionalization score	Legislative session length limit	Annual salary	Salary on non-annualized basis	Per diem
1	California	0.629	Constitution: even-numbered years, November 30; odd-numbered years, none Chamber Rule: even-numbered years, August 31; odd-numbered years, September 12	$114,877.00		$ 206.00
2	Massachusetts	0.431	Odd-numbered years, 3rd Wednesday in November; even-numbered years, July 31	$66,256.00		None
3	New York	0.430	None	$110,000.00		$61/$176 (depends on overnight stay)
4	Pennsylvania	0.417	None	$90,335.00		$ 178.00
5	Michigan	0.401	None	$71,685.00		$10,800 per year
6	Ohio	0.384	None	$65,528.00		None
7	Hawaii	0.321	60 legislative days	$62,604.00		$10/$225
8	Alaska	0.296	90 calendar days	$50,400.00		$ 287.00
9	Illinois	0.294	None	$69,464.00		$ 151.00
10	Maryland	0.278	90 calendar days	$50,330.00		$ 165.00
11	Washington	0.272	Odd-numbered years, 105 calendar days; even-numbered years, 60 days	$52,766.00		$ 120.00
12	Colorado	0.268	120 calendar days	$40,242.00		$45/$219
13	Connecticut	0.267	Odd-numbered year, Wednesday after the first Monday in June; even-numbered years, Wednesday after the first Monday in May	$28,000.00		None
14	Arizona	0.264	Saturday of the last week in which the 100th calendar day falls	$24,000.00		$35/$60
15	Florida	0.245	60 calendar days	$29,697.00		$ 152.00
16	Missouri	0.243	January 6 through May 28	$35,915.00		$ 121.00
17	Iowa	0.241	Odd-numbered year, 110 days; even-numbered years, 100 days	$25,000.00		$ 169.00

18	North Carolina	0.238	None	$13,951.00		$ 104.00
19	Texas	0.234	140 calendar days in two years	$7,200.00		$ 221.00
20	New Jersey	0.233	None	$49,000.00		None
21	Nebraska	0.230	Odd-numbered years, 90 legislative days; even-numbered years, 60 days	$12,000.00		$55/$151
22	Oklahoma	0.229	Last Friday in May	$35,021.00		$ 166.00
23	Oregon	0.214	Odd-numbered years, 160 calendar days; even-numbered years, 35 calendar days	$31,200.00		$ 151.00
24	Arkansas	0.207	Odd-numbered years, 60 days; even-numbered years, 30 days	$42,428.00		$55/$151
25	Minnesota	0.204	120 legislative days in 2 years, or the 1st Monday after the 3rd Saturday in May each year	$46,500.00		$86 senators; $66 representatives
26	Wisconsin	0.204	None	$52,999.00		$115 Senate; $81/$162 Assembly (depends on overnight stay)
27	Delaware	0.203	2nd Tuesday in January through June 30	$47,291.00		None
28	Rhode Island	0.200	None	$15,959.00		None
29	Louisiana	0.187	Odd-numbered years, 45 legislative days in 60 calendar days; even-numbered years, 60 legislative days in 85 calendar days	$16,800 Senate		$ 161.00
30	Nevada	0.182	120 calendar days in two years		$164.69/day	$ 151.00
31	Kansas	0.181	Odd-numbered years, none; even-numbered years, 90 days		$88.66/day	$ 151.00
32	Virginia	0.178	Odd numbered years, 30 calendar days; even-numbered years, 60 days	$18,000 Senate; $17,640 House		$ 210.00
33	Vermont	0.178	None		$742.92/week	$ 198.00
34	Alabama	0.175	30 legislative days in 105 calendar days	$49,861.00		100 (depends on length of trip)
35	Idaho	0.169	None	$18,415.00		$71/$139

Legislative professionalization rank	State	Legislative professionalization score	Legislative session length limit	Annual salary	Salary on non-annualized basis	Per diem
36	Kentucky	0.162	Odd-numbered years, 30 legislative days or March 30; even-numbered years, 60 legislative days or April 15		$188/day	$ 166.00
37	Mississippi	0.161	90 calendar days, except after a gubernatorial election then 125 days	$23,500.00		$ 151.00
38	West Virginia	0.157	60 calendar days	$20,000.00		$ 131.00
39	South Carolina	0.156	First Thursday in June	$10,400.00		$ 140.00
40	Indiana	0.156	Odd-numbered years, 61 days (April 29); even-numbered years, 30 days (March 14)	$26,490.00		$ 181.00
41	Maine	0.154	Odd-numbered years, 3rd Wednesday in June; even-numbered years, 3rd Wednesday in April	$14,862 for first session, $10,582 for second		$ 70.00
42	Georgia	0.149	40 legislative days	$17,342.00		$ 173.00
43	New Mexico	0.140	Odd-numbered years, 60 days; even-numbered years, 30 days			$192/day
44	Tennessee	0.136	90 legislative days	$24,316.00		$61/$284
45	Montana	0.116	90 legislative days in two years		$92.46/day	$ 120.11
46	Utah	0.115	45 calendar days		$285/day	N/A
47	North Dakota	0.112	80 legislative days in two years		$505/month	$181
48	South Dakota	0.103	40 legislative days	$11,892.00		$ 151.00
49	Wyoming	0.081	Odd-numbered years, 40 legislative days; even-numbered years, approximately 20 days		$150/day	$ 109.00
50	New Hampshire	0.048	45 legislative days or July 1	$100.00		None

Note: For salary data, when two numbers are given under per diem, amount available to members is based upon how close they live to state capital. Salary data is for 2020.

Source: Legislative session data: National Conference of State Legislatures, "Legislative Session Length," (August 6, 2020), https://www.ncsl.org/research/about-state-legislatures/legislative-session-length.aspx; Salary data: National Conference of State Legislatures, "2020 Legislator Compensation," (June 17, 2020), https://www.ncsl.org/research/about-state-legislatures/2020-legislator-compensation.aspx; Professionalization data: Peverill Squire, "A Squire Index Update." *State Politics and Policy.* 17(4): 361–371, Table 2 (2017).

A Data Literacy Lesson

Analyzing Legislative Professionalism

Imagine one state legislature where the two houses are in session more or less year-round—the session begins in early January of an odd-numbered year and continues until November of the following even-numbered year. There is no limit on how much the legislature can be in session. Each member is given their own staff allowance for both the legislative office and the district office, and that staff is employed year-round. Member salaries approach $90,000 per year, with bonuses available to those holding leadership positions.

Contrast this with another state legislature, where sessions are limited by law to ninety days, every other year. Members share staff, who are only employed during the legislative session. Members receive a per diem of around $92 per legislative day, plus a per diem allowance of $120 per day (in addition to reimbursement for mileage to the legislature).

If we told you that these are descriptions of the state legislatures of Pennsylvania and Montana, we do not imagine you would have a hard time guessing which is which. A high population state such as Pennsylvania, with all of the challenges that confront urban and rural areas, a wide range of industry, and a very diverse population, is likely to require more state legislative work than would a less populated, less diverse state such as Montana. The western ethos that favors a more limited government might also be acting upon preferences around legislative organization in Montana but wouldn't in Pennsylvania.

The categories of legislatures we are discussing are often summed up as being professional vs. amateur legislatures; some refer to these two types as being full-time versus part-time legislatures. In our heads, we can probably form pictures of what each of these types mean. Full-time legislators work year-round at their job, which is probably the only job they have. They are well-supported by staff, have offices both at the capital and in the district, and are more likely to see politics as a career. Part-time legislators are working in other jobs, from which they take time off for short legislative sessions. They lack the staff to work full-time at their legislative jobs, nor do they make enough money to devote all their time to such a job.

We may have images of what these types are, but doing careful analysis and developing theories concerned with this distinction requires more than just a picture; it requires a carefully operationalized method of measuring where a particular legislature is on the continuum. Peverill Squire has come up with a well-known formula for scoring various legislatures; his scores for 2017 are in the third column of Table 8-5. The Squire measure uses the U.S. Congress as the epitome of a professional legislature, and compares each state legislature to the Congress on three measures—number of legislative staff, legislator salary, and number of days the legislature is in session. If the legislature is the same as the U.S. Congress on one dimension, they get a 1.0 for the dimension; if they are completely different (i.e., they are in session for zero days), they get a 0.0 for that dimension—scores this low are, of course, not feasible. Scores are averaged

(Continued)

(Continued)

across all three dimensions, which results in a value from 0 to 1 for each legislature. (See Squire 2017 for more details, including on the challenges in constructing this index.)

Table 8-5 reveals some interesting patterns—more populous states generally have more professionalized legislatures (Alaska and Hawaii are significant exceptions), as do states that tend to have Democratic majorities. Interested observers can form their own hypotheses and test them effectively using these data. One approach would be to ask questions to explain variation in professionalization across the states (using professionalization as a dependent variable)—is there a systematic relationship between state size, or state partisanship, and legislative professionalization? Moreover, a researcher could also explore how the professionalization of a legislature affects other political phenomena (using professionalization as an independent variable). Examples of this second type could be questions about whether professional legislatures are more or less popular with voters, whether officeholders from professional or amateur legislatures are more likely to end up pursuing higher office, or how effective the different types of legislatures are in addressing the challenges facing their states.

All of the above are interesting questions for scholars of public opinion, or campaigns and elections, or public policy. What they have in common, of course, is that they require measurement of legislative type that goes beyond "knowing it when we see it"—the Squire measure offers scholars an easy-to-apply way to describe and evaluate the fifty state legislatures, opening the door to many other important research questions.

Figure 8-1 Initiatives in the States, 1900–2019

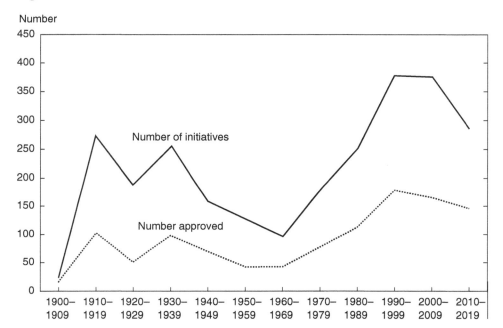

Note: Only initiatives—new laws placed on the ballot by petition—are included. The numbers do not include popular referendums nor measures placed on the ballot by the legislature. From 2010 to 2014, there were 144 initiatives; 61 were approved.

Sources: Initiative and Referendum Institute, "Overview of Initiative Use, 1900–2019," (December 2019), http://www.iandrinstitute.org/docs/IRI-Initiative-Use-(2019-2).pdf.

Table 8-6 Incorporation of Bill of Rights to Apply to State Governments

Amendment	Incorporated / Issue	Supreme Court case	Year	Vote
[1868 Fourteenth Amendment to Constitution passed][a]				
First	Yes, fully			
	Freedom of speech	*Fiske v. Kansas,* 274 U.S. 380	1927	9–0
	Freedom of press	*Near v. Minnesota,* 283 U.S. 697	1931	5–4
	Free exercise of religion	*Hamilton v. Regents of the U. of California,* 293 U.S. 245	1934	9–0
	Freedom of assembly and petition	*De Jonge v. Oregon,* 299 U.S. 353	1937	8–0
	Separation of church and state	*Everson v. Board of Education of Ewing Township,* 330 U.S. 1	1947	5–4
Second	Yes, fully			
	Bear arms	*McDonald v. Chicago,* 561 U.S. 742	2010	5–4
Third	No			
	Safeguards against forced quartering of troops			
Fourth	Yes, fully			
	Unreasonable searches and seizures	*Mapp v. Ohio,* 367 U.S. 643	1961	6–3
	Warrant requirements	*Aguilar v. Texas,* 378 U.S. 108	1964	6–3
Fifth	Yes, partially			
	Eminent domain	*Chicago, Burlington & Quincy RR v. Chicago,* 166 U.S. 266	1897	9–0
	Self-incrimination	*Malloy v. Hogan,* 378 U.S. 1	1964	5–4
	Double jeopardy	*Benton v. Maryland,* 395 U.S. 784	1969	7–2
	Grand jury indictment	Not incorporated		
Sixth	Yes, partially			
	Counsel in capital criminal cases	*Powell v. Alabama,* 287 U.S. 45	1932	7–2
	Public trial	*In re Oliver,* 333 U.S. 257	1948	7–2
	Notice of accusations	*Cole v. Arkansas* 333 U.S. 196	1948	8–0
	Counsel in all criminal cases	*Gideon v. Wainwright,* 372 U.S. 335	1963	9–0
	Confront adverse witnesses	*Pointer v. Texas,* 380 U.S. 400	1965	7–2
	Impartial jury	*Parker v. Gladden,* 385 U.S. 363	1966	8–1

Table 8-6 Incorporation of Bill of Rights to Apply to State Governments

Amendment	Incorporated / Issue	Supreme Court case	Year	Vote
	Obtaining and confronting favorable witnesses	*Washington v. Texas*, 388 U.S. 14	1967	9–0
	Speedy trial	*Klopfer v. North Carolina*, 386 U.S. 213	1967	9–0
	Jury trial in non-petty criminal cases	*Duncan v. Louisiana*, 391 U.S. 145	1968	7–2
Seventh	No Jury trial in civil cases			
Eighth	Yes, fully			
	Cruel and unusual punishment	*Robinson v. California*, 370 U.S. 660	1962	6–2
	Excessive bail	*Schilb v Kuebel*, 404 U.S. 357	1971	6–3
	Excessive fines	*Timbs v. Indiana*, 586 U.S.	2019	9–0
Ninth[b]	No Non-enumerated rights			
Tenth[b]	No States rights			

[a] The Fourteenth Amendment's due process clause is the basis for applying the Bill of Rights to the states.

[b] The 9th and 10th Amendments have not been incorporated, nor is it likely that they will be based on the scope of these amendments.

Sources: Legal Information Institute, "Incorporation Doctrine," https://www.law.cornell.edu/wex/incorporation_doctrine; Additional verification from M. Curiale, "Constitutional law eighth amendment fourteenth amendment excessive bail," *Duquesne Law Review*, 20(4), 689–700, (1982); S. Chhablani, "Disentangling the sixth amendment." *University of Pennsylvania Journal of Constitutional Law*, 11(3), 487–494, footnote 23 (2009); J. H. Israel, "Selective incorporation revisited." *Georgetown Law Journal*, 71(2), 253–338, footnote 670, (1982).

Table 8-7 Length of Time between Congressional Approval and Actual Ratification of the Twenty-Seven Amendments to the U.S. Constitution

Amendment		Time required for ratification	Year ratified
I–X	Bill of Rights	2 years, 2.5 months	1791
XI	Lawsuits against states	11 months	1795
XII	Presidential elections	6.5 months	1804
XIII	Abolition of slavery	10 months	1865
XIV	Civil rights	2 years, 1 month	1868
XV	Suffrage for all races	11 months	1870
XVI	Income tax	3 years, 6.5 months	1913
XVII	Senatorial elections	11 months	1913
XVIII	Prohibition	1 year, 1 month	1919
XIX	Women's suffrage	1 year, 2 months	1920
XX	Terms of office	11 months	1933
XXI	Repeal of prohibition	9.5 months	1933
XXII	Limit on presidential terms	3 years, 11 months	1951
XXIII	Washington, D.C., vote	9 months	1961
XXIV	Abolition of poll taxes	1 year, 4 months	1964
XXV	Presidential succession	1 year, 10 months	1967
XXVI	Eighteen-year-old suffrage	3 months	1971
XXVII	Congressional salaries	203 years	1992

Sources: Congressional Research Service, *The Constitution of the United States: Analysis and Interpretation* (Washington, D.C.: Government Printing Office, 1973), 23–44 (92nd Cong., 2nd sess., S. Doc. 92-82); *Congressional Quarterly Weekly Report* (1992), 1423.

Figure 8-2 Government Employees: Federal, State, and Local, 1929–2019

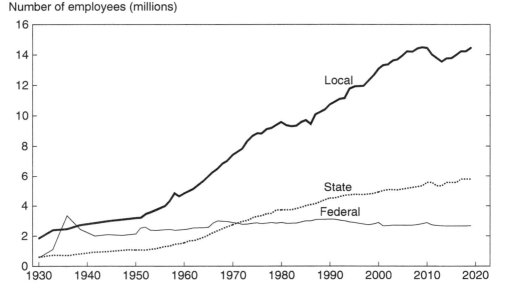

Note: No annual survey of government employment and payroll was conducted in 1996.

Source: 1929–1944, 1949, 1952, 1954, 1959, 1964, 1969–1992: U.S. Advisory Commission on Intergovernmental Relations, *Significant Features of Fiscal Federalism*, 1994, vol. 2 (Washington, D.C.: U.S. Advisory Commission on Intergovernmental Relations, 1994), 151; 1993–1994: 1995, 159; 1995–2013: U.S. Bureau of the Census, www.census.gov/govs/apes.html; other years: U.S. Bureau of the Census, *Historical Statistics of the United States*, Series Y189–198 (Washington, D.C.: Government Printing Office, 1975), 1100; Federal employment data 2013–2019: Congressional Research Service, *Federal Workforce Statistics Sources: OPM and OMB*, October 23, 2020, https://fas.org/sgp/crs/misc/R43590.pdf; State and Local employment data 2013–2019: U.S. Bureau of the Census, *Annual Survey of Public Employment and Payroll State Government Employment and Payroll, Local Government Employment & Payroll*, https://www.census.gov/programs-surveys/apes/data.html.

Table 8-8 Federal, State, and Local Governments: Number of Units and Employees, 1942–2025

Year	Federal government	State government	Local government					Local Gov't. Total	Total
			County	Municipal	School district	Township and town	Special district[a]		
1942									
Number	1	48	3,050	16,220	108,579	18,919	8,299	155,067	155,116
Employees (thousands)[b]	2,664	503[c]	333[c]	872[c]	—	223[c,d]	[d]	1,428[c]	5,915
1952[d]									
Number	1	50	3,052	16,807	67,355	17,202	12,340	116,756	116,807
Employees (thousands)	2,583	1,060	573	1,341	1,234	312[c]	[c]	3,461	7,105
1962									
Number	1	50	3,043	18,000	34,678	17,142	18,323	91,186	91,237
Employees (thousands)	2,539	1,680	862	1,696	2,161	449[c]	[c]	5,169	9,388
1972									
Number	1	50	3,044	18,517	15,781	16,991	23,885	78,218	78,269
Employees (thousands)	2,832	2,957	1,369	2,376	3,587	348	327	8,007	13,759
1982									
Number	1	50	3,041	19,076	14,851	16,734	28,078	81,780	81,831
Employees (thousands)	2,862	3,744	1,824	2,397	4,194	356	478	9,249	15,841
1992									
Number	1	50	3,043	19,279	14,422	16,656	31,555	84,955	85,006
Employees (thousands)	3,047	4,595	2,253	2,665	5,134	424	627	11,103	18,745
2002									
Number	1	50	3,034	19,429	13,506	16,504	35,052	87,525	87,576
Employees (thousands)	2,690	5,072	2,729	2,972	6,367	488	721	13,277	21,039

2012								
Number	1	50	3,031	19,519	12,880	16,360	38,266	90,107
Employees (thousands)	2,793	5,286	—	—	—	—	—	22,040
2017								
Number	1	50	3,031	19,495	12,754	16,253	38,542	90,126
Employees (thousands)	2,653	5,462	—	—	—	—	—	22,228

Note: "—" indicates not available. A census of governmental units is conducted every five years. Subdivisions in local government employment were last reported in 2007. Data for additional years can be found in previous editions of *Vital Statistics on American Politics*.

[a] Special districts include independent public housing authorities, local irrigation units, power authorities, and other such bodies.
[b] Month for employee counts varies across years. For details, see sources. Numbers include full- and part-time employees.
[c] Employees in other than education.
[d] Townships and special districts are combined.

Sources: 1942–1962: U.S. Bureau of the Census, *Historical Statistics of the United States* (Washington, D.C.: Government Printing Office, 1975), 1086, 1100; 1972–1992 governmental units: U.S. Bureau of the Census, *Census of Governments, 1987* (Washington, D.C.: Government Printing Office, 1988), vi; 1993, 3; 1972–1992 employees: U.S. Office of Personnel Management, *Federal Manpower Statistics, Federal Civilian Workforce Statistics* (Washington, D.C.: Government Printing Office, various years); U.S. Bureau of the Census, *Public Employment in 1985* (Washington, D.C.: Government Printing Office, 1986), 2; *1989*, vi; *1992*, vi, ix; 2002 governmental units and employees: U.S. Bureau of the Census, *2002 Census of Governments*, vol. 3, no. 2, "Compendium of Public Employment: 2002" (Washington, D.C.: Government Printing Office, 2002), ix, 2, 34; 2012 governmental units: U.S. Bureau of the Census, "Local Governments by Type and State: 2012"; 2012 employees: *Employment and Payroll Data, 2012 Census of Governments*, https://www.census.gov/library/publications/2014/econ/g12-cg-emp.html; 2017 governmental units: U.S. Bureau of the Census, "Local Governments by Type and State: 2017," https://www.census.gov/data/tables/2017/econ/gus/2017-governments.html, Table 2; 2017 federal employees: U.S. Office of Management and Budget, *Budget of the United States Government, Analytical Perspectives* (Washington, D.C.: Government Printing Office, 2019), "Total Federal Employment," Table 7.4; 2017 state and local employees: U.S. Bureau of the Census, *2017 ASPEP Datasets and Tables*, https://www.census.gov/data/datasets/2017/econ/apes/annual-apes.html.

A Data Literacy Lesson

What Does "Big Government" Mean, Anyway?

How often have you heard people talk about "big government?" We hear the phrase used a lot but notice that people use it to mean different things, from the number of government regulations to the number of people employed by the government. When we talk about the size of the government workforce, it would be easy to focus on the last column in Table 8-8 and say that the government has increased by over 250 percent in the past 75 years. It is true that the number of people in the United States whose paycheck comes from a government entity has increased by that amount. But do the data really support using this as proof of government bloat? What if we look at the total number of government units? If we looked only at that change, we could say that the government is less than 60 percent the size it was in 1942. How can two different conclusions be drawn from the same table? Tables like this demonstrate the importance of looking at the individual components that make up the total, rather than jumping to broad conclusions from the final numbers.

This table presents two important pieces of information: the number of government units, and the number of government employees. It further breaks each of these down by the three levels of government: federal, state, and local. The two categories offer different information that, together, helps us understand the size and scope of where government has grown and where it has contracted. In order to understand the relationship, first consider each category on its own.

The simplest data point is the number of federal governments. There is only one, and that is a constant. Similarly, with the exception of an increase from forty-eight to fifty states when Alaska and Hawaii were admitted as states, there is overall consistency in the number of state governments. Fluctuation and changes become apparent under the umbrella of local government, though, and there are a lot of types of local units that you might not instinctively think of as part of the government. For example, school districts are a unit of local government, and we observe a great deal of change over time in this type of government. We observe the number of school districts decreased nearly 40 percent from 1942 to 1952 (108,579 to 67,355), by another 50 percent in each of the following ten-year periods, until the rate in decrease slowed (but continued to decline) in the 1970s to 1980s. For the most recent year for which we have data (2017), the Census reports 12,754 school districts, only 12 percent of the number of school districts that were in the United States in 1942.

While the number of school districts has dropped dramatically, the number of school district employees has increased as dramatically, if a bit more steadily. This helps us recognize that the two datasets contribute different perspectives on what it means to talk about the size of government and highlights the need for more information before drawing conclusions. Before we made any claims about the role of government in schools, we think we'd need a lot more information. How does the increase in school district employees compare with the population of school-aged children? Moreover, we don't know from these data who the employees are: is the increase primarily more teachers, or administrators, or maintenance and food service workers? As for the number of school districts, has the average geographic size of a district or number of students served increased and what effect has that had on the number and type of employees needed by districts?

The example of school districts demonstrates how looking at different measures within one type of government provides opportunities for thinking critically about data. We also think this table provides a great opportunity to understand the importance of looking across different levels and categories of government employees.

If we turn our attention to the number of government employees, we can observe that since 1942, there's been an increase in government employees from just under 6 million to well over 21 million. However, this increase in employment has not been consistent across all levels of government. The number of federal government employees has stayed relatively stable over the decades, particularly given the overall growth in employment. Much greater increases can be found in the number of state government employees.

Breaking down total numbers to even the three broadest categories begins to give us a clearer picture of where growth in government employment occurs but, again, is useful in developing new questions. What types of occupations account for the growth in government employment? Are the increases in state and local government evenly distributed across the various state and local government units? Do they correspond with changes in population? We can't answer those questions from this table, but by carefully examining the components that make up the totals, we can better understand what depths are available for scholars to explore.

Table 8-9 State Lottery Revenues (in millions)

		Sales		Transfers[a]	
State	Year established	Fiscal year 2019	Change from previous year (percent)	Fiscal year 2018	Change from previous year (percent)
Arizona	1982	$1,076.79	9.7	$211.91	6.9
Arkansas	2009	$515.49	3.2	$91.84	7.9
California	1985	$7,388.05	6.1	$1,698.35	9.9
Colorado	1983	$679.78	11.1	$140.74	5.4
Connecticut	1972	$1,333.91	5.2	$347.30	4.5
Delaware	1975	$649.65	7.2	$214.91	4.5
District of Columbia	1982	$213.06	1.3	$46.10	1.1
Florida	1987	$7,151.24	6.7	$1,758.33	6.2
Georgia	1993	$4,776.01	3.9	$1,143.91	3.9
Idaho	1989	$287.91	8.6	$53.50	10.3
Illinois	1974	$2,977.59	1.7	$722.38	−0.1
Indiana	1989	$1,347.76	6.1	$306.08	6.3
Iowa	1985	$390.90	5.4	$87.10	7.8
Kansas	1987	$295.28	9.8	$74.73	−0.7
Kentucky	1989	$1,129.66	8.4	$263.27	5.9
Louisiana	1991	$523.97	6.7	$171.96	8.0
Maine	1974	$299.45	1.8	$63.03	7.4
Maryland	1973	$3,957.32	6.3	$1,148.85	10.4
Massachusetts	1972	$5,490.37	4.0	$997.06	−4.1
Michigan	1972	$3,884.16	8.6	$935.39	1.2
Minnesota	1989	$636.81	6.8	$145.10	4.3
Mississippi	2018[b]	—	—	—	—
Missouri	1986	$1,466.00	4.7	$306.07	5.0
Montana	1987	$61.26	8.2	$10.70	16.0
Nebraska	1993	$192.18	4.8	$45.25	9.6
New Hampshire	1964	$384.37	15.5	$87.39	14.8
New Jersey	1970	$3,482.35	5.5	$1,030.30	3.7
New Mexico	1996	$143.63	7.2	$40.22	6.3
New York	1967	$10,290.55	3.2	$3,371.87	3.2
North Carolina	2006	$2,859.63	9.8	$671.26	7.5
North Dakota	2004	$35.35	12.9	$8.04	15.8
Ohio	1974	$4,419.40	6.6	$1,087.72	4.2
Oklahoma	2005	$241.69	9.3	$63.98	18.9
Oregon	1985	$1,346.53	3.4	$726.09	9.6
Pennsylvania	1972	$4,884.79	15.7	$1,093.65	4.6
Rhode Island	1974	$956.34	8.0	$364.97	0.6
South Carolina	2002	$1,980.94	13.2	$430.98	5.0

Table 8-9   *(Continued)*

		Sales		Transfers[a]	
State	Year established	Fiscal year 2019	Change from previous year (percent)	Fiscal year 2018	Change from previous year (percent)
South Dakota	1989	$293.23	5.2	$124.75	5.6
Tennessee	2004	$1,812.60	4.4	$421.68	9.0
Texas	1992	$6,251.48	11.1	$1,450.48	8.7
Vermont	1978	$139.25	5.2	$27.15	5.9
Virginia	1988	$2,293.56	7.2	$606.22	8.6
Washington	1982	$803.28	9.4	$182.97	13.0
West Virginia	1986	$1,224.06	5.5	$473.95	−1.3
Wisconsin	1988	$713.13	6.9	$170.66	−7.1
Wyoming	2013	$36.93	28.5	$5.03	84.8
Total United States		$91,317.69	6.7	$23,423.19	5.0

Note: "—" indicates not available. Amounts in current dollars. Data for additional years can be found in previous editions of *Vital Statistics on American Politics*.

[a] Transfers to beneficiaries are generally equivalent to "profits" (used in earlier reports) and refer to funds transferred to state-designated programs including state general funds. However, these transfers may not equal current-year profits due to individual reporting requirements and accounting policies in each jurisdiction.

[b] Mississippi lottery sales began in December 2019.

Source: North American Association of State and Provincial Lotteries, www.naspl.org.

Table 8-10 State and Local Government Expenditures, by Function, 1902–2018 (percent)

Function	1902	1952	1962	1972	1982	1992	2002	2012	2016	2017	2018
Education	23.3	27.0	31.5	34.6	29.4	28.5	29.1	27.6	27.6	27.7	27.5
Highways	16.0	15.1	14.7	10.0	6.6	5.8	5.6	5.0	5.0	5.0	4.9
Public welfare	3.4	9.0	7.2	11.1	11.1	13.5	13.7	15.4	18.5	18.5	18.8
Health	1.6	1.4	0.9	1.4	2.0	2.6	2.9	2.7	2.7	2.7	0.3
Hospitals	3.9	5.7	5.2	5.5	5.8	5.1	4.3	4.9	5.1	5.2	5.2
Police	4.6	3.0	3.0	3.2	3.2	3.0	3.2	3.1	3.1	3.1	3.1
Fire protection	3.7	1.9	1.6	1.4	1.3	1.3	1.3	1.3	1.4	1.4	1.4
Natural resources	0.8	2.5	1.9	1.6	1.3	1.1	1.1	0.9	0.9	0.9	0.8
Corrections	—	1.1	1.1	1.1	1.6	2.5	2.7	2.3	2.2	0.0	2.1
Sanitation and sewerage	4.7	3.2	2.8	2.5	2.9	2.8	2.5	2.4	2.3	2.2	2.2
Housing and community development	—	2.0	1.6	1.4	1.6	1.5	1.5	1.7	1.4	1.4	1.4
Parks and recreation	2.6	1.0	1.3	1.2	1.4	1.4	1.5	1.2	1.2	1.2	1.2
Financial administration	12.9	3.9	1.5	1.3	1.5	1.6	1.6	1.2	1.3	1.2	1.2
Other government administration[a]	—	—	1.8	1.8	2.7	2.8	2.9	2.7	2.7	2.7	2.7
Employment security administration[b]	—	0.6	0.6	0.6	0.4	0.3	0.2	0.2	0.1	0.1	0.1
Interest on general debt	6.2	1.8	2.9	3.2	3.8	4.8	3.7	3.5	3.0	2.9	2.9
Utilities	7.5	9.9	7.7	6.0	9.2	7.1	6.8	6.6	6.3	6.3	6.3

Liquor store expenditure	—	—	—	—	0.3	0.2	0.2	0.2	0.2
Insurance trust expenditure[c]	—	5.5	6.9	5.5	7.9	8.3	11.0	9.6	9.5	9.5
Other	8.8	5.4	5.8	6.6	6.7	6.2	7.0	6.0	5.5	7.5	8.0
Total direct expenditure (millions)	$1,095	$30,863	$70,547	$190,496	$524,817	$1,147,075	$2,044,331	$3,147,545	$3,529,616	$3,661,619	$3,810,632

Note: "—" indicates not available. Amounts in current dollars. For 1902 to 1952, financial administration includes other government administration. For 1902 to 1982, the category utilities includes liquor store expenditures. Data for additional years can be found in previous editions of *Vital Statistics on American Politics*.

[a] Includes judicial and legal, general public buildings, and other governmental administration.
[b] Formerly social insurance administration.
[c] Includes unemployment compensation, employee retirement, workers' compensation, and other insurance trust.

Sources: 1902–1982: U.S. Bureau of the Census, *Census of Government, 1982* (Washington, D.C.: Government Printing Office, 1985), 32–33; 1987: *Governmental Finances in 1987–88* (Washington, D.C.: Government Printing Office, 1990), 13; 1992–2018: "United States State and Local Government Finances by Level of Government," https://www.census.gov/data/datasets/2018/econ/local/public-use-datasets.html.

Table 8-11 Disposable Personal Income per Capita, by State, 1950–2019

State	1950	1960	1970	1980	1990	2000	2010	2016	2017	2018	2019
Alabama	$852	$1,403	$2,662	$6,955	$13,943	$21,355	$31,279	35,690	37,171	38,790	39,995
Alaska	—	2,703	4,559	13,057	19,937	27,081	41,984	51,474	52,805	55,735	57,936
Arizona	1,257	1,841	3,379	8,418	14,932	22,966	31,413	36,614	38,249	40,164	41,340
Arkansas	798	1,287	2,548	6,701	12,928	20,031	29,496	36,415	37,612	39,213	40,321
California	1,703	2,493	4,266	10,420	18,614	27,669	37,651	49,895	52,092	55,045	57,389
Colorado	1,383	2,055	3,550	9,288	17,003	28,865	37,538	45,698	48,644	51,895	53,702
Connecticut	1,695	2,438	4,398	10,551	22,815	33,837	47,594	59,259	60,747	63,737	65,920
Delaware	1,705	2,358	3,819	8,977	18,262	26,428	37,047	43,266	44,965	46,842	48,121
District of Columbia	2,009	2,379	4,273	10,378	22,400	33,441	61,900	66,315	67,471	69,494	71,330
Florida	1,204	1,822	3,559	8,752	17,398	25,392	35,537	41,371	42,740	45,214	46,370
Georgia	997	1,523	2,990	7,397	15,424	24,614	31,288	38,148	39,836	41,857	42,906
Hawaii	—	2,002	4,372	9,959	18,901	25,454	38,315	45,617	47,678	49,256	50,753
Idaho	1,239	1,683	3,183	7,708	13,868	21,577	29,691	36,427	38,031	40,375	41,679
Illinois	1,659	2,350	3,928	9,439	18,180	27,885	37,894	45,853	47,695	50,417	51,687
Indiana	1,403	1,964	3,319	8,168	15,331	23,983	31,327	39,077	40,729	42,771	43,952
Iowa	1,431	1,850	3,448	8,307	15,330	24,129	35,802	41,573	42,659	45,086	46,575
Kansas	1,354	1,921	3,377	8,616	15,921	24,833	35,274	42,511	43,899	46,020	47,898
Kentucky	914	1,459	2,811	7,173	13,544	21,725	30,097	35,480	36,640	38,032	39,279
Louisiana	1,037	1,534	2,787	7,669	13,687	21,059	34,405	38,546	40,032	42,202	43,245
Maine	1,114	1,724	3,069	7,450	15,222	23,230	34,073	40,007	41,776	43,933	45,508
Maryland	1,474	2,041	3,857	9,488	19,420	29,229	44,501	51,070	52,730	54,559	56,127
Massachusetts	1,503	2,177	3,861	9,021	19,549	30,795	45,103	55,685	58,052	61,208	62,964
Michigan	1,569	2,175	3,654	8,961	16,368	25,293	32,072	39,406	40,750	42,507	43,778
Minnesota	1,316	1,909	3,565	8,810	17,123	27,781	38,059	45,743	47,619	49,920	51,083
Mississippi	729	1,135	2,381	6,303	11,938	19,491	28,656	32,657	33,609	34,890	35,816
Missouri	1,308	1,948	3,381	8,124	15,492	24,330	33,480	39,400	40,484	42,209	43,551
Montana	1,535	1,861	3,228	7,936	13,693	20,770	31,694	39,283	41,346	43,226	44,513
Nebraska	1,464	1,950	3,364	8,010	15,996	25,063	36,493	44,424	45,492	47,663	49,035

State	1950	1960	1970	1980	1990	2000	2010	2016	2017	2018	2019
Nevada	1,780	2,572	4,356	10,279	17,562	26,875	33,715	40,352	42,719	45,169	46,114
New Hampshire	1,242	1,958	3,406	8,664	18,016	29,286	41,296	50,363	52,607	55,301	57,022
New Jersey	1,646	2,358	4,218	10,053	21,163	32,334	45,227	54,166	56,148	58,881	61,086
New Mexico	1,110	1,715	2,849	7,467	13,313	20,196	30,784	35,548	36,280	38,127	39,493
New York	1,659	2,452	4,177	9,395	20,371	28,618	43,024	51,545	55,294	57,874	60,359
North Carolina	1,007	1,472	2,884	7,160	15,145	24,246	32,333	37,887	39,468	41,254	42,567
North Dakota	1,310	1,724	2,948	6,920	14,380	23,092	39,617	46,620	47,619	50,625	51,782
Ohio	1,467	2,115	3,591	8,746	16,341	24,758	32,815	40,228	41,788	43,646	44,867
Oklahoma	1,057	1,728	3,098	8,260	14,170	21,721	33,103	37,904	39,713	41,700	43,031
Oregon	1,495	1,986	3,427	8,705	15,709	24,544	32,337	40,412	42,469	45,058	46,369
Pennsylvania	1,417	2,037	3,563	8,725	17,091	26,002	37,606	45,741	47,149	49,788	51,461
Rhode Island	1,404	2,011	3,647	8,445	17,453	25,351	39,177	44,744	46,636	48,345	50,024
South Carolina	862	1,306	2,741	6,840	14,044	22,161	30,192	36,376	37,972	39,630	40,945
South Dakota	1,222	1,751	3,025	7,298	14,725	23,876	38,010	44,312	45,592	48,460	49,600
Tennessee	957	1,477	2,833	7,374	15,004	24,009	33,222	39,749	41,413	43,426	44,731
Texas	1,240	1,755	3,216	8,553	15,463	25,168	35,141	41,456	43,516	46,284	47,690
Utah	1,261	1,826	3,032	7,575	13,131	21,453	29,765	37,559	39,305	41,977	43,498
Vermont	1,073	1,719	3,162	7,593	15,527	24,535	36,833	45,102	46,308	48,019	49,511
Virginia	1,159	1,692	3,267	8,732	17,735	26,775	40,091	46,915	48,608	50,829	52,144
Washington	1,584	2,163	3,746	9,464	17,449	27,954	39,254	49,577	52,077	55,924	58,070
West Virginia	980	1,483	2,753	7,077	12,908	19,815	29,181	33,599	35,344	37,484	38,466
Wisconsin	1,376	1,982	3,463	8,764	15,716	25,079	35,114	41,951	43,675	45,956	47,282
Wyoming	1,591	2,062	3,472	10,167	16,056	25,312	41,047	48,863	50,778	54,841	55,989
United States	1,378	2,013	3,581	8,779	16,985	25,956	36,296	43,959	45,830	48,233	49,788

Note: "—" indicates not available. Amounts in current dollars. Data for additional years can be found in previous editions of *Vital Statistics on American Politics*.

Source: U.S. Department of Commerce, Bureau of Economic Analysis, Regional Economic Data, "Per Capita Disposable Personal Income," www.bea.gov.

A Data Literacy Lesson

Finding Meaning in a Sea of Data

Do you look at a collection of data like we see in Table 8-11 and get overwhelmed by *all those numbers*? So do we. There are a lot of numbers there, and it is hard to know where to look first. What makes this table even harder to interpret is the thing it purports to measure— "Disposable Personal Income per Capita, by State." How would one define what this means, or calculate it? The two of us don't know what our own disposable incomes are, or how we would calculate them, so we lack an anchor to use as a comparison. If we showed you the average income per state, you could use your own income, or your parents' income, to identify a baseline and evaluate accordingly. But we don't know how many of you could quickly calculate your own disposable personal income, so when we look at the table, it is even harder to interpret.

One technique we could use to make sense of data like this would be to look at differences. For example, we are both interested in how disposable personal income might have taken a hit in light of the Great Recession, which began in late 2008. Given this, if we took the 2010 disposable personal income and compared it to 2013, that would let us see which states are showing larger increases, and which are showing smaller increases. We might not have a full understanding of the basic measure (we recommend you learn more about how economists measure this concept before beginning complex data analysis!), but we would at least be able to make state-by-state comparisons. This is one benefit of a federal system; we can look at cross-state differences to help us gain a deeper understanding of the phenomenon in question.

It took us just a couple of minutes to download these data, create a new column to show changes in disposable personal income between 2010 and 2013, and then rank-order the state. The states that experienced the smallest growth were Nevada, Florida, Maryland, Alabama, and New Jersey; the five that experienced the highest growth were North Dakota, Nebraska, Oklahoma, Arkansas, and Texas. Some patterns might immediately be relevant—the slow-growth states tend to be more populated, and have many more urban centers, than the high-growth states. Perhaps this might lead us to hypotheses about states with more urban economies rather than those with more rural economies.

We decided to consider two additional explanatory factors. First, we looked at unemployment. As noted, the Great Recession began in 2008. Unemployment peaked in 2010 and was slowly subsiding through 2013. Perhaps unemployment in 2010 might affect income growth by 2013. To test this, we compared the 2010 unemployment rates for the low-growth states to that for the higher-growth states (using data from the Bureau of Labor Statistics). The former had an average unemployment rate of 10.26 percent, while the latter experienced average unemployment of 7 percent. It seems that unemployment at the beginning of this time period had lingering effects for disposable income growth in the states.

We also wondered about mortgage foreclosures. A large reason for the Great Recession was over-speculation in real estate, but that did not happen across all states. We both recalled reading articles about the real estate boom in Nevada, in which many people took large mortgages (that they could not afford) to buy over-priced homes; the economy collapsed when home prices fell and people could not pay their mortgages. We recall reading no such articles about overheated real estate prices in North Dakota. We did a quick Google search for number of real estate foreclosures by state and discovered that Nevada (our slowest growth state) had the most foreclosures, and that Florida (our second-to-lowest-growth state) was #3 in foreclosures. The #2 state in foreclosures, Arizona, was #7 from the bottom in income growth. None of our fastest-growing states were anywhere near the top in mortgage foreclosures.

Table 8-11 presents a great deal of data, which at first glance can be intimidating. A simple task, such as looking at growth rate between columns, helps us to see patterns not immediately visible when we look at the raw data. This leads us to wonder about factors that might be affecting these patterns. A few quick Google searches yield some interesting data, and then we're off and running to help explain what drives personal disposable income growth across the states. There's more work to be done to develop comprehensive answers to these questions, of course. But a few quick and easy calculations, and data searches, have helped us to crack this table just a little bit, and to clear a path for future investigation.

380   Federalism

Figure 8-3   Surpluses and Deficits in Federal, State, and Local Government Finances, 1948–2019

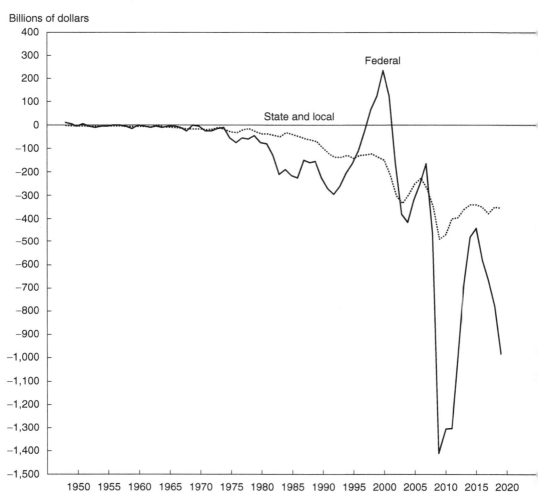

Note: Amounts in current dollars. State and local receipts and expenditures were subject to major revisions in 2003. The revisions made National Income and Product Accounts (NIPA) state and local government receipts and expenditures more comparable to the federal unified budget receipts and outlays. For details, see source and Brent R. Moulton and Eugene P. Seskin, "Preview of the 2003 Comprehensive Revision of the National Income and Product Accounts," *Survey of Current Business* (June 2003): 17–34.

Source: U.S. Office of Management and Budget, *Budget of the U.S. Government, Fiscal Year 2021, Historical Tables* (Washington, D.C.: Government Printing Office, 2020), Table 14.6.

Intergovernmental Revenue Flows 381

Figure 8-4 State and Local Government Deficits Compared with Federal Grants-in-Aid, 1948–2019

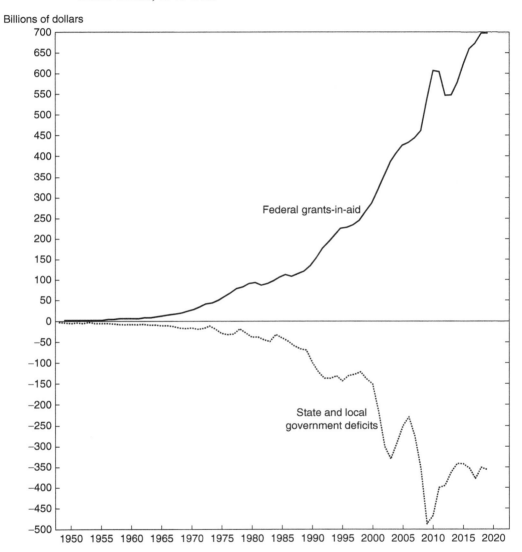

Note: Amounts in current dollars. See note to Figure 8-3, this volume.

Source: U.S. Office of Management and Budget, *Budget of the U.S. Government, Fiscal Year 2021, Historical Tables* (Washington, D.C.: Government Printing Office, 2020), Tables 12.1 and 14.6.

Table 8-12 Federal Grants-in-Aid Outlays, 1940–2025

		Federal grants as a percentage of			
		Federal outlays[a]		State and	Gross
	Total grants-		Domestic	local	domestic
Year	in-aid (billions)	Total	programs[b]	expenditures[c]	product
1940	$0.9	9.2	—	—	0.9
1945	0.9	0.9	—	—	0.4
1950	2.3	5.3	—	—	0.8
1955	3.2	4.7	—	—	0.8
1960	7.0	7.6	18.0	14.3	1.3
1965	10.9	9.2	18.3	15.5	1.5
1970	24.1	12.3	23.2	19.6	2.3
1975	49.8	15.0	21.7	24.0	3.1
1980	91.4	15.5	22.2	27.3	3.3
1985	105.9	11.2	18.2	22.0	2.5
1990	135.3	10.8	17.1	18.7	2.3
1995	225.0	14.8	21.6	22.8	3.0
2000	285.9	16.0	22.0	21.8	2.8
2001	318.5	17.1	22.9	25.2	3.0
2002	352.9	17.5	23.2	26.3	3.2
2003	388.5	18.0	23.7	26.1	3.4
2004	407.5	17.8	23.9	25.0	3.4
2005	428.0	17.3	23.5	23.5	3.3
2006	434.1	16.3	22.4	23.3	3.2
2007	443.8	16.3	—	—	3.1
2008	461.3	15.5	21.2	22.0	3.1
2009	538.0	15.3	17.6	—	3.7
2010	608.4	17.6	23.4	26.4	4.1
2011	606.8	16.8	22.4	27.5	3.9
2012	544.6	15.4	16.2	24.5	3.4
2013	546.2	15.8	20.6	23.2	3.3
2014	577.0	16.5	21.2	23.6	3.3
2015	624.4	16.9	21.2	23.9	3.4
2016	660.8	17.2	21.5	25.5	3.6
2017	674.7	16.9	21.3	26.8	3.5
2018	696.5	17.0	21.8	24.3	3.4
2019	721.1	16.2	21.0	24.1	3.4
2020 est.	790.7	16.5	21.1	—	3.6
2021 est.	810.0	16.8	21.5	—	3.5
2022 est.	837.6	16.7	—	—	3.4
2023 est.	844.2	16.5	—	—	3.3
2024 est.	857.8	16.5	—	—	3.2
2025 est.	848.0	15.6	—	—	3.0

Note: "—" indicates not available. Amounts in current dollars. Data for additional years can be found in previous editions of *Vital Statistics on American Politics*.

[a] Includes off-budget outlays; all grants are on-budget.
[b] Excludes outlays for national defense, international affairs, and net interest and undistributed offsetting receipts.
[c] As defined in the National Income and Product Accounts.

Sources: Total grants, total federal outlays, and GDP: U.S. Office of Management and Budget, *Budget of the United States Government, Fiscal Year 2012, Historical Tables* (Washington, D.C.: Government Printing Office, 2011), 249–250; 2014, 257–258; 2016–2025, Table 12.1; domestic programs and state and local expenditures: U.S. Office of Management and Budget, *Budget of the United States Government, Analytical Perspectives* (Washington, D.C.: Government Printing Office, various years), "Trends in Federal Grants to State and Local Governments."

Table 8-13 Federal Grants-in-Aid to State and Local Governments, by Function, 1950–2025 (percent)

Function	1950	1955	1960	1965	1970	1975	1980	1985	1990	1995	2000	2005	2010	2015	2020 (est.)	2025 (est.)
Health	5	4	3	6	16	18	17	23	32	42	44	46	48	55	56	57
Income security	59	54	38	32	24	19	20	26	27	24	22	21	19	17	17	17
Education, training, employment, and social services	7	10	8	10	27	24	24	17	17	15	15	13	16	10	10	9
Transportation	21	19	43	38	19	12	14	16	14	11	11	10	10	11	10	10
Natural resources and environment	1	1	2	2	2	5	6	4	3	2	2	1	2	1	1	1
Community and regional development	—	2	2	6	7	6	7	5	4	3	3	5	3	2	3	2
General-purpose fiscal assistance	2	3	2	2	2	14	9	7	2	1	1	1	1	1	1	1
Agriculture	5	7	4	5	3	1	1	2	1	—	2	1	1	1	—	—
Other	—	—	—	—	—	1	2	1	1	1	—	—	—	1	1	1
Allowances[a]																5
Total	100	100	102	101	100	100	100	101	101	99	100	98	100	100	101	100

Note: "—" indicates 0.5 percent or less. Due to rounding, percentages may not sum to 100 percent. Data for additional years can be found in previous editions of *Vital Statistics on American Politics*.

[a] Tracking for "Allowances" starts in the 2021 estimates.

Sources: U.S. Office of Management and Budget, *Historical Tables*, Table 12.2 "Total Outlays for Grants to State and Local Governments, by Function and Fund Group: 1940–2025," https://www.whitehouse.gov/omb/historical-tables.

Table 8-14 Fiscal Dependency of Lower Levels on Higher Levels of Government, 1927–2018

	Intergovernmental revenue as a percentage of total revenue		
Year	State from federal	Local from federal	Local from state[a]
1927	5.0	[b]	9.4
1934	27.3	1.3	20.7
1940	11.6	3.6	21.4
1946	9.4	0.1	21.9
1952	13.9	1.2	26.0
1957	14.2	1.2	25.2
1962	18.9	1.8	25.2
1965	20.2	2.2	32.5
1967	22.3	2.7	28.5
1970	21.6	2.9	30.2
1973	24.2	6.1	31.0
1977	22.4	8.4	30.7
1980	22.3	8.2	31.5
1983	19.3	6.2	29.1
1986	19.3	4.7	29.2
1989	18.4	3.3	29.6
1990	18.7	3.2	29.7
1991	20.4	3.1	29.8
1992	21.4	3.1	30.3
1993	22.0	3.1	30.3
1994	22.7	3.3	30.2
1995	22.3	3.5	30.7
1996	21.5	3.3	30.3
1997	20.7	3.4	30.5
1998	20.3	3.4	30.3
1999	20.7	3.3	31.1
2000	20.6	3.2	31.3
2001	24.4	3.3	31.9
2002	28.9	4.0	32.8
2003	26.5	4.0	32.5
2004	23.5	4.0	30.5
2005	23.5	4.0	30.6
2006	22.4	3.9	29.7
2007	20.4	3.7	29.0
2008	26.6	3.8	30.4
2009	42.0	4.3	32.4
2010	27.2	4.2	29.1
2011	25.4	4.3	28.8
2012	27.0	4.4	29.0
2013	23.1	4.1	27.5
2014	22.7	3.7	27.2
2015	27.4	3.7	28.3
2016	29.3	3.7	28.9
2017	25.4	3.5	27.5
2018	25.5	3.4	26.9

Note: Data for additional years can be found in previous editions of *Vital Statistics on American Politics*.

a Includes indirect federal aid passed through the states.
b Less than 0.1 percent.

Sources: 1927–1992: Calculated by the authors from U.S. Advisory Commission on Intergovernmental Relations, Significant Features of Fiscal Federalism, 1994, vol. 2 (Washington, D.C.: U.S. Advisory Commission on Intergovernmental Relations, 1994), 44; 1993–2018: U.S. Bureau of the Census, "State and Local Government Finance Historical Datasets and Tables," https://www.census.gov/programs-surveys/gov-finances/data/datasets.html.

Table 8-15 Variations in Local Dependency on State Aid, 2018

Rank	State	Percentage	Rank	State	Percentage
1	Vermont	64.7	27	North Carolina	30.9
2	Arkansas	52.1	28	Tennessee	30.9
3	New Mexico	44.1	29	Ohio	29.5
4	Michigan	43.4	30	Utah	29.2
5	Wisconsin	43.2	31	Georgia	28.9
6	Minnesota	40.7	32	Oklahoma	28.1
7	Indiana	39.8	33	Illinois	28.0
8	Idaho	39.7	34	Rhode Island	27.5
9	North Dakota	39.3	35	Massachusetts	27.1
10	Nevada	39.3	36	New York	27.0
11	California	38.0	37	Connecticut	26.7
12	Wyoming	37.4	38	Maryland	26.5
13	Kansas	36.0	39	South Carolina	26.4
14	Mississippi	35.5	40	Maine	26.3
15	Pennsylvania	35.5	41	Louisiana	26.2
16	Oregon	34.8	42	Missouri	26.0
17	Alaska	34.1	43	Texas	24.1
18	Arizona	33.5	44	South Dakota	23.8
19	Kentucky	33.1	45	Nebraska	23.7
20	Iowa	33.1	46	New Jersey	22.9
21	Washington	32.0	47	Florida	22.6
22	Montana	31.9	48	New Hampshire	22.5
23	Delaware	31.8	49	Colorado	22.4
24	Virginia	31.8	50	Hawaii	7.0
25	West Virginia	31.7			
26	Alabama	31.3		Total	31.5

Note: Percentages reflect state transfers (including "pull-through" monies from the federal government) as a percentage of total local general revenues. Where ties occur, the rank order was determined by the second decimal. Data for earlier years can be found in previous editions of *Vital Statistics on American Politics*.

Source: U.S. Bureau of the Census, "State and Local Government Finances, by Level of Government and by State: 2018," https://www.census.gov/data/datasets/2018/econ/local/public-use-datasets.html.

9
Foreign and Military Policy

- **Treaties and Agreements**
- **Military Engagements**
- **Military Personnel**
- **Expenditures**
- **Military Sales and Assistance**
- **Foreign Aid**
- **Investment and Trade**

One of the enduring debates in the United States has been the appropriate way to engage with the rest of the world. With fluctuations over time between isolationist and interventionist tendencies among American politicians and public opinion, data on international relations are vital even to understanding domestic politics. One of the notable characteristics of Donald Trump's presidency was an explicit focus on unilateralism and a doctrine of "America First" guiding foreign policy decisions. America's trade deficit, economic relations among allies, and membership in international groups such as the World Health Organization all took center stage over the course of an administration focused on minimizing international entanglements. The decades-long debate over the appropriate role of the use of military force in international conflicts has long played a role in domestic political decisions, from protests over the Vietnam War to concerns about the length of the Afghanistan War and the scope of powers granted to presidents in the aftermath of September 11, 2001, and the resulting so-called "War on Terror."

As we consider how foreign and military policy are informed by and better understood through data, there are a few overarching considerations we think are noteworthy. First, statistical data related to foreign policy, especially its military aspects, are not always publicly available. You might notice that none of our data report on the number of covert operations carried out by the

CIA or the specific measures taken to prevent cyberattacks. There is an obvious need for some secrecy in defense-related areas.

Despite that, there are still many types of data that are readily available and useful in understanding the domestic contexts that shape, and are shaped by, foreign and military policy decisions. Underlying both diplomatic and military decisions are the economic costs associated with them. The economic costs of foreign and military policy, through aid, trade, and military involvement are presented in several tables throughout this chapter. The costs associated with military involvement (Tables 9-4, 9-5, and 9-10) are presented both in actual dollars and as a percentage of GDP and federal outlays. A student or scholar interested in the basic question of whether there is a fundamental tension between "guns and butter" could consider the data presented in this chapter in conjunction with tables in Chapter 10, Social Policy. Is it true that a dollar spent on defense translates to a dollar less spent on social programs? Economic indicators are important in understanding diplomatic efforts as well, including foreign aid provided to other countries (Table 9-12) or the roles of global investment and trade (Tables 9-13 and 9-14). Somewhere in the middle lays the question of diplomatic work done to aid other countries' military efforts and military sales (Table 9-11).

The costs of military policy extend beyond financial matters. Carrying out military policy relies on the personnel of the United States Armed Forces. Consider who comprises the military and how representative they are of the U.S. population as a whole (Table 9-8) and the perils that they face by serving the country (Tables 9-4 through 9-6). Beyond military personnel and their families, these decisions affect all Americans. Consider these tables in conjunction with Chapter 3, specifically those that provide some insights into perspectives of whether the American public consider foreign or domestic problems as more important, or whether peace can be ensured by military strength.

Whether through public opinion and its myriad effects on policy, or questions about balancing budgets between domestic and international spending, or the costs of military action for military personnel, foreign and military policy are clearly important elements of domestic politics in the United States, and the place of the United States in the world. The tables in this chapter present some of the publicly available data that help us begin to understand the relevance and importance of these elements for a more complete picture of the American political system.

Table 9-1 Treaties and Executive Agreements Concluded by the United States, 1789–2020

Years	Number of treaties	Number of executive agreements
1789–1839	60	27
1839–1889	215	238
1889–1929	382	763
1930–1932	49	41
1933–1944 (F. Roosevelt)	131	369
1945–1952 (Truman)	132	1,324
1953–1960 (Eisenhower)	89	1,834
1961–1963 (Kennedy)	36	813
1964–1968 (L. Johnson)	67	1,083
1969–1974 (Nixon)	93	1,317
1975–1976 (Ford)	26	666
1977–1980 (Carter)	79	1,476
1981–1988 (Reagan)	125	2,840
1989–1992 (G. H. W. Bush)	67	1,350
1993–2000 (Clinton)	209	2,048
2001–2008 (G. W. Bush)	136	1,998
2009–2017 (Obama)	24	825
2017–2020 (Trump)	8	286

Note: Number of treaties includes those concluded during the indicated span of years. Some of these treaties did not receive the consent of the U.S. Senate. Because of varying definitions of what comprises an executive agreement and their entry-into-force date, the numbers in the table are approximate. Since 2006, the *Treaties and International Agreements Series* has published exclusively online. With some exceptions such as national security, agreements to which the U.S. is a party must be recorded in TIAS within 180 days. Due to the change in reporting systems, comparisons before and after 2006 may not be comparable.

Sources: 1789–1992: *Congressional Quarterly's Guide to Congress*, 5th ed. (Washington, D.C.: CQ Press, 2000), 219; 1993–2008: Office of the Assistant Legal Adviser for Treaty Affairs, U.S. Department of State; 2009–2020: U.S. Department of State, *Treaties and Agreements by Year*, https://www.state.gov/tias.

Table 9-2 Major Arms Control and Disarmament Agreements

Issue	Participants
Nuclear weapons	
To prevent the spread of nuclear weapons	
Antarctic Treaty, 1959	54 nations
Outer Space Treaty, 1967	110 nations
Latin American Nuclear-Free Zone Treaty, 1967	33 nations[a]
Nuclear Non-proliferation Treaty, 1968	191 nations[a]
Seabed Treaty, 1971	94 nations
Joint Comprehensive Plan of Action (JCPOA), 2015[b]	United States, China, Russia, France, Germany, United Kingdom, and Iran
To reduce the risk of nuclear war	
Hot Line and Modernization Agreements, 1963	United States and Soviet Union
Accidents Measures Agreement, 1971	United States and Soviet Union
Prevention of Nuclear War Agreement, 1973	United States and Soviet Union
To limit nuclear testing	
Limited Test Ban Treaty, 1963	125 nations
Threshold Test Ban Treaty, 1974	United States and Soviet Union
Peaceful Nuclear Explosions Treaty, 1976[c]	United States and Soviet Union
Comprehensive Test Ban Treaty, 1996	185 nations[d]
To limit nuclear weapons	
ABM Treaty (SALT I) and Protocol, 1972	United States and Soviet Union
SALT I Interim Agreement, 1972[e]	United States and Soviet Union
SALT II, 1979[f]	United States and Soviet Union
Intermediate Range Nuclear Forces (INF) Treaty, 1987	United States and Soviet Union
Strategic Arms Reduction Treaty (START), 1991	United States, Russia, Belarus, Kazakhstan, Ukraine[g]
Strategic Arms Reduction Treaty, II (START II), 1993	United States and Russia[h]
Moscow Treaty on Strategic Offensive Reductions, 2002	United States and Russia
New Strategic Arms Reduction Treaty (New START), 2010[i]	United States and Russia
Other weapons	
To prohibit use of gas	
Geneva Protocol, 1925	145 nations[a]
To prohibit biological weapons	
Biological Weapons Convention, 1972	183 nations[j]
To prohibit techniques changing the environment	
Environmental Modification Convention, 1977	78 nations

(Table continues)

Table 9-2 *(Continued)*

Issue	Participants
To control use of inhumane weapons	
Convention on Conventional Weapons, 1981	125 nations[k]
To limit conventional weapons	
Conventional Forces in Europe Treaty, 1990	30 nations[l]
To ban use, development, production, stockpiling of chemical weapons	
Chemical Weapons Convention, 1993	193 nations[m]
To regulate the international trade of conventional arms	
Arms Trade Treaty, 2014	130 nations[n]

Note: "Participation" does not necessarily imply signing without reservations or ratification. In some instances, an agreement is no longer in force. For details, see sources.

[a] Number of parties and signatories as of June 2021.
[b] Not explicitly disarming or controlling arms, JCPOA is intended to prevent nuclear arms buildup. JCPOA is a multilateral agreement of six countries, endorsed as a UNSC Resolution, calling for Iran to take confidence building measures related to their nuclear infrastructure in exchange for economic sanctions relief and other concessions.
[c] Ratified by the United States and entered into force December 1990.
[d] Number of parties and signatories as of June 2021. Not yet entered into force as of June 2021.
[e] Expired by its terms October 3, 1977.
[f] Never ratified. If the treaty had entered into force, it would have expired by its terms December 31, 1985.
[g] Ratified by the United States October 1992; entered into force December 1994. President Barack Obama and President Dmitry A. Medvedev of Russia signed an agreement on July 6, 2009, to cut deployed nuclear warheads and to reduce delivery systems, setting the stage for negotiations to replace the 1991 Strategic Arms Reduction Treaty that expired in December 2009.
[h] Ratified by the United States as of January 1996. Ratified by Russia in April 2000, but with amendments not approved by the U.S. Senate.
[i] In March 2021, the United States and Russia agreed to a five-year extension of New START, extending it through 2026.
[j] Entered into force March 1975; number of parties and signatories as of June 2021.
[k] Entered into force December 1983. Number of parties and signatories as of June 2021. Full title of treaty is Convention on Prohibitions or Restrictions on the Use of Certain Conventional Weapons Which May Be Deemed to Be Excessively Injurious or to Have Indiscriminate Effects (and Protocols).
[l] Ratified by the United States December 1991; entered into force November 1992.
[m] Ratified by the United States April 25, 1997; took effect April 29, 1997. Number of parties and signatories as of June 2021.
[n] The United States signed the pact in 2013 before it went into force in 2014. In July 2019, the United States formally communicated to the UN secretary general that its signature was nonbinding and that the US does not intend to become a party to the treaty.

Sources: U.S. Department of State, www.state.gov; notes "a," "d," "l," and "n": United Nations Office for Disarmament Affairs, https://treaties.unoda.org; notes "i" and "k": United Nations Office at Geneva, "Disarmament," www.unog.ch.

Table 9-3 Use of U.S. Armed Forces Abroad, 1798–2020

Decade	Number of instances	Selected use of U.S. armed forces abroad
1798–1800	1	Undeclared naval war with France
1801–1810	4	Tripoli—First Barbary War, Mexico, West Florida (Spanish territory)
1811–1820	11	Caribbean; Second Barbary War; War of 1812
1821–1830	7	Cuba and Greece
1831–1840	7	Fiji Islands, Falkland Islands, Sumatra
1841–1850	8	China, Ivory Coast, Samoa, Mexican American War
1851–1860	22	Nicaragua, Turkey, China, Uruguay, Fiji Islands, Japan
1861–1870	13	Japan, Mexico, Colombia, Hawaiian Islands
1871–1880	5	Colombia, Hawaiian Islands, Korea, Mexico
1881–1890	7	Hawaii, Haiti, Argentina, Samoa, Egypt
1891–1900	18	Philippine Islands, Korea, China, Samoa, Brazil, Hawaii, Spanish American War
1901–1910	15	Colombia, Panama, Dominican Republic, Honduras, Nicaragua, Morocco, Syria
1911–1920	28	Honduras, China, Turkey, Mexico, Soviet Russia, World War I
1921–1930	11	Panama, Costa Rica, China, Nicaragua
1931–1940	5	China, Cuba, Caribbean
1941–1950	11	Trieste, Palestine, Germany, Iceland, Netherlands, Germany, World War II
1951–1960	6	Formosa, China, Egypt, Lebanon, Korean War
1961–1970	8	Congo, Laos, Cambodia, Dominican Republic, Vietnam War
1971–1980	11	Vietnam, Cambodia, Cyprus, Zaire, Iran
1981–1990	23	Libya, Grenada, Saudi Arabia, Bolivia, Italy, Chad, Honduras, El Salvador
1991–2000	73	Persian Gulf War, Iraq, Zaire, Somalia, Bosnia, Macedonia, Haiti, Rwanda, Yugoslavia, Kosovo, Yemen
2001–2010	43	Afghanistan, Haiti, Iraq, Kosovo, Macedonia, Pakistan, Lebanon, Bosnia, Liberia
2011–2020	117	Afghanistan, Iraq, Libya, Pakistan, Somalia, Yemen

Note: The count of instances is necessarily approximate, and intended as an approximate survey of use of force abroad. Five of the instances were declared wars with formal declarations against eleven nations: War of 1812 (1812–1815); Mexican War (1846–1848); Spanish–American War (1898); World War I (1917–1918); World War II (1941–1945). Others might be considered undeclared wars: undeclared naval war with France (1798–1800); First Barbary War (1801–1805); Second Barbary War (1815); Korean War (1950–1953); Vietnam War (1964–1973); Persian Gulf War (1991); Iraq War (2003). Covert actions, domestic disaster relief, routine alliance stationing and training exercises, and the continual use of U.S. troops in the exploration, settlement, and pacification of the Western United States are not included in this table. Actions that covered more than one decade are counted as occurring in each decade.

Sources: Barbara Salazar Torrean and Sofia Plagakis, *Instances of Use of United States Armed Forces Abroad, 1798–2020* (Washington, D.C.: Congressional Research Service, 2020).

Table 9-4 U.S. Personnel in Major Military Conflicts

Item	Civil War[a]	Spanish-American War	World War I	World War II	Korean War	Vietnam War	Persian Gulf War	Iraq War	Afghanistan War
Personnel serving (thousands)	2,213	307	4,735	16,113	5,720	8,744	2,233	1,500	776[b]
Average duration of service (months)	20	8	12	33	19	23	—	—	—
Casualties (thousands)									
Battle deaths	140	[c]	53	292	34	47	[c]	4.4	2.4[d]
Wounds not mortal	282	2	204	671	103	153	[c]	40.0	20.1[d]
Draftees: classified (thousands)	777	0	24,234	36,677	9,123	75,717	0	0	0
Examined	522	0	3,764	17,955	3,685	8,611	0	0	0
Rejected	160	0	803	6,420	1,189	3,880	0	0	0
Inducted	46	0	2,820	10,022	1,560	1,759	0	0	0
Cost (millions)[e]									
Current	$3,183	$283	$20,000	$296,000	$30,000	$111,000	$7,000[f]	$1,279,000[g]	$1,435,000[h]
Constant (2020)	68,610	10,394	384,295	4,722,005	392,350	849,133	13,462	—	—

Note: "—" indicates not available. For the Revolutionary War, the number of personnel serving is not known, but estimates range from 184,000 to 250,000; for the War of 1812, 286,730 served; for the Mexican–American War, 78,718 served. Periods covered are as follows: Spanish–American War: April 21, 1898, to August 13, 1898; World War II: December 1, 1941, to December 31, 1946; Korean War: June 5, 1950, to July 27, 1953; Vietnam War (personnel and draftees): August 4, 1964, to January 27, 1973; Vietnam War (deaths and wounded): January 1, 1961, to January 27, 1973; Persian Gulf War: August 1, 1990, to April 30, 1992; Iraq War: from March 19, 2003, (deaths as of June 8, 2021, cost through 2020); Afghanistan War: from October 7, 2001, (deaths as of June 8, 2021, cost through 2020).

[a] Union forces only. Estimates of the number serving in Confederate forces range from 600,000 to 1.5 million; cost for the Confederacy estimated at $1,000 million (current dollars) and $23,139 million (constant 2020 dollars).
[b] As of February 2019. Includes deployments from active-duty, reserve, and National Guard units. More than half served two or more deployments.
[c] Fewer than five hundred.
[d] As of June 8, 2021. Combines casualties from both Operation Enduring Freedom and Operation Freedom's Sentinel.
[e] Original direct costs only. Excludes service-connected veterans' benefits and interest payments on war loans.
[f] Total costs estimated at $61.0 billion (in current dollars). Shown is the portion of that amount estimated to have been paid by the United States.
[g] Does not include "complementary" costs such as spending for continuing care of returning veterans or interest payments.
[h] Estimate of cost through fiscal year 2019. Costs are approximations. Does not include "complementary" costs such as spending for continuing care of returning veterans.

(Table continues)

Table 9-4 *(Continued)*

Sources: Noncost items, Civil War–Vietnam: U.S. Bureau of the Census, *Statistical Abstract of the United States, 2001* (Washington, D.C.: Government Printing Office, 2001), 332; personnel serving (Iraq): U.S. Senate Democratic Policy and Communications Center, "Iraq by the Numbers" (December 19, 2011); (Afghanistan): Dan Lamothe, "U.S. deployments to Afghanistan by the Numbers" (*The Washington Post*, September 11, 2019); casualties (Iraq and Afghanistan): Defense Casualty Analysis System, dmdc.osd.mil; cost (through Vietnam): Congressional Research Service, "Costs of Major U.S. Wars," (June 29, 2010), www.crs.gov; cost (Persian Gulf): National Defense University, "Conduct of the Persian Gulf War, Final Report to Congress, April 1992," 725; cost (Iraq): Neta C. Crawford, "The Iraq War has cost the US nearly $2 trillion," (*Military Times*, February 6, 2020); cost (Afghanistan): Brown University, Watson Institute for International and Public Affairs, Costs of War Project, Figure "U.S. Costs to Date for the War in Afghanistan 2001–2021," https://watson.brown.edu/costsofwar.

Table 9-5 U.S. Military Forces and Casualties by Conflict 1950–2020

Conflict	Military forces serving[a]	Hostile Deaths					Wounded, nonfatal
		Killed in Action	Died of wounds	Missing in Action, Declared Dead	Captured, Declared Dead	Total Deaths[b]	No remains
Korean War	5,720,000	23,613	2,460	4,817	2,849	54,246	8,075	103,284
Vietnam War	8,744,000	40,934	5,299	1,085	116	58,220	1,741	153,303
Persian Gulf War	2,225,000	143	4	0	0	1,947	14	467
Afghanistan War	776,000	1,409	497	[d]	[d]	2,442	[d]	20,719
Iraq War	1,500,000	2,697	815	1	6	4,492	[d]	32,292

Note: Inclusive dates by conflict: Korean War: June 25, 1950–July 27, 1953; Vietnam War: November 1, 1955–May 15, 1975; Persian Gulf War (includes Desert Shield and Desert Storm): August 7, 1990–January 15, 1991; Afghanistan War (includes Operation Enduring Freedom and Operation Freedom's Sentinel): October 7, 2001– (updated as of July 16, 2020); Iraq War (includes Operation Iraqi Freedom and Operation New Dawn): March 20, 2003–December 31, 2011. Includes servicemembers who later died from wounds incurred during the period and servicemembers who were involved in an incident and later declared dead.

[a] Estimated number.
[b] Includes hostile, nonhostile, in-theater, and non-theater deaths. For more details, see original source.
[c] Includes service members on active duty and those recalled through involuntary activation of members of Selected Reserve and Individual Ready Reserve.
[d] None reported.

Sources: Military forces serving in Afghanistan and Iraq: Table 9-4, this volume. All other data: David A. Blum and Nese F. DeBruyne, *American War and Military Operations Casualties: Lists and Statistics* (Congressional Research Service, July 29, 2020).

A Data Literacy Lesson
Measuring the Cost of War

How do you measure the costs of entering and continuing a war? Tables 9-4 and 9-5 provide some insights into the ways that scholars have attempted to measure those costs. In the broadest terms, the data shared here show aspects of both financial and human costs to the government and for the armed forces who serve in the conflicts.

Using the data in Table 9-4, you could make some simple comparisons: what were the financial costs of each conflict? Do the number of troops correlate with the length of the conflict? Did certain conflicts carry a higher risk of death to military personnel? Is there a correlation between the amount of money the government spent on the war and the death rate? But, as we've cautioned throughout this book, drawing conclusions without context is risky.

Table 9-5 offers more context to two lines in Table 9-4, specifically deaths and injuries. We think of it like zooming in a bit to see more detail. When we look at this additional detail of the hostile deaths of military forces, we can see the effects of different styles of warfare fairly clearly. Not only are there fewer deaths overall, and a smaller likelihood that each individual solder will be killed, but we also see almost a complete absence of deaths resulting from captured or missing in action status. Zooming back out to Table 9-4, we can take that new information and use it to ask questions about the tradeoffs. Is the lower risk of death and capture related to the higher costs? The data indicate that it is less financially costly to have boots on the ground instead of drones in the sky, but the data also indicate that it is more hazardous to the personnel who wear those boots.

The number of ancillary tables that could be provided for additional information is extensive. We could zoom in on any one of the rows in Table 9-4 to get more information and context. Considering these individual components of bigger tables of data provides one step toward getting the context that is essential to draw conclusions.

As we've noted elsewhere, though, another essential question to ask when going through the process of getting context for data is the question of what's not included. The Costs of War Project housed at Brown University is one organization of scholars, legal and human rights experts, and physicians that is working toward quantifying a wide variety of the various costs of war, including economic costs, human costs (military and civilian alike), and social and political costs. It's worth noting that Tables 9-4 and 9-5 focus on specific defined conflicts but don't included the costs in either financial or human terms of other military involvement. And, at the risk of throwing yet another table in the mix, a quick look at Table 9-3 reminds us that there are dozens of other uses of U.S. Armed Forces abroad each decade, particularly in the post-9/11 era with the "War on Terror."[1]

Quantifying elements such as social and political costs of war is no easy task, to be sure, but it is an effort that can be undertaken with rigorous work and careful consideration. We think it's also important to consider the nonquantifiable questions of justification, though. In terms of dollars spent, World War II was extraordinarily expensive, with a cost in constant (2020) dollars exceeding the costs of all the other conflicts listed here combined. However, the human and financial costs of war must be weighed against the other interests a nation might have (such as, in World War II, stopping Adolf Hitler) when making decisions to enter or stay out of a war.

The data in these tables certainly don't provide the answers to the fundamental question of when a war is worth the costs, or what justifies those costs in dollars and human sacrifice, but they do provide us some basis for beginning to understand the stakes and costs of war.

---

1. The Costs of War Project estimates that the overall financial costs of the post-9/11 War on Terror spending exceeded $6.4 trillion between 2001–2019. For details, see https://watson.brown.edu/costsofwar/figures/2019/budgetary-costs-post-911-wars-through-fy2020-64-trillion.

Table 9-6 Sexual Assaults, Amputations, Suicides, and Traumatic Brain Injuries Sustained by U.S. Military Personnel, 2001–2020

Year	Sexual assaults[a]	Sexual assaults at MSAs[b]	Amputations[c]	Suicides[d]	Traumatic brain injuries[e]
2001	—	—	4	147	11,619
2002	—	—	3	141	12,407
2003	—	—	95	160	12,815
2004	1,700	—	162	171	14,519
2005	2,374	—	169	152	15,531
2006	2,947	42	165	190	17,037
2007	2,846	40	218	197	23,217
2008	3,109	35	105	268	28,462
2009	3,472	29	97	309	28,877
2010	3,327	41	213	295	29,188
2011	3,393	65	273	301	32,625
2012	3,604	79	151	522	30,406
2013	5,518	69	37	474	20,250
2014	6,131	59	8	446	25,068
2015	6,083	91	1	479	22,672
2016	6,172	86	2	482	18,342
2017	6,769	112	2	511	17,841
2018	7,623	117	—	541	18,949
2019	7,823	149	—	498	20,128
2020	7,816	129	—	—	16,198

Note: "—" indicates not available.

[a] Numbers are total reports of sexual assault made to the Department of Defense in the fiscal year ending in the year shown. Total reports include unrestricted reports (reports that are provided to command and/or law enforcement for investigation) as well as reports remaining restricted (reports that allow victims to confidentially access medical care and advocacy services without triggering an investigation).

b Numbers are the total reports of sexual assaults involving enrolled cadets and misdshipmen at the military service academies during the academic program year ending in the year shown.

c Number of service members with deployment-related amputations. Some service members had more than one amputation.

d Numbers are death by suicide among active, reserve, and guard service members. Source prior to 2008 presented graphs only; numbers as read from graphs may contain slight inaccuracies. Cases in 2020 may be underreported due to restrictions placed on hospitals and clinics, impacting case seeking behaviors due to COVID-19.

e Numbers represent actual medical diagnoses of TBI anywhere U.S. forces are located, including the United States, and range from mild concussions to severe and penetrating (or open head injury) TBIs.

Sources: Sexual assaults: Department of Defense, Annual Report on Sexual Assault in the Military, Fiscal Years 2014 and 2020, www.sapr.mil; sexual assaults at MSAs: Department of Defense, Annual Report on Sexual Harassment and Violence at the Military Service Academies, Academic Program Year 2013–2014 and 2019–2020, Appendix D; Amputations: Shawn Farrokhi, Katheryne Perez, Susan Eskridge, and Mary Clouser, "Major deployment-related amputations of lower and upper limbs, active and reserve components, U.S. Armed Forces, 2001–2017," (National Library of Medicine, PubMed Central, July 2018, 25(7):10–16); Armed Forces Health Surveillance Branch, Medical Surveillance Monthly Report, July 2018: Suicides, 2001–2007: June 2012, 8; Suicides, 2008–2019: Department of Defense, Suicide Event Reports, 2008–2019; Traumatic brain injuries, 2001–2013: Congressional Research Service, A Guide to U.S. Military Casualty Statistics: Operation Inherent Resolve, Operation New Dawn, Operation Iraqi Freedom, and Operation Enduring Freedom, RS22452, November 20, 2014, 4; Traumatic brain injuries, 2014–2020: Department of Defense, TBI Worldwide Numbers Annual Reports.

A Data Literacy Lesson
Data Collection and Self-Reporting

As we look at Table 9-6, we see a number of different dangers that members of the military face, both on and off the battle field. What unifies these categories is that they all report on risks faced by military personnel; however, there are differences in both substance and in data interpretation as we consider what conclusions we can draw from the data presented.

When it comes to data interpretation, we think this table provides an excellent example of the importance of understanding the context in which data were collected. As you go through the table left to right, ask yourself where those numbers came from. Who asked what questions to be able to report those final numbers? We know that footnotes aren't always the most exciting things to read, but they can provide a lot of valuable information. In data tables like this, for example, you can learn about where the data are from. In this case, the numbers of sexual assaults are based on reports that are filed by the victims of the assault; the number of deployment-related amputations and traumatic brain injuries are based on medical diagnoses and reports; and the number of deaths by suicide are based on cases when the cause of death is known to be suicide.

In many ways, TBIs and amputations present the most clear-cut data collection. A patient receives a diagnosis or procedure and medical personnel report it. While there are still nuances that can be drawn out, such as what percentage of TBIs are mild concussions compared to open head wounds from combat and how that affects our understanding of TBIs in the military, interpretations are still generally clear: fewer amputations and TBIs is good. As those numbers go down, we can feel more confident that the safety of military personnel is increasing.

There are more questions about the accuracy of the completeness of data reporting death by suicide. Suicide is talked about more and named as a cause of death as a way to help others and encourage them to seek help. We wonder if that willingness to acknowledge suicide as a cause of death has introduced some error in the overall reporting rates. In some cases, the cause of death may be unclear or unknown and cannot be accurately or fully counted. More attention has been paid to suicide rates among personnel and veterans in recent years. However, the effect of that uncertainty is likely to be fairly constant over time and we can say that fewer cases of death by suicide is a positive indication for military personnel.

We note, though, a different interpretation in the data reporting sexual assaults in the military and military service academies. To highlight what we mean, look at the reports of sexual assault among military personnel. From FY 2012 to FY 2013, there was a 53 percent increase in victims' reports of sexual assault. That might actually be a positive step toward a safer environment with fewer sexual assaults. How is that possible?

If you look at footnotes a and b, you'll see that sexual assaults data are from self-reports of assault victims. Historically, sexual assaults have been underreported. Reporting provides access to care and services, and the potential to hold offenders accountable. However, it also increases the risk of retaliation and perhaps, historically, victim blaming that led to shame and reduced the likelihood of self-reporting. In a 2017 report, the Department of Defense estimated that in 2006 as few as 1 in 14 sexual assaults were reported. However, there have been efforts not only to reduce the number of sexual assaults in the military but also to make victims feel safer and more supported in reporting assaults when they do happen. By 2016, the Department of Defense estimates that the number of assaults reported had grown from 1 in 14 to 1 in 3. There's certainly a lot of room for improvement, both in reducing assaults and in increasing reports. Still, we think that for a ten-year period, it's a big improvement to see that increase in reporting. It is possible, then, that increased numbers of sexual assaults is indicative of a better environment for reporting, rather than indicating that there have been more assaults. But that is speculation based on estimates and we have to acknowledge that we know how many reports are made, not how many assaults there were.

When numbers are based on self-reports, particularly when it relies on victims or members of vulnerable populations to come forward, consider the conditions that might affect the numbers reported before drawing broad conclusions from them.

Table 9-7 U.S. Military Personnel Abroad or Afloat, by Country, 1972–2020 (thousands)

Country	1972	1975	1980	1985	1990	1995	2000	2005[a]	2010[a]	2015	2020
Outside United States	628	517	502	515	609	238	258	291	297	213	169
Europe[b]	298	314	332	358	310	118	117	102	79	64	64
Germany	210	220	244	247	228	73	69	66	54	35	34
Greece	3	4	4	4	2	[c]	1	[c]	[c]	[c]	[c]
Iceland	3	3	3	4	3	2	2	1	[c]	[c]	[c]
Italy	10	12	12	15	14	12	11	12	10	12	12
Spain	9	9	9	9	7	3	2	2	1	3	3
Turkey	7	7	5	5	4	3	2	2	2	2	2
United Kingdom	22	21	24	30	25	12	11	11	9	8	9
Afloat	28	30	22	36	18	8	4	2	[c]	—	—
East Asia and Pacific[a]	275	156	115	125	119	89	101	79	44	82	82
Japan (includes Okinawa)	65	48	46	50	45	43	40	36	34	56	54
Korea, Rep. of	41	42	39	42	41	36	37	31	—	25	26
Philippines	17	15	13	15	14	[c]	[c]	[c]	[c]	[c]	[c]
Thailand	47	20	[c]	[c]	[c]	[c]	[c]	[c]	[c]	[c]	[c]
Vietnam	47	0	0	0	0	[c]	1	[c]	[c]	[c]	[c]
Afloat	51	28	16	20	16	13	23	12	9	—	—
U.S. outlying areas[d]	29	25	2	14	11	9	6	3	3	7	6

Note: "—" indicates not available. Data are for September 30, each year the following troops were deployed in and around Iraq as part of Operation Iraqi Freedom: 192,600 in 2005; 96,200 in 2010. Also deployed in and around Afghanistan as part of Operation Enduring Freedom: 19,500 in 2005; 105,900 in 2010.

[a] In addition, as of September. Data for additional years can be found in previous editions of *Vital Statistics on American Politics*.
[b] Includes troops in countries not shown.
[c] Fewer than five hundred.
[d] Primarily Guam and Puerto Rico.

Sources: 1972–1985: U.S. Bureau of the Census, *Statistical Abstract of the United States, 1977* (Washington, D.C.: Government Printing Office, 1977), 370; 1986, 343; 1990–1995: U.S. Department of Defense, *Selected Manpower Statistics, Fiscal Year 1990* (Washington, D.C.: Government Printing Office, 1991), 44–47, 51, 176; 1995, 1–6; 2000–2010: U.S. Department of Defense, *Worldwide Manpower Distribution by Geographical Area* (Washington, D.C.: Government Printing Office, 2000); (2005), 8–11, 38; (2006–2010); 2015–2020: Defense Manpower Data Center, "Military and Civilian Personnel by Service/Agency by State/Country," quarterly reports, https://dwp.dmdc.osd.mil/dwp/app/dod-data-reports/workforce-reports.

Table 9-8 U.S. Active Duty Forces, by Sex, Race, and Hispanic Origin, 1965–2019

Year	Female Officers	Female Enlisted	Female Total	Black Officers	Black Enlisted	Black Total	Hispanic[a] Officers	Hispanic[a] Enlisted	Hispanic[a] Total	Total[b] Officers (thousands)	Total[b] Enlisted (thousands)
1965	3.1%	0.9%	1.2%	1.9%	10.5%	9.5%	—	—	—	339	2,317
1970	3.3	1.1	1.4	2.2	11.0	9.8	—	—	—	402	2,664
1975	4.6	4.5	4.6	3.2	16.2	14.4	1.4	4.6	4.2%	292	1,836
1976	5.0	5.3	5.2	3.6	17.1	15.2	1.3	4.6	4.2	281	1,801
1977	5.4	5.8	5.7	3.9	17.4	15.6	1.5	4.5	4.1	276	1,798
1978	6.2	6.5	6.5	4.3	19.3	17.3	1.6	4.5	4.1	274	1,788
1979	6.9	7.5	7.4	4.7	21.2	19.0	1.6	4.4	3.8	274	1,753
1980	7.7	8.5	8.4	5.0	21.9	19.6	1.2	4.0	3.6	278	1,759
1981	8.1	9.0	8.9	5.3	22.1	19.8	1.2	4.1	3.7	285	1,783
1982	8.6	9.0	9.0	5.3	22.0	19.7	1.2	4.1	3.7	292	1,804
1983	9.0	9.3	9.3	5.8	21.6	19.4	1.4	4.1	3.7	301	1,811
1984	9.4	9.5	9.5	6.2	21.1	19.0	1.4	3.9	3.6	304	1,820
1985	9.8	9.8	9.8	6.4	21.1	18.9	1.5	3.9	3.6	309	1,828
1986	10.1	10.0	10.1	6.5	21.2	19.1	1.7	4.1	3.7	311	1,845
1987	10.4	10.2	10.2	6.5	21.5	19.4	1.7	4.3	3.9	308	1,856
1988	10.7	10.4	10.4	6.7	22.0	19.8	1.8	4.5	4.1	305	1,819
1989	11.1	11.0	11.0	6.9	22.8	20.3	2.0	4.8	4.4	303	1,814
1990	11.4	10.9	10.9	6.9	22.9	20.5	2.1	5.0	4.6	304	1,762
1991	11.7	10.8	10.9	7.1	22.6	20.3	2.2	5.2	4.8	298	1,711
1992	12.0	11.3	11.4	7.2	22.0	19.8	2.3	5.5	5.0	281	1,551
1993	12.4	11.5	11.7	7.1	21.6	19.4	2.4	5.8	5.3	264	1,466
1994	12.8	12.0	12.1	7.3	21.4	19.2	2.6	6.0	5.4	253	1,380
1995	13.0	12.5	12.6	7.5	21.5	19.3	2.8	6.4	5.8	245	1,295
1996	13.4	13.2	13.2	7.8	21.8	19.6	3.0	6.9	6.3	233	1,225
1997	13.6	13.7	13.7	8.0	22.1	19.8	3.2	7.5	6.8	228	1,198

(Table continues)

Table 9-8 *(Continued)*

Year	Female			Black			Hispanic[a]			Total[b]	
	Officers	Enlisted	Total	Officers	Enlisted	Total	Officers	Enlisted	Total	Officers (thousands)	Enlisted (thousands)
1988	10.7	10.4	10.4	6.7	22.0	19.8	1.8	4.5	4.1	305	1,819
1989	11.1	11.0	11.0	6.9	22.8	20.3	2.0	4.8	4.4	303	1,814
1990	11.4	10.9	10.9	6.9	22.9	20.5	2.1	5.0	4.6	304	1,762
1991	11.7	10.8	10.9	7.1	22.6	20.3	2.2	5.2	4.8	298	1,711
1992	12.0	11.3	11.4	7.2	22.0	19.8	2.3	5.5	5.0	281	1,551
1993	12.4	11.5	11.7	7.1	21.6	19.4	2.4	5.8	5.3	264	1,466
1994	12.8	12.0	12.1	7.3	21.4	19.2	2.6	6.0	5.4	253	1,380
1995	13.0	12.5	12.6	7.5	21.5	19.3	2.8	6.4	5.8	245	1,295
1996	13.4	13.2	13.2	7.8	21.8	19.6	3.0	6.9	6.3	233	1,225
1997	13.6	13.7	13.7	8.0	22.1	19.8	3.2	7.5	6.8	228	1,198
1998	13.9	14.1	14.0	8.2	22.2	20.0	3.4	8.0	7.2	224	1,171
1999	14.0	14.2	14.2	8.3	22.0	19.8	3.7	8.5	7.7	227	1,179
2000	14.3	14.5	14.5	8.5	22.1	19.9	4.0	5.0	8.2	224	1,182
2001	14.6	14.8	14.8	8.8	22.1	20.0	3.9	9.4	8.6	223	1,181
2002	14.7	14.8	14.8	8.8	21.7	19.7	4.0	9.6	8.7	224	1,184
2003	15.2	14.9	14.9	8.9	20.6	18.8	4.5	9.8	9.0	235	1,227
2004	15.3	14.7	14.8	8.9	19.7	18.0	4.8	9.8	9.0	236	1,215
2005	15.3	14.3	14.5	8.9	19.1	17.4	4.9	9.8	9.0	234	1,179
2006	15.2	14.3	14.5	9.1	18.9	17.3	5.1	11.2	10.2	232	1,181
2007	15.1	14.1	14.3	9.1	18.5	17.0	5.2	11.4	10.4	230	1,177
2008	15.3	14.0	14.2	9.2	18.3	16.8	5.3	11.6	9.9	232	1,198
2009	15.5	14.0	14.3	9.3	18.1	16.7	5.4	11.7	10.7	237	1,210
2010	15.7	14.1	14.4	9.5	18.5	17.0	5.8	12.2	11.2	235	1,183
2011	15.9	14.2	14.5	9.5	18.4	16.9	5.8	12.3	11.2	237	1,171
2012	16.1	14.3	14.6	9.5	18.3	16.8	5.8	12.5	11.3	239	1,149
2013	16.4	14.5	14.9	9.4	18.5	17.0	6.0	12.8	11.6	239	1,131

2014	16.7	14.8	15.1	9.3	18.9	17.2	5.9	13.2	12.0	235	1,091
2015	17.0	15.1	15.5	9.1	19.1	17.3	6.3	13.9	12.3	231	1,071
2016	17.3	15.6	15.9	9.0	19.1	17.4	7.7	17.1	15.0	229	1,060
2017	17.7	15.9	16.2	8.9	19.1	17.3	8.0	17.9	15.5	229	1,065
2018	18.0	16.2	16.5	8.9	8.8	17.1	8.3	18.8	16.1	231	1,073
2019	18.4	16.6	16.9	8.1	18.9	17.2	8.7	19.6	16.7	233	1,093

Note: " — " indicates not available. Data for additional years can be found in previous editions of *Vital Statistics on American Politics*.

[a] Hispanics may be of any race. Data on percent Hispanic origin from 1971 to 1979 are based on male armed forces members only. Following OMB directives beginning in 2009, Hispanic is no longer considered a minority race designation and is analyzed separately as an ethnicity.
[b] Includes other races not shown separately.

Sources: 1965–1985: U.S. Bureau of the Census, *Statistical Abstract of the United States, 1976* (Washington, D.C.: Government Printing Office, 1976), 336; 1980, 375–376; *1984*, 353; *1986*, 341; *1987*, 327; 1986–1988: U.S. Department of Defense, unpublished data; 1989 (female, total officers, total enlisted): U.S. Department of Defense, *Selected Manpower Statistics, 1989* (Washington, D.C.: Government Printing Office, 1989), 78, 87, 101; 1989 (other): U.S. Department of Defense, *Defense 90 Almanac* (Washington, D.C.: Government Printing Office,1990), 30; 1990–1998: Defense Equal Opportunity Management Institute, *Semi-Annual Race/Ethnic/Gender Profile of the Department of Defense Active Forces, Reserve Forces, and the United States Coast Guard* (Patrick Air Force Base, Fla.: Defense Equal Opportunity Management Institute—DEOMI, 1990), 24; (1991), 9; (1992)–(1998), 12; 1999–2002: Patrick Air Force Base, www.patrick.af.mil; 2003–2013: "Semiannual [now Annual] Demographic Profile of the Department of Defense and U.S. Coast Guard"; 2014–2019: U.S. Department of Defense, Military One Source, "Demographic Profiles of the Military Community," https://www.militaryonesource.mil. Hispanic officer and enlisted percentages 2014-2019: Populations Representation in the Military Services: Fiscal Year Summary Report. 2014: Table 8; 2015-2016: Table 14; 2017 - 2019: Table 10. https://prhome.defense.gov/M-RA/Inside-M-RA/MPP/Accession-Policy/Pop-Rep/

Table 9-9 U.S. Defense Spending, 1940–2025

	Annual percentage change[a]		Defense outlays as a percentage of	
Year	Current dollars	Constant (2012) dollars	Federal outlays	Gross domestic product
1940	—	—	17.5	1.7
1945	4.8	15.3	89.5	36.6
1950	4.4	3.1	32.2	4.9
1951	72.3	62.0	51.8	7.2
1952	95.3	88.1	68.1	12.9
1953	14.5	3.8	69.4	13.8
1954	−6.6	−8.3	69.5	12.7
1955	−13.4	−16.0	62.4	10.5
1956	−0.5	−6.1	60.2	9.7
1957	6.8	1.5	59.3	9.8
1958	3.1	−1.5	56.8	9.9
1959	4.7	−2.1	53.2	9.7
1960	−1.8	−0.8	52.2	9.0
1961	3.1	1.1	50.8	9.1
1962	5.4	5.4	49.0	8.9
1963	2.1	−2.4	48.0	8.6
1964	2.6	1.2	46.2	8.3
1965	−7.7	−7.3	42.8	7.1
1966	14.8	9.6	43.2	7.4
1967	22.9	19.1	45.4	8.5
1968	14.7	9.5	46.0	9.1
1969	0.7	−4.7	44.9	8.4
1970	−1.0	−5.8	41.8	7.8
1971	−3.4	−9.1	37.5	7.0
1972	0.4	−8.4	34.3	6.5
1973	−3.2	−9.5	31.2	5.7
1974	3.4	−3.1	29.5	5.3
1975	9.1	0.1	26.0	5.4
1976	3.6	−2.5	24.1	5.0
TQ[b]	−75.1	−75.6	23.2	4.7
1977	335.9	312.5	23.8	4.8
1978	7.5	0.6	22.8	4.6
1979	11.3	2.9	23.1	4.5
1980	15.2	4.1	22.7	4.8
1981	17.5	6.0	23.2	5.0
1982	17.7	8.0	24.8	5.6
1983	13.3	8.0	26.0	5.9
1984	8.3	3.0	26.7	5.8
1985	11.1	7.0	26.7	5.9
1986	8.2	5.8	27.6	6.0
1987	3.1	1.7	28.1	5.9
1988	3.0	0.4	27.3	5.6
1989	4.5	0.7	26.5	5.4

(Table continues)

Table 9-9 *(Continued)*

	Annual percentage change[a]		Defense outlays as a percentage of	
Year	Current dollars	Constant (2012) dollars	Federal outlays	Gross domestic product
1990	−1.4	−4.7	23.9	5.1
1991	−8.7	13.0	20.6	4.5
1992	9.1	7.5	21.6	4.6
1993	−2.4	−3.4	20.7	4.3
1994	−3.3	−4.1	19.3	3.9
1995	−3.4	−5.2	17.9	3.6
1996	−2.4	−4.4	17.0	3.3
1997	1.8	0.2	16.9	3.2
1998	−0.9	−2.7	16.2	3.0
1999	2.5	0.4	16.1	2.9
2000	7.1	3.5	16.5	2.9
2001	3.5	0.1	16.4	2.9
2002	14.4	10.7	17.3	3.2
2003	16.1	9.1	18.7	3.6
2004	12.6	8.5	19.9	3.8
2005	8.7	3.7	20.0	3.8
2006	5.4	1.0	19.7	3.8
2007	5.7	2.3	20.2	3.8
2008	11.8	7.6	20.7	4.2
2009	7.3	7.5	18.8	4.6
2010	4.9	3.0	20.1	4.7
2011	1.7	−1.2	19.6	4.6
2012	−3.9	−5.2	19.2	4.2
2013	−6.6	−7.2	18.3	3.8
2014	−4.7	−6.3	17.2	3.5
2015	−2.3	−2.8	16.0	3.3
2016	0.6	0.2	15.4	3.2
2017	0.9	−0.45	15.0	3.1
2018	5.4	2.6	15.4	3.1
2019	8.7	6.7	15.4	3.2
2020	5.6	3.6	11.1	3.5
2021 est.	5.9	3.8	10.3	3.4
2022 est.	2.0	0.0	12.8	3.3
2023 est.	0.3	−1.7	12.8	3.1
2024 est.	0.9	−1.1	12.8	3.1
2025 est.	1.4	−0.6	12.4	3.0

Note: "—" indicates not available.

[a] Change from prior year.
[b] Transition quarter, July–September.

Sources: Annual percentage change calculated from actual dollar amounts of defense spending in Table 11-3, this volume; percentage of federal outlays and GDP: U.S. Office of Management and Budget, *Budget of the U.S. Government*, Historical Tables, Table 6.1, https://www.whitehouse.gov/omb.

Figure 9-1 U.S. Defense Spending as a Percentage of Federal Outlays and of Gross Domestic Product, 1940–2025

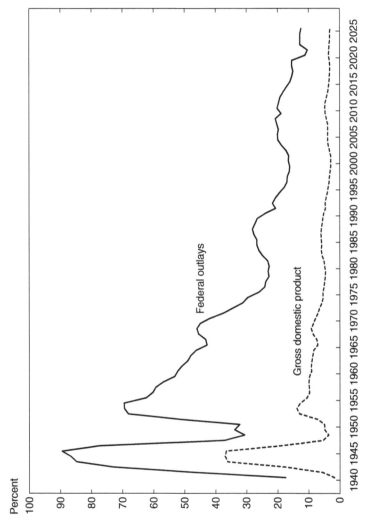

Note: Figures for 2021 through 2025 are estimates.

Source: Table 9-9, this volume.

Table 9-10 Military Expenditures: World, Regional, and Selected National Estimates, 1990–2020

Region[a]	\multicolumn{10}{c}{Estimated expenditure (billions)}	Percentage change, 1990–2020
	1990	1995	2000	2005	2010	2015	2016	2017	2018	2019	2020	
Africa	$14.1	$12.1	$18.6	$22.2	$26.1	$34.8	$34.3	$33.3	$32.4	$32.8	$33.2	135
North	2.1	3.6	5.4	8.6	8.9	14.8	14.9	14.4	14.0	15.0	15.8	671
Sub-Saharan	11.4	8.5	13.2	13.6	17.3	20.0	19.4	18.9	18.4	17.8	17.4	53
Americas	682.7	545.2	525.0	752.3	937.1	760.3	756.9	756.0	778.2	817.2	849.0	24
North	653.6	5,111.1	488.5	713.1	882.8	702.3	700.4	697.3	717.5	756.6	789.4	21
Central	3.8	3.9	4.5	4.2	5.6	7.2	7.9	7.4	8.1	8.9	8.8	133
South	25.3	30.1	31.0	35.0	48.4	50.9	48.6	51.4	52.7	51.8	50.7	101
Asia and Oceania	149.1	167.7	192.3	248.6	337.5	428.1	448.6	469.6	485.6	500.3	512.8	244
Central, South, and Southeast Asia	43.1	49.6	57.0	73.8	96.0	113.9	120.4	127.9	129.7	128.2	131.2	205
East Asia	91.8	103.4	119.3	156.2	218.2	288.3	299.9	313.1	327.8	342.9	350.9	282
Oceania	14.2	14.7	16.0	18.6	82.2	25.9	28.3	28.4	28.0	29.2	30.8	116
Europe[b]	525.1	279.6	284.5	302.9	330.2	335.9	348.3	339.4	345.5	363.4	377.8	−28
Central and Eastern	247.1	44.4	42.7	58.4	74.0	104.7	109.7	96.3	98.0	105.4	109.8	−56
Western[b]	278.0	235.3	241.8	244.4	256.2	231.2	23,865.0	243.1	247.6	258.0	268.1	−4
Middle East[b]	84.9	64.7	91.9	114.8	147.9	166.8	144.4	155.1	158.7	147.0	137.5	62

Top-spending nations in 2020

Country	1990	1995	2000	2005	2010	2015	2016	2017	2018	2019	2020	Percentage change, 1990–2020
United States	$636.2	$511.1	$488.5	$713.1	$882.8	$702.3	$700.4	$697.3	$77.5	$756.6	$789.4	24
China	21.3	25.3	41.2	73.4	129.4	192.8	203.9	216.5	229.2	240.3	244.9	1,051
India	20.6	21.5	30.3	39.5	54.0	56.8	62.6	67.5	69.3	71.5	73.0	254
Russia	220.5[c]	25.6	23.6	35.2	49.8	74.7	80.0	64.9	62.4	65.2	66.8	−70

(Table continues)

Table 9-10 (Continued)

Region[a]	Estimated expenditure (billions)											Percentage change, 1990–2020
	1990	1995	2000	2005	2010	2015	2016	2017	2018	2019	2020	
United Kingdom	60.9	50.1	48.7	58.7	63.2	54.0	53.8	53.5	54.2	56.9	58.5	–4
Saudi Arabia	27.8	20.1	30.8	38.9	53.6	88.5	63.3	70.6	72.9	62.0	55.5	100
France	51.4	47.3	45.0	47.5	48.4	48.0	49.9	50.6	49.3	50.1	51.6	0
Germany	61.4[d]	44.6	42.4	33.3	41.1	40.6	42.3	43.5	45.0	49.0	51.6	–16
Japan	42.7	45.0	46.2	47.1	46.4	47.6	47.3	47.4	47.4	47.6	48.2	13
Korea, Rep. of	15.9	20.4	21.1	26.0	32.2	37.2	38.1	38.8	40.8	43.9	46.1	190
Italy	28.4	25.0	33.1	32.6	29.9	23.0	26.1	26.9	27.1	26.4	28.4	0
Australia	12.0	12.7	14.1	16.7	21.1	23.8	26.1	26.0	25.4	26.1	27.6	131
Brazil	13.0	15.2	16.8	17.7	25.4	25.1	23.8	25.4	27.1	25.9	25.1	93
Canada	17.4	14.7	13.2	15.1	17.5	18.6	18.8	22.7	22.6	22.0	22.9	31
Israel	12.3	12.2	12.8	13.8	15.8	18.3	19.2	20.1	20.1	20.5	21.1	72
World	1,372.0	1,010.0	1,022.0	1,443.0	1,790.0	1,767.0	1,774.0	1,796.0	1,842.0	1,909.0	1,960.0	43
Percentage change from previous year	–5.6	–4.9	3.0	3.9	2.0	1.6	0.4	1.2	2.6	3.7	2.6	

Note: Amounts in constant 2019 U.S. prices and exchange rates. Regional figures do not always add up to totals because of rounding. Figures are estimates for some countries in some years, including China, Iraq, Israel, and Saudi Arabia. Some countries are excluded because of lack of data or of consistent time-series data. Totals exclude Cuba, Haiti, Iraq before 2005, North Korea, Somalia, and Yemen. For details on the derivations of the estimates as well as differences among countries and over time in what counts as military expenditures, see sources.

[a] For the country composition of the regions, see source "Military Expenditure by country," www.sipri.org.
[b] Turkey was reclassified to the Middle East (from Western Europe) in the 1988–2014 SIPRI Military Expenditure database (see sources). The figures for Europe and Western Europe are therefore lower, and figures for the Middle East are higher, than in previous editions of the database and in this table from earlier editions of *Vital Statistics on American Politics*.
[c] Figures for Russia for 1990 refer to the former USSR.
[d] Figures for Germany for 1990 refer to the former Federal Republic of Germany (West Germany).

Sources: Adapted by the editors from Stockholm International Peace Research Institute, Military Expenditure Database, "Military Expenditure by Region in Constant U.S. Dollars, 1949–2020," and "Military Expenditure by Region, in Constant (2019) U.S. Dollars," www.sipri.org/databases/milex. Reprinted by permission of SIPRI.

A Data Literacy Lesson
Using Data for Comparisons

How do you measure a country's military strength? There are many different measures you could consider: number of troops, size of a weapons stockpile, or how quickly troops could be deployed. One means of comparison has been to consider the amount of money that a country invests in its military. Even within that measurement, though, there are plenty of questions that remain before we have clarification regarding our original question.

Table 9-10 presents military expenditures around the world by region, and highlights the countries that spent the most on their military in 2020. A quick glance down the columns highlights some patterns that we suspect aren't all that surprising. By region, North America has the highest expenditures by far—more than twice all of European military spending and more than 150 percent of the expenditures in all of Asia and Oceania. And, looking more closely at the highest-spending nations, we see that the United States spends a great deal more on its military than any other country. Again, not too surprising, we think.

But, while we can say that the United States spends more on their military than any other nation in the world does, what other questions are left unanswered when we measure military expenditures solely by the dollar amounts spent? Can we say that because the United States spent about thirty-seven times more than Israel did in 2020 that the U.S. places thirty-seven times more importance on the military than Israel does? To control for the size of the country's economy, another economic measure that might provide some insights would be to consider what percentage of their GDP a country spends on the military, or what percentage of its overall federal spending is earmarked for the military (both of which are shown over time for the United States in Table 9-9). While the United States spends far more in real dollars, Russia, Israel, and Saudi Arabia all spend more as a percentage of their GDP. That doesn't necessarily change how we interpret overall spending and readiness, but it might change how we interpret the relative importance a country is placing on its military.

Another question we might ask about military expenditures is the importance a country places on the military budget over time, rather than relative to other countries. Here, the final column, which shows percent change in spending, becomes useful. The United States has increased its military spending over the past thirty years by almost 25 percent, which might seem like a lot until you see that China has increased its military spending by over 1,000 percent… of course, we don't know if the amount that China spends as a percent of GDP has grown at a comparable pace. If we're considering relative expenditures over time, it could also be useful to compare a country's increase to the worldwide change. So, the United States' increase of 25 percent is actually less than the global increase of 43 percent while China's increase of 1,051 percent is still significantly outpacing the global growth in military expenditures.

We often turn to data to help answer questions, and when we see patterns that seem to answer the questions quickly, it's easy to stop at that first glance and consider the job done. If we were to take that approach with a question about military strength and support, we might easily stop at the point of identifying that the United States spends more than three times the next-highest spending country. In stopping there, we would miss the complexity and nuance that the data open up to us.

Table 9-11 U.S. Military Sales and Military Assistance to Foreign Governments, Principal Recipients, 1950–2020 (millions)

Country	Military sales[a]					
	1950–2015	2016	2017	2018	2019	2020
Afghanistan	5,264.8	2,755.4	2,525.5	2,698.5	1,576.7	1,071.5
Australia	31,017.9	1,341.9	1,233.6	1,463.0	1,638.8	1,718.4
Canada	9,374.4	95.0	356.5	193.5	1,074.1	517.4
France	4,716.6	1,046.0	190.9	153.1	305.0	246.3
Germany	16,927.2	38.5	222.7	127.8	1,161.0	501.5
Greece	13,396.8	815.5	19.1	1,349.3	39.9	408.1
India	7,418.4	1,030.7	754.5	282.2	6,203.4	3,363.7
Iran	10,715.4	0.0	0.0	0.0	0.0	0.0
Iraq	15,990.2	1,202.0	3,139.2	735.9	1,362.3	367.8
Israel	41,542.5	522.2	2,440.9	598.8	1,489.7	1,058.8
Japan	25,700.7	2,854.1	4,117.1	3,498.9	6,880.4	1,982.6
Netherlands	12,174.8	1,039.6	331.3	1,689.9	324.4	451.0
Saudi Arabia	136,171.8	3,711.5	2,561.0	14,275.0	14,971.8	1,175.2
South Korea	31,365.5	4,232.6	577.1	560.9	2,688.4	2,124.1
Spain	9,471.8	282.5	92.9	129.6	1,788.4	140.1
Taiwan	28,212.6	1,806.5	563.5	1,677.2	875.6	11,777.4
Turkey	20,254.8	228.9	213.4	37.0	134.8	82.2
United Arab Emirates	22,133.2	763.0	759.5	3,217.0	1,087.9	3,568.0
United Kingdom	22,541.2	5,099.6	1,132.3	398.9	572.2	440.8
Total[b]	671,130.5	33,628.9	41,929.5	55,657.9	55,385.9	50,781.5

Note: Figures exclude training. Amounts in current dollars. Data for additional years can be found in previous editions of *Vital Statistics on American Politics*.

[a] Up to FY 2014, sales were counted when the partner signed the case; beginning in FY 2015 sales were counted after the partner signed and provided the initial deposit.
[b] Includes countries not shown.

Source: U.S. Defense Security Cooperation Agency, "Historical Sales Book Fiscal Years 1950–2020," www.dsca.mil.

Table 9-12 U.S. Foreign Aid, Principal Recipients, 1946–2018 (millions)

Region/country	1946–2014	2015	2016	2017	2018
Asia[a]	$68,671	$2,990	2,257	2,240	2,023
China (PRC)	227	14	15	25	13
India	6,391	37	44	34	35
Indonesia	4,688	33	115	108	89
Korea, Rep. of	3,153	0	0	0	0
Pakistan	12,395	612	422	482	363
Philippines	4,780	99	89	89	86
Vietnam	6,263	50	56	65	68
Western Europe[a]	23,397	2	2	41	20
Eastern Europe[a]	8,725	118	131	172	201
Latin America and Caribbean[a]	35,485	1,060	1,047	1,156	1,028
Brazil	1,832	6	3	18	11
Costa Rica	1,832	10	11	10	16
Dominican Republic	1,397	103	50	55	54
El Salvador	4,172	323	65	109	89
Guatemala	1,978	114	264	224	218
Honduras	2,247	82	104	154	107
Jamaica	1,262	19	15	31	15
Middle East and North Africa[a]	107,297	2,492	2,272	3,024	3,359
Egypt/Arab Rep. of Egypt	27,301	191	99	141	188
Israel	32,518	2	3	9	3
Jordan	8,271	848	488	814	983
Lebanon	1,466	350	337	117	230
Morocco	1,175	31	32	34	36
Syria	1,680	666	687	661	665
West Bank/Gaza	4,569	350	319	285	23
Yemen	905	91	131	337	348
Sub-Saharan Africa[a]	42,527	3,555	3,177	3,715	3,502
Kenya	2,134	166	167	168	153
Niger	1,554	135	188	436	435
Senegal	1,302	58	70	76	86
Somalia	1,282	124	183	310	299
South Sudan	968	304	307	430	302
Sudan	4,201	104	103	150	117
The Congo (Kinshasa)[b]	1,942	160	160	200	326
Zambia	1,189	59	52	29	32
Zimbabwe	1,220	43	54	49	60
Eurasia[a]	13,558	297	296	412	469
Russia/Russian Federation	2,952	–2.7	–1.4	0	0
Ukraine	2,242	98	126	196	194
Oceania and other	348	24	73	25	11
Total[c]	366,459	13,183	12,411	14,436	13,473

Note: Amounts in current dollars. Shown are loans and grants made by the U.S. Agency for International Development and its predecessor agencies. Excluded are Economic Support Fund, Development Assistance, International Disaster and Famine Assistance, and other economic assistance. Data for individual years before 2015 can be found in previous editions of *Vital Statistics on American Politics*.

(Table continues)

Table 9-12 *(Continued)*

[a] Includes countries not shown separately.
[b] Formerly Zaire, The Congo (Kinshasa) denotes the Democratic Republic of the Congo, to distinguish it from its neighbor the Republic of Congo (Brazzaville).
[c] Includes interregional aid.

Source: U.S. Agency for International Development, *U.S. Overseas Loans and Grants and Assistance from International Organizations, July 1, 1945–September 30, 2018* (Washington, D.C.: Government Printing Office, 2014), www.usaid.gov.

Table 9-13 Foreign Investment in the United States and U.S. Investment Abroad, 1950–2019 (millions)

Year	All areas	Canada	Europe	Japan
Foreign direct investment in the United States				
1950	$3,391	$1,029	$2,228	—
1960	6,910	1,934	4,707	$88
1970	13,270	3,117	9,554	229
1980	83,046	12,162	54,688	4,723
1985	184,615	17,131	121,413	19,313
1990	396,702	30,037	250,973	81,775
1995	535,553	45,618	332,374	104,997
2000	1,256,867	114,309	887,014	159,690
2005	1,634,121	165,667	1,154,048	189,851
2006	1,840,463	165,281	1,326,738	204,020
2007[a]	1,993,156	201,924	1,421,325	222,695
2009	2,069,438	188,943	1,504,727	238,140
2010	2,280,044	192,463	1,659,774	255,012
2011	2,433,848	205,225	1,732,316	274,283
2012	2,584,708	214,314	1,836,716	301,183
2013	7,272,825	222,989	1,901,471	350,395
2014	7,945,795	273,896	2,004,199	371,874
2015	3,354,907	323,207	2,306,254	401,835
2016	3,561,808	344,929	2,448,305	427,229
2017	3,786,848	395,495	2,565,251	475,864
2018	4,127,175	442,802	2,794,561	493,763
2019	4,458,362	495,720	2,871,431	619,259
U.S. investment abroad				
1950	11,788	3,579	1,733	19
1960	32,778	11,198	6,681	254
1970	78,178	22,790	24,516	1,483
1980	215,578	44,978	96,539	6,243
1985	230,250	46,909	105,171	9,235
1990	430,521	69,508	214,739	22,599
1995	699,015	83,498	344,596	37,309
2000	1,316,247	132,472	687,320	57,091
2005	2,241,656	231,836	1,210,679	81,175
2006	2,477,268	205,134	1,397,704	84,428

Table 9-13 *(Continued)*

2007[a]	2,993,980	250,642	1,682,023	85,224
2009	3,565,020	274,807	1,991,191	91,196
2010	3,741,910	295,206	2,034,559	113,523
2011	4,050,026	330,041	2,246,394	120,482
2012	4,410,015	346,080	2,443,287	125,286
2013	4,579,713	368,297	2,607,204	123,174
2014	4,910,065	357,439	2,796,982	100,823
2015	5,048,773	346,746	2,919,510	104,128
2016	5,518,644	355,394	3,302,727	124,039
2017	6,097,690	371,274	3,654,095	117,134
2018	5,801,025	368,498	3,475,989	113,254
2019	5,959,592	402,255	3,571,710	131,793

Note: "—" indicates not available. Amounts are in current dollars. Data for additional years can be found in previous editions of *Vital Statistics on American Politics*.

[a] There is a discontinuity between 2006 and 2007. See source for details.

Sources: 1950–1960: U.S. Department of Commerce, *Foreign Business Investments in the United States: A Supplement to Survey of Current Business* (Washington, D.C.: Government Printing Office, 1962), 34; 1970–2011: *Survey of Current Business*, August 1973, 50; September 1973, 24; August 1982, 21; August 1985, 63; August 1988, 65, 80; August 1992, 89; August 1994, 134; September 1998, 83; October 1998, 129; September 2003, 67, 119; September 2005, 134; September 2008, D-65, D-67; September 2010, D-69, D-71; September 2011, D-71, D-73; September 2016, Table 14 "Foreign Direct Investment in the U.S.," "U.S. Direct Investment Abroad"; July 2020, Table 1 "U.S. Direct Investment Abroad."

Table 9-14 U.S. Balance of Trade, 1946–2020 (in millions)

Year	Balance on goods[a]	Balance on current account[b]	Year	Balance on goods[a]	Balance on current account[b]
1946	$6,697	$4,885	1984	$112,492	$109,074
1947	10,124	8,992	1985	−122,173	−121,879
1948	5,708	2,417	1986	−145,081	−138,539
1949	5,339	873	1987	−159,557	−151,683
1950	1,122	−1,840	1988	−126,959	−114,566
1951	3,067	884	1989	−117,749	−93,142
1952	2,611	614	1990	−111,037	−80,865
1953	1,437	−1,286	1991	−76,937	−31,136
1954	2,576	219	1992	−96,897	−39,212
1955	2,897	430	1993	−132,451	−70,311
1956	4,753	2,730	1994	−165,831	−98,493
1957	6,271	4,762	1995	−174,170	−96,384
1958	3,462	784	1996	−191,000	−104,065
1959	1,148	−1,282	1997	−198,428	−108,273
1960	4,892	3,508	1998	−248,221	−166,140
1961	5,571	4,194	1999	−337,068	−255,809
1962	4,521	3,371	2000	−446,783	−369,686
1963	5,224	4,210	2001	−422,370	−360,373
1964	6,801	6,022	2002	−475,245	−420,666
1965	4,951	4,664	2003	−541,643	−496,243
1966	3,817	2,939	2004	−664,766	−610,838
1967	3,800	2,604	2005	−782,804	−716,542
1968	635	250	2006	−837,289	−763,533
1969	607	90	2007	−821,196	−710,997
1970	2,603	2,255	2008	−832,492	−712,350
1971	−2,260	−1,301	2009	−509,694	−394,771
1972	−6,416	−5,443	2010	−648,671	−503,087
1973	911	1,900	2011	−740,999	−554,522
1974	−5,505	−4,293	2012	−741,119	−525,906
1975	8,903	12,403	2013	−700,539	−446,861
1976	−9,483	−6,082	2014	−749,917	−483,952
1977	−31,091	−27,247	2015	−761,868	−491,421
1978	−33,927	−29,763	2016	−749,801	−481,475
1979	−27,568	−24,566	2017	−799,343	−512,739
1980	−25,500	−19,407	2018	−878,749	−580,950
1981	−28,023	−16,172	2019	−861,515	−576,341
1982	−36,485	−24,156	2020	−922,026	−676,684
1983	−67,102	−57,767			

Note: Amounts in current dollars and seasonally adjusted.

[a] "Balance on goods" measures the difference between the value of goods the United States imports and the value of goods the United States exports.
[b] "Balance on current account" is the broadest trade gauge, measuring the difference in imports and exports of merchandise trade and trade in services; also includes certain one-way flows of money into the United States such as pension payments.

Sources: 1946–1951: *Economic Report of the President* (Washington, D.C.: Government Printing Office, 2009), Table B-103; 1952: (2011); 1953–1992: (2013), Table B-103; 1960–2020: U.S. Department of Commerce, Bureau of Economic Analysis, "U.S. International Transactions Accounts Data," Table 1, www.bea.gov.

10
Social Policy

- **Population**
- **Immigration**
- **Medicare and Social Security**
- **Income Levels**
- **Public Aid**
- **Health Insurance**
- **Integration in Schooling**
- **Abortion**
- **Crime and Punishment**

Many students' first introduction to political science is through Harold Lasswell's description of politics as the study of "who gets what, when, and how." The study of social policies offers perhaps the clearest example of that definition in practice. Social policy touches nearly every aspect of life, from the health insurance that covers hospital stays at birth to funding for social security in later life. Along the way, it gets at questions we often talk about when we talk about national identity and "the American way." These are inherently controversial questions that people aim to resolve 'in part' through data.

However, it is not only the questions of who gets what, when, and how that are contested. The very data that aim to answer those questions are themselves often controversial. Many of the tables in this chapter, and others throughout the book, rely on data from the Census Bureau. The decennial census was established by Article I, Section 2 of the U.S. Constitution to ensure representation in Congress was appropriately apportioned *(see chapter 5)*. Since 1954, all Census acts and authorizing statutes have been codified in Title 13 of the U.S. Code. Since 2005, data on many socioeconomic characteristics have been gathered in the American Community Survey, which was launched to provide continuous information about these questions separate from the decennial census, but under the authority of the Census Bureau. The Census Bureau explicitly ties the data it collects to policy decisions, writing, "Information from the survey generates data that help determine how more than $675 billion in federal and state funds are distributed each year."

Because these data are used to answer so many fundamental questions, they are themselves subject to controversy. The 2020 Census faced a number of challenges about what information should be collected, particularly around the question of immigration status and whether and how citizenship status should be included in the Census. That question was part of a long history of controversy around who should be counted. (See Wang 2021 for more background on this.) It raised concerns about whether a citizenship questions would dampen immigrant response rates, and lead to undercounting of those populations.

In addition to what questions are asked, there are often questions about when and how those questions are asked. The Census collection fell during 2020, a remarkably unusual year due to the coronavirus pandemic. The Census Bureau indicated early in the spring of 2020 that there would be delays in data collection and release. By fall of that year, the question of the data collection period had made its way to the Supreme Court, with the Court ruling that the Census could be stopped earlier than originally announced amid shifting schedules due to the pandemic and, some argued, political motives.

The amount of public attention given to the data collection in the 2020 Census was not typical, but we think it is highly instructive. The questions of who is asked what questions when, and by what means affect the data that shape our understanding of the country as it is, and as we strive for it to be. Whether the data you encounter are from the decennial Census, the American Community Survey, another government agency, or a nongovernmental organization, we think these questions raised by the 2020 Census apply. This is not to say that the data can't be trusted, or that you should be skeptical of them. Rather, we are encouraging you to consider the context of the data.

The tables in this chapter aim to highlight some of the many types of data that are used to address questions of social policy. These include demographic questions about population by state and nations of origin for immigrants. They also can be used to better understand the effect of policy, as in the application of the death penalty by race. They are often useful when paired with the data in Chapter 3 that provide insights into public opinion around these topics.

In the area of social policy, as in other areas, data do not speak for themselves. They require an understanding of the context in which they were collected, examination of how they are presented, and evaluation of whether the claims being made can be supported by the data that are used.

Figure 10-1 U.S. Population: Total, Urban, and Rural, 1790–2060

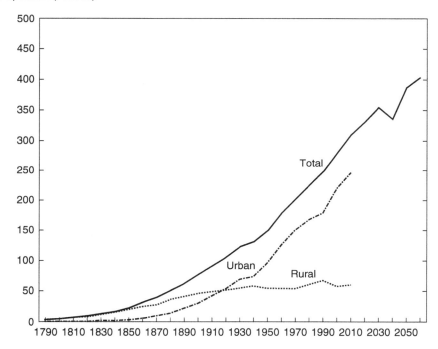

Note: For definitions, see sources. U.S. Census Bureau urban area markers are based on definitions that vary over time. The Census Bureau takes public comments before adjusting criteria definitions. For more details, see 86 Fed. Reg. 10237 (February 19, 2021). The Census Bureau estimates that urban and rural population estimates for the 2020 Decennial Census will be available in summer 2022.

Sources: Population, total, 1790–2000: U.S. Bureau of the Census, "Resident Population of the United States," April 2, 2001; total, 2010: "Resident Population of the 50 States, the District of Columbia, and Puerto Rico: 2010 Census," December 21, 2010; "Resident Population of the 50 States, the District of Columbia, and Puerto Rico: 2020 Census," April 26, 2021; total, 2030–2060: "Projected Population Size and Birthday, Deaths, and Migration: Main Projections Series for the United States, 2017–2060," September 2018; urban and rural, 1790–1990: "Population: 1790 to 1990," March 31, 2001; urban and rural, 2000–2010: "Urban, Urbanized Area, Urban Cluster, and Rural Population, 2010 and 2000: United States," 2010 Census, www.census.gov.

Table 10-1 U.S. Population, 1790–2020, and State Populations, 2010–2040

Year	Resident population[a]	Year	Resident population[a]
1790	3,929,214	1910	92,228,496
1800	5,308,483	1920	106,021,537
1810	7,239,881	1930	123,202,624
1820	9,638,453	1940	132,164,569
1830	12,860,702	1950	151,325,798
1840	17,063,353	1960	179,323,175
1850	23,191,876	1970	203,302,031
1860	31,443,321	1980	226,542,199
1870	38,558,371	1990	248,709,873
1880	50,189,209	2000	281,421,906
1890	62,979,766	2010	308,745,538
1900	76,212,168	2020	334,735,155

	Resident population[a]			Change (percent)	
State	2010	2020	2040	2010–2020	2010–2040
Alabama	4,779,736	5,024,279	5,056,796	5.12	5.80
Alaska	710,231	733,391	819,954	3.26	15.45
Arizona	6,392,017	7,151,502	9,166,279	11.88	43.40
Arkansas	2,915,918	3,011,524	3,217,535	3.28	10.34
California	37,253,956	39,538,223	46,467,001	6.13	24.73
Colorado	5,029,196	5,773,714	7,692,907	14.80	52.96
Connecticut	3,574,097	3,605,944	3,542,707	0.89	−0.88
Delaware	897,934	989,948	1,164,344	10.25	29.67
District of Columbia	601,723	689,545	1,058,820	14.60	75.96
Florida	18,801,310	21,538,187	28,886,983	14.56	53.64
Georgia	9,687,653	10,711,908	12,820,271	10.57	32.34
Hawaii	1,360,301	1,455,271	1,619,703	6.98	19.07
Idaho	1,567,582	1,839,106	2,227,842	17.32	42.12
Illinois	12,830,632	12,812,508	12,397,564	−0.14	−3.38
Indiana	6,483,802	6,785,528	7,095,000	4.65	9.43
Iowa	3,046,355	3,190,369	3,392,783	4.73	11.37
Kansas	2,853,118	2,937,880	3,032,653	2.97	6.29
Kentucky	4,339,367	4,505,836	4,714,761	3.84	8.65
Louisiana	4,533,372	4,657,757	5,062,780	2.74	11.68
Maine	1,328,361	1,362,359	1,326,159	2.56	−0.17
Maryland	5,773,552	6,177,224	6,842,902	6.99	18.52
Massachusetts	6,547,629	7,029,917	7,742,628	7.37	18.25
Michigan	9,883,640	10,077,331	9,960,115	1.96	0.77
Minnesota	5,303,925	5,706,494	6,364,886	7.59	20.00
Mississippi	2,967,297	2,961,279	2,962,160	−0.20	−0.17
Missouri	5,988,927	6,154,913	6,359,970	2.77	6.20
Montana	989,415	1,084,225	1,236,304	9.58	24.95
Nebraska	1,826,341	1,961,504	2,190,918	7.40	19.96
Nevada	2,700,551	3,104,614	4,058,371	14.96	50.28

(Table continues)

Table 10-1 *(Continued)*

State	Resident population[a]			Change (percent)	
	2010	2020	2040	2010–2020	2010–2040
New Hampshire	1,316,470	1,377,529	1,393,451	4.64	5.85
New Jersey	8,791,894	9,288,994	9,470,012	5.65	7.71
New Mexico	2,059,179	2,117,522	2,127,318	2.83	3.31
New York	19,378,102	20,201,249	20,873,488	4.25	7.72
North Carolina	9,535,483	10,439,388	12,658,927	9.48	32.76
North Dakota	672,591	779,094	1,060,457	15.83	57.67
Ohio	11,536,504	11,799,448	11,751,540	2.28	1.86
Oklahoma	3,751,351	3,959,353	4,439,038	5.54	18.33
Oregon	3,831,074	4,237,256	5,164,041	10.60	34.79
Pennsylvania	12,702,379	13,002,700	12,809,150	2.36	0.84
Rhode Island	1,052,567	1,097,379	1,055,318	4.26	0.26
South Carolina	4,625,364	5,118,425	6,352,502	10.66	37.34
South Dakota	814,180	886,667	1,043,032	8.90	28.11
Tennessee	6,346,105	6,910,840	7,823,662	8.90	23.28
Texas	25,145,561	29,145,505	40,015,913	15.91	59.14
Utah	2,763,885	3,271,616	4,344,339	18.37	57.18
Vermont	625,741	643,077	601,865	2.77	–3.82
Virginia	8,001,024	8,631,393	9,876,728	7.88	23.44
Washington	6,724,540	7,705,281	9,776,126	14.58	45.38
West Virginia	1,852,994	1,793,716	1,661,849	–3.20	–10.32
Wisconsin	5,686,986	5,893,718	5,997,137	3.64	5.45
Wyoming	563,626	576,851	615,787	2.35	9.25
United States	308,745,538	331,449,281	379,392,779	7.35	22.88

Note: A counter with the U.S. Census Bureau's estimate of the current U.S. population can be found at www.census.gov. As of December 9, 2020 (2:30 p.m. EST), the count stood at 330,689,317. State and nation projections for 2040 shown are as of 2018.

[a] Resident population differs from apportionment population: "The 2020 Census apportionment population includes the resident population of the 50 states, plus a count of the U.S. military personnel and federal civilian employees living outside the United States (and their dependents living with them) who can be allocated to a home state. The population of the District of Columbia is not included in the apportionment population." United States Census 2021, "2020 Census Apportionment Results," at www.census.gov.

Sources: U.S. Bureau of the Census, "Resident Population of the 50 States, the District of Columbia, and Puerto Rico: 2010 Census," December 21, 2010; "Resident Population of the 50 States, the District of Columbia, and Puerto Rico: 2020 Census," April 26, 2021; University of Virginia Weldon Cooper Center, *Demographics Research Group, 2018, National Population Projections*, https://demographics.coopercenter.org/national-population-projections.

Table 10-2 Foreign-Born and Native-Born U.S. Population, Characteristics, 2017

Nativity	Population	Percent
Total	325,719,178	100.0
Total native born	281,312,807	86.4
Total foreign born	44,406,371	13.6
Mexico	11,236,543	25.3
South and East Asia	12,180,847	27.4
Europe/Canada	5,850,245	13.2
Caribbean	4,405,841	9.9
Central America	3,507,296	7.9
South America	3,219,623	7.3
Middle East[a]	1,829,494	4.1
Sub-Saharan Africa	1,928,329	4.3
All Other	248,153	0.6

English ability by age and country or region of birth (percent)

	Under 18 years			18 years and over		
	English only	English very well	English less than very well	English only	English very well	English less than very well
Total native born	80.4	16.7	3.2	90.8	7.7	1.5
Total foreign born	19.6	48.9	31.5	16.2	35.2	48.7
Mexico	2.8	63.3	33.9	4.3	27.7	68.0
South and East Asia	26.1	46.9	27.0	11.6	43.4	45.0
Europe/Canada	38.6	45.0	16.4	40.9	35.7	23.4
Caribbean	19.6	47.2	33.2	30.7	24.7	44.6
Central America	11.6	37.0	51.4	6.2	26.9	66.9
South America	9.1	53.0	38.0	15.0	38.6	46.4
Middle East[a]	9.5	55.5	35.0	12.6	48.1	39.3
Sub-Saharan Africa	36.5	38.7	24.8	24.8	48.3	26.9
All other	49.0	25.2	25.9	51.9	26.7	21.4

Educational attainment by country or region of birth (percent)

	Less than 9th grade	9th to 12th grade	High school graduate[b]	Two-year degree/Some college	Bachelor's Degree	Advanced degree
Total native born	2.5	6.3	28.0	31.1	20.1	12.1
Total foreign born	17.4	10.0	22.7	18.8	17.8	13.4
Mexico	36.1	18.2	25.7	13.1	5.0	1.8
South and East Asia	9.1	5.8	15.6	16.7	29.0	23.9
Europe/Canada	5.4	4.9	22.2	23.6	21.9	21.9
Caribbean	12.3	10.3	31.8	24.3	14.0	7.3
Central America	31.5	14.6	25.8	17.3	7.8	3.0
South America	8.4	6.0	27.3	26.0	20.6	11.7
Middle East[a]	7.1	5.0	20.0	19.5	26.4	22.0
Sub-Saharan Africa	7.0	4.7	19.8	27.6	23.7	17.3
All other	5.4	8.5	24.6	26.7	20.3	14.5

Note: Table is based on Pew Research Center's Hispanic Trends Project tabulations of the U.S. Census Bureau's 2017 American Community Survey, tables 2, 3, 8, and 17. The universe is the 2017 resident population for nativity and country or region of birth, the 2017 resident population ages five and older for language ability, and the 2017 resident population ages twenty-five and older for educational attainment.

[a] Middle East includes Afghanistan, Algeria, Egypt, Iran, Iraq, Israel/Palestine, Jordan, Kuwait, Lebanon, Morocco, Saudi Arabia, Sudan, Syria, Turkey, and Yemen.
[b] "High school graduate" refers to a person whose highest level of education achievement is a high school diploma or its equivalent, such as a General Educational Development (GED) certificate.

Source: Pew Research Center's Hispanic Trends Project, "Statistical Portrait of the Foreign-Born Population in the United States, 2017," June 3, 2019, www.pewhispanic.org

Table 10-3 Immigrants to the United States, by Region of Origin, 1820–2019

Years	Europe				Asia[e]	Western Hemisphere			Africa and Oceania	Not specified	Total number (thousands)
	Northwestern[a]	Central[b]	Southern[c]	Eastern[d]		Canada	Mexico	Other[f]			
1820–1829	70.2%	4.5%	2.5%	0.1%	—	1.8%	3.0%	2.7%	—	15.2%	128.5
1830–1839	54.2	23.2	1.0	0.1	—	2.2	1.3	2.4	—	15.5	538.4
1840–1849	68.6	27.0	0.3	—	—	2.4	0.2	0.9	—	0.5	1,427.30
1850–1859	57.7	34.7	0.7	—	0.0	2.3	0.1	0.6	—	2.6	2,814.60
1860–1869	54.2	35.0	0.9	0.1	2.6	5.7	0.1	0.5	—	0.9	2,081.30
1870–1879	48.4	30.0	2.4	1.3	4.9	11.8	0.2	0.6	0.0	—	2,742.10
1880–1889	44.9	34.4	5.5	3.6	1.4	9.4	0.1	0.6	0.2	—	5,248.60
1890–1899	33.8	33.0	17.6	12.4	1.7	0.1	—	0.9	0.1	0.4	3,694.30
1900–1909	18.1	28.4	26.4	19.4	3.7	1.5	0.4	1.5	0.2	0.4	8,202.40
1910–1919	14.8	20.9	24.6	18.2	4.2	11.2	2.9	2.8	0.3	—	6,347.40
1920–1929	21.0	19.1	15.9	3.6	3.0	22.1	11.6	3.3	0.4	—	4,295.50
1930–1939	20.2	26.0	14.7	2.7	2.7	23.3	4.7	5.0	0.8	—	699.4
1940–1949	28.6	17.7	8.0	0.9	4.0	18.8	6.6	13.0	2.4	—	856.6
1950–1959	17.4	28.2	10.0	0.5	5.4	14.1	11.0	11.8	1.0	0.5	2,499.30
1960–1969	13.1	9.8	12.0	0.4	11.2	13.5	13.7	24.9	1.5	—	3,213.70
1970–1979	5.0	4.0	9.4	1.1	33.1	4.2	14.6	26.0	2.6	—	4,248.20
1980–1989	4.1	3.1	2.5	1.0	38.3	2.5	16.2	24.5	2.9	4.9	6,244.40
1990–1999	3.2	3.7	1.5	5.4	29.3	2.0	28.2	22.4	4.1	0.3	9,775.40
2000–2009	2.9	4.1	0.7	5.3	33.7	2.3	16.6	24.3	8.0	2.1	10,299.40
2010–2019	2.4	2.0	0.8	3.3	38.2	1.7	14.2	25.8	10.3	1.2	10,633,446

Note: "—" indicates less than 0.1 percent. Data for most years are for country of last permanent residence. See source for details.

[a] United Kingdom, Ireland, Finland, Norway, Sweden, Denmark, the Netherlands, Belgium, Switzerland, and France.
[b] Germany, Poland, Czechoslovakia (now the Czech Republic and Slovakia), Yugoslavia (currently includes Bosnia-Herzegovina, Croatia, Kosovo, Macedonia, Montenegro, Serbia, and Slovenia), Hungary, and Austria.
[c] Italy, Spain, Portugal, and Greece.
[d] Russia, Bulgaria, Romania, and "other Europe." Russia and surrounding areas were reported differently in various historical periods. See source for details.
[e] China, Hong Kong (China), India, Iran, Israel, Japan, Jordan, Republic of Korea, Philippines, Syria, Taiwan, Thailand, Turkey, and "other Asia."
[f] Caribbean and Central and South America.

Source: U.S. Department of Homeland Security, Office of Immigration Statistics, *Yearbook of Immigration Statistics* (2013, 2016, and 2019), Table 2.

A Data Literacy Lesson
The Importance of Aggregation

Immigration policy has a long history of complexity and controversy. From the Chinese Exclusion Act of 1882 or 2017's Executive Order 13769: Protecting the Nation from Foreign Terrorist Entry into the United States (often referred to as the Muslim Travel Ban), the question of who can and should have entry into the United States is a key element of social policy. Data about the region of origin of immigrants to the United States can be instructive. Changes can be caused by policy, as when persons from a country are either encouraged or discouraged to enter the United States, but also can show the effects of broader sociopolitical changes. (For those wishing to learn more about this, the Library of Congress introduction to immigration and relocation includes a timeline with a brief overview of some of the global context that affected immigration patterns. You can find it at this website: https://www.loc.gov/classroom-materials/immigration/global-timeline.

Table 10-3 and the accompanying Figure 10-2 demonstrate changes over time in the region of origin of immigrants to the United States. We think this table and figure are useful to investigate a little closer because of the questions we can ask about how categories are aggregated, or grouped together. In many, if not most, cases, data you encounter will have been aggregated in some way for you. Here, we have grouped countries of origin into larger regions: ten in the table and four in the figure. Aggregation is useful; imagine the size of this table if we presented immigration numbers from each non-U.S. country (currently 194) over 200 years. And, when we imagine trying to graph that many data points into a graph like Figure 10-2, we imagine it might look more like an inkblot than a graph. We have aggregated at this level to highlight patterns in immigration since the United States began reporting information about countries of origin in 1819. That broad historical focus can explain the more granular approach to categories from European regions, which is divided into four categories in the table, than Asia, which is consolidated into one category, or the Western Hemisphere, which is divided into Canada, Mexico, and "other." These categories allow us to illustrate the dominance of one region over a long period of time. Beyond that, for long periods in history, U.S. immigration policy made distinctions based on these regions within Europe and these categories reflect that. In other regions, including Asia, such finer distinctions have historically not been made.

However, as you consider these data for the purposes of informing policy or viewing the effects of policy there might be questions that would be better answered by different groupings—or even by looking at each country individually. One example that comes to mind is the U.S. focus on the "Northern Triangle" countries of El Salvador, Guatemala, and Honduras in 2019. The broad historical intent of this table is not well-suited to such a specific point-in-time question about particular countries. For that, it would be useful if not necessary to go back to the original source data and find information about those three countries. Other research questions, such as how immigration from within Asia has changed since the Vietnam War, or in the past twenty years, would similarly require further exploration beyond the current level of aggregation. These data tell a story, ideal for answering some of the questions you might have, but woefully inadequate for some others.

Figure 10-2 Immigrants to the United States, by Region of Origin, 1820–2019

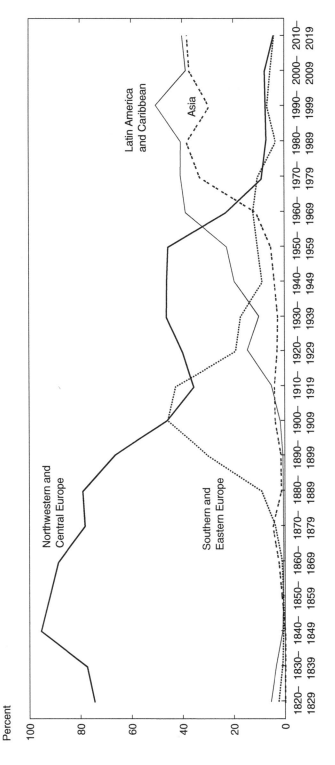

Source: Table 10-3, this volume.

Table 10-4 Legal Status of Immigrants, 2016; Origins of Unauthorized Immigrants, 2016; and State Populations of Unauthorized Immigrants, 1990–2017

	Number (millions)	Percentage of foreign born living in United States
Legal status of immigrants		
Lawful permanent residents	12.2	27.0
Naturalized citizens (former LPRs)	20.2	44.7
Temporary lawful residents (such as students or temporary workers)	2.1	4.6
Unauthorized immigrants[a]	10.7	23.7
Total	45.2	100.0

	Number (millions)	Percentage of unauthorized immigrants
Unauthorized immigrants: country/region of birth, 2016		
Mexico	5.5	51
Central America	1.9	18
South America	0.7	7
Caribbean	0.5	5
Asia	1.3	12
Europe or Canada	0.5	5
Middle East	0.1	1
Africa	0.2	2
Total	10.7	100[b]

	Estimated population (millions)					Percentage of unauthorized immigrants
	1990	2000	2010	2015	2017	2017
Unauthorized immigrants[a]: state of residence						
California	1.5	2.3	2.5	2.4	2.0	19
Texas	0.5	1.1	1.7	1.7	1.6	15
Florida	0.2	0.9	0.9	0.8	0.8	8
New York	0.4	0.7	0.8	0.7	0.7	7
New Jersey	0.1	0.3	0.5	0.5	0.5	5
Illinois	0.2	0.4	0.5	0.4	0.4	4
Remaining states and D.C.	0.6	2.9	4.5	4.6	4.5	43
Total, United States	3.5	8.6	11.4	11.0	10.5	100[b]

Note: Demographic estimates are based on U.S. Census Bureau data, including American Community Survey, March Current Population Survey, and the 1990 Census, with adjustments for survey omissions and corrections for survey errors. See original source for full methodology notes.

[a] "Unauthorized immigrants" are all foreign born noncitizens who reside in the country and are not "lawful immigrants," including those seeking asylum whose cases have not yet been processed, those applying for Temporary Protected Status or Deferred Action for Childhood Arrivals status. According to Pew this "quasi-lawful" group could account for up to 10 percent of all unauthorized immigrants. See original source for full details and definitions.

[b] Due to rounding, the categories shown do not sum to the total or subtotal indicated.

Sources: Estimates of unauthorized immigrants by state of residence: Pew Research Center's Hispanic Trends Project, "Unauthorized immigrant population trends for states, birth countries and regions" (2019), www.pewhispanic.org; Legal status of immigrants and region of birth: Jeffrey S. Passel and D'Vera Cohn, "U.S. Unauthorized Immigrant Total Dips to Lowest Level in a Decade" (2018), https://www.pewresearch.org/hispanic/wp-content/uploads/sites/5/2019/03/Pew-Research-Center_2018-11-27_U-S-Unauthorized-Immigrants-Total-Dips_Updated-2019-06-25.pdf.

Table 10-5 Hospital Insurance Trust Fund: Income, Expenditures, and Balance, 1970–2029 (billions)

Year	Income	Disbursements	Net increase in fund	Fund at end of year
1970	$6.0	$5.3	$0.7	$3.2
1975	13.0	11.6	1.4	10.5
1980	26.1	25.6	0.5	13.7
1985	51.4	48.4	4.8	20.5
1990	80.4	67.0	13.4	98.9
1995	115.0	117.6	−2.6	130.3
2000	167.2	131.1	36.1	177.5
2005	199.4	182.9	16.4	285.8
2006	211.5	191.9	19.6	305.4
2007	223.7	203.1	20.7	326.0
2008	230.8	235.6	−4.7	321.3
2009	225.4	242.5	−17.1	304.2
2010	215.6	247.9	−32.3	271.9
2011	228.9	256.7	−27.7	244.2
2012	243.0	266.8	−23.8	220.4
2013	251.1	266.2	−15.0	205.4
2014	261.2	269.3	−8.1	197.3
2015	275.4	278.9	−3.5	193.8
2016	290.8	285.4	5.4	199.1
2017	299.4	296.6	2.8	202.0
2018	306.6	308.2	−1.6	200.4
2019	322.5	328.3	−5.8	194.6
2020	342.0	351.2	−9.2	85.4
2021	356.0	71.7	−15.7	169.7
2022	372.8	396.1	−23.3	146.4
2023	390.0	422.4	−32.4	114.0
2024	408.3	449.0	−40.7	73.3
2025	427.0	476.9	−49.9	23.4
2026	450.9	505.5	−54.6	−31.2
2027	475.6	536.0	−60.3	−91.5
2028	497.4	567.4	−70.0	−161.5
2029	518.7	596.5	−77.8	−239.3

Note: The Hospital Insurance Program (Medicare Part A) pays for in-patient hospital care and other related care for those ages sixty-five or older and for the long-term disabled. It represents roughly half of all Medicare expenses. Income for the fund is derived from a payroll tax on employees and employers. Figures through 2019 represent actual experience. Figures for 2020 and beyond are "intermediate" projections; see sources for details.

Sources: U.S. Department of Health and Human Services, "Annual Report of the Boards of Trustees of the Federal Hospital Insurance and Federal Supplementary Medical Insurance Trust Funds," Table IIIB, Operations of the HI Trust Fund during Calendar Years 1970–2029," www.cms.hhs.gov.

Table 10-6 Social Security (OASDI)–Covered Workers and Beneficiaries, 1945–2095

Year	Covered workers[a] (thousands)	Beneficiaries[b] (thousands)			Covered workers per OASDI beneficiary	Beneficiaries per 100 covered workers
		OASI	DI	Total		
1945	46,390	1,106	—	1,106	41.9	2
1950	48,280	2,930	—	2,930	16.5	6
1955	65,066	7,564	—	7,564	8.6	12
1960	72,371	13,740	522	14,262	5.1	20
1965	80,539	18,509	1,648	20,157	4	25
1970	92,963	22,618	2,568	25,186	3.7	27
1975	100,193	26,998	4,125	31,123	3.2	31
1980	112,651	30,384	4,734	35,117	3.2	31
1985	120,312	32,763	3,874	36,636	3.3	30
1990	133,123	35,255	4,204	39,459	3.4	30
1995	140,976	37,364	5,731	43,096	3.3	31
2000	154,916	38,556	6,606	45,162	3.4	29
2005	159,212	39,961	8,172	48,133	3.3	30
2010	157,328	43,440	9,958	53,398	2.9	34
2015	167,493	49,377	11,108	60,485	2.8	36
2016	170,853	49,811	10,728	60,539	2.8	35
2017	173,021	50,962	10,517	61,480	2.8	36
2018	175,579	52,168	10,296	62,464	2.8	36
2019	177,864	53,508	10,063	63,570	2.8	36
2020	179,548	54,892	9,867	64,759	2.8	36
2025	182,760	61,346	9,788	71,134	2.6	39
2030	186,135	67,948	9,944	77,893	2.4	42
2035	188,513	72,519	10,321	82,840	2.3	44
2040	190,474	74,728	10,946	85,674	2.2	45
2045	193,973	75,503	11,819	87,322	2.2	45
2050	198,300	76,773	12,398	89,170	2.2	45
2055	202,559	78,891	12,861	91,752	2.2	45
2060	206,369	81,873	13,047	94,920	2.2	46
2065	209,694	84,923	13,322	98,246	2.1	47
2070	213,017	88,233	13,606	101,839	2.1	48
2075	216,806	91,565	13,727	105,291	2.1	49
2080	221,279	93,822	13,943	107,765	2.1	49
2085	226,190	94,909	14,358	109,267	2.1	48
2090	231,159	95,976	15,060	111,036	2.1	48
2095	235,814	98,569	15,488	114,057	2.1	48

Note: "—" indicates not available; "OASI" indicates Old-Age and Survivors' Insurance; "DI" indicates Disability Insurance. Projections (2020–2095) are the "intermediate" projections; see source for details. Data for additional years can be found in previous editions of *Vital Statistics on American Politics*.

[a] Workers who pay OASDI taxes at some time during the year.
[b] Beneficiaries with monthly benefits in current-payment status as of June 30.

Source: U.S. Social Security Administration, "The 2020 Annual Report of the Board of Trustees of the Federal Old-Age and Survivors Insurance and Federal Disability Insurance Trust Funds," (2020), Table IV.B3, www.ssa.gov.

Social Policy 433

Figure 10-3 Social Security Receipts, Spending, and Reserve Estimates, 2020–2030

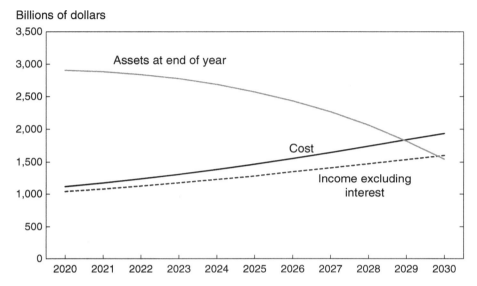

Note: Amounts in current dollars. Based on intermediate economic and demographic assumptions. Under these assumptions it is projected that the combined Old Age and Survivors Insurance (OASI) and Disability Insurance (DI) Trust Funds will become exhausted in 2030.

Source: U.S. Social Security Administration, "2020 OASDI Trustees Report," Table VI.G8, https://www.ssa.gov/oact/tr/2020/VI_G3_OASDHI_dollars.html#23.

Table 10-7 Median Family Income, by Race and Hispanic Origin, 1950–2019

	Median income in current dollars					Median income in constant (2019) dollars					Annual percentage change in median income of all families	
Year	All families[a]	White alone[b]	Black alone[b]	Asian alone[b]	Hispanic origin[c]	All families[a]	White alone[b]	Black alone[b]	Asian alone[b]	Hispanic origin[c]	Current dollars	Constant dollars
1950	$3,319	—	—	—	—	$30,854	—	—	—	—	—	—
1955	4,418	—	—	—	—	36,964	—	—	—	—	6.8	5.5
1960	5,620	—	—	—	—	42,574	—	—	—	—	6	6.3
1965	6,957	—	—	—	—	49,514	—	—	—	—	5.9	4.3
1970	9,867	$10,236	$6,279	—	—	58,137	$60,311	$36,996	—	—	4.6	−0.2
1975	13,719	14,268	8,779	—	$9,551	59,438	61,817	38,036	—	$41,380	6.3	−1.8
1980	21,023	21,904	12,674	—	14,716	62,275	64,885	37,543	—	43,592	7.3	−3.4
1981	22,388	23,517	13,266	—	16,401	60,597	63,653	35,907	—	44,392	6.5	−2.8
1982	23,433	24,603	13,598	—	16,227	59,814	62,800	34,709	—	41,420	4.7	−1.3
1983	24,580	25,757	14,506	—	16,956	60,171	63,053	35,510	—	41,508	4.9	0.6
1984	26,433	27,686	15,431	—	18,832	62,122	65,067	36,266	—	44,259	7.5	3.3
1985	27,735	29,152	16,786	—	19,027	63,019	66,239	38,141	—	43,233	4.9	1.4
1986	29,458	30,809	17,604	—	19,995	65,783	68,799	39,311	—	44,651	6.2	4.3
1987	30,970	32,385	18,406	—	20,300	66,859	69,914	39,735	—	43,824	5.1	1.7
1988	32,191	33,915	19,329	—	21,769	67,072	70,066	40,273	—	45,357	3.9	0.3
1989	34,213	35,975	20,209	—	23,446	68,299	71,816	40,343	—	46,805	6.3	1.9
1990	35,353	36,915	21,423	—	23,431	67,258	70,230	40,757	—	44,577	3.3	−1.6
1991	35,939	37,783	21,548	—	23,895	65,973	69,358	39,555	—	43,864	1.7	−1.9
1992	36,573	38,670	21,103	—	23,555	65,508	69,264	37,799	—	42,191	1.8	−0.8
1993	36,959	39,300	21,542	—	23,654	64,571	68,661	37,636	—	41,326	1.1	−1.3
1994	38,782	40,884	24,698	—	24,318	66,370	69,967	42,267	—	41,617	4.9	2.7
1995	40,611	42,646	25,970	—	24,570	67,865	71,266	43,399	—	41,059	4.7	2.3

Year											
1996	42,300	44,756	26,522	—	26,179	68,854	43,171	—	42,613	4.2	1.5
1997	44,568	46,754	28,602	—	28,142	71,011	45,572	—	44,839	5.4	3.1
1998	46,737	49,023	29,404	—	29,608	73,472	46,224	—	46,545	4.9	3.4
1999	48,831	51,079	31,850	—	31,523	75,163	49,025	—	48,522	4.5	2.3
2000	50,732	53,029	33,676	—	34,442	75,526	50,134	—	51,275	3.9	0.5
2001	51,407	54,067	33,598	—	34,490	74,413	48,634	—	49,925	1.3	−1.4
2002	51,680	54,633	33,525	60,984	34,185	73,647	47,775	86,906	48,716	0.5	−1.1
2003	52,680	55,768	34,369	63,251	34,272	73,405	47,890	88,135	47,755	1.9	−0.3
2004	54,061	56,723	35,148	65,420	35,440	73,348	47,687	88,759	48,083	2.6	−0.1
2005	56,194	59,317	35,464	68,957	37,867	73,744	46,540	90,493	49,693	3.9	0.6
2006	58,407	61,280	38,269	74,612	40,000	74,241	48,644	94,839	50,844	3.9	0.6
2007	61,355	64,427	40,143	77,133	40,566	75,838	49,619	95,340	50,141	5.0	2.2
2008	61,521	65,000	39,879	73,578	40,466	73,230	47,469	8,782	48,168	0.3	−3.4
2009	60,088	62,545	38,409	75,027	39,730	71,774	45,879	89,618	47,457	−2.3	−2.0
2010	60,236	62,914	38,594	75,217	39,300	70,783	45,352	88,387	46,181	0.2	−1.4
2011	60,974	64,081	40,495	72,996	40,061	69,461	46,131	83,156	45,637	1.2	−1.9
2012	62,241	65,880	40,517	77,864	40,764	69,433	45,199	86,862	45,475	2.1	0.0
2013	63,815	67,255	41,588	76,402	42,269	70,150	45,716	83,986	46,465	2.5	1.1
2014	66,632	70,609	43,151	82,732	45,114	72,027	46,645	89,430	48,767	4.4	2.7
2015	70,697	74,291	45,781	90,847	47,328	76,290	49,403	98,034	51,072	6.1	5.9
2016	72,707	76,264	49,365	93,498	51,105	77,459	52,592	99,609	54,445	2.8	1.5
2017	75,938	79,749	50,597	92,784	53,614	79,198	52,769	96,768	55,916	4.4	2.2
2018	78,646	81,976	53,105	101,244	55,093	80,071	54,067	103,078	56,091	3.6	1.1
2019	86,011	89,663	58,518	112,226	60,927	86,011	58,518	112,226	60,927	9.4	7.4

Note: "—" indicates not available. Data for additional years can be found in previous editions of *Vital Statistics on American Politics*.

[a] Includes other races not shown separately.
[b] "White alone," "Black alone," and "Asian alone" refer to the fact that in the 2002 and later Current Population Surveys individuals could describe themselves as being of more than one race.
[c] Persons of Hispanic origin may be of any race.

Source: U.S. Bureau of the Census, "Current Population Reports, Historical Income Tables," (Last updated September 15, 2020), Table F-7, https://www.census.gov/data/tables/time-series/demo/income-poverty/historical-income-families.html.

A Data Literacy Lesson
Current Dollars and Constant Dollars

Measuring the median family income, as in Table 10-7, is a relatively straightforward task. The median income in current dollars, on the left side of the table, tells us what the middle level of income for households was in the dollars of the day. The median income in constant dollars, on the right side of the table, tells us what that amount would translate to in 2019 after accounting for inflation. We discussed in the introduction to this chapter that data are often used to advocate for or against social policies. We think this table is interesting because it offers several examples that highlight what we can—and can't—take away from presentations of data. You will often need to turn to more than one data source to answer policy-driven questions.

First, we turn to what we can learn from the data that is in the categories rather than the numbers themselves. Note that prior to the 1970 entry, the median income is presented for "all families" and aren't separated out by race. So, we can determine that sometime between 1965 and 1970, the government began to recognize that there is both a means and a reason to understand how median family incomes differ by race. Intuitively, that makes sense, given the push toward civil rights legislation and policies during that time period. Similarly, we can see that our understanding of race has evolved over time by seeing the change in different categories (as with the additions of Hispanic origin in 1975 and Asian in 2002). Separating out median household income by race not only reflects an acknowledgement by the government that there are income differences by race, but also provides the means to measure what those gaps are and begin to question how policy might be the solution to—and perhaps cause of—those gaps.

In addition to what we can learn from Table 10-7, we also realized that it raised many additional questions for us as we think about what we can take away from these data. For example, while the inclusion of current dollars helps us to understand what the value of income in 1950 would be today, we don't know whether this translates to understanding buying power. The Bureau of Labor Statistics (BLS) tracks the prices of a "market basket" of everyday expenses such as food, clothing, housing, medical care, and more to calculate the consumer price index (CPI). We don't know from this table alone whether the translation from constant dollars to current dollars accounts for the fluctuations in that market basket. Put more simply, we don't know how much "buying power" these different income amounts would provide.

As we consider this table, we also note that the indicator used is the median family income. In an introductory statistics class, you'll learn that the three indicators of average (mean, median, and mode) provide different insights. By looking at the median, we know what the middle household incomes are, which might give us insights into what is considered "middle class." This raises the questions, though, of whether that is typical for families or what the range of salaries are. In contemporary discussions of family income, one question that it often raised is income inequality, or how income is distributed across the population. This table cannot be used to answer questions about that distribution—it can only answer questions about the central tendency of the data. As in the case of answering questions about buying power, we would need to pull in additional data from other sources if our questions focused on income distribution across society.

> As you encounter new data, we encourage you to consider what information it provides—and what it doesn't. While the measurement of numbers is often straightforward, untangling the very real sociopolitical implications behind those numbers is rarely as simple.

Table 10-8 Persons below the Poverty Line, by Group, 2019

Group	Percentage of group that is poor	Group as a percentage of all poor people
Race/ethnicity		
White alone	9.1	66.2
White alone (not of Hispanic origin)	7.3	41.6
Black alone	18.8	23.8
Asian	7.3	4.3
Hispanic (of any race)	15.7	28.1
Age		
Under 18 years	14.4	30.8
18–64 years	9.4	54.9
65 years and older	8.9	14.3
Residence		
Metropolitan residents	10.0	83.4
Nonmetropolitan residents	13.3	16.6
Region		
Northeast	9.4	15.2
Midwest	9.7	19.2
South	12.0	43.7
West	9.5	21.9
Educational attainment		
Total, aged 25 and older	8.8	57.9
No high school diploma	23.7	14.1
High school, no college	11.5	20.8
Some college	7.8	13.2
Bachelor's degree or higher	3.9	9.7
All persons	10.5	100.0

Note: The Current Population Survey asked respondents to choose one or more races. Shown are people who reported a single race of white or single race of Black or African American. Hispanic origin may be of any race. Data for earlier years can be found in previous editions of *Vital Statistics on American Politics*.

Source: U.S. Bureau of the Census, "Income and Poverty in the United States: 2019," Table B-1, https://www.census.gov/library/publications/2020/demo/p60-270.html.

Table 10-9 Persons below the Poverty Line, by Race and Hispanic Origin, 1959–2019 (percent)

Year	White	Black	Hispanic origin	Total
1959	18.1	55.1	—	22.4
1960	17.8	—	—	22.2
1965	13.3	—	—	17.3
1970	9.9	33.5	—	12.6
1975	9.7	31.3	26.9	12.3
1976	9.1	31.1	24.7	11.8
1977	8.9	31.3	22.4	11.6
1978	8.7	30.6	21.6	11.4
1979	9.0	31.0	21.8	11.7
1980	10.2	32.5	25.7	13.0
1981	11.1	34.2	26.5	14.0
1982	12.0	35.6	29.9	15.0
1983	12.1	35.7	28.0	15.2
1984	11.5	33.8	28.4	14.4
1985	11.4	31.3	29.0	14.0
1986	11.0	31.1	27.3	13.6
1987	10.4	32.4	28.0	13.4
1988	10.1	31.3	26.7	13.0
1989	10.0	30.7	26.2	12.8
1990	10.7	31.9	28.1	13.5
1991	11.3	32.7	28.7	14.2
1992	11.9	33.4	29.6	14.8
1993	12.2	33.1	30.6	15.1
1994	11.7	30.6	30.7	14.5
1995	11.2	29.3	30.3	13.8
1996	11.2	28.4	29.4	13.7
1997	11.0	26.5	27.1	13.3
1998	10.5	26.1	25.6	12.7
1999	9.8	23.6	22.7	11.9
2000	9.5	22.5	21.5	11.3
2001	9.9	22.7	21.4	11.7
2002	10.2	24.1	21.8	12.1
2003	10.5	24.4	22.5	12.5
2004	10.8	24.7	21.9	12.7
2005	10.6	24.9	21.8	12.6
2006	10.3	24.3	20.6	12.3
2007	10.5	24.5	21.5	12.5
2008	11.2	24.7	23.2	13.2
2009	12.3	25.8	25.3	14.3
2010	13.0	27.4	26.5	15.1
2011	12.8	27.6	25.3	15.0
2012	12.7	27.2	25.6	15.0
2013	12.3	27.2	23.5	14.5
2014	12.7	26.0	23.6	14.8
2015	11.6	23.9	21.4	13.5
2016	11.0	21.8	19.4	12.7
2017	10.7	21.2	18.3	12.3
2018	10.1	20.7	17.6	11.8
2019	9.1	18.7	15.7	10.5

Table 10-9 *(Continued)*

Note: "—" indicates not available. Beginning with the 2003 Current Population Survey ASEC, respondents had the option to choose one or more races. White and Black refers to people who did not report any other race category. The use of this single-race population does not imply that it is the preferred method of presenting or analyzing the data. Hispanic origin overlaps across race categories. The Census Bureau uses a variety of approaches and urges caution in interpreting aggregate results for the Hispanic population given the wide variety in socioeconomic characteristics, culture, and recency of immigration. The total includes other races not shown separately. Data for additional years can be found in previous editions of *Vital Statistics on American Politics*.

Source: U.S. Bureau of the Census, "Income and Poverty in the United States: 2019," Table B5, https://www.census.gov/data/tables/2020/demo/income-poverty/p60-270.html.

Figure 10-4 Temporary Assistance for Needy Families (TANF) and Food Stamp (SNAP) Benefit Levels as Percentage of Federal Poverty Line, 2020

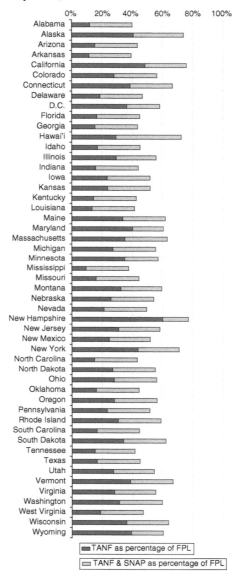

Note: The Temporary Assistance for Needy Families (TANF) program provides monthly cash benefits to eligible families with children. It is run directly by the states. Before 1996, it was known as the Aid to Families with Dependent Children (AFDC) program. The Food Stamp Program (now the Supplemental Nutrition Assistance Program, or SNAP) provides monthly food stamp benefits to individuals living in families or alone, provided their income and assets are below the limits set by federal law. Benefit levels are for a single-parent family of three. For details, see source.

Source: Center on Budget and Policy Priorities, "TANF Benefits Still Too Low to Help Families, Especially Black Families, Avoid Increased Hardship," October 8, 2020, https://www.cbpp.org/research/family-income-support/tanf-benefits-still-too-low-to-help-families-especially-black.

Figure 10-5 U.S. Population Receiving AFDC/TANF and Food Stamps/SNAP, 1970–2018

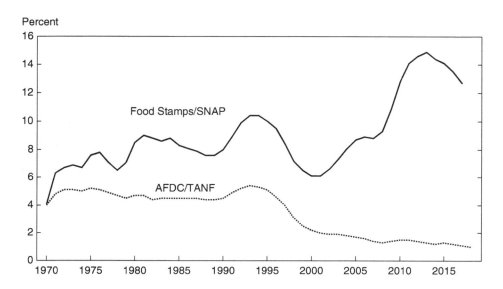

Note: See note to Figure 10-4, this volume.

Sources: 1970–2009: U.S. Department of Health and Human Services, "Indicators of Welfare Dependence: Annual Report to Congress 2008, Appendix A," http://aspe.hhs.gov/hsp/indicators08/index.shtml, and updated by personal communication from HHS; 2010–2018: Gilbert Crouse and Suzanne Macartney, U.S. Department of Health and Human Services, Office of Human Services Policy, Office of the Assistant Secretary for Planning and Evaluation, "Welfare Indicators and Risk Factors, Nineteenth Report to Congress 2020," Table 7 Indicator 3 (TANF) and Table 8 Indicator 3 (SNAP), https://aspe.hhs.gov/system/files/pdf/265031/welfare-indicators-and-risk-factors-19th-report.pdf.

A Data Literacy Lesson
Identifying Patterns with Data Visualization

Data visualizations, whether complex interactive data art or simple line graphs, can be useful for understanding patterns and trends in data that aren't immediately apparent in tables of numbers. Tables such as 10-7 and 10-8 provide useful details about changes over time in median family income and the percentage of the population below the poverty line, but take some consideration to put in context. In contrast, we think Figure 10-5 shows with a quick glance some interesting and noteworthy patterns.

For example, the percent of the population receiving both cash assistance (AFDC/TANF) and nutrition assistance (Food Stamps/SNAP) show a precipitous drop after 1995, and continued to decline for several years. Even if you have no prior experience with or knowledge about government assistance programs, this figure might prompt you to question whether there was a change in policy or a change in the characteristics of the population that led to that drop-off. Some quick investigation would lead you to learn that in 1996, Congress passed the Personal Responsibility and Work Opportunity Reconciliation Act (PRWORA), often referred to broadly as "welfare reform." This sweeping legislation not only changed the names of each program (from Aid to Families with Dependent Children, or AFDC, to Temporary Assistance to Needy Families, or TANF, and from Food Stamps to Supplemental Nutrition Assistance Program, or SNAP), it also introduced new eligibility requirements for both cash and nutrition assistance. The effects of this on the percentage of the population receiving assistance are immediately apparent in this figure. We suspect that effect might not jump out as quickly in a table of numbers.

Data visualization can also lead us to questions that are more complex and take more investigation. For example, as you continue down the timeline in Figure 10-5, you might note that the graphs for TANF and SNAP continue on a relatively similar trajectory until about 2001, when they diverge: enrollment in TANF continues a slight decrease, while SNAP enrollment moves up. Looking deeper into TANF regulations will show you that the changes enacted in 1996 carried a five-year time limit on cash assistance, which would have begun to go widely into effect in 2001. We note that the gradual decline of TANF recipients likely is a function of regulations within PRWORA. Legislative effects are rarely immediate but rather the effects sometimes happen over a few years. As to other changes, including why SNAP enrollment began to go up at that time and has continued to go up so dramatically since then would take additional exploration. Often, when looking at patterns in the outcomes of social policy, it will require a combination of learning more about the changes in the programs themselves and understanding the broader context of the time. We might need to turn to additional data sources to find answers to broader questions, such as whether the number of children in the United States increased, or whether the percentage of families at a certain threshold of the poverty level increased at the same rate, or whether eligibility requirements shifted.

One of the biggest advantages of presenting data in a graphic form is the ability to quickly identify trends and patterns that point to the need for exploration and explanation. However, because we can see these patterns easily, it can be easy to overlook ways in which the data presentation affect how we interpret it. For example, the y-axis in Figure 10-5 is limited to 0–16 percent, highlighting where the change has occurred. Focusing on that interval range amplifies the effect we see in changes over time. How different would this figure look if it were graphed on a y-axis that ranged from 0–100 percent? Would you draw different interpretations or have different questions from that presentation of the same data?

In some extreme cases, the presentation of data can be confusing or misleading. In May 2020, for example, the Georgia Department of Public Health released a graph of COVID-19 cases that seemed to show a clear downward trend in the number of cases. However, looking at dates on the x-axis revealed that they were not placed in chronological order. While the stated intent of this was to highlight the counties and dates of peak cases, the effect was confusion and distrust. When you encounter a data visualization, we encourage you to take a moment to ask yourself questions about how it is presented, what portion of it is presented, and why it's done that way. You might also ask yourself who is presenting the data, and if they have a particular interest in your interpreting the results a particular way.

Table 10-10 Health Insurance Coverage U.S. Population, 1987–2019

Year[a]	Total population (millions)	Uninsured		Insured (percent)		
		Number (millions)	Percent	Employment-based[b]	Government[c]	Military[d]
1987	212.7	30.7	14.4	66.2	9.9	4.4
1988	214.7	32.4	15.1	66.0	10.0	4.2
1989	216.6	33.1	15.3	65.6	10.1	4.0
1990	218.8	34.4	15.7	64.1	11.5	4.0
1991	220.9	35.2	15.9	63.4	12.5	3.9
1992	226.4	38.3	16.9	61.3	13.4	3.7
1993	229.0	39.3	17.2	60.4	14.3	3.6
1994	230.8	39.4	17.1	64.4	14.1	4.2
1995	232.7	40.3	17.3	64.6	14.3	3.5
1996	234.9	41.4	17.6	64.8	14.0	3.3
1997	237.0	43.1	18.2	65.0	13.0	3.1
1998	239.3	43.9	18.4	65.8	12.4	3.2
1999	243.4	38.5	15.8	67.8	12.5	3.0
2000	246.0	38.2	15.5	68.3	12.9	3.1
2001	248.3	39.5	15.9	67.0	13.6	3.0
2002	251.7	41.8	16.6	65.7	14.2	3.1
2003	253.6	43.1	17.0	64.4	15.2	3.1
2004	256.0	43.0	16.8	63.9	16.0	3.2
2005	258.3	44.4	17.2	63.5	15.9	3.3
2006	260.8	46.5	17.8	62.9	15.9	3.0
2007	262.3	45.0	17.1	62.9	16.5	3.2
2008	263.7	45.7	17.3	61.9	17.8	3.3
2009	265.7	50.0	18.8	58.9	19.4	3.5
2010	266.8	49.2	18.4	58.6	19.8	3.6
2011	267.3	47.9	17.9	58.3	20.8	3.7
2012	267.8	47.3	17.7	58.4	21.0	3.7
2013	313.4	41.8	13.3	55.7	30.1	4.5

		Private Plans		Public			
		Employment based	Direct purchase, including marketplace	TRICARE	Medicare	Medicaid	Military	VA or CHAMPVA
2014	316.2	33.0	10.4	55.4	14.6	—	16.0	19.5	4.5	—
2015	318.9	29.0	9.1	55.7	16.3	—	16.3	19.6	4.7	—
2016	320.4	28.1	8.8	55.7	16.2	—	16.7	19.4	4.6	—
2017	323.2	28.5	8.8	56.0	16.0	—	17.2	19.3	4.8	—
2018	323.7	27.5	8.5	55.1	10.8	2.6	17.8	17.9	—	1.0
2019	324.5	26.1	8.0	56.4	10.2	2.6	18.1	17.2	—	1.0

Note: Persons may have more than one type of coverage; percentages may total to more than 100. 2014–2019 data based on CPS ASEC estimates, when individuals are considered to be uninsured at any time of the year. In the CPS ASEC estimate, individuals are considered to be uninsured if they are at the time of the interview. See original source for details.

[a] Because of questionnaire changes in the Current Population Survey in 1994 and 1999, numbers are not strictly comparable over time.
[b] Group health insurance through current or former employer or union.
[c] Medicare or Medicaid. Through 2013, this category also includes other state programs for low-income individuals.
[d] Includes CHAMPUS (Comprehensive Health and Medical Plan for Uniformed Services)/TRICARE, veterans, and military health care through 2017. Beginning in 2018, TRICARE was shifted to being reported as private health care. Through 2013, percent covered by VA care.

Sources: 1987–1998: U.S. Bureau of the Census, Health Insurance, "Historical Health Insurance Tables," Table HI-6; 1999–2009: "Health Insurance Coverage Status and Type of Coverage by State—Persons under 65: 1999 to 2009," Table HIA-6; 2010–2012: "Health Insurance Coverage Status and Type of Coverage by State for All People," Table HI05, available at www.census.gov; 2013–2019: "Health Insurance Coverage in the United States," Table 1, www.census.gov.

Table 10-11 Persons without Health Insurance, by Demographic Characteristics, 2019

	Uninsured	
Group	Number (millions)	Percentage of group population
Race and Hispanic origin		
White	20.0	7.8
White, not Hispanic	10.2	5.2
Black	4.4	9.4
Asian	1.3	6.0
Hispanic origin (any race)	10.1	16.7
Age		
Under 19 years[a]	4.0	5.2
19–25 years[a]	4.2	14.2
26–34 years	5.4	13.3
35–44 years	4.7	11.4
45–54 years	4.0	10.2
55–64 years	3.2	7.6
65 years and older	0.6	1.1
Nativity		
Native born	18.1	6.5
Foreign born	8.0	17.8
Naturalized citizen	2.0	8.7
Not a citizen	6.0	27.1

[a] These age groups are of special interest because of the Affordable Care Act of 2010. Children under the age of 19 are eligible for Medicaid/CHIP and individuals aged 19 to 25 may be a dependent on a parent's health plan.

Source: U.S. Bureau of the Census, "Health Insurance Coverage in the United States: 2019," Tables HHI-01, HHI-02, HHI-04, www.census.gov.

Table 10-12 Persons Who Have Completed High School or College, by Race, Hispanic Origin, and Sex, 1940–2019 (percent)

Level/year	25 years and over							25–29 years						
	White[a]		Black[b]		Hispanic[c]			White[a]		Black[b]		Hispanic[c]	
	Male	Female	Male	Female	Male	Female		Male	Female	Male	Female	Male	Female
Completed four years of high school or more[d]
1940	24.2	28.1	6.9	8.4	—	—		38.9	43.4	10.6	13.6	—	—
1947	33.2	36.7	12.7	14.5	—	—		52.9	56.8	19.6	24.7	—	—
1959	44.5	47.7	19.6	21.6	—	—		66.9	67.4	40.6	38.6	—	—
1970	57.2	57.6	32.4	34.8	—	—		79.2	76.4	54.5	57.9	—	—
1980	71.0	70.1	51.1	51.3	46.4	44.1		86.8	87.0	74.8	78.1	58.3	58.8
1990	79.1	79.0	65.8	66.5	50.3	51.3		84.6	88.1	81.5	81.8	56.6	59.9
2000	84.4	85.0	78.7	78.3	56.6	57.5		86.6	90.0	86.6	85.3	59.2	66.4
2010	86.9	88.2	83.6	84.6	61.4	64.4		87.3	89.9	86.8	91.1	65.7	74.0
2015	88.3	89.3	86.4	87.6	65.5	67.8		90.0	91.8	91.4	93.0	75.7	78.6
2016	88.7	90.1	86.3	87.7	67.2	69.7		90.6	92.7	90.9	90.4	78.3	83.3
2017	89.4	91.1	86.5	87.9	69.5	71.6		90.6	93.7	91.2	92.5	80.7	84.9
2018	89.6	90.8	87.7	88.1	70.7	72.5		91.7	94.1	90.1	93.1	83.4	87.2
2019	89.9	91.0	87.1	88.9	70.1	72.8		93.3	94.3	88.9	93.0	84.5	88.3
Completed four years of college or more[e]
1940	5.9	4.0	1.4	1.2	—	—		7.5	5.3	1.5	1.7	—	—
1947	6.6	4.9	2.4	2.6	—	—		6.2	5.7	2.6	2.9	—	—
1959	11.0	6.2	3.8	2.9	—	—		15.9	8.1	5.6	3.7	—	—
1970	15.0	8.6	4.6	4.4	—	—		21.3	13.3	6.7	8.0	—	—
1980	22.1	14.0	7.7	8.1	9.7	6.2		25.5	22.0	10.5	12.5	8.4	6.9
1990	25.3	19.0	11.9	10.8	9.8	8.7		24.2	24.3	15.1	11.9	7.3	9.1

(Table continues)

Table 10-12 *(Continued)*

	25 years and over								25–29 years					
	White[a]		Black[b]		Hispanic[c]		White[a]		Black[b]		Hispanic[c]	
Level/year	Male	Female	Male	Female	Male	Female	Male	Female	Male	Female	Male	Female
2000	28.5	23.9	16.3	16.7	10.7	10.6	27.8	31.3	18.1	17.0	8.3	11.0
2010	30.8	29.9	17.7	21.4	12.9	15.0	28.8	36.9	14.8	22.9	10.8	16.8
2015	32.6	32.9	20.6	24.0	14.3	16.6	33.2	40.4	16.5	24.2	14.5	18.5
2016	33.4	34.0	21.7	24.6	15.4	17.4	33.6	40.5	20.2	25.1	16.2	21.5
2017	34.0	32.2	22.1	25.4	15.8	18.6	35.0	40.1	20.4	23.9	15.0	22.4
2018	34.9	36.6	23.2	26.9	16.6	20.1	33.5	42.4	18.6	25.7	18.4	23.2
2019	35.7	36.8	24.1	27.7	16.9	20.8	34.7	42.7	28.5	29.5	18.2	23.1

Note: "—" indicates not available. Data for additional years can be found in previous editions of *Vital Statistics on American Politics*.

[a] For 1940 through 2000, data are for white persons only; for 2005 through 2019, data are for people who reported a single race of white.
[b] For 1940 through 1960, data are for Black and other races; for 1970 through 2000, data are for Black persons only; for 2005 through 2019, data are for people who reported a single race of Black or African American.
[c] Persons of Hispanic origin may be of any race.
[d] Beginning in 2000, high school graduate or more.
[e] Beginning in 2000, bachelor's degree or more.

Source: U.S. Bureau of the Census, "Educational Attainment in the United States," Table 1, www.census.gov.

Table 10-13 School Desegregation, by Region, 1968–2017

Region/year	Percentage of black students in schools more than 50 percent minority	Percentage of Hispanic students in schools more than 50 percent minority	Percentage of black students in schools 90–100 percent minority	Percentage of Hispanic students in schools 90–100 percent minority
South				
1968	80.9	69.6	77.8	33.7
1972	55.3	69.9	24.7	31.4
1976	54.9	70.9	22.4	32.2
1980	57.1	76.0	23.0	37.3
1984	56.9	75.4	24.2	37.3
1988	56.5	80.2	24.0	37.9
1991	60.8	76.8	26.6	38.6
1994	63.4	75.6	—	38.0
1996	65.3	75.9	27.9	38.3
1998	67.2	76.1	29.7	39.1
2000	69.0	77.2	30.9	39.5
2001	69.8	77.7	31.0	39.9
2005	72.0	78.0	32.0	40.0
2009	74.0	79.4	33.4	41.3
2011	76.8	81.0	34.2	41.5
2017	81.5	83.8	36.6	41.7
Border				
1968	71.6	—	60.2	—
1972	67.2	—	54.7	—
1976	60.1	—	42.5	—
1980	59.2	—	37.0	—
1984	62.5	—	37.4	—
1988	59.6	—	34.5	8.9
1991	59.3	37.4	33.2	10.8
1994	—	40.8	—	12.3
1996	63.2	43.5	37.3	12.6
1998	64.7	46.1	39.2	13.1
2000	67.0	49.2	39.6	13.4
2001	67.9	52.8	41.6	14.2
2005	70.0	57.0	42.0	17.0
2009	69.9	58.8	39.8	18.4
2011	73.2	59.9	41.0	20.0
2017	75.3	66.5	38.1	25.9
Northeast				
1968	66.8	74.8	42.7	44
1972	69.9	74.4	46.9	44.1
1976	72.5	74.9	51.4	45.8
1980	79.9	76.3	48.7	45.8
1984	73.1	77.5	47.4	47.1
1988	77.3	79.7	48.0	44.2
1991	76.2	78.1	50.1	46.2
1994	—	77.6	—	45.1
1996	77.3	78.2	50.5	46.0
1998	77.5	78.5	50.9	45.7

(Table continues)

Table 10-13 *(Continued)*

Region/year	Percentage of black students in schools more than 50 percent minority	Percentage of Hispanic students in schools more than 50 percent minority	Percentage of black students in schools 90–100 percent minority	Percentage of Hispanic students in schools 90–100 percent minority
2000	78.3	78.5	51.2	45.3
2001	78.4	78.2	51.2	44.8
2005	78.0	77.0	51.0	45.0
2009	77.9	76.3	50.6	43.9
2011	79.4	76.6	51.4	44.1
2017	81.7	77.4	50.5	42.9
Midwest				
1968	77.3	31.8	58.0	6.8
1972	75.3	34.4	57.4	9.5
1976	70.3	39.3	51.1	14.1
1980	69.5	46.6	43.6	19.6
1984	70.7	53.9	43.6	24.2
1988	70.1	52.3	41.8	24.9
1991	69.9	53.5	39.4	21.1
1994	—	53.1	—	21.8
1996	72.0	54.0	43.4	22.3
1998	72.8	55.6	45.5	24.1
2000	73.3	56.3	46.3	24.9
2001	72.9	56.6	46.8	24.6
2005	72.0	57.0	46.0	26.0
2009	71.6	58.8	44.3	27.0
2011	73.7	58.9	43.2	26.2
2017	70.5	60.0	35.8	24.0
West				
1968	72.2	42.4	50.8	11.7
1972	68.1	44.7	42.7	11.5
1976	67.4	52.7	36.3	13.3
1980	66.8	63.5	33.7	18.5
1984	66.9	68.4	29.4	22.9
1988	67.1	71.3	28.6	27.5
1991	69.7	73.5	26.4	29.7
1994	—	75.9	—	32.1
1996	73.5	77.1	27.5	33.0
1998	74.0	78.3	28.8	35.2
2000	75.3	79.4	29.5	36.7
2001	75.8	80.1	30.0	37.4
2005	77.0	82.0	30.0	41.0
2009	78.1	83.7	29.5	43.2
2011	82.4	84.1	34.4	44.8
2017	86.1	85.9	37.6	45.6
Total				
1968	76.6	54.8	64.3	23.1
1972	63.6	56.6	38.7	23.3
1976	62.4	60.8	35.9	24.8
1980	62.9	68.1	33.2	28.8
1984	63.5	70.6	33.2	31.0

Table 10-13 (Continued)

Region/year	Percentage of black students in schools more than 50 percent minority	Percentage of Hispanic students in schools more than 50 percent minority	Percentage of black students in schools 90–100 percent minority	Percentage of Hispanic students in schools 90–100 percent minority
1988	63.2	—	32.1	33.1
1991	66.0	73.4	33.9	34.0
1994	67.1	74.0	33.6	34.8
1996	68.8	74.8	35.0	35.4
1998	70.1	75.6	36.5	36.7
2000	71.6	76.4	37.4	37.4
2002	73.0	77.0	38.0	38.0
2005	73.0	77.0	38.0	39.0
2006	73.1	78.7	38.4	43.1
2009	74.1	79.5	38.1	43.1
2010	76.5	79.1	39.3	41.2
2011	77.1	79.3	39.3	41.2
2012	77.7	79.5	39.6	41.4
2013	78.3	79.8	39.6	41.4
2014	79.0	80.2	39.9	41.7
2015	79.6	80.5	40.2	41.8
2016	80.1	80.7	40.2	41.7
2017	80.6	80.9	40.1	41.6

Note: "—" indicates not available. Data for 1968–1969 to 2011–2012 school years. "Total" data were not available for 2001; regional data were not available for 2002 or 2006. For composition of regions, see Table A-4, this volume. Data for additional years can be found in previous editions of *Vital Statistics on American Politics.*

Sources: 1968–1980: Gary Orfield, testimony before the House Subcommittee on Civil and Constitutional Rights, Civil Rights Implications of the Education Block Grant Program, 97th Cong., 2nd sess., September 9, 1982, 67–72; 1984: Orfield, Franklin Monfort, and Melissa Aaron, "Status of School Desegregation 1968–1986," National School Boards Association, Alexandria, Va., 1989, 5, 7; 1988: Orfield and Monfort, "Status of School Desegregation: The Next Generation," National School Boards Association, Alexandria, Va., 1992, 3, 7–8; 1991: Orfield, "The Growth of Segregation in American Schools: Changing Patterns of Separation and Poverty Since 1968," National School Boards Association, Alexandria, Va., 1993, 9, © 1989, 1992, and 1993 National School Boards Association, all rights reserved; 1994: Orfield et al., "Deepening Segregation in American Public Schools," April 5, 1997, 11, 15; 1996: Orfield and John T. Yun, "Resegregation in American Schools," June 1999, Tables 15, 19; 1998: Orfield, "Schools More Separate: Consequences of a Decade of Resegregation," July 2001, Tables 9, 14, 18; 2000: Erica Frankenberg, Chungmei Lee, and Orfield, "A Multiracial Society with Segregated Schools: Are We Losing the Dream?" January 2003, Tables 11, 29, 33, 37; 2001: Orfield and Lee, "Brown at 50: King's Dream or Plessy's Nightmare?" January 2004, Tables 8, 9; 2002: Orfield and Lee, "Why Segregation Matters: Poverty and Educational Inequality," January 2005, Table 4, www.civilrightsproject.harvard.edu; 2005: Orfield and Lee, "Historic Reversals, Accelerating Resegregation, and the Need for New Integration Strategies," August 2007, Tables 10, 14, 16, 17; 2006–2009: Orfield, John Kucsera, and Genevieve Siegel-Hawley, "E Pluribus… Separation: Deepening Double Segregation for More Students," September 2012, Tables 2, 11; 2011: Orfield and Frankenberg, with Jongyeon Ee and Kuscera, "Brown at 60: Great Progress, a Long Retreat and an Uncertain Future," May 2014, Tables 8, 11, B-1, B-3, http://civilrightsproject.ucla.edu, reprinted with permission of The Civil Rights Project/Proyecto Derechos Civiles at UCLA; 2010–2017 totals for students in majority minority districts: National Center for Educational Statistics, "Digest 2019," Table 216.50, nces.ed.gov; Data for intensely segregated schools from U.S. Department of Education, National Center for Education Statistics, Common Core of Data (CCD), "Public Elementary/Secondary School Universe Survey", 2018–19 vol.1a, "Public Elementary/Secondary School Universe Survey Geographic Data (EDGE)", 2018–19 vol.1a; 2018: Orfied and Danielle Jarvie, "Black segregation matters: School resegregation and black educational opportunity," 2020, Tables 11, 12.

Table 10-14 Frequency of Legal Abortions, 1972–2017

	Total	
Year	Number of abortions (thousands)	Ratio
1972	587.0	15.5
1973	744.6	19.3
1974	898.6	22.0
1975	1034.2	24.9
1976	1179.3	26.5
1977	1316.7	28.6
1978	1409.6	29.2
1979	1497.7	29.6
1980	1553.9	30.0
1981	1577.3	30.1
1982	1573.9	30.0
1983	1575.0	30.4
1984	1577.2	29.7
1985	1588.6	29.7
1986	1574.0	29.4
1987	1559.1	28.8
1988	1590.8	28.6
1991	1556.5	27.4
1992	1528.9	27.5
1993	1495.0	27.4
1994	1423.0	26.6
1995	1359.4	25.9
1996	1360.2	25.9
1997	1335.0	25.5
1998	1319.0	25.1
1999	1314.8	24.6
2000	1313.0	24.5
2001	1291.0	24.4
2002	1269.0	23.8
2003	1250.0	23.3
2004	1222.1	22.9
2005	1206.2	22.4
2006	1242.2	22.9
2007	1209.6	21.9
2008	1212.4	22.5
2009	1151.6	22.2
2010	1102.7	21.7
2011	1058.5	21.2
2012	1011.0	20.4
2013	958.7	19.4
2014	926.2	18.8
2015	899.5	18.5
2016	874.1	18.3
2017	862.3	18.4

Note: Ratio indicates the percentage of pregnancies resulting in live birth or abortion that are terminated by abortion. The percentage is based on births occurring during the twelve-month period starting in July of that year. Figures in 1983, 1986, 1993, 1994, 1997, 1998, 2001, 2002, 2003, 2006, 2009, 2012, and 2015 are estimated by interpolation of numbers of abortions.

Sources: 1973–1988: Stanley K. Henshaw and Jennifer Van Vort, eds., *Abortion Factbook, 1992 Edition: Readings, Trends, and State and Local Data to 1988* (New York: Alan Guttmacher Institute, 1992), 174–175; total, 1991–2011: Rachel K. Jones and Jenna Jerman, Guttmacher Institute, "Abortion Incidence and Service Availability in the United States, 2011," *Perspectives on Sexual and Reproductive Health*, (2014) 46: 1, 3–14; 2012–2017: Rachel K. Jones, Elizabeth Witwer, and Jenna Jerman, Guttmacher Institute, "Abortion Incidence and Service Availability in the United States, 2017, https://www.guttmacher.org/report/abortion-incidence-service-availability-us-2017.

Table 10-15 Crime Rates, 1960–2019

	Violent crime						Property crime				
Year	Murder	Rape[a]	Robbery	Aggravated assault	Total		Burglary	Larceny theft	Vehicle theft	Total	Total
1960	5	10	60	86	161		509	1,035	183	1,727	1,888
1965	5	12	72	111	200		663	1,329	257	2,249	2,449
1970	8	19	172	165	364		1,085	2,079	457	3,621	3,985
1975	10	26	218	227	481		1,526	2,805	469	4,800	5,281
1980	10	37	251	299	597		1,684	3,167	502	5,353	5,950
1985	8	37	209	303	557		1,287	2,901	462	4,650	5,207
1990	9	41	256	423	730		1,232	3,185	656	5,073	5,803
1995	8	37	221	418	685		987	3,043	560	4,591	5,276
2000	6	32	145	324	507		729	2,477	412	3,618	4,125
2005	6	32	141	291	469		727	2,288	417	3,432	3,901
2010	5	28	119	253	405		701	2,006	239	2,946	3,351
2015	5	39[a]	102	238	374		495	1784	222	2,501	2,875
2016	5	41	103	248	387		469	1745	237	2,452	2,839
2017	5	42	99	249	384		430	1696	238	2,363	2,747
2018	5	44	86	248	370		378	1602	230	2,210	2,580
2019	5	43	82	250	367		341	1550	220	2,110	2,477

Note: Figures are rates per 100,000 inhabitants. For definitions of crimes, see the sources. Data for additional years can be found in previous editions of *Vital Statistics on American Politics.*

[a] The URC SRS definition of rape was updated in 2012 to more accurately report rape statistics. See https://www.justice.gov/archives/opa/blog/updated-definition-rape for details.

Sources: 1960–1985: U.S. Bureau of the Census, *Statistical Abstract of the United States, 1976* (Washington, D.C.: Government Printing Office, 1976); 153; 1987, 155; 1990: U.S. Department of Justice, Federal Bureau of Investigation, "Uniform Crime Reports: Crime in the United States, 2009," Table 1, www.fbi.gov; 1995–2013: "2013"; 2015–2019: "2019," https://ucr.fbi.gov/crime-in-the-u.s.

453

Table 10-16 Death Penalty in the States: Number of Executions, 1930–2020, and Number on Death Row, 2021

State	Methods of execution authorized by state[a]	1930s	1940s	1950s	1960s	1970s	1980s	1990s	2000s	2010s	2020	Number awaiting execution[b]
Alabama	lethal injection, lethal gas, or electrocution	60	50	20	5	0	7	12	25	22	1	170
Alaska	none	0	0	0	0	0	0	0	0	0	0	0
Arizona	lethal injection[c]	17	9	8	4	0	0	19	4	14	0	119
Arkansas	lethal injection[d]	53	8	18	9	0	0	21	6	4	0	31
California	lethal injection or lethal gas	108	80	74	30	0	0	7	6	0	0	711
Colorado	none[e]	25	13	3	6	0	0	1	0	0	0	0[e]
Connecticut	none	5	10	5	1	0	0	0	1	0	0	0[f]
Delaware	none[g]	8	4	0	0	0	0	10	4	2	0	0[g]
District of Columbia	none	20	16	4	0	0	0	0	0	0	0	0
Florida	electrocution or lethal injection	44	65	49	12	1	20	23	24	31	0	347
Georgia	lethal injection	137	130	85	14	0	14	9	23	30	0	45
Hawaii	none	0	0	0	0	0	0	0	0	0	0	0
Idaho	lethal injection	0	0	3	0	0	0	1	0	2	0	8
Illinois	none	61	18	9	2	0	0	12	0	0	0	0
Indiana	lethal injection	31	7	2	1	0	2	5	13	0	0	8
Iowa	none	8	7	1	2	0	0	0	0	0	0	0
Kansas	lethal injection	0	5	5	5	0	0	0	0	0	0	10
Kentucky	lethal injection	52	34	16	1	0	0	2	1	0	0	28
Louisiana	lethal injection	58	47	27	1	0	18	7	2	1	0	68
Maine	none	0	0	0	0	0	0	0	0	0	0	0
Maryland	none	16	45	6	1	0	0	3	2	0	0	0

State	Method									
Massachusetts	none	18	9	0	0	0	0	0	0	0
Michigan	none	0	0	0	0	0	0	0	0	0
Minnesota	none	0	0	0	0	0	0	0	0	0
Mississippi	lethal injection[h]	48	60	36	10	4	0	6	11	49
Missouri	lethal injection or lethal gas	36	15	7	4	1	40	26	23	39
Montana	lethal injection	5	1	0	0	0	2	1	0	2
Nebraska	lethal injection	0	2	2	0	0	3	0	1	11
Nevada	lethal injection	8	0	9	2	1	4	4	0	78
New Hampshire	none[i]	1	0	0	0	0	0	0	0	1[i]
New Jersey	none	40	14	17	3	0	0	0	0	0[j]
New Mexico	none	2	2	3	1	0	0	1	0	0[j]
New York	none	153	114	52	10	0	0	0	0	0
North Carolina	lethal injection	131	12	19	1	3	12	28	0	141
North Dakota	none	0	0	0	0	0	0	0	0	0
Ohio	lethal injection	82	1	32	7	0	1	32	23	141
Oklahoma	lethal injection[h]	34	13	7	6	0	19	72	21	45
Oregon	lethal injection	2	12	4	1	0	2	0	0	24
Pennsylvania	lethal injection	82	6	31	3	0	3	0	0	142[k]
Rhode Island	none	0	0	0	0	0	0	0	0	0
South Carolina	electrocution or lethal injection	67	61	26	8	2	22	18	1	39
South Dakota	lethal injection	0	1	0	0	0	0	1	4	1
Tennessee	lethal injection	47	37	8	1	0	0	6	6	51
Texas	lethal injection	120	74	74	29	33	166	248	123	210
Utah	lethal injection or firing squad	2	4	6	1	2	3	0	1	7
Vermont	none	1	1	0	0	0	0	0	0	0
Virginia	none[l]	28	35	23	6	8	65	32	8	0
Washington	none[m]	23	16	6	2	0	3	1	1	0
West Virginia	none	20	11	9	0	0	0	0	0	0
Wisconsin	none	0	0	0	0	0	0	0	0	0

(Table continues)

Table 10-16 (Continued)

State	Methods of execution authorized by state[a]	Number executed								Number awaiting execution[b]
		1930s	1940s	1950s	1960s	1970s	1980s	1990s	2000s	2010s	2020	
Wyoming	lethal injection or lethal gas	4	2	0	1	0	0	1	0	0	0	1
U.S. government	lethal injection	10	13	9	1	0	0	0	3	0	13	49
U.S. military	lethal injection	n	148	11	1	0	0	0	0	0	0	4

[a] In some states, method depends on when sentenced. For details, see sources.
[b] As of February 1, 2021, figures include persons whose death sentences have been overturned but who still face the possibility of being resentenced to death after a new trial or new sentencing hearing. The number of prisoners in the United States facing active death sentences is lower. Four prisoners on death row in two different states had been sentenced as juveniles (under age eighteen at time of crime) as of December 31, 2004.
[c] Those sentenced before 1992 may select between lethal injection or lethal gas.
[d] If lethal injection is "invalidated by a final and unappealable court order," then electrocution will be used.
[e] Colorado abolished the death penalty in 2020, and commuted the sentences of the three prisoners who were on death row at that time.
[f] On April 25, 2012, Connecticut repealed the death penalty. Eleven men remained on death row until 2015 when the Connecticut Supreme Court ruled that the death penalty violated the state constitution.
[g] Delaware's Supreme Court declared capital punishment unconstitutional in 2016 and retroactively applied the ruling to earlier death sentences.
[h] If lethal injection is held unconstitutional or "otherwise unavailable," then lethal gas, electrocution, and firing squad are possible options.
[i] New Hampshire abolished the death penalty in 2019. One person remains on death row, but the state does not have a death chamber.
[j] In March 2009, New Mexico repealed the death penalty. However, the act was not retroactive, leaving two people on the state's death row. In 2019, the New Mexico Supreme Court vacated their death sentences and resentenced them to life in prison.
[k] Pennsylvania's governor declared a moratorium on executions in 2015 that was still in effect as of 2020. Capital crimes are still prosecuted and death warrants are still issued.
[l] Virginia abolished the death penalty in 2021, and commuted the sentences of the two prisoners who were on death row at that time.
[m] The Washington Supreme Court declared the state's death penalty statute unconstitutional in 2018.
[n] 160 executions have been carried out under military authority since 1930. The last execution carried out by the U.S. military was in 1961.

Sources: Number executed in 1930s–1970s: U.S. Department of Justice, Bureau of Justice Statistics, Sourcebook of Criminal Justice Statistics—1989 (Washington, D.C.: Government Printing Office, 1990), 631; method, number executed in 1980s–2020s, number awaiting execution: Death Penalty Information Center, www.deathpenaltyinfo.org; military executions: U.S. Bureau of the Census, https://www.census.gov/prod/2001pubs/statab/sec05.pdf.

Table 10-17 Number of Executions 1977–2020, by Race of Defendant and Race of Victim(s)

	Number of Executions by Race of Defendant						Number of Executions by Race of Victims						Multiple victims (including white)	Multiple victims (not including white)
Year	White	Black	Latinx	Asian	Native American	Other	White	Black	Latinx	Asian	Native American	Other		
1977	1						1							
1978														
1979	2						2							
1980														
1981	1						1							
1982	1	1					2							
1983	4	1					4	1						
1984	13	8					19	1						
1985	9	7	2				14	3					1	
1986	9	7	2				16		2	1				
1987	11	12	2				21	2	1	1				
1988	6	5					8	3						
1989	7	8	1				12	3	1					
1990	16	7					21	2						
1991	6	7	1				11	3						
1992	18	11	2				26	2	1	2			1	
1993	19	14	4				32	2	3					
1994	19	11	1				25	4	1	1				
1995	31	22	2	1	1		39	11	3	1			1	
1996	29	13	2		2		39	4	1				2	
1997	40	26	5	1	1		63	8	2	1			1	
1998	39	18	9	1	3		50	10	4					
1999	53	33	7	2	2		79	10	4	3			4	
2000	42	35	6		2		68	12	2	1	1	1	2	
2001	43	17	2		3	1	47	10	5			1	2	

(Table continues)

Table 10-17 *(Continued)*

	Number of Executions by Race of Defendant						Number of Executions by Race of Victims							
Year	White	Black	Latinx	Asian	Native American	Other	White	Black	Latinx	Asian	Native American	Other	Multiple victims (including white)	Multiple victims (not including white)
2002	46	18	6			1	56	9	5				1	
2003	41	20	3		1		45	11	6				1	
2004	36	19	3	1			48	7	3	1				
2005	37	19	3			1	43	8	4			1	4	
2006	24	21	7				35	10	6				1	
2007	22	14	6		1		29	2	7	3			1	
2008	17	17	3				25	8	1	2			1	
2009	23	22	7				34	9	7				1	
2010	27	13	5		1		30	7	7	1			1	
2011	23	15	5				28	6	5	2			2	
2012	25	11	7				28	7	5				3	
2013	23	13	3				27	4	2	1			5	
2014	12	18	5				25	5	2	1			2	
2015	11	10	7				17	6	3				2	
2016	16	2	2				18	1					1	
2017	13	8	2				16	1	2					1
2018	14	6	5				18	3	3	1			1	
2019	14	7	1				16	6						
2020	10	5	1		1		13	2	1		1			

Source: Death Penalty Information Center, "Race and the Death Penalty by the Numbers" (2021), https://deathpenaltyinfo.org/policy-issues/race/race-and-the-death-penalty-by-the-numbers.

Table 10-18 Sentenced Federal and State Prisoners, 1925–2019

Year	Number of prisoners	Rate (per 100,000 population)[a]	Year	Number of prisoners	Rate (per 100,000 population)[a]
1925	91,669	79	1999	1,304,074	463
1930	129,453	104	2000	1,334,174	478
1935	144,180	113	2001	1,345,217	470
1940	173,706	131	2002	1,380,516	476
1945	133,649	98	2003	1,408,361	482
1950	166,123	109	2004	1,433,728	486
1955	185,780	112	2005	1,462,866	491
1960	212,953	117	2006	1,504,598	501
1965	210,895	108	2007	1,532,851	506
1970	196,429	96	2008	1,547,742	504
1975	240,593	111	2009	1,553,574	504
1980	315,974	139	2010	1,552,669	500
1985	480,568	202	2011	1,538,847	492
1990	739,980	297	2012	1,512,430	480
1991	789,610	313	2013	1,520,403	479
1992	846,277	332	2014	1,507,781	472
1993	932,074	359	2015	1,476,847	459
1994	1,016,691	389	2016	1,459,948	450
1995	1,085,022	411	2017	1,439,877	442
1996	1,137,722	427	2018	1,413,370	432
1997	1,194,581	444	2019	1,380,427	419
1998	1,245,402	461			

Note: Definition of prisoners has varied somewhat over the years. See source for details. Data for additional years can be found in earlier editions of *Vital Statistics on American Politics*.

[a] Prisoners with sentences of more than one year.

Source: 1925–2010: U.S. Department of Justice, Bureau of Justice Statistics, *Sourcebook of Criminal Justice Statistics*, Kathleen Maguire, ed., University at Albany, Hindelang Criminal Justice Research Center, Table 6.28.2011, www.albany.edu/sourcebook; 2011–2012: U.S. Department of Justice, Bureau of Justice Statistics, "Prisoners in 2013," revised September 30, 2014, Tables 1, 6, www.bjs.gov; 2013–2019: E, Ann Carson, Bureau of Justice Statistics, "National Prisoner Statistics, 1989–2019" and U.S. Census Bureau, post-censal resident population estimates for January 1 of the following calendar year.

Table 10-19 Estimated Number of Persons Supervised by Adult Correctional Systems, by Correctional Status, 2000–2018 (thousands)

Year	Total correctional population[a]	Community Supervision			Incarcerated[b]		
		Total[a,c]	Probation	Parole	Total[d]	Local jail	Prison
2000	6,468	4,565	3,840	726	1,945	621	1,394
2005	7,056	4,947	4,163	784	2,200	748	1,526
2010	7,089	4,888	4,056	841	2,279	749	1,614
2015	6,741	4,651	3,790	871	2,174	728	1,527
2016	6,616	4,537	3,673	875	2,165	741	1,508
2017	6,550	4,509	3,647	875	2,154	745	1,489
2018	6,410	4,399	3,540	878	2,123	738	1,465
Average annual percent change, 2008–2018	−12.3	−13.6	−17.1	6.3	−8.1	−6	−8.9
Percent change, 2017–2018	−2.1	−2.4	−2.9	0.3	−1.4	−0.9	−1.6

Note: Counts are rounded to the nearest 100 and include estimates for nonresponding jurisdictions. Estimates for 2016 and earlier may have been revised based on updated reporting and may differ from numbers in past reports. All probation, parole, and prison counts are for December 31, while jail counts are for the last weekday in June. Details may not sum to totals due to rounding and because estimates were adjusted to exclude persons with dual correctional statuses (probationers and parolees held in prisons or local jails, parolees who were also on probation, and prisoners who were held in local jails). See Table 5 and Methodology for more details. See the Key Statistics page on the BJS website for correctional-population statistics prior to 2008. Significance testing was conducted for local jail estimates because counts are based on a sample of jails in the Annual Survey of Jails. Other counts presented are based on a full census of the population.

[a] Total was adjusted to account for offenders with multiple correctional statuses.
[b] Includes inmates held in local jails or under the jurisdiction of state or federal prisons.
[c] Estimates were adjusted to exclude parolees who were also on probation.
[d] Estimates were adjusted to exclude prisoners who were held in local jails.

Sources: U.S. Department of Justice, Bureau of Justice Statistics, "Annual Probation Survey," "Annual Parole Survey," "Annual Survey of Jails," and "National Prisoner Statistics program, 2008–2018," https://www.bjs.gov/index.cfm? ty=pbdetail&iid=7026.

11
Economic Policy

- **Gross Domestic Product (GDP)**
- **Consumer Price Index (CPI)**
- **Federal Budget**
- **National Debt**
- **Tax Rates and Breaks**
- **Income Inequality**
- **Labor Unions**
- **Minimum Wages**
- **Unemployment**

From Martin Luther King Jr's 1967 Riverside Church speech about the Vietnam War to then-representative Mike Pence's 2009 op-ed in Townhall arguing that Planned Parenthood should be defunded, leaders have long explicitly tied the federal budget and economy to the underlying political values, morals, and priorities of the nation. Economic conditions are often used to provide evidence for the United States' relative strength or weakness compared to other countries in the world. Political strategists recognize the importance of economic conditions in swaying voters toward their candidates, as when James Carville famously pegged Bill Clinton's presidential campaign around the mantra "It's the economy, stupid." How do we measure, report, and understand an area of policy that is held up to represent and sway election outcomes, power in the world, and our core values?

Many people tend to look at the budget and just see numbers—political science students, we suspect, might sometimes pay little attention to budget issues because "I study political science so I don't have to do math." We urge you not to do this. The budget, we would argue, is where our values are best expressed. Decisions about how much, or how little, to spend in an area, or about how large a share of revenue will come from the wealthy or the working class, are important. The budget is not esoteric math; it is where the rubber meets the road in policy making.

What is beyond dispute, of course, is that economic policy generates lots of numbers. There are an abundance of economic indicators that, together, provide a piece of the puzzle that is the economy as a whole. What data are best suited to highlight the depth and breadth of economic policy as vital in American politics?

We start with measures of the size and scope of the economy. Between March 2020 and March 2021, three separate stimulus packages totaling over $5 trillion were passed to boost the economy as a response to economic effects of the COVID-19 pandemic. Five trillion dollars is an unimaginable amount of money in the abstract—how do we put it in the context of the economy as a whole to begin to comprehend its relative size and impact? The Gross Domestic Product, or GDP, is the measure usually used to measure the size of the economy as a whole, which we have shared over time in Table 11-1. As we look at the economy over a long period of time, though, it is important to understand the value of a dollar today compared to twenty or thirty or ninety years ago. The Consumer Price Index (CPI, Table 11-2) helps us understand the changing value of a dollar.

If, as we noted above, leaders often claim that budgets are useful for understanding the values of a country, what does our federal budget say about our country's priorities? Tables 11-3 through 11-5 explore different budgetary outlays, or whether and how we collectively put our money where our mouth is. Related to the political questions of how much we spend on what areas is the question of how to raise that money, whether through taxes or taking on additional debt (Tables 11-6 and 11-7, Figure 11-2), and from whom. The decision of when to collect and when not to (Table 11-8) have implications of political consequence.

Finally, we turn our attention to statistics about the labor force and labor market. If the economy is a measure of production, consumption, and trade of goods and services, who is producing what and how do they have the means to purchase those goods and services?

As you read this chapter, we urge you to heed the warning above. Don't view these as just cold, dispassionate numbers. Instead, view the figures we present, and the contentious arguments they generate, as important data on fundamental beliefs about the role of government and our values in the nation. They are, we note again, where the rubber meets the road. The debates that center around these data are often heated and contentious because they reflect the vital political questions of our system.

Table 11-1 Gross Domestic Product, 1929–2020 (billions)

Year	Current dollars	Annual percentage change	Chained (2012) dollars	Annual percentage change
1929	$104.6		$1,109.4	
1930	92.2	–11.9	1,015.1	–8.5
1935	74.2	11.1	986.3	8.9
1940	102.9	10.1	1,330.2	8.8
1945	228.0	1.6	2,328.6	–1
1946	227.5	–0.2	2,058.4	–11.6
1947	249.6	9.7	2,034.8	–1.1
1948	274.5	10.0	2,118.5	4.1
1949	272.5	–0.7	2,106.6	–0.6
1950	299.8	10.0	2,289.5	8.7
1951	346.9	15.7	2,473.8	8.0
1952	367.3	5.9	2,574.9	4.1
1953	389.2	6.0	2,695.6	4.7
1954	390.5	0.3	2,680.0	–0.6
1955	425.5	8.9	2,871.2	7.1
1956	449.4	5.6	2,932.4	2.1
1957	474.0	5.5	2,994.1	2.1
1958	481.2	1.5	2,972.0	–0.7
1959	521.7	8.4	3,178.2	6.9
1960	542.4	4.0	3,260.0	2.6
1961	562.2	3.7	3,343.5	2.6
1962	603.9	7.4	3,548.4	6.1
1963	637.5	5.6	3,702.9	4.4
1964	684.5	7.4	3,916.3	5.8
1965	742.3	8.4	4,170.8	6.5
1966	813.4	9.6	4,445.9	6.6
1967	860.0	5.7	4,567.8	2.7
1968	940.7	9.4	4,792.3	4.9
1969	1,017.6	8.2	4,942.1	3.1
1970	1,073.3	5.5	4,951.3	0.2
1971	1,164.9	8.5	5,114.3	3.3
1972	1,279.1	9.8	5,383.3	5.3
1973	1,425.4	11.4	5,687.2	5.6
1974	1,545.2	8.4	5,656.5	–0.5
1975	1,684.9	9.0	5,644.8	–0.2
1976	1,873.4	11.2	5,949.0	5.4
1977	2,081.8	11.1	6,224.1	4.6
1978	2,351.6	13.0	6,568.6	5.5
1979	2,627.3	11.7	6,776.6	3.2
1980	2,857.3	8.8	6,759.2	–0.3
1981	3,207.0	12.2	6,930.7	2.5
1982	3,343.8	4.3	6,805.8	–1.8
1983	3,634.0	8.7	7,117.7	4.6
1984	4,037.6	11.1	7,632.8	7.2
1985	4,339.0	7.5	7,951.1	4.2

(*Continued*)

Table 11-1 *(Continued)*

Year	Current dollars	Annual percentage change	Chained (2012) dollars	Annual percentage change
1986	4,579.6	5.5	8,226.4	3.5
1987	4,855.2	6.0	8,511.0	3.5
1988	5,236.4	7.9	8,866.5	4.2
1989	5,641.6	7.7	9,192.1	3.7
1990	5,963.1	5.7	9,365.5	1.9
1991	6,158.1	3.3	9,355.4	−0.1
1992	6,520.3	5.9	9,684.9	3.5
1993	6,858.6	5.2	9,951.5	2.8
1994	7,287.2	6.3	10,352.4	4.0
1995	7,639.7	4.8	10,630.3	2.7
1996	8,073.1	5.7	11,031.4	3.8
1997	8,577.6	6.2	11,521.9	4.4
1998	9,062.8	5.7	12,038.3	4.5
1999	9,630.7	6.3	12,610.5	4.8
2000	10,252.3	6.5	13,131.0	4.1
2001	10,581.8	3.2	13,262.1	1.0
2002	10,936.4	3.4	13,493.1	1.7
2003	11,458.2	4.8	13,879.1	2.9
2004	12,213.7	6.6	14,406.4	3.8
2005	13,036.6	6.7	14,912.5	3.5
2006	13,814.6	6.0	15,338.3	2.9
2007	14,451.9	4.6	15,626.0	1.9
2008	14,712.8	1.8	15,604.7	−0.1
2009	14,448.9	−1.8	15,208.8	−2.5
2010	14,992.1	3.8	15,598.8	2.6
2011	15,542.6	3.7	15,840.7	1.6
2012	16,197.0	4.2	16,197.0	2.2
2013	16,784.9	3.6	16,495.4	1.8
2014	17,527.3	4.4	16,912.0	2.5
2015	18,238.3	4.1	17,432.2	3.1
2016	18,745.1	2.8	17,730.5	1.7
2017	19,543.0	4.3	18,144.1	2.3
2018	20,611.9	5.5	18,687.8	3.0
2019	21,433.2	4.0	19,091.7	2.2
2020	20,936.6	−2.3	18,426.1	−3.5

Note: Data for additional years can be found in previous editions of *Vital Statistics on American Politics*.

Source: U.S. Department of Commerce, Bureau of Economic Analysis, "Gross Domestic Product," as of May 23, 2021, www.bea.gov.

Table 11-2 Consumer Price Index, 1950–2020

Year	All items	Food	Shelter	Energy	Apparel and upkeep	Transportation Private[a]	Transportation Public	Medical care	All commodities	All services
1950	24.1	25.4	—	19.2	40.3	24.5	13.4	15.1	29.0	16.9
1955	26.8	27.8	22.7	20.7	42.9	26.7	18.5	18.2	31.3	20.4
1960	29.6	30.0	25.2	22.4	45.7	30.6	22.2	22.3	33.6	24.1
1965	31.5	32.2	27.0	23.0	47.8	32.5	25.2	25.2	35.2	26.6
1970	38.8	39.2	35.5	25.5	59.2	37.5	35.2	34.0	41.7	35.0
1975	53.8	59.8	48.8	42.1	72.5	50.6	43.5	47.5	58.2	48.0
1980	82.4	86.8	81.0	86.1	90.9	84.2	69.0	74.9	86.0	77.9
1981	90.9	93.6	90.5	97.7	95.3	93.8	85.6	82.9	93.2	88.1
1982	96.5	97.4	96.9	99.2	97.8	97.1	94.9	92.5	97.0	96.0
1983	99.6	99.4	99.1	99.9	100.2	99.3	99.5	100.6	99.8	99.4
1984	103.9	103.2	104.0	100.9	102.1	103.6	105.7	106.8	103.2	104.6
1985	107.6	105.6	109.8	101.6	105.0	106.2	110.5	113.5	105.4	109.9
1986	109.6	109.0	115.8	88.2	105.9	101.2	117.0	122.0	104.4	115.4
1987	113.6	113.5	121.3	88.6	110.6	104.2	121.1	130.1	107.7	120.2
1988	118.3	118.2	127.1	89.2	115.4	107.6	123.3	138.6	111.5	125.7
1989	124.0	125.1	132.8	94.3	118.6	112.9	129.5	149.3	116.7	131.9
1990	130.7	132.4	140.0	102.0	124.1	118.8	142.6	162.8	122.8	139.2
1991	136.2	136.3	146.3	102.5	128.7	121.9	148.9	177.0	126.6	146.3
1992	140.3	137.9	151.2	103.0	131.9	124.6	151.4	190.1	129.1	152.0
1993	144.5	140.9	155.7	104.2	133.7	127.5	167.0	201.4	131.5	157.9
1994	148.2	144.3	160.5	104.7	133.4	131.4	172.0	211.0	133.8	163.1

(Table continues)

465

Table 11-2 (Continued)

Year	All items	Food	Shelter	Energy	Apparel and upkeep	Transportation		Medical care	All commodities	All services
						Private[a]	Public			
1995	152.4	148.4	165.7	105.2	132.0	136.3	175.9	220.5	136.4	168.7
1996	156.9	153.3	171.0	110.1	131.7	140.0	181.9	228.2	139.9	174.1
1997	160.5	157.3	176.3	111.5	132.9	141.0	186.7	234.6	141.8	179.4
1998	163.0	160.7	182.1	102.9	133.0	137.9	190.3	242.1	141.9	184.2
1999	166.6	164.1	187.3	106.6	131.3	140.5	197.7	250.6	144.4	188.8
2000	172.2	167.8	193.4	124.6	129.6	149.1	209.6	260.8	149.2	195.3
2001	177.1	173.1	200.6	129.2	127.3	150.0	210.6	272.8	150.7	203.4
2002	179.9	176.2	208.1	121.7	124.0	148.8	207.4	285.6	149.7	209.8
2003	184.0	180.0	213.1	136.7	120.9	153.6	209.3	297.1	151.2	216.5
2004	188.9	186.2	218.8	151.5	120.4	159.4	209.1	310.1	154.7	222.8
2005	195.3	190.7	224.4	177.1	119.5	170.2	217.3	323.2	160.2	230.1
2006	201.6	195.2	232.1	196.6	119.5	177.0	226.6	336.2	164.0	238.9
2007	207.3	202.9	240.6	207.8	119.0	180.8	230.0	351.1	167.5	246.8
2008	215.3	214.1	246.7	236.2	118.9	191.0	250.5	364.1	174.8	255.5
2009	214.5	218.0	249.4	193.4	120.1	174.8	236.3	375.6	169.7	259.2
2010	218.1	219.6	248.4	211.7	119.5	188.7	251.4	388.4	174.6	261.3
2011	224.9	227.8	251.6	243.7	122.1	207.6	269.4	400.3	183.9	265.8
2012	229.6	233.8	257.1	246.0	126.3	212.8	271.4	414.9	187.6	271.4
2013	233.0	237.0	263.1	244.3	127.4	212.4	278.9	425.1	187.7	277.9
2014	236.7	242.7	270.5	243.3	127.5	211.0	276.4	435.3	187.9	285.1
2015	237.0	246.8	278.8	202.6	126.0	193.6	268.8	446.8	181.7	291.7
2016	240.0	247.7	288.2	189.5	126.1	189.5	265.3	463.7	179.2	299.9
2017	245.1	249.8	297.8	204.7	125.6	196.7	263.1	475.3	181.3	308.1
2018	251.1	253.4	307.7	219.9	125.7	206.4	258.8	484.7	184.6	316.6
2019	255.7	258.0	318.0	215.2	124.1	205.7	259.4	498.4	185.3	325.1
2020	258.8	266.6	325.9	197.3	118.1	198.8	227.6	518.9	184.9	332.0

Note: "—" indicates not available. Data for 1982 through 1984 equal 100. Data beginning in 1978 are for all urban consumers; earlier data are for urban wage earners and clerical workers. Data beginning in 1983 incorporate a rental equivalence measure for homeowners' costs and therefore are not strictly comparable with earlier figures. Data for additional years can be found in previous editions of *Vital Statistics on American Politics*.

[a] Includes direct pricing of new trucks and motorcycles beginning with September 1982.

Sources: 1950–1955: *Economic Report of the President* (Washington, D.C.: Government Printing Office, 1995), Tables B-59, B-60, B-61; 1960–1965: (2011), Tables B-60, B-61, B-62; 1970–2012: (2013), Tables B-60, B-61, B-62; 2013–2014: Table 1.A; 2015–2020: U.S. Bureau of Labor Statistics, www.bls.gov, accessed through Federal Reserve Economic Data, https://fred.stlouisfed.org.

A Data Literacy Lesson

What Is the Consumer Price Index?

Have you ever had an older person tell you that back when they were young, they were able to buy a house with the same amount of money you just spent on your lunch? (Annoying, huh?) If you're older, have you ever found yourself reminiscing that back when you were younger, you could go to a baseball game, park the car, get great seats, and buy a whole bunch of food and souvenirs, for less than the price of parking today? (Brace yourself—this will be you one day!) Clearly, musing about how much things cost today relative to how much they cost years ago is part of how we relate to the economic concept of inflation, which refers to the rise in prices (and the decline in how much you can purchase with your money) over time.

Table 11-2 presents some data on inflation by showing the components of the *consumer price index* (CPI), the best-known measure of the inflation rate. The table is not intuitive, but once you get the hang of it, you can see a lot. The rows in the table represent years, while the columns represent a variety of different items, including food, shelter, energy, medical care, and other categories of expenses. The number in each cell represents the ratio that the average urban consumer spent on each of these items compared to the period from 1982–1984, which represents the baseline period (and gets a score of 100). Thus, if we look at the Food category for 2020, we see the value is 266.6. This meant the average urban consumer spent 2.666 times as much on food in 2020 as they did annually in the 1982 to 1984 period. So, if one of the authors of this book recalls buying a bagel for fifteen cents in 1982, he would be expected to pay, on average, about forty cents for a bagel today! The index is not meant to be this precise, of course, but hopefully this example gives you an idea how these values work.

One clear use of this table is that it allows us to see, in broad categories, where costs have gone up and where they have stayed relatively steady. The first column tells us that the overall cost of all items has gone up by 2.588 times since the baseline period, suggesting that food costs are basically tracking the overall rate of inflation. Clothing costs, however, are almost the same as they were back in the early 1980s, increasing by less than 20 percent over that period. It may well be that outsourcing clothing manufacturing (including to infamous sweatshops in the developing world) have reduced clothing costs significantly. And, we would imagine that to nobody's great surprise, the sector that has seen the highest increase has been healthcare—consumers are spending more than five times on health items as they were from 1982 to 1984. When politicians invoke the high costs of healthcare to justify action in this policy area, they're not making this stuff up.

While seeing the overall trends over four decades is interesting, most of us are more concerned with inflation from year to year. Armed with these data, we can perform simple calculations to determine how much costs have gone up from year to year. For example, to see the rate of inflation from 2019 to 2020, we would take the difference of the two, divide it by the earlier figure, and multiply by 100 to convert the figure to a percentage. The calculations would look like this:

2019 CPI = 255.7
2020 CPI = 258.8
Difference = 258.8 − 255.7 = 3.1
Divide by the 2019 figure and multiply by 100: (3.1/255.7) * 100 = 1.2 percent

This inflation rate of 1.2 percent is, historically, an extremely low figure. These numbers are useful, for example, when determining how much one's salary is, or is not, keeping up with the rate of inflation. A 5 percent raise might sound good, for example, but if the rate of inflation is 7 percent, the person getting that raise is actually, in the end, losing purchasing power.

These data might also shed some light on political issues, including the minimum wage debate (for an extended discussion of this issue, see the essay accompanying Figure 11-4). We'll leave it to you to sort out your opinion on this topic—we will just note that the federal minimum wage ($7.25 per hour as we write this) was last raised in 2009. Since then, the overall CPI has increased by 20.7 percent. So, someone earning the minimum wage today has significantly less purchasing power than they did twelve years ago; this is useful data we might want to have in considering this political issue.

The calculation of the CPI is a complicated endeavor, and this essay has not even scratched the surface of the choices made in doing these calculations.[1] It is clear, however, that understanding the CPI, and the rate of inflation, is important for understanding both an individual's personal finances, and the overall economic conditions in the nation. This essay should also make clear that as valuable as Table 11-2 might be, a table like this often requires the researcher to do some exploration to figure out just what all these numbers mean, and by extension how to use this information to learn more about the issues informed by the table.

---

[1] A good place to start learning more about these calculations is found on the FAQ page for the Bureau of Labor Statistics: https://www.bls.gov/cpi/questions-and-answers.htm.

Table 11-3 Federal Budget: Total, Defense, and Nondefense Expenditures, 1940–2025 (billions)

	Current dollars			Constant (2009) dollars		
Year	National defense	Non-defense	Total	National defense	Non-defense	Total
1940	$1.7	$7.8	$9.5	$27.0	$117.9	$145.0
1945	83.0	9.7	92.7	1,050.2	125.0	1,175.1
1950	13.7	28.8	42.6	178.9	273.1	451.8
1951	23.6	21.9	45.5	289.9	190.7	480.6
1952	46.1	21.6	67.7	545.4	171.5	717.0
1953	52.8	23.3	76.1	565.9	183.7	749.8
1954	49.3	21.6	70.9	519.1	158.0	676.7
1955	42.7	25.7	68.4	436.0	196.9	633.2
1956	42.5	28.1	70.6	409.3	216.0	625.1
1957	45.4	31.1	76.6	415.6	230.2	645.7
1958	46.8	35.6	82.4	409.2	247.0	656.1
1959	49.0	43.1	92.1	400.8	303.4	704.1
1960	48.1	44.1	92.2	397.8	296.5	694.2
1961	49.6	48.1	97.7	402.3	317.4	719.6
1962	52.3	54.5	106.8	424.2	362.0	786.0
1963	53.4	57.9	111.3	414.0	370.8	785.0
1964	54.8	63.8	118.5	419.0	403.6	822.5
1965	50.6	67.6	118.2	388.5	421.0	809.2
1966	58.1	76.4	134.5	425.7	470.6	896.3
1967	71.4	86.0	157.5	506.9	519.6	1,026.5
1968	81.9	96.2	178.1	555.1	564.9	1,120.3
1969	82.5	101.1	183.6	528.8	557.0	1,086.0
1970	81.7	114.0	195.6	498.1	597.6	1,096.1
1971	78.9	131.3	210.2	452.8	648.4	1,101.0
1972	79.2	151.5	230.7	415.0	719.7	1,134.7
1973	76.7	169.0	245.7	375.5	780.4	1,155.7
1974	79.3	190.0	269.4	363.8	805.1	1,169.1
1975	86.5	245.8	332.3	364.1	950.6	1,314.6
1976	89.6	282.2	371.8	354.9	1017.6	1,372.4
TQ[a]	22.3	73.7	96.0	86.5	259.2	345.7
1977	97.2	312.0	409.2	356.8	1051.1	1,408.2
1978	104.5	354.3	458.7	359.0	1126.8	1,485.6
1979	116.3	387.7	504.0	369.5	1,132.3	1,501.9
1980	134.0	456.9	590.9	384.5	1,207.9	1,592.4
1981	157.5	520.7	678.2	407.5	1,238.1	1,645.4
1982	185.3	560.4	745.7	440.2	1,239.9	1,680.0
1983	209.9	598.5	808.4	475.2	1,260.7	1,735.8
1984	227.4	624.4	851.8	489.5	1,256.1	1,745.5
1985	252.7	693.6	946.3	523.6	1,346.8	1870.6
1986	273.4	717.0	990.4	553.9	1,363.7	1,917.5
1987	282.0	722.0	1,004.0	563.1	1,326.3	1,889.4
1988	290.4	774.1	1,064.4	565.6	1,371.0	1,936.4
1989	303.6	840.2	1,143.7	569.3	1,432.3	2,001.7

Table 11-3 *(Continued)*

	Current dollars			Constant (2009) dollars		
Year	National defense	Non-defense	Total	National defense	Non-defense	Total
1990	299.3	953.7	1,253.0	542.7	1,588.4	2,130.9
1991	273.3	1,050.9	1,324.2	472.2	1,683.4	2,155.7
1992	298.3	1,083.2	1,381.5	507.4	1,653.7	2,161.0
1993	291.1	1,118.3	1,409.4	490.1	1,651.1	2,141.3
1994	281.6	1,180.1	1,461.8	469.8	1,712.5	2,182.4
1995	272.1	1,243.7	1,515.7	445.2	1,752.4	2,197.7
1996	265.7	1,294.7	1,560.5	425.7	1,790.3	2,216.0
1997	270.5	1,330.6	1,601.1	426.7	1,800.1	2,226.9
1998	268.2	1,384.3	1,652.5	415.2	1,864.1	2,279.3
1999	274.8	1,427.1	1,701.8	417.0	1,901.7	2,318.9
2000	294.4	1,494.6	1,789.0	431.6	1,945.8	2,377.3
2001	304.7	1,558.1	1,862.8	432.0	1,980.6	2,412.4
2002	348.5	1,662.4	2,010.9	478.4	2,086.1	2,564.6
2003	404.7	1,755.2	2,159.9	521.9	2,156.5	2,678.4
2004	455.8	1,837.0	2,292.8	566.4	2,204.8	2,771.1
2005	495.3	1,976.7	2,472.0	587.5	2,300.9	2,888.5
2006	521.8	2,133.2	2,655.1	593.5	2,405.0	2,998.7
2007	551.3	2,177.4	2,728.7	607.0	2,392.0	2,998.9
2008	616.1	2,366.5	2,982.5	653.2	2,515.1	3,168.2
2009	661.0	2,856.7	3,517.7	702.3	3,034.5	3,737.0
2010	693.5	2,763.6	3,457.1	723.7	2,884.5	3,608.3
2011	705.6	2,897.5	3,603.1	715.3	2,959.4	3,674.7
2012	677.9	2,859.1	3,537.0	677.9	2,848.7	3,526.6
2013	633.4	2,821.2	3,454.6	629.0	2,777.2	3,406.5
2014	603.5	2,902.6	3,506.1	589.7	2,813.9	3,403.5
2015	589.7	3,102.2	3,691.9	573.3	2,991.8	3,565.3
2016	593.4	3,259.2	3,852.6	574.5	3,121.6	3,695.9
2017	598.7	3,382.9	3,981.6	571.8	3,185.4	3,757.3
2018	631.1	3,477.9	4,109.0	586.4	3,204.6	3,791.0
2019	686.0	3,762.3	4,448.3	625.5	3,407.9	4,033.3
2020 est.	724.5	4,065.3	4789.7	647.9	3,602.0	4,250.0
2021 est.	767.1	4,062.3	4,829.4	672.8	3,520.8	4,193.6
2022 est.	782.8	4,222.7	5,005.4	673.0	3,578.0	4,250.9
2023 est.	785.1	4,320.3	5,105.3	661.7	3,579.6	4,241.4
2024 est.	792.0	4,416.5	5,208.5	654.4	3,577.8	4,232.1
2025 est.	803.4	4,647.4	5,450.8	650.8	3,682.5	4,333.2

Note: Data for additional years can be found in previous editions of *Vital Statistics on American Politics*.

[a] Transitional quarter when fiscal year start was shifted from July 1 to October 1.

Source: U.S. Office of Management and Budget, *Budget of the United States Government, Fiscal Year 2021, Historical Tables* (Washington, D.C.: Government Printing Office, 2020), Table 6.1.

Table 11-4 Federal Budget Outlays, by Function, 2000–2025 (billions)

Function	2000	2005	2010	2015	2020 est.	2022 est.	2025 est.
National defense	$294.4	$495.3	$693.5	$589.7	$724.5	$782.7	$803.4
Human resources	1,115.5	1,586.0	2,386.6	2,706.9	3,377.3	3,550.6	3,935.5
Education, training, employment, and social services	53.8	97.6	128.6	122.0	195.5	98.6	96.8
Health	154.5	250.5	369.1	482.3	640.9	649.4	647.4
Medicare[a]	197.1	298.6	451.6	546.2	699.3	786.4	906.7
Income security	253.7	345.8	622.2	508.9	529.3	530.8	554.5
Social Security[a]	409.4	523.3	706.7	887.8	1,097.2	1,221.9	1,445.2
Veterans' benefits and services	47.0	70.1	108.4	159.8	215.1	263.5	285.0
Physical resources	84.9	130.1	88.8	115.2	180.0	173.2	161.7
Energy	–0.8	0.4	11.6	6.8	4.6	–3.3	–0.2
Natural resources and environment	25.0	28.0	43.7	36.0	42.8	45.9	41.8
Commerce and housing credit[a]	3.2	7.6	–82.3	–37.9	0.7	–12.4	–12.8
Transportation	46.9	67.9	92.0	89.5	101.6	105.2	111.2
Community and regional development	10.6	26.3	23.9	20.7	30.3	37.7	21.8
Net interest[a]	222.9	184.0	196.2	223.2	376.2	398.7	499.1
Other functions[b]	113.8	141.7	174.0	172.8	241.1	211.2	169.5
International affairs	17.2	34.6	45.2	52.0	58.3	49.3	44.7
General science, space, and technology	18.6	23.6	30.1	29.4	35.0	38.8	38.6
Agriculture	36.5	26.6	21.4	18.5	38.3	24.0	21.6
Administration of justice	28.5	40.0	54.4	51.9	79.6	75.2	72.7
General government	13.0	17.0	23.0	21.0	29.5	30.5	32.1
Undistributed offsetting receipts	–42.6	–65.2	–82.1	–115.8	–109.2	–111.0	–118.5
Total outlays[a]	1,789.0	2,472.0	3,457.1	3,691.9	4,789.7	5,005.4	5,450.8

Note: Amounts in current dollars. Fiscal year ending September 30. Due to rounding, numbers for individual categories may not sum to the subtotals and totals. Data for additional years can be found in previous editions of *Vital Statistics on American Politics.*

[a] Includes both on- and off-budget amounts.
[b] Includes other outlays not shown separately.

Source: U.S. Office of Management and Budget, *Budget of the United States Government, Fiscal Year 2021, Historical Tables* (Washington, D.C.: Government Printing Office, 2020), Table 3.1.

Figure 11-1 Federal Outlays as a Percentage of GNP/GDP, 1869–2025

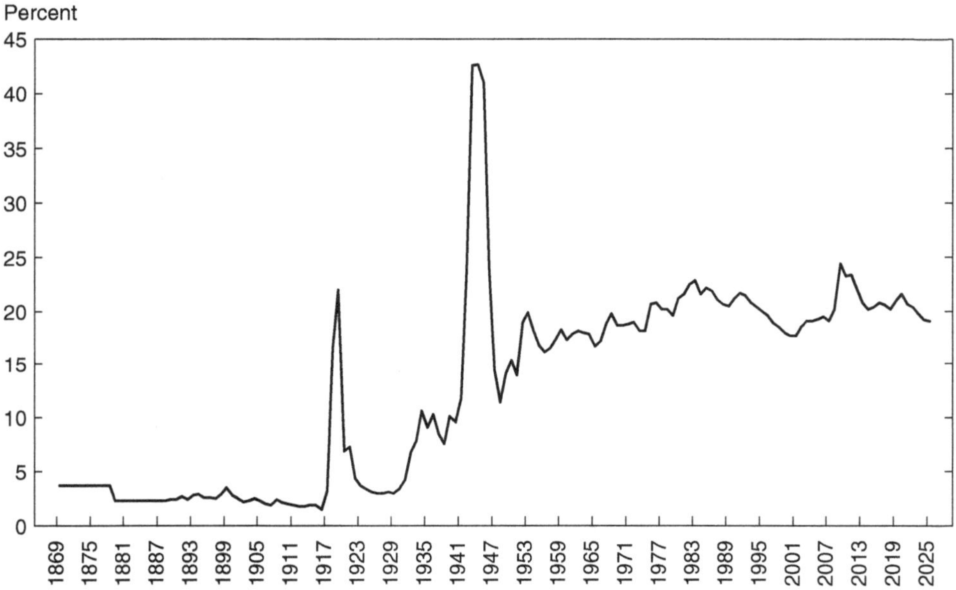

Note: Averaged by decade for 1869 through 1888. Percentage of gross national product (GNP) is shown through 1929, percentage of gross domestic product (GDP) thereafter. Figures for 2020 through 2025 are estimates.

Sources: 1869–1929: U.S. Bureau of the Census, *Historical Statistics of the United States* (Washington, D.C.: Government Printing Office, 1975), 224, 1,114; 1930–1940: U.S. Office of Management and Budget, *Budget of the United States Government, Fiscal Year 2016, Historical Tables* (Washington, D.C.: Government Printing Office, 2015), Table 1.2; 1941–2025: U.S. Office of Management and Budget, *Budget of the United States Government, Fiscal Year 2021, Historical Tables* (Washington, D.C.: Government Printing Office, 2020), Table 1.3

Table 11-5 Mandatory and Discretionary Federal Budget Outlays, 1975–2025 (billions)

Outlay	1980	1985	1990	1995	2000	2005	2010	2015	2020 est.	2022 est.	2025 est.
Mandatory and related program outlays, total[a]	$314.6	$530.6	$752.4	$971.0	$1,174.3	$1,503.4	$2,109.9	$2,519.7	$3,351.5	$3,528.30	$4,023.10
Health	14.7	23.9	42.8	93.4	124.6	200.1	303.7	426.4	568.0	577.0	576.6
Income security	75.8	109.8	125.2	184.6	212.3	291.6	552.6	443.5	454.5	456.9	483.6
Medicare	31.0	64.1	95.8	156.9	194.1	294.3	446.5	539.9	693.4	778.8	899.1
Social Security	117.1	186.4	246.5	333.3	406.0	518.7	700.8	881.9	1,091.6	1,216.2	1,439.5
Veterans' benefits and services	14.0	15.9	16.0	20.4	26.2	39.6	57.5	92.1	124.6	153.5	174.2
Undistributed offsetting receipts[b]	−19.9	−32.7	−36.6	−36.8	−42.4	−65.1	−81.9	−85.7	−106.1	−110.6	−112.3
Net interest[b]	52.5	129.5	184.3	232.1	222.9	184.0	196.2	223.2	376.2	398.7	499.1
Discretionary program outlays, total[a]	276.3	415.8	500.6	544.8	614.6	968.5	1,347.2	1,172.1	1,438.2	1,477.1	1427.7
Domestic, total[a]	128.9	145.3	181.4	251.1	298.4	435.9	612.7	558.8	696.7	693.2	631.6
Education, training, employment, and social services	25.8	21.8	27.9	38.9	49.0	79.1	134.3	89.4	101.2	92.5	91.0
General science, space, and technology	5.8	8.6	14.4	16.7	18.6	23.6	30.0	29.4	34.9	38.6	38.4
Health	8.5	9.6	14.9	22.0	29.9	50.5	65.4	55.9	72.9	72.4	70.8
Income security	10.8	19.2	23.7	39.2	41.4	54.2	69.6	65.3	74.9	73.9	70.9
Natural resources and environment	15.5	15.1	17.8	21.9	24.9	30.4	42.5	36.2	39.7	40.6	36.8
Transportation	20.7	24.8	27.9	37.0	44.8	66.1	89.9	88.5	100.8	103.7	109.6
International affairs	12.8	17.4	19.1	20.1	21.2	39.0	45.6	55.3	60.6	51.5	45.1
National defense	134.6	253.1	300.1	273.6	295.0	493.6	688.9	558.0	680.9	732.4	751.0
Total outlays[c]	590.9	946.3	1,253.0	1,515.7	1,789.0	2,472.0	3,457.1	3,691.8	4,789.7	5,005.4	5,450.8
Mandatory program outlays as a percentage of total outlays	53.2	56.1	60.0	64.1	65.6	60.8	61.0	68.3	70.0	70.5	73.8

Note: Amounts in current dollars. Due to rounding, numbers for individual categories may not sum to the subtotals and totals. Data for additional years can be found in previous editions of *Vital Statistics on American Politics*.

[a] Includes other outlays not shown separately.
[b] Includes both on- and off-budget amounts.
[c] Beginning in 2011, total outlays includes an allowance for future costs that is not displayed in the table by category.

Source: U.S. Office of Management and Budget, *Budget of the United States Government, Fiscal Year 2021, Historical Tables* (Washington, D.C.: Government Printing Office, 2020), Tables 8.1, 8.5, and 8.7.

Table 11-6 The National Debt, 1940–2025

Year	Debt held by the public (millions)	As a percentage of GDP	Year	Debt held by the public (millions)	As a percentage of GDP
1940	$42,772	43.6	1987	$1,889,753	39.5
1945	235,182	103.9	1988	2,051,616	39.8
1950	219,023	78.5	1989	2,190,716	39.3
1951	214,326	65.5	1990	2,411,558	40.8
1952	214,758	60.1	1991	2,688,999	44.0
1953	218,383	57.1	1992	2,999,737	46.6
1954	224,499	57.9	1993	3,248,396	47.8
1955	226,616	55.7	1994	3,433,065	47.7
1956	222,156	50.6	1995	3,604,378	47.5
1957	219,320	47.2	1996	3,734,073	46.8
1958	226,336	47.7	1997	3,772,344	44.5
1959	234,701	46.4	1998	3,721,099	41.6
1960	236,840	44.3	1999	3,632,363	38.2
1961	238,357	43.5	2000	3,409,804	33.6
1962	248,010	42.3	2001	3,319,615	31.4
1963	253,978	41.0	2002	3,540,427	32.5
1964	256,849	38.7	2003	3,913,443	34.5
1965	260,778	36.7	2004	4,295,544	35.5
1966	263,714	33.7	2005	4,592,212	35.6
1967	266,626	31.8	2006	4,828,972	35.3
1968	289,545	32.2	2007	5,035,129	35.2
1969	278,108	28.3	2008	5,803,050	39.3
1970	283,198	27.0	2009	7,544,707	52.3
1971	303,037	27.1	2010	9,018,882	60.9
1972	322,377	26.4	2011	10,128,187	65.9
1973	340,910	25.1	2012	11,281,131	70.4
1974	343,699	23.1	2013	11,982,713	72.3
1975	394,700	24.5	2014	12,779,899	73.7
1976	477,404	26.7	2015	13,116,692	72.5
TQ[a]	495,509	26.2	2016	14,167,624	76.4
1977	549,104	27.1	2017	14,665,439	76.0
1978	607,126	26.6	2018	15,749,567	77.4
1979	640,306	24.9	2019	16,800,746	79.2
1980	711,923	25.5	2020 (est.)	17,881,181	80.5
1981	789,410	25.2	2021 (est.)	18,912,085	81.0
1982	924,575	27.9	2022 (est.)	19,890,747	81.0
1983	1,137,268	32.1	2023 (est.)	20,688,338	80.2
1984	1,306,975	33.1	2024 (est.)	21,283,677	78.5
1985	1,507,260	35.3	2025 (est.)	21,848,263	76.7
1986	1,740,623	38.4			

Note: Amounts in current dollars. "GDP" indicates gross domestic product. Data for additional years can be found in previous editions of *Vital Statistics on American Politics*.

[a] Transitional quarter when fiscal year start was shifted from July 1 to October 1.

Source: U.S. Office of Management and Budget, Historical Tables, Table 7.1 "Federal Debt at the End of Year 1940–2025," https://www.whitehouse.gov/omb/historical-tables.

Figure 11-2 National Debt as a Percentage of GDP, 1940–2025

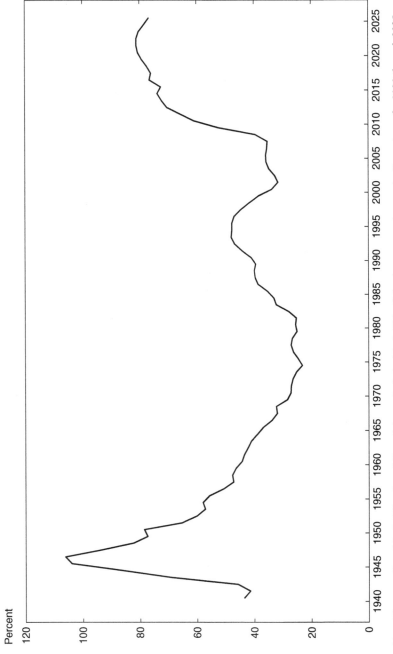

Note: Figures reflect debt held by the public and do not include debt held by federal government accounts. Percentages for 2020 through 2025 are estimates.

Source: U.S. Office of Management and Budget, *Budget of the United States Government, Fiscal Year 2021, Historical Tables* (Washington, D.C.: Government Printing Office, 2020), Table 7.3.

Table 11-7 Cost of Selected Tax Breaks: Revenue Loss Estimates for Selected Tax Expenditures, 2019–2029 (millions)

Type of tax expenditure	2019	2020	2021	2022	2023	2024	2025	2026	2027	2028	2029
Commerce and housing											
Exclusion of life insurance death benefits	13,210	13,760	14,340	14,870	15,470	16,090	16,680	17,550	18,590	19,200	19,690
Exclusion of net imputed rental income	121,320	125,990	130,430	134,570	138,710	142,840	147,500	189,930	200,620	211,550	212,650
Deductibility of mortgage interest on owner-occupied homes	25,130	27,090	29,580	32,290	34,960	37,510	40,110	85,520	112,580	119,280	125,820
Deductibility of property tax on owner-occupied homes[a]	6,010	6,270	6,650	7,030	7,400	7,740	8,090	39,930	58,030	61,630	65,340
Capital gains (except agriculture, timber, iron ore, and coal)	111,470	104,920	103,790	104,580	107,170	111,200	116,250	129,410	143,110	149,840	157,060
Capital gains exclusion on home sales	43,610	45,750	48,040	50,330	52,670	55,090	57,650	64,840	70,000	73,110	76,230
Step up basis of capital gains at death	49,980	51,750	53,640	56,200	59,130	62,650	66,360	70,340	74,740	79,640	84,860
"Accelerated depreciation of machinery and equipment"	49,280	43,460	40,610	38,030	22,830	4,660	−9,700	−24,360	−40,690	−32,810	−16,970
Education, training, employment, and social services											
Deductibility of charitable contributions (education)	4,140	4,450	4,790	5,100	5,410	5,720	6,020	7,160	9,200	9,620	10,070
Credit for child and dependent care expenses	4,260	4,360	4,440	4,540	4,690	4,780	4,890	5,100	5,320	5,390	5,400
Deductibility of charitable contributions, other than education and health	36,660	39,540	42,760	45,510	48,270	51,040	53,750	64,790	84,810	88,800	92,980
Health											
Exclusion of employer contributions for medical insurance premiums and medical care	202,290	214,420	227,880	242,230	258,730	276,820	295,050	348,700	389,240	413,090	438,240
Deductibility of medical expenses	6,500	6,640	7,310	8,140	9,050	10,030	11,090	17,270	21,690	23,780	25,990
Exclusion of interest on hospital construction bonds	2,660	2,820	2,790	2,870	3,060	3,120	3,150	3,390	3,500	3,520	3,540

(*Table continues*)

Table 11-7 (Continued)

Type of tax expenditure	2019	2020	2021	2022	2023	2024	2025	2026	2027	2028	2029
Deductibility of charitable contributions (health)	7,540	8,080	8,650	9,180	9,690	10,200	10,710	12,150	14,590	15,260	15,950
Social Security and Medicare											
Exclusion of Social Security benefits for retired and disabled workers and spouses, dependants, and survivors	29,100	30,900	32,490	33,990	35,640	36,330	36,430	41,480	48,460	50,590	52,670
Income security											
Exclusion of workers' compensation benefits	9,680	9,770	9,870	9,970	10,070	10,170	10,270	10,370	10,470	10,570	10,680
Net exclusion of pension contributions and earnings											
Defined benefit employer plans	71,653	73,831	75,807	78,012	79,560	80,979	81,129	83,516	84,065	85,124	86,795
Defined contribution employer plans	75,680	83,520	90,680	100,410	109,170	117,650	125,990	149,560	162,650	173,070	184,180
Individual Retirement Accounts	20,520	21,650	22,760	23,990	25,490	27,220	29,300	33,310	36,390	39,840	43,430
Self-employed plans	24,150	26,580	29,250	32,070	34,900	38,560	42,770	50,570	62,750	69,180	75,380
Veterans' benefits and services											
Exclusion of veterans' death benefits and disability compensation	7,590	8,340	8,910	9,200	9,500	9,820	10,150	10,950	12,380	12,790	13,230
General-purpose fiscal assistance											
Deductibility of nonbusiness state and local taxes other than on owner-occupied homes[a]	4,430	7,110	7,510	7,920	8,310	8,660	8,990	78,340	117,330	124,170	131,130

Note: Amounts in current dollars. Fiscal year basis. Tax expenditures are defined as revenue losses attributable to provisions of the federal tax laws that allow a special exclusion, exemption, or deduction from gross income or that provide a special credit, a preferential rate of tax, or a deferral of liability. Data for additional years can be found in previous editions of *Vital Statistics on American Politics*.

[a] Because of interactions with the $10,000 cap on state and local tax decuctions for years 2018–2025, these estimates understate the combined effects of repealing deductions for both property taxes on owner occuped housing and other nonbusiness taxes.

Sources: U.S. Department of the Treasury, *Tax Expenditures, FY 21*, Table 1, https://home.treasury.gov/policy-issues/tax-policy/tax-expenditures.

Income Inequality 479

Figure 11-3 Mean Income Received by Each Fifth and Top 5 Percent of Families, 1966–2019

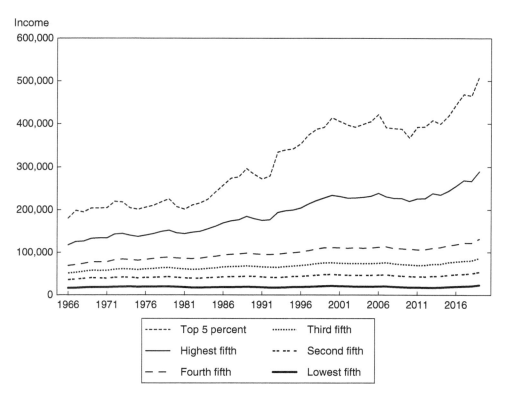

Note: Income is in 2019 CPI-U-RS adjusted dollars.

Source: U.S. Census Bureau, Historical Income Tables, Table F-3, from *Current Population Survey, Annual Social and Economic Supplements*, www.census.gov.

A Data Literacy Lesson
Analyzing Economic Policy Impacts through Data

Issues of social and economic policy often go hand in hand. Economic policies influence social conditions, and social policies have economic outcomes. Questions of who benefits from policies to what effect in the greater economy, and to what extent that's driven by government policy are commonly asked... and commonly divisive. This figure can shed some light on that debate. You may notice that some of the data that we present here in Chapter 11 partner with data in Chapter 10. Figure 11-3, for example, presents the mean income by families in each quintile of the population, and the mean income of the top 5 percent of the population. This is closely related to Table 10-7 in Chapter 10, which presented the median family income as a whole since 1955.

John F. Kennedy popularized the phrase "a rising tide lifts all boats" and used it often in his approach to economic policy. That is, when economic policy is good at the macro level, it will have good outcomes for all at the micro level. How would you go about assessing whether that's true? We noted in the essay accompanying Table 10-7 that we could not make inferences about income inequality or the distribution of income over time based on that data, and that to begin to explore that question we would need more information. Figure 11-3 allows us to investigate that question more fully.

We saw in Table 10-7 that the median family income for all families saw a fairly steady increase over time. The tide, so to speak, has been rising. However, looking at Figure 11-3, we can clearly see that the increase in income is not distributed evenly across the whole population. Indeed, the first four fifths, or 80 percent of the population, saw relatively flat trends over more than fifty years. The top fifth, or 20 percent of the population, experienced more growth in the same time period and the gap between the top fifth and the second fifth grew more than the gaps between any of the first four fifths. Taking that even further, we can see that the income growth for the top 5 percent of families increased the most dramatically over time, with an even bigger gap between the top 5 percent and the top fifth.

We want to exercise some caution, though. In the same way that there were inferences we could not make from Table 10-7 alone, our ability to draw sweeping conclusions from Figure 11-3 is similarly limited. For example, are there systematic patterns that help us understand which families represent each fifth of the population? What type of mobility is there between the different quintiles, and what social policies might drive that mobility or lack thereof? To answer some of those questions, we need to turn back to data such as that in Chapter 10, which focuses on the social aspects of data.

Data on its own can answer questions about "who" and "what" and "where," and "when." More complicated questions such as the "why" and "how" that are at the heart of academic and policy research require data-informed theories and hypotheses, and usually rely on data from a variety of sources rather than a single table. We think that pairing Table 10-7 and Figure 11-3 illustrates how we can start to answer different pieces of a bigger puzzle by pulling in multiple data sources. When attempting to answer the question of whether a rising tide really does lift all boats, you might need to do some digging to answer whose boat is being lifted, under what circumstances, and to what effect.

Table 11-8 Membership in Labor Unions, 1900–2020

		Percentage in unions		
Year	Membership (thousands)	Nonagricultural employment	Employed wage and salary workers	Labor force
1900	932.4	6.5	—	3.3
1905	1,947.1	10.8	—	6.0
1910	2,168.5	10.3	—	5.9
1915	2,597.6	11.5	—	6.6
1920	4,823.3	17.6	—	11.7
1925	3,685.1	12.8	—	8.2
1930	3,749.6	12.7	—	7.5
1935	3,649.6	13.5	—	6.9
1940	7,296.7	22.5	—	13.1
1945	12,254.2	30.4	—	22.8
1950	14,294.2	31.6	—	23.0
1955	16,126.9	31.8	—	24.8
1960	15,516.1	28.6	—	22.3
1965	18,268.9	30.1	—	24.5
1970	20,990.3	29.6	—	25.4
1975	22,207.0	28.9	—	23.7
1976	22,153.0	27.9	—	23.0
1977	21,632.1	26.2	—	21.8
1978	21,756.5	25.1	—	21.3
1979	22,025.4	24.5	—	21.0
1980	20,968.2	23.2	—	19.6
1981	20,646.8	22.6	—	19.0
1982	19,571.4	21.9	—	17.8
1983	18,633.6	20.7	—	16.6
1984	18,306.0	19.4	—	16.1
1985	16,996.0	—	18.0	14.7
1986	16,975.0	—	17.5	14.4
1987	16,913.0	—	17.0	14.1
1988	17,002.0	—	16.8	14.0
1989	16,960.0	—	16.4	13.7
1990	16,740.0	—	16.1	13.3
1991	16,568.0	—	16.1	13.1
1992	16,390.0	—	15.8	12.8
1993	16,389.0	—	15.8	12.7
1994	16,748.0	—	15.5	12.8
1995	16,360.0	—	14.9	12.4
1996	16,269.0	—	14.5	12.1
1997	16,110.0	—	14.1	11.8
1998	16,211.0	—	13.9	11.8
1999	16,477.0	—	13.9	11.8
2000	16,258.0	—	13.5	11.4
2001	16,387.0	—	13.4	11.4
2002	16,107.0	—	13.2	11.1
2003	15,776.0	—	12.9	10.8

(Table continues)

Table 11-8 *(Continued)*

		Percentage in unions		
Year	Membership (thousands)	Nonagricultural employment	Employed wage and salary workers	Labor force
2004	15,472.0	—	12.5	10.5
2005	15,685.0	—	12.5	10.5
2006	15,359.0	—	12.0	10.1
2007	15,670.0	—	12.1	10.2
2008	16,098.0	—	12.4	10.4
2009	15,327.0	—	12.3	9.9
2010	14,715.0	—	11.9	9.6
2011	14,764.0	—	11.8	9.6
2012	14,366.0	—	11.3	9.3
2013	14,528.0	—	11.3	9.3
2014	14,576.0	—	11.1	9.3
2015	14,795.0	—	11.1	9.4
2016	14,555.0	—	10.7	9.1
2017	14,817.0	—	10.7	9.2
2018	14,744.0	—	10.5	9.1
2019	14,574.0	—	10.3	8.9
2020	14,253.0	—	10.8	8.9

Note: "—" Comparisons of 1983 and 1984 show that the counts by Troy and Sheflin are about one million members higher per year than the counts based on the Current Population Surveys reported by the U.S. Bureau of Labor Statistics in *Employment and Earnings*. In 1985–1996, self-employed workers whose businesses are incorporated are excluded from the union member count. After 1996, all self-employed workers are excluded. Wage and salary workers are workers who receive wages, salaries, commissions, tips, payment-in-kind, or piece rates in both the public and private sectors. Data for additional years can be found in previous editions of *Vital Statistics on American Politics*.

Sources: 1900–1984: Leo Troy and Neil Sheflin, *U.S. Union Sourcebook* (West Orange, N.J.: Industrial Relations Data and Information Services, 1985), 3–10, A-1, A-2; 1985–2000, membership and percentage of employed wage and salary workers: U.S. Department of Labor, Bureau of Labor Statistics, *Employment and Earnings, January 1987* (Washington, D.C.: Government Printing Office, 1987), 219; (1988), 222; (1990), 232; (1992), 228; (1996), 214; (1997), 211; (1999), 219; (2001), 218; 2001–2020, membership and percentage of employed wage and salary workers: Bureau of Labor Statistics, www.bls.gov; 1985–2020, size of labor force: "Labor Force Statistics," available at www.bls.gov.

Figure 11-4 Federal Minimum Wage Rates, 1938–2021

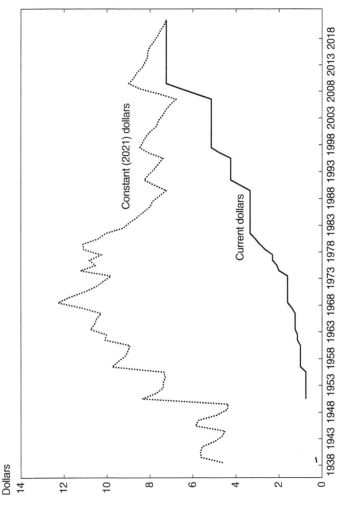

Note: A federal minimum wage was introduced in 1938 and was applicable generally to employees engaged in interstate commerce. Coverage was expanded in 1961 and again in 1966. In 1996, a subminimum wage was established for employees under twenty years of age during their first ninety consecutive calendar days of employment with an employer. In 2007, a bill was signed into law increasing the minimum wage to $7.25 over a two-year period, with the first increase in the summer of 2007. Tipped employees (those who receive more than $30 in tips monthly) are subject to a different minimum hourly cash (non-tipped) wage of $2.13, as of January 2021. Constant (2021) dollars are derived using the CPI Inflation Calculator, set to compare buying power in January of each year to January 2021.

Sources: Minimum wage: U.S. Department of Labor, "History of Federal Minimum Wage Rates Under the Fair Labor Standards Act, 1938–2009," https://www.dol.gov/agencies/whd/minimum-wage/history/chart; Minimum Wage for Tipped Employees," https://www.dol.gov/agencies/whd/state/minimum-wage/tipped; Consumer Price Index Calculator, https://www.bls.gov/data/inflation_calculator.htm.

A Data Literacy Lesson
Contextualizing Economic Indicators

As the last legislative push of the New Deal, the Fair Labor Standards Act of 1938 established a standard forty-hour work week, eliminated child labor, and introduced a federal minimum wage of $0.25 an hour. While there are few debates over the appropriate number of hours in the work week, or whether children should be working in factories, debates over the appropriate level of the federal minimum wage have remained largely constant since its introduction. Advocates for a strong minimum wage argue that it will improve the overall economy by increasing the buying power of workers. Advocates against raising the minimum wage argue that it will harm the overall economy by reducing the number of employees business owners can employ, thus increasing unemployment.

The debate over the minimum wage rate took center stage in early 2021 with the shift from the Trump administration to the Biden administration; there was contention over whether the minimum wage should be included as part of the $1.9 trillion economic relief bill passed to alleviate the economic effects of the COVID pandemic. Substantive debates over minimum wage increases were avoided when the Senate Parliamentarian ruled that Senate rules did not allow the plan to raise the minimum wage to $15 an hour to be included as part of the budget bill.

Fundamental to the debate over what the appropriate minimum wage should be is the question of whether it provides an acceptable level of pay. (We note that this is related to, but separate from, the debate over a living wage). We know that inflation changes the real value of dollars over time and that the federal minimum wage of $0.25/hour introduced in 1938 is not the same as $0.25/hour in today's market. Figure 11-4 provides one table of data that is often used to contextualize the value of the minimum wage and to provide comparative frameworks for economic indicators. By presenting the minimum wage in current dollars (that is, the federally mandated amount at the time) and then in constant dollars (that is, the value of that amount indexed to the same level) we can better understand what the value of previous levels of minimum wage might mean to us today.

This figure highlights that the value of the minimum wage has not been constant over time. The value of the minimum wage peaked in 1968, when the minimum wage of $1.60/hour was worth the equivalent of $12.20/hour in 2021. Put another way, the minimum wage of $7.25/hour in 2021 has 59 percent of the buying power of the minimum wage in 1968.

There are other ways that comparing current dollars to constant dollars can be instructive and help us make comparisons. While we present the minimum wage over the years in constant dollars pegged to 2021, we might want to find what the value of today's minimum wage would be at a previous period in time using the U.S. Bureau of Labor Statistic's CPI Inflation Calculator (https://www.bls.gov/data/inflation_calculator.htm). For example, Congress last passed legislation increasing the minimum wage in 2007, when the minimum wage was $5.15/hour, with a graduated plan to land at $7.25 by 2009. The 2021 minimum wage of $7.25 had a buying power of $5.61 in 2007. We can use that understanding to make comparisons to the situation when Congress last deemed an increase necessary.

Economic indicators can be daunting at first glance and making a case for or against changes in economic policy relies on understanding what those indicators mean to us. Tools such as the inflation calculator and comparing current dollars to

> constant dollars can help us contextualize those values. Your grandfather may tell you stories about how he could buy a hot dog for a nickel and a car for $100, but sometimes, it is useful to have hard data to put these stories in context.

Table 11-9 Civilian Labor Force Participation Rate, Overall and by Sex and Race, 1948–2020 (percent)

Year	Total	Male	Female	White	Black or African American[a]	Asian
1948	58.8	86.6	32.7	—	—	—
1950	59.2	86.4	33.9	—	—	—
1955	59.3	85.4	35.7	58.7	64.2	—
1960	59.4	83.3	37.7	58.8	64.5	—
1965	58.9	80.7	39.3	58.4	62.9	—
1970	60.4	79.7	43.3	60.2	61.8	—
1975	61.2	77.9	46.3	61.5	58.8	—
1980	63.8	77.4	51.5	64.1	61.0	—
1985	64.8	76.3	54.5	65.0	62.9	—
1990	66.5	76.4	57.5	66.9	64.0	—
1991	66.2	75.8	57.4	66.6	63.3	—
1992	66.4	75.8	57.8	66.8	63.9	—
1993	66.3	75.4	57.9	66.8	63.2	—
1994	66.6	75.1	58.8	67.1	63.4	—
1995	66.6	75.0	58.9	67.1	63.7	—
1996	66.8	74.9	59.3	67.2	64.1	—
1997	67.1	75.0	59.8	67.5	64.7	—
1998	67.1	74.9	59.8	67.3	65.6	—
1999	67.1	74.7	60.0	67.3	65.8	—
2000	67.1	74.8	59.9	67.3	65.8	67.2
2001	66.8	74.4	59.8	67.0	65.3	67.2
2002	66.6	74.1	59.6	66.8	64.8	67.2
2003	66.2	73.5	59.5	66.5	64.3	66.4
2004	66.0	73.3	59.2	66.3	63.8	65.9
2005	66.0	73.3	59.3	66.3	64.2	66.1
2006	66.2	73.5	59.4	66.5	64.1	66.2
2007	66.0	73.2	59.3	66.4	63.7	66.5
2008	66.0	73.0	59.5	66.3	63.7	67.0
2009	65.4	72.0	59.2	65.8	62.4	66.0
2010	64.7	71.2	58.6	65.1	62.2	64.7
2011	64.1	70.5	58.1	64.5	61.4	64.6
2012	63.7	70.2	57.7	64.0	61.5	63.9
2013	63.3	69.7	57.2	63.5	61.2	64.6
2014	62.9	69.2	57.0	63.1	61.2	63.6
2015	62.7	69.1	56.7	62.8	61.6	62.8
2016	62.8	69.2	56.8	62.9	61.6	63.3
2017	62.9	69.1	57.0	62.8	62.3	63.7
2018	62.9	69.0	57.1	62.8	62.3	63.5
2019	63.1	69.2	57.5	63.1	62.5	64.0
2020	61.7	67.7	56.2	61.8	60.5	62.7

Note: "—" indicates not available. Figures are for persons sixteen years of age and older. The participation rate is the percentage of adults who are either working or looking for work. For details on how employment and unemployment are measured, see "How the Government Measures Unemployment" (*www.bls.gov*). Labor force statistics, which are from the Current Population Survey, have included different categories of race and ethnicity over time. For details on how these categories have changed over time, the Current Population Survey Design and Methodology Technical Paper 77 from October 2019 has an interesting appendix with the History of the Current Population Survey. Data for additional years can be found in previous editions of *Vital Statistics on American Politics*.

[a] Black and other nonwhite prior to 1975.

Source: 1948: *Economic Report of the President* (Washington, D.C.: Government Printing Office, 1997), Table B-37; 1950: (2001); 1955–1960: (2003); 1965: (2011); 1970–2012: (2013), Table B-39; 2013–2014: Federal Reserve Bank of St. Louis, http://research.stlouisfed.org; 2015–2020 and all data for Asian Americans): U.S. Department of Labor, Bureau of Labor Statistics, "Labor Force Statistics from the Current Population Survey," https://data.bls.gov/PDQWeb/ln.

Table 11-10 Unemployment Rate Overall, 1929–2019, and by Sex and Race, 1948–2019 (percent)

Year	Civilian workers	Male	Female	White	Black or African American[a]	Asian	Hispanic or Latinx ethnicity
1929	3.2	—	—	—	—	—	—
1933	24.9	—	—	—	—	—	—
1939	17.2	—	—	—	—	—	—
1940	14.6	—	—	—	—	—	—
1941	9.9	—	—	—	—	—	—
1942	4.7	—	—	—	—	—	—
1943	1.9	—	—	—	—	—	—
1944	1.2	—	—	—	—	—	—
1945	1.9	—	—	—	—	—	—
1946	3.9	—	—	—	—	—	—
1947	3.9	—	—	—	—	—	—
1948	3.8	3.6	4.1	3.5	5.9	—	—
1949	5.9	5.9	6.0	5.6	8.9	—	—
1950	5.3	5.1	5.7	4.9	9.0	—	—
1951	3.3	2.8	4.4	3.1	5.3	—	—
1952	3.0	2.8	3.6	2.8	5.4	—	—
1953	2.9	2.8	3.3	2.7	4.5	—	—
1954	5.5	5.3	6.0	5.0	9.9	—	—
1955	4.4	4.2	4.9	3.9	8.7	—	—
1956	4.1	3.8	4.8	3.6	8.3	—	—
1957	4.3	4.1	4.7	3.8	7.9	—	—
1958	6.8	6.8	6.8	6.1	12.6	—	—
1959	5.5	5.2	5.9	4.8	10.7	—	—
1960	5.5	5.4	5.9	5.0	10.2	—	—
1961	6.7	6.4	7.2	6.0	12.4	—	—
1962	5.5	5.2	6.2	4.9	10.9	—	—
1963	5.7	5.2	6.5	5.0	10.8	—	—
1964	5.2	4.6	6.2	4.6	9.6	—	—
1965	4.5	4.0	5.5	4.1	8.1	—	—
1966	3.8	3.2	4.8	3.4	7.3	—	—
1967	3.8	3.1	5.2	3.4	7.4	—	—
1968	3.6	2.9	4.8	3.2	6.7	—	—
1969	3.5	2.8	4.7	3.1	6.4	—	—
1970	4.9	4.4	5.9	4.5	8.2	—	—
1971	5.9	5.3	6.9	5.4	9.9	—	—
1972	5.6	5.0	6.6	5.1	10.4	—	—
1973	4.9	4.2	6.0	4.3	9.4	—	—
1974	5.6	4.9	6.7	5.0	10.5	—	—
1975	8.5	7.9	9.3	7.8	14.8	—	12.2
1976	7.7	7.1	8.6	7.0	14.0	—	11.5
1977	7.1	6.3	8.2	6.2	14.0	—	10.1
1978	6.1	5.3	7.2	5.2	12.8	—	9.1
1979	5.8	5.1	6.8	5.1	12.3	—	8.3
1980	7.1	6.9	7.4	6.3	14.3	—	10.1

(*Continued*)

Table 11-10 *(Continued)*

Year	Civilian workers	Male	Female	White	Black or African American[a]	Asian	Hispanic or Latinx ethnicity
1981	7.6	7.4	7.9	6.7	15.6	—	10.4
1982	9.7	9.9	9.4	8.6	18.9	—	13.8
1983	9.6	9.9	9.2	8.4	19.5	—	13.7
1984	7.5	7.4	7.6	6.5	15.9	—	10.7
1985	7.2	7.0	7.4	6.2	15.1	—	10.5
1986	7.0	6.9	7.1	6.0	14.5	—	10.6
1987	6.2	6.2	6.2	5.3	13.0	—	8.8
1988	5.5	5.5	5.6	4.7	11.7	—	8.2
1989	5.3	5.2	5.4	4.5	11.4	—	8.0
1990	5.6	5.7	5.5	4.8	11.4	—	8.2
1991	6.8	7.2	6.4	6.1	12.5	—	10
1992	7.5	7.9	7.0	6.6	14.2	—	11.6
1993	6.9	7.2	6.6	6.1	13.0	—	10.8
1994	6.1	6.2	6.0	5.3	11.5	—	9.9
1995	5.6	5.6	5.6	4.9	10.4	—	9.3
1996	5.4	5.4	5.4	4.7	10.5	—	8.9
1997	4.9	4.9	5.0	4.2	10.0	—	7.7
1998	4.5	4.4	4.6	3.9	8.9	—	7.2
1999	4.2	4.1	4.3	3.7	8.0	—	6.4
2000	4.0	3.9	4.1	3.5	7.6	3.6	5.7
2001	4.7	4.8	4.7	4.2	8.6	4.5	6.6
2002	5.8	5.9	5.6	5.1	10.2	5.9	7.5
2003	6.0	6.3	5.7	5.2	10.8	6.0	7.7
2004	5.5	5.6	5.4	4.8	10.4	4.4	7.0
2005	5.1	5.1	5.1	4.4	10.0	4.0	6
2006	4.6	4.6	4.6	4.0	8.9	3.0	5.2
2007	4.6	4.7	4.5	4.1	8.3	3.2	5.6
2008	5.8	6.1	5.4	5.2	10.1	4.0	7.6
2009	9.3	10.3	8.1	8.5	14.8	7.3	12.1
2010	9.6	10.5	8.6	8.7	16.0	7.5	12.5
2011	8.9	9.4	8.5	7.9	15.8	7.0	11.5
2012	8.1	8.2	7.9	7.2	13.8	5.9	10.3
2013	7.4	7.6	7.1	6.5	13.1	5.2	9.1
2014	6.2	6.3	6.1	5.3	11.3	5.0	7.4
2015	5.3	4.9	4.8	4.6	9.6	3.8	6.6
2016	4.9	4.5	4.4	4.3	8.4	3.6	5.8
2017	4.4	4	4	3.8	7.5	3.4	5.1
2018	3.9	3.6	3.5	3.5	6.5	3.0	4.7
2019	3.7	3.4	3.3	3.3	6.1	2.7	4.3

Note: "—" indicates not available. Figures for 1929 through 1947 are for persons fourteen years of age and older; 1948 and later figures are for persons sixteen years of age and older; 2015 and later figures by sex are for persons twenty years and older.

[a] Black and other nonwhite prior to 1972.

Source: 1929–1949: *Economic Report of the President* (Washington, D.C.: Government Printing Office, 1997), Table B-33; 1950–1954: (2001); 1955–1958: (2003); 1959: (2007); 1960–1963: (2009); 1964–1965: (2011); 1966–1969: (2013), Table B-42; 1970–2014: (2015), Table B-12; 2015–2019 and all data for Asians and Hispanic and Latino ethnicity: (2021), Table B-27, https://www.govinfo.gov/content/pkg/ERP-2021/pdf/ERP-2021-table27.pdf.

> # A Data Literacy Lesson
> ## The Importance of Definitions
>
> When we see a percentage sign, it's natural to start thinking in terms of 100 percent to understand totals. If you look at Table 11-10, which presents the overall unemployment rate, you will see that in 2019 the unemployment rate in the United States was 3.7 percent. We can understand if you make the assumption from that number that 96.3 percent of the population was employed. However, looking back to Table 11-9, you will see that in 2019, 63.1 percent of the civilian population was in the labor force. What is going on here? What happened to the other 33 percent of the population?
>
> The answer to this question lies in how the categories are defined and highlights the importance of understanding what is being measured. In this case, we found the data for the unemployment rate in the Economic Report of the President. While this report includes a great deal of information about the unemployment situation, we found that it doesn't include a definition of unemployment. We weren't surprised by this: the audience of this report is likely to already have a baseline understanding of what unemployment means. However, we wanted to explore further. We noted that the unemployment data presented in the Economic Report of the President was originally from the Bureau of Labor Statistics (BLS), so we turned to them to find how they defined it. We found that the BLS has a very clear definition of unemployment. In order to be classified as unemployed, a person must
>
> - Not have a job
> - Have actively looked for work in the prior four weeks (with another set of requirements to be considered "actively looking" for a job)
> - Be currently available for work
>
> This definition of unemployment does not include all people who are not currently working. Those who are neither employed nor meeting the criteria for unemployment are not considered part of the labor force. In other words, the missing 33 percent are simply not included in this calculation.
>
> We think this is important to highlight because these types of data are often used to understand the relative strength or weakness of the economy, and to make economic policy decisions. Is a 3.7 percent unemployment rate always an indicator of a better economy than a 4.5 percent rate? Economists have recognized that there are people who aren't well represented by either the definition of "unemployed" but also aren't employed. For many years, the BLS has also gathered data on "alternative measures of labor underutilization." The definitions used in those measures offer different, broader conceptions of what it means to be unemployed. For instance, some people who have not actively looked for work in the past four weeks have not done so for labor market-related reasons. They might have given up their job search because they do not have the necessary skills to be hired, or they might have faced discrimination that led them to stop their job search. These people, known as "discouraged workers," are people who might actively want to work but are not considered unemployed. Thus, during times of our greatest economic upheaval, the unemployment rate probably systematically underrepresents the number of people unemployed.

Alternative definitions also provide the ability get more nuanced information about what is represented. For example, someone working twenty hours per week at a part-time job is considered employed. Some part-time workers are only interested in part-time work; others, however, might be actively searching for a full-time job. These workers who are involuntarily part-time are designated as "underemployed" in the alternative measures available.

As we've talked about elsewhere in this book, the data that you need will depend on the questions you're exploring. As the labor force participation and unemployment data highlight, it's worth taking the additional steps of tracking back to the original source to make sure that you understand what the data you're using are actually measuring.

Table 11-11 Unemployment, by Race, Sex, and Age, 1955–2020 (percent)

	White				Black or African American[a]				Asian			
	Male		Female		Male		Female		Male		Female	
Year	16–19	20 and older	16–19	20 and older	16–19	20 and older	16–19	20 and older	16–19	20 and older	16–19	20 and older
1955	11.3	3.3	9.1	3.9	13.4	8.4	19.2	7.7	—	—	—	—
1960	14.0	4.2	12.7	4.6	24.0	9.6	24.8	8.3	—	—	—	—
1965	12.9	2.9	14.0	4.0	23.3	6.0	31.7	7.5	—	—	—	—
1970	13.7	3.2	13.4	4.4	25.0	5.6	34.5	6.9	—	—	—	—
1975	18.3	6.2	17.4	7.5	38.1	12.5	41.0	12.2	—	—	—	—
1980	16.2	5.3	14.8	5.6	37.5	12.4	39.8	11.9	—	—	—	—
1985	16.5	5.4	14.8	5.7	41.0	13.2	39.2	13.1	—	—	—	—
1990	14.3	4.3	12.6	4.1	31.9	10.4	29.9	9.7	—	—	—	—
1991	17.6	5.8	15.2	5.0	36.3	11.5	36.0	10.6	—	—	—	—
1992	18.5	6.4	15.8	5.5	42.0	13.5	37.2	11.8	—	—	—	—
1993	17.7	5.7	14.7	5.2	40.1	12.1	37.4	10.7	—	—	—	—
1994	16.3	4.8	13.8	4.6	37.6	10.3	32.6	9.8	—	—	—	—
1995	15.6	4.3	13.4	4.3	37.1	8.8	34.3	8.6	—	—	—	—
1996	15.5	4.1	12.9	4.1	36.9	9.4	30.3	8.7	—	—	—	—
1997	14.3	3.6	12.8	3.7	36.5	8.5	28.7	8.8	—	—	—	—
1998	14.1	3.2	10.9	3.4	30.1	7.4	25.3	7.9	—	—	—	—
1999	12.6	3.0	11.3	3.3	30.9	6.7	25.1	6.8	—	—	—	—
2000	12.3	2.8	10.4	3.1	26.2	6.9	22.8	6.2	15.1	3.2	13.3	3.1
2001	13.9	3.7	11.4	3.6	30.4	8.0	27.5	7.0	14.6	4.2	11.1	4.1
2002	15.9	4.7	13.1	4.4	31.3	9.5	28.3	8.8	19.9	5.5	11.2	5.4
2003	17.1	5.0	13.3	4.4	36.0	10.3	30.3	9.2	20.3	5.8	13.8	5.5
2004	16.3	4.4	13.6	4.2	35.6	9.9	28.2	8.9	14.0	4.2	8.7	4.2
2005	16.1	3.8	12.3	3.9	36.3	9.2	30.3	8.5	17.0	3.7	7.8	3.8
2006	14.6	3.5	11.7	3.6	32.7	8.3	25.9	7.5	13.6	2.8	14.4	2.8

(*Continued*)

Table 11-11 *(Continued)*

Year	White Male 16–19	White Male 20 and older	White Female 16–19	White Female 20 and older	Black or African American[a] Male 16–19	Black or African American[a] Male 20 and older	Black or African American[a] Female 16–19	Black or African American[a] Female 20 and older	Asian Male 16–19	Asian Male 20 and older	Asian Female 16–19	Asian Female 20 and older
2007	15.7	3.7	12.1	3.6	33.8	7.9	25.3	6.7	11.2	3.0	14.3	3.1
2008	19.1	4.9	14.4	4.4	35.9	10.2	26.8	8.1	16.6	3.9	11.6	3.6
2009	25.2	8.8	18.4	6.8	46.0	16.3	33.4	11.5	25.9	7.5	25.2	6.2
2010	26.3	8.9	20.0	7.2	45.4	17.3	40.5	12.8	25.7	7.5	23.7	6.8
2011	24.5	7.7	18.9	7.0	43.1	16.7	39.4	13.2	30.0	6.4	20.6	7.0
2012	24.6	6.7	18.5	6.6	41.4	14	35.5	11.9	22.7	5.5	19.1	5.8
2013	22.5	6.2	18.2	5.7	44.5	12.9	33.3	11.3	21.0	5.3	17.8	4.6
2014	19.2	4.9	15.4	4.8	36.8	11.3	29.9	9.8	18.4	5.1	10.5	4.5
2015	16.2	4.3	13.2	4.2	30.7	9.5	25.9	8.3	17.4	3.7	11.3	3.5
2016	14.9	4	13.2	3.8	30.9	8.2	22.8	7.3	13.4	3.3	8.4	3.8
2017	13.3	3.5	11.1	3.5	30	7.2	19	6.5	12.0	3.2	11.3	3.2
2018	12.6	3.2	10	3.2	25.7	6.2	18.2	5.6	6.9	2.9	10.7	2.9
2019	12.9	3.0	10.1	3.0	22.1	6.1	19.6	5.1	8.4	2.6	7.7	2.5
2020	17.4	6.7	16.5	7.3	25	11.7	23.4	10.5	14.5	7.8	16.0	9.5

Note: "—" indicates not available. Data for additional years can be found in previous editions of *Vital Statistics on American Politics*.

[a] Black and other nonwhite prior to 1972.

Source: 1955–1960: *Economic Report of the President* (Washington, D.C.: Government Printing Office, 2003), Table B-43; 1965: (2009); 1970: (2011); 1975–2012: (2013), Table B-43; 2012–2020 and Asian, 2000–2020: U.S. Department of Labor, Bureau of Labor Statistics, "Labor Force Statistics from the Current Population Survey," https://data.bls.gov/PDQWeb/ln.

Table 11-12 Consumer Confidence, Unemployment, and the Stock Market

Date	Consumer Confidence	Dow-Jones Industrial Average	Unemployment
July 1, 2011	59.7	11647.55	9.0
October 1, 2011	64.8	11798.65	8.6
January 1, 2012	75.5	12847.53	8.3
April 1, 2012	76.3	12760.67	8.2
July 1, 2012	75.0	13113.50	8.0
October 1, 2012	79.4	13140.36	7.8
January 1, 2013	76.7	13994.44	7.7
April 1, 2013	81.7	14958.95	7.5
July 1, 2013	81.6	15285.61	7.2
October 1, 2013	76.9	15735.65	6.9
January 1, 2014	80.9	16177.21	6.7
April 1, 2014	82.8	16603.50	6.2
July 1, 2014	83.0	16954.39	6.1
October 1, 2014	89.8	17344.80	5.7
January 1, 2015	95.5	17808.30	5.5
April 1, 2015	94.2	18004.35	5.4
July 1, 2015	90.7	17076.92	5.1
October 1, 2015	91.3	17475.44	5.0
January 1, 2016	91.6	16663.03	4.9
April 1, 2016	92.4	17763.71	4.9
July 1, 2016	90.3	18372.32	4.9
October 1, 2016	93.1	18864.77	4.8
January 1, 2017	97.2	20405.68	4.6
April 1, 2017	96.4	20993.82	4.4
July 1, 2017	95.1	21890.75	4.3
October 1, 2017	98.4	23689.23	4.1
January 1, 2018	98.9	25127.20	4.0
April 1, 2018	98.3	24555.88	3.9
July 1, 2018	98.1	25594.50	3.8
October 1, 2018	98.1	24948.45	3.8
January 1, 2019	94.5	25147.44	3.9
April 1, 2019	98.5	26095.56	3.7
July 1, 2019	93.8	26675.74	3.6
October 1, 2019	97.2	27537.41	3.6
January 1, 2020	96.6	26554.48	3.8
April 1, 2020	74.1	24570.83	13.1
July 1, 2020	75.7	27299.04	8.8
October 1, 2020	79.8	29091.59	6.8
January 1, 2021	80.2	31550.58	6.2

Source: U.S. Bureau of Labor Statistics, Consumer Price Index for All Urban Consumers: Shelter in U.S. City Average [CUSR0000SAH1], retrieved from FRED, Federal Reserve Bank of St. Louis; https://fred.stlouisfed.org/series/CUSR0000SAH1, May 24, 2021.

Figure 11-5 Linking Consumer Confidence to Unemployment and the Stock Market

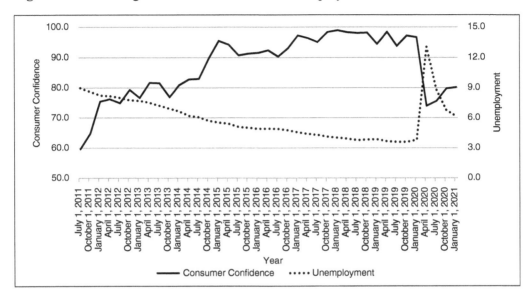

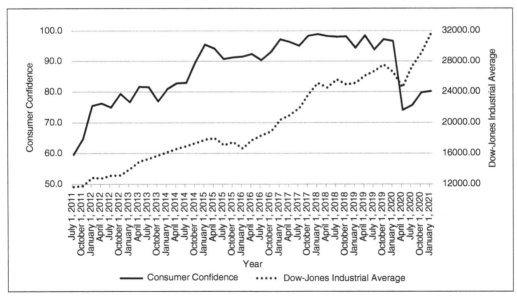

Sources: Table 11-12, this volume.

A Data Literacy Lesson
Thinking about Consumer Confidence

So many of the economic decisions people make—Should I buy a new car? Can we afford a vacation this year?—are made based on their perceptions of how economic conditions will be in the future. These decisions reflect consumer confidence—our general level of optimism or pessimism about where the economy is headed. If we believe things are looking up, we might buy that new car. If not, we may wait. Since all of these individual-level decisions drive the overall economy—the more people who buy new cars, for example, the better the automotive sector does—understanding consumer confidence is an important tool for understanding the overall health of any nation's economy.

So how healthy is the economy at any point in time? Answering this question brings to mind the paradox of the blind men and the elephant. When confronting something as vast as an elephant, each was able to offer his best guess what they were encountering, based on the piece of the elephant that they could touch. While most of us can "see" the economy more than the blind man could see the elephant, something so large as the nation's economy is typically encountered just one piece at a time.

As one example of this, ask yourself how well the economy is doing. That question can be answered at an individual level—how are things going for you? On the one hand, if you are out of work, and many other members of your social network are also unemployed or under-employed, you might be tempted to say that the economy is performing poorly. If, on the other hand, things are going well—your job pays well, your needs are secured, and your investments are doing well—you might say that the economy is doing very well. Voters who heavily weight their own economic situation when voting or evaluating candidates in this way have come to be called "pocketbook voters."

It is not hard to see the flaw in pocketbook voting, however: you are just one person, and your own situation might not reflect how the economy as a whole is doing. For example, during the early days of the COVID-19 pandemic, many people were losing their jobs or having their hours slashed, while others were doing quite well. There is no doubt that the economy took a hit in the spring of 2020, but if you were working as a shelf-stocker at a grocery store, or you were fortunate to have invested in Zoom (or toilet paper manufacturers), the national economic shock might have passed you by. When voters choose to vote based not so much on their pocketbooks, but instead on how the broad economy is doing, such voters would be called "sociotropic voters."

Perhaps you see the challenge in sociotropic voting: when we look at something as big as the economy, we're stumbling around like the blind men. How do we judge the state of the economy? Table 11-13 and Figure 11-5 explore this a little bit by using the consumer confidence index and comparing it to two very different measures of the economy. The first, shown at the top of Figure 11-5, is unemployment. We assume, logically, that the more people who are out of work, the weaker the economy is. The second, shown at the bottom of Figure 11-5, is the stock market, measured by the Dow Jones Industrial Average.[1]

These measures are related, but not perfectly. After COVID hit, the stock market tanked, and unemployment soared. The stock market returned to its high levels quickly—the market began a decline in mid-February 2020 but had pretty much erased those declines by the end of August 2020 and had gained over 20 percent by May 2021. Unemployment, however, soared in April of 2020, peaking at 14.8 percent; job losses reversed themselves quickly, but as of May 2021, unemployment remained about 70 percent higher (6.1 percent versus 3.6 percent) than it had been before COVID entered our vocabulary.

The table and accompanying figures show that consumer confidence does map well onto unemployment and the stock margin; the graphs move much as one might expect over time. But, when we look at recent months, we see that while the stock market has more than recovered from COVID, unemployment has not completed the recovery. And, while consumer confidence is recovering from its post-COVID dip, it is nowhere near where it had been at the beginning of 2020. What happens on Wall Street, it seems, does not fully reflect (or influence) what is felt on Main Street. The public, it appears, had not regained the same sense of optimism at the beginning of the year as investors had. So, when President Trump pointed to the stock market as a measure of how well the economy is doing, Table 11-13 and Figure 11-5 suggest to us why the public might have been somewhat skeptical of his argument; the longitudinal way we present these data help to address this issue and invite us to ask other questions of the data we present.

---

[1] Although it is beyond the scope of this essay, we will just briefly note that the Dow, while the best-known indicator of how the stock market is doing, tends to focus more on the performance of large companies. A broader-based, although lesser-known, index like the S & P 500 might give a more discerning picture of the overall market.

Appendix
Definitions of Regions

Table A-1 Regions as Defined by the U.S. Census Bureau and by Pew Research

Northeast	Midwest	South	West
New England	East North Central	South Atlantic	Mountain
Connecticut	Illinois	Delaware	Arizona
Maine	Indiana	District of	Colorado
Massachusetts	Michigan	Columbia	Idaho
New Hampshire	Ohio	Florida	Montana
Rhode Island	Wisconsin	Georgia	Nevada
Vermont	West North Central	Maryland	New Mexico
Middle Atlantic	Iowa	North Carolina	Utah
New Jersey	Kansas	South Carolina	Wyoming
New York	Minnesota	Virginia	Pacific
Pennsylvania	Missouri	West Virginia	Alaska
	Nebraska	East South Central	California
	North Dakota	Alabama	Hawaii
	South Dakota	Kentucky	Oregon
		Mississippi	Washington
		Tennessee	
		West South Central	
		Arkansas	
		Louisiana	
		Oklahoma	
		Texas	

Sources: U.S. Census Bureau, "Census Regions and Divisions of the United States," www.census.gov; and Pew Research, unpublished data.

Table A-2 Regions as Defined by Congressional Quarterly, *New York Times*/CBS News Poll, and Voter Research and Surveys

East	Midwest	South	West
Connecticut	Illinois	Alabama	Alaska
Delaware	Indiana	Arkansas	Arizona
District of Columbia	Iowa	Florida	California
Maine	Kansas	Georgia	Colorado
Maryland	Michigan	Kentucky	Hawaii
Massachusetts	Minnesota	Louisiana	Idaho
New Hampshire	Missouri	Mississippi	Montana
New Jersey	Nebraska	North Carolina	Nevada
New York	North Dakota	Oklahoma	New Mexico
Pennsylvania	Ohio	South Carolina	Oregon
Rhode Island	South Dakota	Tennessee	Utah
Vermont	Wisconsin	Texas	Washington
West Virginia		Virginia	Wyoming

Table A-3 Regions for Party Competition Table (Table 1-4) and Apportionment Map (Figure 5-1)

New England	Middle Atlantic	Midwest	Plains
Connecticut	Delaware	Illinois	Iowa
Maine	New Jersey	Indiana	Kansas
Massachusetts	New York	Michigan	Minnesota
New Hampshire	Pennsylvania	Ohio	Nebraska
Rhode Island		Wisconsin	North Dakota
Vermont			South Dakota

South	Border	Rocky Mountain	Pacific Coast
Alabama	District of Columbia	Arizona	Alaska
Arkansas	Kentucky	Colorado	California
Florida	Maryland	Idaho	Hawaii
Georgia	Missouri	Montana	Oregon
Louisiana	Oklahoma	Nevada	Washington
Mississippi	West Virginia	New Mexico	
North Carolina		Utah	
South Carolina		Wyoming	
Tennessee			
Texas			
Virginia			

Table A-4 Regions for School Desegregation Table (Table 10-13)

South	Border	Northeast	Midwest	West	Excluded
Alabama	Delaware	Connecticut	Illinois	Arizona	Alaska
Arkansas	District of Columbia	Maine	Indiana	California	Hawaii
Florida		Massachusetts	Iowa	Colorado	
Georgia	Kentucky	New Hampshire	Kansas	Idaho	
Louisiana	Maryland	New Jersey	Michigan	Montana	
Mississippi	Missouri	New York	Minnesota	Nevada	
North Carolina	Oklahoma	Pennsylvania	Nebraska	New Mexico	
South Carolina	West Virginia	Rhode Island	North Dakota	Oregon	
Tennessee		Vermont	Ohio	Utah	
Texas			South Dakota	Washington	
Virginia			Wisconsin	Wyoming	

Source: Gary Orfield and Franklin Monfort, "Status of School Desegregation: The Next Generation" (Alexandria, VA: National School Boards Association, 1992), 2.

Index

Abortion
  legal, frequency of, 452
  public opinion on, 166, 168–169
Age
  Congressional composition and, 229–231
  Congressional vote and, 144
  Democratic presidential primary vote and, 140
  health insurance, persons without, 446
  media use and, 194, 197
  partisan identification and, 126
  persons below poverty line and, 437
  presidential vote and, 137
  Republican presidential primary vote and, 142
  unemployment rate and, 491–492
  voter registration/turnout and, 10
Aggregation, 427
Aid to Families with Dependent Children (AFDC) program, 440–442
American National Election Studies survey, 120
Article III of the Constitution, 315, 334

Balance of trade, 418
Bipartisan Campaign Reform Act (BCRA), 87
Blacks
  Congressional composition and, 229–233
  state legislators and voting-age population, 62–63
  See also Race/ethnicity
Budget. *See* Federal budget

Cabinet
  nominations rejected by Senate, 306
  president, 292–293

Campaign finance, 87–89
  contribution limits, state election, 91–92
  incumbency advantage and, 117–118
  law, 87
  presidential, 93–95
  public funding, 98
  "soft" and "hard" money, 103
  See also Political action committees (PACs)
Campaign Finance Institute (CFI), 96
Campaign news, 200
Citizen voting-age population, 5
Civil liberties, public opinion on, 161–163
Community, partisan identification and, 127
Confidence
  consumer, 493–496
  government, in, 152
Congress/Congressional elections, 219–220
  age, composition by, 229–231
  apportionment, 221–226
  Black members of, 229–233
  committees and majority party chair positions, 239–241
  divided government, 40–41
  Hispanics, composition by, 229–231
  legislative districting, 78–79
  "majority-minority" districts, 56–60
  marital status, composition by, 229–231
  measures introduced and enacted, 242–243
  open seat, 46–47
  PACs, campaign contributions, 114–116
  party-line voting, 148

501

party unity and polarization in voting, 248–250
presidential victories on votes in, 296–298
presidential vote and, 138
press corps, 186
public bills, 244
rating of, public opinion on, 151
reapportionment, 227–228
record votes, 246
seats and shifts in party, 46–47
seniority and previous legislative service, 238
sex, composition by, 229–231
split districts outcomes, 42
split-ticket voting, 149
voting in general elections, 144–145
voting in support of president, 299–300
women, composition by, 229–231, 234–235
See also House/House election; Senate/Senate election
Connected PACs, 110
Constitutions
ratification, U.S. amendments, 366
state, 351–353
Consumer confidence, 493–496
Consumer price index (CPI), 465–469
Convention, national
location and size, 77
states methods for choosing delegates, 67–70
television coverage and viewership, 208–210
Corporations and contribution limits on state election, 91–92
Costs of War Project, 398–399
Courts
appeals caseload, 340
federal court appointees characteristics, 328–330
judicial selection methods of state, 319
system, 317
See also District courts; Supreme courts
CPI. *See* Consumer price index (CPI)
CQ Roll Call, 268, 275
Crime rates, 453

Data
availability, xxiv–xxv
information literacy, xxvii–xxviii
political, xxvi–xxvii
reporting, ways of, xxv–xxvi
statistical literacy, xxvii–xxviii
Data literacy
aggregation, 427
apolitical judiciary, 334–335
big government, 370–371
consumer confidence, 495–496
consumer price index, 468–469
counting, data, 187–188
current dollars and constant dollars, 436–437
data visualization, 442–443
descriptive representation, 64–65
dichotomies and public opinion, 168–169
divided government, 38–39
economic indicators, 484–485
economic policy, analyzing, 480
economy and vote, 159–160
executive orders, 311–312
group voting, 146–147
incumbency advantage and campaign finance, 117–118
independent leaners and partisanship, 134–135
interest group ratings, 276–277
issues of, xxii–xxiv
judicial characteristics, 331–332
legislative professionalism, 361–362
newspaper endorsements, 216–217
nonconnected PACs, 110–111
political issue questions, 155–156
presidential nominations/rejected/withdrawn, 307–308
presidential ratings, 288–289
presidential success in Congress, 301–302
reapportionment data, 227–228
split districts, 43–44
surveys, 201–202
unemployment, definition of, 489–490
using data for comparisons, 413
voter turnout, 8–9

Index   503

war cost measurement, 398–399
women in elective office, 236–237
Death penalty
   number of executions, 457–458
   public opinion on, 164
   states, in, 454–456
Defense spending, 408–410
Descriptive representation, 64–65
Digital media, 203
District courts, 318
   caseload, 341
   circuit court nominations and
      confirmed, 333
   civil and criminal cases, 342–343
   See also Courts
Divided government, 38–39
   Congress, by, 40–41

Economic policy, 461–462
   analyzing, 480
   consumer confidence, 493–494
   consumer price index, 465–467
   federal budget, 470–474
   federal minimum wage, 483
   gross domestic product, 463–464
   labor force participation rate, 485–486
   labor union membership, 481–482
   national debt, 475–476
   tax expenditures, 477–478
   unemployment rate, 487–488, 491–494
Economy
   public opinion on, 158
   vote and, 159–160
Education
   Congressional vote and, 144
   media use and, 194, 197
   partisan identification and, 126–127
   persons below poverty line and, 437
   presidential vote and, 137
   voter registration/turnout and, 11
Elections
   federal preclearance and minority
      language provisions, 80
   group voting in, 146–147
   open-seat, 118
   primary, 66, 74–75
   voter turnout, 4–11

voting equipment types, 85–86
See also Congress/Congressional
   elections; Presidential elections
Electoral votes, 19–23
Employment
   labor force participation rate, 485–486
   voter registration and turnout, 10
   See also Unemployment
Ethnicity. *See* Race/ethnicity
Executive branch, 280

Federal budget
   defense and nondefense, 470–471
   mandatory and discretionary outlays, 474
   outlays, 472–473
Federal Election Commission (FEC), 87
Federal government
   employees, 367
   number of units and employees,
      368–369, 371
   surpluses and deficits, 380
Federal grants-in-aid
   local government, 384
   outlays, 382–383
   state government, 384
   state/local government deficits *vs.*, 381
Federalism, 347–349
Federal Judicial Center, 316
Federal judicial circuits, 318
Federal minimum wage, 483–484
Federal preclearance, Voting Rights Act, 80
Federal prisoners, sentenced, 459
Federal Register, number of pages, 314
Female. *See* Sex; Women
Food Stamp, 440–442
Foreign aid, 415–416
Foreign investment, 416–417
Foreign policy, 389–390
   economic cost of, 390
   executive agreements, 391
   treaties, 391
Full-time legislators, 361

Gender. *See* Sex
Generation
   partisan identification and, 127
   religious unaffiliation by, 173

Gerrymandering, 43, 117
Government employees
  civilian federal, 309–310
  number of, 367–369, 371
Governors
  item veto, 354–355
  partisan division, 16–18
  reelection rates, 52–55
  term limits, 354–355
Gross domestic product (GDP), 463–464
  federal outlays as, 473
  national debt as, 476
Gun control, public opinion on, 167–169

"Hard" money, 103
Health insurance, 444–446
Hispanics
  Congressional composition
    and, 229–231
  high school/college, persons completed, 447–448
  median family income, 434–435
  military personnel, 405–407
  persons below poverty line, 438–439
  state legislators and voting-age population, 62–63
  See also Race/ethnicity
Hospital insurance trust fund, 431
House/House election
  apportionment of membership, 221–226
  Black members of, 232–233
  committees and majority party chair positions, 239
  Congress, by, 29–33
  117th Congress, 251–268
  party-line voting, 148
  party unity and polarization in voting, 248–250
  party victories by state, 34–35
  party vote in, 247
  popular vote and seats, 36–37
  presidential victories on votes in, 296–298
  president's party losses in midterm elections, 48
  race/ethnicity, by, 34–35, 56–60
  record votes, 246

reelection rates, 52–55
retired/defeated/reelected incumbents, 49
seats and shifts in party, 46
split districts and outcomes, 42
voting in support of president, 299–300
women, composition by, 234–235
See also Congress/Congressional elections; Senate/Senate election

Ideology
  college freshmen, self-identification, 130
  Congressional vote and, 145
  Democratic presidential primary vote and, 140
  liberal/conservative self-identification, 129
  liberal/moderate/conservative self-identification, 130
  presidential vote and, 138
  religious affiliation, by, 172
  Republican presidential primary vote and, 142
Immigrants, 426, 428
  legal status and unauthorized, 429
Income
  Congressional vote and, 145
  disposable personal income by states, 376–379
  median family, 434–435
  media use and, 194
  partisan identification and, 127
  presidential vote and, 138
Incumbency advantage, 117–118
Initiative, 356–357
Interest group ratings, 268, 275–277
Internet, 201
  utilization of, 183, 190–191

Judicial characteristics, 331–332
Judiciary, 315–316

Labor unions
  contribution limits, state election, 91–92
  membership, 481–482
Latino elected officials, 61
Legislative professionalism, 361–362

Local government
  deficits, 380–381
  employees, 367
  expenditures by function, 374–375
  federal grants-in-aid, 384
  number of units and employees, 368–369, 371
  surpluses, 380

"Majority-minority" congressional districts, 56–60
Male. *See* Sex
Marijuana legalization, public opinion on, 171
Marital status
  Congressional composition and, 229–231
  partisan identification and, 127
Media, 181–182
  digital, 203
  misinformation in election, perceptions of, 195–197
  partisan differences in utilization of, 198
  political news, for, 194
  public's use, presidential campaigns, 204–205
  utilization of, 183
  See also Internet; Newspaper; Social media; Television
Midterm elections
  president's party losses in, 48
  voter turnout of, 6, 8–9
Military conflicts
  casualties by, 397
  personnel in, 395–396
Military expenditure, 408–409, 413
  federal outlays, as, 410
  gross domestic product, as, 410
  region and, 411–412
Military personnel
  abroad/afloat, 404
  amputations, 400–401
  major conflicts, in, 395–396
  sex/race/Hispanic origin, by, 405–407
  sexual assaults, 400–401
  suicides, 400–401
  traumatic brain injuries, 400–401

Military policy, 389–390
  arms control and disarmament agreements, 392–393
  economic cost of, 390
  use of abroad, 394
Military sales, 414
Military veteran and Republican presidential primary vote, 143
Minority language provisions, 80
Mortgage foreclosures, 378–379

National convention delegates, 67–70
National debt, 475–476
National Institute on Money in Politics, 96
News
  campaign, sources of, 200
  conferences, presidential, 187
  endorsements, 214–218
  internet for, 190–191
  newspapers for, 190–192
  political, 194
  preference with point of view, 199
  radio for, 192
  television for, 189, 192
Newspaper
  circulation, 184–185
  news, utilization for, 190–192
Nonconnected PACs, 110–111

117th Congress
  House of Representatives, 251–268
  Senate, 269–275
Open Secrets, 96

PACs. *See* Political action committees (PACs)
Parties. *See* Political parties
Partisan gerrymandering, 43
Partisan identification, 123–128, 134–135
  American National Election Studies, 123–124
  groups, by, 126–128
  media use and, 194
  Pew surveys, 125
  presidential vote and, 132–133
Partisanship, 134–135
Part-time legislators, 361

Party-line voting, 148
Personal Responsibility and Work Opportunity Reconciliation Act (PRWORA), 442
Pew survey, 120
Pocketbook voters, 495
Political action committees (PACs), 87–88
- Congressional campaign contributions, 114–116
- connected, 110
- contribution limits, 90
- contribution limits, state election, 91–92
- contributions, 105, 107–109
- expenditures, 105, 107–109
- nonconnected, 110–111
- number and type, 104
- receipts, 105
- spending and type, 106
- top twenty, 112–113
- *See also* Campaign finance

Political parties
- competition by region, 14
- competition by states, 13, 15
- Congressional vote and, 145
- Democratic presidential primary vote and, 140
- digital media usage by, 203
- favorable opinion of, 157
- financial activity, 99
- financial activity, committees, 100
- popular vote in House elections, 36–37
- presidential vote and, 138
- president's party losses in midterm elections, 48
- Republican presidential primary vote and, 142
- seats in House elections, 36–37
- since 1789, 12
- "soft" and "hard" money, 103
- victories in House election, 34–35
- winning presidential elections by state, 24–25

Popular votes
- House election, 36–37
- president, for, 19–23

Population
- foreign-born, 424–425
- health insurance coverage, 444–445
- "majority-minority" districts, 56–60
- native-born, 424–425
- rural, 421
- state, 422–423
- urban, 421
- voting-age. *See* Voting-age population

Poverty line, persons below, 437–439
Preclearance, Voting Rights Act, 80
Presidential elections
- campaign finance, 93–95
- campaign length, nomination, 71–73
- candidate preferences during, 136
- caucus results, Republican, 76
- electoral vote, 26–27
- general election, 26–28
- party-line voting, 148
- party winning by state, 24–25
- popular vote, 26–27
- primaries, 66, 140–143
- public funding, 98
- Republican primary returns, 74–75
- split Congressional districts, 42
- voter turnout, 6, 8–9

Presidential general election, 26–28
- vote in, 137–139

Presidential vote
- Congressional vote and, 145
- general elections, in, 137–139
- partisan identification and, 132–133

President/presidency, 279–284
- approval, public opinion on, 150
- cabinet, 292–293
- civilian federal government employees, 309–310
- Congressional vote victories, 296–298
- Congressional voting in support, 299–300
- executive office, 294–295
- executive orders, 309–312
- federal judicial appointments of same party, 332
- news conferences, 187
- newspaper endorsements of, 214–215, 218

nominees rejections by Senate, 306
popular and electoral votes, 19–23
preferences, public opinion on, 136
public positions/office previously held, 290–291
ratings, 285–289
Senate action on nominations of, 305
signing statements, 303–304
vetoes, 303–304
White House staff, 294–295
Press corps, Congressional, 186
Primary elections, presidential, 66
Democratic, 140–141
Republican, 74–75, 142–143
Print media, credibility of, 206–207
PRWORA. *See* Personal Responsibility and Work Opportunity Reconciliation Act (PRWORA)
Public opinion, 119–122
abortion, 166, 168–169
civil liberties, 161–163
college freshmen, self-identification, 131
confidence in government, 152
Congress rating, 151
courts handling of criminals, 174
death penalty, 164
dichotomies and, 168–169
economy, 158
favorable opinion of political party, 157
gun control, 167–169
integrated neighborhood people, 165
liberal/conservative self-identification, 129
liberal/moderate/conservative self-identification, 130
marijuana legalization, 171
military involvement in Iraq, 177
partisan identification, 123–128
peace through military strength, 176
personal financial situations, 158
political issues importance, 154
polling, 119
presidential approval, 150
presidential preferences, 136
religious affiliation/unaffiliation, 172–173
same-sex marriage, 170

sampling error in surveys, 120–121
satisfaction with country development, 153
surveys, 119
terrorism, 178–179
world affairs, involvement in, 175

Race/ethnicity
Congressional vote and, 144
Democratic presidential primary vote and, 140
health insurance, persons without, 446
high school/college, persons completed, 447–448
House of Representatives by, 56–60
labor force participation rate by, 485–486
median family income by, 434–435
media use and, 194
military personnel by, 405–407
partisan identification and, 126
poverty line, persons below, 437–439
presidential vote and, 137
Republican presidential primary vote and, 142
school desegregation by region, 449–451
unemployment rate by, 487–488, 491–492
voter registration/turnout and, 10
Radio, utilization of, 192
Reelection rate, 49–50, 52–55
Referendum, 356–357
Region
Congressional apportionment, 226
Congressional vote and, 144
definitions of, 497–499
digital media use and, 203
foreign aid by, 415–416
immigrants by, 426, 428
military expenditure by, 411–412
partisan identification and, 126
party competition by, 14
persons below poverty line, 437
presidential vote and, 137
school desegregation by, 449–451
voter registration and, 10
voter turnout and, 4–5, 7, 10

Regulatory agencies, 313
Religion
    Congressional vote and, 144
    Democratic presidential primary vote and, 140
    partisan identification and, 127
    presidential vote and, 137
    religious affiliation/unaffiliation, public opinion on, 172–173
    Republican presidential primary vote and, 142

Same-sex marriage, public opinion on, 170
School desegregation, 449–451
Section 5 of Voting Rights Act, 80
Senate/Senate election
    action on presidential nominations, 305
    Black members of, 232–233
    cabinet nomination rejections, 306
    committees and majority party chair positions, 239
    Congress, by, 29–33
    117th Congress, 269–275
    party-line voting, 148
    party unity and polarization in voting, 248–250
    presidential victories on votes in, 296–298
    president's party losses in midterm elections, 48
    record votes, 246
    reelection rates, 52–55
    retired/defeated/reelected incumbents, 49–50
    seats and shifts in party, 46–47
    voting in support of president, 299–300
    See also Congress/Congressional elections; House/House election
Sex
    Congressional composition and, 229–231
    Congressional vote and, 144
    Democratic presidential primary vote and, 140
    high school/college, persons completed, 447–448

labor force participation rate and, 485–486
media use and, 194, 196
military personnel and, 405–407
partisan identification and, 126
presidential vote and, 137
Republican presidential primary vote and, 142
unemployment rate and, 487–488, 491–492
voter registration/turnout and, 10
See also Women
SNAP. See Supplemental Nutrition Assistance Program (SNAP)
Social media, 213
Social policy, 419–420
    crime rates, 453
    death penalty in states, 454–456
    Food Stamp, 440–441
    health insurance, 444–446
    high school/college, persons completed, 447–448
    hospital insurance trust fund, 431
    immigrants, 426, 428–430
    legal abortions, 452
    median family income, 434–435
    persons below poverty line, 437–439
    population, 421–425
    prisoners, 459–460
    school desegregation, 449–451
    social security, 432–433
    Temporary Assistance for Needy Families, 440–441
Social security
    beneficiaries, 432
    covered workers, 432
    receipts, 433
    spending, 433
Sociotropic voters, 495
"Soft" money, 103
Split districts, 42–44
Split-ticket voting, 149
State(s)
    aid, local dependency on, 387
    Bill of Rights, incorporation of, 364–365
    constitutions, 351–353
    death penalty in, 454–456

disposable personal income, 376–377
governors, 16–18
historical data, 349–350
initiative, 356–357, 363
legislative professionalism, 358–360
lottery revenues, 372–373
methods for national convention delegates, 67–70
party competition, 13, 15
party victories in House election by, 34–35
party winning presidential elections by, 24–25
population, 422–423
presidential general election returns, 26–27
referendum, 356–357
sentenced prisoners, 459
split-ticket voting, state-local, 149
term limits on legislators, 81–82
voting-age population by, 62–63
voting equipment types by, 85–86
State government
deficits, 380–381
employees, 367
expenditure by function, 374–375
federal grants-in-aid, 384
number of units and employees, 368–369, 371
surpluses, 380
State legislatures
districting, 78–79
partisan division, 16–18
termed out members of, 83–84
term limits on legislators, 81–82
Super PACs, 87, 105
Supplemental Nutrition Assistance Program (SNAP), 440–442
Supreme courts
caseload, 336–337
case's path, 338
economic and civil liberties laws, 345
failed nominations, 327
filed cases, 339
justices, 320–326
unconstitutional laws, 344
See also Courts

Surveys, 119, 201–202
American National Election Studies, 120
"interval" scale, 134
Pew, 120
sampling error in, 120–121

TANF. *See* Temporary Assistance for Needy Families (TANF)
Tax expenditures, 477–478
Television
credibility, 206–207
national nominating conventions, coverage and viewership, 208–210
presidential/vice-presidential debates, viewership of, 211–212
utilization of, 183, 189, 192
viewing, 183
Temporary Assistance for Needy Families (TANF), 440–442
Term limits
governors, 354–355
state legislators, 81–82
Terrorism, public opinion on, 178–179

Unemployment, 378
consumer confidence and, 493–494
definition of, 489–490
sex/race/age, by, 487–488, 491–492
See also Employment
Union household
Congressional vote and, 144
Democratic presidential primary vote and, 141
presidential vote and, 138

Vice presidents, 282–284
Voter turnout
presidential and midterm elections, 6, 8–9
United States, South, and Non-South, 4–5, 7
voter registration and, 10–11
Voting
Congressional, 144–145
Democratic presidential primary, 140–141

equipment, 85–86
group, 146–147
party-line, 148
pocketbook, 495
presidential. *See* Presidential vote
Republican presidential primary, 142–143
sociotropic, 495
split-ticket, 149
Voting-age population, 5
Blacks/Hispanics/women, 62–63
registered and voting, 10–11

Voting Rights Act, 8, 80

Welfare reform, 442
Women
Congressional composition and, 229–231, 234–235
elective office, in, 236–237
state legislators and voting-age population, 62–63
See also Sex